中国—阿拉伯国家博览会
معرض الصين والدول العربية
CHINA-ARAB STATES EXPO

中阿经贸关系发展进程
2023年度报告

中国—阿拉伯国家博览会秘书处／编
李绍先／主编

The Development Process of
China-Arab States Economic and Trade
Relations Annual Report

—————— 2023 ——————

社会科学文献出版社
SOCIAL SCIENCES ACADEMIC PRESS (CHINA)

图书在版编目(CIP)数据

中阿经贸关系发展进程2023年度报告/中国—阿拉伯国家博览会秘书处编；李绍先主编. -- 北京：社会科学文献出版社，2024.12. -- ISBN 978-7-5228-4799-3

Ⅰ.F125.537.1

中国国家版本馆CIP数据核字第20245LB399号

中阿经贸关系发展进程2023年度报告

编　　者 / 中国—阿拉伯国家博览会秘书处
主　　编 / 李绍先

出 版 人 / 冀祥德
责任编辑 / 周志静
责任印制 / 王京美

出　　版 / 社会科学文献出版社·人文分社（010）59367215
　　　　　 地址：北京市北三环中路甲29号院华龙大厦　邮编：100029
　　　　　 网址：www.ssap.com.cn
发　　行 / 社会科学文献出版社（010）59367028
印　　装 / 三河市东方印刷有限公司

规　　格 / 开　本：787mm×1092mm　1/16
　　　　　 印　张：32.75　字　数：590千字
版　　次 / 2024年12月第1版　2024年12月第1次印刷
书　　号 / ISBN 978-7-5228-4799-3
定　　价 / 198.00元

读者服务电话：4008918866

版权所有 翻印必究

《中阿经贸关系发展进程2023年度报告》编委会

主　任　徐晓平

副主任　杨文辉　聂　丹　李绍先

委　员（按姓氏笔画排序）

　　　　丁　隆　王广大　王林聪　牛新春
　　　　毛小菁　朱　东　李绍先　苏　鸿
　　　　杨文辉　杨春泉　吴思科　张前进
　　　　陆如泉　唐志超　徐晓平　聂　丹
　　　　崔彦祥

主　编　李绍先

副主编　苏　鸿　张前进

前　言

在世界格局深刻变化、国际环境变乱交织背景下，中东地区也在经历着深刻的时代之变和历史之变。2023年，中东地区国家求稳定、谋发展意愿持续上升，地区国家纷纷将发展置于优先位置。沙特阿拉伯和伊朗在中国斡旋下实现历史性和解，催生了中东地区"和解潮"：阿拉伯国家间关系回暖，伊朗同海合会成员国关系出现明显缓和；土耳其改善与阿拉伯国家和伊朗关系，总统埃尔多安先后访问阿联酋、卡塔尔和沙特，推动与相关国家建立新的安全和外交伙伴关系，土耳其还与埃及恢复大使级外交关系，地区形势总体呈缓和态势。但与此同时，2023年10月7日新一轮巴以冲突爆发并持续升级，冲突对世界经济造成较大冲击，并对中东地区格局产生深远影响。

2023年也是首届中阿峰会后的第一年，在元首外交的战略引领下，中阿关系不断提质升级，中国同阿拉伯国家关系处于历史上最好时期，双方政治互信持续增强，高层交往持续扩大，经贸合作持续拓展，文明互鉴持续深化，共同推进共建"一带一路"高质量发展和践行三大倡议的落地，不断推进中阿命运共同体建设。

经贸合作是深化中阿关系的"压舱石"和"助推器"。阿拉伯国家是中国推进"一带一路"建设的重要合作伙伴。在双方共同努力下，截至2023年底，中国已同全部22个阿拉伯国家和阿盟签署共建"一带一路"合作文件，实现了全覆盖。双方在共建"一带一路"框架内，实施了200多个大型项目，合作成果惠及双方近20亿人民。贸易方面，中国连续多年稳居阿拉伯国家第一大贸易伙伴地位。中阿贸易额从 2013 年的 2388.9 亿美元增长至 2022 年创纪录的 4314 亿美元，10 年间增长了 80.6%。中国对阿投资存量从 2013 年的 85.7 亿美元增长至 2023 年的 276 亿美元，增长 2.2 倍。与此同时，阿拉伯国家也在加大对华投资力度，2023 年阿拉伯国家对华直接投资达 23 亿美元，同比增长 120%。阿联酋、沙特阿拉伯是对华投资最活跃的阿拉伯国家。截至 2023 年底，阿拉伯国家对华投资累计已超过 70 亿美元。基础设施建设方面，2023 年中国企业在该地区的新签合同额 472 亿美元，同比增长 28.8%，占新签合同总额的 17.8%；完成营业额 277 亿美元，同比增长 9.5%，占完成营业额总额的 17.2%。其中在沙特阿拉伯新签合同额达 168 亿美元，同比增长 72.6%，位居阿拉伯国家第一。从具体领域来看，中阿在能源、产能合作、农业、数字经济、航空航天等诸多领域取得丰硕成果，金融、绿色、数字经济等新兴领域合作不断拓展和深化，成为新亮点。2024 年 5 月，习近平主席出席中阿合作论坛第十届部长级会议并发表主旨演讲，提出同阿方构建"五大合作格局"，推动中阿命运共同体建设跑出加速度，为下一阶段中阿合作指明了方向，提供了根本遵循。

中国—阿拉伯国家博览会（以下简称中阿博览会）作为国家级、国际性综合博览会经过十年发展，已成为中阿共建"一带一路"的重要平台，为深化中阿务实合作、推动共建"一带一路"高质量发展发挥了积极作用。2023 年第六届中阿博览会共形成合作成果 403 个，其中合作类项目 50 个，投资类项目 218 个，贸易类项目 135 个，金额达 1709.7 亿元，项目涉及现代农业、清洁能源、医疗健康、数字经济、旅游合作等多个领域。

鉴于此，宁夏大学中国阿拉伯国家研究院组织相关领域权威专家学者编写《中阿经贸关系发展进程 2023 年度报告》，介绍中国与阿拉伯国家经贸合作发展历程，展示 2023 年中国与阿拉伯国家的经贸合作状况和成果，剖析存在的机遇和挑战。我们希望本书能够为政府决策部门、学者、企业家、学生等提供有价值的参考。

最后，我们要感谢所有为本书撰写、翻译、编辑、校对等方面做出贡献的人员，感谢广大读者的关注和支持。

李绍先

2024 年 12 月于宁夏

目 录

第1章　中阿经贸合作总体形势 ……………………………… 001

　1.1　中阿经贸合作总体情况 ……………………………… 001

　1.2　中阿经贸合作领域态势 ……………………………… 005

　1.3　中阿经贸合作趋势展望 ……………………………… 012

第2章　中阿贸易合作专题报告 ……………………………… 017

　2.1　中国对阿拉伯国家贸易状况 ………………………… 017

　2.2　阿拉伯国家对中国贸易状况 ………………………… 024

　2.3　中国与阿拉伯国家的贸易关系 ……………………… 033

第3章　中阿投资合作专题报告 ……………………………… 043

　3.1　中国对阿拉伯国家投资趋势 ………………………… 043

　3.2　阿拉伯国家对中国投资趋势 ………………………… 051

　3.3　中阿投资合作面临的机遇和挑战 …………………… 057

第4章　中阿金融合作专题报告 ……………………………… 063

　4.1　阿拉伯国家金融环境 ………………………………… 063

　4.2　中阿金融合作进展 …………………………………… 067

中阿经贸关系发展进程2023年度报告

4.3　中阿金融合作的发展趋势 ·· 075

4.4　中阿金融合作展望 ·· 077

第5章　中阿农业合作专题报告 ·· 081

5.1　阿拉伯国家农业发展现状 ·· 081

5.2　中阿农业合作现状 ·· 085

5.3　中阿农业合作展望 ·· 095

第6章　中阿能源合作专题报告 ·· 098

6.1　阿拉伯国家能源资源概况 ·· 098

6.2　中阿传统能源合作现状 ·· 106

6.3　中阿新能源合作现状 ·· 109

6.4　中阿能源合作前景 ·· 112

第7章　中阿数字经济合作专题报告 ·· 115

7.1　阿拉伯国家数字经济水平现状 ·· 115

7.2　中阿数字经济合作现状 ·· 123

7.3　中阿数字经济合作展望 ·· 127

第8章　中阿科技合作专题报告 ·· 131

8.1　阿拉伯国家科技发展现状 ·· 131

8.2　中阿科技合作的具体实践 ·· 137

8.3　中阿科技合作展望 ·· 144

第9章　中阿生态环境治理合作专题报告 ·· 147

9.1　阿拉伯地区生态环境现状 ·· 148

9.2　中阿生态环境治理合作现状 ·· 151

9.3 中阿生态环境治理合作展望 ·········· 156

第10章 中阿旅游合作专题报告 ·········· 161

10.1 全球旅游业发展情况 ·········· 161

10.2 阿拉伯国家旅游发展情况 ·········· 163

10.3 中阿旅游合作进展 ·········· 167

第11章 中阿博览会专题报告 ·········· 178

11.1 中阿共建"一带一路"以来中阿博览会发展回顾 ·········· 179

11.2 新形势下中阿博览会面临多重发展机遇 ·········· 185

11.3 新形势下办好中阿博览会的思路 ·········· 187

11.4 新形势下办好中阿博览会的路径 ·········· 189

第12章 宁夏对外开放专题报告 ·········· 192

12.1 宁夏推进高水平对外开放现状 ·········· 192

12.2 宁夏推进高水平开放发展趋势展望 ·········· 203

2023年中阿经贸合作大事记 ·········· 211

后 记 ·········· 223

第1章 中阿经贸合作总体形势

2023年，全球经济增速放缓，地缘格局加速调整，地区冲突多点爆发，人道危机持续恶化，粮食、能源、灾害、生态等传统安全与非传统安全风险交错叠加。2023年，中东地区局势亦在曲折动荡中复杂演进。一方面，以沙伊和解、叙利亚重返阿盟为标志的外交和解持续推进；另一方面，以新一轮巴以冲突为主线的地区冲突持续升级。在这种和解与动荡交织的背景下，2023年，中国和阿拉伯国家经贸合作以元首外交为引领，首届中国—阿拉伯国家峰会（以下简称"中阿峰会"）和首届中国—海湾阿拉伯国家合作委员会峰会（简称"中海峰会"）经贸成果后续落实为主线，实现平稳健康发展。中阿贸易量稳质升，双向投资持续升温，基础设施建设合作稳步推进，金融、绿色、数字经济等新兴领域合作不断拓展和深化。中阿经贸合作为推动共建"一带一路"高质量发展、构建面向新时代的中阿命运共同体做出重要贡献。

1.1 中阿经贸合作总体情况

1.1.1 共建"一带一路"合作实现全覆盖

2023年，适逢中国国家主席习近平提出共建"一带一路"倡议十周年。过去十年，阿拉伯国家日益成为"一带一路"建设的重要战略支点、成果富集地带和增量显著区域。2023年10月18日，第三届"一带一路"国际合作高峰论坛在北京举行，埃及总理、阿联酋总统特别代表等阿拉伯

001

领导人参会。2023 年 11 月 29 日，中国和约旦两国政府签署关于共同推进"一带一路"建设的谅解备忘录，标志着中国已同全部 22 个阿拉伯国家和阿盟签署了共建"一带一路"合作文件，实现了"全覆盖"。此外，中国国家发展改革委与巴林外交部签署了关于共同编制共建"一带一路"合作规划的意向书，将共建"一带一路"倡议与巴方"2030 经济发展愿景"深度对接，描绘了两国在金融、信息通信技术、物流、先进制造、可再生能源等领域务实合作的"路线图"，有助于推动双边关系更高质量发展。

1.1.2 中阿博览会充分展现桥梁纽带作用

经过十年的发展，中阿博览会形成了一批具有影响力和示范意义的中阿经贸合作成果，已成为中阿共建"一带一路"的重要平台。2023 年 9 月 21—24 日，第六届中阿博览会全面恢复线下举办，围绕落实中阿务实合作"八大共同行动"和中海未来 3—5 年重点合作的五大领域，在原有新兴材料展、品牌商品展、医疗康养展的基础上，首次设置了中央企业展、智慧气象展、装备制造及技术展，进一步展现中阿在经贸、能源、基础设施等领域的合作优势，并取得丰硕成果。博览会共形成合作成果 403 个，计划投资和贸易总额达 1709.7 亿元人民币，其中合作类项目 50 个，投资类项目 218 个、投资额 1571 亿元人民币，贸易类项目 135 个、贸易额 138.7 亿元人民币。其间，签订了《中卡"一园两中心"建设及光伏智慧农业技术转移合作协议》《吉赞产业集聚区战略合作协议》等合作协议 36 份，促成各类项目 58 个、金额 528.2 亿元人民币。沙特作为本届博览会的主宾国，派出 150 多人的庞大经贸代表团参会参展。其间，中沙双方围绕金融合作、能源合作、园区国际合作等方面开展了一系列推介和交流洽谈活动，达成合作项目 15 个、金额为 124 亿元人民币[①]。

---

① 《第六届中阿博览会共形成合作成果 403 个金额超 1700 亿元》，央视新闻，https://news.cctv.com/2023/09/24/ARTIGsUsNVvohybnYmZYYBpR230924.shtml，2023 年 9 月 24 日。

1.1.3　中阿贸易额略有回落

受国际油价回落等因素影响，2023 年，中阿贸易额为 3981 亿美元，同比下降 7.7%。中国继续保持阿拉伯国家最大贸易伙伴国的地位，沙特、阿联酋、伊拉克、阿曼、卡塔尔是中国在阿拉伯国家中的前五大贸易伙伴。进口方面，中国自阿拉伯国家进口额为 2167.9 亿美元，同比下滑 16.06%。在中国从阿拉伯国家进口原油总量小幅减少 2.29% 的背景下，中国进口阿拉伯国家原油累计金额为 1649.09 亿美元，同比下降 17.25%。出口方面，中国对阿拉伯国家出口额为 1812.97 亿美元，同比增长 4.69%。在中国出口整体萎缩 4.6% 的情况下，中国对 12 个阿拉伯国家实现了出口增长，表现亮眼。特别是对沙特、阿尔及利亚、摩洛哥、利比亚、毛里塔尼亚五国的出口增幅均达到两位数，其中阿尔及利亚、利比亚两国的增幅分别高达 52.4% 和 68.2%。

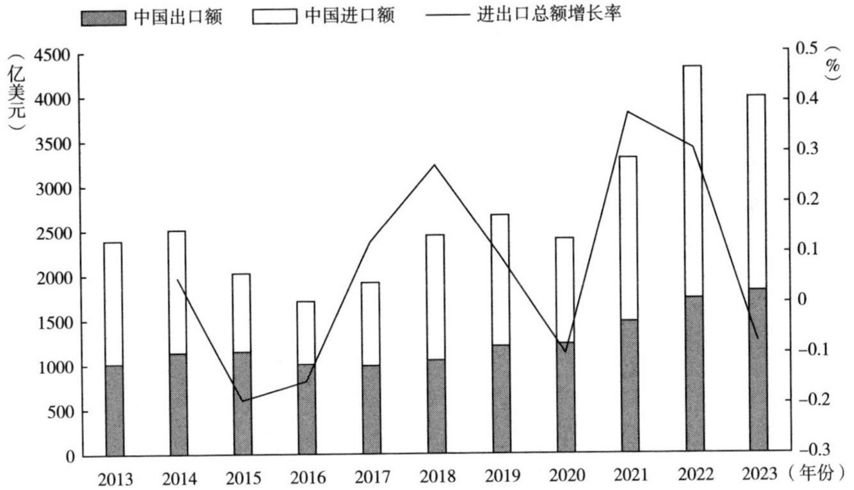

图 1.1　2013—2023 年中国同阿拉伯国家进出口总额

资料来源：海关总署。

1.1.4 双向投资持续升温

2023 年，中国对阿拉伯国家新增全行业直接投资 26.9 亿美元，同比增长 2.7%，继续保持对阿拉伯国家投资的增长态势。阿联酋、沙特和埃及是 2023 年中国在阿拉伯国家前三大投资目的地，对三国的新增直接投资分别达到 17.89 亿美元、2.79 亿美元和 2.03 亿美元。此外，阿尔及利亚、摩洛哥、毛里塔尼亚等国对中国企业的投资吸引力不断提升，2023 年新增投资同比增幅分别达到 86.47%、20.22% 和 79.92%。中国企业在阿拉伯国家投资的油气项目、加工制造项目平稳运营，建设运营的工业园区稳步推进。

2023 年，阿拉伯国家新增来华实际投资 23 亿美元，同比增长 120%。新增投资中的 99% 来自海湾阿拉伯国家。阿拉伯国家普遍看重中国的超大市场规模，在石油化工领域加大投资布局；看好中国高新产业、数字经济等市场空间和发展潜力，积极加大在半导体、新材料、新能源等领域的资产配置力度。阿联酋、沙特阿拉伯是对华投资最活跃且力度最大的阿拉伯国家。在公司层面，沙特阿拉伯国家石油公司（沙特阿美公司）在华累计投资已超千亿元人民币，成为截至 2023 年底在华累计投资最多的外国企业。

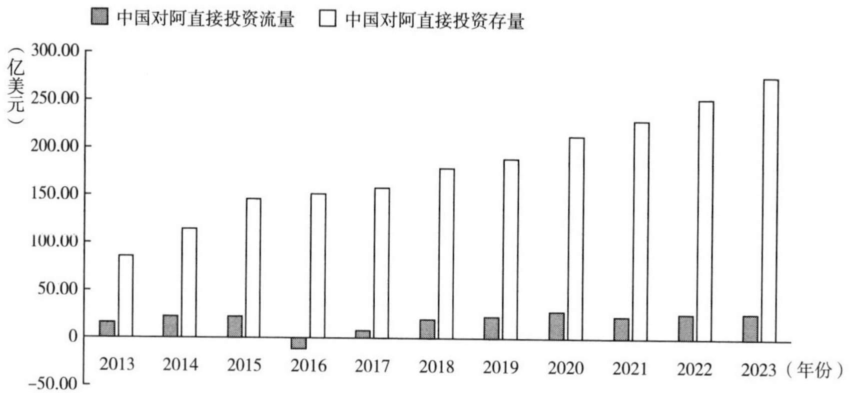

图 1.2 2013—2023 年中国对阿拉伯国家直接投资流量和存量情况

资料来源：商务部历年中国对外直接投资统计公报。

第1章　中阿经贸合作总体形势

1.2　中阿经贸合作领域态势

1.2.1　油气上下游合作持续巩固

2023 年，中阿双方携手努力，积极落实 2022 年 12 月首届中阿峰会、中海峰会精神，持续扩大在石油、天然气等传统能源领域的合作规模，不断提升合作水平。

双边交流机制日益完善。2023 年 5 月，中国国家能源局局长章建华应邀率团访问阿联酋、沙特、卡塔尔，与三国政府部门和公司负责人就油气等领域合作深入交换意见。2023 年 9 月，第七届中阿能源合作大会在海南省海口市成功举行。大会期间，中阿双方与会嘉宾围绕"秉承高质量高标准可持续　开创中阿能源合作黄金期"主题进行了深入探讨。大会还发布了成果《中阿能源合作回顾与展望》，全面回顾和梳理了中阿能源合作的历程和成果，总结了经验和启示，分析了中阿能源合作形势，提出未来合作建议。

传统贸易中油减气增。油气贸易合作始终是中阿经贸合作的"压舱石"。2023 年，中国自阿拉伯国家进口原油总量约 2.6 亿吨，同比下降 2.29%，占中国自全球原油进口总量的 47%。在前十大原油进口来源国中，阿拉伯国家占据半壁江山，依次是沙特（第二）、伊拉克（第三）、阿联酋（第五）、阿曼（第六）和科威特（第九）。天然气方面，中国自阿拉伯国家进口液化天然气总量为 1898 万吨，同比增长 10.5%，占中国自全球进口总量的 26%，金额合计为 118.9 亿美元。卡塔尔已成为中国第二大液化天然气进口来源国，液化天然气对华出口量为 1666 万吨，仅次于澳大利亚（2416 万吨）。更具里程碑意义的是，2023 年 5 月，来自阿联酋的 6.5 万吨 LNG 在广东大鹏接收站完成接卸，这是中国首单以人民币结算的进口液化天然气，标志着中国在油气贸易领域的跨境人民币结算交易探索迈出实质性一步。阿布扎比国家石油公司与新奥集团签署 15 年液化天然气供应合同，自 2028 年起每年向中国供应 100 万吨液化天然气。

005

中阿经贸关系发展进程2023年度报告

上游合作稳中有进。在上游资源开发方面，中石油、中石化、中海油、振华石油等公司在伊拉克、阿联酋、阿曼等国参与开发的油田均较好完成了生产经营指标，收获了可观的权益产量。2023年11月，美国埃克森美孚公司对外转让其在伊拉克西古尔纳-1油田的股份，中石油成为该油田的牵头作业者，中国和伊拉克石油合作进一步深化。中石化与卡塔尔能源集团于2023年4月和11月连续签署两项协议，参股获得卡塔尔北部气田扩能项目东扩新增液化天然气生产线的1.25%权益和南扩新增液化天然气生产线的1.875%权益，标志着中国油气企业首次进入卡塔尔液化天然气上游开发领域，并将自2028年起带动新增进口卡塔尔液化天然气约1100万吨/年。

下游合作升温明显。2023年3月，浙江荣盛石化和沙特阿美公司签订战略合作协议，沙方以34亿美元现金收购荣盛10%股份，双方同时签订原油及原料供应、原油储备、下游先进石化技术共享等一揽子协议。沙特阿美公司还与江苏东方盛虹、山东裕龙石化等企业先后签署了合作框架协议，有意收购这些中国民营炼化企业10%战略股权，在中国下游一体化产业布局力度持续加大。2023年4月，中沙古雷乙烯项目前期工程开工仪式在福建漳州举行，标志着这个总投资约448亿元人民币的项目正式启动。该项目由福建省能源石化集团和沙特基础工业公司共同投资开发，是福建省迄今为止一次性投资规模最大的中外合资项目，预计乙烯年产能最高可达180万吨，处于当前世界最高水平。[①]

配套合作成绩亮眼。沪东中华造船（集团）有限公司与卡塔尔石油集团自2022年建立起良好合作关系，正在执行12艘常规型17.4万立方米液化天然气船订单，合同总金额为24亿美元，进展十分顺利。在此基础上，卡方于2023年下半年启动包括44艘17.4万立方米常规型液化天然气船及18艘27.1万立方米超大型液化天然气船的招标。沪东中华造船

---

① 《中沙古雷乙烯项目又实现一重要里程碑》，福建省人民政府国有资产监督管理委员会网站，https：//gzw.fujian.gov.cn/zwgk/gzdt/gzyw/fjsnyjtyxzrgs_31446/202401/t20240122_6384411.htm#：~：text=中沙古雷乙烯项目,合作的重大项目%E3%80%82，2024年1月22日。

006

（集团）有限公司凭借领先的设计建造能力一举拿下全部 18 艘 QC Max 型 LNG 船订单，总金额逾 59 亿美元，成为全球单一造船厂赢得的最大单笔造船订单。

1.2.2 绿色能源合作成为亮点

中阿双方均面临能源结构转型和绿色发展的挑战，开展绿色清洁能源领域的合作，不仅有助于推动各自能源结构的多元化，还能为全球应对气候变化做出贡献。2023 年，中阿双方不断拓展在光伏、风能、水电、氢能、核电等清洁能源领域的合作，展现出这一合作领域的广阔发展前景。

大型合作项目不断涌现。中国企业在阿拉伯国家承建的光伏电站、风电站等已成为当地清洁能源供给的主力。中国企业承建的埃及康翁波 500 兆瓦光伏电站、苏伊士湾 500 兆瓦风电站和阿曼 Manah Ⅰ 号、Manah Ⅱ 号两个 500 兆瓦光伏电站如期开工，突尼斯凯鲁万 100 兆瓦光伏电站项目进入临建状态；沙特阿尔舒巴赫 2.6 吉瓦光伏项目进展顺利；阿布扎比风电示范项目、阿布扎比艾尔达芙拉光伏电站项目、迪拜马克图姆太阳能园光伏电站项目（4 期）先后完工；迪拜哈斯彦清洁燃煤电站 4 台机组完工并进入商业运行阶段，摩洛哥丹吉尔 34 兆瓦光伏项目开始调试并网。此外，中国企业还积极开拓新项目。中国能源建设集团有限公司、中国南方电网有限责任公司在埃及分别就绿氢项目、抽水蓄能项目与当地合作伙伴签署意向协议，中石油与中国能建洽谈组建联合体参与阿曼绿氢项目竞标。

贸易投资带动技术转移。科威特公交系统中约 95% 的传统能源公交车从中国进口，中国金龙公司生产的电动公交车于 2023 年 1 月 1 日在科威特正式投入使用，助力当地绿色交通发展。在卡塔尔，纯电动公交车占比超过 80%，几乎全部为中国制造。中国企业已不满足于单纯的贸易合作，有意通过投资建厂、技术转移等升级合作模式深化与阿拉伯国家在绿色能源领域合作，希望在阿拉伯国家减少碳排放、推动能源战略转型方面发挥重要作用。宇通客车计划与卡塔尔公交公司共同投资 2000 万美元，在卡塔尔自由区内建设新能源客车组装厂，设计年产电动大客车 500 辆。在摩洛哥，中国企业积极布局电动汽车全产业链合作，涉及电池正负极、电解液、隔膜等各环节，国轩高科就投资 64 亿美元建设电动汽车超级工厂项目与摩洛哥政府签署谅解备忘录，中伟新材料拟在摩洛哥打造绿色新能源产业园并与摩方合作伙伴组建了合资公司，上海艾郎风电已进入厂房建设的地勘阶段，宁德时代、华友钴业等公司纷纷前往摩洛哥发掘市场潜力。

1.2.3 金融合作多彩纷呈

资金融通是中阿双方共建"一带一路"的重要内容。2023 年，中国同多个阿拉伯国家在金融合作方面"多点开花"，为促进中阿各领域务实合作、实现中阿共同发展提供了有力支撑。

机制建设迈出新步伐。本币互换和人民币清算合作方面，沙特央行、阿联酋央行与中国人民银行新签、续签了双边本币互换协议，互换规模分别达到 500 亿元人民币/260 亿里亚尔、350 亿元人民币/180 亿迪拉姆，将在便利双边贸易和投资、维护金融体系稳定等方面发挥积极作用；阿联酋央行与中国人民银行签署了《关于加强央行数字货币合作的谅解备忘录》，将在金融技术创新和央行数字货币方面深化合作；中国进出口银行同沙特国民银行完成首单人民币贷款合作，贷款资金优先用于中沙两国贸易项下的资金需求；中国进出口银行同摩洛哥非洲银行于 2023 年 10 月签署合作协议，将通过项目融资、平行融资、贸易融资等方式积极推动经贸往来与金融合作，同时加强信息共享和人员交流，共同探讨使用人民币贷款。资本市场合作方面，香港交易所与沙特证交所签署合作备忘录，将在金融科技、互挂上市等领域探索合作机遇；上海证交所和迪拜金融市场签署合作谅解备忘录，计划共同探索开发 ESG（环境、社会和公司治理）和可持续发展相关产品，以及跨境指数、交易型开放式基金（ETF）等金融产品。

融资合作跨上新台阶。中国、埃及两国政府签署债转发展合作谅解备忘录；中国银行助力埃及成功发行 35 亿元人民币可持续发展熊猫债；中国国家开发银行完成与埃及中央银行 70 亿元人民币贷款协议的全额发放工作，重点支持埃及国民银行及埃及银行非洲中小企业专项贷款、埃及

500 千伏输电线路工程和中埃·泰达苏伊士经贸合作区等项目。中国出口信用保险公司承保首单中长期险新能源电力融资项目，为阿曼 Manah Ⅱ 号 500 兆瓦光伏电站项目提供中长期出口买方信贷保险支持。沙特财政部委任中国工商银行独家牵头为其筹集 110 亿美元，用于基础设施建设项目，还与中国进出口银行就"大陆桥"铁路项目混合贷款融资进行多轮磋商。

合作领域实现新突破。中国银联积极拓展阿拉伯国家支付市场，在卡塔尔等国家实现了银联卡 POS 终端全覆盖和 ATM 机 90% 以上覆盖，推动部分阿拉伯国家公交系统受理银联信用卡支付，还吸纳科威特国民银行等阿拉伯国家商业银行成为银联会员。中国工商银行迪拜分行在迪拜纳斯达克上市"一带一路"主题绿色债券，中国银行迪拜分行、中国建设银行迪拜分行各自成功发行 5.34 亿美元、6 亿美元绿色浮息债券。海湾阿拉伯国家主权财富基金扩大在华布局，阿联酋穆巴达拉投资公司北京办事处于 2023 年 9 月正式挂牌成立。科威特、卡塔尔、沙特阿拉伯和阿联酋等国主权财富基金在中国密集开展直接投资和并购交易，全年投资总金额高达 23 亿美元。2023 年第四季度，沙特未来新城（NEOM）旗下基金 NIF 向小马智行投资 1 亿美元，阿联酋科技公司 G42 通过旗下基金 CYVN 向蔚来汽车先后两次投资总计逾 30 亿美元，卡塔尔投资局宣布投资约 2 亿美元认购金蝶国际的普通股。

1.2.4　高质量产业合作有序前行

工业制造业领域的合作是中阿务实合作的重要组成部分，也是推动中阿合作取得突破的重点方向。近年来，随着阿拉伯国家经济多元化战略、工业化进程有所加快，中阿双方依托中国企业打造的境外经贸合作区等重要合作平台，围绕产业合作的高质量发展不断拓宽合作领域，不断涌现合作新趋势和新亮点。

产业集聚效应逐步显现。截至 2023 年底，中阿共建各类经贸合作区超过 16 个，帮助轻工业、重工业、农业、物流等诸多领域的中国企业实现"抱团出海"。中埃·泰达苏伊士经贸合作区已成为埃及综合环境最优、投资密度最大、单位产出最高的工业园区，累计吸引中方投资 18 亿美元、入驻企业近 150 家，初步形成新型建材、石油装备、高低压电器等产业集群，累计销售额超 43 亿美元，向埃及缴纳税费超 2 亿美元，为当地直接创造就业岗位 5000 余个，间接带动就业约 5 万人。海尔获得埃及政府颁发的"黄金许可"，投资 1.06 亿美元在当地打造家电生态园，主体工程已建设完工，2024 年第一季度投产运营后将进一步带动中国家电行业上下游企业整体"走出去"。宁夏在阿曼杜库姆经济特区打造的中国—阿曼（杜库姆）产业园一期项目明晰思路，重点聚焦油气设备产业。园内重点企业鸿通管业一期投资 600 万美元后，于 2023 年投资 200 万美元上马二期扩建项目，新增一条复合输油管生产线。天津荣亨泵业计划在园内投资 200 万美元建设年产 2000 台油田专用泵项目，已获得阿曼政府颁发的投资许可证。

产业合作主体更趋多元。2023 年，中国对阿产业投资合作主体呈现国企民企协同发力的态势。中国能源建设集团有限公司、联合能源集团有限公司、中国玻璃控股有限公司等分别与埃及苏伊士运河经济区签署产能合作协议，涉及建设氯化钾厂等重点项目，计划投资总额达 150 亿美元；宝山钢铁股份有限公司与沙特合资的总投资额 41.54 亿美元厚钢板厂项目举行开工仪式。中国巨石股份有限公司、海尔智家股份有限公司、奥特佳新能源科技股份有限公司、宁波艾尔克林电子科技有限公司等企业在埃及、约旦、摩洛哥、巴林等国投资设立玻璃纤维、洗衣机、汽车零件、空调铜管等生产加工项目，有效助力当地产业多元化发展。洛阳钼业计划投资 15 亿美元在沙特建设 50 万吨电解铝项目，协鑫科技计划与沙特共同投资 160 亿元人民币上马颗粒硅项目，二者均待沙方审批。2023 年 4 月，华新水泥以 1.9 亿美元完成对阿曼水泥公司 59.58% 股权的收购后，对其生产组织和工艺进行优化，将阿曼水泥公司产量从收购前的 4300 吨/天大幅提升至 5400 吨/天。

1.2.5 基础设施大项目合作稳步推进

阿拉伯国家是中国企业开展承包工程业务最早和最重要的市场之一。近年来，为改善民生和增加就业，阿拉伯国家普遍加大基础设施投入，中阿承包工程合作快速发展。

新签合同额稳步增长。在共建"一带一路"基础设施建设合作框架下，中国企业在阿拉伯国家新签承包工程合同额稳步增长，2023年签约额为472亿美元，同比增长28.8%，占中国企业在外新签合同总额的17.8%。沙特、阿尔及利亚、阿联酋、伊拉克、埃及是前五大市场，其中在沙特阿拉伯新签合同额高达168亿美元，同比增长72.6%，位居阿拉伯国家第一。中国企业中标了总合同额为20.5亿美元的沙特利雅得大型房地产项目，签署了价值20亿美元的伊拉克炼油厂EPC总承包合同，参与联合体中标了合同额15亿美元的阿尔及利亚石化项目。[1]

重点项目取得积极进展。2023年，中国企业在阿拉伯国家完成营业额277亿美元，同比增长9.5%，占中国企业在外完成营业总额的17.2%。中国企业承建的大型项目为沙特"2030愿景"、阿尔及利亚"新阿尔及利亚"等发展战略提供重要支撑。埃及新行政首都中央商务区内"非洲第一高楼"拔地而起，位于沙特红海新城的全球最大储能项目稳步推进，绵延1216公里的阿尔及利亚东西高速公路由"断头路"变为"致富路"，伊拉克米桑、萨拉赫丁、鲁迈拉等电站项目正式投入使用，巴林东锡特拉保障房的落成极大改善了当地民众居住条件。此外，中国北斗卫星导航系统还为阿拉伯国家提供优质应用服务，在交通运输、精准农业、国土测绘、环境监测等领域为当地民众提供便利；华为等企业积极参与埃及等国5G网络等电信基础设施建设，以人工智能、信息通信技术等帮助阿联酋、阿尔及利亚等国建设智慧城市，开展国际数字产业合作。

1.2.6 贸易结构不断优化

在中阿双方共同努力下，贸易规模不断扩大，商品结构日趋合理。中国的机电产品、高新技术产品等高附加值商品在阿拉伯国家市场上越来越受欢迎。2023年，中国对阿拉伯国家出口"新三样"（电动汽车、锂电

---

[1] 数据来源：中华人民共和国商务部。

池、太阳能电池）总额达到 48 亿美元，同比增长 10.4%，成为中阿贸易的新增长点。其中，太阳能电池、锂电池出口额分别增长 21.3% 和 6.6%，电动汽车出口量增长 32.7%。约旦海关统计显示，2023 年进口汽车中近半为电动汽车，其中 80% 产自中国。

中国积极扩大进口阿拉伯国家的非油气产品。2023 年，中国自阿拉伯国家进口果蔬类产品 1.2 亿美元，同比增长 21.1%，埃及柑橘等阿拉伯特色农产品在中国市场持续热销。目前，埃及芒果、阿联酋骆驼奶、沙特干椰枣、阿曼水产品等相继获得输华准入；中阿双方已就阿联酋生蚝输华议定书达成一致，未来将实现规模贸易。

1.3 中阿经贸合作趋势展望

2024 年是中阿合作论坛成立 20 周年，论坛第十届部长级会议在北京举办。此次部长级会议通过了《北京宣言》，回顾首届中阿峰会重要共识及峰会成果落实进展，阐明推进中阿命运共同体建设的实践路径；通过了《中国—阿拉伯国家合作论坛 2024 年至 2026 年行动执行计划》，就未来两年中阿加强论坛机制建设，推进多双边政治、经贸、投资、金融、基础设施、资源环境、人文交流、航空航天、教育卫生等各领域合作做出规划。站在新的历史起点上，中阿双方将持续深化经贸合作，积极推动高质量共建 "一带一路"，为中阿战略伙伴关系发展和中阿命运共同体建设注入新动力、谱写新篇章。

1.3.1 中阿经贸合作面临新的发展机遇

当前，阿拉伯国家正处在 "后美国时代" "后石油时代" 叠加的历史方位上。随着美国在中东地区影响力减弱，阿拉伯国家 "向东看" 势头更加明显。在经历了多年地缘冲突和意识形态对抗后，阿拉伯国家 "求稳定、谋发展" 的愿望更加迫切，将发展经济作为优先任务和突出关切，希望通过深化改革、扩大开放，实现产业发展 "弯道超车"。阿联酋、沙特

和埃及 "2030 愿景"，卡塔尔 "2035 愿景"，阿曼和科威特 "2040 愿景"，摩洛哥 "经济起飞计划" 等重大发展战略持续推进，各国改善贸易投资环境、加大对外开放力度、推进社会世俗化改革决心更加坚定，内生发展动力和自主发展能力持续提升。

未来一个时期，阿拉伯国家在基础设施、能源转型、数字经济、医疗健康等领域依然有着较强的外在需求和内在动力，与中国产业互补性和契合度极高，将成为中阿经贸合作高质量发展的发力点和新蓝海。在 2024 年 5 月召开的中阿合作论坛第十届部长级会议开幕式上，习近平主席发表的主旨讲话强调，中方愿同阿方守望相助、平等互利、包容互鉴、紧密协作，把中阿关系建设成维护世界和平稳定的标杆、高质量共建 "一带一路" 的样板、不同文明和谐共生的典范、探索全球治理正确路径的表率。[1] 习近平主席还在讲话中提出，中方愿同阿方构建 "五大合作格局"[2]，推动中阿命运共同体建设跑出加速度。"五大合作格局" 契合中阿双方共同意愿和需要，系统提出中阿在创新驱动、投资金融、能源合作、经贸互惠、人文交流等领域务实合作新倡议新举措，既统筹了双方合作优势领域，又进一步挖掘了中阿合作新潜能，拓展了中阿合作的深度和广度，助力中阿合作不断取得新突破。

1.3.2 中阿经贸合作面临的风险与挑战

展望 2024 年，中东地区形势复杂多变的基本面并未改变，不确定性、不稳定性仍较为突出，中阿经贸合作仍面临诸多困难和挑战。

一是安全风险。2023 年 10 月爆发的新一轮巴以冲突延宕未决，影响持续外溢，引发外界担忧。同时，苏丹内战再起，也门、利比亚问题陷入

---

[1] 《习近平在中阿合作论坛第十届部长级会议开幕式上的主旨讲话》，中国政府网，https://www.gov.cn/yaowen/liebiao/202405/content_6954511.htm，2024 年 5 月 30 日。

[2] "五大合作格局"，是指更富活力的创新驱动格局、更具规模的投资金融格局、更加立体的能源合作格局、更为平衡的经贸互惠格局和更广维度的人文交流格局。参见习近平《中方愿同阿方构建 "五大合作格局"》，新华网，http://www.news.cn/politics/leaders/20240530/4d0361664d6f4348aeb2f15b7bb17a91/c.html，2024 年 5 月 30 日。

僵局，地区安全局势持续恶化。特别是红海等关键航道面临严重安全危机，已对中阿货物贸易、能源贸易构成威胁，中国在部分阿拉伯国家的投资和人员财产安全等利益保护难度进一步加大。

二是政策风险。从经济发展和社会稳定看，沙特、阿联酋等海湾阿拉伯国家加速推进经济多元化，但受国际油价相对低迷等影响，经济增速放缓；埃及、突尼斯、黎巴嫩等国饱受货币贬值、通胀高企、债台高筑等冲击，发展问题严重；摩洛哥遭遇史上罕见地震，利比亚遭遇飓风，自然灾害的频发对多个阿拉伯国家的生存构成威胁。从政治格局和社会思潮看，阿拉伯国家强人政治回潮态势凸显，政党派系斗争白热化，各种新旧政治势力加速分化组合。这些因素叠加导致阿拉伯国家的贸易投资保护主义和经济政策内顾倾向有所加重，税赋水平和用工本地化比例要求居高不下，或转嫁推高外国企业在当地贸易投资等商业活动成本，对中阿经贸合作造成消极影响。

三是外部干扰风险。美国的中东战略以服务大国博弈竞争为目标，推动"印度—中东—欧洲经济走廊"（IMEC）等谋求在中东构建排华包围圈，推动多个阿拉伯国家在高科技、军工军贸、关键基础设施等领域对华脱钩。在美国威逼利诱下，个别阿拉伯国家企业被迫剥离中国业务、撤离中国市场。下阶段，美国如何调整其中东战略及在中东地区的遏华战略，沙特、阿联酋、埃及等地区大国是否会在美国"胡萝卜+大棒"政策下削减对华合作势必将对中阿经贸合作产生不可忽视的影响，值得高度关注。

1.3.3　中阿经贸合作的未来重点方向

展望未来，中国与阿拉伯国家经贸合作前景广阔。双方将继续秉持互利共赢的原则，加强贸易往来和投资合作，不断发掘传统和可再生能源、数字经济、高新技术等领域的合作潜力，不断改善贸易结构和投资合作，实现双边经贸合作的高质量发展。

在中阿合作论坛第十届部长级会议开幕式的主旨发言中，习近平主席提出："中方将同阿方进一步加强油气领域战略合作，对接供应安全和市场安全；愿同阿方联合开展新能源技术研发和装备生产。中方将支持中国能源企业和金融机构在阿拉伯国家参与总装机容量超过 300 万千瓦的可再生能源项目。"① 在此指引下，中国将与阿拉伯国家加强石油、天然气等传统领域合作，继续扩大石油和天然气进口，加强油气上游开发、工程服务、储运炼化合作；积极因应阿拉伯国家"能源清洁化"转型诉求，探索新能源领域合作机会，加强氢能、储能、风电、光伏、智能电网等清洁低碳能源技术合作和新能源设备本地化生产合作，共同推动能源结构的转型和升级，实现双方绿色可持续发展。

习近平主席还提出："中方将同阿方在生命健康、人工智能、绿色低碳、现代农业、空间信息等领域共建 10 家联合实验室；愿同阿方加强人工智能领域合作，共同促进人工智能赋能实体经济，推动形成具有广泛共识的全球人工智能治理体系；愿同阿方共建空间碎片联合观测中心、北斗应用合作发展中心，加强载人航天、民用客机等合作。"② 中国将与阿拉伯国家继续加强在跨境电商、智慧城市、信息通信等数字经济和人工智能、生物制药、航空航天等高新技术领域的"产学研"一体合作，促进中国与阿拉伯国家在高新技术领域的共同发展。

在经贸互惠方面，习近平主席提出："中方将继续积极推动实施 30 亿元人民币的发展合作项目；愿同阿方加快双边和区域自由贸易协定谈判，推动电子商务合作对话机制建设。中方欢迎阿方积极参加中国国际进口博览会，愿扩大自阿方进口非能源类产品特别是农食产品。"③ 中阿双方将努力改善双边贸易结构，促进贸易均衡发展；提升贸易自由化、便利化水平，为双边贸易投资创造更为广阔的发展空间。

在投资合作方面，习近平主席提出："中方愿同阿方设立产业与投资

---

① 习近平：《深化合作，继往开来：推动中阿命运共同体建设跑出加速度——在中阿合作论坛第十届部长级会议开幕式上的主旨讲话》，人民出版社，2024，第 5 页。

② 习近平：《深化合作，继往开来：推动中阿命运共同体建设跑出加速度——在中阿合作论坛第十届部长级会议开幕式上的主旨讲话》，人民出版社，2024，第 4—5 页。

③ 习近平：《深化合作，继往开来：推动中阿命运共同体建设跑出加速度——在中阿合作论坛第十届部长级会议开幕式上的主旨讲话》，人民出版社，2024，第 5 页。

合作论坛，继续推进中阿银联体扩容，加快实施中东工业化专项贷款、中阿金融合作专项贷款合作项目。中方支持双方金融机构加强合作，欢迎阿拉伯国家在华发行'熊猫债'，欢迎阿方银行机构加入人民币跨境支付清算系统，愿同阿方深化央行数字货币领域交流合作。"[1] 中阿双方金融机构可就此探索更为灵活多样的合作模式，为贸易、投资、基础设施各领域务实合作提供更为便利、高效的金融服务支撑。

---

[1] 习近平：《深化合作，继往开来：推动中阿命运共同体建设跑出加速度——在中阿合作论坛第十届部长级会议开幕式上的主旨讲话》，人民出版社，2024，第5页。

第2章　中阿贸易合作专题报告

2023 年以来，全球经济和需求复苏不及预期，多边贸易规则受到冲击，贸易保护主义抬头，全球产业链供应链加快重构，贸易格局呈现日益动荡和不稳定局面。乌克兰危机、巴以冲突及其外溢加剧了地缘政治局势紧张，使得国际经贸环境日趋严峻复杂，国际贸易风险和成本急剧上升。经历新冠疫情冲击后，中国经济运行逐渐好转，但是周期性和结构性问题逐渐显化，内需不足叠加外需收缩，外贸发展面临巨大的挑战和不确定性。在如此复杂严峻的背景下，中国加强顶层设计，不断完善外贸政策体系，提升外贸企业活力和韧性，培育外贸竞争新优势，积极推动外贸转型，外贸规模和质效持续提升，稳中有进，实现了新的突破。

2.1　中国对阿拉伯国家贸易状况

2.1.1　中国对外贸易基本状况

面对复杂严峻的外部形势，中国外贸承压前行，总体呈现平稳发展态势，展现出较强的发展韧性和创新活力，为国民经济持续恢复向好做出了积极贡献。

2023 年，中国进出口总额为 58322 亿美元，领先第二名美国 0.75 万亿美元，连续 7 年保持全球货物贸易第一大国地位。具体来看，中国出口总额为 33797.48 亿美元，尽管同比下降 5.95%，但仍占据 14.2% 的国际市场份额，与 2022 年持平，连续 15 年保持全球出口第一。同时，中国进口总额也达到 24524.67 亿美元，同比下降 5.42%，国际市场份额为 10.6%，较 2022 年略有增长，连续 15 年位列全球进口第二。在世界经济艰难复苏的大背景下，中国保持了国际市场份额的总体稳定，显示出较强的发展韧性。

表 2.1　2013—2023 年中国对外贸易额及增长速度

年份	进出口贸易		出口贸易		进口贸易		贸易差额	
	总额（亿美元）	同比（%）	金额（亿美元）	同比（%）	金额（亿美元）	同比（%）	金额（亿美元）	同比（%）
2013	40014	7.45	22090.07	7.82	17924.51	6.99	4165.56	11.52
2014	41566	3.88	23422.93	6.03	18143.54	1.22	5279.39	26.74
2015	38096	−8.35	22734.68	−2.94	15361.95	−15.33	7372.73	39.65
2016	36855	−3.26	20976.37	−7.73	15879.21	3.37	5097.16	−30.86
2017	39747	7.85	22633.71	7.90	17114.24	7.78	5519.47	8.29
2018	44828	12.78	24942.30	10.20	19886.01	16.20	5056.29	−8.39
2019	45675	1.89	24985.78	0.17	20689.50	4.04	4296.20	−15.03
2020	46462	1.72	25906.01	3.68	20555.91	−0.65	5350.10	24.53
2021	60467	30.14	33623.02	29.79	26843.63	30.59	6779.39	26.72
2022	61867	2.31	35936.01	6.88	25931.14	−3.40	10004.87	47.58
2023	58322	−5.73	33797.48	−5.95	24524.67	−5.42	9272.81	−7.32

注：以中国为报告国。

分类依据：HS2007。

资料来源：根据联合国国际贸易数据库数据整理计算。

2023 年以来，中国外贸市场多元化成效显著，区域合作步伐加快，与共建"一带一路"国家的贸易规模不断扩大。2023 年，中国前十位贸易伙伴分别为东盟、欧盟、美国、阿拉伯国家、日本、韩国、俄罗斯、越南、澳大利亚和德国，中国对其贸易额占贸易总额的比重达到 75.31%，其中，对东盟、欧盟、美国、阿拉伯国家贸易比重分别为 15.63%、15.11%、11.43%、6.82%，合计占贸易总额的 48.99%。与 2022 年相比，阿拉伯国家依旧稳居中国第四大贸易伙伴，俄罗斯则跃居中国第七大贸易伙伴。

出口方面，欧盟依然是中国最大出口目的地，东盟超过美国居第二，美国、阿拉伯国家和日本分别位居第三、第四、第五，阿拉伯国家稳居中国第四大出口贸易伙伴。进口方面，排名依次是东盟、欧盟、阿拉伯国家、美国、韩国、日本、俄罗斯、巴西、德国和马来西亚。阿拉伯国家稳居中国第三大进口贸易伙伴。

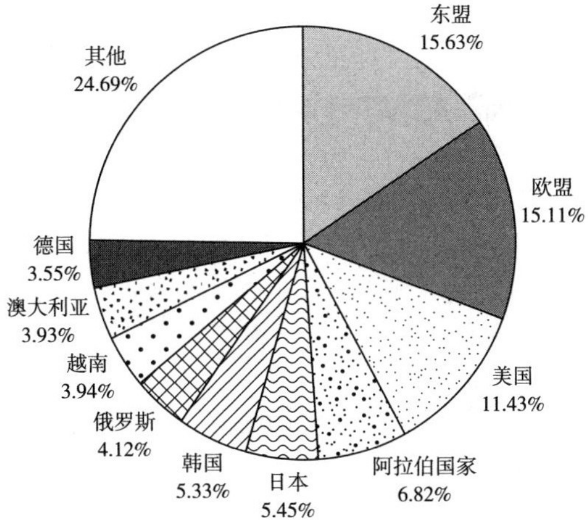

图 2.1　2023 年中国对前十位贸易伙伴贸易额占总贸易额比重
注：以中国为报告国。
分类依据：HS2007。
资料来源：根据联合国国际贸易数据库数据整理计算。

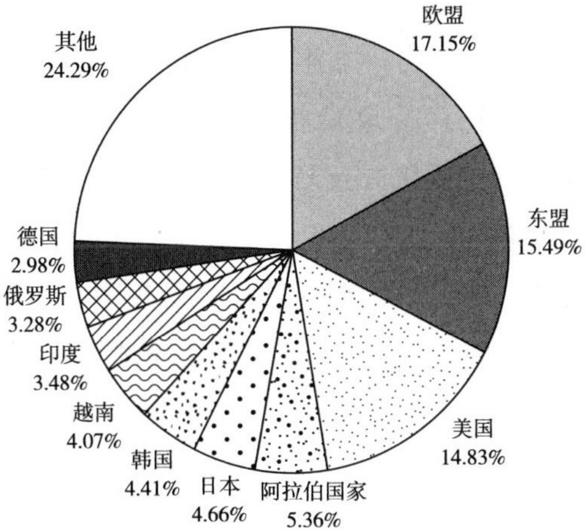

图 2.2　2023 年中国对前十位出口贸易伙伴出口额占总出口额比重
注：以中国为报告国。
分类依据：HS2007。
资料来源：根据联合国国际贸易数据库数据整理计算。

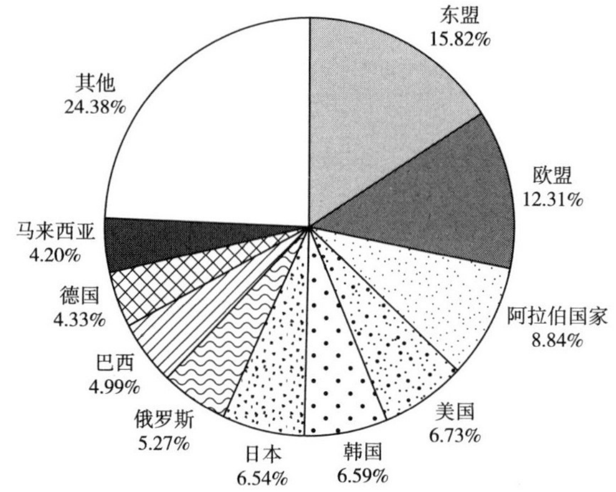

中阿经贸关系发展进程2023年度报告

图 2.3 2023 年中国对前十位进口贸易伙伴进口额占总进口额比重

注：以中国为报告国。

分类依据：HS2007。

资料来源：根据联合国国际贸易数据库数据整理计算。

2.1.2 中国对外服务贸易状况

2022 年，中国服务贸易稳中有增，规模创历史新高。由表 2.2 可知，中国服务贸易进出口总额、出口总额、进口总额从 2013 年到 2022 年发展趋势以上升为主，服务贸易规模整体不断扩大。根据世界贸易组织（WTO）数据，2022 年中国服务贸易进出口总额为 8477 亿美元，同比增长 1.7%。其中，出口额为 4543 亿美元，同比增长 15.8%；进口额为 3934 亿美元，同比下降 10.8%。中国服务贸易主要集中在与贸易有关的服务，运输服务，其他商业服务，电信、计算机和信息服务，知识产权服务，保险和金融服务等方面。与上一年相比，服务贸易分类结构变化不大。出口方面，与贸易有关的服务占比最高，达到 29.90%，运输服务占比为 27.66%，其他商业服务占比为 19.59%，电信、计算机和信息服务占比为 17.73%，知识产权服务占比为 2.98%，保险和金融服务占比为 2.14%。进口方面，运输服务占比最高，达到 33.81%，与贸易有关的服务占比为 26.53%，其他商业服务占比为 12.30%，知识产权服务占比为 11.29%，

020

电信、计算机和信息服务占比为 9.81%，保险和金融服务占比为 6.26%。

由于所处经济发展阶段和技术水平等因素，中国服务贸易竞争力相对欧美发达国家而言较弱，一直以来贸易额呈现逆差状态。据表 2.2 可知，2013 年中国服务贸易逆差额为 1236 亿美元，2018 年逆差额最大，为 2550 亿美元，2019 年以来逆差额以逐年收窄趋势为主，2022 年服务贸易逆差额下降为 609 亿美元，与 2018 年相比逆差额下降幅度较大。

表 2.2　2013—2022 年中国对外服务贸易额及增长速度

年份	进出口贸易		出口贸易		进口贸易		净出口额	
	金额（亿美元）	同比（%）	金额（亿美元）	同比（%）	金额（亿美元）	同比（%）	金额（亿美元）	同比（%）
2013	5376	11.3	2070	2.7	3306	17.5	−1236	55.08
2014	6520	21.3	2191	5.9	4329	30.9	−2138	72.98
2015	6541	0.3	2186	−0.2	4355	0.6	−2169	1.45
2016	6616	1.1	2095	−4.2	4521	3.8	−2426	11.85
2017	6957	5	2281	8.9	4676	3.4	−2395	−1.28
2018	7822	12.4	2636	15.5	5186	10.9	−2550	6.47
2019	7839	0.2	2832	7.4	5007	−3.5	−2175	−14.71
2020	6617	−14.9	2806	−0.9	3811	−23.9	−1005	−53.79
2021	8335	24.9	3922	39.8	4413	25.8	−491	−51.14
2022	8477	1.7	4543	15.8	3934	−10.8	−609	24.03

资料来源：根据 WTO（世界贸易组织）网站数据整理计算。

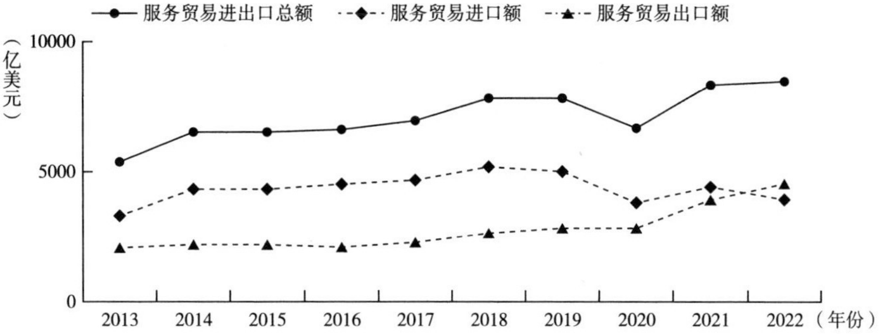

图 2.4　2013—2022 年中国服务贸易趋势

资料来源：根据 WTO（世界贸易组织）网站数据整理计算。

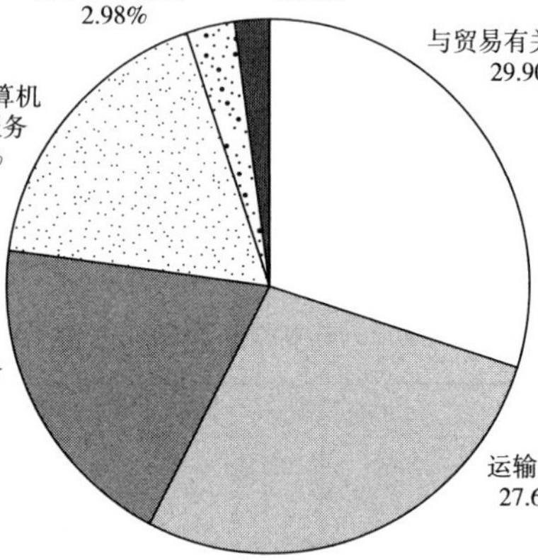

中阿经贸关系发展进程2023年度报告

知识产权服务 2.98%

保险和金融服务 2.14%

电信、计算机和信息服务 17.73%

与贸易有关的服务 29.90%

其他商业服务 19.59%

运输服务 27.66%

图 2.5 2022 年中国出口各服务贸易额占总出口服务贸易额比重

注：以中国为报告国。

资料来源：根据 WTO（世界贸易组织）网站数据整理计算。

保险和金融服务 6.26%

电信、计算机和信息服务 9.81%

运输服务 33.81%

知识产权服务 11.29%

其他商业服务 12.30%

与贸易有关的服务 26.53%

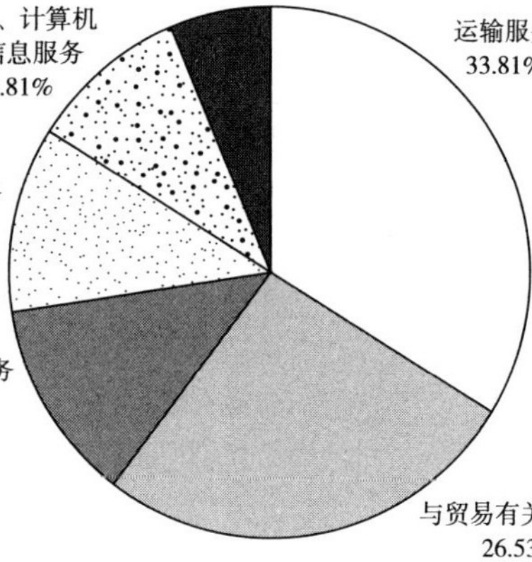

图 2.6 2022 年中国进口各服务贸易额占总进口服务贸易额比重

注：以中国为报告国。

资料来源：根据 WTO（世界贸易组织）网站数据整理计算。

2.1.3 中国对阿拉伯国家贸易基本状况

虽然 2023 年对外经贸环境复杂多变，但是中阿贸易合作持续稳定推进，双方贸易关系进一步深化。

2023 年，中国对阿拉伯国家的进出口贸易总额达到 3981.00 亿美元，较 2022 年下降 7.69%。其中，中国对阿拉伯国家出口贸易总额为 1813.00 亿美元，较 2022 年增长 4.79%；中国从阿拉伯国家进口贸易总额为 2168.00 亿美元，较 2022 年下降 16.06%（见表 2.3）。如图 2.7 所示，虽然 2023 年中国对阿拉伯国家的进出口总额、进口额有小幅下降，但中阿贸易总体呈波动上升趋势。面对百年变局叠加世纪疫情带来的全球挑战，中阿合作并没有暂停，而是展现出旺盛活力，中国已连续多年成为阿拉伯国家的最大贸易伙伴国。

表 2.3　2013—2023 年中国对阿拉伯国家贸易额

年份	进出口贸易		出口贸易		进口贸易		净出口额	
	总额（亿美元）	同比（%）	金额（亿美元）	同比（%）	金额（亿美元）	同比（%）	金额（亿美元）	同比（%）
2013	2388.97	7.41	1013.52	11.03	1375.45	4.88	−361.93	−9.20
2014	2510.51	5.09	1138.21	12.30	1372.30	−0.23	−234.09	−35.32
2015	2025.41	−19.32	1150.40	1.07	875.01	−36.24	275.38	117.64
2016	1710.29	−15.56	1006.74	−12.49	703.56	−19.59	303.18	10.10
2017	1917.57	12.12	986.73	−1.99	930.84	32.30	55.89	−181.57
2018	2445.67	27.57	1053.10	6.70	1392.57	49.60	−339.47	−807.39
2019	2662.01	8.85	1205.21	14.44	1456.82	4.61	−251.61	−25.88
2020	2393.43	−10.09	1227.99	1.89	1165.44	−20.00	62.55	124.86
2021	3301.90	37.96	1473.12	19.96	1828.78	56.92	−355.66	−668.60
2022	4312.84	30.62	1730.14	17.45	2582.69	41.22	−852.55	139.71
2023	3981.00	−7.69	1813.00	4.79	2168.00	−16.06	−355.00	−58.36

注：以中国为报告国。

分类依据：HS2007。

资料来源：2013—2022 年数据根据联合国国际贸易数据库整理计算，2023 年数据根据中华人民共和国商务部发布的数据整理计算。

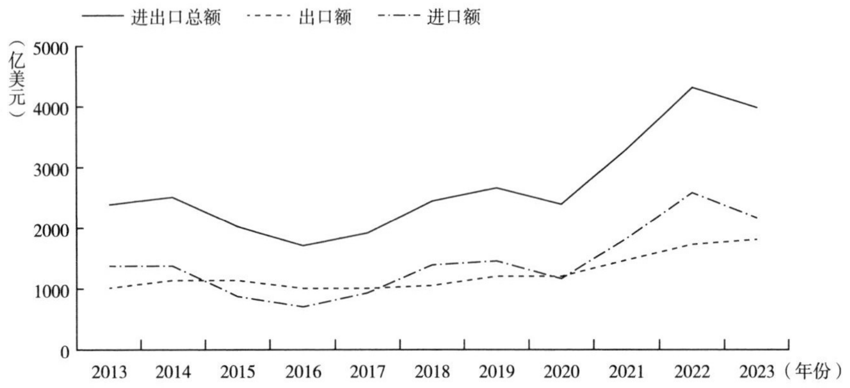

图 2.7　2013—2023 年中国与阿拉伯国家贸易趋势

注：以中国为报告国。

分类依据：HS2007。

资料来源：2013—2022 年数据根据联合国国际贸易数据库数据整理计算，2023 年数据根据中华人民共和国商务部发布的数据整理计算。

2.2　阿拉伯国家对中国贸易状况

2.2.1　阿拉伯国家对外贸易基本状况

阿拉伯国家对外贸易额于 2013 年达到 19903.86 亿美元后，由于石油价格下降、地区局势动荡等，其对外贸易额从 2014 年到 2017 年连续四年下跌（见表 2.4）。油价在持续数年走低后，于 2018 年上涨，而后又因复杂多变、动荡不安的局势以及新冠疫情等影响，2019 年、2020 年都出现了不同程度的下跌。2021 年，全球经济开始复苏，原油价格整体呈现震荡上行走势，阿拉伯国家对外贸易总额大幅度上升，2021 年对外贸易总额为 16607.35 亿美元，相比 2020 年上升了 45.70%。相对来说，石油减产等可能是重要原因。2022 年，阿拉伯国家的对外贸易总额为 15916.44 亿美元，相比 2021 年下降了 4.16%，特别是出口额，下降至 8002.35 亿美元，同比减少了 8.54%。2023 年，阿拉伯国家的对外贸易总额继续下降至 14205.02 亿美元，相比 2022 年下降了 10.75%；出口额下降至

6667.90 亿美元，同比减少 16.68%；进口额下降至 7537.13 亿美元，同比减少 4.76%。

表 2.4　2013—2023 年阿拉伯国家对外贸易额及增长速度

年份	进出口贸易		出口贸易		进口贸易		贸易差额	
	总额（亿美元）	同比（%）	金额（亿美元）	同比（%）	金额（亿美元）	同比（%）	金额（亿美元）	同比（%）
2013	19903.86	2.35	12088.30	-1.64	7815.56	9.21	4272.74	-16.76
2014	19208.59	-3.49	11205.41	-7.30	8003.18	2.40	3202.23	-25.05
2015	14392.32	-25.07	7091.00	-36.72	7301.32	-8.77	-210.33	-106.57
2016	13007.05	-9.63	6264.12	-11.66	6742.93	-7.65	-478.80	-127.64
2017	12838.43	-1.30	6744.69	7.67	6093.74	-9.63	650.95	235.95
2018	18598.23	44.86	9974.09	47.88	8624.14	41.52	1349.95	107.38
2019	14080.79	-24.29	7335.58	-26.45	6745.21	-21.79	590.37	-143.73
2020	11398.47	-19.05	5712.96	-22.12	5685.51	-15.71	27.45	-95.35
2021	16607.35	45.70	8749.95	53.16	7857.40	38.20	892.55	3151.52
2022	15916.44	-4.16	8002.35	-8.54	7914.10	0.72	88.25	-90.11
2023	14205.02	-10.75	6667.90	-16.68	7537.13	-4.76	-869.23	-10.85

注：以阿拉伯国家为报告国。

分类依据：HS2007。

资料来源：根据联合国国际贸易数据库数据整理计算。

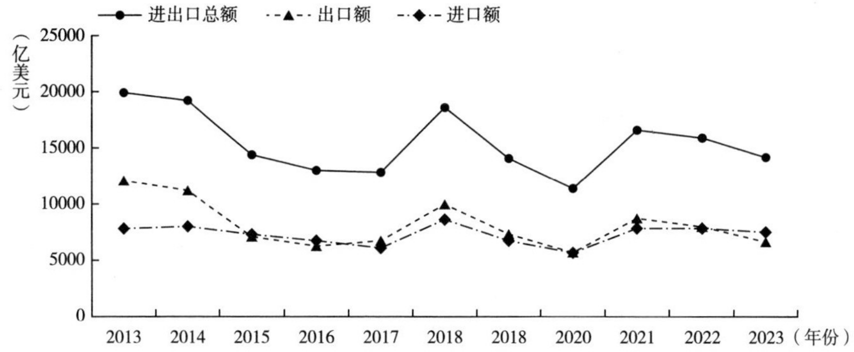

图 2.8　2013—2023 年阿拉伯国家对外贸易趋势

注：以阿拉伯国家为报告国。

分类依据：HS2007。

资料来源：根据联合国国际贸易数据库数据整理计算。

中阿经贸关系发展进程2023年度报告

2023 年，阿拉伯国家前四位贸易伙伴分别为欧盟、中国、印度、美国，进出口额分别占阿拉伯国家贸易总额的 14.44%、9.75%、5.20%、4.35%，合计占进出口总额的 33.74%（见图 2.9）。与 2022 年相比，阿拉伯国家前四位贸易伙伴位次未发生变化。

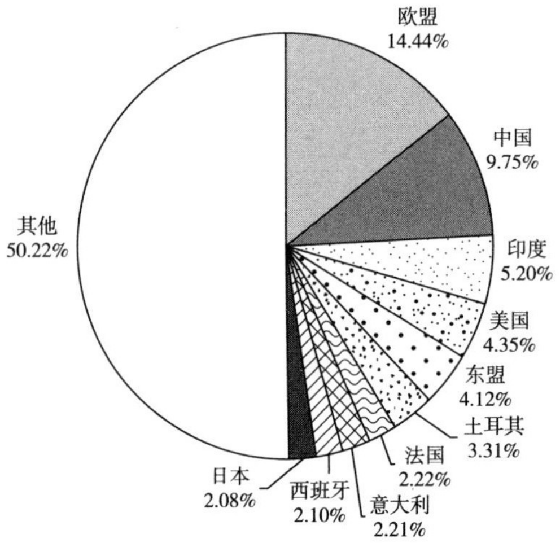

图 2.9　2023 年阿拉伯国家对前十位贸易伙伴进出口总额占比
注：以阿拉伯国家为报告国。
分类依据：HS2007。
资料来源：根据联合国国际贸易数据库数据整理计算。

2.2.2　阿拉伯国家服务贸易基本状况

2022 年，阿拉伯国家服务贸易进出口总额为 4555.35 亿美元，其中，出口额为 2144.99 亿美元，进口额为 2410.36 亿美元。服务贸易的进出口总额、进口额与 2021 年相比都出现不同程度的下降，进出口总额同比下降 5.81%，进口额同比下降 12.37%。服务贸易出口表现较好，2022 年同比增长 2.85%（见表 2.5、图 2.10）。2022 年，阿拉伯国家服务贸易出口额占世界服务贸易出口总额的比重为 3.51%，较 2021 年的 3.43% 上升 0.08 个百分点，总体变化不大，基本保持稳定。

026

阿拉伯国家服务贸易自 2013 年以来就一直处于逆差状态，2014 年逆差额达到峰值 1684 亿美元，此后逆差在波动中逐年缩小，2022 年服务贸易逆差额为 265.37 亿美元，较 2021 年逆差额下降 60.10%。从出口结构来看，阿拉伯国家服务贸易出口主要集中在运输服务（34.02%），与贸易有关的服务（26.94%），保险和金融服务（17.13%），电信、计算机与信息服务（10.26%）等方面。从进口结构来看，阿拉伯国家服务贸易进口主要是：运输服务（36.85%），保险和金融服务（25.58%），与贸易有关的服务（17.21%），其他商业服务（11.45%），电信、计算机与信息服务（5.84%）。

表 2.5　2013—2022 年阿拉伯国家服务贸易进出口额及增长速度

年份	进出口贸易		出口贸易		进口贸易		差额（亿美元）
	总额（亿美元）	同比（%）	金额（亿美元）	同比（%）	金额（亿美元）	同比（%）	
2013	4220.32	3.5	1324.40	1.4	2895.92	4.5	−1571.52
2014	5268.17	24.8	1792.08	35.3	3476.09	20.0	−1684.00
2015	5029.84	−4.5	1812.73	1.2	3217.12	−7.5	−1404.39
2016	4859.74	−3.4	1825.64	0.7	3034.10	−5.7	−1208.46
2017	4846.27	−0.3	1910.41	4.6	2935.87	−3.2	−1025.46
2018	4810.82	−0.7	2027.81	6.1	2783.01	−5.2	−755.20
2019	5263.35	9.41	2174.80	7.25	3088.54	10.98	−913.74
2020	4018.71	−23.65	1595.00	−26.66	2423.71	−21.53	−828.71
2021	4836.16	20.34	2085.51	30.75	2750.65	13.49	−665.14
2022	4555.35	−5.81	2144.99	2.85	2410.36	−12.37	−265.37

资料来源：根据 WTO（世界贸易组织）网站数据整理计算。

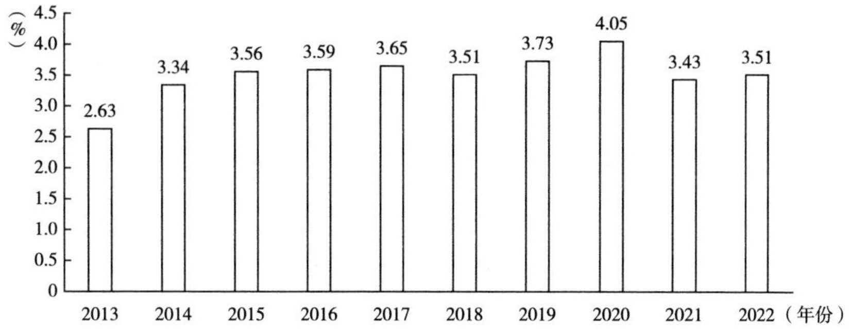

图 2.10　2013—2022 年阿拉伯国家服务贸易出口额占世界服务贸易出口总额比重

资料来源：根据 WTO（世界贸易组织）数据库数据整理计算。

中阿经贸关系发展进程2023年度报告

从阿拉伯国家服务贸易出口看，2022年，服务贸易出口额居前五位的国家依次是阿联酋、卡塔尔、沙特、埃及、科威特。阿联酋是该地区服务贸易出口规模最大的国家，出口额达到934.72亿美元，较2021年下降0.82%；卡塔尔位列第二，排名较2021年上升了一位，出口额294.09亿美元，较2021年增长60.30%；沙特居第三位，排名较2021年上升了四位，出口额226.88亿美元，较2021年增长120.21%；埃及位列第四，排名较2021年下降了两位，出口额167.00亿美元，较2021年下降23.73%；科威特位居第五，排名较2021年上升了一位，出口额为119.43亿美元，较2021年增长10.20%。2022年，除数据缺失外，服务贸易出口最少的阿拉伯国家是科摩罗，出口额为0.18亿美元（见表2.6）。

表2.6　2015—2022年阿拉伯各国服务贸易出口额

单位：亿美元

国别	2015年	2016年	2017年	2018年	2019年	2020年	2021年	2022年
阿尔及利亚	34.55	34.33	32.61	30.40	—	32	30.25	48.53
巴林	91.13	109.98	111.3	119.15	115.78	114.68	132.25	109.37
科摩罗	0.84	—	—	—	—	0.68	0.51	0.18
吉布提	4.55	4.06	—	2.09	11.04	—	—	8.85
埃及	185.39	136.06	200.33	229.06	209.32	150.53	218.97	167.00
伊拉克	62.60	48.35	—	53.06	66.37	38.03	43.73	65.20
约旦	62.69	60.35	67.20	70.21	79.65	24.59	44.03	21.50
科威特	60.56	55.29	51.63	76.17	82.39	72.55	108.38	119.43
黎巴嫩	159.1	151.93	160.8	152.95	150.68	50.06	—	—
利比亚	4.83	0.86	—	—	1	—	—	12.40
毛里塔尼亚	2.46	2.70	—	—	—	1.83	1.93	2.33
摩洛哥	146.74	153.79	172.61	178.94	193.7	138.55	154.61	112
阿曼	33.79	36.04	—	—	—	18.30	—	40.70
卡塔尔	149.97	151.76	177.06	177.80	190.80	194.29	183.46	294.09

续表

国别	2015 年	2016 年	2017 年	2018 年	2019 年	2020 年	2021 年	2022 年
沙特	144.74	172.53	180.21	173.86	241.82	102.48	103.03	226.88
索马里	3.55	3.73	3.93	4.05	—	—	—	2.79
苏丹	17.27	15.45	15.17	14.86	13.68	12.30	18.80	1.87
叙利亚	—	—	—	—	—	—	—	—
突尼斯	32.94	32.49	32.60	36.43	42.73	22.75	27.18	20.1
阿联酋	607.76	655.96	704.97	708.78	734.65	621.38	1018.38	934.72
也门	7.28	—	—	—	—	—	—	2.06

注:"—"代表数据缺失。

资料来源:根据 WTO(世界贸易组织)网站数据整理计算。

从服务贸易进口来看,2022 年阿联酋依然位居第一,服务贸易进口额为 732.10 亿美元;沙特居第二位,进口额为 479.86 亿美元;卡塔尔位居第三,进口额为 232.59 亿美元。埃及位居第四,伊拉克超过科威特位居第五,它们的进口额分别为 220.72 亿美元和 129.51 亿美元。其中,海合会依然是阿拉伯国家服务贸易进口总额占比最高的区域一体化组织,高达 71.96%。2022 年,除数据缺失外,服务贸易进口额最少的国家为科摩罗,仅为 1.42 亿美元(见表 2.7)。

表 2.7 2015—2022 年阿拉伯各国服务贸易进口额

单位:亿美元

国别	2015 年	2016 年	2017 年	2018 年	2019 年	2020 年	2021 年	2022 年
阿尔及利亚	110.77	108.81	115.99	104.52	—	80.03	66.64	68.67
巴林	65.92	75.3	76.42	79.39	80.83	92.63	102.89	84.32
科摩罗	0.83	—	—	—	—	0.97	1.14	1.42
吉布提	2.30	1.99	—	2.02	6.20	—	—	8.73
埃及	175.19	170.32	173.99	178.34	209.32	181.99	229.51	200.72
伊拉克	126.20	100.37	—	177.85	244.93	137.96	132.55	129.51

029

续表

国别	2015 年	2016 年	2017 年	2018 年	2019 年	2020 年	2021 年	2022 年
约旦	45.28	45.65	46.70	46.62	47.85	30.10	41.08	45.95
科威特	237.96	263.48	285.66	335.67	300.67	189.92	206.75	112.01
黎巴嫩	136.93	132.80	138.53	143.38	144.49	57.46	—	—
利比亚	46.58	28.83	—	—	62.67	—	—	44.09
毛里塔尼亚	6.41	6.05				8.45	7.82	9.82
摩洛哥	79.13	86.04	97.94	92.97	101.84	70.88	85.26	99.59
阿曼	102.14	99.46	—	—	—	55.39	—	93.54
卡塔尔	307.75	315.41	314.27	307.35	354.16	346.98	343.40	232.59
沙特	880.36	702.67	768.18	554.77	749.73	538.83	732.81	479.86
索马里	13.28	13.35	14.52	14.78	—	—	—	21.53
苏丹	17.79	15.07	19.06	6.07	14.23	13.22	13.91	6.00
叙利亚	—	—	—	—	—	—	—	—
突尼斯	30.76	30.11	29.62	29.41	30.98	23.67	25.83	25.89
阿联酋	818.79	838.39	855	709.87	740.64	595.23	761.06	732.10
也门	12.75	—	—	—	—	—	—	14.01

注："—"代表数据缺失。

资料来源：根据 WTO（世界贸易组织）网站数据整理计算。

2.2.3 阿拉伯国家对中国出口状况

自 2013 年"一带一路"倡议提出以来，阿拉伯国家积极响应，双方充分发挥资源禀赋和产业互补优势，贸易合作取得了飞速发展。2023 年，中阿双边贸易总额实现强势增长，贸易总额首次突破 4312.84 亿美元，阿拉伯国家对中国出口额达到 2582.69 亿美元，较 2021 年增长 41.22%；进口额为 1730.14 亿美元，较 2021 年增长 17.45%。2023 年，中阿双边贸易总额为 3981.00 亿美元，其中，出口额为 2168.00 亿美元，较 2022 年下降 15.97%，进口额为 1813.00 亿美元，较 2022 年增长 4.79%。虽然 2023 年

030

贸易总额和出口额相比 2022 年有所减少，但是，总的来说，2013—2023
年，中国与阿拉伯国家的平均贸易增速高于中国对外贸易增速，同时，平
均增速也高于中国对共建"一带一路"国家的平均增速，显示出双方贸易
增长具有强劲动力。自 2013 年起，中国成为阿拉伯国家的第一大贸易伙
伴国，阿拉伯国家对中国的贸易额占阿拉伯国家全部贸易额的 12.00%，
2022 年这一比重上升到 27.10%，2023 年上升到 28.02%（见图 2.11）。
双方贸易伙伴地位进一步提升和加强。

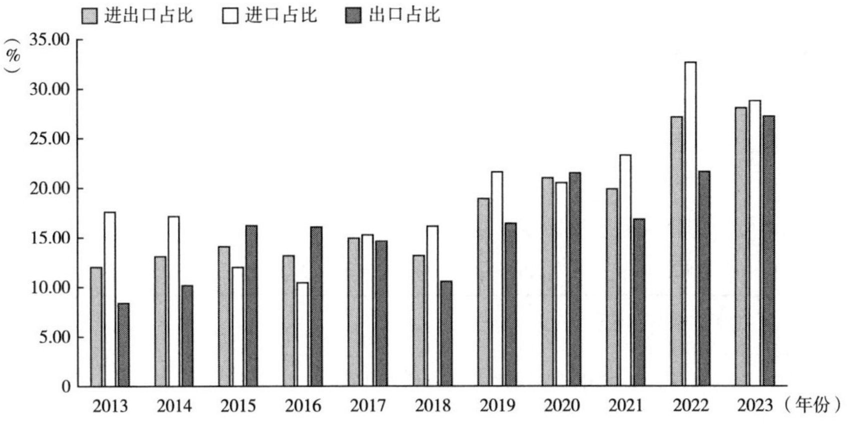

图 2.11 2013—2023 年阿拉伯国家对中国贸易额占阿拉伯国家贸易额比重

　　注：以阿拉伯国家为报告国。

　　分类依据：HS2007。

　　资料来源：根据联合国国际贸易数据库数据整理计算。

　　中国与海合会国家经贸互补性强，海合会国家是中国能源的重要供给
方。近年来，双方经贸往来日益密切，经贸合作不断深化拓展。2023 年，
海合会国家与中国贸易进出口总额达到 2859.77 亿美元，占中阿贸易进出
口总额的 71.83%。其中海合会国家对中国出口 1732.33 亿美元，占阿拉
伯国家对中国出口的 79.90%；进口 1127.44 亿美元，占阿拉伯国家对中
国进口的 62.19%（见表 2.8、图 2.12、图 2.13）。海合会国家在中阿贸
易合作中占据最为重要的地位。

中阿经贸关系发展进程2023年度报告

表 2.8　2013—2023 年海合会国家对中国贸易总体情况

年份	进出口贸易		进口贸易		出口贸易	
	总额（亿美元）	占比（%）	金额（亿美元）	占比（%）	金额（亿美元）	占比（%）
2013	1653.47	69.21	596.77	58.88	1056.70	76.83
2014	1751.83	69.78	685.90	60.30	1065.93	77.67
2015	1366.15	67.45	678.10	58.98	688.05	78.63
2016	1122.8	65.65	561.73	55.83	561.08	79.75
2017	1280.29	66.77	551.13	55.89	729.16	78.33
2018	1628.91	66.60	572.88	54.40	1056.03	75.83
2019	1792.59	67.34	681.50	38.02	1111.06	61.98
2020	1614.06	67.44	905.78	77.72	708.28	57.68
2021	2328.97	70.53	874.15	59.34	1454.82	79.55
2022	3158.00	73.22	1067.88	61.72	2090.12	80.93
2023	2859.77	71.83	1127.44	62.19	1732.33	79.90

注：以海合会国家为报告国。

分类依据：HS2007。

资料来源：根据联合国国际贸易数据库数据整理计算。

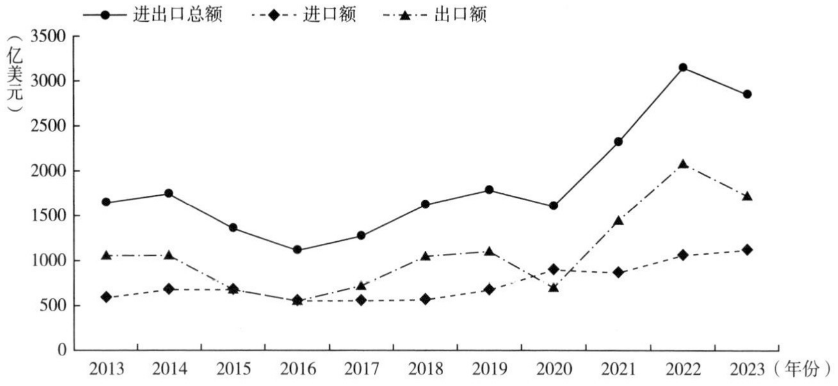

图 2.12　2013—2023 年海合会国家对中国贸易趋势

注：以海合会国家为报告国。

分类依据：HS2007。

资料来源：根据联合国国际贸易数据库数据整理计算。

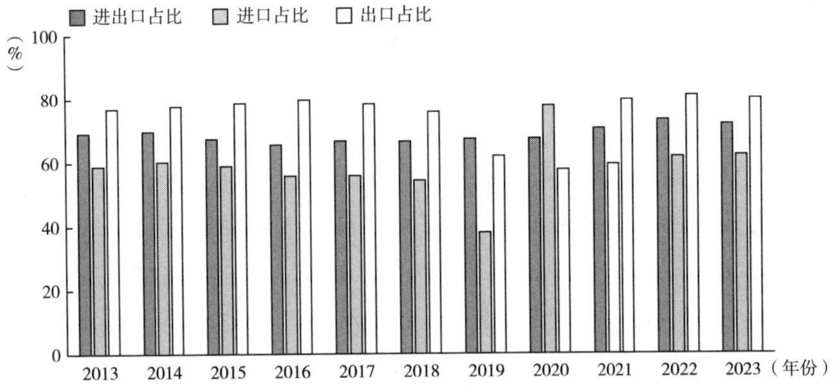

第2章 中阿贸易合作专题报告

图 2.13 2013—2023 年海合会国家对中国贸易额占阿中贸易额比重

注：以海合会国家为报告国。

分类依据：HS2007。

资料来源：根据联合国国际贸易数据库数据整理计算。

2.3 中国与阿拉伯国家的贸易关系

中阿贸易合作是中阿携手构建面向新时代的中阿命运共同体的重要内容。目前，中国是阿拉伯国家第一大贸易伙伴国，阿拉伯国家则是中国最大的能源进口来源地。

2.3.1 中国与阿拉伯国家主要贸易伙伴的贸易关系

2023 年，中国在阿拉伯国家的第一大贸易伙伴是沙特，贸易额为 1072.16 亿美元；第二是阿联酋，贸易额为 949.92 亿美元。伊拉克、阿曼、卡塔尔、科威特、埃及、阿尔及利亚、摩洛哥和利比亚分别居第三位至第十位，其中，伊拉克、阿曼、卡塔尔、科威特、埃及和阿尔及利亚与中国的贸易额均超过了 100 亿美元，分别为 497.52 亿美元、350.77 亿美元、245.64 亿美元、223.89 亿美元、158.16 亿美元和 103.04 亿美元。在前十大贸易伙伴中，与中国贸易额增幅最大的是阿尔及利亚，增速达 38.87%。

033

从出口来看，中国对阿联酋出口额最多，达到 556.83 亿美元。其次是沙特，达到 428.55 亿美元。埃及、伊拉克和阿尔及利亚紧随其后，分别为 149.35 亿美元、142.86 亿美元、94.58 亿美元。在前十大贸易伙伴中，中国对利比亚的贸易出口额增幅最大，达到 64.41%。

从进口来看，中国在该地区最大的进口来源国是沙特，进口额为 643.61 亿美元。其次是阿联酋、伊拉克、阿曼、卡塔尔和科威特，进口额分别达到 393.09 亿美元、354.66 亿美元、312.79 亿美元、209.28 亿美元和 171.65 亿美元。在前十大贸易伙伴中，进口增幅最大的是摩洛哥，达到 7.68%（见表 2.9）。

总体来看，与 2022 年相比，2023 年中国与阿拉伯国家前十大贸易伙伴没有发生显著变化，只是科威特与卡塔尔排名互换，卡塔尔超越科威特成为中国与阿拉伯国家贸易额排名第五的贸易伙伴。

表 2.9　2023 年中国与阿拉伯国家前十大贸易伙伴情况

序号	国家	金额（亿美元）			同比增长（%）		
		进出口	出口	进口	进出口	出口	进口
1	沙特	1072.16	428.55	643.61	−7.60	12.81	−17.53
2	阿联酋	949.92	556.83	393.09	−4.31	3.38	−13.43
3	伊拉克	497.52	142.86	354.66	−6.79	2.13	−9.95
4	阿曼	350.77	37.98	312.79	−13.27	−9.68	−13.69
5	卡塔尔	245.64	36.36	209.28	−7.47	−8.85	−7.23
6	科威特	223.89	52.25	171.65	−28.88	5.12	−35.25
7	埃及	158.16	149.35	8.81	−13.05	−13.02	−13.59
8	阿尔及利亚	103.04	94.58	8.47	38.87	50.70	−26.00
9	摩洛哥	74.34	64.54	9.80	11.77	12.42	7.68
10	利比亚	61.01	39.01	21.99	14.96	64.41	−25.02

注：以中国为报告国。
分类依据：HS2007。
资料来源：根据联合国国际贸易数据库数据整理计算。

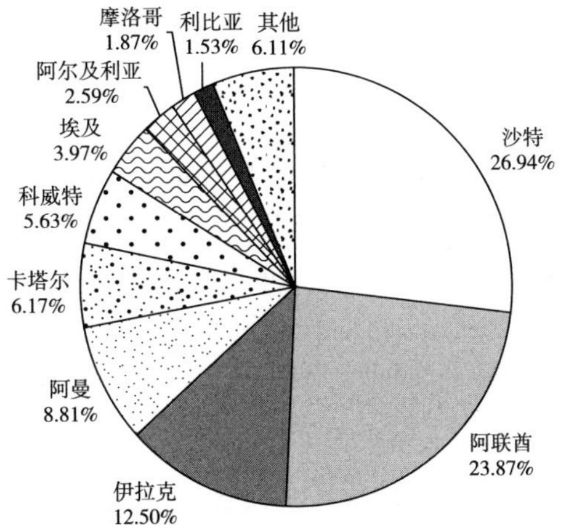

图 2.14　2023 年中阿前十大贸易伙伴进出口额占中阿贸易进出口总额比重

注：以中国为报告国。

分类依据：HS2007。

资料来源：根据联合国国际贸易数据库数据整理计算。

2.3.2　中阿双边商品贸易结构

根据联合国贸易和发展会议对贸易商品的分类方法，对 2023 年中阿双边贸易结构进行分析，发现双边商品贸易结构呈现如下特点。

2023 年，中国对阿拉伯国家的出口主要是消费品和资本品，出口额分别为 718.24 亿美元和 624.56 亿美元，这两大类出口商品总额为 1342.80 亿美元，占中国对阿拉伯国家全部出口商品的 75.96%，较 2022 年增长 2.29%。这反映出中国对阿拉伯国家出口以制成品为主，主要原因是中国在制成品上具有明显竞争优势且产品升级趋势明显。中国的产品满足了阿拉伯国家不断增长的消费需求。

中国从阿拉伯国家进口的商品以原材料为主，2023 年进口额达到 1700.18 亿美元，占中国从阿拉伯国家进口总额的 78.53%；其次是消费品，进口额为 276.65 亿美元，占比 12.78%。中国从阿拉伯国家进口的中间品和资本品分别占全部进口额的 8.27% 和 0.43%。自 2017 年以来，中阿双边商品贸易结构变化不大，一直呈现上述特征（见表 2.10、图 2.15、图 2.16）。

表 2.10　2019—2023 年中国与阿拉伯国家大类商品贸易结构

UNCTAD 分类产品	贸易额和比重	2019 年	2020 年	2021 年	2022 年	2023 年
原材料	出口额（亿美元）	13.15	13.22	13.78	14.87	17.46
	比重（%）	1.11	1.09	0.94	0.87	0.99
	进口额（亿美元）	1090.45	858.22	1378.79	2047.38	1700.18
	比重（%）	74.94	73.85	75.39	79.37	78.53
中间品	出口额（亿美元）	236.02	224.92	327.45	420.57	407.34
	比重（%）	19.86	18.60	22.23	24.87	23.04
	进口额（亿美元）	207.85	185.84	244.54	215.58	178.99
	比重（%）	14.28	15.99	13.37	8.40	8.27
消费品	出口额（亿美元）	549.84	569.63	636.41	722.68	718.24
	比重（%）	46.27	47.11	43.20	42.73	40.63
	进口额（亿美元）	152.44	113.38	195.40	308.76	276.65
	比重（%）	10.48	9.76	10.68	11.97	12.78
资本品	出口额（亿美元）	389.39	401.29	465.29	533.00	624.56
	比重（%）	32.77	33.19	31.59	31.52	35.33
	进口额（亿美元）	4.35	4.68	5.92	7.84	9.24
	比重（%）	0.30	0.40	0.32	0.30	0.43

商品分类：根据联合国贸易和发展会议的分类整理。

注：以中国为报告国。

分类依据：HS2007。

资料来源：根据联合国国际贸易数据库数据整理计算。

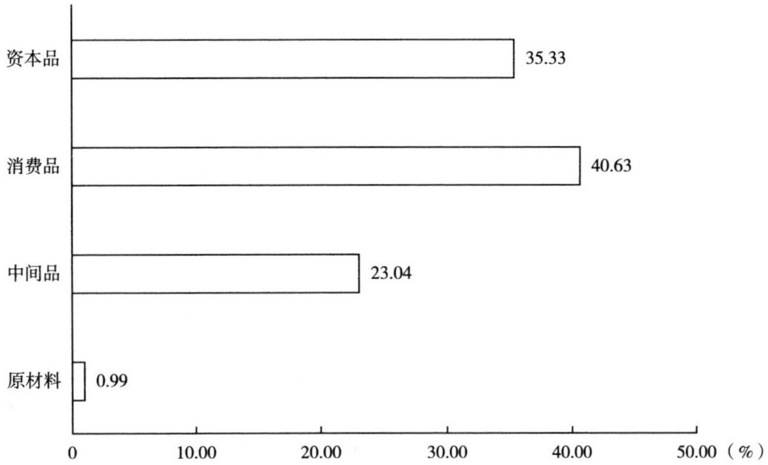

资本品　35.33

消费品　40.63

中间品　23.04

原材料　0.99

0　10.00　20.00　30.00　40.00　50.00（%）

图 2.15　2023 年中国对阿拉伯国家出口四大类商品占比

分类依据：HS2007。

资料来源：根据联合国国际贸易数据库数据整理计算。

资本品　0.43

消费品　12.78

中间品　8.27

原材料　78.53

0　20.00　40.00　60.00　80.00　100.00（%）

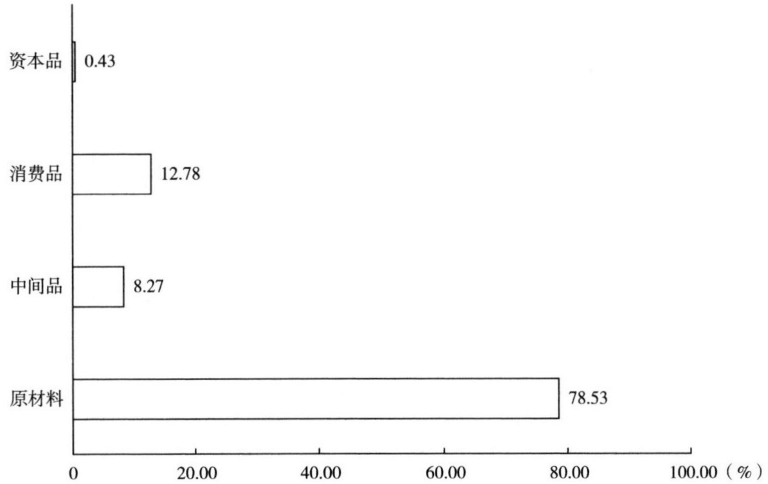

图 2.16　2023 年中国对阿拉伯国家进口四大类商品占比

分类依据：HS2007。

资料来源：根据联合国国际贸易数据库数据整理计算。

从更为具体的产品分类来看，2023 年，中国对阿拉伯国家主要出口产品是机械设备和电气产品、金属产品、纺织和服装以及杂项制品，这些商品出口额占出口总额比重较高，分别达 32.58%、13.52%、11.17% 和 10.84%，上述四类产品占中国对阿拉伯国家出口总额的 68.11%。此外，中国还向阿拉伯国家出口塑料和橡胶产品、运输设备、矿石和玻璃以及化学制品等。与 2022 年相比，2023 年出口结构没有变化（见表 2.11）。

表 2.11 2019—2023 年中国对阿拉伯国家的出口商品结构

单位：亿美元

产品编码	大类产品名称	2019 年出口额	2020 年出口额	2021 年出口额	2022 年出口额	2023 年出口额
84-85	机械设备和电气产品	368.35	387.76	443.16	518.82	590.08
72-83	金属产品	146.26	144.64	174.41	242.08	244.91
50-63	纺织和服装	192.32	180.57	207.08	204.24	202.30
90-99	杂项制品	127.02	161.57	187.07	195.10	196.35
86-89	运输设备	72.59	68.04	95.8	137.12	159.94
39-40	塑料和橡胶产品	76.63	79.47	98.62	121.21	121.68
28-38	化学制品	41.89	46.02	85.79	89.10	80.11
68-71	矿石和玻璃	57.65	54.52	56.31	67.38	60.84
64-67	鞋靴类产品	37.68	32.92	41.01	45.81	43.21
44-49	木及木制品	29.25	27.85	30.53	44.48	40.18
41-43	皮革和毛皮制品	18.67	12.31	16.84	20.58	20.71
06-15	蔬菜	14.34	14.84	14.98	15.84	18.03
27-27	矿物燃料和矿物油	9.93	6.28	9.63	14.50	15.70
16-24	食品	9.34	8.5	7.99	11.24	14.45
25-26	矿产品	1.13	1.65	1.82	1.38	1.42
01-05	动物产品	2.14	1.04	1.17	1.27	1.33

注：以中国为报告国。

分类依据：HS2007。

资料来源：根据联合国国际贸易数据库数据整理计算。

2023 年，中国从阿拉伯国家进口商品排名第一的依然是矿物燃料和矿物油，为 1926.25 亿美元，占中国从阿拉伯国家进口总额的 88.83%，较 2022 年的 2307.86 亿美元下降 16.54%；第二是化学产品，进口额为 81.32 亿美元，较 2022 年的 95.73 亿美元下降 15.05%；第三是塑料和橡胶产品，进口额为 69.14 亿美元（见表 2.12）。综上分析，除进口额排名前三的大类产品外，其他产品进口额所占比重一直较低。这种贸易结构反映出阿拉伯国家产业结构相对单一，制造业和农业相对薄弱，石油产业为其主要产业支柱的特征没有变化，产业体系有待完善。近年来，海湾产油国已充分认识到经济多元化的重要意义，一直在推行经济现代化，以阿联酋为首的国家大力发展金融、旅游和会展等现代服务业，经济转型取得积极进展；埃及、摩洛哥等国家积极争取国外投资，发展轻工纺织等产业，加强产品生产能力。在这些领域，这些国家与中国从贸易合作延伸到投资、金融等领域合作，以互利共赢推动产能合作和经济增长取得积极成效。

表 2.12　2019—2023 年中国对阿拉伯国家进口商品结构

单位：亿美元

产品编码	大类产品名称	2019 年进口额	2020 年进口额	2021 年进口额	2022 年进口额	2023 年进口额
27-27	矿物燃料和矿物油	1205.03	941.58	1524.2	2307.86	1926.25
28-38	化学产品	100.44	78.36	106.92	95.73	81.32
39-40	塑料和橡胶产品	91.24	83.98	92.79	92.05	69.14
25-26	矿产品	26.73	20.75	36.54	31.92	31.83
72-83	金属产品	9.69	14.5	35.6	21.85	22.10
06-15	蔬菜	6.85	10.9	12.39	10.93	11.03
84-85	机械设备和电器产品	4.37	4.76	5.91	7.87	9.17
68-71	矿石和玻璃	2.46	0.62	2.55	2.03	4.99
50-63	纺织和服装	4.17	3.82	3.76	4.28	4.74
16-24	食品	2.19	3.66	5.15	5.27	4.68

中阿经贸关系发展进程2023年度报告

续表

产品编码	大类产品名称	2019年进口额	2020年进口额	2021年进口额	2022年进口额	2023年进口额
01-05	动物产品	2.16	0.65	1.05	1.47	1.58
90-99	杂项制品	0.33	0.43	0.68	0.61	0.65
41-43	皮革和毛皮制品	0.39	0.28	0.57	0.50	0.54
86-89	运输设备	0.21	0.17	0.19	0.17	0.18
44-49	木及木制品	0.51	0.94	0.44	0.09	0.15
64-67	鞋靴类产品	0.05	0.04	0.04	0.04	0.05

注：以中国为报告国。

分类依据：HS2007。

资料来源：根据联合国国际贸易数据库数据整理计算。

2.3.3 中国与阿拉伯国家服务贸易合作

在商品贸易带动下，中阿服务贸易不断拓展，尤其是在共建"一带一路"倡议及中阿合作论坛、中阿博览会的带动下，中国与阿拉伯国家服务贸易不断取得突破，其中，双方在金融、高科技和技术服务、新能源开发和电子商务等服务贸易领域表现出了较大合作潜力。

双方货币金融合作持续深化。2012年以来，中国陆续与阿联酋、卡塔尔和沙特等国家签署双边货币互换协议，之后又多次续签，截至2023年，仅中国与沙特签署的双边本币互换协议规模就达到500亿元人民币。2022年12月，浙江义乌和沙特完成了首单跨境人民币支付业务，同时中国人民银行与阿联酋中央银行在内的多家机构一同加入多边央行数字货币桥（m-CBDC Bridge）项目，探索中央银行数字货币在跨境支付中的应用。中阿双边货物和服务贸易中，以人民币结算的份额从2013年的11%增长至2022年的25%，人民币国际化在中东地区认可度逐渐提升。金融合作机制建设持续完善，截至2022年7月，阿拉伯国家已有16个国家成为亚投行成员国。2023年8月，沙特、阿联酋和埃及先后成为金砖国家新开发银行成员，实现中阿金融合作的重大突破。双方金融机构不断增开分支机

040

构，2022 年阿联酋阿布扎比第一银行在上海的办事处转为分行，科威特国家银行、卡塔尔国家银行均在上海有分支机构。资本市场合作不断拓展，2022 年 12 月，中国银行 3 亿美元债券在迪拜纳斯达克正式上市，中国农业银行、中国工商银行和中国银行分别在迪拜发行债券。阿联酋主权财富基金在中国银行、中国工商银行、中国农业银行等中资银行的 H 股上市和海外 IPO 过程中也积极参与交易，为从更深层面推进双方经贸、产能合作创造了便利条件。

高科技和技术合作领域不断突破。近年来，中阿双方通过发展战略的深度对接，在相关高科技领域取得突破性进展。在中阿科技伙伴计划框架下，共同实施"一带一路"科技创新行动计划，2023 年 9 月 21 日，第五届中阿技术转移与创新合作大会在宁夏银川召开。大会以"中阿科技合作，共享创新未来"为主题，以视频形式面向阿拉伯国家发布 300 项先进适用技术，涉及生态环境保护、资源能源利用、污染控制等领域。此外，8 个中阿科技合作与技术转移重点项目进行了集中签约。在 5G 通信领域，中国公司成为阿拉伯国家 5G 通信领域关键合作伙伴，在埃及、沙特、阿联酋、阿曼、巴林等国占据较高市场份额。中国的数字化技术帮助各国在交通、电力、教育和人工智能等方面推进数字化转型，中国帮助沙特阿拉伯建设数据中心、提供具有国际领先水准的云服务成为典型案例。在核能领域，中国企业与阿联酋、沙特、苏丹等国签署了和平利用核能协定，并在铀矿勘探、核燃料供应、核电站运维等领域达成合作意向。在航天卫星领域，中国同阿拉伯国家建立中阿北斗合作论坛，在突尼斯落成北斗卫星导航系统首个海外中心——中阿北斗/GNSS 中心。中国同阿尔及利亚、苏丹、埃及、沙特等国签署航天卫星领域多个合作文件，成功将阿尔及利亚一号通信卫星、"沙特—5A/5B"卫星、苏丹科学实验卫星一号等发射升空。生态和农业技术合作成效显著。宁夏、甘肃等西部省区发挥自身技术比较优势，依托中阿合作论坛及中阿技术转移中心，积极推进与阿方在环境保护、节水、农业、荒漠化防治等方面的合作。宁夏大学实施的"中阿绿色智能节水关键技术研究和示范"等项目，建成节水灌溉国际联合实验室两个，培养了一批阿方技术人员，实现了科技成果在阿曼、阿联酋、埃及等国家典型旱区的规模化应用。2022 年在卡塔尔世界杯球场草坪应用的宁夏大学的节水技术受到世人瞩目。

中阿清洁能源合作大幅提速，中阿能源合作已形成"油气合作、低碳能源合作"的"双轮"驱动模式，有效助力阿方能源转型和可持续发展。2023 年，中国与沙特合作建设的红海综合智慧能源项目，是全球最大规模离网型综合智慧能源项目和最大规模在建储能项目；中国能源建设股份有限公司与埃及新能源管理局，国家电投黄河公司分别与阿曼、摩洛哥相关公司签署绿氢项目合作开发备忘录，中国核工业集团有限公司与阿联酋、沙特、阿尔及利亚等国签署了和平利用核能协定。

当前，中东地区电子商务蓬勃发展，市场规模持续扩大，增长势头强劲。中国电商，如希音等品牌，敏锐捕捉这一机遇，凭借独特的商业模式和技术优势，迅速在中东市场崭露头角。京东、阿里巴巴等电商巨头通过与当地平台合作或升级跨境物流服务，进一步加强了在中东的影响力。同时，中国物流企业如极兔速递在中东市场也取得了显著成就，有效提升了当地的物流效率，为中国商品在中东的流通提供了有力支持。未来，双方合作前景广阔，中国将继续助力中东电商市场繁荣，也为自身电商国际化发展开辟新路径。

第3章 中阿投资合作专题报告

由于全球经济增长放缓，贸易摩擦加剧，2023年全球外国直接投资持续下滑。阿拉伯国家在推行经济多元化的进程中，不断完善基础设施、制定并营造开放的政策和经贸环境，为该地区的发展带来新机遇。经贸合作是中阿关系的"压舱石"和"推进器"，中国连续多年成为阿拉伯国家最大的贸易伙伴。由于经济结构互补性强、发展战略契合度高，双方在多领域的合作中展现出活力。阿拉伯国家日益将目光投向东方，积极寻求与中国和印度等快速增长经济体的合作机会。近年来，中阿加速产能和投融资合作，投资合作呈现新的发展特征和趋势。从2023年中国的科技、能源等企业相继出海中东，国内GP（普通合伙人）纷纷前往中东募资，到包括沙特阿美、主权财富基金等阿拉伯国家资本在中国一、二级市场的投资，中国和中东的"双向奔赴"在2024年仍然延续。然而，由于历史的原因，中阿相互投资仍处于起步阶段，未来发展潜力巨大。

3.1 中国对阿拉伯国家投资趋势

阿拉伯国家经济多元化进程保持韧性，非石油部门逐渐成为该地区经济增长的重要支撑。近年来，中国和阿拉伯国家加速推进产业与投资合作，也为经济转型提供了蓬勃动能。[①] 中阿投资合作超越能源与贸易领域，

[①] 杨啸林：《中东多国推动经济多元化，中阿合作提速升级》，《中国经济》2024年6月7日。

并逐步向可再生能源、建筑、金融、互联网科技（电子支付、云计算、数据中心）、文化（电子游戏与娱乐）领域扩展，越来越具有综合性和多元性。

3.1.1 阿拉伯国家投资环境持续改善

联合国贸易和发展组织 2024 年 6 月发布的《世界投资报告》显示，2023 年全球外国直接投资下降 2%，至 1.3 万亿美元。全球外资（包括直接和间接投资）连续第二年降幅超过 10%。融资条件收紧、投资者意愿不定、金融市场波动以及监管措施趋严是造成这一趋势的主要原因。2023 年，流向发展中国家的外国直接投资下降 7%，至 8670 亿美元。[①]报告还指出，国际投资环境在 2024 年仍将充满挑战，受增长前景乏力、贸易和地缘紧张、工业政策调整和供应链重塑等因素影响，外国直接投资模式正在发生剧变，导致一批跨国企业在海外业务拓展上采取更加谨慎的态度。

在阿拉伯国家推行经济多元化进程中，不断完善的基础设施、开放的政策和经贸环境，正为该地区的发展带来新机遇。阿拉伯各国政府积极引导外资流向新兴科技和战略产业。2024 年上半年以来，尽管受到油价波动和地区形势动荡影响，国际机构对阿拉伯国家的经济增长预期依然表现出乐观态度。根据联合国贸易和发展会议 2024 年 6 月发布的报告数据，2023 年流入阿拉伯国家的外国直接投资下降了 12.3%，至 677 亿美元，占发展中国家总流入量的 7.8%，占全球总流入量约 1.33 万亿美元的 5.1%（见图 3.1）。流入阿拉伯国家的外国直接投资继续集中在五个国家，份额超过 95%。总流入量最高的是阿联酋，吸引了 307 亿美元，占 45.4%；其次是沙特，吸引了 124 亿美元，份额为 18.2%；埃及以 98 亿美元排名第三，占流入阿拉伯国家总额的 18.2%；巴林以 68 亿美元排名第四，占总额的 10%；然后是阿曼的 47 亿美元，科威特的 21 亿美元，分

---

① UNCTAD, *2024 World Investment Report*, June 2024, p. 3.

别占总额的 6.9% 和 3.1%。①

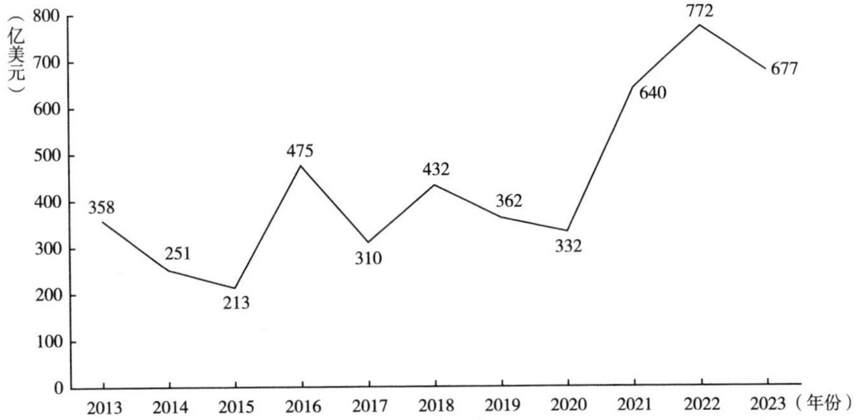

图 3.1　2013—2023 年阿拉伯国家吸引 FDI 流量

资料来源：UNCTAD，*2024 World Investment Report*，June 2024，pp. 152-156。

　　根据阿拉伯投资和出口信贷担保公司（Dhaman）2024 年 7 月发布的《阿拉伯国家投资环境年度报告 2024》，阿拉伯国家正成为各行业公司和商业投资者寻求增长机会的主要目的地。2023 年，流入阿拉伯国家的绿地外国直接投资项目数量增长了 20.3%，达到 2001 个，总资本支出 1810 亿美元（占全球绿地项目资本支出的 13.6%）。绿地项目创造了 266000 多个工作岗位（占全球总数的 8.1%），比 2022 年增长 17.7%，平均每个项目创造 113 个工作岗位。② 就绿地项目资本支出而言，阿联酋以 437 亿美元的投资额排名第一，占 24.1%。就绿地项目数量而言，美国以 302 个项目位居第一（资本支出约 64 亿美元），占项目总数的 15.1%。中国在阿拉伯国家绿地投资项目数量排名第五（87 个项目，占 4.3%）。在资本支出方面中国内地排名第二（资本支出 364 亿美元，占 20.1%），但在创造就业方面其高居榜首，创造就业岗位 65423 个，占 28.8%（见表 3.1）。

---

①　UNCTAD，*2024 World Investment Report*，June 2024，p. 156.

②　Dhaman，*The Investment Climate in Arab Countries 2024*，July 2024，p. 60.

中阿经贸关系发展进程2023年度报告

表 3.1　2023 年阿拉伯国家绿地投资来源国（地区）

排名	国家/地区	项目数（个）	占比（%）	国家/地区	资本支出（亿美元）	占比（%）	国家/地区	创造就业岗位（个）	占比（%）
1	美国	302	15.1	阿联酋	437	24.1	中国内地	65423	28.8
2	英国	269	13.4	中国内地	364	20.1	美国	16801	7.4
3	印度	234	11.7	中国香港	197	10.9	阿联酋	13132	5.8
4	阿联酋	144	7.2	英国	131	7.2	英国	13116	5.8
5	中国	87	4.3	卡塔尔	112	6.2	德国	12090	5.3
6	法国	86	4.3	爱尔兰	98.9	5.5	法国	11362	5.0
7	德国	65	3.2	美国	64	3.5	土耳其	10453	4.6
8	意大利	60	3.0	沙特	63	3.5	中国香港	9960	4.4
9	瑞士	56	2.8	印度	44	2.4	印度	8040	3.5
10	新加坡	55	2.7	法国	41	2.2	意大利	6541	2.9

资料来源：Dhaman，*The Investment Climate in Arab Countries 2024*，July 2024，p. 63。

3.1.2　中国不断加大对阿拉伯国家的投资布局

中国投资遍布全球。2023 年中国对外直接投资流量 1772.9 亿美元，比上年增长 8.7%；对外直接投资存量 29554 亿美元，分布在全球 189 个国家（地区），近八成流向商务服务、批发零售、制造、金融领域。[①] 面对严峻的国际形势，中国构建新发展格局，积极参与全球投资治理体系改革和建设，"一带一路"投资合作走深走实，多双边投资合作机制日益完善。根据联合国贸发会议（UNCTAD）《2024 年世界投资报告》，2023 年全球对外直接投资流量 1.55 万亿美元，年末存量 44.38 万亿美元。[②] 以此

[①] 中华人民共和国商务部、国家统计局、国家外汇管理局：《2023 年度中国对外直接投资统计公报》，中国商务出版社，2024，第 3—4 页。

[②] UNCTAD, *2024 World Investment Report*, June 2024, p. 157.

046

为基数计算 2023 年中国对外直接投资分别占全球投资流量、存量的 11.4% 和 6.7%，均列全球国家（地区）排名的第三位。[①]

尽管受到地缘政治紧张、全球直接投资低迷等不利因素影响，中国对阿拉伯国家直接投资逆势上扬，从 2022 年的 20.3 亿美元上升至 2023 年的 26.4 亿美元，同比上升 29.6%。截至 2023 年末，中国对阿拉伯国家直接投资存量 216.9 亿美元。与此同时，中国对阿拉伯国家直接投资在中国对外投资流量和存量总额的占比仍然很低，2023 年分别为 1.5% 和 0.7%（见表 3.2）。

表 3.2　2023 年中国对世界主要经济体直接投资情况

经济体	流量			存量	
	金额（亿美元）	同比（%）	比重（%）	金额（亿美元）	比重（%）
世界	1772.9	8.7	100	29554.0	100
中国香港	1087.7	11.5	61.3	17525.2	59.3
东盟	251.2	34.7	14.2	1756.2	5.9
欧盟	64.8	-6.1	3.7	1024.2	3.5
美国	69.1	-5.2	3.9	836.9	2.8
澳大利亚	5.5	-80.4	0.3	347.7	1.2
阿拉伯国家	26.4	29.6	1.5	216.9	0.7
以上经济体合计	1504.7	11.3	84.9	21707.1	73.4

资料来源：中华人民共和国商务部、国家统计局、国家外汇管理局《2023 年度中国对外直接投资统计公报》，中国商务出版社，2024，第 30 页。

海合会国家及埃及、苏丹等阿拉伯国家是中国对阿拉伯国家直接投资主要目的地。截至 2023 年末，阿联酋在中国对外直接投资流量前 20 位国家中排名第 10 位，投资流量 17.8 亿美元，占比 1%。[②] 阿联酋保持中国在

[①]　中华人民共和国商务部、国家统计局、国家外汇管理局：《2023 年度中国对外直接投资统计公报》，中国商务出版社，2024，第 4 页。

[②]　中华人民共和国商务部、国家统计局、国家外汇管理局：《2023 年度中国对外直接投资统计公报》，中国商务出版社，2024，第 15 页。

阿拉伯国家第二大贸易伙伴、第一大投资目的地、第一大出口市场、第三大工程市场地位。双边合作"上天入地""点多面广"，超过 8000 家中资企业在阿联酋投资兴业，覆盖基础设施、金融货币、新能源、生命科学、人工智能等行业。[①] 令人欣喜的是，资本、货币为主的投资合作正成为新亮点和增长点。中国已成为阿联酋的第三大投资来源国。就投资流量来看，2023 年，阿联酋、沙特阿拉伯和摩洛哥为中国对阿拉伯国家直接投资前三大目的地，其次是阿尔及利亚、埃及和苏丹（见图 3.2）。2023 年，除了埃及，中国对上述几个阿拉伯国家的投资均实现较大幅度的增长。阿联酋一直保持中国对阿投资第一大投资目的地，占中国对阿直接投资流量总额的 67.3%。就投资存量来看，2023 年，中国对阿联酋直接投资存量为 89.1 亿美元，占中国对阿拉伯国家直接投资存量总额的比重为 41.1%。其次是沙特 31.86 亿美元、伊拉克 21.69 亿美元、阿尔及利亚 16.99 亿美元、埃及 12.87 亿美元。[②]

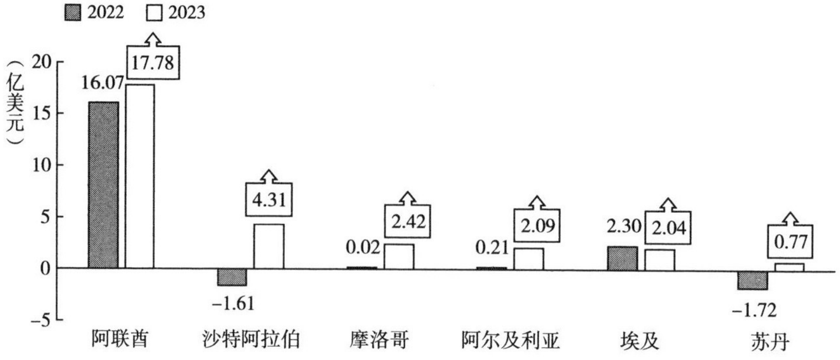

图 3.2　2022 年和 2023 年中国对阿拉伯国家直接投资流量主要目的地

资料来源：中华人民共和国商务部、国家统计局、国家外汇管理局《2023 年度中国对外直接投资统计公报》，中国商务出版社，2024，第 47—54 页。

---

① 《2024 中阿企业家峰会在阿布扎比开幕》，新华网，http://www.xinhuanet.com/world/20240516/770238424adf4460b7d43274c12344f8/c.html，2024 年 5 月 16 日。

② 中华人民共和国商务部、国家统计局、国家外汇管理局：《2023 年度中国对外直接投资统计公报》，中国商务出版社，2024，第 52—54 页。

中国对阿拉伯国家投资日益多元化。2023 年以来，中阿关系互动加速深化，越来越具有综合性和多元性。中阿关系已超越经贸领域，进入第二阶段。资本、人才和技术的流动远超以往，成为双方关系的新主题。"中国方案+本土产能"有利于中国与阿拉伯国家投资合作实现双赢。中国投资中东较为集中的是能源和基建两大传统领域。国有企业是中国投资阿拉伯国家的主体，投资领域集中在能源、基础设施和建材等。民营企业投资也在迎头赶上，主要投向信息技术业、制造业、建筑业、商贸服务业和生活服务业等。此外，后续新增投资领域还包括金融、新能源、航空航天、生物制药、数字经济、现代农业等。中国高附加值的优势产能和科技解决方案的输出，也正在给中东带来积极变化。越来越多的中国企业加速"出海"中东，由中企总承包的全球最大单体光伏电站在阿联酋全面竣工，极兔速递在阿联酋、沙特为中国电商出海企业打通网购"最后一公里"，华为云、商汤科技等一批高科技企业奔赴中东市场，隆基绿能参与了沙特红海新城、新未来城的多个光伏电站的建设，美团进军沙特，国内游戏公司已悉数布局中东市场[1]……阿联酋、沙特、埃及和伊拉克是中国投资比较活跃和潜力较大的阿拉伯市场。

阿拉伯国家正以其独特的优势吸引着 A 股上市公司前往掘金。据《经济观察报》不完全统计，2024 年上半年，已有超过 15 家上市公司透露将加大对中东地区的布局投资。[2] 这一数字创近五年同期新高。2024 年7 月以来，中国电建（601669.SH）、盛视科技（002990.SZ）、风光股份（301100.SZ）、阳光电源（300274.SZ）、晶科能源（688223.SH）、TCL 中环（002129.SZ）、海南矿业（601969.SH）、荣盛石化（002493.SZ）等多家 A 股上市公司将目光投向中东地区，展开战略投资和市场布局。石油资源和新能源资源丰富的中东正在成为中国清洁能源企业的海外扩产重

---

[1] 在沙特，TOP App 流行排行前 30 名里，中企占了 12 个席位；在阿联酋，TOP App 流行排行前 39 位中，中企占了 13 个席位。

[2] 蔡越坤：《中企投资中东潮起》，经济观察网，http://www.eeo.com.cn/2024/0726/675638.shtml，2024 年 7 月 26 日。

镇，多家上市公司签下海外大单，这是中国新能源产业新一轮出海需求与中东绿色转型渴求的双向奔赴。[1] 2024 年 7 月 16 日，中国新能源行业的三大巨头——晶科能源、TCL 中环与远景科技集团宣布与沙特王国公共投资基金签署了在沙特成立合资企业的战略协议，推动中东清洁能源转型。

中企布局阿拉伯国家主要分为两类。一类是追求多元化融资来源，以增强二级市场的活跃性和融资能力，部分公司考虑向中东地区拓展；另一类则是那些寻求海外市场增长机会的公司，这些公司通过业务落地和国际化实现增长。在一级市场，国内数家知名风险投资机构在阿拉伯国家开设办公室，其主要诉求为：一是寻找更多的退出渠道，以应对国内市场退出形势的挑战；二是探索新的资金来源；三是协助中国企业在中东落地和拓展业务。[2] 在公募基金领域，2023 年 11 月 29 日，南方东英沙特 ETF 以超过 10 亿美元的初始投资额在香港交易所上市；2024 年 6 月首批 2 只境内投资沙特市场的 ETF 分别在上交所和深交所上市，满足中国投资者布局沙特市场、实现投资多元化的需求，也有助于沙特资本市场多元化和增强对外资吸引力。中国主权财富基金也积极走向中东。2024 年 4 月，中国主权财富基金中投公司和总部位于巴林的投资公司 Investcorp 合作，推出了一个 10 亿美元的投资平台 Investcorp Golden Horizon，用来投资海湾地区和中国的高成长公司，重点关注消费品、医疗保健、物流和商业服务等领域。此前，Investcorp 和中国香港私人投资公司冯氏资本于 2022 年携手成立了一个规模达 500 亿美元的基金，专门用于投资中国粤港澳大湾区的中型公司。

中国企业将投资视野聚焦至中东地区，与中资企业加速国际化的步伐息息相关。与此同时，中东国家正积极推动经济多元化，加快能源转型步伐，降低对石油产业的依赖，而中国持续保持世界第一制造大国和出口大

---

[1] 杨漾：《四大清洁能源企业同日宣布揽下沙特重磅大单》，澎湃新闻网，https://m.thepaper.cn/newsDetail_forward_28098736，2024 年 7 月 17 日。

[2] 蔡越坤：《7 月近 10 家上市公司官宣　中企投资中东潮起》，《经济观察报》2024 年 7 月 27 日。

国地位，拥有先进的 5G、新能源技术等，双方紧密合作有望实现双赢。寻求与中国建立更加紧密的政治和经贸关系，以及通过技术合作实现能源多元化和经济转型是阿拉伯国家加大对华投资的主要原因。此外，由于全球地缘政治和经济格局的转变，欧美国家对华投资增速有所放缓，而中阿国家经贸联系越发紧密，阿拉伯国家对华投资呈现快速增长的势头。

3.2　阿拉伯国家对中国投资趋势

2023 年，全球跨境投资在 2021 年强劲反弹和 2022 年出现下滑后，继续下降 1.8%。2020—2023 年中国吸引外国直接投资整体表现不弱，但高位回落的压力明显，受到全球 FDI 趋势变化、中国产业结构变化，以及制造业逆全球化等多重因素影响。2023 年全年外商直接投资新设立企业53766 家，比上年增长 39.7%。实际使用外商直接投资额 1632.5 亿美元（下降 13.7%），占全球比重为 12.3%，稳居世界第二。其中，共建"一带一路"国家对华直接投资（含通过部分自由港对华投资）新设立企业13649 家，增长 82.7%；对华直接投资额为 176 亿美元，下降 16.7%。高技术产业实际使用外资额为 610 亿美元，下降 10.8%。[1] 2022 年中国实际使用外商直接投资额为 1891.3 亿美元，同比增长 4.5%。2022 年在主要投资来源地前 15 位国家中，阿联酋位居第 13 位，对华直接投资 9.6 亿美元，占比 0.5%。[2] 2023 年，阿联酋对华直接投资额为 22 亿美元，占当年中国吸引外资流量总额的 1.4%，位居第 10 位。[3]

3.2.1　阿拉伯国家对华直接投资大幅增加

近两年，中国式现代化加速发展新质生产力，不断加快改革开放步伐，营商环境和外资吸引力逐渐增强。与此同时，伴随阿拉伯国家石油美

---

[1]　中华人民共和国商务部：《中国外资统计公报 2024》，中国商务出版社，2024，第 1 页。
[2]　中华人民共和国商务部：《中国外资统计公报 2023》，中国商务出版社，2023，第 7 页。
[3]　中华人民共和国商务部：《中国外资统计公报 2024》，中国商务出版社，2024，第 7 页。

中阿经贸关系发展进程2023年度报告

元收入增加、对中国市场潜力的巨大认可，阿拉伯国家向东看趋势加强，对华直接投资大幅增加。2022年，中国吸引阿拉伯国家直接投资流量从2021年的1.1亿美元大幅增加至10.4亿美元，同比增长近10倍（见图3.3）。2023年继续保持大幅上升态势，达到23.0亿美元，同比增长两倍多，[1] 接近甚至超过了近年来中国对阿拉伯国家的投资规模。阿拉伯国家对华投资从无到有再到比肩中国对阿投资，仅仅用了三年时间。[2]

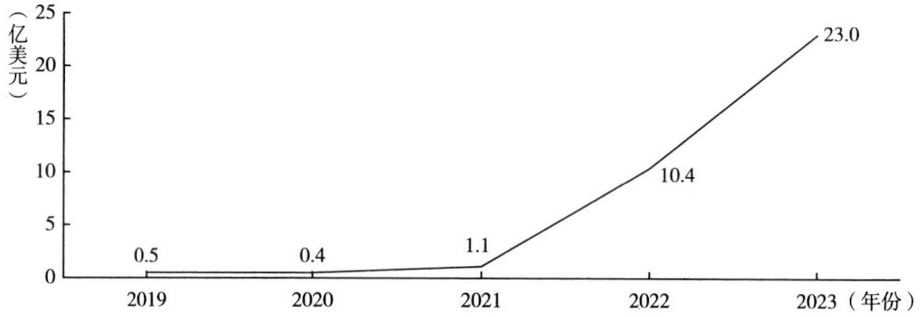

图 3.3　2019—2023 年阿拉伯国家对华直接投资流量

资料来源：中华人民共和国商务部《中国外资统计公报2024》，中国商务出版社，2024，第27—30页。

2003—2022年，阿联酋在中国进行了大量投资，总额高达114亿美元，主要涉及房地产、金融服务、绿色能源和交通等关键领域。[3] 随着两国关系加强，2023年，阿联酋对华直接投资从2022年的9.6亿美元大幅增加至22亿美元，同比增长129.2%，占阿拉伯国家对华投资流量的95.7%。[4] 中国已成为沙特资本最重要的投资目的地之一。庞大的沙特财团，在对外行动时实际上动作高度集中，对外投资依赖于两大支柱——沙

---

[1]　中华人民共和国商务部：《中国外资统计公报2024》，中国商务出版社，2024，第27—30页。

[2]　牛新春：《阿拉伯国家对华投资激增，既有经济账，也有政治账》，《中国日报》2024年4月2日。

[3]　阿联酋驻华大使侯赛因·本·易卜拉欣·哈马迪：《中阿建交40年：走向全球合作，共促经济增长》，《中国日报》2024年6月19日。

[4]　中华人民共和国商务部：《中国外资统计公报2024》，中国商务出版社，2024，第28页。

特主权财富基金公共投资基金（PIF）和沙特阿美，分别对应资本投资和实业投资。中沙两国建立全面战略伙伴关系之后，沙特资本逐步开始直接进入中国，投资范围也从早期看重互联网独角兽、初创科技企业，逐步切换到石化、新能源等实体产业。由于沙特资本的特殊投资方式，沙特对华直接投资流量仍比较低。2022年，沙特对华直接投资流量从2021年的0.7亿美元略增至0.8亿美元，2023年为0.9亿美元。[1]

就投资存量来看，截至2023年末，阿拉伯国家对华直接投资存量从2022年的49.9亿美元增至72.9亿美元，前三大投资来源国为阿联酋（45亿美元，占比61.7%）、沙特（18.9亿美元，占比25.9%）、科威特（3.3亿美元，占比4.5%）。尽管阿拉伯国家对华直接投资大幅增加，占中国吸引FDI流量的比重从2022年的0.5%增加至2023年的1.5%，但由于起点低，阿拉伯国家对华直接投资仍处于起步阶段，2023年阿拉伯国家对华直接投资存量占比仅为0.26%，且主要集中于阿联酋、沙特和科威特等海合会国家。[2]

3.2.2　阿拉伯资本频繁大手笔布局中国

阿拉伯资本中较为常见的是各国主权财富基金、家族办公室以及企业投资部。中东资本对华投资最早可以追溯至2006年，科威特投资局、卡塔尔投资局参与了当时全球最大IPO工商银行的认购。近年来，中东财团越发青睐中国新经济的投资机遇，在中国区域投资方向的选择上，阿拉伯资本保持了自身长期以来的倾向，将自身国家产业发展规划与中国优势产业综合考虑，主要聚焦人工智能、生物医药、新能源与智能汽车等领域，同时习惯性地关注传统能源项目（主要是炼化一体化项目）。2023年6月，在中阿合作论坛第十届企业家大会上，中国企业与中东投资者签署了约30项投资协议，总价值达100亿美元。2024年3月，沙特阿美公司总

---

[1]　中华人民共和国商务部：《中国外资统计公报2024》，中国商务出版社，2024，第28页。

[2]　中华人民共和国商务部：《中国外资统计公报2024》，中国商务出版社，2024，第27—37页。

裁在 2024 年"投资中国"首场标志性活动上发表演讲，强调沙特阿美将加大对华投资，重点关注化学工业、数字技术创新和新能源领域。此前中东资金大多以 LP（有限合伙人）的角色，通过头部 VC/PE（风险投资/私募股权投资）参与对中国的投资。而现在则是绕过投资机构，直接在中国设立办公室，组建本土投资团队，开展直接投资业务。此前，科威特投资局、卡塔尔投资局和阿布扎比投资局均在中国设立办公室。2023 年 9 月，穆巴达拉投资公司在北京设立办公室，沙特公共投资基金继在中国香港开设办事处后，计划 2024 年底或 2025 年初在北京成立办公室，开展直投业务。

全球主权财富基金（SWFs）2023 年的总投资额为 1247 亿美元。在投资规模排名前十的主权财富基金之中，有五家来自阿拉伯国家，分别为：阿联酋阿布扎比投资局（ADIA）、科威特政府投资局（KIA）、沙特公共投资基金（PIF）、卡塔尔投资局（QIA）、阿联酋迪拜投资公司（ICD）。2023 年，沙特公共投资基金（PIF）、阿联酋穆巴达拉投资公司（Mubadala）、阿联酋阿布扎比投资局、阿联酋阿布扎比发展控股公司（ADQ）和卡塔尔投资局总计投资 740 亿美元，占全球主权财富基金投资总额的 58.34%。其中，沙特公共投资基金投资 316 亿美元，位居全球第一。Global SWF 数据显示，在阿拉伯国家主权财富基金 2022 年近 890 亿美元投资中，有 516 亿美元流向了欧洲和北美洲，只有 1%—2% 投向亚洲，主要是中国。截至 2023 年，中东五大主权财富基金的资产管理规模达 4.1 万亿美元，其中对华累计投资规模约为 400 亿美元。[1]

沙特公共投资基金多点布局中国。从 1971 年成立至今，PIF 投资成立了上百家公司，资产管理规模超过 9250 亿美元，是沙特政府"2030 愿景"的重要推手。在本国经济战略转型要求和中国市场不断发展的双重吸引力下，PIF 近年将投资触角伸向中国，PIF 公开表示"中国是重要战略市场"，在华投资额已达 220 亿美元，聚焦可持续发展、科技、汽车、卫

---

[1] 张传捷：《中东国家对华投资的机遇和挑战》，《世界知识》2024 年第 9 期。

生保健、文娱等消费领域。① PIF 接触中国投资主要包括成为共同基金管理人、通过沙特实体企业间接投资、投资二级市场等渠道。但目前来看，PIF 直接在中国私募股权一级市场配置的资产较少。PIF 投资取向与"沙特 2030 愿景"保持一致——推动能源转型，改变沙特的经济结构和国际形象；其投资既是为了收益，更为实现国家战略目的服务。

阿联酋穆巴达拉投资公司和阿布扎比投资局、卡塔尔投资局和科威特投资局均已开展对华投资，计划长期深耕中国市场。穆巴达拉投资公司关注与互联网搭边的商业模式，目前已投资快手、BOSS 直聘、小鹏汽车、商汤科技、自如等企业，涵盖科技、消费、医疗、生活服务多个领域。阿布扎比投资局于 2023 年 12 月通过旗下投资基金 CYVN 向蔚来汽车投资 22 亿美元。卡塔尔投资局于同年 12 月宣布投资约 2 亿美元认购金蝶国际的普通股，2024 年 6 月宣布将经由春华资本收购中国第二大公募基金公司华夏基金 10% 的股份，成为其第三大股东。科威特投资局于 2022 年第四季度增持深圳机场集团的股份。在二级市场，中东主权财富基金在华投资保持较高活跃度，通过 QFII 渠道大量持有 A 股上市公司的股份。

传统能源、石化领域合作走向纵深。沙特阿美公司以股权投资方式成为对华投资最多的外企之一，分布在传统能源的上游、下游、AI 和新能源等领域②：沙特阿美以 246 亿元人民币收购了荣盛石化 10% 的股权，和浙江石化达成每天供应 48 万桶石油（20 年期限）的合同。2024 年 7 月，沙特阿美与荣盛石化签署合作框架协议，拟相互收购对方下属实体公司各 50% 股权并扩建工程；耗资 122 亿美元联合北方工业、盘锦鑫诚成立合资公司，建设日产 30 万桶的大型炼油化工联合装置。随后，沙特阿美和另外三大石化巨头（盛虹石化、恒力石化、裕龙石化）达成协议，计划收购盛虹石化、恒力石化、裕龙石化 10% 的股权，以锁定下游炼化企业的长期原油供给，并扩大与中石化的战略合作伙伴关系。中国炼化企业和沙特阿

---

① 吴娟娟：《沙特公共投资基金：中国是重要战略市场》，《中国基金报》2024 年 7 月 12 日。

② 2024 年，沙特阿美与吉利集团签订意向书，投资智谱 AI 等，布局新能源和 AI 行业。

美合作有利于发挥双方资源优势，互利共赢。目前，沙特阿美拥有上游资源优势，中国则拥有成熟配套产业及广泛的市场优势，这不仅能够整合资源、降低成本，在市场竞争中获得价值体现，而且能够带动国内炼化企业迎来资产价值重估。沙特基础工业公司（SABIC）参与投资的年产26万吨聚碳酸酯工厂在天津投入商业运营。卡塔尔和中国在油气领域的合作也在不断延伸。卡塔尔能源公司与中国合作方在北京签署两项协议：一是中国船舶集团有限公司将建造18艘超大型液化天然气（LNG）运输船，用于满足卡塔尔北方气田扩产后的运输需求；二是卡塔尔能源公司和招商轮船等三家中资船东签署9艘超大型LNG船舶的长期运输租约。

中国新能源汽车也是阿拉伯资本热衷投资的领域，包括可再生能源、电动汽车和电池技术等领域。2022年11月，PIF宣布将和富士康合作推出自己的第一个电动汽车品牌Ceer，并在当地建设100万平方米的工厂。一个月后，新能源车企天际汽车宣布将同沙特公司Sumou Holding成立合资公司，共同在沙特投资5亿美元，设立新能源汽车的生产制造和研发基地。2023年6月，阿布扎比主权基金的投资机构CYVN Holdings，通过定向增发新股和老股转让的方式，向蔚来汽车进行总计约11亿美元的战略投资，成为持股7%的大股东。目前经营不佳的高合汽车、恒大汽车，以及小鹏汽车、小马智行、长城华冠、宾理汽车、天际汽车等都获得过中东资本的青睐。2024年6月，沙特阿美还收购了吉利和雷诺的合资公司——全球动力总成技术公司（HORSE Powertrain Limited）10%的股权，将专注于燃油发动机和混合动力总成技术。阿拉伯投资者希望通过投资以及合资伙伴的返投，把中国汽车制造业领域的专业知识、技术经验带回到本国，促进本国汽车产业的发展。例如，小马智行获得沙特新未来城投资基金（NIF）1亿美元投资，作为交换条件，小马智行需要与NEOM成立合资公司，Robotaxi车队、自动驾驶生产制造及研发中心都要在新未来城落地。

阿拉伯资本对华投资方向主要聚焦新能源、大消费、生物医药、信息技术等多个领域，倾向于配置与本国产业结构相关的制造业、公用事业、原材料与必选消费等。随着产业升级战略的推进，阿拉伯国家主要经济体后续有望加大对新能源、先进制造等中国优势产业的布局，与其本国发展战略形成呼应。中国作为全球第二大经济体，具有庞大的市场规模和潜在的消费能力，吸引着来自全球的投资者。中东国家出于产业多元化的需求，开始加速在中国的投资布局。中东资本在二级市场投资，可能更多是为了财务回报。但主权财富基金无论是直投还是做 LP（有限合伙人），更注重被投企业是否对自己国家的产业发展有帮助。例如，阿布扎比主权财富基金会关注新能源、前沿科技、新材料和医疗等领域。

阿拉伯资本将继续加大对华布局。正如宁夏大学中国阿拉伯国家研究院执行院长牛新春所言："摆脱对石油的过度依赖，摆脱对美国的单一依赖，拥抱新兴国家、新兴产业和新兴市场，是阿拉伯国家投资转向的根源。"[1] 这种战略转向会持续数十年，而中国作为世界第二大经济体经济发展潜力巨大，营商环境日益完善，投资吸引力日益增强，阿拉伯国家对华投资长期向好。

3.3　中阿投资合作面临的机遇和挑战

当前，百年未有之大变局加速演进，世界进入新的动荡变革期，外部环境的复杂性、严峻性、不确定性上升，政治、经济、法律、安全、舆情、经营风险叠加，对外投资合作发展面临的形势依旧错综复杂。同时，中国经济长期向好的基本面没有改变，产业结构不断优化升级，新质生产力催生新业态、新模式、新动能，国际影响力、感召力、塑造力不断提升，相关国家热切期盼分享中国发展红利，为投资合作带来了新机遇。阿拉伯国家的人口红利和经济多元化转型，为中国企业出海带来良好机遇。中国是全球经济增长的重要引擎，拥有先进的技术和经验以及优势产能，仍是包括阿拉伯资本在内所有外资重要的投资目的地。

---

① 牛新春：《阿拉伯国家对华投资激增，既有经济账，也有政治账》，《中国日报》2024 年 4 月 2 日。

3.3.1 中阿投资合作新机遇

中国将向世界释放更多开放红利。党的二十届三中全会吸引了国内外高度关注，会议审议通过的《中共中央关于进一步全面深化改革、推进中国式现代化的决定》（以下简称《决定》）紧扣中国式现代化这一主题，对进一步全面深化改革做出全面部署，共提出 300 多项重要改革举措，进一步阐释了中国主张和中国方案，向世界传递了中国理念和中国声音。《决定》提出到 2029 年这些改革任务要全部完成，制度红利会进一步释放出来。这将为中国经济带来新的机遇和新的动力。发展新质生产力成为推动经济增长的重要抓手，其中一个重要方面是构建现代化产业体系。这次会议的一个重点是扩大中国高水平对外开放。《决定》就对外开放做出专门部署，提出开放是中国式现代化的鲜明标识，必须坚持对外开放基本国策，坚持以开放促改革，建设更高水平开放型经济新体制。当前，经济全球化面临巨大挑战，反对单边主义、保护主义，维护全球经济秩序和产业链、供应链安全稳定，是各国的共同责任。中国推进高水平对外开放，不仅来自以开放促改革、促发展的成功实践，也是把握经济发展规律、顺应时代潮流的必然之举，展现出与世界共享机遇的决心与担当。

阿拉伯国家持续向外国投资者展示开放姿态，投资环境总体趋势向好。发展成为阿拉伯国家的第一要务，各国政府制定了规模宏大的经济发展战略，出台一系列招商引资优惠政策，努力改善营商环境，积极吸引外资流入。根据阿拉伯投资和出口信贷担保公司（Dhaman）2024 年 7 月发布的《阿拉伯国家投资环境年度报告 2024》，在过去三十年里，流入阿拉伯国家的资金量明显从 1994—2003 年的 66 亿美元增加到 2004—2013 年的约 450 亿美元，然后在 2014—2023 年略有下降到 446 亿美元。2014—2023 年，阿拉伯国家在发展中国家吸引 FDI 总流入中的份额平均为 5.7%（2023 年达到 7.8%）。[①] 当前，阿拉伯国家吸引外资有两个特点：一是全

---

① Dhaman, *The Investment Climate in Arab Countries 2024*, July 2024, p. 8.

球南方国家的投资占比日益升高；二是吸引直接外来投资的领域更加多元，除了传统的能源与基础设施领域，新能源、大数据、人工智能、人造卫星等领域成为近年来新的投资热门领域。[1]

中阿经济结构互补。中国拥有广阔的消费市场、完备的工业体系，阿拉伯国家能源资源丰富，经济多元化发展方兴未艾，双方是天然合作伙伴。随着共建"一带一路"深入推进，中阿经贸合作不断扩展，绿色经济和高科技领域等合作迎来新发展。

中阿命运共同体建设取得积极进展。[2] 2024 年 5 月 30 日，中共中央政治局委员、外交部部长王毅在出席中国—阿拉伯国家合作论坛第十届部长级会议时表示，首届中阿峰会举办以来，在习近平主席和阿拉伯国家领导人的指引下，中阿命运共同体建设取得明显进展，中阿关系进入了历史最好时期。5 月 30 日，中阿合作论坛第十届部长级会议在京成功举行，取得丰硕成果。会议通过《北京宣言》《中国—阿拉伯国家合作论坛 2024 年至 2026 年行动执行计划》《中国和阿拉伯国家关于巴勒斯坦问题的联合声明》三份成果文件。行动执行计划就未来两年中阿加强论坛机制建设，推进多双边政治、经贸、投资、金融、基础设施、资源环境、人文交流、航空航天、教育卫生等领域合作做出规划。会议期间，中方还同与会各国及阿盟秘书处签署了多份双多边合作文件。国家主席习近平出席中阿合作论坛第十届部长级会议开幕式并发表主旨讲话，提出四方面目标和构建"五大合作格局"，引发阿拉伯国家各界人士热烈反响。中国将继续同阿拉伯国家高质量共建"一带一路"，给古老的丝绸之路注入鲜活时代动力。中国将同阿拉伯国家进一步筑牢能源合作主轴，强化能源供求伙伴关系。中国欢迎阿拉伯国家加大投资中国发展，同时将继续支持在阿拉伯国家实施标志性的大项目、"小而美"

---

[1] 《阿拉伯国家吸引外资磁力增强》，《人民日报》（海外版）2023 年 8 月 10 日。

[2] 王毅：《做中阿命运共同体建设的行动派实干家——王毅在中阿合作论坛第十届部长级会议上的讲话》，中阿合作论坛网站，http://www.chinaarabcf.org/chn/zyfw/202405/t20240531_11366647.htm，2024 年 5 月 31 日。

的好工程，同阿方合力打造更具科技含量的高新产业增长极。[①] 习近平主席宣布，中方将于2026年在中国举办第二届中阿峰会。阿拉伯各国人士对此充满期待，认为中阿峰会将进一步引领阿中命运共同体建设阔步前行。

3.3.2 中阿投资合作新挑战

当前，中国发展面临复杂严峻的国际环境和艰巨繁重的国内改革发展稳定任务。全球经济增长动能偏弱，通胀具有黏性，地缘政治冲突、国际贸易摩擦等问题频发，国内有效需求不足，企业经营压力较大，重点领域风险隐患较多，推动经济稳定运行面临诸多困难和挑战。与此同时，阿拉伯国家也面临较大下行风险和不确定性，包括巴以冲突升级和苏丹武装冲突持续、红海危机、债务危机激增、石油减产和紧缩的财政政策、生活成本高和增长率缓慢等。受全球增长前景乏力、贸易和地缘政治局势紧张、工业政策调整和供应链重塑等因素影响，国际投资环境在2024年仍将充满挑战。

中阿投资合作面临的新挑战主要体现在地缘政治、国际竞争，以及融入国际主流的ESG（环境、社会和公司治理）标准等领域。新一轮巴以冲突和该地区潜在的军事升级所带来的不确定性，给初创企业生态系统蒙上了一层阴影，促使地区和国际风险投资公司采取观望的态度，也对阿拉伯国家外资流入造成负面影响。中美关系是影响中阿投资合作的重要地缘政治因素。中美的紧张关系不仅体现在政治和安全领域，也对两国的经济合作产生了间接影响。美国秉持冷战思维，把经贸问题"政治化""安全化"，加大了对阿拉伯主权财富基金的审查力度，尤其对高新技术融资项目、金融科技等领域，阻挠中阿合作。对于中东资本而言，这些博弈可能增加其在华投资的不确定性风险和政治成本。中美关系对高科技领域的影响尤为显著。从长期看，中美关系的变化对于中东资本进入中国投资既是

---

① 王毅：《加快构建面向新时代的中阿命运共同体》，《人民日报》2024年5月30日。

挑战也是机会。美西方与中国"脱钩、断链",导致中国外商投资与资本市场下行压力加大。阿拉伯国家日益意识到美元霸权的潜在风险,在产业多元化和摆脱对美国依赖的动机下,阿拉伯金融资本加大对中国的投资布局,看好中国经济发展巨大潜力,"向东看"到"向东行"不断加速。此外,阿拉伯国家投资门槛高,倾向欧洲标准,中国企业面临来自欧美、印度以及日本和韩国等新兴经济体的激烈竞争。

对于那些考虑在阿拉伯国家进行投资的中国企业来说,重要的是设定合理的预期。同时,由于文化上存在的显著差异,投资者在决策过程中需要对可能出现的认知偏差和潜在风险保持警觉。中企主要面临以下四方面风险。第一,政治风险,这往往体现为投资所在国政局是否稳定。第二,政策与法律风险,一个行业的发展与政策法律的支持息息相关。因此,政策与法律的稳定性,对于出海企业判断长期的发展机遇与风险,整合、优化资源配置有重要作用。同时,阿拉伯地区其法律体系与大陆法系、英美法系均有所不同,出海企业要避免陷入过往经验的怪圈。第三,要考虑商业风险、汇率风险等变化,给国内企业投资带来不确定因素的增加。第四,合规风险。中国企业在"出海"过程中面临海外市场进入战略、税务筹划、成本控制、文化融入、本土化、数据安全合规等一系列挑战。尽管阿拉伯主权财富基金被视为替代美国 LP(有限合伙人)的上乘选择,但实际上,其目前投资重心仍在欧美地区。投资已经成为中东国家获取技术、人才的敲门砖,阿拉伯人千年商业文化底蕴令他们更加专业、务实,会更多注重投资是否会对国家发展战略有帮助。中企出海到中东,必须具备国际化视野和跨文化能力,能够理解对方想法。

中国和阿拉伯国家的"双向奔赴"正在加速。过去几十年,在中阿经济关系中,主要是中国向阿拉伯国家单向投资,阿拉伯国家巨额石油美元主要投向欧美市场。但最近两年形势发生重大变化,中国成为阿拉伯资本的新兴目的地,中阿双向投资流量基本持平。更值得关注的是,这种变化不是暂时的策略调整,而是一种长期的战略转向,背后既有政治原因,亦有经济考虑。① 展望未来，中阿投资合作热的趋势还将持续。中国与阿拉伯国家不断强化的政治与经济合作，是全球地缘政治发展、中国经济巨大发展潜力、阿拉伯国家多元化转型、全球能源转型、中国与阿拉伯国家经济产业结构高度互补以及中国与中东国家长期相对友好与认同等多种因素叠加而形成的客观结果。这些趋势在未来几年内将持续并不断深化。目前，中国经济面临的内外压力与结构性因素叠加，也让中国企业有更多动力去开拓中东新市场。"中国方案+本土产能"有利于中国中东投资实现双赢。②

当前发展优先、和解合作与平衡外交成为阿拉伯国家政府优先要务，中国式现代化提出加快发展新质生产力，进一步加大对外开放步伐。2022年12月首届中阿峰会召开标志着中阿合作进入新时代。2024年5月在中阿合作论坛第十届部长级会议开幕式上，习近平主席指出：在推进中阿务实合作"八大共同行动"的基础上，"同阿方构建'五大合作格局'，推动中阿命运共同体建设跑出加速度"。③ 中阿双方的合作空间进一步打开，无论是在传统能源、基建、经贸领域，还是在人工智能、投融资、新能源等新领域，都体现出中阿合作的新潜力和新动能，持续推动中阿关系跨越式发展，将为推动中阿命运共同体建设注入强大动力。

---

① 牛新春：《阿拉伯国家对华投资激增，既有经济账，也有政治账》，《中国日报》2024年4月2日。

② 李明珠：《深化中东投资　中国方案+本土产能实现双赢》，《证券时报》2024年3月13日。

③ 一是更富活力的创新驱动格局；二是更具规模的投资金融格局；三是更加立体的能源合作格局；四是更为平衡的经贸互惠格局；五是更广维度的人文交流格局。参见习近平《深化合作，继往开来：推动中阿命运共同体建设跑出加速度——在中阿合作论坛第十届部长级会议开幕式上的主旨讲话》，人民出版社，2024，第4—6页。

第4章　中阿金融合作专题报告

中国在产业和技术方面同阿拉伯国家形成优势互补，金融合作在促进中国与阿拉伯国家之间的经贸、基建和产能项目发展进程中扮演关键角色。得益于中阿合作论坛及"一带一路"倡议，双方的金融协作日益紧密，取得显著进展，并不断创新突破。阿拉伯国家持续向东寻求多元化投资市场，致力于减少对石油收入的依赖并优化金融结构，在中国市场加强布局资本配置的意愿持续增强；金融实力较强的阿拉伯国家不但是中国新兴产业融资来源的重要补充，也是进一步推动人民币国际化的重要合作伙伴。展望未来，双方的金融合作有着极大的发展潜力。

4.1　阿拉伯国家金融环境

4.1.1　阿拉伯国家金融发展呈现两极分化

在国际金融领域，资金的流动突破国家界限。一国的金融体系并不是孤立的，其国内经济增长是否持续、金融政策是否稳定、金融体系是否安全等宏观因素决定了金融发展内生动力的强弱，而对外开放程度的高低，以及国际信誉是否良好则影响着一国配置外部金融资产的实际能力。阿拉伯国家金融发展的主要力量来自资金雄厚的海合会各成员国，人均 GDP均达到世界领先水平，并且实现了大量资本积累和财政盈余；中低收入水平的阿拉伯国家金融整体发展水平相对薄弱，金融体系开放程度普遍较低。

中阿经贸关系发展进程2023年度报告

表 4.1　阿拉伯国家金融开放程度及债务水平

国别	金融开放指数	外债存量总额（百万美元）	外债存量总额占 GNI 比重（%）	偿债额占出口比重（%）
高收入经济体				
巴林	1.00			
科威特	0.70			
阿曼	0.94			
卡塔尔	1.00			
沙特	0.70			
阿联酋	1.00			
中等偏上收入经济体				
利比亚	0.16			
阿尔及利亚	0.16	7129	3.7	0.4
伊拉克	—	22588	8.6	5.3（2021）
中等偏下收入经济体				
科摩罗	0.16	368.7	29.5	2.7
吉布提	0.70	3170	88.5	1.6
埃及	0.42	163104	35.4	23.2
约旦	1.00	41204	85.6	21.4
黎巴嫩	0.45	67109	309.4（2021）	32.7
突尼斯	0.16	39652	88.0	17.8
毛里塔尼亚	0.16	4604	47.4	8.0
摩洛哥	0.16	64713	50.1	10.1
低收入经济体				
索马里	—	4164	40.1	1.1
苏丹	0.55	22433	44.2	2.9
叙利亚	0.00	4848	58.8（2021）	3.1（2010）
也门	1.00	7351	32.6（2018）	14.6（2016）

注：金融开放指数更新至 2021 年，债务相关数据更新至 2022 年。如 2022 年数据缺失，则报告可获得的最近时期数据，引用的年份在标号中标出。

资料来源：Chinn-Ito 金融开放指数，世界银行国际债务统计（IDS）数据库，世界发展指标（WDI）数据库。数据库访问日期为 2024 年 9 月。

阿拉伯国家的金融发展呈现明显的两极分化特征。Chinn-Ito 金融开放指数是衡量各国资本账户开放程度的常用指标，属于高收入经济体的海合会各成员国金融开放指数均居于前列，吉布提和约旦等国的资本账户开放程度也相对较高（见表 4.1），其余多数阿拉伯国家金融开放程度较低。从外部融资角度看，如果外债负担比例过高且不断增加，将影响国家主权信誉和抵御外部冲击的能力，尤其是对于低收入国家而言，该国对外融资会变得难以持续。分别以外债存量占国民总收入（GNI）的比重衡量一国负债率，以偿债额占出口额比重衡量一国偿债压力，前者在国际上公认的安全线是 20%，后者一般设定在 15%～25%。综合来看，埃及、约旦、吉布提和黎巴嫩的外债负担十分突出，埃及的外债存量规模更是在阿拉伯国家中居于首位，达到 1631 亿美元。

随着外债负担和偿债成本攀升，发展中国家可选择的融资渠道日益受限，特别是中低收入国家，因长期经济落后和财政实力不足，整体经济抵御风险能力较差，当外汇大量流出、本国货币大幅贬值时，往往出现流动性危机，极有可能陷入主权债务困境。世界银行发布的《2024年国际债务报告》显示，2023 年，全球低收入和中等收入国家（LMICs）的外部债务总额达 8.8 万亿美元，较上年增长 2.4%；全球利率上升加大了债务负担，当年的总偿债支出达 1.4 万亿美元，其中利息支付达到 2723亿美元，增幅达 41.7%，许多发展中国家面临沉重偿债压力。阿拉伯国家中，苏丹长期进入全球主权违约债务集中程度最高的前十国家名单之列，伊拉克和黎巴嫩等国家也有主权债务违约的较大风险。这些债务负担沉重的阿拉伯国家，不但难以在国际上实现顺利融资，甚至无法获得国际援助；索马里、苏丹和也门等低收入国家，以及巴勒斯坦、利比亚等受地区争端影响而陷入战乱和社会危机的国家，金融体系十分脆弱；美国对叙利亚的经济制裁，更导致了该国经济发展停滞不前，难以融入国际金融体系。

4.1.2 主要阿拉伯国家的国际金融中心地位日益突出

阿拉伯国家拥有多个重要的国际金融枢纽，排名呈上升趋势。根据2023年9月发布的第34期全球金融中心指数报告（GFCI 34），阿拉伯国家在全球121个金融中心占有7个席位，除摩洛哥卡萨布兰卡来自非洲，其余六大金融中心均来自亚洲（见表4.2）。阿联酋金融业非常发达，迪拜和阿布扎比是阿拉伯国家中最有影响力的金融中心，在区域内排名前二，迪拜金融市场也是中东最活跃的股票市场之一。沙特正积极转化其首都利雅得为中东金融中心。

从得分看，阿拉伯国家七大金融中心评分均有所提高，整体平均得分比上期提高了5.9%，显现出在营商环境、人力资本、基础设施、税收和声誉等相关金融业发展水平的综合竞争力不断上升。在GFCI 34的次级指数排名中，迪拜在投资管理的部门排名中位列全球第13位，专业服务位列第15位，金融科技位列第11位，是阿拉伯国家中最为领先的金融中心，吸引了大量跨国企业和境外投资者。

表4.2 阿拉伯国家地区金融中心排名情况

金融中心	GFCI 34 地区排名	GFCI 34 全球排名	GFCI 34 得分	排名变化	得分变化
迪拜	1	21	719	↑1	↑17
阿布扎比	2	35	702	0	↑13
卡萨布兰卡	3	54	682	↑3	↑40
巴林	4	74	660	↑8	↑51
利雅得	5	75	659	↑13	↑56
多哈	6	78	656	↓14	↑28
科威特城	7	82	646	↑20	↑57

资料来源：全球金融中心指数（Global Financial Centres Indes，GFCI）。

4.2　中阿金融合作进展

中阿双方在中阿合作论坛和共建"一带一路"框架下进一步加强资金融通，不断推进金融合作的平台与机制建设，合作形式与范围不断拓展，在央行合作、人民币国际化，以及吸收阿拉伯主权财富基金对华融资等方面都取得了积极成果。

4.2.1　平台建设

中海合作不断推进落实。2023年10月22日，中国—海合会6+1经贸部长会在中国广州举行。会议聚焦首届中国—海湾阿拉伯国家合作委员会峰会经贸举措落实，就共同维护多边贸易体制、促进双向投资、深化产业链供应链合作、提升互联互通水平、推动能源转型等议题达成广泛共识，通过了《中华人民共和国与海湾阿拉伯国家合作委员会成员国经贸部长关于深化经贸合作的联合声明》。

中阿企业各领域交流平台日益增多，发挥着带动投融资的积极作用。2023年2月，在沙特首都利雅得举行的LEAP 2023峰会上，中国—沙特企业联合会正式成立，旨在连接两国高层政府机构、企业、非营利组织以及学术机构。2023年6月，沙特利雅得举办中阿合作论坛第十届企业家大会暨第八届投资研讨会，围绕贸易、金融、能源、绿色产业等议题展开交流，中阿双方签署了价值超过700亿元人民币的30多项经济与投资合作协议。2023年8月，中国—沙特商业论坛举办期间，中沙双方签署了12项价值超50亿沙特里亚尔（13亿美元）的合作协议。2023年12月15日，中沙投资峰会在北京举行，双方签署了60多份合作协议和备忘录，涉及能源、农业、旅游、矿业、金融、物流、医疗保健等众多领域。

中东成为深圳打造国际财富管理中心，进行业务联动和产业布局的目标地区。2023年1月，为加快建设国际财富管理高地，探索多渠道增加居民财产性收入，贯彻"守望相助，平等互利，包容互鉴"的中阿友好精神，深圳首次引入沙特公共投资基金，在境内成立蓝海太库（深圳）私募股权投资基金有限公司，并发起首支中东合作基金，首支基金规模超过 10亿美元。

香港凭借其独特的国际金融地位，助力中国内地和沙特市场的联结。2023 年 2 月，中国香港特别行政区行政长官李家超率团访问沙特后，双方积极推动经贸合作，取得首批成果。沙特通信与信息技术部部长 Abdullah Al-Swaha 访问香港期间，11 家中国内地和香港公司与易达资本签署了关于进军沙特市场及加入中沙企业联合会的合作备忘录，旨在促进香港领先的金融和技术公司进入沙特市场。中国—沙特阿拉伯企业联合会通过香港办公室连接中国内地、中国香港和沙特，加强人才交流、商业合作和创新科技领域的合作，推动沙特公司在沙特和香港交易所上市。2023 年 9 月，香港举办"一带一路"高峰论坛，并首次设立中东论坛。

4.2.2　中央银行合作

中国与阿拉伯国家中央银行间进一步加强双边本币互换和人民币清算合作，促进本币直接兑换结算，缓解贸易融资压力，有效应对短期流动性波动的问题，推动双方贸易与投资往来，在维护地区金融稳定与健康发展方面发挥了积极作用。

双边本币结算。2023 年，在银行间外汇市场即期交易中，人民币/沙特里亚尔交易量为 28.5 亿元人民币，较 2022 年 33.2 亿元人民币的规模有所下降；人民币/阿联酋迪拉姆交易量为 7.2 亿元人民币，较 2022 年1.6 亿元人民币规模提高了 3.5 倍。[①]

双边本币互换。至 2023 年末，中国人民银行共与 41 个国家和地区的中央银行或货币当局签署规模超过 4 万亿元人民币的双边本币互换协议，

[①]　中国人民银行：《2024 年人民币国际化报告》，http：//www.pbc.gov.cn/huobizhengceersi/214481/3871621/5472873/index.html，2024 年 9 月 30 日。

其中同阿拉伯国家签署的有效协议包括：2023 年 2 月 20 日，中国人民银行与埃及中央银行续签规模为 180 亿元人民币/807 亿元埃及镑的双边本币互换协议；2023 年 11 月 20 日，中国人民银行与沙特中央银行签署双边本币互换协议，互换规模为 500 亿元人民币/260 亿沙特里亚尔，协议有效期三年；2023 年 11 月 28 日，中国人民银行与阿联酋中央银行续签双边本币互换协议，协议有效期 5 年，互换规模为 350 亿元人民币/180 亿阿联酋迪拉姆。双边本币互换安排，有助于加强两国金融合作，扩大本币使用并促进双方贸易和投资便利化。

境外清算机制安排。2023 年，设立人民币清算行的国家和地区增至 33 个，中国工商银行多哈分行和中国农业银行迪拜分行分别是卡塔尔和阿联酋唯一的人民币业务清算行，业务辐射周边更广泛区域，在满足中东与北非客户跨境人民币资金清算需求方面发挥了重要作用。人民币跨境支付系统（CIPS）运行平稳，为境内外金融机构提供资金清算与结算服务。截至 2023 年末，共有 139 家直接参与者，阿拉伯国家中的中国银行（吉布提）有限公司、中国银行股份有限公司迪拜分行、中国银行股份有限公司阿布扎比分行、中国银行卡塔尔金融中心分行、中国工商银行股份有限公司多哈分行、中国工商银行股份有限公司利雅得分行、中国农业银行迪拜分行，以及中国农业银行股份有限公司迪拜国际金融中心分行成为 CIPS 直参行。

4.2.3　金融机构及业务开展

设立分支机构。2023 年，中国工商银行与中国银行在沙特阿拉伯开设分行，成为落地沙特的第二家和第三家中资银行。设立分支机构进一步拓展了中资金融服务的覆盖面，显示出中方对沙特金融监管、投资环境以及区位优势的高度认可，标志着两国金融领域合作迈上新台阶，为共建"一带一路"和沙特"2030 愿景"深入对接的双边务实合作提供更有力支持。

中阿经贸关系发展进程2023年度报告

互发债券。"熊猫债"① 稳步提升人民币融资货币功能，有序推进人民币国际化进程。近年来，在主要发达经济体大幅加息的环境下，人民币融资成本相对下降。随着中国债券市场规模提升和开放水平提高，境外主体境内发债的便利性和规范性进一步优化，注册地在境外的发行人在境内发行的以人民币计价的"熊猫债"呈较快增长态势。Wind 数据显示，2022 年全年熊猫债发行共计 850.7 亿元人民币，2023 年全年增长到 1554.5 亿元人民币。阿联酋于 2018 年在中国银行间债券市场成功发行了规模达 20 亿元人民币的中东首支主权"熊猫债"；2023 年 10 月，埃及成功发行 35 亿元人民币可持续发展"熊猫债"，也是非洲首单"熊猫债"。2023 年 11 月，中国工商银行"一带一路"主题绿色债券在纳斯达克迪拜交易所成功上市，此次绿色债券的成功使工商银行在纳斯达克迪拜交易所上市的债券规模达到 74 亿美元，成为该交易所领先的中资债券发行人。这些债券的成功发行，显示了中国与阿拉伯国家在资本募集、投资方面的合作潜力。

人民币贷款。2023 年 3 月，中国进出口银行与沙特国家银行落地首笔人民币贷款合作，资金优先用于中沙双边贸易，促进了中国与阿拉伯国家资金融资、贸易畅通，为双边贸易和投资往来提供更有力支持。2023 年 10 月，中国进出口银行与摩洛哥非洲银行签署合作协议，双方将通过项目融资、平行融资、贸易融资等方式积极推动经贸往来与金融合作，同时加强信息共享和人员交流，共同探讨使用人民币贷款。标志着中阿之间的贸易和支付体系更加多样化，有助于减少对美元的依赖，降低外汇风险，为两国之间的商业交易提供更多便利。

资本市场平台合作。2023 年 2 月，香港交易所与沙特证交所集团签署合作备忘录，探讨在多个领域展开合作，包括互挂上市的安排。9 月 3 日，上海证券交易所与沙特交易所集团在利雅得签署合作备忘录，致力于促进企业上市和 ETF 双重上市。9 月 28 日，上海证券交易所与沙特交易所集

---

① "熊猫债"是指境外机构在中国发行的以人民币计价的债券。参见中国银行间市场交易商协会《熊猫债产品手册》，https://www.nafmii.org.cn/xhdt/202407/P0202407055339 54859021.pdf，2024，第 3 页。

070

团香港交易所全资附属公司香港联合交易所有限公司宣布，已将沙特交易所纳入其认可证券交易所名单，此后在沙特交易所主板市场上市的公司可以在香港申请第二上市。上海证券交易所和迪拜金融市场于 2023 年 11 月签署合作谅解备忘录，计划共同探索开发 ESG（环境、社会和公司治理）和可持续发展相关产品。香港交易所在 2023 年底引入亚太地区首个追踪沙特股票的交易所交易基金（ETF），标志着双方在加强国际合作、促进资本市场发展关键领域合作上迈出重要一步。

信贷保险业务。2023 年 10 月 9 日，中国出口信用保险公司承保首单中长期险新能源电力融资项目，为阿曼马纳 2 号 500 兆瓦光伏电站项目提供中长期出口买方信贷保险支持。

数字货币桥。自 2022 年参与数字货币桥试点以来，中国工商银行阿布扎比分行利用货币桥平台，在货物贸易、服务贸易、银行间资金调拨和资金拆借等场景下开展央行数字货币试点，取得良好效果。其中，通过数字货币桥开展的跨境人民币发薪业务，拓展了人民币国际化实际应用场景，更好地服务中资企业海外发展。

4.2.4　主权财富基金

作为国家公共部门的投资主体，主权财富基金迅速发展意味着发展中国家在国际金融体系的话语权和重要性在不断提高。主权财富基金研究所（SWFI）的最新排名显示，沙特公共投资基金（PIF）、阿联酋的阿布扎比投资局（ADIA）、科威特投资局（KIA）和卡塔尔投资局（QIA）均排在全球前列（见表 4.3）。近年来，阿拉伯国家主权财富基金不断增加在华投资。

表 4.3　全球十大主权财富基金排名

排名	主权财富基金	总资产（亿美元）	地区
1	挪威政府全球养老基金	16314	欧洲
2	中国投资有限责任公司	13500	亚洲

续表

排名	主权财富基金	总资产（亿美元）	地区
3	华安投资公司	10900	亚洲
4	阿布扎比投资局	9930	中东
5	沙特公共投资基金	9250	中东
6	科威特投资局	9234.5	中东
7	GIC 私人有限公司	7700	亚洲
8	卡塔尔投资局	5261	中东
9	香港金融管理局投资组合	5142	亚洲
10	淡马锡控股	4922	亚洲

资料来源：主权财富基金研究所（SWFI），查询时间为 2024 年 6 月。

在华资产配置。中国是科技创新和新经济领域的参与者和引领者。随着中国经济在创新领域的成果不断增加，中东主要主权财富基金在中国初创投资和风险投资市场加大投入，为具有增长潜力的新经济企业提供了资金支持和更多机遇。为寻求经济多元化发展和产业升级，中东主权基金在中国的一级市场加快资本配置。主权财富基金研究所（SWFI）数据显示，2023 年海湾六国的主权财富基金直接在华并购和投资额达到 23 亿美元。从行业分布来看，生物医药、人工智能和电动汽车是最有吸引力的投资领域（见表 4.4）。实力雄厚的中东主权财富基金选择直接参与中国高科技企业股权融资，一方面是因为可观的投资回报，另一方面有助于吸引中国高科技企业到阿拉伯国家发展业务，扶持当地科技产业升级发展。

表 4.4　阿拉伯国家主权财富基金投资中国企业代表案例

中方企业	时间	行业	阿拉伯投资方	融资情况
滴滴	2017 年 12 月	出行平台	穆巴达拉投资公司（MIC）	参与新一轮超 40 亿美元融资
陆金所	2019 年 3 月	财富管理	卡塔尔投资局（QIA）	领投 13.3 亿美元 C 轮融资

续表

中方企业	时间	行业	阿拉伯投资方	融资情况
旷视科技	2019 年 5 月	人工智能	阿布扎比投资局（ADIA）	领投 7.5 亿美元 D 轮融资
小鹏汽车	2020 年 8 月	电动汽车	卡塔尔投资局（QIA）、穆巴达拉投资公司（MIC）	MIC 和 QIA 认购小鹏汽车 C++轮融资中 1 亿美元优先股
创胜集团	2020 年 12 月	生物医药	卡塔尔投资局（QIA）	QIA 作为新投资者参与 1.05 亿美元交叉轮融资
商汤科技	2022 年 9 月	人工智能	沙特人工智能公司（SCAI）	达成合作协议，向商汤科技与 PIF 的合资公司 SenseTime MEA 投资 7.76 亿沙特里亚尔
英雄体育 VSPO	2023 年 2 月	娱乐	Savvy Games Group	PIF 旗下子公司 Savvy Games Group 向英雄体育 VSPO 投资 2.65 亿美元，成为单一最大股东
京东工业	2023 年 3 月	流通	穆巴达拉投资公司（MIC）、阿布扎比增长基金旗下 42X 基金	领投 3 亿美元融资
原启生物	2023 年 3 月	生物医药	卡塔尔投资局（QIA）	领投 4500 万美元的 B1 轮融资
海森生物	2023 年 4 月	生物医药	穆巴达拉投资公司（MIC）	由康桥资本和穆巴达拉领投 3.15 亿美元的融资
Shein	2023 年 5 月	电子商务	穆巴达拉投资公司（MIC）	领投新一轮 20 亿美元融资

续表

中方企业	时间	行业	阿拉伯投资方	融资情况
国动集团	2023 年 5 月	通信研发	穆巴达拉投资公司（MIC）	全资控股子公司 MIC Capital Management 投资的 1.5 亿美元融资
蔚来	2023 年 7 月	电动汽车	阿布扎比 CYVN Holdings	完成总计约 11 亿美元的战略投资
	2023 年 12 月			约 22 亿美元的战略投资
小黄鸭德盈	2023 年 7 月	娱乐	沙特公共投资基金（PIF）	投资总额 2.5 亿美元
中国生命科学产业设施基金	2023 年 10 月	医疗健康	穆巴达拉投资公司（MIC）	领投 8.75 亿美元募资
小马智行	2023 年 10 月	自动驾驶	新未来城投资基金（NIF）	投资总额 1 亿美元
易达资本	2023 年 12 月	投资机构	沙特公共投资基金（PIF）	投资总额达到约 2 亿美元

资料来源：根据公开报道整理。

除了一级市场私募股权投资之外，中东主权财富基金在中国资产配置也包括 A 股和 H 股市场。穆巴达拉投资公司更倾向于直接参与中国高科技企业股权融资，在 A 股证券市场的投资活动相对较少。A 股上市公司的十大股东中，频繁出现了阿布扎比投资局和科威特投资局等中东投资机构，这两大基金在行业选择上存在明显差异，阿布扎比投资局更偏重能源领域。

在华设立办事处。中东主权财富基金在中国境内设立分支机构，以便追踪了解中国高科技企业最新发展情况，做出投资决策。目前，阿布扎比投资局、科威特投资局、卡塔尔投资局、沙特公共投资基金等中东主权基金都已经在中国设立办事处。2022 年成立的阿联酋 42X 基金已在上海设立办事处。2023 年 9 月，穆巴达拉中国办公室在北京设立。沙特投资部（MISA）正在筹办粤港澳大湾区办公室。

4.3　中阿金融合作的发展趋势

2018 年 7 月，在中阿合作论坛第八届部长级会议开幕式上，中方提出中阿合作要牢牢抓住互联互通的"龙头"，积极推动油气合作、低碳能源合作"双轮"转动，努力实现金融合作、高新技术合作"两翼"齐飞。中阿金融的务实合作基于"一带一路"倡议与阿拉伯国家发展战略的对接，依托基础设施建设与产能建设的深化，正从国家战略高度建设机制和搭建平台的宏观层面，面向和吸引更广泛的金融市场参与主体，以多种创新形式扎实推动中阿金融合作。

主要阿拉伯国家的长期发展战略为中阿金融合作创造了更多机遇。实现经济发展多元化与可持续增长是阿拉伯国家未来一段时期的重大发展愿景。沙特作为世界上最大的石油出口国之一，经济实力雄厚，加快金融业转型是该国"2030 愿景"的重要组成部分，沙特正积极将首都利雅得转化为中东金融中心。阿联酋为减少对石油的依赖，发展了极具竞争力的金融服务业和新型基础设施。卡塔尔《2030 年国家愿景规划》提出把资源转化为国家金融财富，加速实现经济多元化。埃及作为非洲第三大经济体，近年来通过实施经济改革，致力于在通货膨胀和债务负担的压力下增强宏观经济的韧性。近年来，阿拉伯国家不断推出产业转型和开放政策，改善融资和政策环境，力求为国际金融投资创造更多合作空间，以实现经济多元化的发展目标。

中阿金融合作持续为基础和能源项目赋能。在共建"一带一路"倡议下，中国企业在全球范围内投资建设了大量基建项目，涉及 5G、高铁、公路、港口和能源等领域，为发展中国家提供了良好的产业基础。大部分阿拉伯国家处在国家转型关键时期，本国经济和社会发展所需的资金和金融服务不足，来自中国的技术和经验弥补了其发展短板，促进了本国基础设施建设和产业升级。围绕能源基建，中阿之间持续开展多个金融合作项目。2023 年 10 月 9 日，中国出口信用保险公司承保首单中长期险新能源电力融资项目，为阿曼马纳 2 号 500 兆瓦光伏电站项目提供中长期出口买方信贷保险支持。同月，由丝路基金、哈电集团与阿联酋投资机构共同投资建设的迪拜哈斯彦电站项目全部投入商业运行，该电站也是丝路基金在中东地区的首单投资，将为迪拜提供 20% 的电力能源，助力当地实现能源结构多元化发展。截至 2023 年底，国家开发银行在埃及累计发放贷款超过 64.8 亿美元，在基建金融领域重点支持了埃及 500 千伏输电线路工程、中埃·泰达苏伊士经贸合作区等项目。

具有前瞻性的新能源等高新技术产业成为阿拉伯国家在华投资的新亮点。阿拉伯资本参与中国境内金融市场的目的更加清晰，诉求更加积极主动，中阿金融合作也成为阿拉伯资本加快产业布局、实现经济多元化的重要渠道。中国新经济企业日益受到阿拉伯国家主权财富基金以及大型企业资本的青睐，在新能源、数字科技、医疗健康等高新技术领域的投资项目积极推进。以新能源汽车为例，阿拉伯国家正加快与中国新能源汽车企业的合作，以获得更为快速的发展。2023 年 10 月 9 日，北汽新能源与阿联酋的本奥米尔控股集团有限公司达成合作共识，对车型进行智能化技术的升级与改进，并在市场推广方面进行深度合作。2023 年 10 月 11 日，西菱动力披露与阿布扎比本奥米尔控股集团有限公司签订《战略合作框架备忘录》，本奥米尔将作为西菱动力战略投资人，双方计划设立合资公司投资 7 亿元人民币用于开发新能源汽车零部件。金融领域合作将为双边产业务实合作提供更有力支持。

中国香港在推进金融开放方面领先一步，成为联系中国内地与主要海湾国家资金融通的重要通道。境外参与者对人民币利率风险管理需求持续增加，中国金融市场双向开放稳步推进。2022 年 7 月，中国人民银行、香港证券及期货事务监察委员会（香港证监会）、香港金管局发布联合公告，宣布中国内地与中国香港利率互换市场互联互通合作（简称"互换通"）启动建设。2023 年 5 月 15 日，"互换通"正式上线，便利境外投资者参与境内人民币利率互换市场，支持构建高水平金融开放格局。2023 年以来，中国香港与沙特在深化两地资本市场的互联互通方面取得了显著进展。2023 年，阿布扎比投资办公室与香港 Arte Capital 合作，帮助中国企业在中东和北非地区扩张，进一步促进了中阿两国的经济联系。中国香港在金融服务领域与以沙特和阿联酋为代表的中东国家建立了更加紧密的合作关系，促进监管层面的对话和理解，为未来资本市场的深入合作奠定了坚实基础。

4.4　中阿金融合作展望

中国与阿拉伯国家在金融领域的深入合作，是中阿全面协作的关键成就之一。阿拉伯国家为了扩大海外投资市场、降低对石油经济的依赖、完善金融体系以及促进国内产业升级等实际发展需求，与中国的金融合作意愿持续上升，并与中国进一步扩大对外开放的发展战略相契合。积极推动"一带一路"倡议、中海经贸合作、金砖机制与阿拉伯国家经济发展愿景等中长期战略和规划的对接，深化金融合作，有利于共同促进双方的产业升级和发展。

现阶段的中阿金融合作，主要由中资金融机构进行的贸易结算、跨境投资和银团贷款等业务构成，金融市场主体的积极性和参与度还处于起步阶段，金融机构对于"走出去"中小企业的融资支持力度尚显不足。展望未来，应加强金融监管的合作与风险防范，促进资本市场的进一步开放，推动包括证券和债券发行在内的多级金融服务平台的构建，进一步提高在货币互换安排和离岸人民币清算中心的建立，以期通过金融合作的深化来促进和带动贸易与投资。

在更多层次的机制建设中加强与主要阿拉伯国家金融政策的对接。长期以来，中国在很大程度上将阿拉伯世界视为一个整体，而实际上阿拉伯各国的发展程度有着极大差异，中阿金融方面的主要合作项目更多地集中于经济增长积极且金融体系完善的国家。除了中阿合作论坛和"一带一路"倡议的平台及框架，中国与主要阿拉伯国家的小范围合作，并以此为基础辐射到其他阿拉伯国家也是重要的路径选择。首先是加强建设中海合作平台。中国与海合会各成员国发展战略进行对接，强化经贸合作机制建设，依托中国—海合会6+1经贸部长会和双边经贸联（混）委会等平台，深化贸易投资、数字经济、可持续发展、基础设施等领域交流合作，积极推进中海共同投资联合会运作。其次是金砖框架下的共同合作。2023年8月24日，在南非举行的金砖国家领导人第十五次会晤宣布金砖国家合作机制第二次扩员，沙特、埃及、阿联酋、伊朗、埃塞俄比亚于2024年1月1日正式成为金砖国家成员。其中，沙特是中国面向中东和北非地区投资与贸易的重要支点，阿联酋作为主要转口贸易枢纽，能够对周边阿拉伯国家和地区起到更多的辐射和带动作用，埃及掌管着沟通红海和地中海的苏伊士运河，在地理位置上极具重要性。加强沟通与协调，充分利用金砖机制推动金融市场开放，借助沙特、阿联酋和埃及在阿拉伯国家的影响力，将促使中阿建立贸易投资和金融的高效联系。

以金融技术创新促进市场互联互通，建立更顺畅的人民币境内外循环机制，以能源合作为基础推动人民币国际化进程。便利化贸易和支付体系，将有效降低外汇风险，为中阿经贸往来提供更多便利。继续推进央行数字货币的应用试点，积极参与多边支付系统的对接以及区域性结算平台的构建，促进在多边货币桥框架下的跨境支付互联，以减少对当前美元支付体系的依赖。2023年11月，中国人民银行与阿联酋中央银行签署了《关于加强央行数字货币合作的谅解备忘录》，中国银行与阿联酋第一阿布扎比银行签署了数字货币合作协议，双方在金融技术创新和央行数字货币方面开展合作。在大宗商品交易领域，人民币结算货币功能不断深化。2022年，大宗商品贸易领域人民币跨境收付保持较快增长，全年主要大宗商品贸易跨境人民币结算金额合计为9857.3亿元。上海期货交易所的可交割国外原油品种均来自阿拉伯国家，2022年原油期货总成交量为5358.1万手，已成为全球第三大原油期货交易中心，人民币原油期货影响力逐渐增加。中东产油国正寻求减少对美元的依赖，增强与包括中国在

第4章 中阿金融合作专题报告

内的全球主要经济体的货币合作。中阿双方以深厚的能源合作为基础，为人民币继续扩大在国际结算和交易中的使用创造了条件。在重构大宗商品结算和定价机制的过程中，人民币作为国际货币的角色将得到持续加强。

对接阿拉伯国家能源转型和金融科技等新技术领域的诉求，促进双边融资和政策环境的提升，加快企业"走出去"，抢占新兴产业全球布局的重要机遇。当前，阿拉伯国家大力推进能源转型，在多个阿拉伯国家的发展战略愿景中，经济多元化和数字化转型的需求频繁出现，减少石油经济比重而转向数字经济和高科技领域的呼声越来越高。在此背景下，新能源和金融科技等行业发展迅速，大量的传统产业转型升级也不断加快。拥有大量可再生能源资源的中东地区，成功落地一系列代表世界先进水平的项目。中阿不断探索在新能源、数字经济等创新领域的金融合作，在全球绿色低碳发展倡导下，积极推动能源转型，不断释放光伏、风电、核能、氢能、物质能等清洁能源，以及动力电池、智能充电桩等新能源汽车产业合作潜能。宝钢股份在 2023 年 5 月 1 日与沙特阿拉伯国家石油公司、沙特公共投资基金正式签约，共同在沙特建设全球首家绿色低碳全流程厚板工厂。2023 年 6 月 19 日，前途汽车母公司长城华冠与约旦最大的私营公司 Manaseer Group 签署战略合作协议，双方将共同在约旦建立合资公司，以服务中东和北非电动汽车市场。在数字化转型背景下，中国企业将数字支付技术和金融服务扩展到阿拉伯商家，通过提供跨境移动支付、数字化技术解决方案、商家支付服务、跨境贸易的数字支付和金融服务以及数字批发银行等服务获得更大的市场前景。例如迪拜金融科技生态系统的快速扩展，为中国金融科技公司提供了与当地金融机构合作、测试新产品和服务的机会；iPayLinks 拥有成熟的支付解决方案，也是国内首家获得沙特服务投资许可的金融科技公司。阿拉伯国家的商业社会和资本市场逐步向中国开放，为行业领先的创新企业提供财政激励政策和投资者帮扶支持。中国积极鼓励和支持企业和金融机构深化同阿拉伯国家在新技术领域的合作，逐步扩大项目运营和合作规模，也有助于中国企业完善全球产业链，增强国际竞争力和影响力。

中阿经贸关系发展进程2023年度报告

吸引主权财富基金为代表的阿拉伯资本在中国境内金融市场中发挥更大作用。国家主权财富基金因其较高的风险承受能力而迅速崛起，成为21世纪国际金融市场的一个重要新兴力量。阿拉伯国家主权财富基金传统上聚焦欧美市场，近年来显示出对中国金融市场的关注，以及对中国经济长期增长前景的积极评价。沙特公共投资基金在2017—2021年对华股权投资总金额达到约122亿美元，占其海外股权投资总额的约1/5。以阿布扎比穆巴达拉投资公司为例，计划将其管理的亚洲资产占总资产的比重，从约12%提升至2030年的25%，这将促使数百亿美元规模的资金流入亚洲市场。中国在工业制造体系中，无论是技术还是供应链上下游的建立，与阿拉伯国家相比都形成了明显的产业优势，得到阿拉伯资本融资支持的创新型企业利用广泛的网络和资源优势，可以更好地创造协同效应，助力阿拉伯国家当地经济转型和技术发展，有利于实现双赢。

中阿金融合作展现出巨大的潜力和前景。中阿金融合作的不断加强，不仅展现了彼此之间的深厚信任和对加强经济贸易及投资合作的强烈意愿，促进金融以及各行业的务实合作达到新的高度，为双边关系提供持久而强大的推动力，共同提高发展中国家话语权，促进全球金融治理向更加平衡和多元化的方向发展。

080

第5章 中阿农业合作专题报告

农业合作是中阿经贸合作的重要组成部分。在元首外交战略引领下，中阿务实合作越走越实，农业合作正不断结出丰硕果实，农产品贸易额持续增长，农业科技合作稳步推进，交流合作不断增强。

5.1 阿拉伯国家农业发展现状

农业是国民经济的基础，社会稳定的基石。重视农业不仅可以消除许多危机，还可以为各国增加经济和战略优势。农业具有重要的战略性，农业生产被阿拉伯国家视为国家经济的重点，也体现在其国家发展战略之中，如埃及"2030 愿景"、沙特"2030 愿景"、阿曼"2020 愿景计划"、苏丹"五年经济改革规划（2015—2019）"、吉布提"2015—2019 年加快经济发展与促进就业战略"、科摩罗"2017—2021 年加快经济增长战略"等。这些发展战略都将促进农业生产视为国家经济建设和改善民生的主要议题。例如，突尼斯主要生产谷物和橄榄油，是世界上生产和出口橄榄油的主要国家之一。以海合会国家为代表的非粮食生产国则通过将部分农业产业转移至其他国家发展，利用他国富余的土地资源发展本国农业，从而为本国人民提供所需粮食，缓解粮食安全危机。农业部门对阿拉伯国家的经济贡献率因国家而异。在沙特，农业部门的贡献率约为 3.2%；在阿联酋，2022 年农业部门的贡献约为 153 亿迪拉姆，预计 2025 年将增长 28%，达到 190 亿迪拉姆；在埃及，2022 年农业部门

081

中阿经贸关系发展进程2023年度报告

的贡献率为 15%。[1]

阿拉伯地区农业普遍不发达，阿拉伯国家总面积约为 14.02 亿公顷，约占世界总土地面积的 10.2%，可耕地面积约为 1.97 亿公顷。制约阿拉伯地区农业可持续发展的一个主要问题是农业用地和水资源短缺。此外，该地区还面临着水土流失、沙漠化、涝渍和盐碱化导致的自然资源退化的严重问题。由于可耕地面积不足、水资源严重短缺、气候变化以及持续的地缘政治冲突，阿拉伯地区面临巨大的粮食安全问题，而人口的快速增长则加剧了这一问题。阿拉伯地区人口年增长率超 2%，高于全球中等收入国家的年平均增长率（1.3%）。

阿拉伯国家高度依赖粮食进口，尤其是小麦。人口增长和气候变化只会增加阿拉伯国家对小麦进口的依赖，从而使其更易遭受国际市场波动的影响。因此，保障粮食安全不仅是在解决人民温饱问题，更是在维护统治者的执政根基。从表 5.1 可知，埃及是世界上第二大小麦进口国。2023 年，全球小麦进口额最高的 15 个国家中，阿拉伯国家有 3 个，分别为埃及、摩洛哥和阿尔及利亚。与 2022 年相比，阿尔及利亚排名从第 6 名下降至第 11 名，摩洛哥从第 8 名下降至第 10 名。[2] 在全球小麦进口前 100 个国家中，阿拉伯国家有 14 个，其中仅伊拉克进口小麦为增幅，增长了 90.4%，这主要是缺水、沙漠化等导致小麦产量下降，迫使伊拉克不得不通过进口弥补缺口。冬季缺雨是伊拉克小麦、大米和大麦等农作物生产面临的最大挑战。

表 5.1 2023 年部分阿拉伯国家小麦进口情况

世界市场排名	进口国	进口额（亿美元）	变化幅度（%）
2	埃及	37.73	-11.6
10	摩洛哥	19.11	-25.3

---

[1] Ali Mohamed Al-Khouri, "The Agricultural Sector, the Interest and Challenges It Faces in the Middle East", *Al-Wafd Newspaper*, October 12, 2023, https://arab-digital-economy.org/language/en/9095.

[2] https://www.worldstopexports.com/wheat-imports-by-country/?expand_article=1.

续表

世界市场排名	进口国	进口额（亿美元）	变化幅度（%）
11	阿尔及利亚	18.41	−31.3
24	突尼斯	7.92	−10.8
31	沙特	5.63	−66.1
32	也门	5.59	−44.7
33	伊拉克	5.45	+90.4
43	阿联酋	3.30	−49.1
60	毛里塔尼亚	1.82	−43.7
64	约旦	1.47	−65.2
65	科威特	1.30	−19.4
70	苏丹	1.21	−76.8
80	黎巴嫩	0.85	−62.7
87	阿曼	0.65	−81.8

资料来源：Wheat Imports by Country，https：//www. worldstopexports. com/wheat-imports-by-country/？ expand_article＝1。

2023 年，阿拉伯国家粮食安全状况持续恶化，营养不足率再创新高。2023 年，阿拉伯国家营养不足率达 14%，比 2022 年增加了 0.6%，营养不良人数达 6610 万，比 2022 年增加了 400 万。其中，低收入国家和最不发达国家的营养不足发生率分别达 31.1% 和 28.8%。2023 年，受冲突影响的国家与未受冲突影响的国家之间的食物不足差距继续扩大。受冲突影响的国家（26.4%）的营养不良率是未受冲突影响的国家（6.6%）的四倍。索马里的粮食不安全发生率最高（51.3%），其次是也门（39.5%）、叙利亚（34%）和科摩罗（16.9%）。2023 年，阿拉伯地区的中度或重度粮食不安全发生率达到 39.4%（1.865 亿人），比上一年增加 1.1 个百分点，15.4% 的人口（7270 万人）面临严重的粮食不安全。[1] 战乱和冲突也

---

[1] Food and Agriculture Organization of the United Nations, International Fund for Agricultural Development, United Nations Children's Fund, World Food Programme & World Health Organization, " 2024 Regional Overview of Food Security and Nutrition: Financing the Transformation of Agrifood Systems", Cairo, 2024, p. 1.

极大影响了阿拉伯国家的粮食获取量。《2023 年全球粮食危机报告》显示，2022 年 1—5 月，也门有 1737 万人面临严重的粮食不安全问题。[1] 在叙利亚和伊拉克，战争、抵抗和冲突常导致粮援等任务延期或取消。[2] 联合国粮农组织和世界粮食计划署联合发布的《饥荒热点地区早期预警（2023 年 11 月—2024 年 4 月）》指出，2023 年苏丹内乱导致的粮食不安全将对周边国家产生外溢效应，巴勒斯坦粮食安全问题或将随巴以冲突升级而加重。[3] 苏丹冲突严重影响了苏丹粮食生产和谷物收成，1800 万人（占总人口的 37%）面临严重的粮食不安全问题。与冲突前相比，面临严重粮食安全问题的人数增加了 1000 万人，其中包括 500 万人面临灾难性饥饿风险，70 多万名苏丹儿童患有严重营养不良。[4] 此外，由于俄罗斯退出黑海粮食运输协议，[5] 全球粮食供应受到影响，尤其是小麦市场。与此同时，自印度于 2023 年 7 月决定停止非巴斯马蒂品种的出口以来，全球大米价格一路飙升。外部不确定性导致许多中低收入国家的粮食安全状况不断恶化。最脆弱的国家包括突尼斯、利比亚、黎巴嫩、伊拉克和埃及，更不用说饱受战乱的叙利亚、苏丹和也门。埃及和黎巴嫩严重依赖大米和小麦进口，目前正面临粮食融资挑战，而深陷饥荒和内乱的苏丹则无力进口昂贵的粮食。粮食协议的破裂只会加剧这些国家已面临的供应挑战和价格压力。黎巴嫩、埃及、叙利亚等国家经历了货币大幅贬值，导致食品价格上涨了三位数，现在这些国家面临的风险更大。事实上，由于冲突和干旱等气候相关挑战，三年来中东地区粮食不安全人口数量激增了 20%。

---

[1] Food Security Information Network, 2023, Global Report on Food Crisis, Online Publishing, 2023, p. 149.

[2] Food Security Information Network, 2023, Global Report on Food Crisis, Online Publishing, 2023, pp. 43–44.

[3] WFP and FAO, Hunger Hotspots, FAO-WFP Early Warnings on Acute Food Insecurity: November 2023 to April 2024 Outlook, Rome: FAO, 2023, pp. 5–8.

[4] "Crisis in Sudan: What is Happening and How to Help", International Rescue Committee, June 24, 2024, https://www. rescue. org/article/crisis-sudan-what-happening-and-how-help.

[5] 2022 年 7 月，联合国与土耳其促成了黑海粮食运输协议。根据该协议，穿越黑海的粮食中约有 1/3 运往埃及、利比亚、以色列、突尼斯、阿尔及利亚、土耳其和伊朗。该协议生效仅一年后，俄罗斯就宣布退出该协议。

5.2 中阿农业合作现状

不论从国家稳定的安全视角还是从国家发展的经济视角看，粮食安全和农业发展都是阿拉伯国家治理的重点关切，但农业发展缓慢和粮食不安全已在阿拉伯地区呈区域性聚集，地区内有重要影响力的大国都不具备凝聚各方力量构建区域粮食安全机制以解决区域共有安全问题的能力。因此，对外农业合作成为阿拉伯国家集体应对农业和粮食安全问题的有效路径。[①] 中阿农业合作是中阿务实合作的重要组成部分，是中阿交往的重要领域。

2022 年，中华人民共和国农业农村部发布的《"十四五"时期农业农村国际合作规划》指出："十四五"期间，"对西亚国家以开展粮食安全、防灾减损、贸易投资领域合作为主，丰富农业经贸合作形式，提升双方农业综合发展能力"；"继续推动从阿联酋引进椰枣苗试种研究，丰富我国市场椰枣产品供应，并在现代农业、草畜一体化和粮食安全方面深化合作"；"以经贸合作、经验分享、能力建设、技术转移等形式，推进与北非国家在粮食安全、可持续农业、数字农业等领域的深入合作"。[②] 2022 年 12 月首届中阿峰会上，习近平主席首次提出中阿务实合作"八大共同行动"，其中有关粮食安全共同行动中指出，中方愿帮助阿方增强粮食安全水平，提升农业综合生产能力；同阿方共建 5 个现代农业联合实验室，开展 50 个农业技术合作示范项目，向阿方派遣 500 名农业技术专家，帮助阿方增加粮食产量、提高收储减损能力、提升农业生产效率；为阿方优质农食产品开辟输华准入"绿色通道"。2024 年 5 月，第十届中阿合作论坛部长级

[①] 孙德刚：《中阿合作论坛框架下中国对阿拉伯国家整体外交研究》，新星出版社，2024，第 393 页。

[②] 农业农村部：《"十四五"农业农村国际合作规划》，http://www.moa.gov.cn/zxfile/reader?file=http://www.moa.gov.cn/govpublic/GJHZS/202201/P020220128632546567867.pdf，2022 年 1 月 18 日，第 22—23 页。

会议上，习近平主席提出了"五大合作格局"，在建立更为平衡的贸易互惠格局中指出："中方欢迎阿方积极参加中国国际进口博览会，愿扩大自阿方进口非能源类产品特别是农食产品。"[①] 这些重要文件精神为未来中阿农业合作指明了方向，擘画了蓝图。近年来，中国与阿拉伯国家不断加强农业贸易往来、深化农业技术合作。随着中阿合作论坛、中阿博览会、"一带一路"倡议等平台机制的建立，中阿农业合作不断迈上新台阶，为双方农业发展增添了新动能。中阿农业合作主要包括农产品贸易、农业技术合作、农业人才交流与培训，以及农业合作项目签署等。

5.2.1 中阿农产品贸易往来

5.2.1.1 中阿农产品贸易规模

根据商务部 2023 年 12 月发布的农产品统计报告，2023 年，中国农产品进出口额为 3330.3 亿美元，同比下降 0.4%，其中出口额为 989.3 亿美元，同比增长 0.7%；进口额为 2341.1 亿美元，同比下降 0.8%。中阿农产品贸易额为 56.66 亿美元，同比增长 12.8%，出口额为 36.92 亿美元，同比增长 21.4%，进口额为 19.74 亿美元，同比下降 0.3%。一些阿拉伯国家也成为中国农产品进出口的重要来源国和目的地。例如，摩洛哥人偏爱中国绿茶，摩洛哥也是中国绿茶出口的第一大目标国，摩洛哥是中国出口茶叶的第三大市场，2023 年为 59830.5 吨 19006.5 万美元，2022 年为 75439.9 吨 23949.8 万美元，同比下降 20.7% 和 20.6%。叙利亚是中国小麦出口的第三大市场，2023 年出口小麦 2336.0 吨 132.9 万美元。阿联酋是中国烟草第三大出口市场，2023 年共出口 27400.0 吨 7130.4 万美元，2022 年为 31005.1 吨 7988.4 万美元，同比下降 11.6% 和 10.7%。阿联酋还是中国菜籽油进口的第二大市场，2023 年为 284257.4 吨 31921.8

---

① 习近平：《深化合作，继往开来：推动中阿命运共同体建设跑出加速度——在中阿合作论坛第十届部长级会议开幕式上的主旨讲话》，人民出版社，2024，第 5 页。

万美元，2022 年为 185410.1 吨 27921.7 万美元，同比增长 53.3% 和 14.3%。[1]

5.2.1.2 中阿农产品贸易结构

从表 5.2 可以看出，2023 年，中国从阿拉伯国家进口的主要农产品依次为："（12）含油子仁及果实；杂项子仁及果实；工业用或药用植物；稻草、秸秆及饲料""（23）食品工业的残渣及废料；配制的动物饲料""（15）动、植物油、脂及其分解产品；精制的食用油脂；动、植物蜡"，进口额都在 3 亿美元以上；"（03）鱼、甲壳动物、软体动物及其他水生无脊椎动物""（08）食用水果及坚果；甜瓜或柑橘属水果的果皮"进口额超 1 亿美元；此外，有 4 类农产品未从阿拉伯国家进口。与 2022 年相比，2023 年进口涨幅最大的农产品为"（22）饮料、酒及醋"，涨幅达 227.86%，还有 4 类农产品涨幅超 100%。降幅最大的农产品为"（14）编结用植物材料；其他植物产品"，降幅为 91.78%。

2023 年，中国向阿拉伯国家出口的前五类农产品依次为"（20）蔬菜、水果、坚果或植物其他部分的制品""（09）咖啡、茶、马黛茶及调味香料""（24）烟草、烟草及烟草代用品的制品""（12）含油子仁及果实；杂项子仁及果实；工业用或药用植物；稻草、秸秆及饲料""（07）食用蔬菜、根及块茎"，出口额均在 2 亿美元以上；出口最少的农产品为"（01）活动物"，出口额仅为 9.13 万美元。与 2022 年相比，2023 年涨幅最大的农产品为"（14）编结用植物材料；其他植物产品"，增幅为 77.80%，降幅最大的农产品为"（15）动、植物油、脂及其分解产品；精制的食用油脂；动、植物蜡"，降幅为 30.43%。

---

[1] 中华人民共和国商务部对外贸易司：《中国进出口月度统计报告农产品（2023 年 12 月）》，中华人民共和国商务部网站，http://wms.mofcom.gov.cn/cms_files/filemanager/1077459795/attach/20247/fc1e6d927252464ab24b9e53b391c4a1.pdf? fileName = % E4% B8% AD%E5%9B%BD%E5%86%9C%E4%BA%A7%E5%93%81%E8%BF%9B%E5%87%BA E5%8F%A3%E6%9C%88%E5%BA%A6%E7%BB%9F%E8%AE%A1%E6%8A%A5%E5% 91%8A2023%E5%B9%B412%E6%9C%88. pdf，2024 年 2 月 8 日。

中阿经贸关系发展进程2023年度报告

表5.2 2023年中国与阿拉伯国家进出口农产品情况

（代码）产品名称	进口		出口	
	金额（万美元）	同比（％）	金额（万美元）	同比（％）
第一类活动物；动物产品				
（01）活动物	0	0	9.13	34.66
（02）肉及食用杂碎	0	0	2373.41	35.44
（03）鱼、甲壳动物、软体动物及其他水生无脊椎动物	15938.79	8.49	8451.93	7.91
（04）乳品；蛋品；天然蜂蜜；其他食用动物产品	118.81	118.81	1922.30	-15.41
（05）其他动物产品	226.86	-5.17	840.38	-22.23
第二类植物产品				
（06）活树及其他活植物；鳞茎、根及类似品；插花及装饰用簇叶	0.74	0.74	2243.38	48.52
（07）食用蔬菜、根及块茎	5.27	-27.41	29275.05	29.91
（08）食用水果及坚果；甜瓜或柑橘属水果的果皮	11631.85	15.31	25912.58	38.44
（09）咖啡、茶、马黛茶及调味香料	150.68	-23.26	63388.41	17.87
（10）谷物	0	0	13631.25	-24.56
（11）制粉工业产品；麦芽；淀粉；菊粉；面筋	0	0	1904.11	9.65
（12）含油子仁及果实；杂项子仁及果实；工业用或药用植物；稻草、秸秆及饲料	60996.80	-7.57	39000.95	6.46
（13）虫胶；树胶、树脂及其他植物液、汁	647.10	-42.17	2348.76	20.80
（14）编结用植物材料；其他植物产品	14.02	-91.78	343.60	77.80

第5章 中阿农业合作专题报告

续表

（代码）产品名称	进口		出口	
	金额（万美元）	同比（%）	金额（万美元）	同比（%）
第三类动、植物油、脂及其分解产品；精制的食用油脂；动、植物蜡				
（15）动、植物油、脂及其分解产品；精制的食用油脂；动、植物蜡	36838.73	15.96	2259.60	−30.43
第四类食品；饮料、酒及醋；烟草及烟草代用品的制品				
（16）肉、鱼、甲壳动物、软体动物及其他水生无脊椎动物的制品	8.23	−86.29	12681.51	5.03
（17）糖及糖食	600.60	−52.46	15404.38	35.00
（18）可可及可可制品	1094.27	105.67	3232.39	12.39
（19）谷物、粮食粉、淀粉或乳的制品；糕饼点心	293.33	107.99	5348.70	33.21
（20）蔬菜、水果、坚果或植物其他部分的制品	222.48	192.97	69979.82	50.70
（21）杂项食品	92.30	−27.78	17619.95	14.96
（22）饮料、酒及醋	711.72	227.86	5140.91	11.58
（23）食品工业的残渣及废料；配制的动物饲料	42340.84	−14.22	3249.83	−18.58
（24）烟草、烟草及烟草代用品的制品	998.65	27.71	45132.11	37.12

资料来源：根据中国海关总署数据整理计算。

5.2.1.3 中国与阿拉伯国家农产品贸易来源国和目的国

从表5.3可看出，中国主要的农产品进口来源国为苏丹、阿联酋、埃及、毛里塔尼亚、沙特等。2023年，中国从上述五国进口农产品金额占从阿拉伯国家进口农产品的96.08%。从农产品结构的进口国来说，"（03）鱼、甲壳动物、软体动物及其他水生无脊椎动物"的主要进口国为沙特（8736.8630万美元）、索马里（316.0422万美元）和科摩罗

089

（0.9462 万美元）；"（08）食用水果及坚果；甜瓜或柑橘属水果的果皮"的主要进口国为埃及（10171.2559 万美元）和伊拉克（60.0956 万美元）；"（12）含油子仁及果实；杂项子仁及果仁；工业用或药用植物；稻草、秸秆及饲料"主要进口国为苏丹（60706.0305 万美元）；"（15）动、植物油、脂及其分解产品；精制的食用油脂；动、植物蜡"主要进口国为摩洛哥（2889.0461 万美元）和叙利亚（22.7821 万美元）；"（18）可可及可可制品"的主要进口国为黎巴嫩（878.6603 万美元）；"（23）食品工业的残渣及废料；配制的动物饲料"的主要进口国为毛里塔尼亚（10184.1530 万美元）。

表 5.3 　2022 年、2023 年中国从阿拉伯国家进口农产品来源国

国家	排名	2022 年进口额（万美元）	2023 年进口额（万美元）	同比（%）
苏丹	1	81265.3	77294.5	-4.9
阿联酋	2	50500.2	53955.0	6.8
埃及	3	33412.3	31883.0	-4.6
毛里塔尼亚	4	16044.9	16554.2	3.2
沙特	5	11645.5	9996.2	-14.2
摩洛哥	6	3327.6	5803.5	74.4
黎巴嫩	7	507.7	967.9	90.6
索马里	8	665.7	469.1	-29.5
阿尔及利亚	9	181.6	173.0	-4.8
突尼斯	10	274.6	139.3	-49.3
约旦	11	60.3	69.2	14.6
伊拉克	12	14.5	60.7	317.6
叙利亚	13	188.4	37.2	-80.2
阿曼	14	22.6	13.4	-40.6
科摩罗	15	4.8	6.4	33.9
也门	16	0.0	4.6	105097.7

国家	排名	2022 年进口额（万美元）	2023 年进口额（万美元）	同比（%）
巴林	17	0.1	0.6	434.1
利比亚	18	0.2	0.3	34.9
科威特	19	0.4	0.2	-44.5
卡塔尔	20	1.2	0.1	-88.5
巴勒斯坦	21	—	—	—
吉布提	22	—	—	—

资料来源：中华人民共和国商务部《中国进出口月度统计报告——农产品》，2023，第23—25页。

从表5.4可以看出，2023年，中国向阿拉伯国家出口农产品的十大主要目的地为阿联酋、沙特、伊拉克、摩洛哥、埃及、阿尔及利亚、约旦、利比亚、突尼斯、科威特，出口额占总出口额的86.96%。阿联酋连续多年是中国对阿拉伯国家农产品出口的首要目的地，2023年出口额为103323.3万美元，同比增长13.2%，占中国对阿拉伯国家出口总额的26.91%。中国向伊拉克出口涨幅达106.5%，伊拉克跃升为中国第三大出口目的地。

从农产品结构上来说，2023年，"（09）咖啡、茶、马黛茶及调味香料"和"（20）蔬菜、水果、坚果或植物其他部分的制品"是中国向阿拉伯国家出口最多的农产品。其中"（09）咖啡、茶、马黛茶及调味香料"出口主要目的地为北非阿拉伯国家，分别为摩洛哥（19751.5416万美元）、毛里塔尼亚（6716.1799万美元）、阿尔及利亚（8102.1551万美元）、利比亚（3221.4168万美元）、突尼斯（991.1156万美元）和吉布提（309.3944万美元）。"（20）蔬菜、水果、坚果或植物其他部分的制品"的主要出口目的地为伊拉克（23786.5549万美元）、沙特（15328.4990万美元）、也门（4930.4593万美元）、约旦（4116.0956万美元）、阿曼（2294.7081万美元）、叙利亚（288.4201万美元）、科摩罗（82.7640万美元）。

中阿经贸关系发展进程2023年度报告

表 5.4 2022 年、2023 年中国向阿拉伯国家出口农产品目的国

国家	排名	2022 年出口额（万美元）	2023 年出口额（万美元）	同比（%）
阿联酋	1	91242.9	103323.3	13.2
沙特	2	36762.8	54154.6	47.3
伊拉克	3	24005.9	49581.6	106.5
摩洛哥	4	32846.4	33408.0	1.7
埃及	5	31776.0	24791.2	-22.0
阿尔及利亚	6	14999.6	22888.8	52.6
约旦	7	13703.2	13496.9	-1.5
利比亚	8	5742.3	11155.5	94.3
突尼斯	9	10608.1	11004.7	3.7
科威特	10	10858.9	10031.2	-7.6
黎巴嫩	11	8551.0	8508.6	-0.5
也门	12	8174.0	8329.8	1.9
毛里塔尼亚	13	6542.0	7669.8	17.2
阿曼	14	5513.4	6377.3	15.7
巴林	15	4003.2	5372.0	34.2
苏丹	16	4171.3	5178.3	21.2
卡塔尔	17	3798.2	4422.0	16.4
叙利亚	18	1060.7	1261.2	18.9
索马里	19	1072.0	1204.2	12.3
吉布提	20	1298.7	825.8	-36.4
巴勒斯坦	21	383.7	702.8	83.1
科摩罗	22	212.6	200.8	-5.6

资料来源：中华人民共和国商务部《中国进出口月度统计报告——农产品》，2023，第15—17 页。

5.2.2 中阿农业合作进展

中阿农业合作不仅体现在农产品贸易方面，在技术培训、交流合作、协议签署等方面也取得了新进展。

092

第5章　中阿农业合作专题报告

中阿博览会是中国和阿拉伯国家经贸合作的重要平台，也是中阿共建"一带一路"的重要平台，农业板块是中阿博览会的重要组成部分。2023年9月21—24日，以"携手新时代抢抓新机遇共享新未来"为主题的第六届中阿博览会在宁夏银川召开。作为博览会的重要内容，现代农业高质量发展合作大会聚集了40多个国家的官员和专家学者，围绕农业技术、贸易投资、粮食安全等领域展开讨论。大会为进一步深化中国与共建"一带一路"国家农业务实合作、挖掘合作新潜力、开辟合作新空间搭建了重要平台。会议邀请了国内外350余名嘉宾出席会议，其中国外嘉宾110人，国内嘉宾240人，来自毛里塔尼亚、巴基斯坦、埃及等40多个国家的农业高级官员、专家学者及重点商协会、企业代表以及农业农村部领导，国内知名科研院校的专家学者、重点商协会代表、重点企业代表等参加了此次大会。会议围绕"深化务实合作　共促粮食安全"主题，举办了开幕式、签约仪式、主旨演讲、高端对话、"一带一路"粮食安全及农业合作圆桌会、发展中国家高级官员研修及现代农业考察交流等7项活动。围绕"推动农业合作，保障粮食安全"主题，召开"一带一路"粮食安全及农业合作圆桌会，形成合作共识5项，进一步推动了宁夏乃至中国与阿拉伯国家在内的"一带一路"合作伙伴农业领域交流合作。签署中阿农业技术转移摩洛哥海外分中心建设、种植（养殖）业优新品种引进等国际合作项目8个；围绕"六特"产业，签署国内区域间投资贸易及合作项目26个，进一步深化与共建"一带一路"国家农业多双边交流合作，拓展宁夏特色农产品国际国内市场营销渠道。[①]

2023年8月15—16日，中国农业农村部部长在开罗分别会见埃及农业和土地改良部部长卡斯尔、阿盟首席助理秘书长扎齐。在会见卡斯尔时，中国农业农村部部长表示，近年来，在习近平主席和塞西总统元首外交的战略引领下，中埃全面战略伙伴关系实现跨越式发展，农业合作成效

[①] 《第六届中阿博览会现代农业高质量发展合作大会在银川圆满召开》，宁夏回族自治区农业国际合作项目服务中心网站，2023年9月27日，https：//nynct. nx. gov. cn/xwzx/zwdt/202309/t20230927_4290401. html。

093

显著。中方愿以实际行动落实习近平主席提出的"九项工程"和"八大共同行动"，与埃方一道围绕土壤综合保护利用、耐盐碱作物品种培育和高产栽培、水肥一体化灌溉、农业绿色增长等，加强中埃农业领域联合实验室建设、扩大农业技术和管理人员往来、拓展双边农业经贸合作，促进各自粮食生产和农业可持续发展能力不断迈上新台阶。双方共同签署了《中埃农业合作行动计划2023—2025年》。在会见扎齐时，中国农业农村部部长高度评价中阿农业关系，表示中方愿以落实全球发展倡议为契机，与阿方强化对话交流，加深利益交融，通过开展联合研发、技术示范推广和能力建设等，不断提升国家和地区粮食安全水平，推动中阿农业合作，为构建中阿命运共同体做出积极贡献。2023年9月，由甘肃省治沙研究所举办的"气候变化背景下荒漠化防治国际培训班"在兰州开班。甘肃省科技厅、甘肃省林草局相关负责同志，联合国粮农组织（FAO）驻沙特代办处、沙特植被覆盖和荒漠化防治中心的15名专家学者参加了开班研讨会，旨在提高沙特沙漠化防治和利用水平。通过实地考察和学习，沙方深入了解了甘肃成熟的沙障治沙和沙地造林技术并广泛推广应用，全方位展示中国生态环境建设成果，增进彼此了解，为今后深入开展合作与交流奠定坚实基础。[①] 2023年11月23日，"一带一路"重点农业项目迪拜中国农牧渔产品（欧威尔）批发市场开业仪式暨中国—中东国际农产品流通研讨会在迪拜欧威尔批发市场举办。中国农业农村部农业贸易促进中心主任马洪涛，率中国农产品贸易代表团参加活动并进行产品推介。与会中外企业共签署16份供采对接意向合同，合同额高达97亿元人民币。在农产品贸易持续增长的同时，中阿农业科技合作和技术交流也日益密切。中阿农业技术转移中心在毛里塔尼亚、摩洛哥等多个阿拉伯国家示范运营，取得成果。截至2022年底，中国已为22个阿盟成员国1万名农业官员和技术人员举办培训班近500期，涉及沙漠农

---

① 《甘肃省举办气候变化背景下荒漠化防治国际培训班》，甘肃省科技厅网站，https://www.most.gov.cn/dfkj/gs/zxdt/202309/t20230908_187800.html，2023年9月8日。

业、水产养殖、智慧农业等领域。①

5.3 中阿农业合作展望

在元首外交的战略引领下，中阿政治互信不断增强，经贸务实合作不断深化，中阿农业合作作为中阿务实合作的重要组成部分，保持着良好的发展势头。展望未来，中阿农业合作应以全球发展倡议和高质量共建"一带一路"为契机，对标"八大共同行动"和"五大合作格局"，共同推动中阿农业合作再上新台阶。

第一，加强现代农业技术交流与合作。阿拉伯国家农业产量下降，除客观因素外，缺乏现代农业技术也是导致其农业产量下降的重要原因。世界正经历百年未有之大变局，在农业方面最突出的表现为全球粮食链供应严重短缺，造成粮食安全状况恶化，尤其是阿拉伯国家。因此，阿拉伯世界必须充分利用现有的一切能力，提供所有农业用地，同时利用先进技术，实现地区粮食的自给自足，这也给中阿农业合作提供了契机。一是鼓励双方农业科技人员加强交流。中方可派遣技术专家重点围绕旱作农业、盐碱地综合利用、动物疫病防控等领域开展农业科技交流，同时，加强与阿拉伯国家农业人才经验交流，助力阿拉伯国家农业可持续发展。截至2022年，中方积极为阿盟成员国近万名农业官员和技术人员举办培训班。"八大共同行动"指出，中方愿向阿方派遣500名农业技术专家，帮助阿方增加粮食产量、提高收储减损能力、提升农业生产效率。二是加强联合实验室的建设和联合研究中心的建设。"八大共同行动"和"五大合作格局"均指出，中方愿同阿方共建现代农业联合实验室，愿同阿方设立中阿干旱、荒漠化和土地退化国际研究中心。三是加强对阿拉伯国家农业研究，了解不同阿拉伯国家农业需求，精准对接。四是建设农业技术合作项

---

① Pramod Kumar, "China and Arab States Sign ＄471m Worth of Agri Deals", September 25, 2023, https://www.agbi.com/agriculture/2023/09/china-and-arab-states-sign-471m-worth-of-agri-deals/.

目。利用中阿技术转移中心，将中国成熟的农业技术推广至阿拉伯国家。例如，由商务部和宁夏共同投资援建的毛里塔尼亚畜牧业技术示范中心在非洲撒哈拉沙漠边缘成功种出近千亩饲草，在不毛之地上打造出一片绿洲。该中心还将土壤改良、节水灌溉等技术分享给毛里塔尼亚、阿联酋、苏丹等国的农业技术人员，带动这些国家种植饲草上万亩，成为中国和阿拉伯国家农业合作的一张亮眼名片。[①]

第二，拓展农业合作新增长点。中国与阿拉伯国家在智慧农业、旱作农业、沙漠农业、节水灌溉、畜牧与兽医、绿色农业等方面开展了大量合作，且取得积极成效。未来，中国与阿拉伯国家应积极拓展农业合作新增长点，可在土壤健康、水培农业、无土栽培、农用无人机使用领域加强合作，同阿拉伯国家共享发展成果，帮助阿方改进现有农田灌溉系统，加强农业节水能力，使其谷物和战略性农产品等达到自给自足的安全线，助力阿拉伯国家摆脱粮食安全困境。

第三，持续扩大中阿农产品贸易往来。"八大共同行动"指出，要为阿方优质农食产品建立输华准入"绿色通道"。近年来，阿拉伯国家正优化商品结构，实施经济多元化政策，加大非石油类商品的出口，如埃及的鲜橙、葡萄，沙特的椰枣等。党的二十届三中全会指出，中国扩大高水平对外开放，对于包括阿拉伯国家在内的发展中国家来说意味着更多合作机遇，中国拥有的超大市场规模为阿拉伯国家农产品进入中国提供了新商机。借力中阿合作论坛、中非合作论坛、中阿博览会、中国国际进口博览会等国际性合作平台，扩大自阿方进口非能源类产品特别是农食产品。例如，中国对橄榄油需求旺盛且主要依赖进口，橄榄油是约旦重要的特色农产品，这为中约橄榄油合作提供了广阔合作空间。

第四，推动中阿农业部长级对话机制的建立。农业是国家经济发展的重要基础和保障粮食供给的关键，近年来，在中阿博览会框架下，中阿双

[①] 《中阿农业合作让沙漠变绿洲》，新华社，https://finance.sina.com.cn/jjxw/2023-09-24/doc-imznuqqi0383278.shtml，2023 年 9 月 24 日。

方在农业经贸和农业科技领域建立了合作，然而，在中阿合作论坛框架下，尚未建立中国与阿拉伯国家农业部长级对话机制，这也为中阿农业高层交往与互动增添了困难，制约中阿农业治理经验的交流以及推动中阿农业诸领域的合作。

中阿农业合作拥有广阔的合作空间，但也面临一些困境。首先，巴以问题"世纪难题"久拖不决，新一轮巴以冲突加大了地区经济发展和经济合作的外在风险，特别是巴以冲突外溢明显，战争的风险逐步攀升，直接威胁着地区国家的安全、稳定和发展。与此同时，中东地区地缘政治竞争激烈，美国等西方大国干预频发，恐怖主义活动大有卷土重来的势头，这些都给地区国家的稳定和经济发展带来了严峻的挑战。在此背景下，中国与阿拉伯国家应共同携手应对地区不确定因素等诸多挑战，从而为中阿农业合作创造良好的环境。其次，农业合作具有时间跨度大、收效慢等特征，因此，在农业企业出海阿拉伯地区之前，应加强对合作对象国的实地调研，做好风险防范，制定相应的农业合作规划，避免盲目出海和投资。

第6章　中阿能源合作专题报告

6.1　阿拉伯国家能源资源概况

6.1.1　阿拉伯国家石油资源储量与生产情况

2023 年，阿拉伯国家可探明的原油储量占全球可探明原油储量的 41.42%，原油产量占全球原油总产量的 30.32%（见表 6.1、表 6.2）。在可探明储量方面，近年来，阿拉伯国家可探明原油储量规模及其占全球可探明原油储量比重小幅回升。在原油产量方面，受乌克兰危机引发全球能源危机影响，对俄罗斯的原油需求转移至阿拉伯国家中其他资源国并推动其产量增加，阿拉伯国家原油产量自 2022 年起连续两年增加。

阿拉伯国家石油资源总量丰富，但分布不均衡，集中于沙特、伊拉克、科威特、阿联酋等国家。2023 年末，上述 4 国可探明储量总计占阿拉伯国家原油可探明储量的 85.64%，占全球原油可探明储量的 35.48%。在产量方面，2023 年，上述 4 国原油总产量为 106329 万吨，占阿拉伯国家原油总产量的 78.11%，占全球原油总产量的 23.69%（见表 6.1、表 6.2）。

表 6.1　2020—2023 年阿拉伯国家可探明原油储量

单位：十亿桶，%

国家	2020 年	2021 年	2022 年	2023 年	2023 年占比
阿尔及利亚	12.20	12.20	12.20	12.20	0.71

第6章　中阿能源合作专题报告

续表

国家	2020 年	2021 年	2022 年	2023 年	2023 年占比
巴林	0.09	0.19	0.19	0.19	0.01
埃及	3.30	3.30	3.30	3.30	0.19
伊拉克	145.02	145.02	145.02	145.02	8.47
约旦	0.00	0.00	0.00	0.00	0.00
科威特	101.50	101.50	101.50	101.50	5.93
毛里塔尼亚	0.02	0.02	0.02	0.02	0.00
利比亚	48.36	48.36	48.36	48.36	2.82
摩洛哥	0.00	0.00	0.00	0.00	0.00
阿曼	5.37	5.37	5.37	5.37	0.31
卡塔尔	25.24	25.24	25.24	25.24	1.47
沙特	267.03	258.60	258.60	260.67	15.22
苏丹	1.25	1.25	1.25	1.25	0.07
叙利亚	2.50	2.50	2.50	2.50	0.15
突尼斯	0.43	0.43	0.43	0.43	0.03
阿联酋	97.80	97.80	99.56	100.45	5.86
也门	3.00	3.00	3.00	3.00	0.18
阿拉伯国家总计	713.12	704.78	706.54	709.50	41.42
世界	1661.91	1703.11	1706.88	1712.92	100

注：包括原油和凝析油。

资料来源：ETRI，EIA。

表 6.2　2020—2023 年阿拉伯国家原油产量

单位：万吨，%

国家	2020 年	2021 年	2022 年	2023 年	2023 年占比
阿尔及利亚	5760	5820	6360	6137	1.37
巴林	874.50	874.50	874.50	874.50	0.19
埃及	3110	2960	2990	2966	0.66
伊拉克	20470	20061	22230	22213	4.95
约旦	0.00	0.00	0.00	0.00	0.00

099

续表

国家	2020 年	2021 年	2022 年	2023 年	2023 年占比
科威特	13112	13000	13505	13500	3.01
毛里塔尼亚	0.00	0.00	0.00	0.00	0.00
利比亚	2000	5960	5100	6018	1.34
摩洛哥	0.00	0.00	0.00	0.00	0.00
阿曼	4233	4212	4350	4754	1.06
卡塔尔	7587	7850	7753	7884	1.76
沙特	52316	51750	52530	52493	11.69
苏丹	310	320	310	255	0.06
叙利亚	285	289	474	502	0.11
突尼斯	170	210	180	180	0.04
阿联酋	16562	16649	18129	18123	4.04
也门	408	408	267	224	0.05
阿拉伯国家总计	127198	130364	135053	136124	30.32
世界	417905	423717	438278	448929	100

注：包括原油和凝析油。
资料来源：ETRI，EIA。

6.1.2　阿拉伯国家天然气储量与生产情况

阿拉伯国家天然气资源丰富，但储量和产量在全球占比中显著低于石油资源。2023 年，阿拉伯国家可探明天然气储量为 52.37 万亿立方米，占全球可探明天然气总储量的 26.14%。阿拉伯国家天然气总产量为 6428 亿立方米，占全球天然气总产量的 15.01%（见表 6.3、表 6.4）。

阿拉伯国家中，卡塔尔的天然气可探明储量和产量均最大。2023 年，卡塔尔可探明天然气储量占阿拉伯国家的比例为 47.11%，产量占阿拉伯国家的比例为 28.31%。除卡塔尔外，沙特、阿联酋、阿尔及利亚、伊拉克等国家也拥有较丰富的天然气资源。

第6章 中阿能源合作专题报告

表 6.3 2020—2023 年阿拉伯国家可探明天然气储量

单位：万亿立方米，%

国家	2020 年	2021 年	2022 年	2023 年	2023 年占比
阿尔及利亚	4.50	4.50	4.50	4.50	2.25
巴林	0.00	0.00	0.00	0.00	0.00
埃及	2.14	2.14	2.14	2.14	1.07
伊拉克	3.53	3.53	3.53	3.53	1.76
约旦	0.00	0.00	0.00	0.00	0.00
科威特	1.70	1.70	1.70	1.70	0.85
毛里塔尼亚	0.00	0.00	0.00	0.00	0.00
利比亚	1.50	1.50	1.50	1.50	0.75
摩洛哥	0.00	0.00	0.00	0.00	0.00
阿曼	0.67	0.67	0.67	0.67	0.33
卡塔尔	24.67	24.67	24.67	24.67	12.31
沙特	6.02	6.02	6.50	6.66	3.32
苏丹	0.08	0.08	0.08	0.08	0.04
叙利亚	0.27	0.27	0.27	0.27	0.13
突尼斯	0.07	0.07	0.07	0.07	0.03
阿联酋	5.94	6.30	6.31	6.31	3.15
也门	0.27	0.27	0.27	0.27	0.13
阿拉伯国家总计	51.36	51.72	52.21	52.37	26.14
世界	192.20	193.45	199.51	200.37	100

资料来源：ETRI。

表 6.4 2020—2023 年阿拉伯国家天然气产量

单位：亿立方米，%

国家	2020 年	2021 年	2022 年	2023 年	2023 年占比
阿尔及利亚	851	1050	1005	1063	2.48
巴林	184	184	184	184	0.43
埃及	585	678	645	615	1.44

101

续表

国家	2020 年	2021 年	2022 年	2023 年	2023 年占比
伊拉克	120	122	124	95	0.22
约旦	2	2	2	2	0.00
科威特	173	181	191	157	0.37
毛里塔尼亚	0.00	0.00	0.00	0.00	0.00
利比亚	124	145	148	153	0.36
摩洛哥	1	1	1	1	0.00
阿曼	354	389	406	430	1.00
卡塔尔	1753	1780	1833	1820	4.25
沙特	1068	1105	1228	1252	2.92
苏丹	0.00	0.00	0.00	0.00	0.00
叙利亚	35	35	27	32	0.07
突尼斯	13	22	23	20	0.05
阿联酋	551	557	574	603	1.41
也门	5	5	4	1	0.00
阿拉伯国家总计	5819	6256	6395	6428	15.01
世界	40228	42295	42485	42824	100

资料来源：ETRI。

6.1.3 阿拉伯国家其他能源开发利用情况

在传统能源资源方面，阿拉伯国家的煤炭资源稀缺，2023 年，全球煤炭可探明储量为 12851.8 亿吨，阿拉伯国家煤炭可探明储量为 5.52 亿吨，占全球的比重为 0.04%。

除传统能源外，随着全球应对气候变化压力不断增加，阿拉伯国家也积极推进可再生能源发展。2019—2023 年，阿拉伯国家可再生能源发电能力由 19284 兆瓦增加至 32430 兆瓦，年均增长 17.04%，高于全球 12.93% 的年均增速（见表 6.5）。

在可再生能源中，由于阿拉伯国家地处西亚北非地区，气候炎热干燥，水资源短缺，水电发展潜力有限。除埃及、苏丹尼罗河流域，伊拉克底格里斯河流域和叙利亚等建有水力发电设施外，其他阿拉伯国家水能资源缺乏。2023 年，阿拉伯国家水力发电能力为 9852 兆瓦，占世界水力发电能力的比例仅为 0.70%（见表 6.6）。

表 6.5　2019—2023 年阿拉伯国家可再生能源发电能力

单位：兆瓦，%

国家	2019 年	2020 年	2021 年	2022 年	2023 年	2023 年占比
阿尔及利亚	604	585	505	590	590	0.02
巴林	10	11	22	48	59	0.00
埃及	5690	5934	6258	6322	6709	0.17
伊拉克	1594	1594	1594	1599	1599	0.04
约旦	1374	2088	2460	2597	2621	0.07
科威特	97	97	97	114	114	0.00
黎巴嫩	368	382	482	1167	1297	0.03
毛里塔尼亚	122	122	122	123	260	0.01
利比亚	5	5	6	6	8	0.00
摩洛哥	3272	3522	3638	3725	4105	0.11
阿曼	76	179	205	705	722	0.02
巴勒斯坦	82	118	178	192	192	0.00
卡塔尔	24	24	24	824	824	0.02
沙特	113	113	443	843	2689	0.07
索马里	11	19	27	51	54	0.00
苏丹	1761	1798	1817	1871	1871	0.05
叙利亚	1500	1509	1530	1557	1557	0.04
突尼斯	391	406	406	508	817	0.02
阿联酋	1936	2334	3003	3597	6052	0.16
也门	254	258	258	264	290	0.01
阿拉伯国家总计	19284	21098	23075	26703	32430	0.84
世界	2550319	2822931	3088809	3396323	3869705	100

资料来源：国际可再生能源署。

103

中阿经贸关系发展进程2023年度报告

表 6.6 2019—2023 年阿拉伯国家水力发电能力

单位：兆瓦，%

国家	2019 年	2020 年	2021 年	2022 年	2023 年	2023 年占比
阿尔及利亚	228	209	129	129	129	0.01
埃及	2832	2832	2832	2832	2832	0.20
伊拉克	1797	1797	1797	1797	1797	0.13
约旦	6	6	4	4	4	0.00
黎巴嫩	282	282	282	282	282	0.02
摩洛哥	1770	1770	1770	1770	1770	0.13
苏丹	1482	1482	1482	1482	1482	0.11
叙利亚	1490	1490	1490	1490	1490	0.11
突尼斯	66	66	66	66	66	0.00
阿拉伯国家总计	9953	9934	9852	9852	9852	0.70
世界	1313071	1335280	1360923	1395266	1407754	100

资料来源：国际可再生能源署。

阿拉伯国家风力发电能力目前也较小，2023 年风力发电能力为 5334 兆瓦，仅占全球风力发电能力的 0.52%（见表 6.7）。西亚北非地区是全球光热资源最丰富的地区之一，太阳能开发在阿拉伯国家可再生能源资源开发中占据重要地位。2023 年，阿拉伯国家光伏发电能力占可再生能源发电能力总量的比例为 54.10%。2019—2023 年，阿拉伯国家光伏发电能力由 6598 兆瓦增加至 17544 兆瓦，年均增长率处于 41.47%的高位，高于全球 34.57%的年均增速。阿拉伯国家的太阳能资源开发呈显著的不均衡趋势，2023 年，光伏发电以阿联酋、沙特、约旦、埃及和黎巴嫩等国家为主，上述五国的光伏发电能力占阿拉伯国家光伏发电能力总量的比例为 74.45%（见表 6.8）。

104

第6章 中阿能源合作专题报告

表 6.7 2019—2023 年阿拉伯国家风能发电能力

单位：兆瓦，%

国家	2019 年	2020 年	2021 年	2022 年	2023 年	2023 年占比
阿尔及利亚	10	10	10	10	10	0.00
巴林	1	1	1	3	3	0.00
埃及	1132	1380	1640	1643	1890	0.19
约旦	384	529	632	614	614	0.06
科威特	12	12	12	12	12	0.00
黎巴嫩	3	3	3	3	3	0.00
毛里塔尼亚	34	34	34	34	137	0.01
摩洛哥	1225	1435	1471	1558	1858	0.18
阿曼	50	50	50	50	50	0.00
沙特	3	3	3	403	403	0.04
索马里	4	4	4	4	4	0.00
叙利亚	1	1	1	1	1	0.00
突尼斯	245	245	245	245	245	0.02
也门	0	0	0	0	104	0.01
阿拉伯国家总计	3104	3707	4106	4580	5334	0.52
世界	622773	733719	824602	901231	1017199	100

资料来源：国际可再生能源署。

表 6.8 2019—2023 年阿拉伯国家光伏发电能力

单位：兆瓦，%

国家	2019 年	2020 年	2021 年	2022 年	2023 年	2023 年占比
阿尔及利亚	366	366	366	451	451	0.03
巴林	10	10	21	46	57	0.00
埃及	1647	1643	1663	1724	1856	0.13
伊拉克	37	37	37	42	42	0.00
约旦	971	1541	1811	1966	1990	0.14
科威特	84	84	84	102	102	0.01
黎巴嫩	76	90	190	875	1005	0.07

105

续表

国家	2019 年	2020 年	2021 年	2022 年	2023 年	2023 年占比
毛里塔尼亚	88	88	88	89	123	0.01
利比亚	5	5	6	6	8	0.00
摩洛哥	734	774	854	854	934	0.07
阿曼	26	129	155	655	672	0.05
巴勒斯坦	82	117	178	192	192	0.01
卡塔尔	5	5	5	805	805	0.06
沙特	109	109	439	440	2285	0.16
索马里	7	16	24	47	51	0.00
苏丹	80	117	136	190	190	0.01
叙利亚	2	12	33	60	60	0.00
突尼斯	80	95	95	197	506	0.04
阿联酋	1935	2333	3002	3588	5925	0.42
也门	254	258	258	264	290	0.02
阿拉伯国家总计	6598	7829	9445	12593	17544	1.24
世界	595492	728405	873858	1073136	1418969	100

资料来源：国际可再生能源署。

6.2 中阿传统能源合作现状

6.2.1 中阿油气贸易情况

油气贸易是中国与阿拉伯国家贸易合作的顶梁柱。阿拉伯国家是中国油气进口的重要贸易伙伴，2023 年，中国累计进口原油 56429.11 万吨，排名前十的进口来源国分别是俄罗斯、沙特、伊拉克、马来西亚、阿联酋、阿曼、巴西、安哥拉、科威特和美国。其中，阿拉伯国家有 5 个（沙特、伊拉克、阿联酋、阿曼和科威特），占进口总量的 44.43%（见表 6.9）。

第6章 中阿能源合作专题报告

表 6.9 2019—2023 年中国自阿拉伯国家进口原油情况

单位：万吨

国家	2019 年	2020 年	2021 年	2022 年	2023 年
沙特	8332.12	8492.20	8757.58	8750.01	8598.38
伊拉克	5179.72	6011.62	5412.45	5548.47	5924.35
阿联酋	1528.89	3117.51	3194.94	4281.84	4180.63
阿曼	3386.99	3784.38	4479.36	3938.43	3915.95
科威特	2268.86	2749.58	3016.37	3327.93	2453.07
卡塔尔	85.83	619.89	785.17	770.44	1046.40
利比亚	940.43	169.67	613.78	374.20	333.67
阿尔及利亚	54.14	40.44	3.99	0.00	14.69
也门	175.52	182.57	94.30	84.05	0.00
埃及	79.55	132.41	49.00	18.94	0.00

资料来源：GTT。

天然气进口贸易方面，2023 年，中国进口天然气 1656 亿立方米，同比增加 9.5%，其中，进口液化天然气占比为 59.4%，进口量同比增加 12.35%。中国从阿拉伯国家进口天然气以液化天然气为主，2023 年，中国从阿拉伯国家进口液化天然气 1907.35 万吨，同比增加 10.69%，占中国液化天然气进口总量的 26.55%。中国从阿拉伯国家进口天然气主要集中于卡塔尔，2023 年从卡塔尔进口液化天然气占中国从阿拉伯国家进口液化天然气的 87.65%（见表 6.10）。

表 6.10 2019—2023 年中国自阿拉伯国家进口液化天然气（LNG）情况

单位：万吨

国家	2019 年	2020 年	2021 年	2022 年	2023 年
卡塔尔	832.90	816.75	907.96	1573.33	1671.85
阿曼	109.21	106.95	165.37	96.28	104.52
阿联酋	11.99	30.09	72.87	11.92	67.49
阿尔及利亚	6.16	12.24	25.14	6.83	34.65
埃及	18.55	6.43	132.87	34.85	28.84

资料来源：GTT。

107

6.2.2 中阿油气全产业链投资合作

除油气贸易业务外，中国与阿拉伯国家在油气田建设、油气基础设施、油气炼化等领域也开展了全方位的投资合作。

在上游勘探开发领域，中国与卡塔尔、沙特、阿尔及利亚、伊拉克等多个重点国家开展了合作，2023 年签署了多项合作协议。

2023 年 4 月，中国石化与卡塔尔能源（Qatar Energy）签署北方气田东扩项目（NFE）5% 的参股协议，该项目总投资达 287.5 亿美元，建成投产后卡塔尔 LNG 年出口能力将从当前的 7700 万吨提升至 1.1 亿吨。6月，中国石油与卡塔尔能源公司签署协议，成为北方气田扩容项目首个增值合作伙伴，卡塔尔能源公司将在未来 27 年向中国石油供应 400 万吨/年的 LNG，并向中国石油转让北方气田扩容项目 1.25% 的股份。11 月，中国石化与卡塔尔能源公司（Qatar Energy）签署了卡塔尔北部气田扩能项目二期（NFS）一体化合作协议，包括为期 27 年的 LNG 长期购销协议和上游参股协议。根据该协议，卡塔尔能源公司将每年向中国石化供应 300万吨 LNG，并向中国石化转让其合资公司 5% 的股权（折合 NFS 项目 1.875% 股权）。这是双方签署的第三个 LNG 长期购销协议，也是继北部气田扩能项目一期后双方达成的第二个一体化合作项目。

2023 年 5 月，中国石化、道达尔能源与沙特阿美石油公司就沙特 Jafurah 天然气开发项目进行谈判，有望达成价值 100 亿美元的投资协议，包括建设 LNG 出口设施。Jafurah 气田是世界上未开发的大气田之一，也是沙特提高天然气产量的关键项目。目前，谈判仍在进行中，尚未做出最终投资决定。

2023 年 11 月，伊拉克石油部与埃克森美孚达成和解协议，为埃克森美孚退出西古尔纳 1 号油田铺平了道路，中国石油持有该油田最大股份，并于 2024 年 1 月 1 日正式成为该油田的牵头合同者。伊拉克于 2024 年 5 月举行第 5 轮+和第 6 轮油气招标，振华石油、中海油、安东石油、中曼、中石化等 5 家中国石油企业共获得多个区块。其中，振华石油中标 Abu Khema、

Qurnain 两个区块，中海油中标 Block 7 区块，安东石油中标 Dbufriyah 区块，中曼中标 Middle Furat（Euphrates）和 Northern Extension of East Baghdad 区块。

在油气下游炼化加工领域，2023 年 3 月 26 日，沙特阿美公司联手中国北方工业集团、盘锦鑫诚实业集团，成立名为华锦阿美石化有限公司的合资公司，三方持股比例分别为 30%、51% 和 19%，计划在辽宁省盘锦市建设大型炼油化工一体化联合装置，包括一座加工能力为 30 万桶/日的炼油厂和一座年产 165 万吨乙烯、200 万吨对二甲苯的化工厂。27 日，沙特阿美石油公司宣布，将以 246 亿元人民币的价格收购中国荣盛石化 10% 的股份。2024 年 1 月，荣盛石化发布公告称拟收购沙特朱拜勒 SASREF 炼厂 50% 的股权，并通过扩建增加产能。同时，双方也正在讨论沙特阿美对荣盛石化子公司宁波中金石化不超过 50% 股权的收购，并联合参与中金石化现有装置的升级扩建，开发新建下游荣盛新材料金塘项目。

6.2.3 其他能源基础设施建设

2023 年 6 月，中英合资公司 Petrofac-HQC 财团与阿尔及利亚国家石油公司（Sonatrach）旗下全资石化子公司（Step Polymers Spa）签署了石化项目工程的总承包合同（EPC），价值 15 亿美元。该项目位于阿尔及利亚 Arzew 港口，占地面积 88 公顷，聚丙烯产能达 55 万吨/年，计划 42 个月后投产。

6.3 中阿新能源合作现状

6.3.1 中阿新能源合作的驱动力

气候变化议题持续引发全球普遍关注。2023 年 11 月 30 日至 12 月 12 日，《联合国气候变化框架公约》第二十八次缔约方大会（COP28）在阿联酋迪拜召开。这是继埃及沙姆沙伊赫后，联合国气候变化大会连续第二年在阿拉伯地区召开，凸显了阿拉伯国家致力于全球气候治理的强烈意愿。当前，能源绿色转型已成为发展大势，新能源合作符合中阿共同愿景，日益成为中阿共同诉求。

首先，能源转型与经济多样化需求是中阿新能源合作的原动力。推动绿色低碳转型是应对气候变化的一致行动，目前已有约140个国家提出了碳中和发展目标，覆盖全球88%的温室气体排放、90%的世界经济体量和85%的世界人口。作为全球气候治理的积极参与者，中国在低碳减排领域持续做出努力，非化石能源消耗比重逐年上升，能效提升速度居世界前列，建成了全球规模最大的电力供应系统和清洁发电体系，水电、风电、光伏、生物质发电和在建核电规模多年位居世界第一。阿拉伯国家普遍具有较为迫切的发展转型和能源转型需求，纷纷提出中长期国家发展规划，以沙特"2030愿景"、阿联酋"2071百年规划"、阿曼"2040年愿景"等政策文件的出台为标志，多个阿拉伯油气资源国启动了以"去石油化""市场化""私有化""国际化"为主要特征的经济转型战略，减少对石油和天然气的依赖，发展可再生能源，创造新的就业机会和经济增长点，以实现能源多样化和经济可持续发展。在阿拉伯国家中，走在能源转型最前列的是阿联酋、沙特等富裕的油气资源国，埃及、摩洛哥等地区大国也在积极推进能源转型，这些国家都是中阿开展新能源合作的重点国家。

其次，技术与投资的互补是中阿新能源合作的加速器。新能源与新技术紧密融合，能源领域的绿色化、电动化、市场化、数字化趋势加速推进，共同推动能源系统根本性变革。中国正在形成新质生产力，支持高质量共建"一带一路"的八项行动中提出"促进绿色发展""持续深化绿色基建、绿色能源、绿色交通等领域合作"，红海公用基础设施等项目被列入务实合作清单。中国拥有全球领先的新能源产业体系，在光伏、风能、储能等行业具有领先的技术优势和丰富的项目建设经验，可以为阿拉伯国家提供先进的技术和管理支持，帮助其快速发展新能源产业。在资源禀赋方面，阿拉伯国家拥有丰富的太阳能和风能资源，且分布均匀，为大规模新能源项目开发提供了理想条件。同时，阿拉伯国家对外资的需求和开放的市场环境为中国企业提供了投资和合作机会，中阿双方在新能源领域的合作潜力巨大，中国"资源+技术"是中阿新能源合作的重要领域。中国与沙特合作成立的中沙可再生能源技术研究中心，专注于光伏发电和储能技术的研发及应用，中国电建集团在阿布扎比投资建设的光伏电站项目为阿联酋提供大量清洁能源。

6.3.2　中阿新能源合作的新进展

2023 年，中国与阿拉伯国家在新能源合作领域取得重要进展，体现了双方在经济多样化、技术创新、政策支持和环境保护等方面的共同努力。

2023 年 5 月，中国石油天然气集团有限公司与卡塔尔能源公司（Qatar Energy）签署北部气田扩容项目合作文件。11 月，中国石油化工集团有限公司与卡塔尔能源公司签署卡塔尔北部气田扩容项目二期合作协议。卡塔尔能源公司在此后 27 年内分别向中国石油和中国石化供应 400 万吨/年和 300 万吨/年的 LNG 资源，并分别向两家公司转让项目 1.25% 和 1.875% 的股份。

2023 年 5 月，中国—阿拉伯国家合作论坛（CASCF）第十八次高官会（The 18th Senior Official's Meeting）在四川成都举行。6 月，中阿合作论坛第十届企业家大会暨第八届投资研讨会在沙特利雅得举行。9 月，第七届中阿能源合作大会在海南海口举行。10 月，中阿合作论坛第十届中阿关系暨中阿文明对话研讨会在阿联酋阿布扎比举行。这些会议召开期间，与会各方多次就太阳能、风能和储能技术等领域合作进行了专题讨论，达成一系列能源合作协议，涵盖了可再生能源项目投资、技术转让和联合研发等方面，进一步深化了中阿新能源合作关系。

2023 年 6 月，沙特投资部与中国电动汽车制造商华人运通汽车公司（Human Horizons）签署了价值 56 亿美元的协议，双方将合作开发、制造和销售高合品牌电动汽车。

2023 年 10 月，由中国电力建设集团有限公司承建的阿联酋风电示范项目投入运营，项目总装机容量为 117.5 兆瓦，由 4 座风电场组成，可为

2.3 万多户家庭供电，每年将减少 12 万吨二氧化碳排放。作为阿联酋首个建成的风电项目，对阿联酋全境风能可利用程度和风能开发性能指标验证有重要意义，是中阿合作带动中国技术和设备出口的具体实践。

2023 年 11 月，晶科电力科技股份有限公司就 Tabarjal400 兆瓦太阳能光伏项目与沙特电力采购公司签署购电协议。该项目位于沙特焦夫省塔巴哈尔市东北约 17 公里处，计划在开工后两年内完成建设并实现商业运营。项目投入运营后，预计每年减少超过 717 万吨的二氧化碳排放量。

2023 年 11 月，由中国机械设备工程股份有限公司承建的阿联酋艾尔达芙拉 PV2 光伏电站完工。这是目前已建成的世界最大单体光伏电站，占地约 21 平方公里，主要包括装机容量 2.1 吉瓦的光伏发电区、33/400千伏升压站和 400 千伏开关站。发电量可满足阿联酋约 20 万户家庭用电需求，每年可减少超过 240 万吨二氧化碳排放量，使清洁能源在阿联酋总能源结构中的比重提高到 13% 以上。

6.4 中阿能源合作前景

6.4.1 中阿双方共建多样化能源供应链

中阿双方将开创能源安全与绿色发展的双赢局面，在共建多样化能源供应链方面展现了巨大的合作潜力，在可再生能源领域更加深入和多样化的合作体现了共同应对气候变化的决心。沙特、卡塔尔和阿联酋等阿拉伯国家拥有丰富的石油和天然气资源以及得天独厚的太阳能和风能资源，中国是全球最大的能源消费国，能源需求巨大且多样化。资源互补性为双方的能源合作和长远的绿色转型奠定坚实基础，可再生能源合作是中阿双方能源合作的新亮点。阿拉伯国家可以更好地利用其丰富的自然资源，实现能源结构多样化，推动本国的经济多样化和可持续发展。中国可以推动能源供应来源的多样化，减少对单一能源进口的依赖，增强能源安全。沙特、阿联酋与中国合作建设的太阳能发电项目都是新能源领域的典范工程。

技术转让和投资合作是实现多样化能源供应链的重要手段。中国在可再生能源技术和设备制造方面具有全球领先的优势，通过技术转让和投资合作，搭建光伏发电、储能技术和智能电网等领域的研发技术交流平台，可以帮助阿拉伯国家提升技术水平和管理能力，为当地培养大量技术人才，推动当地新能源产业的发展。共建多样化能源供应链的合作模式，不仅有助于双方共享经验和技术，应对当前和未来的能源安全挑战和全球能源市场的不确定性，在能源领域实现互利共赢，还将为全球能源市场的稳定和可持续发展做出贡献。

6.4.2 中阿双方推动双向投资与市场开拓

推动双向投资与市场开拓是中阿能源合作的核心内容之一。通过双向投资，双方不仅能够分享经济发展成果，还能够实现技术交流和产业升级。2023 年，中阿双方在新能源项目上的投资总额达到 150 亿美元，涵盖太阳能、风能和储能等多个领域。中国电建集团在阿布扎比投资建设的光伏电站项目，不仅为当地提供了大量清洁能源，还创造了约 5000 个直接就业岗位和上万个间接就业岗位。阿拉伯国家通过与中国的合作，可以更好地利用丰富的自然资源，实现经济多样化。沙特"2030 愿景"和阿联酋"2050 能源战略"等都强调了经济多样化和可持续发展的重要性。通过双向投资，双方在能源技术研发和创新领域的合作将得到进一步深化。

市场开拓是实现双向投资成果的重要保障。通过市场开拓，中阿双方企业不仅可以提升自身的市场竞争力，还能够实现资源的优化配置和效益的最大化。2023 年，中阿在新能源市场上的合作进一步提升了双方在全球新能源市场的影响力。中国企业通过在阿拉伯国家投资建设太阳能和风能项目，推动了当地新能源市场的发展，扩大了自身的市场空间。在未来，随着能源技术研发和创新领域的合作不断深入和拓展，中阿双方将共同应对全球能源市场的挑战和机遇，提升在全球新能源市场的竞争力并获得经济发展的强大动力。

6.4.3 中阿双方促进经济与财政的可持续发展

促进经济与财政的可持续发展，是中阿能源合作的重要目标之一。通过新能源合作，阿拉伯国家有效改善了财政状况，实现财政收入的多样化和稳定化。沙特通过与中国的合作，开发了多个大型太阳能和风能项目，为当地提供了清洁能源，创造了大量就业机会，推动了当地经济发展。据统计，2023年，沙特通过新能源项目获得的财政收入占总财政收入的比例达到10%，相比2022年增长了3个百分点。中国通过在阿拉伯国家的投资，获得了长期稳定的回报，推动了国内经济的增长和产业升级，提升了中国企业的国际竞争力。2023年，中国在阿拉伯国家的新能源项目投资回报率平均达到12%，其中部分项目如卡塔尔的太阳能发电项目回报率高达15%，大大超过了全球平均水平。

就业机会和社会稳定是新能源合作带来的重大社会效益。中阿能源合作项目创造了大量就业机会，改善了当地居民的生活水平，促进了社会的稳定和繁荣。经济与财政的可持续发展，也体现在对相关产业的带动作用上。新能源项目的发展带动了制造业、服务业等相关产业的发展，推动了区域经济的全面改善。据统计，2023年，中阿新能源合作项目共创造了超过40万个直接和间接就业岗位，有效促进了阿拉伯国家的社会稳定和经济发展，中阿新能源合作实现了更广泛的经济效益。

通过经济与财政的可持续发展，中阿双方不仅实现了经济利益，还为未来的合作奠定了坚实的基础。随着新能源项目的不断发展和成熟，双方在经济和财政上的合作将会更加紧密和深入，不仅有助于提升双方在全球新能源市场的地位和影响力，也将为全球能源市场的稳定和繁荣提供有力支持。

第7章 中阿数字经济合作专题报告

数字经济是一种以数字化知识和信息为关键生产要素、数字技术为核心驱动力、现代信息网络为重要载体的新型经济形态，通过数字技术与实体经济深度融合，提升经济社会的数字化、网络化、智能化水平。[1] "数字丝绸之路"作为共建"一带一路"的重要组成部分和未来国际合作的突破口，促使数字经济成为国际合作的新领域和新竞争赛道。[2] 在此背景下，中国需密切关注阿拉伯国家数字经济发展的新态势新趋势，不断深化与阿拉伯国家在数字经济领域的交流与合作，共同推动双方经济的发展和繁荣，为全球数字经济健康发展注入新动力。

7.1 阿拉伯国家数字经济水平现状

科学测度数字经济是分析数字经济发展现状的前提，需要综合考虑多维度、多层次的指标体系，为推动数字经济高质量发展、制定科学合理的数字战略、提升国家和地区的数字竞争力提供有力支撑。综合考虑指标数据的权威性和可得性等条件，本章主要从数字经济发展硬实力、软实力和市场支撑环境三个层面，分析阿拉伯国家的数字经济水平现状。

---

[1] 《以数字贸易激活外贸发展新引擎》，人民网，http://finance.people.com.cn/n1/2021/0719/c1004-32161520.html，2021年7月19日。

[2] 中国社会科学院金融研究所、国家金融与发展实验室、中国社会科学出版社：《全球数字经济发展指数报告（TIMG 2023）》，中国社会科学院金融研究所网站，http://ifb.cass.cn/newpc/sjk/202306/P020230601501807198861.pdf。

115

7.1.1 数字经济发展硬实力： ICT 基础设施

信息通信技术（ICT）产业是数字经济的重要组成部分和数字化转型的基础。一国的 ICT 发展情况直接影响该国数字化转型进程和数字经济发展潜力[①]，是考察一国数字经济发展的重要前提。加快数字基础设施建设也成为世界各国重构生产力新形态，拓展新应用场景，打造新业态的重要举措。[②]

（1）地区层面

阿拉伯地区 ICT 发展总体水平不高，国际电联年度报告《衡量数字发展：事实与数据 2023》[③] 调查显示，虽然近些年各指标基本都呈现增长趋势，但仍有很多方面低于世界平均水平（见表 7.1）。2023 年，阿拉伯地区互联网渗透率为 68.9%，略高于世界平均水平（67%）；固定电话订阅率为 9.2%，低于世界平均水平（11%）；移动蜂窝电话订阅率为 103.1%，低于世界平均水平（111%）；活跃移动宽带订阅率为 75.4%，低于世界平均水平（87%）。细分不同类型的移动网络渗透率发现，2023 年阿拉伯地区 3G 及以上移动网络渗透率为 95.4%，略高于世界平均水平（95%）；4G 及以上移动网络渗透率为 77.3%，低于世界平均水平（90%）；5G 及以上移动网络渗透率为 12.2%，低于世界平均水平（38%）。此外，固定宽带网络作为"信息高铁"，直接反映国家信息通信技术发展水平，是衡量国家综合国力的重要指标[④]，而阿拉伯地区固定宽带订阅率为 11.7%，距离世界平均水平（19%）还有明显差距。

与此同时，阿拉伯地区存在不同层面的"数字鸿沟"。例如，城乡差

[①] 蔡跃洲、牛新星：《中国信息通信技术产业的国际竞争力分析——基于贸易增加值核算的比较优势及技术含量测算》，《改革》2021 年第 4 期。

[②] 焦勇、齐梅霞：《数字经济赋能新质生产力发展》，《经济与管理评论》2024 年第 3 期。

[③] ITU, "Measuring digital development: Facts and Figures 2023", https://www.itu.int/en/ITU-D/Statistics/Pages/facts/default.aspx.

[④] 《中国联通发布〈家庭组网终端高质量发展白皮书〉，拉开家庭网络高质量发展序幕》，新浪财经网，https://finance.sina.com.cn/tech/roll/2022-12-21/doc-imxxmspu4037828.shtml，2022 年 12 月 21 日。

异上，2023 年阿拉伯地区城市互联网渗透率为 81.6%，乡村互联网渗透率为 50.8%。人口性别差异上，女性互联网渗透率为 63.8%，男性互联网渗透率为 73.7%。2019—2023 年，互联网渗透率性别均等得分[①]的世界平均水平从 0.9 上升到 0.92，而阿拉伯地区仅从 0.79 上升到 0.87。

阿拉伯地区网民人口结构虽然呈现年轻化特征，但是其他年龄结构人口的互联网渗透率增加明显，由 2020 年的 58% 上升到 2023 年的 66.4%，这也是促进阿拉伯地区网络渗透率水平提升的重要原因之一。

表 7.1　2019—2023 年阿拉伯地区 ICT 基本情况汇总

ICT		2019 年	2020 年	2021 年	2022 年	2023 年
互联网渗透率（%）		55.3	61.6	64.2	66.9	68.9
城乡	城市	N/A	73.7	76.4	79.1	81.6
	乡村	N/A	44.6	46.7	49.4	50.8
性别	女性	49.4	55.6	58.6	61.5	63.8
	男性	62.2	67.2	69.5	71.9	73.7
年龄	青年人口（15—24 岁）	N/A	74.5	76.5	77.8	78.4
	青年之外人口	N/A	58.0	61.7	64.1	66.4
固定电话订阅率（%）		8.4	8.7	9.0	9.1	9.2
固定宽带订阅率（%）		7.5	8.6	9.7	10.5	11.7
移动蜂窝电话订阅率（%）		96.7	96.2	99.2	101.6	103.1
活跃移动宽带订阅率（%）		60.8	64.0	67.6	71.4	75.4
移动蜂窝网络渗透率（%）		96.8	97.1	97.1	97.6	97.6
3G 及以上移动网络渗透率（%）		91.2	92.5	94.1	94.5	95.4
4G 及以上移动网络渗透率（%）		61.8	73.6	74.8	76.4	77.3
5G 及以上移动网络渗透率（%）		N/A	N/A	7.3	8.5	12.2
手机普及率（%）		75.4	77.2	79.2	81.0	82.6

注："N/A"表示缺失值。
资料来源：根据《衡量数字发展：事实与数据 2023》整理。

---

① 当性别均等得分（定义为女性百分比除以男性百分比）小于 1，表示男性比女性更有可能使用互联网，而分数大于 1 则表示相反。介于 0.98 和 1.02 之间时，则认为实现了性别均等。

除渗透率外，宽带可及性[①]也是考量 ICT 发展水平的重要参考指标。总体上，2021—2023 年，阿拉伯地区移动宽带的使用成本虽然有所下降，且低于世界平均水平，但固定宽带的费用成本还有不小的压缩空间。例如，2021—2023 年，阿拉伯地区移动宽带可负担性分别为 1.2%、1% 和 0.9%，分别低于世界平均水平 1.9%、1.5% 和 1.3%，并呈现逐年降低趋势，但固定宽带可负担性分别为 3.5%、3.7% 和 3.1%，持平或高于世界平均水平 3.5%、3.2% 和 2.9%。

（2）国别层面

国际电联《衡量数字发展：信通技术发展指数 2023》[②] 调查显示，阿拉伯地区不同国家之间的 ICT 水平存在较大的差异（见表 7.2）。互联网渗透率方面，阿尔及利亚、伊拉克、吉布提、毛里塔尼亚、索马里低于世界平均水平（70.5%），再加上埃及、突尼斯，均低于中国水平（73.1%）。固定互联网普及率方面，吉布提、突尼斯、索马里低于世界平均水平（70.8%），伊拉克、阿尔及利亚、黎巴嫩、埃及，均低于中国水平（80.9%）。移动宽带渗透率方面，阿联酋、卡塔尔、科威特、巴林、利比亚、沙特、阿曼高于中国平均水平（101.6%），阿尔及利亚高于世界平均水平（92.5%）。4G 移动网络渗透率方面，科威特、巴林、沙特高于中国平均水平（99.9%），阿尔及利亚、叙利亚、利比亚、毛里塔尼亚、索马里、巴勒斯坦低于世界平均水平（82.9%）。手机普及率方面，只有巴勒斯坦、伊拉克、吉布提、毛里塔尼亚、索马里等国低于中国（81.5%）和世界平均水平（80.7%）。

---

① 宽带可及性是联合国宽带促进可持续发展委员会（简称"联合国宽带委员会"）制定的一个目标：到 2025 年发展中国家的入门级宽带服务应做到价格可承受，即不超过其月人均国民总收入（GNI）的 2%。参见《宽带促进可持续发展委员会到 2025 年实现的具体目标》，宽带委员会官网，https://broadbandcommission.org/Documents/Translated%20Documents/Targets/Targets2025%20Chinese.pdf。

② ITU, "Measuring digital development ICT Development Index 2023", https://www.itu.int/itu-d/reports/statistics/IDI2023/.

第7章 中阿数字经济合作专题报告

表 7.2　2023 年阿拉伯国家和中国的 ICT 基本情况

国别	互联网渗透率（%）	固定互联网普及率（%）	移动宽带渗透率（%）	3G 及以上移动网络渗透率（%）	4G 及以上移动网络渗透（%）	手机普及率（%）
阿尔及利亚	66.2†	78.3†	97.1	98.2	79.9	83.3†
巴林	100	100	135.2	100	100	100
吉布提	64.0†	65.9†	35.9	90	90	74.3†
埃及	71.9‡	73‡	61.6	99.5	98	99.4‡
伊拉克	65.0†	79.8†	47.5	96.9	95.9	75.3†
约旦	86	90.1	65.3	99.8	99	89.9†
科威特	99.7	99.4	136.6	100	100	99.2
黎巴嫩	87.9†	75.8†	76.8‡	99.6‡	99.2‡	89.1†
利比亚	84.3†	N/A	120.9	72	40	85.4†
毛里塔尼亚	43.8†	N/A	70.8	43.7	34.7	60.9†
摩洛哥	88.1	86.2	82.6	99.3	99.1	96.2
阿曼	95.2‡	94.4‡	112.6	100	97.8	97.1‡
巴勒斯坦	81.8	87.6†	20.1	59	0	77.8†
卡塔尔	99.7‡	95.0‡	144	100	99.8	99.6‡
沙特	100	99.8	119.5	100	100	100
索马里	19.9†	11.9‡	2.6	70	30	18.9†
叙利亚	N/A	N/A	17.4	97	42	N/A
突尼斯	71.9†	55.5†	81.3	99	95	86.4†
阿联酋	100	99.9	241.2	100	99.8	100
中国	73.1	80.9†	101.6	99.9	99.9	81.5†

注："†"表示 ITU 估计值；"‡"表示 2020 年的滞后值；"N/A"表示缺失值。
资料来源：根据《衡量数字发展：信通技术发展指数 2023》整理。

　　另外，根据知名网络测速软件 SPEEDTEST 发布的《全球网速指数》[①]，全球 144 个国家参与移动网速测评，181 个国家参与固定宽带网

---

① SPEEDTEST, Speedtest Global Index（Median Country Speeds January 2024），https://www.speedtest.net/global-index.

119

速测评。综合移动网速和固定宽带网速两个指标来看（见表 7.3），阿拉伯地区仅阿联酋进入世界前 10，卡塔尔、科威特、沙特 3 个国家进入世界前 50。进一步分析单项指标发现，阿联酋、卡塔尔、科威特、巴林、沙特和阿曼等 6 国的移动网速超过世界平均水平（50Mbps），其中阿联酋、卡塔尔、科威特的移动网速分别位居世界前三名，且超过中国的平均网速（164.58Mbps）；阿联酋、卡塔尔、科威特、约旦和沙特 5 国的固定宽带网速超过世界平均网速（91.93Mbps），但都没有超过中国平均网速（259.7Mbps）。

表 7.3　2023 年阿拉伯国家和中国的互联网速度及排名

国别	移动网络		固定宽带		国别	移动网络		固定宽带	
	速度（Mbps）	世界排名	速度（Mbps）	世界排名		速度（Mbps）	世界排名	速度（Mbps）	世界排名
阿联酋	302.38	1	249.87	6	索马里	21.8	112	13.63	151
卡塔尔	285.84	2	137.07	33	阿尔及利亚	20.86	115	12.28	158
科威特	196.94	3	158.68	26	约旦	19.78	116	126.47	35
巴林	128.74	9	80.25	69	利比亚	15.09	127	9.56	166
沙特	126.14	11	107.19	44	叙利亚	11.35	134	3.48	179
阿曼	71.58	38	61.18	86	也门	7.94	139	7.27	174
摩洛哥	35.51	68	26.58	130	苏丹	4.82	142	8.66	170
黎巴嫩	30.95	78	10.47	163	巴勒斯坦	N/A	N/A	62.87	83
伊拉克	27.46	89	32.62	122	吉布提	N/A	N/A	22.18	136
埃及	24.26	106	62.94	82	毛里塔尼亚	N/A	N/A	21.77	137
突尼斯	22.25	111	9.02	168	中国	164.58	4	259.7	5

注："N/A"表示缺失值。

资料来源：根据 SPEEDTEST 整理。

7.1.2　数字经济发展软实力：创新潜力与人力资本

创新潜力是数字经济发展的动力源泉，直接影响着数字经济的可持续发展。只有不断推动创新，才能不断提升数字技术的应用水平。而数字经济的发展也需要大量具备创新能力的人才参与其中，让人力资本成为数字经济时代国家实现技术创新的主体，以及拉开国家间技术水平差距的重要因素。据此，本章从创新潜力与人力资本两个方面衡量阿拉伯国家数字经济发展软实力水平。

全球创新指数是由康奈尔大学、欧洲工商管理学院和联合国专门机构世界知识产权组织共同发布的一个衡量经济创新能力的指标。全球创新指数在2007年首次推出，每年发布一次。《全球创新指数2023》[①] 对世界132个经济体进行排名和梯队划分：1—33名为第一梯队，34—66名为第二梯队，67—99名为第三梯队，100—132名为第四梯队。调查数据显示（见表7.4），阿拉伯国家仅阿联酋属于第一梯队，居世界第32名，但与中国第12名的水平还存在不小差距，中国也是第一梯队中唯一的中等收入经济体。沙特、卡塔尔、科威特属于第二梯队，其余国家都处于世界后一半水平。科研和创新是促进数字经济发展所必需的重要基础，近些年处在第一、第二梯队的阿拉伯国家不断重视加大创新研发投入。

全球创新指数中的人力资本指数是对基础教育、高等教育、研发三个方面的综合考量。阿拉伯国家人力资本水平普遍偏低，2023年只有阿联酋超过中国的世界排名，再加上沙特，该地区只有两个国家位列世界前1/3水平。究其原因，阿拉伯数字人才短缺主要受三方面因素影响：一是阿拉伯地区公共教育水平普遍偏低，尤其在科学、技术、工程和数学等学科领域实力单薄；二是青年人口红利流失严重，地区青年失业问题日益严峻，约有18%的青年人处于"不升学、不就业、不进修"状态；三是全民数字素养整体偏低，严重依赖外籍技术人员。[②]

---

① WIPO, "Global Innovation Index 2023", https://www.wipo.int/edocs/pubdocs/en/wipo-pub-2000-2023-en-main-report-global-innovation-index-2023-16th-edition.pdf.

② 王晓宇：《新发展格局下中阿数字经济合作的基础与前景》，《西亚非洲》2022年第3期。

中阿经贸关系发展进程2023年度报告

表 7.4　2023 年阿拉伯国家和中国的创新指数和人力资本指数及排名

国别	全球创新指数	世界排名	人力资本指数	世界排名	国别	全球创新指数	世界排名	人力资本指数	世界排名
阿联酋	43.2	32	54.3	16	约旦	28.2	71	26.8	82
沙特	34.5	48	40.6	35	突尼斯	26.9	79	36.1	46
卡塔尔	33.4	50	33.8	54	埃及	24.2	86	21.9	95
科威特	29.9	64	33.6	55	黎巴嫩	23.2	92	29.9	72
巴林	29.1	67	28.1	77	阿尔及利亚	16.1	119	16	113
阿曼	28.4	69	34.2	52	毛里塔尼亚	13.5	127	14.2	119
摩洛哥	28.4	70	25.6	86	中国	55.3	12	49.8	22

资料来源：根据《全球创新指数 2023》整理。

7.1.3　数字经济发展市场支撑：数字产业进出口贸易

数字经济发展的硬实力和软实力主要从自身发展水平考虑，而以高科技产业和 ICT 产业为代表的数字产业进出口贸易有助于形成国内外市场联动，为一国数字经济的健康持续发展提供重要支撑力。一方面，通过进口先进的 ICT 设备和技术，提升国内数字产业的水平和竞争力，促进数字经济与其他产业的融合发展；另一方面，通过出口数字产品和服务拓展国际市场，提升一国在全球数字经济发展中的影响力，促进数字经济的国际化发展。

根据《全球创新指数 2023》调查结果（见表 7.5），2023 年，阿拉伯地区贸易总额中高科技出口占比排名前五的国家依次为阿联酋、突尼斯、阿曼、摩洛哥、巴林，但都落后于中国；高科技进口占比排名地区前五的国家依次为阿联酋、阿尔及利亚、突尼斯、摩洛哥、沙特，也均落后于中国；ICT 服务出口占比排名地区前五的国家依次为科威特、巴林、摩洛哥、黎巴嫩、阿联酋，仅前三名超过中国；ICT 服务进口占比排名地区前五的国家依次为卡塔尔、埃及、摩洛哥、阿联酋、黎巴嫩，仅卡塔尔超过中国，埃及、摩洛哥与中国持平。进一步分析阿拉伯各国高科技制造业在

122

制造业总额的占比发现，仅摩洛哥、卡塔尔、阿联酋、沙特四国的世界排名位列前50名，但均不及中国的发展水平。由此看来，高科技制造业生产力水平不高，是导致阿拉伯国家数字产业贸易发展水平落后的关键原因之一。

表7.5　2023年阿拉伯国家和中国数字产业贸易及高科技制造业占比情况

国别	高科技出口占贸易总额（%）		高科技进口占贸易总额（%）		ICT服务出口占贸易总额（%）		ICT服务进口占贸易总额（%）		高科技制造占制造业总额（%）	
	占比	排名	占比	排名	占比	排名	占比	排名	占比	排名
阿联酋	10.6	16	14.3	17	2	59	1.1	78	29.3	42
沙特	0.8	76	7.5	74	0.6	98	0.5	111	26.3	47
卡塔尔	0.2	103	6	102	1.1	84	2.7	25	37.7	30
科威特	0.3	99	7.1	86	6.8	11	0.2	128	20.9	62
巴林	1.4	68	4.7	118	4.2	26	0.5	107	9.8	93
阿曼	2.2	56	5	116	1.2	80	0.7	97	17	72
摩洛哥	2.1	57	8.1	68	3.7	30	1.2	75	42.8	23
约旦	1.2	71	7.2	82	0.1	125	0.2	125	17.7	67
突尼斯	4.5	40	8.7	55	1.5	71	0.4	120	24.3	53
埃及	0.7	81	7.4	75	1.7	65	1.2	72	22.6	57
黎巴嫩	0.4	94	5.1	113	2	58	0.9	89	N/A	N/A
阿尔及利亚	0	131	8.9	53	0.2	121	0.4	115	4.1	104
毛里塔尼亚	0	126	7.4	79	0.4	107	0.4	113	N/A	N/A
中国	28	5	22.6	6	2.3	52	1.2	76	48.5	13

注："N/A"表示缺失值。

资料来源：根据《全球创新指数2023》整理。

7.2　中阿数字经济合作现状

新时代中阿合作日益密切，数字经济合作成为中阿合作新的增长极，涵盖数字基础设施建设、跨境电商、数字人才培养等关键合作领域。一方面，第四次工业革命推动阿拉伯国家纷纷制订数字化转型方案，发展潜力巨大；另一方面，中国企业凭借在大数据、云计算、人工智能和电子商务领域的优势与阿拉伯国家深入合作，推动中阿数字经济合作进入新阶段，拓展并延伸中阿"设施联通""贸易畅通"的合作内涵。

7.2.1 数字基础设施建设合作稳扎稳打

中国已经走在数字经济领域前列，以华为、中兴为代表的中国科创巨头企业深耕阿拉伯市场，共同推进中阿基础设施建设合作向高新技术和数字领域延伸，通过提供高品质的技术和解决方案，赢得了阿拉伯国家的欢迎与信任，推动双方在数字经济领域合作不断向好。与此同时，阿拉伯国家也积极加大对数字基础设施建设的投入。以沙特、阿联酋等为代表的阿拉伯国家在高科技应用技术方面持务实态度，看重以 5G 为代表的数字新基建及其广阔的应用前景，反对西方大国的高科技垄断，欢迎中国企业参与本国的 5G 基建，并认可中国企业在阿拉伯国家信息与通信技术产业建设中发挥的积极作用。

2023 年 3 月，中国成功斡旋沙特和伊朗复交，助力地区和平稳定。随着地区经济发展，沙特加快落实"2030 愿景"，试图降低西方国家的设备与组件对其数字基础设施造成的安全风险，再加上中国正在突破西方国家对其数字产业"出海"的围堵，中沙在数字基础设施领域合作意愿不断上升。2023 年 4 月 10 日，中国信息通信科技集团旗下公司——烽火通信与中信科移动完成沙特 5G FWA 网络建设项目移交，将为沙特实现"2030愿景"中的数字化目标铺平道路。[①] 4 月 13 日，沙特宣布新建 4 个经济特区，以提升本国在全球科技产业以及供应链中的地位。其中，阿卜杜勒阿齐兹国王科技城将成为云计算和新兴技术中心，允许投资者建立数据中心

[①] 《中国信科集团承建沙特 5GFWA 网络建设项目正式移交》，中国经济网，http://www.ce.cn/xwzx/gnsz/gdxw/202304/17/t20230417_38502964.shtml，2023 年 4 月 17 日。

124

和云计算基础设施，为中国企业提供更多合作机会。[①] 此外，华为助力沙特未来新城 5G 网络、骨干传输网络、数据中心、云和 AI 平台建设。[②] 2023 年 9 月，华为云利雅得节点正式开服，成为华为云服务中东、中亚和非洲的核心节点，加速沙特开启数字时代的无限机遇。[③] 除中沙合作外，2023 年 9 月，第六届中阿博览会"网上丝绸之路大会"以"创新驱动 数引未来"为主题，围绕数字创新展开讨论，促进中阿数字经济合作，并将中阿经济合作推向新高度。[④] 2023 年 10 月，中东中亚数字能源在迪拜举办数据中心 Partner Connect 2023 伙伴大会，华为深化与伙伴合作，共创绿色智能数据中心。[⑤]

7.2.2 跨境电商合作呈现鲜明发展特色

电子商务作为数字经济的一个重要应用场景，是数字经济最活跃、最集中的表现形式之一，通过互联网和数字技术实现在线购物、支付和营销，成为促进中阿数字经济合作蓬勃发展的重要抓手。近年来，阿拉伯国家电子商务发展迅猛，主要得益于该地区数字基础设施水平的提升、偏好数字技术的年轻化人口结构、社交媒体消费趋势增长、民众对数字支付信任度的上升、当地政府的政策支持等因素。中国在电子支付、数字生态和电商方面的先进经验，推动了中阿跨境电商和海外仓服务发展，加速了传统贸易的数字化转型，覆盖电商平台、物流服务和电子支付等领域，形成特色鲜明的合作特点。

---

① 《沙特正式发放 4 个新经济特区许可证》，中华人民共和国商务部网站，http://sa.mofcom. gov. cn/article/sqfb/202306/20230603414941. shtml，2023 年 6 月 7 日。

② 《沙特新未来城："全球追梦者之地"》，环球网，http://www.news.cn/globe/2023-04/ 27/c_1310711435. htm，2023 年 4 月 27 日。

③ 《"与沙特一起，共赴全球"——华为云在沙特正式开服》，华为云网站，https:// www. huaweicloud. com/news/2023/20230904160120957. html，2023 年 9 月 4 日。

④ 《第六届中阿博览会·特刊丨丝绸之路》，中国—阿拉伯国家博览会网，https://www. cas-expo. org. cn/zh/newsDet. html？ id=1841，2023 年 9 月 24 日。

⑤ 《中东中亚数据中心伙伴大会 Partner Connect 2023 在迪拜成功举办》，华为官网，https:// digitalpower. huawei. com/cn/data-center-facility/news/detail/1393. html，2023 年 10 月 24 日。

第一，中国电商平台成为推动中东电商发展的有生力量。中东地区以跨境进口为主，中国的 AliExpress（阿里速卖通）、Shein（领添）、TikTok Shop（抖音商店）、Temu（跨境版拼多多）等平台已在中东崭露头角。据统计，中国电商平台在海湾六国的互联网用户覆盖率已达 80%[1]，助推中东电子商务增速水平居世界前茅。第二，中国社交电商模式的兴起成为中东线上购物的重要推动力。随着中东地区的电商渠道已然成熟并迅速多样化，社交渠道已迅速成为该地区线上购物的基石，尤其是 TikTok（抖音国际版）出海中东，使得直播行业为当地电商发展注入了巨大活力，网红和 KOL 营销也成为十分受欢迎的营销方式。第三，中国跨境电商物流依托电商行业迅速发展。中国物流数字化领先企业注重中东地区电商物流网络布局，其中，以 iMile、极兔为代表的中国快递公司凭借其覆盖范围广泛、物流运营高效和本地化运营能力强等优势，极大拓展了中东客户群体和市场份额。第四，中国金融科技公司在中东推广移动支付和电子钱包解决方案受到欢迎。例如，2022 年 12 月，义乌义特网络科技有限公司通过快捷通"义支付"（Yiwu Pay）与沙特完成了首单跨境人民币支付业务[2]；2023 年 3 月，"义乌付"与中国工商银行阿布扎比分行跨境支付业务的落地，完成了首单与迪拜市场直接进行货币结算的外贸订单[3]。

7.2.3 青年交流为双边合作注入新生动力

中阿青年科技合作具有明显的人力资源优势，当前在中国科技人力资源中，39 岁及以下人口约占 3/4[4]，青年才俊已经挑起中国科技创新大梁。

---

[1] 沈小晓：《中东电子商务发展势头强劲（国际视点）》，人民网，http：//world.people.com.cn/n1/2022/0715/c1002-32475935.html，2022 年 7 月 15 日。

[2] 《义乌和沙特完成首单跨境人民币支付业务，外交部：中阿经贸合作不断迈上新台阶》，中国日报网，https：//cn.chinadaily.com.cn/a/202212/09/WS6393057ba3102ada8b226067.html，2022 年 12 月 9 日。

[3] 《义支付首单迪拜跨境人民币业务落地》，中华人民共和国商务部网站，http：//ae.mofcom.gov.cn/article/ztdy/202403/20240303486777.shtml，2024 年 3 月 28 日。

[4] 《中国科协：中国科技人力资源年轻化特点和趋势明显》，人民网，http：//finance.people.com.cn/n1/2022/0625/c1004-32456472.html，2022 年 6 月 25 日。

与此同时，阿拉伯国家青年人口占比高，各国都开始重视青年科技人才培养，部分阿拉伯国家的高等教育入学率明显提升，更多阿拉伯国家青年人才承担起推动国家工业化、数字化转型建设的重任。中阿青年科技人才数量快速增长，为双方数字经济合作注入新的发展动能。

青年人才是科技创新的新生动力，扩大数字人才交流规模，重视数字技能培养和共同开发人力资源对中阿数字经济合作至关重要。2022年12月，习近平主席在首届中国—阿拉伯国家峰会上提出中阿务实合作"八大共同行动"，其中"青年成才共同行动"专门提及邀请阿方100名青年科学家来华开展科研交流。[①] 2023年9月21日，第六届中阿博览会青年创新发展论坛在银川开幕，主题为"中阿青年携手，共同创新成才"，通过举办开幕式、主题论坛、互动交流等系列活动，组织中阿青年围绕科技创新、绿色低碳、青年发展等内容开展交流对话，促进中阿青年深化合作、共同成才。[②] 11月30日，以"加强中阿青年伙伴关系，推动构建开放型世界经济"为主题的首届中阿青年发展论坛在海口成功举办，中阿青年围绕科技创新驱动绿色发展等议题展开热烈讨论。[③]

7.3　中阿数字经济合作展望

中国与阿拉伯国家在数字经济领域的合作日益深入，特别是数字经济发展靠后的阿拉伯国家，正在努力通过数字经济国际合作来提升本国数字经济发展水平。据估计，2022—2027年将是中东国家"数字经济加速

[①] 《习近平在首届中国—阿拉伯国家峰会上提出中阿务实合作"八大共同行动"》，中华人民共和国中央人民政府网，https://www.gov.cn/xinwen/2022-12/10/content_5731138.htm，2022年12月10日。

[②] 《第六届中阿博览会中阿青年创新发展论坛暨二〇二三中阿青年交流营开幕》，《中国青年报》2023年9月22日，第1版。

[③] 《首届中阿青年发展论坛聚焦推动构建开放型世界经济》，人民网，http://world.people.com.cn/n1/2023/1130/c1002-40129265.html，2023年11月30日。

中阿经贸关系发展进程2023年度报告

期"。[①] 在高质量共建"一带一路"背景下，双方合作在数字经济的传统领域、新兴领域和前沿领域都有巨大的提升空间。

7.3.1 弥合传统领域数字鸿沟：以数字基建与人才培养为基础

从数字"一带一路"可持续发展的角度来看，普遍、安全和负担得起的网络是"数字丝绸之路"的基本推动力。发展5G、互联网、大数据中心、云计算中心等数字基础设施，推动传统产业的数智化转型，是中阿共享数字经济收益的必经之路，双方应共同努力弥合"数字鸿沟"。第一，对阿拉伯欠发达国家提供政策、资金和技术援助，推动宽带网络覆盖和提高服务质量，并以可负担的价格扩大高速互联网接入。第二，与阿拉伯国家分享数字化转型成功经验，借助中国数字经济发展优势，帮助提升阿拉伯国家的自主发展能力。第三，共同搭建数字技术人才培训平台，加强人员往来和交流，提升阿拉伯国家民众的数字素养和应用技能，为双方数字经济合作与可持续发展提供长期人力资本支持。

7.3.2 巩固壮大新兴领域合作：以电子商务为发展范式

电子商务作为数字经济的新兴领域，渗透到数字经济的诸多方面，包括数据利用、数字支付、智慧物流、网红经济、产业数字化转型等，不仅对全球经济产生了深远影响，还重塑了人们的工作和生活方式，已成为推动中阿数字经济新业态合作发展的重要引擎。未来，中阿跨境电商合作可重点关注以下方面。第一，"社媒+"是电商发展的重要突破口。直播电商和KOL营销不仅能解决商品信任问题，还能满足阿拉伯国家消费者的娱乐需求，具有广阔市场。中国社交电商可借助技术手段和社交平台影响力，将线上购物从功能型消费转向符合阿拉伯国家风俗习惯的体验型消费，创造独特的品牌价值和竞争优势。第二，提升阿拉伯地区数字支付信

---

① 《中东地区国家大力发展数字经济（国际视点）》，《人民日报》2023年11月22日，第14版。

128

任。中东地区约60%的网购是以货到付款（COD）为付款方式。[1] 随着技术成熟和政府推广，数字支付逐渐普及，电子钱包和支付应用也在快速增长，中国金融科技公司可积极寻求与本地资本合作，助力解决支付本地化难题。第三，加快中东地区数字化和智慧物流创新。一些阿拉伯国家新的电商法规要求更详细的商品和配送信息，中国物流公司应提供先进的技术解决方案，结合智能技术和传统物流，提升追踪和数据分析能力。第四，洞见中东地区女性消费者的"她经济"前景。年轻女性是阿拉伯电商的主要用户群体，购买力强，特别是在女装、母婴用品和珠宝首饰等领域，需求潜力巨大，为专注于美妆服饰的中国垂直电商平台带来无限"钱景"。

7.3.3 培育布局前沿领域合作：以新能源汽车为延伸

近年来，在能源多样化倡议推动下，阿拉伯地区正在成为一个重要的电动汽车市场。中国电动车企业积极拓展海外市场，得益于中阿双边政策支持、阿拉伯国家市场需求量大以及其新能源汽车产业政策友好等优越条件，阿拉伯国家成为中国电动汽车的主要出口市场，使得以新能源汽车、锂电池、光伏产品为代表的中国制造"新三样"（相较于服装、家具、家电"老三样"）在阿拉伯世界广受欢迎。虽然新能源汽车本身不是数字经济，但其发展和应用高度依赖于数字经济的技术和理念，成为数字经济的重要组成部分。新能源汽车涉及智能网联技术、大数据和人工智能、智能制造等领域，体现了数字技术在现代经济中的广泛应用和深远影响。中国电动车企注重提升产品科技感，为汽车搭载智能辅助驾驶、智能语言交互、智能车身控制等系统，并能够与手机等移动终端连接，在阿拉伯市场备受青睐。目前，阿联酋与中国企业共建了中东最大、最健全的中国新能

---

[1] 《中东电商大战，一触即发》，澎湃网，https：//www.thepaper.cn/newsDetail_forward_22400823，2023年4月10日。

源车中东服务总部基地[1]，比亚迪、奇瑞、长安、吉利等20余家中国车企进驻中东市场[2]。通过新能源汽车合作，中阿双方未来有望在更多以智能网联、工业物联网、算法推荐、数字孪生、智能交通为代表的数字经济新疆域展开更深入的合作。

---

[1] 《中国新能源车中东服务总部基地，助力中国新能源车品牌"加速"出海》，中国日报网，https：//qiye.chinadaily.com.cn/a/202208/24/WS6305c8aaa3101c3ee7ae556a.html，2022年8月24日。

[2] 《中国品牌汽车中东出海记》，环球网，http：//www.xinhuanet.com/globe/2023-07/03/c_1310729581.htm，2023年7月3日。

第8章 中阿科技合作专题报告

中阿科技合作是符合中阿双方共同利益的发展之策。近年来，在"一带一路"倡议的推动下，在中国扩大对外开放、阿拉伯国家加速转型发展的时代需要下，中阿科技合作顺利开展并取得了丰硕成果。首届中阿峰会以来，中阿务实合作"八大共同行动"为中阿科技合作提出了更加明确的政策引领和时代要求。2023年，中阿科技合作加速推进，在合作模式、合作领域和合作成果等方面都有了较大突破。2024年，中阿合作论坛第十届部长级会议提出了以创新驱动格局为首的中阿"五大合作格局"，为新时代中阿关系擘画出"向新而行"的美好蓝图。从当前看，中阿科技合作将成为未来中阿合作的"主力军"、中阿共同发展的"发动机"。

8.1 阿拉伯国家科技发展现状

8.1.1 战略布局逐步完善

进入21世纪，全球技术革新和科技竞争不断加剧，"科技兴国"成为阿拉伯各国寻求产业转型、经济增长和可持续发展的重要路径。对此，阿拉伯各国高度重视在地区和国家层面制订多层级的战略计划，以实现国家的科技创新发展和战略自主。

中阿经贸关系发展进程2023年度报告

2018年，阿盟建立阿拉伯数字经济联合会①，并发布"阿拉伯数字经济共同战略愿景"。作为推动地区发展数字经济的行动指南，该愿景围绕"数字创新""数字公民""数字基础设施""数字业务""数字政府"五大主题，针对20项战略目标制订了50项规划项目。②在国家经济结构转型过程中，海湾地区的科技发展走在阿拉伯国家前列，发挥了区域领头羊作用。海合会作为区域组织，也将行动重点转向经济多元化和数字技术转型。近年来，海合会主权财富基金重点关注高新技术、可再生能源、数字智能产业投资。截至2023年，该基金资产总额达到3.6万亿美元，相比2018年增长超70%，为海湾国家的科技创新和经济转型打下坚实基础。③

除区域层面的战略支持外，阿拉伯各国也根据本国科技创新的条件特点和目标侧重，定制了本国的科技创新发展计划。首先，科技创新作为阿拉伯国家可持续发展的重要部分，是国家整体发展计划的关键组成。科威特"2035国家愿景"、沙特"2030愿景"、阿曼"2040愿景"、阿联酋"面向未来50年国家发展战略"、埃及"振兴计划"等，均将科技创新作为阿拉伯国家发展计划的重要组成部分，为国家发展方向给予明确设置和清晰谱绘。其次，为应对个性化需求，阿拉伯各国也制定了专项战略计划以服务国家科技创新。例如，2023年巴林推出"智能编程员"计划，计划至2027年培养10000名程序员进入巴林科技创新行业；阿联酋"智能数字"战略、沙特"开放大数据"战略、巴林"开放数据"战略等，均重点围绕提升数据转化效能和信息处理技术专题开展战略布局。

---

① 该组织建立于2018年，隶属于阿盟并由阿盟秘书长直接监督管理，旨在支持和加强阿拉伯各国数字经济领域的合作。

② Arab Commission for Digital Economy, *Arab Digital Economy Vision Towards A Sustainable Inclusive And Secure Digital Future*, January 2020.

③ 中国贸促会驻海湾代表处：《海湾合作委员会主权财富基金管理的资产增长到3.6万亿美元》，中国国际贸易促进委员会网，https：//www.ccpit.org/gulf/a/20230927/20230927axs7.html，2022年9月27日。

8.1.2　科技创新实践卓有成效

近几年，阿拉伯国家科技创新快速发展，引发全球关注。联合国西亚经济社会委员会《可持续发展目标年度审查报告》分析认为，过去几年，阿拉伯国家的创新格局得到显著改观，阿拉伯国家通过政府、私营企业、学术机构共同发力，在清洁能源、新型技术设施、航天科技、数字卫星等领域开展多元探索，挖掘出巨大的社会和经济发展潜力。[①] 对比近五年《全球创新指数报告》（见表8.1），阿拉伯国家排名整体呈动态上升趋势。沙特被评为2019—2023年全球创新增长最快的五大杰出经济体之一。阿联酋近五年科技创新进展稳定，至2023年已接近全球前30名。2019—2023年，沙特（48）、卡塔尔（50）排名分别提升20、15个名次，成功跻身全球前50名。巴林（67）、阿曼（69）、约旦（71）和埃及（86）创新指数也显著提高，巴林和阿曼成功跻身全球前50名。其中，阿曼在2022—2023年，跃升幅度最大，排名晋升10个名次。整体看，阿拉伯国家呈现出系统性和整体性并进的创新发展趋势。[②]

表 8.1　2019—2023 年阿拉伯国家创新指数全球排名

国家	2019 年	2020 年	2021 年	2022 年	2023 年
阿联酋	36	34	33	31	32
沙特	68	66	66	51	48
卡塔尔	65	70	68	52	50
科威特	60	78	72	62	64
巴林	78	79	78	72	67
阿曼	80	84	76	79	69
摩洛哥	74	75	77	67	70
约旦	86	81	81	78	71

---

①　UN Economic and Social Commission for Western Asia, Annual SDG Review 2024: Skill Development, Innovation and the Private Sector in the Arab Region, February 2024, p. 35.

②　WIPO, Global Innovation Index 2023: Innovation in the Face of Uncertainty, 2023, pp. 50–52.

续表

国家	2019 年	2020 年	2021 年	2022 年	2023 年
突尼斯	70	—	71	73	79
埃及	92	96	94	89	86
黎巴嫩	88	87	92	—	92
阿尔及利亚	113	121	120	115	119
毛里塔尼亚	—	—	—	129	127
伊拉克	—	—	—	131	—
也门	129	131	131	128	—

注：无数据年份为当年统计未覆盖国家。
资料来源：根据世界知识产权组织《全球创新指数》数据统计整理。

相比而言，海湾地区阿拉伯国家科技创新速度更快、进步更大，处于阿拉伯国家的领先地位。根据《全球网络就绪指数 2023 年报》统计（见表 8.2），阿联酋、沙特、卡塔尔、巴林、阿曼、科威特占据阿拉伯国家前 6 名，进入全球排位前 65 名，比较优势较为明显。[1] 此外，海湾国家在全球人才竞争力指数、政府人工智能就绪指数、全球创新指数和联合国电子政务发展指数中均排名前列。[2]

表 8.2 2023 年海湾国家全球网络就绪指数排名

国家	阿联酋	沙特	卡塔尔	巴林	阿曼	科威特
总体得分	62.4	56.1	54.2	52.5	52.1	48.4
排名	30	41	46	51	54	64

资料来源：根据《全球网络就绪指数 2023 年报》数据统计整理。

具体来看，阿拉伯国家在信息通信、智能开发、能源转型、航天技术等多维度，均开展了多元发展并取得显著成就。在信息通信方面，近年来，海合会国家对 5G 移动网络的发展进行了大量投资以构建智能互联城

---

[1] Portulans Institude, Network Readiness Index 2023, 2023, pp. 32-40.

[2] P. Mokshita , "Digital Giants: GCC Countries Lead the Charge in Global Tech Rankings", https://www.sme10x.com/10x-industry/digital-giants-gcc-countries-lead-the-charge-in-global-tech-rankings, 2024-01-09.

市，以提升各行业领域的连通性。2023 年第二季度数据显示，阿联酋已成为全球增长速度最快的 5G 市场；巴林的光纤普及率也名列全球前 20 位。[1] 在智能开发方面，根据奥维咨询报告，人工智能政务服务正在阿拉伯国家广泛应用，该项目将为海湾国家每年节省超 70 亿美元。2023 年，阿拉伯国家仍将进一步推进人工智能发展。预计至 2030 年，人工智能技术将为巴林、科威特、阿曼和卡塔尔 GDP 贡献 459 亿美元。[2] 在能源转型方面，阿拉伯国家坚持油气产业的低碳转型，沙特、卡塔尔、阿联酋等多家能源公司均设置了明确的碳减排目标。同时，各国均高度重视开发可再生能源，推进可再生能源装机容量大幅增长。阿联酋马克图姆太阳能发电园区、卡塔尔首家全容量并网发电光伏项目、阿曼首家共用事业规模光伏项目，均已建成投运。预计 2030 年建成的迪拜穆罕默德·本·拉希德太阳能园区，将成为全球最大的太阳能园区，总装机规模预计高达 5GW。此外，各国已投运部分蓝氢设备和实验性的绿氢设备，其他大型氢能项目也投产建设。[3] 在航天技术方面，2020 年，沙特政府拨款 21 亿美元开展太空计划，国家通信空间技术委员会宣布成立太空创业联盟以服务航空技术的可持续发展。此外，巴林、科威特分别于 2021 年、2022 年成功发射纳米卫星；阿联酋"希望号"探测器成功进入火星轨道，完成了阿拉伯国家的首次星际任务，阿曼也正在建设中东地区首个太空港。[4]

8.1.3 科技创新前景仍存挑战

阿拉伯国家正经历着快速数字转型过程，并已取得可观成效。但实现

---

[1] Telecom Review, "From Deserts to Digital Dominance: Tech Transformation in the GCC", https://www.telecomreview. com/articles/reports-and-coverage/7409 – from-deserts-to-digital-dominance-tech-transformation-in-the-gcc, 2023 – 10 – 09.

[2] Oliver Wyman, "7 Insights into Digital Trends in the GCC Digital Evolution", https://www.oliverwyman. com/our-expertise/insights/2024/apr/7-digital-trends-gcc. html, 2024 – 03 – 01.

[3] 张瑞、相均泳：《海合会国家能源融合转型：内涵、进展与挑战》，《阿拉伯世界研究》2023 年第 4 期。

[4] Omar Qaise, "Will Arab Countries Become the New Space-Tech Powerhouse?", https://interactive. satellitetoday. com/via/june – 2023/will-arab-countries-become-the-new-space-tech-powerhouse/, 2023 – 05 – 23.

数字转型和科技创新需要汇集国家财政实力、治理能力和人力资本等多重合力。从阿拉伯地区当前的产业结构、治理模式、社会基础等维度分析，阿拉伯国家的科技创新发展路径仍存在现实挑战。

第一，地区科技发展水平不均衡，缺乏区域协同共创的有力支撑。科技创新作为复合型发展目标，需要周边国家在科技、政治、文化、安全等多方面协调共进，形成双边或多边的合作框架，共同推动科技创新的可持续发展。然而，受各国国情影响，阿拉伯国家间科技创新发展水平差距较大，且"数字鸿沟"在未来仍有被扩大趋势。近年来，沙特、阿联酋、巴林、卡塔尔等海湾阿拉伯国家通过对数字基础设施建设、5G和云技术投资，成为阿拉伯国家科技发展的领航者。此外，埃及、摩洛哥等北非地区的阿拉伯国家也积极尝试通过发挥人口结构优势和有限的资本注入，来实现国家的科技创新愿景。相比之下，伊拉克、黎巴嫩、叙利亚等阿拉伯国家在技术水平和发展愿景上远远落后于前者，形成了国家间不平衡的科技创新发展结构，难以构建区域内强有力的创新合作体系和可匹配的协同合作关系。从全球创新指数分析，2023年，阿联酋、沙特、科威特位居全球前50名，远远领先于其他阿拉伯国家。相反，阿尔及利亚、毛里塔尼亚则位居132个参评国家的末位，伊拉克、也门等阿拉伯国家甚至不在排序范围内。[①]

第二，科技创新能力仍较薄弱，亟须强化科研产出和产业提升。目前，阿拉伯国家主要的科技成果还依靠国际合作，科技创新的主体性尚未充分发挥。科技创新作为国家发展转型和可持续发展的关键环节，提升独立自主的科技创新能力是阿拉伯国家的当务之急。数据表明，尽管阿拉伯国家科技创新表现呈现出波动性提升，但多数国家的科技成果转换率仍然较低。2022年，全球专利申请量达到346万项，阿拉伯国家共申请专利17260项，其中获批5786项，但其知识产权专利仅占全球总量的0.5%。并且，专利项目仅集中于沙特（34%）、摩洛哥（30%）、阿联酋（17%）、

[①] WIPO, Global Innovation Index 2023: Innovation in the Face of Uncertainty, 2023, pp. 58-61.

埃及（11%）和阿尔及利亚（6%），其他阿拉伯国家尚未有突出表现。[1]
在成果产出方面，全球顶尖科技创新专利的持有者均为 IBM、三星等私营
企业，成果转换效率较高。反之，阿拉伯国家专利主要由公共投资和国有
企业推动，专利能否有效及时地开展商业化转换还有待观望。[2]

第三，人才支撑基础和科技创新产业模式仍不成熟，导致国家缺乏长
效发展的内生动力。在全球人才激烈竞争的时代，专业人才资本匮乏是阿
拉伯国家面临的现实挑战。据统计，阿拉伯国家完成中等教育的青年人不
足 60%。此外，仅有不到 1/3 的青年熟练掌握数学技能、不到 2/3 的青年
具有识字阅读能力；只有约 30%的青年接受过大学教育，其中科学、技
术、工程和数学专业毕业生仅占 28%。[3] 可见，专业人才资源匮乏是制约
阿拉伯国家科技创新的重要因素。同时，当前阿拉伯国家主要依靠公共部
门和国有企业推动科技创新产业转型发展，私营企业的参与度仍然较低。
私营部门作为科技创新、成果转化、应用实践的核心支撑，是国家成功开
展创新性转型的决定性因素。但当前，除了参与度较低外，私营部门在自
身人才梯队建设、运营资金保障以及同政府政策对接等事项上均存在现实
障碍。

8.2 中阿科技合作的具体实践

8.2.1 整体趋势

中阿科技合作已晋升为中阿整体外交的重要组成部分，其作为中阿双
方激活合作潜能、拓展合作增量，推动构建中阿命运共同体的重要支撑，
正持续为中阿关系提质升级注入充沛动能。对此，中阿双方均高度关注科

---

[1] WIPO, World Intellectual Property Report 2022: The Direction of Innovation, 2022, pp. 79-87.

[2] International Monetary Fund, Promoting Inclusive Growth in the Middle East and North Africa: Challenges and Opportunities in a Post-Pandemic World, 2022, p. 93.

[3] UN Economic and Social Commission for Western Asia, Annual SDG Review 2024: Skill Development, Innovation and the Private Sector in the Arab Region, February 2024, p. 6.

技合作。当前，在战略有效对接的基础上，中阿科技合作在合作方式、合作领域、合作深度上不断拓展，合作潜能正在被有效激发。

中阿科技合作的顶层设计不断完善。2022年12月，习近平主席在首届中阿峰会提出中阿务实合作"八大共同行动"，科技合作成为不可或缺的实践维度。2023年10月，习近平主席在第三届"一带一路"国际合作高峰论坛提出支持高质量共建"一带一路"的八项行动，其中构建"一带一路"立体互联互通网络、建设开放型世界经济、促进绿色发展等行动，进一步深化了对中阿科技合作的战略引领。目前，除科摩罗外，中国已与21个阿拉伯国家签署了双边经济、贸易和技术合作协定，为中阿科技合作赋予有力支撑。[1] 总体来看，在元首外交的高度引领下，在中阿共建"一带一路"的时代背景下，中阿科技合作在理念引领、政策支撑、发展方向上均不断完善。

中阿科技合作的实践成果不断丰富。一是科技合作形式逐步多元。随着中阿科技合作的深入，除传统科技合作形式外，中阿双边在技术成果转移、科技创业园共建、科技人文交流等多维度，开展了互促、共建、同享的中阿科技合作。二是科技合作领域不断拓展。中阿科技合作覆盖多维领域（见表8.3），已形成"巩固存量、扩大增量"的特点，双方在新能源、航天卫星、5G技术、人工智能、无人机、数字经济等新兴领域开展了深入交流合作。[2] 三是科技合作潜能持续释放。开展中阿科技合作不仅是为了应对当前社会信息化、经济全球化等现实挑战，也有助于互促双方治理现代化的新探索。中阿双方在交通互联、农业科技、政务服务、信息通信、人口健康、卫星导航、资源环境等多领域也尝试创新合作，合作前景广阔。

---

[1] 李绍先主编《中阿经贸关系发展进程2022年度报告》，社会科学文献出版社，2023，第147页。

[2] 孙德刚、武桐雨：《第四次工业革命与中国对阿拉伯国家的科技外交》，《西亚非洲》2020年第6期。

第8章 中阿科技合作专题报告

表 8.3 中国与阿拉伯国家或地区组织科技合作的领域分布

国家/地区组织 ＼ 科技领域	核能	能源科技	太空航天	人工智能	数字经济	农业技术	生物医药	智慧通信
阿盟	√	√	√	√	√	√	√	√
海合会	√	√	√	√	√	√	√	√
阿联酋	√	√	√	√	√	√	√	√
沙特	√	√	√	√	√	√		√
卡塔尔		√						
阿尔及利亚	√	√			√			
埃及	√	√	√		√	√		
突尼斯	√	√			√			√
伊拉克			√	√				
约旦	√	√				√		
苏丹	√					√	√	
阿曼		√	√	√		√		√
摩洛哥		√		√				
黎巴嫩	√					√		√
科威特						√	√	√
巴林			√					√

资料来源：根据商务部、科技部及国内外公开报道信息统计整理。

8.2.2 主要途径

中阿技术转移网络越发牢固，助力双边科技合作。2015 年，中阿技术转移中心在中国科技部和宁夏回族自治区人民政府的共同推动下建立。近 10 年间，作为国家级国际技术转移中心，其通过推进中阿技术转移双边中心建设、构建国内国际技术转移协作网络、打造中阿技术转移综合信息服务平台、组织开展技术转移培训与推介对接活动，在中阿科技合作中发挥了积极作用。2023 年 9 月 21—24 日，第五届中阿技术转移与创新合作大会在宁夏银川举办。大会围绕"中阿科技合作，共享创新未来"的主题，邀请阿盟秘书处、阿盟农业发展组织、摩洛哥高教科研创新部、埃及科研与技术研究院及中国有关专家共计 700 余人，集中发布 300 项先进技术成果对接活动，签署重点合作协议 10 项。[①] 通过开展中阿科技合作高层论坛、中阿绿色创新发展技术成果推介会等多项活动，中阿技术转移中心不仅有效推动一批先进适用技术与装备走出国门，还成功联动中阿建立了一批重要创新平台，助力推动中阿落实了一批重要科技示范项目，切实成为推动中阿科技合作不可或缺的实践路径。

中阿创新合作规模不断扩大，提升双边发展动能。除技术转移外，中阿双方发挥优势互补的效力，积极开展创新合作实践，在数字科技、新能源、生态环境治理、医疗卫生等多个领域开展共谋共建、合作研发、人才培养等科技合作交流。为共同提升科研能力，中国已与近 20 个阿拉伯国家签署科技合作协定、5G 技术协定和人才培养协定。为加强中阿科技产业互促，中阿双方在航天卫星、数字通信、农业生态、医疗卫生等领域，建设多家联合创新实验室和海外科技合作中心，切实推进了中阿创新链、产业链、人才链的融合发展。为促进中阿科技交流，中阿开展全方位的科技往来活动，特别是中国资助阿拉伯青年科学家来华开展短期交流培训，有效夯实了阿拉伯国家科技人才梯队。

8.2.3　重点领域

在中阿共谋发展的时代背景下，在中阿合作论坛、中阿博览会等合作平台的助推下，中阿科技合作不断走深走实，合作领域更加扩展、合作内容更加丰富。在传统能源合作之外，围绕绿色能源开发、航天卫星应用、数字通信建设、卫生健康升级和农业生态提质等领域的科技合作，成为赋能中阿关系发展的新基点。

绿色能源合作助推中阿构建低碳能源体系，推进阿拉伯国家能源模式

---

① 中阿博览会秘书处：《中阿技术转移与创新合作大会》，中国—阿拉伯国家博览会网，https：//www.cas-expo.org.cn/zh/cloudSummitDet.html？createTime＝2023－09－21&id＝730，2023 年 9 月 21 日。

和经济结构转型。作为中阿务实合作"八大共同行动"的重要组成，绿色创新共同行动和能源安全共同行动推动中阿能源科技合作，中阿能源合作已覆盖太阳能、氢能、风能、核能等多项领域。凭借中国清洁能源领域的技术优势，中企深度参与摩洛哥、阿联酋、沙特等阿拉伯国家大型清洁能源项目。2023年以来，包括天合光能、中信博、协鑫科技等中国多家光伏企业宣布在阿拉伯国家投资，规划产能涉及硅片、电池组、多晶硅等。2023年5月，由哈尔滨电气集团承建的阿联酋迪拜哈斯彦清洁燃煤电站项目4号机组首次并网发电，其是中东首个清洁燃煤电站，预计全部投运后可为迪拜提供20%的电力能源。[①] 2023年11月，由国机工程集团总承包的艾尔达芙拉PV2太阳能电站在阿布扎比全面竣工，为全球已建成的最大单体光伏电站，可供20万户居民用电，每年将减少碳排放240万吨，使清洁能源在阿联酋总能源结构中的比重提高到13%以上。截至2023年底，该项目已为阿联酋累计贡献清洁电力36亿度。[②] 此外，摩洛哥努奥三期光热电站、卡塔尔哈尔萨电站等项目作为中阿绿色能源领域合作的重要成果，也在阿拉伯国家能源转型中发挥了积极作用。

航天卫星合作助推中阿打造"太空丝路"，增添中阿科技合作新进展。近年来，中国航天在遥感卫星、通信导航、深空探测等太空航天领域，为阿拉伯国家提供了有国际竞争力的技术和研发支持。2023年6月，由航天科技集团五院承担建设的埃及卫星总装集成测试中心（AIT中心）圆满完成，这是中国首个援外航天地面基础设施建设项目，切实为埃及提供了卫星自主研制的基础能力。2023年12月，由中埃联合研制的埃及二号低轨高分辨率光学遥感卫星在酒泉卫星发射中心成功发射，切实为埃及的环境危害监测、国土资源评估、城市发展规划等评估活动提供技术支持。[③] 此

---

① 新华社：《综述：中国与中东国家携手应对气候变化》，中华人民共和国中央人民政府网，https：//www.gov.cn/yaowen/liebiao/202312/content_6919310.htm，2023年12月9日。

② Global Times, "China, Arab Countries Eye Technology Cooperation for High-Quality Development", https：//www.globaltimes.cn/page/202405/1313252.shtml, 2024-05-29.

③ 今日中国：《以"星"相连，中阿航天合作纪实》，中阿合作论坛网，http：//www.chinaarabcf.org/chn/zagx/gjydyl/202406/t20240613_11435348.htm，2024年6月13日。

外，2023 年 10 月，第四届中阿北斗合作论坛在埃及成功举办。会议期间，阿拉伯国家和企业均期望通过突尼斯的中阿北斗/GNSS 中心使用北斗系统服务，以提升在精准农业、自然开采、渔业监控等方面的产业效率。[①] 2023 年以来，中国已同阿拉伯多国签署和平利用外层空间合作谅解备忘录，包括《中埃关于空间合作及和平利用外层空间的谅解备忘录》《中苏关于加强空间合作的谅解备忘录》《中阿（联酋）和平利用外层空间合作的谅解备忘录》等，为中阿航天科技合作打下坚实的政策基础。

数字通信合作助推中阿构建数字联通，成为中阿科技合作的重要领域。近年来，中国企业已成为阿拉伯国家在 5G 通信领域的重要合作伙伴，其在沙特、阿联酋、埃及、阿曼、巴林等国家都占据明显的市场优势。中国企业已帮助中东 14 个国家电信运营商部署 5G 网络。2023 年 3 月，沙特电信（STC）与华为签署了迈向 F5.5G 时代构建全光战略合作伙伴关系的合作备忘录；同月，华为与沙特领先的电信运营商 Zain KSA 签署战略合作谅解备忘录，共同发布 "5.5G City" 联合创新项目。[②] 此外，科威特 STC、阿联酋 Du 和科威特 Zain Group 等电信运营商与华为达成了 5.5G 领域的合作协议，共同推动 5.5G 技术的研发与实地测试。同月，深圳市大数据研究院、香港中文大学（深圳）与沙特阿卜杜拉国王科技大学签署合作备忘录，共建科学计算与机器学习联合实验室，并在科学研究、人才培养等方面开展深度合作，共同激发中阿科技创新活力。此外，阿里巴巴、京东、希音等中国电商企业也加快进入阿拉伯国家市场，"丝路电商" 成为激活阿拉伯地区经济的新路径。当前，极兔速递已实现沙特全境覆盖，日单配送量超 10 万件。

卫生健康合作助推构建中阿 "互联网+医疗健康" 智慧平台，成为中阿务实合作的龙头领域。2023 年 9 月 22 日，中阿博览会开设大健康产业

---

① 《专访：中阿北斗合作为 "一带一路" 倡议增添新维度——访阿拉伯信息通信技术组织秘书长》，搜狐网，https://www.sohu.com/a/733132535_121687414，2023 年 10 月 26 日。

② Middle East Economy, Huawei: Leading the Next Phase of 5G Advances in the GCC, https://economymiddleeast.com/news/huawei-leading-5g-advances-gcc/, 2023-12-19.

论坛，并围绕宁夏"互联网+医疗健康"、国家区域医疗中心、妇幼健康、健康管理、远程医疗、智慧医疗、中医中药、医械智造、智慧康养等 9 个主题进行展览展示，启动了中阿中医"互联网+医疗健康"智慧平台和中非对口医院合作机制建设项目，推动了中阿企业、医疗机构在区域医疗中心建设、中医药传承创新发展、慢性综合病防控和医疗装备智能产业发展等领域的合作，促成了埃及艾因夏姆斯大学同宁夏卫生健康委签订合作谅解备忘录。此外，为落实中阿务实合作"八大共同行动"之"青年成才共同行动"，中阿实施"中阿高校 10+10 合作计划"，包括天津中医药大学、首都医科大学、天津医科大学等在内的 39 所院校成为卫生健康领域成员高校，进一步促进中阿在卫生健康领域的人才交流、学术交往、临床实践。

农业生态合作推进中阿粮食安全，成为宁夏发挥地方优势开展中阿合作的重要领域。2023 年 9 月 22—23 日，第六届中阿博览会举办现代农业高质量发展合作大会，大会以"深化务实合作、共促粮食安全"为主题，旨在促进中阿农业科技创新、农业投资合作和农业科技交流，进一步夯实中阿双边在农业领域的务实合作。大会成功落实农业合作项目 34 个，包括现代农业技术培训合作、种养业新品种引进等研发、贸易、投资合作项目。① 其中，宁夏农林科学院与埃及国家研究中心签订科技合作备忘录，双方将围绕农作物育种、盐碱地改良、农业生物技术等领域开展科技合作。② 近年来，除传统的农业灾害防治、节水灌溉技术、农业生态提升等领域，中阿围绕提升农业多样性方面的合作进一步增多。2023 年 3 月，中国同阿联酋签署《椰枣种植可持续发展谅解备忘录》，双方将在椰枣再生及遗传转化体系、现代生物育种和病虫害防治等方面开展联合研究和产业

---

① 《第六届中阿博览会现代农业高质量发展合作大会在银川召开》，人民网，http：//nx.people.com.cn/n2/2023/0922/c192493-40581410.html，2023 年 9 月 22 日。

② 宁夏农林科学院：《埃及国家研究中心代表团访问我院并签订科技合作备忘录》，宁夏农林科学院网，https：//www.nxaas.com.cn/xwzx/ynyw/202309/t20230928_4291969.html，2023 年 9 月 28 日。

合作。2023 年 8 月，中国国家林业和草原局与阿拉伯国家联盟秘书处共同签署《关于建立中阿干旱、荒漠化和土地退化国际研究中心的谅解备忘录》，计划整合中阿资金、技术、人才资源，为中阿应对土地荒漠化、退化干旱提供理论和决策支撑，共同为全球 2030 年土地退化零增长和 2040 年土地退化减少 50% 的目标做出贡献。[①]

8.3 中阿科技合作展望

开展中阿科技合作是迎合时代之变、应对现实之需、服务中阿发展的现实之策。近年来，依托科技合作，中阿合作已成功从能源贸易、工程承包等传统模式，升级成为涵盖新能源、高新技术、航天通信等新兴模式。首届中阿峰会提出中阿务实合作"八大共同行动"，其中在粮食安全、卫生健康、绿色创新、能源安全等多项行动中均对中阿科技合作提出了更高的要求和期待。在此基础上，中阿合作论坛第十届部长级会议提出以创新驱动格局为首的中阿"五大合作格局"，擘画出新时代中阿关系"向新而行"的美好蓝图。展望未来，中阿科技合作将成为推动中阿命运共同体建设跑出加速度的核心引擎和关键动能。

发挥优长，持续深化中阿科技合作。过去 10 年间，中阿科技合作的蓬勃发展主要归因于中阿双方存在较强的互补优势。一方面，中国在技术水平上全球领先，是阿拉伯国家开展国家技术革新、经济转型的重要支撑。另一方面，阿拉伯国家又掌握着可观的资本积累和广阔的潜力市场，是中国技术、中国企业"走出去"的理想选择。据联合国《全球科技创新 2023 年度报告》预测，中国将长期是人工智能、物联网、区块链、5G通信、3D 打印、机器人、无人机、基因工程、纳米技术、太阳能光伏、

[①] 宁夏回族自治区科技厅：《荒漠化防治技术成果推介对接会在银川召开》，中华人民共和国科学技术部网，https://www.most.gov.cn/dfkj/nx/zxdt/202310/t20231009_188350.html，2023 年 10 月 9 日。

生物燃料、绿色氢能、电动汽车等高新技术行业的主导者和领先者。[①] 同时，阿拉伯国家拥有全球最大的主权财富基金，掌握着占全球36%，总计3.7万亿美元的资产。沙特、阿联酋、卡塔尔、科威特、阿曼和巴林等海湾国家还拥有6000万人的高收入人群。在知识经济的时代浪潮下及国家全面转型的迫切需求下，阿拉伯国家将加大对科技创新的投入。可见，中阿双方在技术、资本、市场三个维度，均体现出了更高的契合性。在已有合作的成功经验上，中阿双方可继续紧密供需对接，发挥各自优长，形成发展合力，共济中阿利益。

织密网络，拓宽筑牢中阿科技合作。近年来，中阿科技合作仍主要依托政府单位和国有企业引导推动，私营部门参与中阿科技合作的潜力仍待开发。当前，中阿"五大合作格局"已将科技创新提上了前所未有的高度，要求中阿科技合作朝着深入、多元、常态化的方向推进。合作主体多元化、合作方式丰富化是中阿科技合作长效开展的重要保障。虽然，已有中国私人企业出海进入阿拉伯市场，但在合作领域、合作层次、合作对象上仍存在较大的局限性，未能在市场中营造"由下至上""以点带面"的市场氛围。相似地，阿拉伯国家私营部门也极少参与中阿科技合作，仍面临科技创新能力薄弱、人才资源短缺、资金筹集困难、信息获取不畅等现实困难，亟须在政策资源上加以扶持。因此，中阿科技合作需要在固有合作模式之外，增加企业、科研机构的政策沟通和技术交流，将不同层级的实践主体纳入合作视野，依靠全覆盖的市场机制和内生长效的民间力量，正向推动中阿科技合作。

培养梯队，长效推进中阿科技合作。回顾历史，中阿科技合作发展迅速、势头迅猛。但中阿科技合作模式仍以中国向阿拉伯国家的技术转移和技术援助为主，基于技术研发合作的双向互动仍较为欠缺。这主要归因于阿拉伯国家在科技发展水平、专业人才存量上仍有待提升，特别是海湾地区以外的阿拉伯国家自身资源更为薄弱。未来，中阿科技合作长久有序推

[①] United Nations, "Technology and Innovation Report 2023", 2023, pp. 136-151.

进，亟须倚靠科研人才队伍建设。阿拉伯国家拥有 30 岁以下青年人口近 3.7 亿人，占阿拉伯社会总人口的 60%以上，是决定国家未来发展走向、发展水平、发展前景的关键因素。汇集青年人才、培育新生力量、完善科研梯队，切实依据中阿青年成才共同行动，有效落实"中阿高校 10+10 合作计划"，加密中阿高校、科研机构的青年人才交流，方可从根源上稳固中阿科技合作。

共商共享，和平共促中阿科技合作。"一带一路"倡议提出以来，中国秉持的"共商、共享、共建"和平发展理念已被阿拉伯国家广泛接受。中国是当今世界经济发展的"发动机"。阿拉伯国家在战略定位调整、发展结构转型的改革过程中，已明显展现出"向东看"的趋势。[1] 除了中国在清洁能源、数字经济、高新技术、新型工业化的技术优势外，开放包容、和平共享、独立自主的理念优势也是吸引阿拉伯国家的关键要素。当前，中东战略环境正加速演进，大国博弈将辐射至中东政治、经济、外交、安全等多方领域。对此，中国和阿拉伯国家均面临巨大的战略竞争压力，中阿科技合作或将受到干扰和影响。在此局面下，中国和阿拉伯国家更需以构建中阿命运共同体为目标，加强多元合作，维护战略共识，加强战略互信，进而打造更为高效、稳固、持久的中阿科技合作。

---

[1] 李伟健、唐志超、丁俊、王广大：《中阿峰会成果丰硕，中阿关系谱写新篇》，《阿拉伯世界研究》2023 年第 1 期。

第9章　中阿生态环境治理合作专题报告

党的十八大以来，在习近平新时代中国特色社会主义思想的引领下，中国紧跟时代、放眼世界，承担大国责任、展现大国担当，推动构建人类命运共同体，实现由全球环境治理参与者到引领者的重大转变。生态文明建设是新时代的主题之一，共谋生态文明建设更是习近平生态文明思想的重要理念之一。2023 年 12 月 13 日，《联合国气候变化框架公约》第二十八次缔约方大会（COP28）在阿联酋迪拜落下帷幕。来自 198 个缔约方的谈判代表齐聚迪拜，对《巴黎协定》进行了首次全球盘点，并最终针对在最近 10 年加大气候行动力度的决定达成共识。

阿拉伯国家位于干旱、半干旱地区，生态环境类型多样。气候干旱少雨，水资源匮乏，生态脆弱。该地区 68% 的地域为沙漠和丘陵，且大部分地区气候炎热，干旱少雨，有限的土地资源面临沙漠化的危险，引发土壤和森林的进一步退化。此外，随着大规模工业化、石油开采、海洋污染、环境破坏的日益突出，生态环境和可持续发展问题成为阿拉伯地区普遍面临的重大挑战。[①]

中国一直以来致力于推动构建人类命运共同体，加强国际合作，维护多边秩序和规则，推动落实《巴黎协定》。作为负责任的发展中大国，中国一直是气候变化南南合作的积极倡导者和务实实践者，持续通过气候变化南南合作为其他发展中国家，特别是小岛屿国家、最不发达国家、阿拉

[①] 王林伶：《中国与阿拉伯国家生态环境领域合作研究——兼论防沙治沙合作与技术输出》，《宁夏党校学报》2013 年第 6 期。

147

中阿经贸关系发展进程2023年度报告

伯国家和非洲应对气候变化提供支持。

9.1 阿拉伯地区生态环境现状

阿拉伯地区生态环境十分脆弱。该地区地形大部分是高原，高原的边缘有较高的山岭。平原面积狭小，主要分布在埃及的尼罗河谷地和河口三角洲、伊拉克的两河流域，它们分别是古代埃及文化和古巴比伦文化的摇篮。阿拉伯地区大部分地处北纬20°—30°，北回归线从中部穿过，气候炎热。这里又受到副热带高压和来自亚洲内陆干旱地区东北信风的控制，常年干旱少雨。同时，闭塞的高原地形，阻挡了海洋湿润空气的进入，更加剧了地区干旱，所以形成了以热带沙漠气候为主的气候特点。

9.1.1 水资源分布与利用格局

阿拉伯地区是世界上最干旱的地区之一。近年来，由于气候变化、人口增长和经济社会环境变化等因素，阿拉伯国家水资源日益短缺。据统计，全球17个最缺水的国家中，有14个在中东北非地区，其中包括阿尔及利亚、利比亚、沙特和也门等12个阿拉伯国家。[①] 就水资源的分布而言，阿拉伯地区水资源分布不均，主要分布在尼罗河谷地、底格里斯河和幼发拉底河流域，以及约旦河等地区，许多河流是跨国界的国际河流，多国共有，存在因水资源利用而出现的国际争端。此外，拥有河流和地下水资源的地区也存在水资源分布不均的问题。就水资源的利用而言，一是农业对水资源的需求占据了主导地位。阿拉伯地区大部分是灌溉农业，过度灌溉和低效用水问题严重。二是工业和城市发展对水资源的需求不断增加。阿拉伯地区的城市人口呈爆发式增长，导致对水资源的需求不断上升。

[①] Jeannie Sowers, "Climate Change, Water Resources, and the Politics of Adaptation in the Middle East and North Africa", *Climatic Change*, 2011, Vol. 104, p. 604.

世界银行相关报告指出，预计到 2050 年，阿拉伯地区每年的水资源缺口将达到 250 亿立方米。2023 年，世界银行发布的《中东和北非地区水资源短缺经济学：制度解决方案》指出，中东和北非地区正面临前所未有的水资源短缺情况，并提出了一系列水资源管理及制度改革建议，以减轻该地区用水压力。方案的预测结果表明：到 2029 年末，中东和北非地区人均年可用水量将降至 500 立方米这一世界公认的严重缺水阈值以下；到 2050 年，该地区每年水资源缺口将达到 250 亿立方米，相当于 65 座沙特修建的世界最大海水淡化厂的供水量。方案指出，在中东和北非的很多国家，对于水资源在农业和城市间不同部门的分配，通常由中央政府部门集中管理，地方层面难以协调和解决不同用水需求的矛盾。方案建议在阿拉伯各国全国性水资源战略框架下，在水资源分配决策过程中应给予地方政府更多管理权限，以更有效地协调部门的水资源分配和利用。[①]

9.1.2 干旱与荒漠化

阿拉伯地区地处低纬度的副热带高压地带，形成了广泛的干旱气候。地形以高原、盆地和山脉为主，缺乏大规模的水源，降水量稀缺，尤其是沙特、也门、埃及、阿联酋等国，经常面临干旱、干燥和高温天气。该地区水资源管理能力弱、灌溉技术不成熟，导致水资源利用率低。随着人口不断增长，用水需求增加，城市化进程加快，该地区本就薄弱的水利基础设施承受了更大的压力，导致人道主义危机加剧。[②] 值得警惕的是，干旱会导致粮食、水和能源价格上涨，令情况进一步恶化。2023 年，联合国世界粮食计划署的一份报告显示，叙利亚超过 1200 万人面临饥饿，还有近 300 万人面临粮食不安全的风险。

受严峻气候环境的影响，阿拉伯地区的土壤和植被持续退化，荒漠化严重。阿拉伯地区荒漠化不断扩大，已成为全球荒漠化最严重的地区之

---

① 管克江：《中东北非国家加大应对水危机》，《人民日报》2023 年 5 月 18 日。

② Nasrat Adamo, "Cliamate Change: Droughts and increasing Desertification in the Middle East, With Special Reference to Iraq", *Engineering*, 2022, No. 14, p. 237.

一。饱受荒漠化和沙尘暴肆虐之苦的阿拉伯国家，期盼能够借鉴中国成功的治沙技术和经验，共同防沙治沙。高温、降水减少、土地沙漠化导致沙尘暴频发。全世界 15%—20% 的沙尘源自中东地区。[①] 2020 年 3 月，埃及遭遇 26 年来最严重的沙尘暴；2022 年 3 月，阿尔及利亚北部地区遭遇沙尘暴，一度影响地中海北岸的欧洲国家。伊拉克环境部的预测显示，伊拉克境内每年遭遇的沙尘日将逐渐增长，从目前的 272 天最终将增至 2050 年的近 300 天。联合国的数据显示，中东北非地区沙尘暴出现的频率正大幅增加，影响全球 151 个国家的近 3.3 亿人，造成巨大的经济损失。沙尘暴导致空气质量下降，影响大气环流，进而对生态环境以及人的身体健康造成危害。地球科学期刊《大气》发布的统计报告显示，近年来中东和北非地区每年因沙尘暴灾害造成的损失近 1500 亿美元，约占 2022 年该地区各国国内生产总值的 2.5% 以上。[②]

9.1.3 极端天气

纵观 2023 年全年，极端天气和严重自然灾害不断发生，给相关国家及其民众带来巨大损失，也不断提醒人们保护环境，珍惜地球资源。极端天气在中东和北非地区频繁发生，揭示了当前全球气候变化的严峻现实。从高温天气导致的持续干旱、沙尘暴到飓风所引发的严重洪灾，气候变化影响着中东国家民生乃至整体稳定，也为全世界敲响了警钟。2023 年，阿拉伯地区多个国家遭遇高温天气，一些国家的气温创下了历史新高。中东北非多国 2023 年夏季气温达新峰值。

世界气象组织在《联合国气候变化框架公约》第二十八次缔约方大会开幕前夕发布的《全球气候状况临时报告》显示，中东和北非地区气温均值为目前全球最高的地区，2023 年入夏以来，地区内多个国家历史高温

[①] 闫伟、刘爱娇：《气候变化对中东的复合安全威胁及其应对》，《世界社会科学》2023 年第 4 期。

[②] Nasrat Adamo, "Cliamate Change: Droughts and increasing Desertification in the Middle East, With Special Reference to Iraq", *Engineering*, 2022, vol. 14, p. 239.

纪录被打破。^① 伊拉克交通部下属的气象局统计，巴格达、纳杰夫、迪瓦尼耶、济加尔和穆萨纳 5 省在 2023 年 8 月中旬的最高气温达 51℃，伊拉克北部省份气温峰值也突破 44℃。与高温天气及严重干旱一同到来的，是水资源的缺乏。地处两河流域的伊拉克水资源原本相对丰沛，但近年来情况急转直下，特别是 2023 年夏季，迪瓦尼耶和米桑两省多地旱情极为严重。邻近底格里斯河的果园面临水资源短缺，很多果农遭受大量经济损失。由于缺水严重，伊拉克农业部在 2023 年 9 月宣布停止全国水稻种植，不少农产品从出口优势产品被迫变成了进口商品。遭遇极端高温天气的不仅仅是伊拉克。叙利亚西北部城市伊德利卜 8 月 13 日和 14 日气温突破 46℃；位于北非地区的突尼斯、阿尔及利亚两国首都和摩洛哥城市阿加迪尔夏季最高气温分别创下 49.0℃、49.2℃ 和 50.4℃ 的历史新高。海湾国家阿联酋 7 月、8 月也曾经历极端高温天气，阿布扎比和迪拜等多地气温超过 50℃。^②

9.2　中阿生态环境治理合作现状

所谓生态合作治理，是指在当前生态环境问题日益复杂化和跨区域发展情势下，通过强化不同政治权力主体之间的合作，打破狭隘的区域生态保护主义，发挥治理的整体效应和协同效应，以政治手段推动其他相关主体，共同寻求生态环境问题的协同治理，最终达到整体改善生态环境的目的。^③ 中阿生态环境治理合作已经形成了较为完善的机制和多层次、多领域的合作局面。2023 年，第六届中阿博览会中阿技术转移与创新合作大会在宁夏银川举行。大会以"中阿科技合作 共享创新未来"为主题，通

---

① 《多项气候记录打破和再生能源成为解题关键》，中国气象局网，http://www.cma.gov.cn，2024 年 3 月 26 日。

② 《中东 2023：多国面临极端天气威胁，应对危机势在必行》，《北京日报》2023 年 12 月 24 日。

③ 杨美勤、唐鸣：《生态合作治理：促进"一带一路"国际合作的新动力》，《当代世界社会主义问题》2020 年第 1 期。

中阿经贸关系发展进程2023年度报告

过视频形式面向阿拉伯国家发布了 300 项先进适用技术，涉及生态环境保护、资源能源利用、污染控制等领域。同时，签订了 8 个中阿科技合作与技术转移合作协议，包括防沙治沙、节水灌溉、生态保护等项目。大会还开设了 4 场技术对接及研讨会，涉及荒漠化防治、绿色创新发展等，供中阿科研工作人员进行科学技术成果推介与研讨。

9.2.1　土地荒漠化治理技术合作

荒漠化、土地退化与干旱是人类面临的共同挑战。中国始终是推动全球荒漠化防治的坚定力量。2023 年 8 月 26 日，第九届库布其国际沙漠论坛在内蒙古鄂尔多斯市开幕，论坛主题是"以科技引领治沙 让荒漠造福人类"。在库布其国际沙漠论坛上，中国国家林业和草原局与阿拉伯国家联盟秘书处共同签署了《关于建立中阿干旱、荒漠化和土地退化国际研究中心的谅解备忘录》。中国和阿盟干旱、荒漠化和土地退化国际研究中心成立揭牌，并启动首批项目。研究中心旨在服务和增强中阿干旱、荒漠化与土地退化领域的创新研究与国际合作，力争成为中阿绿色发展领域的典范式合作成果。中国和阿拉伯国家联盟力争将研究中心打造成集科学研究、技术创新与转移转化、人才培养与能力建设于一体的国际研究机构，将重点整合中阿在人才、技术、资金等方面的资源，聚焦关键技术创新、成果转化和经验分享，为中阿双方抵御干旱影响、防治荒漠化与土地退化提供科技支撑、决策支持和智库服务。

建立中阿干旱、荒漠化和土地退化国际研究中心是中国国家主席习近平在 2022 年 12 月首届中阿峰会上提出的中阿务实合作"八大共同行动"内容之一，旨在加强和深化中国与阿拉伯国家在荒漠化防治等领域的合作，为中阿抵御干旱影响、防治荒漠化和土地退化提供科技支撑、决策支持和智库服务；整合中阿人才、技术、资金等资源，聚焦关键技术创新、成果转化和经验分享，促进治理理念和实践创新；推动中阿双方履行《联合国防治荒漠化公约》并服务全球履约事业；推动区域及全球绿色发展和民生改善，为实现全球 2030 年土地退化零增长和 2040 年土地退化减少

152

50%目标做出贡献。① 未来，中阿双方将根据该备忘录，依托中阿干旱、荒漠化和土地退化国际研究中心，举办国际论坛、联合研发创新技术、打造科学智库、构建技术共享与成果转移平台、开展能力建设活动。

中国非常重视生态环境治理教育培训和科技交流。2023 年 9 月 20—24 日，2023 年荒漠化防治技术与实践国际研修班在宁夏银川举办。来自巴基斯坦、尼日利亚、阿尔及利亚等 13 个国家、地区及国际组织的 20 名国际学员和近 50 名宁夏林草部门技术人员参加了学习。研修班开班期间恰逢第六届中阿博览会在银川举办，学员们借此机会参加了第五届中阿技术转移与创新合作大会，《联合国防治荒漠化公约》秘书处科技创新项目负责人受邀围绕加快荒漠化防治、推动可持续发展发表主题演讲。在荒漠化防治经验分享与技术成果专场推介国际研讨会上，专家学者聚焦荒漠化防治这一国际性难题做主题报告，学员开展座谈交流。国际学员一致表示，中国在荒漠化防治上取得显著成效，他们会把学到的好经验好做法带回去，造福自己的国家；同时也希望借助国际荒漠化防治知识管理中心网络平台，进一步共享中国在荒漠化防治方面取得的新成果，推进技术成果转化和科技项目合作。

9.2.2　节水灌溉和现代农业技术合作

互联网时代，大数据、云计算、物联网等数字技术让更多国家拥有了实现水资源高效管理的"新工具"。国际灌溉排水委员会秘书长阿什温·潘迪亚说，现今，世界各国应充分促进水管理领域的科技运用，形成适合本国的系统和机制，增进彼此之间水管理知识的传播分享，在全球层面衡量水资源安全。

第六届中阿博览会水资源论坛现场发布了中国与"一带一路"共建国家取得的水利合作成果。本届论坛以"科技赋能水资源节约集约利用"为

---

① 《中阿干旱、荒漠化和土地退化国际研究中心成立》，国家林业和草原局政府网，http：//www.forestry.gov.cn，2024 年 5 月 20 日。

主题，以水为脉搭建通道，针对促进贸易、增加投资、提高人民生活水平等需求，创新对外合作服务渠道，加强与共建"一带一路"国家在水资源方面的信息交流，鼓励先进技术转移，推动政府和企业间的对话协作，提供中国治水思路和相关标准、产品、服务，促成贸易订单和项目落地，争取将中阿博览会水资源论坛建成水事合作、水科技交流、水经济合作的新通道。

此外，2023年是"一带一路"倡议提出十周年，其中科技合作是共建"一带一路"的重要组成部分。近年来，在"一带一路"科技创新行动计划和中阿科技伙伴计划框架下，中国与阿拉伯国家在科技领域的合作交流不断拓宽，在农业水管理技术等多领域取得务实成果，助推中国与阿拉伯国家共建"一带一路"。2023年6月9—16日，中国科学院空天信息创新研究院遥感科学国家重点实验室副研究员朱伟伟带队，联合北京雨根科技有限公司、黎巴嫩国家科学研究委员会国家遥感中心、黎巴嫩农业研究所的工作人员，通过走访调研和讨论完成了4个通量观测站的选址。[①]在黎巴嫩贝卡河谷北部Kfrdan LARI农场（果树林）、中部黎巴嫩农业研究所灌溉实验站（农田）、南部贝鲁特阿拉伯大学环境与发展研究中心野外实验站（混合林与农田），完成了涡动相关仪观测系统、茎秆液流计观测系统等观测仪器的安装建设，与各实验站原有的蒸渗仪、气象站及波文比观测系统共同形成了黎巴嫩不同下垫面水热通量观测网络。其间，中方团队对黎方技术人员开展了地面站定期维护、数据接收与数据处理的技术培训。2023年10月30日至11月10日，项目组举办"联合实验室第一期蒸散遥感监测方法与地面观测技术、灌区农业水管理线上培训班"。课题承担单位中国灌溉排水发展中心组织协调有关灌区、企业专家，为黎巴嫩国家遥感中心、黎巴嫩农业部农业研究所、黎巴嫩大学、约旦西亚地区空间科学和教育技术中心、突尼斯阿拉伯农业发展组织以及也门、利比亚等

---

① 《国家重点研发计划"中黎现代农业水管理联合实验室"项目完成黎巴嫩不同下垫面水热通量观测站建设与培训》，中国科学院空天信息创新研究院网，http：//www. aircas. ac. cn/dtxw/hzjl/202306/t20230621_6784348. html，2024年6月1日。

5 个国家有关机构技术人员，开展了灌区农业水管理培训，为黎巴嫩等共建"一带一路"阿拉伯国家农业水管理提供良好实践。本次技术培训为黎巴嫩等共建"一带一路"阿拉伯国家提供了中国蒸散遥感监测和灌区农业水管理方面的创新技术和成功经验，促进了中国农业水管理方法在阿拉伯地区推广应用，为共建"一带一路"阿拉伯国家农业和生态系统可持续发展、提升阿拉伯国家的气候风险抵御能力、改善阿拉伯国家农业水管理系统提供了技术支撑，促进了中国农业水管理技术与企业走向共建"一带一路"阿拉伯国家，并为今后开展类似工作积累了重要经验。

9.2.3　极端气候应对与气象合作

极端天气在气候变暖的情况下日益频繁，正在对人类健康、生态系统、经济、农业、能源和水供应产生重大影响。正如世界气象组织秘书长佩特里·塔拉斯所言，日渐频发的极端气候正在给全球经济社会发展带来持续威胁。气候适应与减少碳排放不仅考验阿拉伯国家的治理能力，更是一个宏观经济问题，需要经济发展模式的绿色转型、相应的科学和工程技术支持，以及大量的经济投入。[①]

2022 年 12 月，中国国家主席习近平在首届中阿峰会上提出中阿务实合作"八大共同行动"，其中就包括绿色创新共同行动和能源安全共同行动。中国提出共建中阿清洁能源合作中心等具体举措，展现出持续深化应对气候变化合作的决心。中国拥有世界最大的清洁发电体系，水电、风电、太阳能发电装机容量均居世界第一。凭借在清洁能源领域的技术优势，中国与阿拉伯国家在清洁燃煤、太阳能等领域积极展开合作，中国企业深度参与阿联酋、摩洛哥、沙特等国大型清洁能源项目，助力当地能源转型。除了能源领域合作，中国还为中东国家在海水淡化、绿色金融、绿色农业等领域发展提供助力，以共同应对气候变化带来的挑战。

---

① 闫伟、刘爱娇：《气候变化对中东的复合安全威胁及其应对》，《世界社会科学》2023 年第 4 期。

此外，"八大共同行动"聚焦绿色创新共同行动，"利用中国风云气象卫星和北京世界气象中心，支持阿方防灾减灾"，为中阿气象合作指明方向、路径。中国气象局局长陈振林指出，中国高度重视与阿拉伯国家的气象合作。2023年上半年，中国气象局和阿联酋国家气象局签署了双边政府间气象科技合作备忘录。论坛期间，双方再次举行双边会谈，希望在人工影响天气、气象卫星遥感监测与应用、人工智能、信息和通信、观测仪器设备、教育培训等领域深化务实合作。

近年来，高温、台风、暴雨、沙尘暴等在全球范围内频发，应对气候变化和防灾减灾成为全人类共同的挑战，呼吁加强气象国际合作。据了解，目前中国风云气象卫星服务国家129个，风云气象卫星国际防灾减灾应急保障机制注册国家达到32个。其中，3个阿拉伯国家注册成为风云气象卫星国际用户防灾减灾应急保障机制成员，10个阿拉伯国家成为风云气象卫星数据国际用户；中国为22个阿盟成员国的2000多人次提供了短期国际气象培训，不少人还来华进修气象硕士或博士研究生学位。

9.3　中阿生态环境治理合作展望

中国和阿拉伯国家之间的关系源远流长，和平合作、开放包容、互学互鉴、互利共赢始终是中阿历史交往的主旋律。新时代的中阿合作，共建"一带一路"就是要建设一条开放发展之路，同时也必须是一条绿色发展之路。在共建"一带一路"过程中，中国始终将生态保护放在重要位置，始终坚持绿色发展，在生态环境治理、生物多样性保护和应对气候变化等领域加强国际合作，致力于建设人与自然和谐共生的生态文明。绿色基建、绿色能源、绿色交通、绿色金融等项目正不断从愿景变为行动和成果，绿色正成为共建"一带一路"的底色。中国和阿拉伯国家拥有各自不同的资源禀赋和发展路径，但都处于绿色发展转型的阶段，双方在生态环境治理理念和实践方面有相同之处。

9.3.1 弘扬中阿生态协同治理的命运共同体理念，加强对阿生态理念宣传

习近平总书记指出："人与自然共生共存，伤害自然最终将伤及人类。"[1] 人类生产与生活正在对赖以生存的自然环境造成广泛的影响。极端天气、生态恶化带来的农业、经济、环境、贸易、安全等问题不是一个国家、一个地区所能应对和解决的。在生态文明建设方面，世界上每一个国家都不能独善其身和置身事外，都是人类生态文明建设进程中的一员，每个国家都承担应尽的国际义务，与其他国家深入展开交流合作，弥补生态文明的国际合作赤字，分享生态文明建设成果，携手共建生态环境优美的地球美好家园，充分释放生态文明红利，让每个国家的人民都能获得高水平的生态福祉。

具有中国特色的全球治理方案日益受到国际社会的认可。2016 年 5 月，联合国环境规划署发布《绿水青山就是金山银山：中国生态文明战略与行动》报告，充分认可中国生态文明建设的举措和成果。2018 年在第 26 次"基础四国"气候变化部长级会议发表的联合声明中，首次将"构建人类命运共同体"理念体现在应对气候变化领域的多边性国际文件中。2020 年 9 月，习近平主席指出，"中国将提高国家自主贡献力度，采取更加有力的政策和措施，二氧化碳排放力争于 2030 年前达到峰值，努力争取 2060 年前实现碳中和"[2]。2021 年，习近平主席在领导人气候峰会上首次提出构建"人与自然生命共同体"。

讲好中国故事，加强对阿生态理念的宣传。夯实共建"一带一路"生态共同体民心民意根基，突破"传播困境"和"认同障碍"，是推动"一带一路"生态共同体建设的关键环节。一是构建对阿多元化传播体系。在具体实践中，着重挖掘民间外交在"一带一路"生态共同体理念国际传播

---

[1] 习近平：《共同构建人类命运共同体》，《求是》2021 年第 1 期。

[2] 习近平：《在第七十五届联合国大会一般性辩论上的讲话》，求是网，http://www.qstheory.cn/yaowen/2020-09/22/c_1126527766.htm，2020 年 9 月 22 日。

中的潜在效用，系统展开分层次、立体式传播，形成政府、媒体、学界、群众多元互动的人文交流大格局。二是打造对阿普适性传播内容。选取在阿拉伯国家认可度较高的普适性内容进行传播，把刚性刻板的话语叙事转变为富有感染力和亲和力的柔性叙事，以立体、生动、鲜活的方式宣传"一带一路"生态共同体理念的价值核心。三是搭建对阿创新化传播平台。开发阿拉伯国家人民易于接受的数字影音传播平台，以人们喜闻乐见的方式促进"一带一路"生态共同体理念传播，打破国别、信仰的藩篱，触及共建"一带一路"国家人民的心灵，凝聚高质量建设"一带一路"生态共同体国际共识。

9.3.2 依托多边机制，逐步完善中阿环保合作机制，深化全球南方生态环境合作

阿拉伯国家与中国同属发展中国家，在应对全球环境问题上立场一致、责任相当。虽然起步较晚，但中阿双方需求互补，合作潜力很大。要充分利用中阿合作论坛、中阿博览会等平台，提前规划，充分准备，适时举办环保合作会议，增加交流机会，积极推动中阿环保合作不断深化，并以此为依托，建立起稳定通畅的交流渠道，逐步完善中阿环保合作机制。

从双边关系的视角来看，阿拉伯关键国家如沙特、埃及、阿尔及利亚和苏丹等与中国的双边战略合作关系内涵不断丰富。适时推进中阿双边环保合作，将有助于进一步发展平等互利、真诚友好的中阿双边关系，对于深化全球南方环保合作、谋求共同绿色发展、促进地区和平稳定具有重要意义。

9.3.3 生态合作共赢的中阿生态保护与治理的现代化模式

生态兴则文明兴。中国始终坚持生态优先、绿色发展，实现在发展中保护、在保护中发展，为广大发展中国家实现可持续发展提供了借鉴。建设"一带一路"生态共同体是构建人类命运共同体的重要内容。十年来，中国秉持人类命运共同体理念，推动"一带一路"生态共同体建设取得了

显著成效。生态共治，推动"一带一路"生态共同体协同治理。面对生态环境持续恶化的威胁，阿拉伯国家必须冲破生态合作的政治阻碍，以命运休戚与共的自觉参与到区域生态治理行动之中。中国政府依托现有的双边、多边合作机制，建立了一系列深化双方交流合作的平台机制，举办了一系列以绿色"一带一路"建设为主题的对话交流活动，与阿拉伯国家和地区开展生态文明和绿色发展的交流合作与经验分享。① 一是充分利用中阿合作论坛机制，持续推进中国与阿拉伯国家在生态环保领域的合作机制建设，共筑生态环保合作新格局。二是持续加强与阿拉伯国家在温室气体排放、核与辐射安全、水污染、土壤污染等方面的协同治理，推动在森林、草原、海洋、湿地、生物多样性等领域形成系统性保护共识，强化生态环保领域的科技交流与合作，携手阿拉伯国家构建环境公约履约合作长效机制。三是大力推进环保社会组织与海合会及阿盟的合作，发挥其在区域生态保护和治理中的积极作用。

9.3.4 为中阿携手治理生态环境贡献中国方案和中国智慧

生态文明建设关乎人类未来，建设绿色家园是人类的共同梦想。在习近平生态文明思想的科学指引下，我们实现由重点整治到系统治理的重大转变、由被动应对到主动作为的重大转变。生态文明建设的成就举世瞩目，成为新时代党和国家事业取得历史性成就、发生历史性变革的显著标志。构建人类命运共同体为推进全球环境治理、维护全球生态安全指明了方向与路径。其中，共谋全球生态文明建设、建设清洁美丽世界，是构建人类命运共同体的重要内容与目标。中国秉持共商共建共享的全球治理观，倡导国际关系民主化，坚持国家不分大小、强弱、贫富一律平等，支持联合国发挥积极作用，支持扩大发展中国家在国际事务中的代表性和发言权。中国将继续发挥负责任大国作用，积极引导国际秩序变革方向，形

---

① 杨美勤、唐鸣：《生态合作治理：促进"一带一路"国际合作的新动力》，《当代世界社会主义问题》2020年第1期。

成世界环境保护和可持续发展的解决方案。

2023年恰值"一带一路"倡议提出十周年，在经济全球化、区域一体化的国际背景下，中国应以全球环境问题的治理为契机，倡导与阿拉伯国家加强交流互动，在合作发展经济的同时，致力于环境的治理与保护，以建设绿色"一带一路"助力碳中和承诺如期实现，推动阿拉伯国家人民携手共建人类命运共同体，尽显中国智慧和大国担当。

尽管生态文明建设是全世界面对的共同课题，但不同国家在生态文明建设过程中需要处理的主要问题和所处的阶段不同，由此立足国情会形成不同的经验。中国作为发展中大国，既要处理好发展问题，又要处理好生态环境保护问题，这使得中国必须将生态环境保护和经济社会发展视为有机整体而不是对立关系，在协同推进中实现经济社会显著发展和生态环境优先保护。响应"一带一路"发展倡议，中国与阿拉伯国家持续深化新发展理念和领域合作，为推动阿拉伯国家发展转型，构建中阿命运共同体贡献坚实力量，为阿拉伯国家解决好生态文明建设问题贡献中国经验、中国智慧和中国方案。

第10章　中阿旅游合作专题报告

10.1　全球旅游业发展情况

10.1.1　全球旅游业总体呈强势复苏态势

2023 年，全球国际旅游人数约为 12.9 亿人次，恢复到 2019 年的 88%。全球旅游业收入达到 1.4 万亿美元，相当于 2019 年水平的 93%。[①] 全球旅游业总体呈明显复苏态势。

表 10.1　2019 年与 2023 年全球各区域的入境旅游人次对比

单位：百万

区域	2019 年	2023 年	百分比变化
美洲	123	117	−4%
欧洲	440	428	−3%
亚太	213	149	−30%
中东	29	33	+0.13%
非洲	49	43	−13%

资料来源：牛津经济研究院，http：//www.economics.ox.ac.uk。

[①] 《全球休闲旅游业报告，2023 年 11 月 8 日（2023 年度）》，牛津经济研究院，搜狐网，https：//www.sohu.com/a/736843840_118838。

10.1.2　国际旅游与国内旅游的复苏水平不平衡

新冠疫情期间国际旅行受到严格限制，全球范围均产生了国内游替代出境游的效应，并且目前仍然存在一定影响。2023 年，全球入境旅游接待人次增长最快的 3 个国家分别为沙特、阿尔巴尼亚和波兰，但是全球大部分国家国际旅游的恢复速度明显落后于国内旅游。

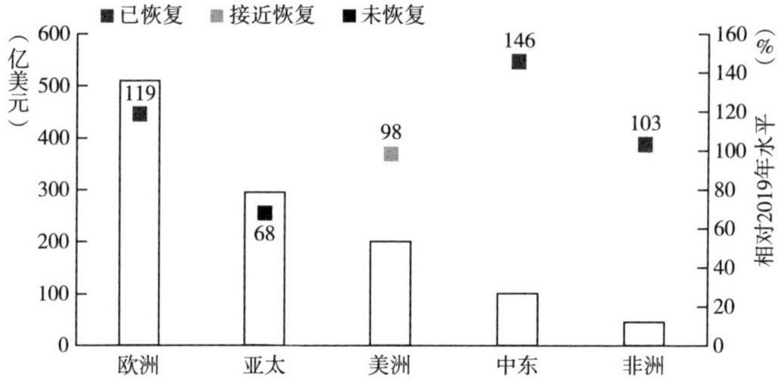

图 10.1　2019 年与 2023 年全球各区域主要入境旅游目的地对比

资料来源：牛津经济研究院，http：//www.economics.ox.ac.uk。

10.1.3　国内旅游需求持续增加，呈现明显替代效应

2023 年，全球大部分地区的国内旅游支出恢复到 2019 年的水平。不少幅员辽阔、人口众多，且拥有大量有旅行支付能力人口的国家，国内旅游业发展更快。全球各大区域国内旅游复苏情况表现最为突出的还是中东地区，与 2019 年相比，国内旅游消费额增长 276％；其次是美洲地区，国内旅游消费额上涨 131％；欧洲和非洲地区的国内旅游额消费分别增长 116％和 113％；亚太地区虽未完全复苏，但也恢复到了 2019 年水平的 99％[1]（见图 10.2）。

---

[1]　牛津经济研究院，http：//www.economics.ox.ac.uk。

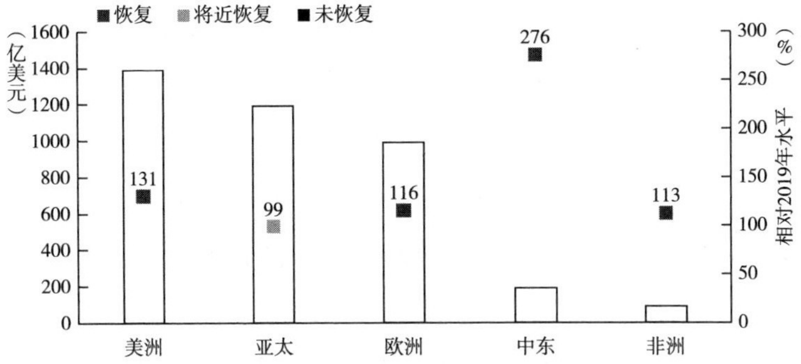

第10章 中阿旅游合作专题报告

图 10.2 2019 年与 2023 年全球各区域国内旅游消费对比

资料来源：牛津经济研究院，http：/www.economics.ox.ac.uk。

10.2 阿拉伯国家旅游发展情况

10.2.1 阿拉伯国家旅游业成为新冠疫情后复苏最快的区域

相较 2019 年，阿拉伯国家 2023 年接待的国际旅游人次整体上涨 13%。其中，接待国际旅游者最多的国家是沙特和阿联酋，分别比 2019 年上涨了 66% 和 21%。这两个国家都把发展旅游业当作一项国家战略，在近几年大力投资建设旅游基础设施。旅游接待人次增速最快的国家是科威特，2023 年的旅游者接待量比 2019 年增长 90%。[①]

与 2019 年相比，阿拉伯国家 2023 年的国际旅游消费整体上涨 46%，除伊拉克之外的其他阿拉伯国家的入境旅游消费均超过 2019 年的水平。阿拉伯国家成为新冠疫情之后国际旅游业复苏最快的地区。

10.2.2 2023 年阿拉伯国家旅游业表现良好

2023 年，大部分阿拉伯国家在国际旅游收入和接待旅游人次方面依旧展示了较好的发展态势。

---

① 牛津经济研究院，http：/www.economics.ox.ac.uk。

163

2023 年第一季度，埃及旅游业收入已达到 41 亿美元，同比增长 43.5%。全年旅游业收入达到 136 亿美元，相较 2022 年 41 亿美元的国际旅游收入，增幅达到 231.7%，成为阿拉伯国家旅游业发展速度最快的国家之一。[①] 约旦国际旅游收入从 2022 年的 15.837 亿美元迅速提升至 20.176 亿美元，增速达 27.39%。摩洛哥接待游客 1450 万人次，同比增长 34%，较 2019 年增长 12%；旅游总收入为 98 亿美元，同比增长 15.8%。[②] 2022 年，阿联酋国际旅游表现良好，借助迪拜世博会，吸引了超过 192 个国家和地区的 2400 万名游客，国际旅游收入达 370.91 亿美元。但是在 2023 年，阿联酋国际旅游收入依旧提升至 408 亿美元，增速接近 9%。[③] 2022 年，沙特国际旅游收入为全球第 11 位；2023 年，国际旅游收入在阿拉伯国家旅游业发展中仅低于阿联酋（见图 10.3、图 10.4）。[④]

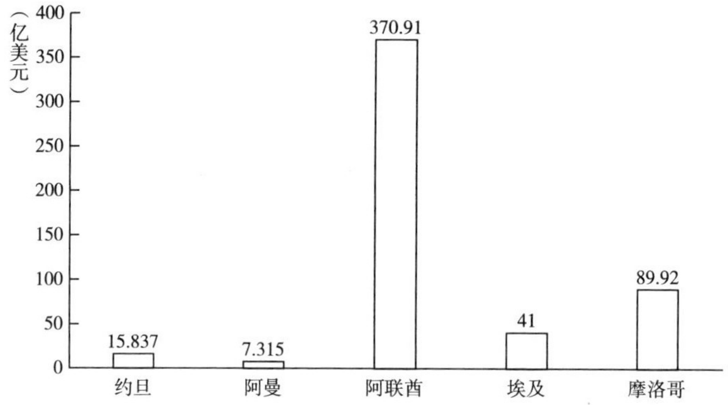

图 10.3 2022 年部分阿拉伯国家国际旅游收入

资料来源：牛津经济研究院，http://www.economics.ox.ac.uk。

[①] 《中东地区旅游业加速恢复》，人民日报网，https://m.gmw.cn/baijia/2023-02/28/36396044.html，2023 年 2 月 28 日。

[②] 《2023 年摩洛哥接待游客 1450 万》，中华人民共和国驻摩洛哥王国大使馆经济商务处，http://ma.mofcom.gov.cn/jmxw/art/2024/art_3f4d0b382f3c492cb08b18229e5f4eee.html，2024 年 2 月 2 日。

[③] 《阿联酋多举措发展旅游业》，人民网，http://www.people.cn/，2023 年 11 月 21 日。

[④] 《沙特宣布将投资 8000 亿美元发展旅游业 计划到 2030 年接待 1 亿游客》，网易网，https://www.163.com/dy/article/IHTFQUEJ05198CJN.html?spss=dy_author，2023 年 10 月 25 日。

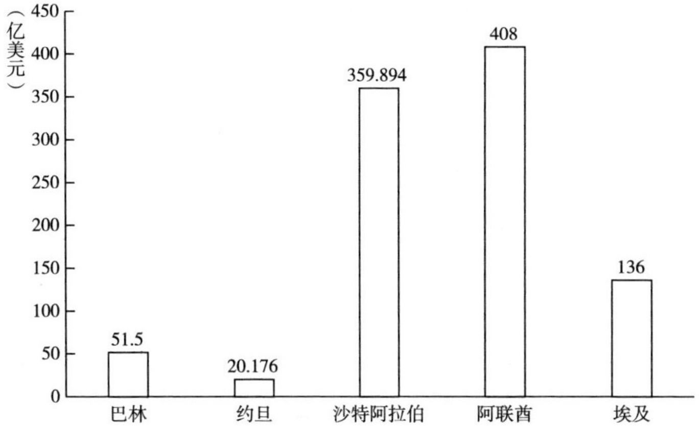

第10章　中阿旅游合作专题报告

图10.4　2023年部分阿拉伯国家国际旅游收入

资料来源：牛津经济研究院，http：//www.economics.ox.ac.uk。

2022年，沙特共接待游客9350万人次，较2019年增长121%，居阿拉伯国家之首。其中，接待入境游客1756.41万人次，为全球第13位；接待当地游客7700万人次，较2021年增长21%。2023年第一季度，沙特接待国际游客约780万人次，较2019年增长64%，创历史最高记录。显然，沙特的总体战略与举措初见成效，旅游业对GDP的贡献大大提升。[①]

2022年，迪拜吸引了1436万人次的国际游客，比2021年增长97%。2023年，阿联酋各机场的旅客吞吐量达6279万人次，同比增长46%。同期，迪拜游客数量达到855万人次，同比增长20%，创下历史新高；阿布扎比、沙迦、哈伊马角等酋长国接待的游客也都有两位数增长。阿联酋旅游业快速复苏得益于在该领域的长期投资和创新举措。统计显示，2018—2022年，阿联酋旅游业在吸引外国直接投资方面位列全球第五，占全球的4.7%。中东地区新增旅游项目中，约有35%落户阿联酋。2022年，埃

———————————

[①] 《沙特宣布将投资8000亿美元发展旅游业 计划到2030年接待1亿游客》，网易网，https：//www.163.com/dy/article/IHTFQUEJ05198CJN.html？spss＝dy_author，2023年10月25日。

及共接待国际游客 1170 万人次，仅在 7—9 月，埃及国际游客就达到 340 万人次，同比增加 52%。2023 年，埃及国际游客达 1490 万人次，比上年增长 27.35%。借助 2022 年国际足联俱乐部世界杯（以下简称"世界杯"）的举办，卡塔尔旅游业发展迅速，这是首次在中东地区举办世界杯赛事，共吸引全球约 150 万名游客到访。统计数据显示，举办世界杯为卡塔尔带来约 170 亿美元的收益，此外，卡塔尔为举办世界杯而进行的基础设施建设将为旅游业长期发展提供支撑。[①]

2023 年摩洛哥旅游业发展创历史新高，全年共接待国际游客 1450 万人次，较 2019 年增长 12%，较 2022 年增长 33.02%。[②] 此外，巴林、约旦旅游接待人次均有所上升（见图 10.5、图 10.6）。

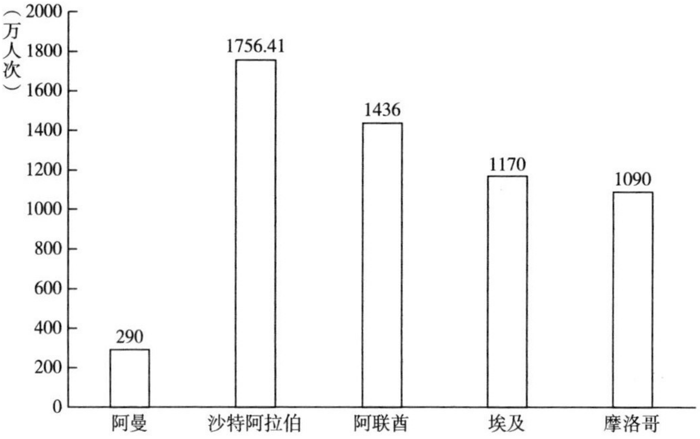

图 10.5　2022 年部分阿拉伯国家接待国际游客人次

资料来源：牛津经济研究院，http：／www.economics.ox.ac.uk。

---

① 《中东地区旅游业加速恢复》，光明网，https：//m.gmw.cn/baijia/2023－02/28/36396044.html，2023 年 2 月 28 日。

② 中华人民共和国驻摩洛哥王国大使馆经济商务处，http：//ma.mofcom.gov.cn/article/jmxw/202402/20240203471621.shtml。

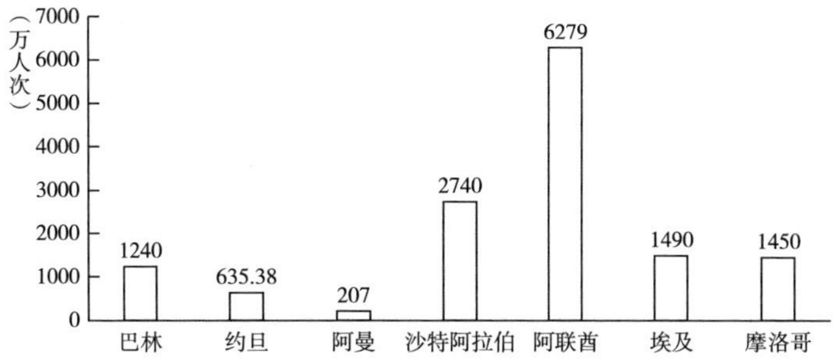

第10章　中阿旅游合作专题报告

图10.6　2023年部分阿拉伯国家接待国际游客人次

资料来源：牛津经济研究院，http：//www.economics.ox.ac.uk。

10.3　中阿旅游合作进展

2024年是中国—阿拉伯国家合作论坛成立20周年，在中阿合作论坛推动下，中阿在旅游方面的合作逐渐深入。包含旅游服务贸易在内的中阿贸易额从2012年的2224亿美元，增长到2022年的4314亿美元，十年间增长近一倍。2016—2019年，中国公民首站出境阿拉伯国家的人数保持平均10%的增长，并在2019年达到历史峰值；其间入境中国大陆的阿拉伯国家公民人数也保持稳定增长。旅游在中阿命运共同体建构中发挥着日益重要的作用。

中国是全球最大的国内旅游市场，连续多年保持世界第一大出境客源国地位，新冠疫情前后，中国都是世界旅游经济繁荣的关键力量。游客是流动的文化，繁荣的旅游经济背后是文化平等和合作交流。培育更有韧性的旅游产业生态，以旅游赋能中阿合作成为加强中阿交往的重要途径之一。

10.3.1　平台新动能不断增强，提升对外开放影响力

中阿博览会、葡萄酒文化旅游博览会、"西部数谷"算力产业大会等

167

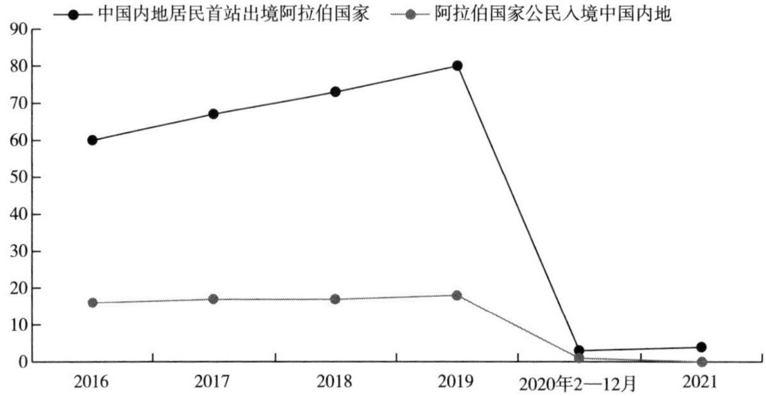

中阿经贸关系发展进程2023年度报告

图 10.7　2016—2021 年中国—阿拉伯国家入出境旅游情况

资料来源：中国旅游研究院（文化和旅游部数据中心）。

开放平台成果落实落地。中阿博览会、葡萄酒之都、"西部数谷"等特色开放品牌，持续提升平台载体的影响力和号召力。建设葡萄及葡萄酒产业开放发展综合试验区，举办三届国际葡萄酒文化旅游博览会，贺兰山东麓产区葡萄酒获得 1100 多个国际大奖，远销 40 多个国家和地区，作为国礼赠送多国政要。开创性发力数字经济和算力产业，高规格举办两届"西部数谷"算力产业大会和 2023 中国算力大会，搭建"东数西算"交流合作桥梁。[①]

10.3.1.1　中阿博览会在中阿旅游合作中持续发挥重要作用

2023 年 9 月，宁夏回族自治区成功举办第六届中阿博览会。共有 65 个国家、地区和区域性组织，20 个中央和国家部委，29 个省（自治区、直辖市）的嘉宾出席，工商界和企业、商协会参会人数占 82%，参会参展总人数超过 1.12 万人，全网浏览量 25 亿人次，境外浏览量超 1.5 亿人次，两个微博话题阅读总量超过 17 亿次，在嘉宾规格、参展规模以及覆盖范围等方面均远超往届，得到了国际社会和与会嘉宾的广泛赞誉。第六

---

① 《共建"一带一路"十周年 宁夏内陆开放添异彩》，宁夏回族自治区发展和改革委员会网，https：//fzggw．nx．gov．cn/zwdt/202310/t20231012_4307691．html，2023 年 10 月 12 日。

168

届中阿博览会共形成合作成果 403 个，计划投资和贸易总额达 1709.7 亿元人民币，中阿共签署了 18 项文旅合作协议，经贸务实合作硕果累累，旅游合作不断深入①。中阿博览会在服务共建"一带一路"、加强国内各省区市和大型企业拓展经贸合作，以及促进宁夏经济高质量发展，提升高水平向西开放等方面的作用进一步凸显。

10.3.1.2　召开中阿旅行商大会

2023 年，中阿旅行商大会举办，国内有关地区文化和旅游行政部门、企业代表，伊朗、沙特、瑞士、土耳其、印度尼西亚等国家旅行商代表参加大会。宁夏回族自治区党委常委、宣传部部长李金科表示：宁夏将文化和旅游高质量发展融入"一带一路"建设，大力实施文旅融合提升、赋能行动计划，推动中阿文明交流互鉴，大会将进一步促进宁夏与共建"一带一路"国家和地区在文旅领域的交流合作。萨尔瓦多驻华大使阿尔多·阿尔瓦雷斯、摩尔多瓦驻华大使杜米特鲁·贝拉基什在致辞中一致表示，将在共建"一带一路"倡议下抓住机遇，深化与中国在文化和旅游领域的交流合作。文化和旅游部国际交流与合作局有关负责人表示，大会必将增进中阿友谊、推动民心相通，为共建"一带一路"贡献力量，希望中阿旅行商以大会为契机，在旅游政策对接、产业合作、人才培养、市场推广等方面深化合作，发挥旅游在推动中阿文明交流互鉴中的重要作用。

旅行商大会以"共享发展机遇·共促旅游合作·共建'一带一路'"为主题，以"1+4"为方式（"1"即中阿旅行商大会开幕式，"4"即在大会期间将分别举办中阿旅游合作论坛、"一带一路"文旅合作推介会、宁夏文旅资源推介暨美食品鉴活动、"塞上江南·神奇宁夏"文旅资源考察等活动），中阿旅行商企业代表签署了多项战略合作协议，② 为增进中

---

① 《中阿旅行商大会将搭建中外文旅资源推介新平台》，新华网，https：//www.gov.cn/yaowen/liebiao/202309/content_6903323.htm，2023 年 9 月 11 日。

② 《第六届中阿博览会中阿旅行商大会开幕》，中华人民共和国文化和旅游部网，https：//www.mct.gov.cn/preview/whzx/qgwhxxlb/nx/202309/t20230920_947360.htm，2023 年 9 月 20 日。

中阿经贸关系发展进程2023年度报告

外旅游业界务实合作搭建有效平台。可以说，中阿旅行商大会在增强国内国际两个市场文旅资源有效联动，推进国际国内旅游领域共享共赢发展机遇，推动游客互访，促进中阿民心相通等方面发挥了重要的平台作用。

10.3.1.3　举办中阿旅游合作论坛

作为2023年中阿旅行商大会的重要板块，中阿旅游合作论坛力求打造新时代中国与阿拉伯国家之间交流分享、务实合作的高端平台，探索新时代中阿旅游交流与合作的多样化路径，推动中阿战略伙伴关系迈上更高水平。论坛围绕"新时代中阿旅游交流与合作的多样化路径"主题，邀请外国驻华使节以及国内旅游业界知名专家、企业代表等进行交流对话。[①]

萨尔瓦多驻华大使表示：文化是一个国家的灵魂，文化交流是中萨关系的源泉和重要内容，在两国政府的大力支持下，两国友谊历久弥新，他将一如既往地促进两国在文化、经济、政治和学术领域的交流与合作，增进相互了解。中国旅游研究院（文化和旅游部数据中心）副院长唐晓云指出：旅游是联结中阿友谊的桥梁，是新时代中阿文明交流互鉴、增进了解的重要渠道，为中阿深化交流合作带来新机遇，建议通过推动建立中阿旅游合作联盟、出台更便捷的综合出行政策、深化中阿人民的文化交往、推动以新媒体为主导的立体营销和推广等途径，广泛且深入地开展中阿旅游合作。中国旅游协会休闲度假分会秘书长、北京联合大学中国旅游经济与政策研究中心主任曾博伟以"一带一路"倡议下中阿旅游新发展为主题，从"一带一路"倡议的推进、中阿国际旅游合作等背景切入，为宁夏旅游的国际化、品质化、联动化高质量发展提出建议。他认为，发展出入境旅游是中阿国际旅游合作的重点，未来应制订中阿国际游客往来计划，扩大双方国际旅游规模。中阿之间凝聚成的"守望相助、平等互利、包容互鉴"的友好精神，将成为推动世界和平发展的重要力量。新时代文化旅游研究院院长、中国劳动关系学院文化旅游政策研究中心副主任吴若山指

---

① 《中阿旅行商大会将搭建中外文旅资源推介新平台》，中华人民共和国中央人民政府网，https：//www.gov.cn/yaowen/liebiao/202309/content_6903323.htm，2023年9月11日。

170

出：在"一带一路"国际共识持续扩大的背景下，丝路文旅合作成绩喜人，合作机制与平台建设稳步扎实推进，品牌活动全面展开，旅游交流不断深化，文化遗产交流紧密。在新发展格局下，持续提升中阿丝路旅游合作的发展质量，可通过强化丝路旅游品牌建设、做好精准营销推广、完善旅游服务人才队伍等方面发力。建议中阿双方可开展国际旅游相关课题的联合研究，以理论成果指引市场行为，这也将是深耕中阿旅游合作的关键一步。[1]

10.3.1.4 举办"一带一路"文旅合作推介会

2023 年，包括阿拉伯国家在内的与会国家、地区以及中国部分省区市文化和旅游部门共同举办"一带一路"文旅合作推介会，这是首次搭建的国际与国内文化旅游资源联合推介新平台。宁夏、福建、甘肃、四川、新疆等 7 个省区文化和旅游部门以及部分"一带一路"共建国家，以"文艺节目创意视频+特色资源"的方式，开展文化旅游资源的联合推广活动，推介当地特色文化旅游资源。会议有力推动了中阿双方在旅游政策对接、旅游产业合作、旅游人才培养和旅游推广等方面的合作，为进一步落实中阿"文明对话行动"助力添彩，为中阿旅游业界深度合作搭建平台，进一步发挥了旅游在推动中阿文明交流互鉴中的重要作用。[2]

10.3.1.5 宁夏文旅资源推介暨美食品鉴活动

2023 年，宁夏文旅资源推介暨美食品鉴活动采取"文艺节目+创意视频+特色资源"的方式，创意开展宁夏文化旅游资源推介活动；采取"视频推广+美食品鉴"的方式，展示宁夏"枸杞+文旅"融合发展新成果。在"塞上江南·神奇宁夏"文旅资源考察活动中，组织与会嘉宾实地考察"紫梦贺兰微醺之旅"和"黄河文化探寻之旅"两条新线路，宣传推介宁夏在打造黄河生态文旅绿色岸线、贺兰山东麓生态文旅紫色廊道等举措中

---

[1] 《中阿旅游合作论坛今日在宁夏银川举行》，中国日报网，https：//baijiahao.baidu.com/s?id=1777461822242418804&wfr=spider&for=pc，2023 年 9 月 19 日。

[2] 《中阿旅游界共商文旅合作新前景》，中华人民共和国中央人民政府网，https：//www.gov.cn/yaowen/liebiao/202309/content_6904932.htm，2023 年 9 月 19 日。

推出的一些文旅新项目、特色新产品。[1]

10.3.2 中阿在旅游、广电等文化领域的交往与合作不断加强

2023 年，中国境外投资目的地由欧美发达国家向沙特、哈萨克斯坦、蒙古国等共建"一带一路"国家拓展，投资领域由矿产开发、进出口贸易向农业、制造业、境外园区等多元化方向发展，中阿在文化、旅游、广电等领域的交往与合作不断加强。

2023 年，第十届中阿关系暨中阿文明对话研讨会在阿联酋阿布扎比举行。中国政府中东问题特使翟隽、阿联酋国务部部长萨耶赫、阿盟文化和文明对话司司长玛哈等，中国外交部、文化和旅游部等机构以及 18 个阿拉伯国家和阿盟的近 80 名代表出席研讨会。研讨会旨在加强人文交流合作，推动双方民心相知相通，共同推动文明交流互鉴，高质量共建"一带一路"，全力构建面向新时代的中阿命运共同体。[2]

2023 年，宁夏本土民营企业智慧宫被中宣部确定为国家对外宣传重点企业。目前，该企业已向"一带一路"共建国家和地区翻译出版了涵盖阿拉伯语、波斯语、乌尔都语等 6 个语种，涉及中国政治、经济、文学、儿童读物等多个类型的图书 1260 余种，销量近 200 万册，成为国内对阿图书输出的龙头企业，也是阿拉伯国家规模最大的中国图书出版机构。智慧宫设立中阿影视服务（迪拜、杭州）中心，向阿拉伯国家出口动漫、影视作品 220 余部，《山海情》等电视剧阿拉伯语版在多家阿拉伯国家电视台播出，《摩洛哥小姐姐带你打卡"山海情"故事发生地》短视频在海外传播量达 1000 万。[3]

2023 年，"陕耀丝路"中阿对外文化国际交流暨《三原印象》合拍纪

---

[1] 《中阿旅行商大会将首次推出"一带一路"文旅合作推介会》，宁夏新闻网，https：//whhlyt. nx. gov. cn/xxfb/hyxx/202309/t20230913_4262841. html，2023 年 9 月 13 日。

[2] 《第十届中阿关系暨中阿文明对话研讨会在阿联酋举行》，新华网，http：//world. people. com. cn/n1/2023/1026/c1002-40103498. html，2023 年 10 月 26 日。

[3] 《共建"一带一路"十周年 宁夏内陆开放添异彩》，宁夏回族自治区发展和改革委员会网，https：//fzggw. nx. gov. cn/zwdt/202310/t20231012_4307691. html，2023 年 10 月 12 日。

录片启动仪式在陕西省咸阳市举行，该记录片表达了中国与阿拉伯国家进行深入、长期交流合作的强烈愿望。立足《视听中国·陕西时间》平台，进一步深挖陕西各地的自然历史文化资源，通过丰富的视听语言，更好地讲好陕西故事、中国故事，把更多三秦大地的好景、好物、好风光呈现给阿拉伯人民，吸引更多阿拉伯国家和地区的朋友们来到陕西留学、旅游、投资、兴业，让中阿广播电视领域的合作结出更加丰硕的成果，为促进中阿文化长远交流搭建新平台、注入新动能、焕发新活力。①

2023年，以"打造经贸交流新平台，拓展中阿合作新领域"为主题的北京中阿经贸文化交流活动在北京朝阳区举办。活动对阿联酋和朝阳区营商环境进行了主题推介，与阿联酋、沙特重点产业开展深度交流合作，并签约4个合作项目，开展多个中阿项目路演，活动内容涉及文旅、金融等多个领域。②

2023年，中阿文化和旅游合作研究中心在北京第二外国语学院成立③，围绕学术交流、人才培养、研修培训、智库研究和产业促进等五个方面展开工作。通过促进中阿文化和旅游企业交流、对阿文化和旅游人才培养和中阿青少年文化交流等项目推动中阿文化和旅游的务实合作交流；通过学术交流、专家座谈会和学术论坛讲座等形式为中阿文化和旅游产业交流合作发展提供有效支持；积极发挥学校学科优势，招收阿拉伯国家来华学生攻读学位，为中阿双方培养文化和旅游领域的高级翻译人才、高层次复合型文化和旅游类人才；定期举办阿拉伯国家文化和旅游行业官员研修班，为来华参与研修培训的阿拉伯官员搭建文明交流互鉴的桥梁；促进产学研交流互动，建立健全中阿文化和旅游产业合作机制和交流平台，鼓励中阿文化和旅游企业交流互访，推动中阿文化和旅游领域交流与合作进一步机制化、常态化。中阿文化和旅游合作研究中心以成为世界一流文化

---

① 《2023"陕耀丝路"中阿对外文化国际交流暨〈三原印象〉合拍纪录片正式启动》，三秦网，https：//www.sanqin.com/2023-09/19/content_10368160.html，2023年9月19日。

② 《2023北京中阿经贸文化交流活动举办》，都市文明网，https：//www.bjwmb.gov.cn/wmdt/cyq/10049277.html，2023年12月6日。

③ 《中阿文化和旅游合作研究中心在北二外揭牌成立》，中国网，https：//news.china.com.cn/txt/2023-08/02/content_97702135.shtml，2023年8月2日。

和旅游发展研究服务平台为建设目标，推动中阿务实合作"八大共同行动"，通过旅游增进互识互信，推动文明交流互鉴，构建面向新时代的中阿命运共同体。

10.3.3 中阿在教育领域的合作不断深化

2023年6月，由沙特苏尔坦亲王大学和深圳大学共建的苏尔坦亲王大学孔子学院在沙特首都利雅得正式揭牌，标志着沙特第一所正式挂牌的孔子学院投入运转。其他多个阿拉伯国家也建有多所孔子学院和独立孔子课堂。沙特教育部门推出一系列奖励措施鼓励中文学习。例如，学生参加中文课程将被视为参与志愿服务；教育部将在全国范围内遴选优秀学生予以表彰，并将赴华研学游作为奖励。除了中外合办的孔子学院之外，多个阿拉伯国家还主动加大中文教育在国民教育体系中的比重。目前，已有沙特、埃及、阿联酋、突尼斯4个阿拉伯国家将中文纳入国民教育体系。

阿拉伯国家的"中文热"持续升温，显示了中阿友好合作日益密切。阿拉伯国家的"中文课堂"越来越多，中文课纳入沙特、埃及、阿联酋等国家学生的课表；摩洛哥、约旦等国家的不少年轻人爱唱中文歌、选择到中国工作；许多阿拉伯国家的青年给自己起了中国名字；沙特巴哈法赫德国王学校的学生用中文进行早会，早会视频不仅在沙特国内引发热议，还被其他阿拉伯国家媒体广为报道。阿联酋《海湾新闻报》称，该校鼓励学生用中文开早会的创新做法是在沙特教育部门启动强化中文教学计划的背景下推出的，旨在提高学生的中文能力，许多社交媒体用户对此表达了鼓励和赞许。

此外，阿拉伯国家兴起的"中文热"还搭上"网上丝绸之路"的建设快车，一些中国互联网企业积极参与打造网络中文课堂、移动智慧教室等，借助互联网平台，建立了面向阿拉伯国家的专用中文学习平台，开放适合阿拉伯国家中文学习者的语言学习、中文考试、"中文+职业技能"等多种课程，将人工智能、虚拟现实、大数据等先进技术融入中文教育创新模式。[1]

2013年以来，中国为阿拉伯国家培训各类人才2.5万人，向阿拉伯国家提供约1.1万个政府奖学金名额，派出医疗队80批次，医疗队员近1700人次。截至2022年10月，已有4个阿拉伯国家宣布将中文纳入国民教育体系，15个阿拉伯国家在当地开设中文院系，13个阿拉伯国家建有20所孔子学院、2个独立孔子课堂。

2023年，中国同阿拉伯国家不断加强旅游人才培养合作，共同探索数字化时代旅游人才核心能力建设的发展方向和实现路径，建设高素质旅游规划、策划和经营、管理人才队伍，提升旅游从业者水平，为双方培养更多国际化复合型人才。中阿在旅游、教育、文化等领域开展了丰富多彩的合作，扩大了人文交流，深化了相互理解。

10.3.4 阿拉伯国家积极开展同中国的旅游合作

2023年2月，中国和阿尔巴尼亚双方签署《中华人民共和国文化和旅游部与阿尔巴尼亚共和国旅游和环境部关于旅游合作的谅解备忘录》，继续深化旅游合作。积极倡导并务实推进旅游共同体的建设，通过组建联盟议事机构，建立稳定的对话机制和定期会议，有针对性地研究、协调并推动联盟体内签证、航班、人才、营销推广等旅游发展的基本问题。搭建旅游企业交流平台，加强人员往来，推进项目合作。搭建联盟内旅游统计和数据体系，建设旅游数据平台，让各国充分了解联盟成员旅游发展情况。

2023年5月，以"迈向净零"为主题的第30届阿拉伯旅游市场展在阿联酋迪拜世界贸易中心举行[2]，来自150多个国家和地区的2000多家展商和34000名参会者参展。阿拉伯旅游市场展是阿拉伯地区最大、全球第三

---

[1] 《"中文热"折射"中阿合作热"》，人民网—人民日报海外版，https://www.chinanews.com/m/gj/2023/05-11/10005120.shtml，2023年5月11日。

[2] 《5月1日—4日，相约第30届阿拉伯国际旅游业展！》，中东新视野网，https://zhuanlan.zhihu.com/p/625780274，2023年4月28日。

的旅游交易展会，本届展会涵盖了旅游技术、航空、酒店、邮轮、景点等领域，探讨全球旅游业创新及可持续发展趋势，研判关键行业的增长方式。

2023 年，沙特宣布在利雅得西北部建设一个 19 平方公里的新城，其核心是 400 米高的立方体建筑新四方宫，与位于利雅得城南的旧四方宫方位相对。建成后这将是世界上最大的单体建筑。新四方宫将用数字和虚拟技术，为游客构建一个立体虚拟空间。5 月，沙特又宣布建设新未来城、阿玛拉、德拉伊耶、红海、奇迪亚等多个超大型综合文旅项目。

2018 年，阿联酋迪拜成立"拥抱中国"执委会后，配合中国政府与阿联酋政府达成互免签证安排，采取一系列政策吸引中国游客并做好相关服务，包括在主要景点设置中文标识、鼓励培训中文导游、开设中文旅游热线等。自中国和阿联酋签署免签证协定和旅游合作谅解备忘录以来，双方积极推动在中阿"一带一路"合作框架下的旅游合作，提升航空公司合作，加强对开通航班的精准决策能力。以特色化、个性化交通解决当地城市与城市、城市内部的小交通问题，极大提升了中阿旅游的便利性。2023年 2 月，迪拜旅游局负责人通过视频表达对中国游客的热切期盼："为欢迎中国游客归来，我们一切准备就绪。更多的新景点和新体验在等待你们，是时候在这里创造新的美好回忆了。"[1] 阿布扎比法拉利世界主题公园总经理表示："我们非常想念中国游客，迫不及待地欢迎大家来到这里。"[2] 2023 年，阿布扎比各机场总客运量达到 2300 万人次，同比增长44.5%。在正式更名为扎耶德国际机场后，60 天内扎耶德国际机场共计接待旅客 448 万人次。截至 2023 年 12 月，扎耶德国际机场已为 117 个旅行目的地提供服务，比 2022 年的 100 个城市增加了近 20%。

2023 年，埃及航空公司宣布从 3 月起将埃中之间的航班数量增加到每周 13 班。埃及航空公司董事长表示：埃中两国都是拥有悠久历史的文明

---

[1] 《迪拜"移民局"局长：欢迎中国游客来到阿联酋》，搜狐网，https：//www.sohu.com/a/722460320_121124399，2023 年 9 月 22 日。

[2] 《非常想念中国游客！时隔三年，阿联酋红毯欢迎中国旅游团回归》，网易网，https：//m.163.com/dy/article/HT53CJQ50530WJIN.html，2023 年 2 月 9 日。

古国，埃方期待中国游客的到来。"我们欢迎中国游客来这里品尝美食。"埃及首都开罗扎马雷克地区一家传统美食餐厅负责人表示：中国游客的回归将大大促进埃及旅游业的发展，推动全球旅游业的繁荣。埃及外交部部长舒凯里说："期待越来越多的中国游客来埃及旅游，参观文明古迹。我们将为中国游客提供良好的服务。"[①]

此外，卡塔尔政府宣布，已把世界杯期间推出的球迷卡申办网站转型为游客入境卡塔尔的门户网站。阿曼首个大型综合设施项目卡赞经济城正在建设，除了港口和经济基础设施，还包括酒店、住宅区和娱乐区。[②] 阿拉伯各国为欢迎中国游客采取了多种举措，提供优质服务，吸引中国游客。

中国和阿拉伯国家之间的关系源远流长，和平合作、开放包容、互学互鉴、互利共赢始终是中阿交往的主旋律。新中国成立后的 70 多年间，中国和阿拉伯国家在争取民族独立、实现民族振兴的道路上肝胆相照、风雨同舟，在世界政治经济舞台上团结守正、合作共赢，双方友好合作的广度和深度都实现历史性跨越。当前，中国和阿拉伯国家面临相似的历史机遇和挑战，更加需要传承历史友好，深化战略合作，携手构建面向新时代的中阿命运共同体，共同创造中阿关系更加美好的未来。[③]

---

① 《中东地区旅游业加速恢复》，人民日报网，http://world.people.com.cn/n1/2023/0228/c1002-32632599.html，2023 年 2 月 28 日。

② 《中东旅游市场强劲复苏 可持续旅游成为关注重点》，中国新闻网，https://www.chinanews.com/m/gj/2023/05-11/10005120.shtml，2023 年 5 月 11 日。

③ 《新时代的中阿合作报告》，中华人民共和国外交部网，https://www.mfa.gov.cn/web/ziliao_674904/tytj_674911/zcwj_674915/202212/t20221201_10983991.shtml，2022 年 12 月 1 日。

第11章 中阿博览会专题报告

构建以国内大循环为主体、国内国际双循环相互促进的新发展格局，是习近平总书记2020年4月在中央财经委员会会议上提出的中长期重大发展战略，对于推动高质量发展、全面建设社会主义现代化国家具有全局性指导意义。党的二十大报告进一步提出"增强国内大循环内生动力和可靠性，提升国际循环质量和水平"[①]。从我国发展经验看，改革开放以来之所以能取得经济长期快速发展的奇迹，积极参与国际大循环是一个决定性因素，这是我们必须坚定参与并不断提升国际循环的根本依据。新发展格局中，国内大循环是基础和主体，参与国际循环则是经济全球化和国际产业分工格局下的必然要求。

习近平总书记多次推动中阿关系跨越式发展，充分说明中阿关系在百年变局中占据特殊重要地位，充分说明中阿关系对推进强国建设、民族复兴伟业具有重要战略意义。2022年12月中旬，习近平主席在沙特首都利雅得出席首届中国—阿拉伯国家峰会，引领中国与阿拉伯国家的整体外交和集体合作迈向历史性新高度。中阿双方扎实有力推进首届中阿峰会成果落实，共建"一带一路"成果显著，实现了阿盟22个阿拉伯国家的全覆盖，表明"一带一路"合作机制和路径得到阿拉伯国家和阿盟的广泛认可，具有强大吸引力。2023年10月18日，习近平主席在北京出席第三届"一带一路"国际合作高峰论坛开幕式并发表主旨演讲，阐述倡议初心，

---

① 习近平：《高举中国特色社会主义伟大旗帜 为全面建设社会主义现代化国家而团结奋斗——在中国共产党第二十次全国代表大会上的报告》，人民出版社，2022，第28页。

回顾建设成绩，总结合作经验，宣布八项行动，得到各方热烈反响和积极支持。2024年5月30日，习近平主席出席中阿合作论坛第十届部长级会议开幕式并发表主旨讲话，进一步提出与阿方构建"五大合作格局"：更富活力的创新驱动格局、更具规模的投资金融格局、更加立体的能源合作格局、更为平衡的经贸互惠格局、更广维度的人文交流格局，推动中阿命运共同体建设跑出加速度。① 中阿关系处于历史最好水平，中阿全方位合作迎来重大战略机遇。中阿博览会理应顺势而为、加速作为，力争在新时代的中阿合作大局中发挥更加重要的作用。

11.1 中阿共建"一带一路"以来 中阿博览会发展回顾

中阿博览会是中华人民共和国商务部、中国国际贸易促进委员会和宁夏回族自治区人民政府共同主办的国家级、国际性综合博览会，其前身是2010—2012年举办的中国·阿拉伯国家经贸论坛（以下简称中阿经贸论坛）。2013年以来，习近平主席连续5次向中阿博览会致贺信，多次指出中阿博览会为深化中阿务实合作、推动共建"一带一路"高质量发展发挥了积极作用，充分体现出党中央对办好中阿博览会的重视和支持。随着中阿关系的深入发展和宁夏实践的不断积累，中阿博览会的功能定位从"高度集成中阿多领域合作"向"深化经贸合作"逐步聚焦，服务范围从促进宁阿合作、中阿合作到"一带一路"国际合作不断拓展。机制建设方面，科技板块活动从地方经验上升为国家认可的中阿科技交流合作机制，中阿博览会成为中阿共建"一带一路"框架下重要的国际经贸合作机制。

---

① 《习近平出席中阿合作论坛第十届部长级会议开幕式并发表主旨讲话》，《人民日报》2024年5月31日，第1版。

11.1.1 中阿共建"一带一路"促使中阿博览会的功能特征由"高度集成多领域合作"向"聚焦经贸合作"转变

进入 21 世纪以来，经党中央、国务院批准同意，中国部分地方政府开始举办区域性涉外会展活动，承担在经贸合作领域服务国家总体外交的职能，办会特色和成效十分突出。但从国家和地方层面来看，始终缺少一个主要面向阿拉伯国家开放合作的国家级经贸会展平台。2004 年中阿合作论坛成立，中阿双方本着"加强对话与合作、促进和平与发展"的宗旨，广泛开展了政治、经贸、文化、环境等领域的交流与合作，很好地发挥了促进中阿经贸合作的平台效应。但从总体来看，仍缺少一个能够充分发挥非官方力量，进而将政府和民间力量整合起来的中阿经贸合作平台。从阿方视角看，国际、地区和国内政治经济形势的变化，为中阿进一步合作提供了发展机遇和空间：国际层面，中国发展模式得到阿拉伯国家的认可，阿拉伯国家普遍出现了"向东看"趋势，2008 年国际金融危机后阿拉伯国家对与中国的经贸合作乃至政治合作有了更多期待；地区层面，2010 年底，西亚北非地区陷入动荡，阿拉伯世界总体处于在变革中求稳定、谋发展、惠民生的历史阶段，中国经济的转型升级给中阿合作提供了更大空间，在探索符合各自国情发展道路的过程中，发展与中国的互利合作符合各国战略利益；国内层面，阿拉伯各国正面临大力加强基础设施建设、实施产业多元化发展战略、加快实现经济转型和改善民生的艰巨任务，深化中阿经贸合作已成为双方实现自身经济发展的战略选择。在此背景下，探索建立深化中阿关系、构建经贸合作平台的现实需要呼之欲出。基于宁夏区位特点、对阿交往实践和经贸合作基础，这一重要使命历史性地落在了宁夏。

中阿经贸论坛的功能呈现高度集成性特征。在中阿经贸论坛机制下，其功能模块（活动内容）包含经贸政策沟通、投资贸易、基础设施建设和能源、金融、农业、科技、教育、广电、生态环保合作等，主要服务于三大功能。一是配合国家对阿战略及政策。主要是邀请党和国家领导人出席中阿经贸论坛开幕式并发表主旨讲话，积极承接中阿合作论坛框架下机制性活动，以体现其规格高、权威性强的特色。二是广泛推进中阿多领域合作。中阿经贸论坛以"传承友谊、深化合作、共同发展"为主题，为中阿政府、企业和民间搭建共商经贸交流的高层对话平台，致力于建设中阿经贸合作的国际性新机制。三是推动宁夏内陆开放型经济发展。

中阿博览会的功能呈现由"高度集成多领域合作"向"聚焦经贸合作"逐步集中的特征。其功能模块以聚焦经贸合作为导向进行优化调整，包括推进中阿共建"一带一路"框架下的经贸促进、产能合作、技术合作等，主要服务于四大功能。一是着力服务国家经贸合作机制和平台建设。积极发挥政府间经贸联委会、中国与阿拉伯国家联合商会等双多边机制作用，充分发挥中阿博览会平台功能，促进中阿双方政府和企业间的互访和交流。二是着力落实中国对阿拉伯国家投资贸易合作政策文件。坚持企业主体、市场主导、政府推动、商业运作的原则，对接中国产能优势和阿拉伯国家需求，与阿拉伯国家开展先进、适用、有效、有利于就业、绿色环保的产能合作，支持阿拉伯国家工业化进程。三是着力构建中阿政府间科技创新合作平台。构建覆盖中国和阿拉伯国家的一体化技术转移协作网络，实施中阿科技伙伴计划，积极推进双方科技成果和先进适用技术在彼此之间的应用和推广。四是着力促进各地方与阿经贸合作。创新活动组织形式，服务全国各省（自治区、直辖市）"走进阿拉伯国家"开拓市场，服务阿方在中国各地投资合作，扩大双向经贸实效。

2013—2023 年，中阿博览会已连续举办 6 届。为实现各项功能及作用，中阿博览会主动落实习近平主席在历届中阿合作论坛部长级会议上的重要讲话精神，积极配合实施中国对阿政策文件，形成了促进中阿经贸合作的一系列重要机制。一是围绕国家经贸合作机制和平台建设，充分发挥中阿博览会的经贸政策沟通和项目对接洽谈作用，举办国家级、国际性、机制化的中阿工商峰会，由中国贸促会、阿拉伯农工商会总联盟组织政府部门、重要商协会和各类企业参会参展，密切中阿双方政府和企业间的互访和交流，积极推进贸易投资便利化，形成政策沟通促共识、经贸合作惠

181

民生的良好态势。二是围绕落实中国对阿投资贸易合作政策文件，充分发挥中阿博览会促成企业与境外产业园区招商和政策协调等作用，盘活部分阿拉伯国家的投资优势与中国的产能优势，推进中阿产业和市场双循环，带动中阿双向投资和经贸可持续发展。三是围绕构建中阿政府间科技创新合作平台，率先落实习近平主席在中阿合作论坛第六届部长级会议开幕式上提出的"探讨设立中阿技术转移中心"重要倡议，宁夏回族自治区人民政府与科学技术部于2015年9月共同创办了"中国—阿拉伯国家技术转移与创新合作大会"，共同组建了中国—阿拉伯国家技术转移中心，成为推进中阿科技创新合作的重要机制和务实平台。四是围绕提升服务地方对阿经贸合作能力，创新办会机制，设立"双主宾国""双主题省"，征集全国对阿经贸合作优质案例，全面展示地方经济特色与实力，汇集阿方经贸合作需求，服务全国各省（自治区、直辖市）开拓阿拉伯国家市场，服务阿方在中国各地投资合作。2016年1月，习近平主席在访问阿盟总部时指出，中阿博览会成为服务中阿共建"一带一路"的重要平台。

11.1.2 中阿共建"一带一路"框架下的中阿博览会举办成效

中国与阿拉伯国家的合作是全方位、多层次、跨领域的合作，中阿博览会始终坚持"服务国家战略、聚焦经贸合作"的目标导向，已逐渐发展成为以中国和阿拉伯国家为主体，集高层对话、经贸促进、会展洽谈等功能于一体，向全世界开放的国际性博览会，成为推进和落实中阿务实合作的重要平台，在国际社会上产生了广泛而深远的影响。2019年9月，阿拉伯农工商会总联盟秘书长哈立德·哈纳菲在接受新华社专访时表示，中阿博览会是推进中阿经贸合作的好平台，中国对包括阿拉伯国家在内的世界各国保持开放姿态，将惠及中阿双方。[①] 中阿博览会为赓续中阿友谊，深化中阿友好合作关系，推动中阿共建"一带一路"合作共识不断凝聚，促

---

① 《中阿务实合作向新领域扬帆起航——访阿拉伯农工商联合会秘书长哈立德》，新华网，http：//www.xinhuanet.com/world/2019-09/06/c_1124968827.htm，2019年9月6日。

进中阿经贸合作高质量发展，深化各省（自治区、直辖市）对阿多领域合作，助力宁夏对外开放和经济全面发展提速做出了积极贡献，取得了丰硕成果。

一是高层对话卓有成效。作为中国与阿拉伯国家高层次的交流平台，中阿博览会不仅是中国与阿拉伯国家间商贸合作的渠道，同时也是中国与阿拉伯国家政策沟通的渠道，为中阿双方高层对话、政策沟通搭建平台，推动双方战略合作对接持续扩容，先后有112个国家和地区、29位中外政要、383位中外部长级嘉宾参会。中阿博览会已成为中国与阿拉伯国家政府间政策沟通、协商以及信息发布的重要平台，多领域、多层次交流的作用日益凸显。2022年12月，习近平主席赴沙特出席中阿、中海、中沙领导人"三环峰会"时，又专门向沙特发出担任第六届中阿博览会主宾国的邀请，并写入《中沙联合声明》《中阿全面合作规划纲要》，掀开了中阿博览会服务元首外交的崭新篇章。阿拉伯国家给予高度评价和积极回应，纷纷表达了借助中阿博览会共建"一带一路"、促进中阿经贸合作的强烈意愿。

二是经贸合作不断深化。中阿博览会始终以经贸合作为重点，为中国与阿拉伯各国的客商进行经贸沟通、投资推介和实现经济互补提供了对接平台，促进了双边经贸快速增长，为双方经济发展和增进人民福祉做出了贡献。签约项目上，中阿博览会以企业为中心，聚焦经贸合作，重点围绕商品贸易、服务贸易和技术贸易设置各类展览会和论坛，促进中阿经贸务实合作。纵观历届中阿博览会经贸成果，签约项目逐渐增多。2013年中阿博览会经贸活动共签订合作项目158个，签约金额2599.0亿元人民币，相比2012年宁洽会暨中阿经贸论坛签约项目增加34个，签约金额增长18.82%。至2023年第六届中阿博览会，签约项目达403个，计划投资和贸易总额1709.7亿元人民币，相比2013年首届中阿博览会，签约项目增长75.32%。合作项目包括商品贸易、投资合作、发布政策报告、友好城市建设等方面，投资合作广泛涉及基础设施建设、产能合作、高新技术、卫生健康、现代农业、物流等领域，为推动共建"一带一路"高质量发展

183

发挥了重要平台作用。科技合作上，在中阿博览会框架下，中阿双方高新技术合作方式更加多元、合作领域更加广阔、合作关系更加紧密。通过多方高质量协作，中阿技术转移中心、中阿技术转移暨创新合作大会，已从地方经验上升为推动中阿科技合作政策及项目的国家级、国际性机制。产能合作上，中阿博览会推动中阿双方共建产业园，促成国内企业与境外产业园区签约，为国内企业开创国际市场、携手阿拉伯国家及"一带一路"共建国家"走出去""请进来"双向投资合作新模式提供了借鉴，有效推动了中阿产能合作。

三是国内省区对阿合作务实发展。中阿博览会作为中阿共建"一带一路"的重要平台，联通中阿双方市场，打造互济开放平台，积极调动国内资源流动，极大地激发了国内省区市的积极参与热情。六届中阿博览会以来，国内省区市参展参会规模不断扩大，参会企业质量、规格不断提升，深化了相关省区市对阿各领域的合作与交流，并为地方政府构建对外经贸合作机制提供了有益借鉴。第六届中阿博览会为各兄弟省区市和国内头部企业创造与阿拉伯国家"零距离"对接、"点对点"洽谈条件，促成与沙特、约旦等国家签约各类项目 37 个，签约金额 206.2 亿元人民币；促成国内投资项目 24 个，投资金额 30.6 亿元人民币；主题省广东与沙特、陕西等有关方面达成合作项目 37 个，签约金额 100.4 亿元人民币。

四是宁夏对外开放迈上新台阶。2013 年以来，宁夏充分利用中阿博览会积极融入和服务"一带一路"建设，搭建合作平台，深挖贸易潜力，优化投资环境，完善政策支撑，建设开放载体，畅通对外通道，坚持整体推进与重点突破相结合，机制创新与政策引领相结合，在更大范围、更高层次上实现高水平对外开放，推动建设向西开放战略高地，参与"一带一路"建设取得了阶段性成效。开放通道功能逐步增强。截至 2023 年底，银川河东国际机场已开通 96 个通航城市的 140 条航线，其中国内航点 85 个，省会城市直飞率达到 100%；国际航点 11 个，已开通 12 条国际（地区）航线。宁夏加强与沿海港口合作，强化与西部陆海新通道省区市交流，初步构建了通边达海、连南接北的陆上开放通道格局，搭建起涵盖国际铁路、铁海联运等多种运输方式于一体的国际货物体系，形成了西北向出境、东南向出海的口岸通道网络，为建设区域性国际物流中心提供了重要支撑。开放型经济发展水平稳步提升。2013—2022年，宁夏累计实际利用外资23.6亿美元，年均增速为8.2%，在全球36个国家和地区设立对外直接投资企业152家，对外投资总额43.9亿美元，其中在6个阿拉伯国家投资设立了23家境外投资企业，总投资额4.35亿美元。从贸易市场看，宁夏与俄罗斯、印度、马来西亚、沙特等59个共建"一带一路"国家开展了经贸往来，市场多元化格局逐步形成。2022年，宁夏主要进出口市场中，对共建"一带一路"国家实现进出口80.20亿元人民币，同比增长23.7%，占全区进出口总额的31.2%。对中东国家实现进出口10.99亿元人民币，增长38.7%。

11.2　新形势下中阿博览会面临多重发展机遇

首届中阿峰会和中阿合作论坛第十届部长级会议成果为创新中阿博览会办会内容带来新机遇。2022年12月，首届中阿峰会发表三份重要成果文件：《首届中阿峰会利雅得宣言》，宣布中阿双方一致同意全力构建面向新时代的中阿命运共同体；《中阿全面合作规划纲要》，就双方在政治、经贸、投资、金融等18个领域的合作提出182项合作举措；《深化面向和平与发展的中阿战略伙伴关系文件》，涉及双方同意深化中阿战略伙伴关系、倡导多边主义、加强在共建"一带一路"框架内合作、加强中阿合作论坛建设等重要内容。二十年来，中阿合作论坛建立起部长级会议、战略政治对话、改革发展论坛、能源合作大会等19项重要机制，发布了85份重要成果文件，树立了发展中国家集体合作标杆。[①] 2024年5月30日，中阿合作论坛第十届部长级会议在北京举行，中阿双方围绕加紧落实首届中阿

---

① 王毅：《加快构建面向新时代的中阿命运共同体——写在中阿合作论坛第十届部长级会议召开之际》，人民网，https://www.gov.cn/yaowen/liebiao/202405/content_6954208.htm，2024年5月29日。

峰会成果、加快推动中阿命运共同体建设深入探讨，签署了《北京宣言》《论坛 2024 年至 2026 年行动执行计划》等合作文件。

阿拉伯国家加入金砖国家会议等多边机制为创新中阿博览会办会机制带来新机遇。阿拉伯国家是"全球南方"国家国际发展的重要合作伙伴。[①]"全球南方"崛起的基础源于长期的经济发展，未来"全球南方"在国际舞台上发挥更加重要的作用依然要靠持续的经济发展。无论是南南合作，还是南北对话，发展问题始终是"全球南方"的核心议题。[②] 当前，金砖国家会议已成为"全球南方"最具实力和活力的国际发展合作机制，在全球治理中的影响力持续提升，对包括中东国家在内的广大发展中国家产生了巨大吸引力。目前，已有埃及、沙特、阿联酋三个阿拉伯国家正式加入金砖大家庭。此外，阿拉伯国家还积极申请加入上海合作组织。2021 年上合组织杜尚别峰会上，上合组织秘书处与阿盟秘书处签署合作谅解备忘录，会议决定吸收沙特阿拉伯、埃及、卡塔尔为对话伙伴。2022 年上合组织撒马尔罕峰会批准埃及、沙特、卡塔尔成为对话伙伴，巴林、阿联酋、科威特则被列入同意吸收的新一批对话伙伴。[③]

新时代推进西部大开发形成新格局为完善中阿博览会平台功能带来新机遇。2020 年 5 月 17 日，《中共中央 国务院关于新时代推进西部大开发形成新格局的指导意见》明确指出，西部地区要积极参与和融入"一带一路"建设，强化开放大通道建设，构建内陆多层次开放平台，办好各类国家级博览会，提升西部地区影响力，发展高水平开放型经济，拓展区际互动合作。2024 年 8 月 23 日，中共中央政治局召开会议，审议《进一步推动西部大开发形成新格局的若干政策措施》，会议指出，西部大开发是党中央做出的重大战略决策，要深刻领会党中央战略意图，准确把握西部大

---

① 刘中民：《"全球南方"的中东板块：历史逻辑与现实价值》，国际合作中心网站，https：//www.icc.org.cn/publications/internationaloberservation/2070.html，2023 年 12 月 8 日。

② 徐秀军等：《国际秩序转型背景下"全球南方"的战略地位和角色作用》，《国际论坛》2024 年第 2 期。

③ 《阿拉伯国家为何希望加入上合组织》，人民网，http：//world.people.com.cn/n1/2023/0707/c1002-40030697.html，2023 年 7 月 7 日。

开发在推进中国式现代化中的定位和使命，保持战略定力，一以贯之抓好贯彻落实，聚焦大保护、大开放、高质量发展，加快构建新发展格局，提升区域整体实力和可持续发展能力。[①]

11.3 新形势下办好中阿博览会的思路

11.3.1 总体思路

未来十年，中阿博览会将高举人类命运共同体旗帜，传承和弘扬丝路精神，坚持目标导向、行动导向，以落实中阿务实合作"八大共同行动"和"五大合作格局"为指引，积极构建功能定位更趋完善、办会机制务实创新、服务水平显著提升、合作基础更加坚实、经贸实效更为突出的升级版中阿博览会，扎实推进中阿高质量共建"一带一路"不断取得新的更大成效，为宁夏高水平开放和高质量发展做出更大贡献。

在习近平主席同阿方领导人战略引领下，当前中阿关系处于历史最好时期，中阿全方位、多层次、宽领域合作格局不断充实和深化。中国共产党宁夏回族自治区第十三届委员会第八次全体会议指出："不断提高内陆开放水平，服务融入共建'一带一路'和西部陆海新通道，建立产业转移承接协作机制，稳步拓展制度型开放。"在此背景下，中阿博览会迎来重大战略机遇，应顺势而为、练好内功、加速作为，力争在新时代的中阿合作大局中发挥更加重要的作用，注重做好"五个统筹"。

一是统筹继承和创新。维护好中阿博览会朋友圈，夯实高质量发展根基，做精做实存量活动；着力提升创新发展能力，聚焦新时代中阿合作格局，打造特色增量活动。二是统筹政府和市场。坚持"政府引导、市场运作、企业主体、合作共赢"的协调推进原则，充分激发各方参与中阿博览

[①] 新华社：《中共中央政治局召开会议 审议〈进一步推动西部大开发形成新格局的若干政策措施〉中共中央总书记习近平主持会议》，中华人民共和国中央人民政府网，https://www.gov.cn/yaowen/liebiao/202408/content_6970134.htm，2024年8月23日。

会的积极性。三是统筹双边和多边。秉持"多边谈合作、双边促落实"工作思路，与阿方共同推动落实中阿峰会和中阿合作论坛部长级会议议定事项，着力提升中阿博览会框架下活动与双边经贸合作议程有效对接、协同增效，以双边促多边，通过双边合作、三方合作、多边合作等各种形式，增强经贸合作的有效性。四是统筹规模和效益。稳步提升中阿博览会的规模和效益，将"小而美"项目作为合作优先事项，多搞投资小、见效快、经济社会环境效益好的项目，形成更多接地气、聚人心的合作成果。五是统筹发展和安全。牢固树立和践行总体国家安全观，完善风险防控制度机制，强化统筹协调，压实各方责任，做好要素保障，不断提高应对风险、迎接挑战、化险为夷的能力水平。

11.3.2 基本原则

坚持战略对接与统筹发展相结合。充分对接落实《中华人民共和国和阿拉伯国家全面合作规划纲要》《中国—阿拉伯国家合作论坛行动执行计划》《中海战略对话行动计划》，统筹协调对接各部门各行业面向阿拉伯国家的经贸合作事务，寻求利益汇合点和合作最大公约数，形成上下联动、内外衔接、互惠共赢的协同发展格局。

坚持市场主导与政府引导相结合。充分发挥市场在中阿博览会机制建设中的主导作用，更好发挥政府在中阿博览会筹办工作中的引导和协调作用，共同促进中阿博览会有效有序运行。

坚持目标导向与问题导向相结合。聚焦中阿高质量共建"一带一路"的目标要求，精准匹配投资贸易、数字经济、科技合作、产能合作、绿色发展等领域合作的供需结构，研究破解中阿博览会发展中存在的突出问题，增强发展的协同性、联动性、整体性、有效性。

11.3.3 功能定位

服务中阿经贸合作的主要机制。加强国家层面中阿经贸合作机制统筹，明确中阿博览会作为对内对外集中统一的对阿经贸合作机制和综合服务平台功能定位；加强省区层面中阿经贸合作机制协同，通过建立互利合作关系、轮流举办机制，优化配置会议论坛等经贸合作资源，着力提升中阿博览会平台功能。

推进中阿高质量共建"一带一路"的重要平台。以推动构建面向新时代的中阿命运共同体为战略目标，聚焦中阿高质量共建"一带一路"重点合作领域，盘活中国对阿经贸合作总体资源，适配阿拉伯国家发展需求，协同落实新时代中阿合作的战略、规划、政策和项目，将中阿博览会打造成为中阿高质量共建"一带一路"的重要平台。

助推宁夏高水平开放的重要引擎。深入贯彻落实习近平总书记历次来宁考察重要讲话重要指示精神，巩固宁夏对阿合作基础，充分发挥对阿合作特色和优势，完善与其他省区开放平台对接机制，抢抓东部地区资金、技术、产业向中西部转移的重大机遇，因地制宜构建特色化、差异化的现代化产业体系，形成高水平开放工作任务与中阿博览会开放平台功能有效融合的发展态势。

11.4　新形势下办好中阿博览会的路径

中阿博览会作为中阿合作论坛在经贸领域的延伸和补充，经过多年发展，不断优化运行机制和顶层设计，逐渐形成了开幕大会、主宾国和主题省系列活动、展览展示、投资贸易促进活动和会议论坛等交流机制，已成为中阿共建"一带一路"的重要平台，对促进中阿经贸合作日益发挥出重要而独特的作用。

在习近平主席和阿方领导人共同引领下，中阿关系处于历史最好水平，中阿全方位合作迎来重大战略机遇。中阿博览会理应顺势而为、加速作为，打造中阿高质量共建"一带一路"的重要平台，力争在新时代的中阿合作大局中发挥更加重要的作用。一是着力服务国家经贸合作机制和平台建设。更大力度协同商务部和中国贸促会支持，积极发挥中阿政府间经贸联委会、中国与阿拉伯国家联合商会等双多边机制作用，充分发挥中阿博览会平台功能，促进中阿双方政府和企业间的互访和交流。二是着力落实中国对阿拉伯国家投资贸易合作政策文件。坚持企业主体、市场主导、政府推动、商业运作的原则，对接中国产能优势和阿拉伯国家需求，与阿拉伯国家开展先进、适用、有效，有利于就业、绿色环保的产能合作，支持阿拉伯国家工业化进程。三是着力构建中阿政府间科技创新合作平台。构建覆盖中国和阿拉伯国家的一体化技术转移协作网络，实施中阿科技伙伴计划，积极推进双方科技成果和先进适用技术在彼此之间的应用和推广。四是着力促进各地方与阿经贸合作。创新活动组织形式，常态化在阿拉伯国家举办投资贸易推介活动，服务全国各省（自治区、直辖市）"走进阿拉伯国家"开拓市场，服务阿方在中国各地投资合作，扩大双向经贸实效，强化中国与阿拉伯国家市场和资源"双循环"联动效应。

在筹办工作思路上，可考虑"政府主导＋市场化"办好中阿博览会。"政府主导"主要突出"定方向""定规则""定任务"。"定方向"，是指在科学制订中阿博览会战略规划和总体方案过程中，确保各项会议论坛、展览展示和对接洽谈活动聚焦经贸合作，始终以落实中国与阿拉伯国家的战略、规划、政策和项目为目标，以铸牢中华民族共同体意识为主线，统领中阿博览会筹办工作全流程，把握好政治方向。"定规则"，是指政府研究出台促进中阿博览会发展的政策举措中，遵循展览业发展规律，借鉴国内外有益经验，建立公开公平、开放透明的市场规则，实现博览会持续健康发展。明确政府为展会提供公共服务的工作职责，在加强财政资金奖补、优化展品出入境监管、改善金融保险服务、健全会展业统计制度、加强知识产权保护等方面，制定好促进展会可持续发展的规则体系。"定任务"，是指政府加强与阿方政府部门、国家部委、各地方政府的对接和协调，全力争取各方支持，积极整合全国对阿经贸合作资源，实事求是设计中阿博览会各项活动应达成的指标和成果，优选市场化合作主体，确保务实办会，增进经贸合作实效。

"市场化"主要突出创新性、专业性和国际性。各行业协会、商会、中介组织和企业，是机制性涉外论坛和博览会的重要合作伙伴，在服务国家发展战略和对外战略全局中具有不可替代的作用。一是发挥好市场化主体创新性优势，加快数字科技赋能的展览形态、展览技术、会展沟通、展览服务等会展要素在中阿博览会中的创新应用，构建数字化的、全流程的会展生态体系。二是发挥好市场化主体专业化优势，精确匹配商品或服务的供需信息，降低国内外采购商、贸易商和供应商的交易成本，全面提升中阿博览会的信息化、数字化、智能化服务的水平和能力。三是发挥好市场化主体的国际性优势，积极开展贸易促进服务，建立合作共享展会协同发展机制，鼓励市场主体与境外专业展览机构和成熟展会项目合作，常态化在境外举办"中阿博览会"专业展，不断扩大中阿博览会在阿拉伯国家及共建"一带一路"国家的影响力和美誉度，将中阿博览会打造成为区域性国际展会品牌。

第12章 宁夏对外开放专题报告

抓住机遇，融入共建"一带一路"，促进开放发展是宁夏健康发展的关键。2013年以来，宁夏回族自治区系统构建融入共建"一带一路"，推进高水平开放"1+X+6"政策体系，有力促进了宁夏更宽领域、更深层次、更高水平对外开放。

12.1 宁夏推进高水平对外开放现状

12.1.1 开放型经济稳步推进

1. 经济质效全面提升

2023年，宁夏整体目标完成情况为历史最好水平，其中地区生产总值增长6.6%，居全国第5位，第一产业、第二产业、规上工业增加值3项增速（分别增长7.7%、8.5%、12.4%）均列全国第二位。由表12.1、12.2、12.3可以看出，2013年宁夏地区生产总值为2327.7亿元人民币，2023年为5315.0亿元人民币，总量增长近1.8倍，年均增长8.61%；人均GDP从2013年的35135元人民币增长至2023年的72957元，绝对值扩大到2.08倍，平均增长6.07%；固定资产投资额由2013年的2681.1亿元人民币增长到2023年的3390.9亿元人民币，总量为2013年的1.26倍，经济发展取得了显著的成就。横向看，宁夏人均国内生产总值排名由2013年的全国第19位上升至2023年的第18位，经济发展实现速度与总量加快增长，质效与格局全面提升。

第12章 宁夏对外开放专题报告

表 12.1 2013—2023 年宁夏地区生产总值发展变化情况

	宁夏地区生产总值（亿元人民币）	宁夏地区生产总值增速（%）	人均 GDP（元人民币/人）	人均 GDP增速（%）
2013 年	2327.7	9.8	35135	8.6
2014 年	2473.9	8.0	36815	6.8
2015 年	2579.4	8.0	37876	6.9
2016 年	2781.4	8.1	40339	7.0
2017 年	3200.3	7.8	45718	6.7
2018 年	3510.2	7.0	49614	6.0
2019 年	3748.5	6.5	52537	5.5
2020 年	3956.3	3.9	55021	3.1
2021 年	4588.2	6.7	63461	6.1
2022 年	5104.6	4.0	70263	3.5
2023 年	5315.0	6.6	72957	6.3

资料来源：根据国家统计局官方数据库、中国与宁夏统计年鉴数据计算所得。

表 12.2 2013—2023 年宁夏固定资产投资变化情况

	固定资产投资（亿元人民币）	固定资产投资增速（%）	人均固定资产投资（元人民币）	人均固定资产投资增速（%）
2013 年	2681.1	27.1	40257.4	25.8
2014 年	3201.0	19.4	47212.2	17.3
2015 年	3532.9	10.4	51651.0	9.4
2016 年	3835.5	8.6	55186.5	6.8
2017 年	3813.4	-0.6	54090.5	-2.0
2018 年	3119.3	-18.2	43934.4	-18.8
2019 年	2773.1	-11.1	38676.4	-12.0
2020 年	2906.2	4.8	40308.0	4.2
2021 年	2984.7	2.7	41167.9	2.1
2022 年	3229.4	8.2	44360.1	7.8
2023 年	3390.9	5.0	46514.0	4.9

资料来源：根据国家统计局官方数据库、中国与宁夏统计年鉴及统计公报数据计算所得。

中阿经贸关系发展进程2023年度报告

表 12.3 2013、2019 年、2023 年全国各省区人均 GDP 排名

	2023 年	2019 年	2013 年
安徽省	13	13	16
北京市	1	1	1
福建省	4	4	6
甘肃省	31	31	30
广东省	7	7	7
广西壮族自治区	29	29	29
贵州省	28	28	31
海南省	17	19	18
河北省	26	27	23
河南省	25	18	20
黑龙江省	30	30	25
湖北省	9	8	10
湖南省	14	14	15
吉林省	27	25	17
江苏省	3	3	3
江西省	21	17	22
辽宁省	19	15	12
内蒙古自治区	8	10	9
宁夏回族自治区	*18*	*21*	*19*
青海省	24	22	26
山东省	11	11	8
山西省	15	24	24
陕西省	12	12	13
上海市	2	2	2
四川省	20	16	21
天津市	6	5	4
西藏自治区	*22*	26	28
新疆维吾尔自治区	16	20	14
云南省	23	23	27
浙江省	5	6	5
重庆市	10	9	11

资料来源：根据国家统计局官方数据库数据计算所得。

194

2. 产业结构不断优化

由表 12.4 看出，2013—2023 年宁夏三次产业结构比例逐渐得到优化。三次产业结构由 2013 年的 9.1∶45.5∶45.4 变为 2014 年的 8.8∶45.0∶46.2，实现了产业结构从"二三一"向"三二一"转变，2021 年产业结构为 7.9∶45.8∶46.3，[①]"三二一"格局比较稳定，走出了一条具有当地特色的产业发展道路。2022 年由于疫情对第三产业影响所致宁夏产业结构为 8.0∶48.3∶43.7，即"二三一"，但占比相差不大。2023 年为疫情之后第一年产业结构为 8.1∶46.8∶45.1，产业结构不断优化并与全国平均水平大体相当，工业和服务业双轮支撑格局基本形成。总体来看，根据美国经济学家西蒙·库兹涅茨的划分标准，宁夏产业结构处在由初级向高级演变的过渡阶段，经济发展处在工业化中期发力阶段。

表 12.4　2013—2023 年宁夏三次产业结构比重发展变化

	第一产业	第二产业	第三产业
2013 年	9.1	45.5	45.4
2014 年	8.8	45.0	46.2
2015 年	9.2	43.3	47.5
2016 年	8.7	42.4	48.9
2017 年	7.8	43.9	48.3
2018 年	8.0	42.4	49.6
2019 年	7.5	42.3	50.2
2020 年	8.5	41.2	50.2
2021 年	7.9	45.8	46.3
2022 年	8.0	48.3	43.7
2023 年	8.1	46.8	45.1

资料来源：根据国家统计局官方数据库、中国与宁夏统计年鉴数据计算所得。

---

① 宁夏回族自治区统计局、国家统计局宁夏调查总队编《宁夏统计年鉴 2022》，中国统计出版社，2023。

中阿经贸关系发展进程2023年度报告

3. 外贸外资较快发展

（1）外贸发展

宁夏外贸经营主体突破 500 家，与 170 多个国家和地区开展贸易往来，由表 12.5 可以看出，2013—2023 年，宁夏外贸总额发展较快，2023 年进出口总额 205.41 亿元人民币，为 2013 年的 1.03 倍。其中对共建"一带一路"国家进出口总额 69.79 亿元人民币，比重达到 34%。外商直接投资企业达 1127 家，累计实际利用外资 27.7 亿美元，年均增速为 8.3%。

从产品出口结构来看，近年来，宁夏加大产业结构调整，重点加强对具有宁夏特色的生物制品、农畜产品以及新材料、新能源等特色产品的出口，出口结构得到不断优化。从"高耗能"到"高新"，从"初加工"到"精加工"和"高端"，[①] 为提升出口产品结构注入强劲内生动力。2023 年，单晶硅、双氰胺、泰乐菌素、金属锰、赖氨酸酯盐酸盐在宁夏外贸出口排前五。

从主要贸易市场来看，近几年来，宁夏积极开拓国际市场，实施市场多元化战略，宁夏与俄罗斯、印度、马来西亚、土耳其、乌兹别克斯坦、沙特、阿联酋等 60 个"一带一路"共建国家开展了经贸往来，市场多元化格局逐步形成。主要进口商品为大宗工业原材料，分别是石油、锰矿砂、木浆、机床和橡胶等。值得注意的是自 2013 年"一带一路"倡议提出以后，宁夏对欧盟、东盟、美国、印度、新加坡进出口实现增长。

表 12.5　2013—2023 年宁夏外贸发展情况

	进出口总额（万元人民币）	进口总额（万元人民币）	出口总额（万元人民币）	贸易差（万元人民币）	外贸依存度（%）
2013 年	1992757	412093	1580664	1168571	8.6
2014 年	3339168	697801	2641367	1943566	13.5
2015 年	2344123	502824	1841299	1338475	9.1

① 《2023，让"宁夏名片"熠熠生辉》，宁夏新闻网，https：//www. nxnews. net/cj/cjtj/202302/t20230221_7863994. html，2023 年 2 月 21 日。

续表

	进出口总额 （万元人民币）	进口总额 （万元人民币）	出口总额 （万元人民币）	贸易差 （万元人民币）	外贸依存度 （％）
2016 年	2147837	501406	1646431	1145025	7.7
2017 年	3412931	935852	2477079	1541227	10.7
2018 年	2491609	686850	1804759	1117909	7.1
2019 年	2406182	916994	1489188	572194	6.4
2020 年	1231665	364914	866752	501838	3.1
2021 年	2140404	392280	1748125	1355845	4.7
2022 年	2573794	606012	1967782	1361770	5.0
2023 年	2054100	556000	1498100	942100	3.9

资料来源：根据国家统计局官方数据库、中国与宁夏统计年鉴及统计公报数据计算所得。

（2）利用外资

2013—2023 年，宁夏累计实际利用外资 27.7 亿美元，年均增速为8.3%，其中，"一带一路"共建国家在宁投资 1.7 亿美元，累计在宁投资设立 37 家外商直接投资企业，全区累计设立外商直接投资企业 1127 家。

外资主要源于美国、新加坡、挪威、日本、韩国、马来西亚等 50 多个国家和地区，主要投向装备制造、煤化工、新能源、现代农业、商贸服务、金融等行业。美国亚马逊、辛普劳，法国路易威登轩尼诗、保乐力加，德国舍弗勒、麦德龙，挪威埃肯，新加坡斯伦贝谢，丹麦嘉士伯，日本山崎马扎克，韩国晓星、泰光等一批世界 500 强和知名跨国企业先后来宁投资建厂。新加坡、马来西亚、阿联酋、伊朗等"一带一路"共建国家在宁夏累计设立外商直接投资企业 124 家，实际投资额 2.2 亿美元，主要涉及旅游、咨询、互联网和饮料生产加工等领域。

总体上看，宁夏实际利用外资规模较小，对经济增长影响能力有限。外资投资结构发展不均衡，投资主要集中在传统的劳动密集型制造业，高附加值的产业和服务业涉及较少。

中阿经贸关系发展进程2023年度报告

表 12.6　2013—2023 年宁夏实际利用外资投资额变化情况

	实际利用外商投资额（亿美元）	外资依存度（％）
2013 年	2.0	0.6
2014 年	1.4	0.4
2015 年	2.2	0.6
2016 年	2.5	0.6
2017 年	3.1	0.7
2018 年	2.1	0.4
2019 年	2.5	0.5
2020 年	2.7	0.5
2021 年	2.9	0.4
2022 年	3.4	0.5
2023 年	4.1	0.5

资料来源：根据国家统计局官方数据库、中国与宁夏统计年鉴及统计公报数据计算所得。

4. 开放环境明显提升

出台融入"一带一路"建设、促进开放型经济发展、推进外贸新业态新模式发展、积极利用外资、支持企业"走出去"、加强口岸建设等一系列政策措施，有效提升了开放型经济的引领作用。复制推广自贸区改革试点经验 260 项，建立外资重点项目专班、外资大项目包抓机制；完善十部门组成的贸易便利化工作机制，建成"宁贸通"外贸综合服务平台和 e 外贸数字贸易服务平台，全面推广国际贸易单一窗口标准版，与西部 12 省（自治区、直辖市）共同签署《合作共建西部陆海新通道框架协议》，有力强化了外向型经济融资担保和供应链服务能力。

区域经济合作及重点招商成效明显提升，宁夏紧盯国内外大企业、大集团投资动向和产业转移趋势，围绕重点企业、优势产业和重点园区，赴京津冀、长三角、粤港澳大湾区、黄河流域重点省区，组织实施了一系列招商引资活动，建立了一系列区域合作机制，构建了一系列交流合作平台。2017—2023 年，累计实施招商引资项目 5000 余个、实际到位资金近

198

9000 亿元人民币，引进世界 500 强和中国 500 强企业 100 余家，招商引资项目形成的固定资产投资占全社会固定资产投资比例连续多年保持在 45% 左右，有力推动了全区经济结构调整和增长动能转换。

12.1.2　对外通道建设不断加强

1. 公路通畅显著提升

截至 2023 年，宁夏已建成"三环四纵六横"高速公路网，省际出口达到 13 个，是西部第 2 个县县通高速的省区，综合立体交通网加速成型。公路网密度 56.59 公里/百平方公里，高于全国平均水平，在我国 31 个省（自治区、直辖市）中排名第 25 位。宁夏高速公路网已实现向西通达阿拉山口、霍尔果斯等沿边口岸，向东顺畅连接天津港、上海港等沿海港口；与周边的兰州、西安、包头、太原等经济中心城市均实现高速公路连通。特别是银昆高速宁夏段全线通车，成为连接宁夏、甘肃、陕西三省区的南北大通道，带动沿线地区特别是宁夏中南部地区的交通路网资源开发和产业发展。目前，宁夏境内公路总里程已达 3.9 万公里，高速公路通车里程突破 2300 公里，国省干线公路网持续完善，农村公路基础网通乡达村，路网韧性持续增强，为宁夏及周边地区的经济发展和人民生活水平的提升提供了坚实的交通基础。

2. 铁路联通扎实推进

截至 2023 年，宁夏有 9 条铁路纳入国家铁路网中长期规划，国家规划的"八纵八横"高速铁路网中有"两横一纵"经过宁夏，为宁夏铁路项目的建设奠定了良好基础。其中，银川至西安高铁、中卫至兰州高铁、包头至银川高速铁路建成后，将实现银川至北京、西安、川渝、兰州等重点城市 2—5 小时到达，使宁夏真正融入全国高速铁路网，宁夏融入"一带一路"、服务全国的路网能力将大幅提升。目前，银西高铁、银（川）兰（州）高铁中（卫）兰（州）段已全线通车，包银高铁惠农至银川段已正式进入运行试验阶段。

国际铁路通道方面，宁夏开通银川至德黑兰的中亚货运班列，与天津港实现铁水联运，打通了中国华北、西北、东北地区面向中亚、西亚的低成本便捷陆路通道；开通银川至哈萨克斯坦等中亚 5 国、至欧洲匈牙利、至蒙古国、至俄罗斯等国际货运班列。宁夏南向陆海新通道班列和东向铁海联运班列，联通中亚、西亚、南亚市场。宁夏新一轮"铁公机"和国家物流示范园区、银川—西安国家综合货运枢纽等项目正在加快建设。

3. 航空枢纽不断夯实

截至 2023 年，银川河东国际机场完成三期扩建，飞行区等级提升至4E 级。银川机场旅客吞吐量跨入千万量级大型机场行列。银川河东国际机场获准开放第三、第四、第五航权，通航城市 79 个、航线 113 余条。开通银川至泰国、越南、马来西亚、新加坡等国家（地区）的 10 条国际航线。直飞迪拜、香港航线稳定运行。银川河东国际机场改扩建项目（四期）稳步推进，已取得了中国民用航空局关于《银川河东国际机场总体规划》的批复，据悉，总体规划按照满足 2035 年旅客 2800 万人次、货邮 20万吨设计，计划新建 3600 米长第二跑道、22 万平方米航站楼、85 万平方米扩建站坪等设施，建成后将迈入现代化西部一流机场行列。

4. 数字通道加快建设

宁夏坚持把数字经济作为宁夏发展的第一增长极，已经建成了我国西部唯一的算力和互联网交换"双中心"。银川已形成智能算力 3000P 以上，政务数据资源 5 亿余条，数据规模 8000 余 TB，着力打造"银川数据港"。截至 2023 年，宁夏亚马逊、中国移动、美团、西云等 100 多家企业在宁夏建立了数据中心或者应用数据中心进行数据储备。与此同时，加快建设国家级银川跨境电子商务综合试验区，在用好中阿博览会和中国（银川）跨境电商综试区金字招牌的基础上，聚焦自治区"六新六特六优"产业布局，以"两平台六体系"为建设目标，打造企业主体集聚、服务体系完备、监管模式创新的跨境电商产业生态，先后在德国、哈萨克斯坦、马来西亚等 6 个国家租用海外仓 19 个，跨境电商企业达到 475 家。

12.1.3 创新驱动成效显著

2023 年宁夏 R&D 经费支出规模达到 79.38 亿元，同比增长 12.7%。这一数据不仅显示了宁夏在研发经费上的持续增长，而且其增速高于全国平均增速 2.6 个百分点，增速排名全国第 8 位、西部第 4 位、西北第 2 位、沿黄九省区第 1 位，完成"研发经费投入年均增长 10% 以上"的目标。此外，R&D 经费投入强度达到 1.57%，排名居全国第 18 位。企业研发经费占比达到 81.4%、高于全国平均水平 3.8 个百分点，带动有研发活动的规上工业企业占比达到 41.2%，高于全国平均水平 4 个百分点，排名全国第 8 位、西北省区第 1 位。这些数据表明，宁夏在创新驱动发展战略上取得了显著的成效，研发经费的持续增长为地区的科技创新和经济发展提供了强有力的支持。同时，宁夏坚持厚植人才沃土，发展是第一要务，人才是第一资源原则，不断创新人才政策措施，先后出台了《宁夏回族自治区支持企业引进和培养人才暂行办法》《宁夏回族自治区引进科技创新团队实施意见》《宁夏回族自治区引进海外华侨华人专家暂行办法》等政策办法，为宁夏实施创新驱动战略高水平开放提供了人才支撑，取得明显成效，如宁夏大学与上海交通大学、北京航空航天大学等建立人才共享和交流机制，先后柔性引进多名学科带头人，新增入选国家重大人才工程人选 15 人，服务自治区化工、材料、能源等产业发展，在西部高校中名列前茅。

表 12.7　2019—2023 年宁夏等沿黄九省区 R&D 经费支出占 GDP 比重对比

单位：%

	2023 年	2022 年	2021 年	2020 年	2019 年
宁夏	1.57	1.56	1.56	1.51	1.45
陕西	2.50	2.35	2.33	2.43	2.27
内蒙古	0.93	0.20	0.20	0.93	0.86
甘肃	1.32	1.30	1.26	1.22	1.26

续表

	2023 年	2022 年	2021 年	2020 年	2019 年
青海	0.80	—	—	0.71	0.70
山西	1.16	1.07	1.12	1.20	1.13
四川	2.26	—	2.26	2.17	1.88
河南	2.05	1.96	1.73	1.66	1.48
山东	2.59	2.49	2.34	2.31	2.10

资料来源：根据国家统计局官方数据库、宁夏等沿黄九省区统计年鉴及宁夏科技厅数据计算所得。

2023 年，共建"一带一路"进入下一个新的十年，面临新的国际国内环境。国际上各类贸易合作协定的签订有望促使"一带一路"成为区域经济和世界经济新的增长极。金融危机后各国为了摆脱经济复苏乏力境况，都在不断谋求新的经济增长点。2023 年 10 月，习近平主席在第三届"一带一路"国际合作高峰论坛开幕式上发表主旨演讲时宣布中国支持高质量共建"一带一路"的八项行动，为宁夏更加深度融入共建"一带一路"大格局指明了方向。宁夏作为"一带一路"的重要支点，肩负着建设内陆改革开放高地、推进高水平开放重要任务。同时，宁夏处于新时代西部大开发、黄河流域生态保护和高质量发展等重大国家战略的叠加区，也是黄河流域生态保护和高质量发展的先行区，在共建"一带一路"高质量发展中需要与新时代推进西部大开发形成新格局、黄河流域生态保护和高质量发展等重大战略互为支撑，具有打通与北向、西向、南向和东部地区之间的流通循环，发展更高层次的开放型经济的地理和经济发展优势。通过 10 年的发展与积累，宁夏对外开放迈上新台阶，宁夏平台、通道、载体、科技创新、外贸外资有一定提升，为深度融入共建"一带一路"筑牢了较坚实的基础。未来，宁夏将以党的二十大精神和习近平总书记历次来宁考察重要讲话重要指示精神为根本遵循，在打造高水平通道、高能级平台、积极融入国内国际双循环新格局、构建更加开放政策体系等方面，扎实推进高质量共建"一带一路"行稳致远，促进内陆高水平开放。

12.2 宁夏推进高水平开放发展趋势展望

12.2.1 强化"一带一路"通道建设

1. 夯实顶层设计

其一，由"基建思维"向"通道思维"转变。宁夏要融入"一带一路"通道建设，需在跨区域合作中坚持全局思维，精准定位，差异化发展，提升自身在顶层设计中的利益契合度。其二，加快统筹编制宁夏参与西部陆海新通道的总体规划，明确宁夏战略定位、发展目标、空间布局与主要任务；强化区域性合作和省区协作联动，按照补断点、强内联、梳堵点的基本思路高位推动通道基础设施建设，共享通道建设发展成果。其三，结合自治区内产业园区布局和物流枢纽发展实际，加快推进重点领域、重点项目、重要节点、重要枢纽建设，借鉴杭州锦江集团氧化铝项目从银川注册走向沙特成功经验，着力推动"通道经济"提质升级，撬动与其他东向、西向、北向和南向国家战略的对接。其四，放大中阿峰会效应，加强与"一带一路"高峰合作论坛、博鳌亚洲论坛等全球性国际组织以及东盟、上海合作组织等区域性国际组织的联系和对话，在这些国际组织的业务范围框架下，探索建立合作平台的可能性与可行性，力争在国际交通设施互联互通、国际运输协定签署、跨境直达通关便利化等方面取得新突破。

2. 加快推进"数字丝绸之路"

宁夏地处内陆，一定要走好"数字丝绸之路"这条新发展格局下高水平对外开放的新路径。其一，不断夯实数字经济发展基础，对标数字经济伙伴关系协定（DEPA）、全面与跨太平洋伙伴关系协定（CPTPP）等国际规则对接，构建具有竞争力的数字经济发展体系，建设西部数字经济示范区，扩大宁夏在世界数字经济发展中的话语权。其二，创新数字合作机制，建设国家数字经济创新发展试验区，加快发展新模式新业态，大力发展智慧物流、数字金融、数字经济总部基地等金融数字经济产业，打造"数字丝绸之路"的产业多态。其三，精心谋划出台新一轮发展规划和建设实施方案，强化中阿峰会在数字经济合作中全局性牵引作用，挖掘阿盟各国在数字贸易竞争中优势和合作利益共同点，延展宁夏在数字贸易发展中的价值链和产业链。

3. 强化通道金融运营协作能力

其一，加强与中央有关部门对接，争取"一带一路"通道建设专项资金、亚洲基础设施投资银行贷款、中央预算内投资等各类资金支持。加快通道关键基础设施 PPP 项目准备，申报列入国家示范项目。其二，培育壮大金融服务主体，组建宁夏"一带一路"通道建设金融服务联合体，开展金融支持宁夏"一带一路"通道建设的融资产品和债券融资创新，探索在宁夏综保区+外贸基地+特色园区设立中外合资的通道建设投资（私募）基金的可能性。其三，强化通道金融运营协作能力建设。在西部陆海新通道现有的合作基础之上，探索金融资源利益共享机制，推进各区域之间利益协调与补偿机制、风险联合防范工作机制。

4. 提升空中筑陆开放通道水平

其一，依托宁夏作为中国—中亚—西亚经济走廊和中蒙俄经济走廊的重要节点，积极争取国家支持推动宁夏增开、加密至沿线国家热点城市的国际航线，构建面向丝绸之路经济带沿线国家，连通东北亚、东南亚地区，辐射我国中西部省区的航线网络，将银川河东国际机场打造成为我国面向中亚、西亚的重要门户机场。其二，推动宁夏班列运营企业利用"中（国）—吉（尔吉斯斯坦）—乌（兹别克斯坦）"国际物流通道，打造自宁夏—新疆伊尔克什坦口岸至中亚、西亚、欧洲的"中阿快线"，开辟面向中亚五国、阿富汗、伊朗等的国际物流"第二通道"。不断夯实通道新支撑，谋划推进疆煤东运、蒙煤入境和中亚能源粮食入境新通道，积极融入对接西部陆海新通道，推动物流枢纽建设。

12.2.2 着力提升对外开放平台能级

1. 中阿博览会平台

其一,加强顶层设计,以"世界眼光、中国平台"来重新审视和定位中阿博览会,做好中长期发展规划,着力建设中国与阿拉伯国家政治对话、经贸合作、商事调节、法律服务、人文交流的总平台、总枢纽、总通道。争取国家发展改革委、商务部、丝路基金、亚投行及相关央企支持,高水平、高质量办好"一带一路"贸易投资促进大会。加强与外交部、商务部协调对接,将中阿合作论坛经贸投资类活动整合在中阿博览会期间举办,并形成机制性运行,提升中阿博览会经贸合作能级。通过打造"两平台、一中心、一引擎"(中阿命运共同体的重要服务平台、"一带一路"经济带有机衔接的核心平台、中国—阿拉伯国家新型投资贸易促进中心、推进内陆开放型经济发展的重要引擎),加快形成"外资+外贸"双向互济的开放合作新机制,助力中阿经贸合作走深走实,推动宁夏回族自治区对阿经贸合作实现新突破。其二,中海自贸区谈判可能会加快完成,在中国建设中海自贸区先行区势在必行,应加快研究并依托银川综合保税区,吸引中国与海合会国家商协会、知名企业以及国际机构等入驻,提供商贸投资、法务服务、金融、物流、数字信息、农业经济合作、文旅合作、专业人才等服务。其三,全面完善中阿轮办和中方主办"主宾国"机制,在中阿博览会下成立"'一带一路'中阿企业家联合会",加快促进中阿企业精英的交流与协作,让政策、资源、资本实现有效对接。加强对阿经贸和涉外法律法规和产业政策系统研究,借鉴广西、重庆有关中国—东盟研究平台经验,成立"中国—阿拉伯国家经贸法律研究中心",为企业"走出去""引进来"提供决策咨询。其四,以中阿博览会为牵引、中国(宁夏)国际葡萄酒文化旅游博览会、"西部数谷"算力产业大会等高层次国际合作平台紧密协同,加快构建国际会展经济新发展格局,深入探索西亚、中亚、北非和东盟等产业体系和宁夏"六新六特六优"产业合作潜能,形成促进宁夏联动发展的长效机制。

中阿经贸关系发展进程2023年度报告

2. 中国（宁夏）国际葡萄酒文化旅游博览会平台

其一，加强总体设计，全力推动宁夏葡萄酒业走向世界，让世界葡萄酒业融入中国，促进世界葡萄酒业相互交流合作。推进葡萄酒与文化深度融合，打造具有宁夏风格、中国特色、世界水平的国际知名葡萄酒业专业展会，成为推动宁夏社会经济发展及对外开放的重要平台。其二，加强内涵发展，制定展会质量发展目标，通过国际展览业协会（UFI）认证和中国质量认证中心ISO9001质量管理体系认证，成为国内经过双认证的国际酒类高质量专业展会。其三，扩大展会影响力。力争每届我国国家领导人，各国政要，国际国内葡萄酒行业商（协）会、重要生产及营销企业负责人和国际国内酒类采购商、经销商等重要客商出席会议，成为国内外酒行业的重要盛会。其四，加强同世界主要葡萄酒国家及国内葡萄酒产区与销区的交流合作，不断提升博览会影响力。探索在法国、美国、德国等国家合作举办中国（宁夏）国际葡萄酒博览会，让国内外更多的消费者了解和关注宁夏贺兰山东麓葡萄酒产区，引领中国葡萄酒更好地融入世界。

3. "西部数谷"算力产业大会平台

其一，"西部数谷"算力产业大会以"全球视野、算力合作，价值创新、驱动未来"为办会理念，推动算力行业深度融合、增强科技创新能力，全面助力西部乃至世界算力产业高质量发展，已成为荟萃行业精英的国际知名盛会、引领前沿趋势的专业展示舞台、汇聚全球资源的商贸合作平台。其二，该产业大会坚持国际化、专业化、市场化的办会方向，紧紧围绕行业最新发展趋势，紧盯前沿技术成果，聚焦大数据应用场景和人才培养，以"算"赋能，全力为企业搭建展示产品、促成合作的广阔舞台，全方位提升算力产业创新力、竞争力、影响力。其三，该产业人会注重营造开放合作生态。推动产学研用深度结合，引导产业链上下游企业有效衔接、融通发展，加快构建软硬件协同发展的产业生态。加强与"一带一路"共建国家交流，拓展合作领域、丰富合作项目，共享算力创新发展成果。

206

12.2.3　拓展区域合作，促进共赢发展

1. 加强黄河"几"字弯城市群合作

其一，加快基础设施互通互联，推进经济一体化。研究和发展经验证明，地理区位对于城市发展的影响是决定性的。企业向港口附近集聚，集聚又导致更高的劳动生产率，实现工资水平的提升。如果距离港口超过500公里，工资水平和到港口的距离就没有明显的关联，这也使黄河流域"几"字弯地区企业对科技含量高、市场需求大的项目产生畏难心理，转而追逐资源型、加工型项目。为此，加强通道建设和区域合作，是降低要素流动成本、产业梯度转移成本的重要途径，其一，加快5G网络建设，扩大千兆及以上光纤覆盖范围，建立物联网和工业互联网基础设施。提高工业互联网、人工智能、大数据的渗透率，推动传统优势产业向绿色化、智能化和数字化转型赋能。其二，协同4省区建设沿黄"几"字形高速城际铁路网，填补缺失线路，畅通瓶颈路段，加快形成至北向、东向、南向大通道建设，优化与内蒙古、陕西煤炭合作协商机制，打通清洁能源互补打捆外送通道。其三，发挥陕甘川宁毗邻地区经济联合会、呼包银榆经济区联席会等平台作用，强化与毗邻省区在产业协同发展、平台联动共建、市场信息共享等领域的合作。大力推动黄河流域"几"字弯地区人才、产业、科技、投资、文化、信息等方面的交流合作，全面融入"几"字弯地区创新链、产业链、供应链、资金链、人才链，实现区域内的互联互通，共享发展成果，推进经济一体化进程。

2. 加强同国家重大战略区域合作

加强京津冀协同发展、长江经济带发展、长三角一体化发展、粤港澳大湾区建设、海南自贸港等国家区域发展战略和区域重大战略对接交流合作，更好融入和支撑新发展格局。深化"国际知名企业入宁""央企入宁"计划机制建设，推动实施一批科技含量高、集聚带动作用大的好项目、大项目、高新技术项目。聚焦闽宁协作，深入贯彻习近平总书记关于深化东西部协作的重要指示精神，拓展产业对接、园区共建、商贸流通、

中阿经贸关系发展进程2023年度报告

展会活动等领域的合作交流，推动闽宁协作向更宽领域、更高水平、更深层次迈进，打造新时期东西部对口协作的新样板，续写"山海情"崭新篇章。

12.2.4 积极构筑对外开放新载体

1. 做好目标设计

围绕争取设立中国（宁夏）自由贸易试验区这个目标，聚焦内陆开放型经济试验区和中国葡萄及葡萄酒开放发展综合试验区建设两个重点，打造高水平对外开放新引擎，做大做强国家级开发区，率先在国家级开发区推行容缺审批、告知承诺制、先建后验等管理模式，强化开发区招商引资平台职能，培育和增强外贸发展新优势和新动能，稳步提升开发区对地区经济增长的贡献作用。

2. 加强制度创新

其一，对标自由贸易试验区目标，着力推进内陆开放型经济试验区制度创新，提升在国际分工中的地位和对外贸易的国际竞争力。借鉴《中国（上海）自由贸易试验区条例》及实施成功经验，进一步探索与国际接轨的全要素对外贸易开放新规则新模式，出台宁夏经济试验区相关法规，并在国家级经开区先试先行，逐步推进，逐步完善。其二，在税收体制创新方面，宁夏可进一步借鉴上海自贸区财政税收政策，大力推广已经在综合保税区试行过的财税政策，实施促进投资、贸易的税收政策，形成区别于试验区外的税收政策，促进贸易投资便利化。同时，还可以直接试行在上海自贸区采取的税收政策。如对试验区内企业以股份或出资比例等股权形式给予企业高端人才和紧缺人才的奖励等。其三，在金融体制创新方面，宁夏进行金融创新可进一步优化"内培外引"的模式，引进具有相当实力和影响力的金融机构，努力建设成为具有国际水平、金融机构集聚、金融业务繁荣的经济试验区。争取中国人民银行同意在宁夏国家级开放型产业园阶段性设立自由贸易账户制度。积极争取允许宁夏设立中外合资金融机构（主要是投资银行、保险公司、基金等），并提供配套政策支持，服务内陆开放型试验区建设。争取央行成立人民币境外结算中心，在离岸网点、离岸数额上给予更多的自由度。积极争取在宁夏设立亚投行代办处和丝路基金代办处，重点支持各种外向型产业园区建设。

3. 加强综保区建设

做强银川综合保税区和石嘴山B保，积极推动设施互联互通、产业优势互补、通关高效对接，重点发展口岸通关、保税加工、保税物流等外向型产业，打造贸易投资便利、功能特色突出、公共服务高效的海关特殊监管区域。加快发展银川跨境电商综试区，合理优化园区布局，强化跨境服务能力，提升产业集聚效应，加快构建集生产、贸易、结算、物流为一体的跨境电商产业链和生态圈。

12.2.5 着力提升产业核心竞争力

1. 强化外向型产业链布局人才链

聚焦"六新六特六优"和"十大产业链"外向型产业新赛道，绘制产业人才开发路线图，加快实施学科引领汇聚高层次人才计划，支持宁夏大学等高校化学工程技术、材料科学与工程材料、区域国别学等一级博士点建设，全面助推外向型产业体系可持续高质量发展。加强国际贸易、知识产权、数字经济和电子商务专业+外语水平的复合型人才培养。

2. 强化产业链构筑出口产品创新链

借鉴重庆引进外国资本和现金技术，提高出口产品附加值和技术含量，突出经济增长的内涵式拉动成功经验，进一步探索提高企业研发投入机制，培育一流出口创新型领军企业，开展未来外向型产业培育"沃土"行动。完善协作机制，建设国内外"飞地"研发中心、科技成果育成平台和离岸孵化器，构建"东部、国外（欧美为主）研发+宁夏转化"科技成果落地新机制。推广宁夏大学绿色技术创新与节能降碳先进技术团队成果商品化和产业化成功经验，推动中阿、中非等绿色经济和绿色产业高质量合作。

中阿经贸关系发展进程2023年度报告

3. 聚焦外向型产业链优化教育链

激发宁夏高校对外向型产业发展的支撑效能，沿出口产业链优化学科设置，新增和调整相关专业，形成覆盖外向型产业的创新平台矩阵。同时，支持高校建立联合实验室，可与沙特、阿联酋、卡塔尔、伊拉克、伊朗等研究机构和大学合作，共同建立新材料、新能源、环保技术、食品技术等领域的联合实验室，推动双方科研资源和创新成果的共享。

2023年中阿经贸合作大事记

1月1日，沙特交通和物流服务大臣萨利赫会见陈伟庆。双方就加强两国交通和物流领域合作交换了意见。

1月12日，驻毛里塔尼亚大使李柏军会见毛外交合作与海外侨民部部长马尔祖克，就双方共同关心的重大问题和推动两国友好关系发展深入交换意见。

1月18日，驻科威特大使张建卫会见科商务国务大臣阿卜杜勒阿齐兹，就落实习近平主席和米沙勒王储会晤成果、加强两国战略对接、深化务实合作等交换意见。

1月19日，驻毛里塔尼亚大使李柏军会见毛内政与地方分权部部长拉明，就双方共同关心的问题和推动两国友好关系发展深入交换意见。

1月26日，驻巴勒斯坦办事处主任郭伟同巴勒斯坦总理府秘书长加尼姆共同签署中国外交部援助巴勒斯坦民生物资交接证书。

2月5日，中国香港特区行政长官李家超开始对沙特阿拉伯进行访问，他先后与沙特投资大臣哈立德·法利赫、沙特公共投资基金副主席土耳基·诺瓦西尔分别会面，就双方建立更密切经贸关系交流意见。

2月6日至7日，香港特别行政区行政长官李家超对阿联酋进行正式访问。由香港贸易发展局组织、来自不同领域的30多位香港商界高级别代表随同访问。

2月8日，驻阿尔及利亚大使李健会见 MADAR 集团总裁阿马拉·沙特，就推动双边企业合作交换了意见。

211

2月9日，中国红十字会向叙利亚援助首批医疗物资运抵大马士革。驻叙利亚大使史宏微及叙地方行政管理与环境部副部长穆阿塔兹、叙红新月会主席哈立德等前往机场迎接。

2月14日，廖力强大使会见埃及农业部部长卡斯尔，就促进中埃合作进行交流。

2月15日，由中国冶金科工股份有限公司（中国中冶）承建的科威特医保医院项目杰赫拉省分院试运营仪式在杰赫拉省举行，标志着该项目整体完成初步交付。

2月15日，第六届埃及石油展览会在埃及首都开罗落下帷幕。展会期间，中国企业展台吸引众多参观者，有望与中东地区油气企业进一步加强合作。

2月16日，驻毛里塔尼亚大使李柏军会见毛卫生部部长达希，双方就进一步加强中毛两国医疗卫生领域交流合作交换了意见。

2月18日，国家主席习近平致电第36届非洲联盟峰会，向非洲国家和人民表示热烈祝贺。

2月20日，廖力强大使应邀出席中埃企业家研讨会，并围绕中国经济形势、中埃经贸合作成果与潜力、"一带一路"倡议框架下推动对埃投资、落实中阿峰会成果等做主旨演讲。

2月21日，伊拉克政府与包括中国企业在内的三家能源公司签署6处油气田的勘探与开发协议。

2月21日，驻科威特大使张建卫会见科财政大臣兼经济事务和投资事务国务大臣阿卜杜勒瓦哈卜，就推动中科务实合作等议题交换意见。

2月23日，中国驻约旦大使陈传东出席在安曼举行的"支持巴勒斯坦国家就业战略"高级别伙伴会议。

2月26日，驻叙利亚大使史宏微拜会叙计划与国际合作署署长哈利勒，就加强双边援助合作交换意见。

2月28日，张益明大使出席中国工商银行"碳中和"主题绿色债券在纳斯达克迪拜交易所上市摇铃仪式。

3月2日，中毛"对口医院"合作项目援毛医疗物资交接仪式在毛首都医院举行。在李柏军大使的见证下，黑龙江省眼科医院院长阚泽与毛首都医院负责人穆克塔尔签署向毛方捐赠药品、器械等医疗物资的交接证书。

3月3日，驻突尼斯大使万黎拜会娜杰拉总理，就双边关系、务实合作和共同关心的国际问题进行交流。

3月5日，科威特金融公司（KFH）举办专场中国汽车展，驻科威特大使张建卫、科威特金融公司代理首席执行官阿卜杜勒瓦哈卜等出席。

3月7日，首届中国工业品展会在阿布扎比中阿产能合作示范园隆重举行。

3月7日，外交部亚非司组织阿拉伯国家驻华使节代表团赴中航技进出口有限责任公司参观考察。17个阿拉伯国家驻华使馆和阿盟驻华代表处大使、临时代办及外交官共20人参加。

3月7日，2023年中东电信资源展在阿联酋迪拜举行。本届展会期间，中国移动国际有限公司（中移国际）宣布，中移国际阿曼MC1网络服务接入点（MC1 PoP）成功投产。

3月15日，驻苏丹使馆临时代办张向华会见苏能源和石油部部长穆罕默德·阿卜杜拉，双方就中苏石油领域合作交换了意见。

3月15日，由中国企业海尔智家投资的海尔埃及生态园在埃及斋月十日城举行奠基仪式。

3月16日，驻叙利亚大使史宏微拜会叙地方行政管理和环境部部长马赫卢夫，就加强双边合作等议题交换意见。

3月17日，由中华人民共和国商务部和阿联酋经济部主办的"投资中国年"暨中国—阿联酋投资论坛在阿联酋迪拜举行，来自中阿两国的70多家企业参加论坛。

3月22日，倪汝池大使到任拜会巴林协商会议主席阿里。双方就中巴关系和深化两国议会合作深入交换意见。

3月22日，驻阿尔及利亚大使李健会见阿经济复兴委员会主席卡梅尔·穆拉，使馆经商参赞陈忠等参加会见。

3月28日，国家主席习近平同沙特王储兼首相穆罕默德通电话。

4月12日，中国能建国际建设集团与沙特阿吉兰兄弟公司和摩洛哥盖亚能源公司签署摩洛哥南部大区绿氢项目合作备忘录。这是继签署埃及绿氢项目合作开发备忘录后，中国能建发挥全产业链一体化优势，加强全球第三方市场合作，在海外新能源及"新能源+"市场开发取得的又一重要成果，实现了西北非区域市场新突破。

5月16日，满载来自阿联酋6.5万吨液化天然气的"马尔文"轮在中国海油广东大鹏液化天然气接收站完成接卸，这船货物是我国首单以人民币结算的进口液化天然气，标志着我国在油气贸易领域的跨境人民币结算交易探索迈出实质性一步。

5月16日，中国工商银行沙特吉达分行开业仪式暨人民币业务推介会在沙特阿拉伯首都利雅得举行。

5月18日，2023年中阿企业家峰会开幕式在迪拜举行。

5月19日，国家主席习近平向阿拉伯国家联盟首脑理事会会议轮值主席沙特国王萨勒曼致贺信，祝贺第32届阿拉伯国家联盟首脑理事会会议在吉达召开。

5月21日，以"美好的时代、共同的愿景"为主题的第六届中阿博览会推介会在沙特阿拉伯首都利雅得举行。

5月24日，沙特愿景工业公司与中国新能源科技公司TCL中环签署战略合作协议，计划成立合资公司，并在沙特投资建设光伏晶体晶片工厂项目。

5月24日，中阿博览会秘书处、自治区商务厅赴阿联酋，在迪拜举办第六届中阿博览会阿联酋推介会。

5月29日，中国—阿拉伯国家合作论坛第十八次高官会在四川成都举行。

6月1日，由宁夏贸促会与广东省贸促会、广州市贸促会共同举办的2023年中国—阿拉伯国家企业合作洽谈会在广州举行。

6月4日，率团访问卡塔尔的中国国家能源局局长章建华在多哈拜会卡塔尔副埃米尔阿卜杜拉·本·哈马德·阿勒萨尼并与卡塔尔能源事务国务大臣、卡塔尔能源公司总裁兼首席执行官萨阿德·卡阿比会谈。

6月11日，中阿合作论坛第十届企业家大会暨第八届投资研讨会在沙特阿拉伯首都利雅得举行，来自20余个国家的逾3000名代表参会。

6月11日，沙特投资部与中国创新型出行科技公司华人运通签署价值56亿美元的合作协议，计划成立从事汽车研发、制造与销售的合资公司。

6月14日，国家主席习近平在人民大会堂同来华进行国事访问的巴勒斯坦总统阿巴斯举行会谈。两国元首宣布建立中巴战略伙伴关系。

6月19日，约旦最大私营公司Manaseer Group与中国汽车公司长城华冠签署战略合作协议，计划在约旦成立从事电动汽车生产、销售的合资公司。

6月20日，中国石油与卡塔尔能源公司在卡塔尔首都多哈签署北方气田扩容项目合作文件。

6月25日，中国政府援助埃及二号卫星初样星交付仪式在埃及航天城卫星总装集成测试（AIT）中心举行。此次交付使埃及成为首个具备卫星总装、集成和测试能力的非洲国家。

6月29日，国家副主席韩正在湖南长沙出席第三届中非经贸博览会开幕式并致辞。

7月6日，中国（甘肃）—沙特阿拉伯荒漠化防治与绿色产业合作对接会在兰州召开。甘肃省政协副主席霍卫平和沙特投资部副部长赛乐·阿里出席活动并致辞。

7月6日，第二十九届兰洽会在金城兰州盛大开幕。本届兰洽会邀请沙特阿拉伯、泰国担任主宾国，天津市、福建省担任主宾省（市）。主宾国、主宾省（市）将举办专题经贸洽谈活动。

7月8日，2023年中国—阿拉伯国家青年领袖对话会在西安市成功举办。

7月13日，由中共中央对外联络部、中央党校（国家行政学院）和宁夏回族自治区党委联合主办的第四届中国—阿拉伯国家政党对话会在银川开幕。

7月13日，阿联酋主权财富基金之一，CYVN Holdings 完成对中国智能电动汽车公司蔚来总计 11 亿美元的战略投资，收购蔚来 7% 股权。

7月13日，由中国铁建承建的阿尔及利亚东西高速公路贝贾亚连接线控制性工程西迪艾什隧道通车。

7月13日，比亚迪在摩洛哥举行品牌发布暨新车型上市发布会，面向摩洛哥市场正式推出三款全新纯电车型——汉 EV、唐 EV 和元 PLUS（海外称 BYD ATTO 3），并公布官方售价，正式开启比亚迪摩洛哥的新格局。

7月18日，国家主席习近平在人民大会堂同来华进行国事访问的阿尔及利亚总统特本举行会谈。

7月21日，沙特阿美石油公司完成对中国民营炼化企业荣盛石化总计 34 亿美元的战略投资，收购荣盛石化 10% 股权。

7月28日，国家主席习近平在成都会见来华出席第 31 届世界大学生夏季运动会开幕式并访华的毛里塔尼亚总统加兹瓦尼。

7月29日，商务部部长王文涛在成都会见毛里塔尼亚经济与可持续发展部部长萨利赫，双方就落实两国领导人重要共识、进一步深化中毛在贸易投资、基础设施、农业以及绿色发展等领域务实合作深入交换了意见。

7月30日，国务院总理李强在人民大会堂会见来华出席第 31 届世界大学生夏季运动会开幕式并访华的毛里塔尼亚总统加兹瓦尼。

8月10日，伊拉克总理穆罕默德·希亚·苏达尼出席由哈电国际总承包的伊拉克阿玛拉 2×125MW 单循环改联合循环电站项目发电剪彩活动。

8月14日，商务部部长王文涛在阿联酋阿布扎比会见阿联酋总统中国事务特使、穆巴达拉投资公司首席执行官哈勒敦，就落实两国元首重要共识，进一步发展全面战略伙伴关系，推动中阿共建"一带一路"经贸合作走深走实深入交换意见。

8月16日2时许，顺丰航空一架载有 90 余吨货物的全货机从我国首个专业货运机场——湖北鄂州花湖机场起飞，前往阿联酋首都阿布扎比。这标志着鄂州至阿布扎比国际货运航线正式开通，鄂州花湖机场货运范围进一步扩大。

8月24日，由中国电力建设集团（中国电建）承建的科威特七环路项目交付仪式在费尔瓦尼耶省举行。

8月27日11时40分，承载260多名旅客的3U3781航班从宁夏银川河东国际机场飞向迪拜，这标志着银川直飞迪拜航线复航。

9月2日至6日，以"开放引领发展，合作共赢未来"为主题的2023年中国国际服务贸易交易会在北京成功举办。中东国家精彩亮相，积极参与，"中东元素"成为本届服贸会上一道靓丽的风景线。

9月5日，中国银行利雅得分行开业。中国银行行长刘金、中国驻沙特大使陈伟庆、沙特央行行长阿依曼·阿尔·萨亚里（Ayman Al-Sayari）、沙特投资部副部长赛乐·哈布提（Saleh Khabti）出席开业仪式并致辞。

9月12日，首届"环境与气候投资论坛"在开罗以东的埃及新行政首都举行。福阿德在论坛期间接受新华社记者采访时表示，中国在环境和气候领域的技术适用于埃及，埃中两国在能源领域合作的机会正在扩大。

9月21日至24日，第六届中阿博览会在银川召开。第六届中阿博览会共形成合作成果403个，总投资金额1709.7亿元，项目涉及现代农业、清洁能源、医疗健康等多个领域。

9月22日，国家主席习近平在杭州西湖国宾馆会见来华出席第19届亚洲运动会开幕式的叙利亚总统巴沙尔。两国元首共同宣布建立中叙战略伙伴关系。

9月22日，国家主席习近平在杭州西湖国宾馆会见来华出席第19届亚洲运动会开幕式的科威特王储米沙勒。

9月25日，国务院总理李强在人民大会堂会见来华出席杭州第十九届亚洲运动会开幕式的叙利亚总统巴沙尔。

9月26日，外交部依托中阿改革发展研究中心在上海举办第四届中国—阿拉伯国家改革发展论坛。来自中国以及17个阿拉伯国家的专家学者参加。

10月17日至18日，第三届"一带一路"国际合作高峰论坛在北京举行。国家主席习近平出席高峰论坛开幕式发表主旨演讲，并为来华出席高峰论坛的嘉宾举行欢迎宴会和双边活动。

10月19日，国家主席习近平在人民大会堂会见来华出席第三届"一带一路"国际合作高峰论坛的埃及总理马德布利。

10月22日，中国—海合会6+1经贸部长会在广州举行。商务部部长王文涛、海合会秘书长布达维和阿曼、阿联酋、巴林、沙特、卡塔尔、科威特等海合会成员国经贸部门负责人出席会议并发言。

10月29日至31日，海合会国家驻华使节、主权财富基金驻华代表访问上海，出席上海—海合会国家投资合作座谈会，并实地考察上海高质量发展成就。

10月30日，为助力推动共建"一带一路"倡议不断走深走实，积极服务加快打造面向新时代的中非、中阿命运共同体，国家开发银行成功完成与埃及中央银行70亿元人民币贷款协议的全额发放工作。这是开发银行落实第三届"一带一路"国际合作高峰论坛合作成果，助力推动中非合作论坛"九项工程"的一项具体举措。

11月4日，中国石化与卡塔尔能源公司签署北部气田扩能项目二期一体化合作协议，包括为期27年的液化天然气长期购销协议和参股协议。

11月13日，第18届迪拜国际航空展在阿联酋迪拜阿勒马克图姆国际机场拉开帷幕。中国航空工业以"旋翼新时代"为主题参展，展示多型高新军贸产品，彰显中国航空工业实力，被航展组委会评为十大展商之一。

11月23日，"一带一路"重点农业项目迪拜中国农牧渔产品（欧威尔）批发市场开业仪式暨中国—中东国际农产品流通研讨会在迪拜欧威尔批发市场举办。

11月24日，北京大兴国际机场临空经济区国际创新中心中阿绿色发展合作中心启动仪式隆重举行，约旦哈希姆王国驻华大使胡萨姆·侯赛尼、阿尔及利亚民主人民共和国驻华参赞、合作主管思迈尔·哈乐发卫、沙特阿拉伯王国驻华大使馆商务处沙特阿拉伯商业专家杨丰等外交官以及20余位外方企业机构出席仪式。

11月26日，驻亚历山大总领事杨易出席在亚历山大商会举办的中国企业与埃及棉花出口商洽谈对接会。

11月26日，由湖北省人民政府、沙特投资部主办的"2023中国湖北—沙特经贸合作对接会"在沙特首都利雅得浓情上演。

11月27日，中国工商银行在纳斯达克迪拜交易所举行债券上市摇铃仪式。李旭航总领事为中国工商银行"一带一路"主题绿色债券成功上市摇铃。

11月27日，HDC·Together华为终端生态合作伙伴高峰论坛中东非专场在著名的迪拜歌剧院举行。此次峰会由华为与迪拜经济和旅游局（DET）以及沙特旅游局（STA）合作举办，旨在结合两者的优势和举措，促进创新、经济增长以及技术和旅游业的变革性发展。

11月27日，驻巴林大使倪汝池拜会巴林水电大臣亚希尔，双方就深化两国水电工程和新能源建设合作交换意见。

11月27日，中国电建集团向毛里塔尼亚努瓦克肖特大区捐赠太阳能灯具交接仪式在毛努瓦克肖特大区总部举行，驻毛里塔尼亚大使李柏军，毛石油、矿业与能源部秘书长布哈德，毛努瓦克肖特大区主席玛丽克，中国电建集团国际工程有限公司毛塔国别代表常云飞、中国驻毛里塔尼亚使馆负责经济事务的参赞席威出席仪式。

11月29日，驻巴勒斯坦办事处主任曾继新同联合国近东巴勒斯坦难民救济和工程处（UNRWA）对外伙伴关系部主任卡里姆签署现汇援助交接证书。

11月30日，中国驻阿尔及利亚大使李健应邀出席阿西部矿业铁路项目奠基仪式。阿总统特本为该项目进行奠基。

11月28日至30日，驻沙特大使陈伟庆应邀访问吉赞省并出席2023年吉赞投资论坛。

11月30日至12月1日，习近平主席特别代表、中共中央政治局常委、国务院副总理丁薛祥在迪拜出席世界气候行动峰会并发表致辞。

11月27日至30日，来自20个阿拉伯国家的驻华使节代表团赴海南参访并出席首届中阿青年发展论坛。使节们考察了三亚、文昌、海口等地，赞赏海南在自贸港建设、热带特色高效农业、航天高新技术和生态文明建设等领域取得的成就，期待同中国在生态、农业和青年交流等领域进一步深化合作。

11月30日，以"加强中阿青年伙伴关系，推动构建开放型世界经济"为主题的中阿青年发展论坛在海口举办。外交部中阿合作论坛事务大使李琛、22个阿拉伯国家驻华使节和外交官、中阿双方各领域青年代表等200余人出席论坛。

12月2日，中国驻阿尔及利亚大使李健、阿高教和科研部秘书长阿卜杜勒卡里姆·本特利斯出席华为阿尔及利亚电讯公司与阿高教和科研部2023年度"未来种子"旗舰项目闭幕式并致辞。

12月4日12时10分，我国在酒泉卫星发射中心使用长征二号丙运载火箭，成功将援埃及二号卫星发射升空，卫星顺利进入预定轨道，发射任务获得圆满成功。

12月5日，中国—阿拉伯国家银行联合体第二届理事会会议在埃及开罗召开。本届理事会由埃及国民银行担任轮值主席行。

12月6日，2023年第二届中约友好对话会在京举行。本届对话会以"'一带一路'十周年：时代成就梦想青年引领未来"为主题，来自中国、约旦、苏丹、埃及等多国青年代表共200余人参加了对话会。

12月6日，中国国家航天局张克俭局长与埃及航天局谢里夫·塞德基局长在北京签署《中华人民共和国政府和阿拉伯埃及共和国政府关于空间合作及和平利用外层空间的谅解备忘录》和《中国国家航天局与埃及航天局关于国际月球科研站的合作协定》。

12月6日，驻毛里塔尼亚大使李柏军出席中国驻毛里塔尼亚使馆向毛基法市捐赠汽油机抽水泵、手压式喷雾器等设备物资仪式，基法市长克布德出席捐赠仪式并同李大使共同签署交接证书。

12月7日，驻科威特大使张建卫会见科商工大臣兼青年事务国务大臣穆罕默德。

12月7日，驻叙利亚使馆援助修缮小学项目竣工仪式在大马士革举

220

行，史宏微大使及叙教育部部长马勒提尼出席仪式。

12月7日，驻阿联酋大使张益明应邀赴迪拜可持续城出席"中阿（联酋）绿色价值峰会——未来可持续城市"主题活动并致辞。第十三届全国政协副主席辜胜阻、万科集团创始人王石出席本次活动。

12月8日，国家国际发展合作署副署长刘俊峰在昆明会见来华出席第二届中国—印度洋地区发展合作论坛的埃及环境部部长助理谢琳。双方就加强中埃发展合作深入交换意见。

12月9日，广东省委常委、常务副省长张虎在广州会见沙特投资大臣哈立德·法利赫一行，并出席沙特"能源、石化及加工业"投资研讨会。

12月10日，商务部部长王文涛在京会见来访的沙特投资大臣法利赫。双方重点就落实两国领导人共识、深化双边经贸合作等交换意见。

12月10日，第六届中国—阿拉伯国家广播电视合作论坛在杭州举行。中共中央政治局委员、中宣部部长李书磊以视频方式出席开幕式并致辞。

12月10日，工业和信息化部部长金壮龙在北京会见沙特投资大臣哈立德·法利赫。双方就加强中沙两国工业和信息化领域合作进行交流。

12月11日0时45分，东航MU223"上海—开罗"航班从上海浦东国际机场起飞，这是中国航空公司首次开通由上海直飞北非的定期客运航线。

12月11日，由北京市贸促会、沙特—中国商务理事会共同主办的"沙特—北京投资贸易洽谈会"在京举办。阿吉兰兄弟控股集团等50多家沙特企业与70余家北京市高新科技企业面对面深入洽谈，涉及人工智能、生物医药、金融服务、商务服务、工程设计、产品贸易等多个领域。

12月12日，上海机场集团与阿布扎比机场集团签署合作谅解备忘录，共同促进在机场经营、管理、运作和营销等方面的交流合作。

12月12日，驻摩洛哥大使李昌林在使馆举办中摩企业家招待会，欢迎中外企业家联合会代表团访摩。

12月13日，深圳证券交易所与阿布扎比交易所在阿联酋首都阿布扎比签署合作谅解备忘录，为两所合作与发展奠定基础。

12月13日，驻吉达总领事王奇敏应邀出席中国品牌商品（沙特）展览会开幕式。

12月17日，国家主席习近平致电科威特新任埃米尔米沙勒，祝贺他继任科威特埃米尔。

12月17日，国家主席习近平就科威特埃米尔纳瓦夫不幸逝世向科威特新任埃米尔米沙勒致唁电。

12月18日，习近平主席特使、全国人大常委会副委员长雪克来提·扎克尔在科威特首都科威特城出席科威特已故埃米尔纳瓦夫吊唁活动，科威特新任埃米尔米沙勒予以会见。

12月18日，由中国建筑股份有限公司埃及分公司（中建埃及）承建的埃及阿拉曼新城超高综合体项目D01住宅楼率先封顶，为整个项目主体结构封顶拉开序幕。

12月19日，国家主席习近平致电阿卜杜勒法塔赫·塞西，祝贺他当选连任阿拉伯埃及共和国总统。

12月20日，由中建集团主办、中建埃及分公司承办的中埃建筑可持续发展论坛在埃及新首都钻石酒店举行。

12月21日，驻亚历山大总领事杨易出席阿盟科技海运学院技能与就业论坛，并现场见证阿盟科技海运学院与中建埃及分公司签署合作协议。

后　记

《中阿经贸关系发展进程年度报告》已成为中阿经贸合作的重要文献和中阿博览会的重要成果之一。《中阿经贸关系发展进程 2023 年度报告》（中英文版）是在中阿博览会秘书处和宁夏回族自治区商务厅指导下，由宁夏大学中国阿拉伯国家研究院组织国内外专家编写完成。本课题系统梳理了 2023 年中阿在贸易、投资、科技、农业、数字经济、生态、旅游等领域取得的新进展，描绘了中阿经贸关系发展的进程特征和发展趋势。

本课题组包括中文撰写团队和英文翻译团队。中文由李绍先、张前进、丁丽萍担任全书统稿工作，英文由宁夏大学外国语学院杨春泉带领的翻译团队完成。衷心感谢课题组每一位成员，他们不计名利，勤恳工作，以良好的学术素养，克服困难，顺利完成报告的撰写和翻译工作。感谢社会科学文献出版社、宁夏商务厅和宁夏大学对本报告给予的支持和帮助。如没有以上团队成员、机构的大力支持，本书不可能顺利出版。

本报告具体分工如下：

统稿

李绍先　宁夏大学中国阿拉伯国家研究院

张前进　宁夏大学中国阿拉伯国家研究院

丁丽萍　阳光出版社

中文章节撰写

前　言　李绍先　宁夏大学中国阿拉伯国家研究院

第一章　王　诚　毛小菁　商务部国际贸易经济合作研究院西亚非洲所

第二章　杨韶艳　宁夏大学经济管理学院

第三章　姜英梅　中国社会科学院西亚非洲研究所

第四章　陈　诚　商务部国际贸易经济合作研究院西亚非洲所

第五章　陈玉香　宁夏大学中国阿拉伯国家研究院

第六章　陆如泉　郎峰翘　段艺璇　刘佳　中国石油集团经济技术研究院

第七章　王晓宇　复旦大学国际问题研究院中东研究中心

第八章　郝诗羽　宁夏大学中国阿拉伯国家研究院

第九章　冯　燚　宁夏大学中国阿拉伯国家研究院

第十章　许丽君　宁夏大学前沿交叉学院

第十一章　杨子实　宁夏师范大学

第十二章　张前进　宁夏大学中国阿拉伯国家研究院

大事记　陈玉香　宁夏大学中国阿拉伯国家研究院

英文章节译者

前　言　冯汝源　宁夏大学外国语学院

第一章　杜　玮　宁夏大学外国语学院

第二章　刘　燕　宁夏大学外国语学院

第三章　洪春梅　宁夏大学外国语学院

第四章　杨春泉　宁夏大学外国语学院

第五章　陈玉香　宁夏大学中国阿拉伯国家研究院

第六章　王军礼　宁夏医科大学外国语学院

第七章　刘艳芬　宁夏大学外国语学院

第八章　李　霞　宁夏大学外国语学院

第九章　杨春泉　宁夏大学外国语学院

后 记

第十章　浦玉吉　自由译者

第十一章　冯汝源　宁夏大学外国语学院

第十二章　马海燕　宁夏立爱教育咨询有限公司

大事记　陈玉香　宁夏大学中国阿拉伯国家研究院

英文审校　杨春泉　Carolyn Stent

225

Chapter 3 Hong Chunmei, School of Foreign Languages and Cultures, Ningxia University

Chapter 4 Yang Chunquan, School of Foreign Languages and Cultures, Ningxia University

Chapter 5 Chen Yuxiang, China Institute for Arab Studies, Ningxia University

Chapter 6 Wang Junli, School of Foreign Languages and Cultures, Ningxia Medical University

Chapter 7 Liu Yanfen, School of Foreign Languages and Cultures, Ningxia University

Chapter 8 Li Xia, School of Foreign Languages and Cultures, Ningxia University

Chapter 9 Yang Chunquan, School of Foreign Languages and Cultures, Ningxia University

Chapter 10 Pu Yuji, Freelance Translator

Chapter 11 Feng Ruyuan, School of Foreign Languages and Cultures, Ningxia University

Chapter 12 Ma Haiyan, Ningxia Li Ai Education Consulting Co., Ltd

Chronology Chen Yuxiang, China Institute for Arab Studies, Ningxia University

English Editors and Proofreaders: Yang Chunquan, Carolyn Stent

Postscript

Zhang Qianjin, China Institute for Arab Studies, Ningxia University

Ding Liping, Sunshine Publishing House

Chapter authors

Preface Li Shaoxian, China Institute for Arab Studies, Ningxia University

Chapter 1 Wang Cheng, Mao Xiaojing, Institute of West-Asian and African Studies, Chinese Academy of International Trade and Economic Cooperation, Ministry of Commerce

Chapter 2 Yang Shaoyan, School of Economics and Management, Ningxia University

Chapter 3 Jiang Yingmei, Institute of West-Asian and African Studies, Chinese Academy of Social Sciences

Chapter 4 Chen Cheng, Institute of West-Asian and African Studies, Chinese Academy of International Trade and Economic Cooperation, Ministry of Commerce

Chapter 5 Chen Yuxiang, China Institute for Arab Studies, Ningxia University

Chapter 6 Lu Ruquan, Lang Fengqiao, Duan Yixuan, Liujia, CNPC Economics and Technology Research Institute

Chapter 7 Wang Xiaoyu, Center for Middle Eastern Studies, Institute of International Studies, Fudan University

Chapter 8 Hao Shiyu, China Institute for Arab Studies, Ningxia University

Chapter 9 Feng Yi, China Institute for Arab Studies, Ningxia University

Chapter 10 Xu Lijun, School of Advanced Interdisciplinary Studies, Ningxia University

Chapter 11 Yang Zishi, Ningxia Normal University

Chapter 12 Zhang Qianjin, China Institute for Arab Studies, Ningxia University;

Chronology Chen Yuxiang, China Institute for Arab Studies, Ningxia University

Translators of the English version

Preface Feng Ruyuan, School of Foreign Languages and Cultures, Ningxia University

Chapter 1 Du Wei, School of Foreign Languages and Cultures, Ningxia University

Chapter 2 Liu Yan, School of Foreign Languages and Cultures, Ningxia University

Postscript

The Development Process of China-Arab States Economic and Trade Relations Annual Report has become an important document of China-Arab States economic and trade cooperation and an important report released by the China-Arab States Expo to the public. Under the guidance of the Secretariat of the China-Arab States Expo and the Department of Commerce of Ningxia, *The Development Process of China-Arab States Economic and Trade Relations 2023 Annual Report* (both in Chinese and the English version) was organized and completed by China Institute for Arab Studies at Ningxia University. The research systematically reviewed the new progress made by China-Arab States in 2023 in the fields of trade, investment, technology, agriculture, digital economy, ecology, tourism, etc. and described the process characteristics and the development trends of China-Arab States economic and trade relations.

The research group included a Chinese writing team and an English translation team. The Chinese version was reviewed by Li Shaoxian, Zhang Qianjin and Ding Liping, and English version was translated by Yang Chunquan from the School of Foreign Languages and Cultures at Ningxia University and his translation team. We want to express our sincere gratitude to all for their diligent work, overcoming difficulties and successfully completing the report with good academic standards, regardless of fame and fortune. We would like to thank Zhou Zhijing, editor at the Social Sciences Academic Press, for her hard work, and the Social Sciences Academic Press, Department of Commerce of Ningxia and Ningxia University for their support and assistance in completing this report. Without the strong support of the team members and institutions mentioned above, this book could not have been successfully published.

The specific division of labor in this report is as follows:
Chief Compiler
Li Shaoxian, China Institute for Arab Studies, Ningxia University

On December 21, Consul General Yang Yi in Alexandria attended the Skills and Employment Forum of the Arab League Science, Technology and Maritime Academy and witnessed the signing of a cooperation agreement between the Arab League Science, Technology and Maritime Academy and Egyptian branch of China State Construction Engineering Corporation (CSCEC Egypt).

a memorandum of understanding on cooperation to jointly promote exchanges and cooperation in airport management, operation and marketing.

On December 12, Ambassador to Morocco Li Changlin hosted a reception for Chinese and Moroccan entrepreneurs at the embassy to welcome the delegation of the China-Foreign Entrepreneurs Federation to visit Morocco.

On December 13, Shenzhen Stock Exchange and Abu Dhabi Securities Exchange (ADX) inked a memorandum of understanding on cooperation in Abu Dhabi, the capital of the United Arab Emirates, laying the foundation for cooperation and development between the two sides.

On December 13, Consul General Wang Qimin in Jeddah was invited to attend the opening ceremony of the Chinese Brand Products (Saudi Arabia) Exhibition.

On December 17, President Xi Jinping sent a congratulatory message to the new Emir Sheikh Meshal Al-Ahmad Al-Jaber Al-Sabah of Kuwait on his succession as Emir of Kuwait.

On December 17, President Xi Jinping sent a message of condolence to the new Emir Sheikh Meshal Al-Ahmad Al-Jaber Al-Sabah of Kuwait over the passing of Emir Sheikh Nawaf Al-Ahmad Al-Jaber Al-Sabah of Kuwait.

On December 18, President Xi Jinping's special envoy and vice chairman of the Standing Committee of the National People's Congress, Shohrat Zakir, attended the mourning event for Kuwait's late Emir Sheikh Nawaf al-Ahmad Al-Sabah in Kuwait City, the capital of Kuwait, and was met by the new Emir of Kuwait, Mishal.

On December 18, a ceremony was held for the capping of the D01 residential building of the high-rise complex project, being constructed by the Egyptian branch of China State Construction Engineering Corporation (CSCEC Egypt) in the Alamein Downtown Towers Project in Egypt's New Alamein City, which has started capping its main structures.

On December 19, 2023, President Xi Jinping sent a congratulatory message to Abdel Fattah El-Sisi on his reelection as President of the Arab Republic of Egypt.

On December 20, the China-Egypt Construction Sustainable Development Forum, hosted by China Construction Group and organized by Egyptian branch of China State Construction Engineering Corporation (CSCEC Egypt), was held at the Diamond Hotel in Egypt's new capital.

Cooperation Agency Liu Junfeng, met with Assistant Minister of the Ministry of Environment of Egypt Xie Lin, who was in China to attend the Second China-Indian Ocean Development Cooperation Forum in Kunming. The two sides had an in-depth exchange of views on strengthening China-Egypt development cooperation.

On December 9, member of the Standing Committee of the Guangdong Provincial Party Committee and Executive Vice Governor Zhang Hu met with Minister of Investment of Saudi Arabia Khalid Al-Falih and his delegation in Guangzhou and attended the Saudi Arabia "Energy, Petrochemical and Processing Industry" Investment Seminar.

On December 10, Minister of Commerce Wang Wentao met with the Minister of Investment of Saudi Arabia Khalid Al-Falih in Beijing. The two sides had an exchange of views on implementing leaders' consensus and deepening bilateral trade and economic cooperation.

On December 10, the 6th China-Arab States Broadcasting and Television Cooperation Forum was held in Hangzhou. Li Shulei, a member of the Political Bureau of the Communist Party of China (CPC) Central Committee and head of the Publicity Department of the CPC Central Committee, addressed the opening ceremony via video link.

On December 10, Minister of Industry and Information Technology Jin Zhuanglong met with Investment Minister of Saudi Arabia Khalid Al-Falih in Beijing. The two sides exchanged views on strengthening cooperation between China and Saudi Arabia in the fields of industry and informatization.

At 00:45 Beijing time on December 11, China Eastern Airlines flight MU223 "Shanghai-Cairo" took off from Shanghai Pudong International Airport. This is the first passenger flight from Shanghai to North Africa operated by a Chinese airline,

On December 11, the "Saudi Arabia-Beijing Investment and Trade Fair," co-organized by Beijing Council for the Promotion of International Trade and Saudi Arabia-China Business Council, was held in Beijing. More than 50 companies from Saudi Arabia including Ajlan Brothers Holding Group held face-to-face in-depth negotiations with more than 70 high-tech companies in Beijing, covering artificial intelligence, biomedicine, financial services, business services, engineering design, product trade and other fields.

On December 12, Shanghai Airport Authority and Abu Dhabi Airports signed

launch mission was a complete success.

On December 5, the second meeting of the Board of Directors of the China-Arab Countries Interbank Association was held in Cairo, Egypt. The National Bank of Egypt served as the rotating chairman of this board.

On December 6, the Second China-Jordan Friendship Dialogue was held in Beijing under the theme "The 10th Anniversary of the Belt and Road Initiative: Times Makes Dreams Come True, and the Youth Leads Us into the Future." More than 200 youth representatives from China, Jordan, Sudan, Egypt and other countries attended the dialogue.

On December 6, Director of the China National Space Administration Zhang Kejian, and Director of the Egyptian Space Agency Sherif Mohamed Sedky, signed *the Memorandum of Understanding on Space Cooperation and the Peaceful Uses of Outer Space between the Government of the People's Republic of China and the Government of the Arab Republic of Egypt* and *the Cooperation Agreement on the International Lunar Research Station between the China National Space Administration and the Egyptian Space Agency* in Beijing.

On December 6, Ambassador to Mauritania Li Baijun attended the ceremony where the Chinese Embassy in Mauritania donated gasoline water pumps, hand-pressure sprayers and other equipment to Kiffa, Mauritania. Kiffa Mayor Kebud attended the donation ceremony and signed the handover certificate with ambassador Li.

On December 7, Ambassador to Kuwait Zhang Jianwei met with Kuwaiti Minister of Commerce and Industry and State Minister for Youth Affairs Mohammed Al-Aiban.

On December 7, the completion ceremony of the primary school renovation project assisted by the Chinese Embassy in Syria was held in Damascus. Ambassador to Syrian Shi Hongwei and Syrian Minister of Education Muhammad Amer Mardini attended the ceremony.

On December 7, Ambassador to the UAE Zhang Yiming was invited to attend the theme event of "China-Arab (UAE) Green Value Summit-Future Sustainable Cities" in Dubai Sustainable City and delivered a speech. Vice Chairman of the 13th National Committee of the Chinese People's Political Consultative Conference Gu Shengzu, and founder of Vanke Group Wang Shi attended the activity.

On December 8, Vice Director of the National International Development

On November 29, Head of Office of the People's Republic of China to the State of Palestine Zeng Jixin and the Director of Partnerships with the UNRWA Department of External Relations Karim Amer signed a certificate for the handover of cash aid.

On November 30, Ambassador to Algeria Li Jian was invited to attend the groundbreaking ceremony of the Western Mining Railway Project in Algeria. Algerian President Tebboune laid the foundation for the project.

From November 28 to 30, Ambassador to Saudi Arabia Chen Weiqing was invited to visit Jizan Province and attend the 2023 Jizan Investment Forum.

From November 30 to December 1, Ding Xuexiang, President Xi Jinping's Special Representative, Member of the Standing Committee of the Political Bureau of the CPC Central Committee and Vice Premier of the State Council, attended the World Climate Action Summit in Dubai and delivered a speech.

From November 27 to 30, a delegation of envoys from 20 Arab countries visited Hainan and attended the first China-Arab Youth Development Forum. The envoys visited Sanya, Wenchang, Haikou and other places, and praised Hainan's achievements in the construction of free trade ports, tropical characteristic high-efficiency agriculture, aerospace high-tech and ecological civilization construction, and looked forward to further deepening cooperation with China in the fields of ecology, agriculture and youth exchanges.

On November 30, the China-Arab Youth Development Forum with the theme of "Strengthening China-Arab Youth Partnership and Promoting the Construction of an Open World Economy" was held in Haikou. More than 200 people attended the forum, including Li Chen, ambassador for China-Arab States Cooperation Forum Affairs of the Ministry of Foreign Affairs, envoys and diplomats from 22 Arab countries to China, and youth representatives from various fields of China and Arab countries.

On December 2, Ambassador to Algeria Li Jian and Secretary General of the Ministry of Higher Education and Scientific Research of Algeria Mr. Abdelhakim Ben Tellis attended the closing ceremony and delivered a speech of the 2023 "Seeds for the Future" flagship project of Huawei Telecom Algeria and the Ministry of Higher Education and Scientific Research of Algeria.

At 12:10 on December 4, China successfully launched the Egypt-aided satellite MISRSAT-2 using the Long March 2C carrier rocket at the Jiuquan Satellite Launch Center. The satellite entered the predetermined orbit smoothly and the

Airside Economic Zone of Beijing Daxing International Airport was grandly held. Ambassador of the Hashemite Kingdom of Jordan to China Hussam Husseini, Counselor and Cooperation Director of the People's Democratic Republic of Algeria in China Simael Khalfawi, Saudi Arabian business expert of the Commercial Department of the Embassy of the Kingdom of Saudi Arabia in China Yang Feng, and other diplomats as well as more than 20 foreign enterprises and institutions attended the ceremony.

On November 26, Consul General Yang Yi in Alexandria attended the negotiation and matchmaking meeting between Chinese companies and Egyptian cotton exporters held at the Alexandria Chamber of Commerce.

On November 26, 2023 China (Hubei)-Saudi Arabia Economic and Trade Cooperation Matchmaking Conference, hosted by the People's Government of Hubei Province and the Ministry of Investment of Saudi Arabia, was held in Riyadh, the capital of Saudi Arabia.

On November 27, ICBC held a bond listing bell ringing ceremony at the Nasdaq Dubai Exchange. Consul General Li Xuhang rang the bell for the successful listing of ICBC's "Belt and Road" themed green bonds.

On November 27, the HDC Together Huawei Terminal Ecosystem Partner Summit Middle East and Africa was held at the famous Dubai Opera House. The summit was jointly organized by Huawei, Dubai Economy and Tourism (DET) and Saudi Arabia Tourism Authority (STA), aiming to combine the advantages and initiatives of both parties to promote innovation, economic growth, and transformative development of technology and tourism.

On November 27, Ambassador to Bahrain Ni Ruchi paid a visit to Bahraini Minister of Electricity and Water Affairs Yasser bin Ibrahim Humaidan. The two sides exchanged views on deepening cooperation in hydropower projects and new energy construction between the two countries.

On November 27, the handover ceremony of solar lamps donated by China Power Construction Group to Nouakchott Region of Mauritania was held at the headquarters of Nouakchott Region. Ambassador to Mauritania Li Baijun, Secretary General of the Ministry of Petroleum, Mines and Energy of Mauritania Bouhad, Chairman of Nouakchott Region of Mauritania Malik, China Power Construction Group International Engineering Co., Ltd. Mauritanian Country Representative Chang Yunfei and our embassy's Counselor in charge of economic affairs Xi Wei attended the ceremony.

was held in Guangzhou. Minister of Commerce Wang Wentao, Secretary General of the Gulf Cooperation Council Jasem Al Budaiwi, and heads of economic and trade departments of GCC countries such as Oman, United Arab Emirates, Bahrain, Saudi Arabia, Qatar and Kuwait attended the opening ceremony of the forum and delivered speeches.

From October 29 to 31, envoys from GCC countries and representatives of sovereign wealth funds in China visited Shanghai, attended the Shanghai-GCC Investment Cooperation Seminar, and conducted on-site inspections of Shanghai's achievements in high-quality development.

On October 30, in order to help promote the joint construction of the "Belt and Road" Initiative to go deeper and more practical, and actively serve to accelerate the creation of a China-Africa and China-Arab community of shared future for the new era, the China Development Bank successfully completed the full disbursement of a loan agreement worth 7 billion yuan with the Central Bank of Egypt. This is a specific measure for the Development Bank to implement the cooperation results of the third "Belt and Road" International Cooperation Summit Forum and help promote the "Nine Projects" of the China-Africa Cooperation Forum.

On November 4, Sinopec and Qatar Energy Company signed an integrated cooperation agreement for the second phase of the North Field South (NFS) expansion project, including a 27-year long-term purchase and sales agreement for liquefied natural gas and an equity participation agreement.

On November 13, the 18th Dubai International Air Show kicked off at Al Maktoum International Airport in Dubai, UAE. China Aviation Industry participated in the exhibition with the theme of "New Era of Rotor Wings," displaying a variety of high-tech military trade products, demonstrating the strength of China's aviation industry, and was rated as one of the top ten exhibitors by the organizing committee of the air show.

On November 23, the opening ceremony of the Dubai China Agricultural, Animal Husbandry and Fishery Products (Owell) Wholesale Market, a key agricultural project of the "Belt and Road" Initiative, and the China-Middle East International Agricultural Products Distribution Seminar were held at the Dubai Owell Wholesale Market.

On November 24, the launching ceremony of the China-Arab States Green Development Cooperation Center of the International Innovation Center of the

Saudi Arabia Chen Weiqing, Saudi Central Bank Governor Ayman Al-Sayari, and Saudi Deputy Minister of Investment Saleh Khabti attended the opening ceremony and delivered speeches.

On September 12, the first "Environment and Climate Investment Forum" was held in Egypt's new administrative capital east of Cairo. During the forum, Fuad told Xinhua News Agency reporters that China's technology in the fields of environment and climate is suitable for Egypt, and the opportunities for cooperation between Egypt and China in the field of energy are expanding.

From September 21 to 24, the 6th China-Arab States Expo was held in Yinchuan. The Expo produced 403 cooperation outcomes with a total investment of 170.97 billion yuan, covering modern agriculture, clean energy, medical health and other fields.

On September 22, President Xi Jinping met at the West Lake State Guesthouse in Hangzhou with President of Syria Bashar al-Assad who is in China to attend the opening ceremony of the 19th Asian Games. The two heads of state jointly announced the establishment of China-Syria strategic partnership.

On September 22, President Xi Jinping met at the West Lake State Guesthouse in Hangzhou with Crown Prince of Kuwait Sheikh Meshal Al-Ahmad Al-Jaber Al-Sabah who is in China to attend the opening ceremony of the 19th Asian Games.

On September 25, Premier Li Qiang of the State Council met at the Great Hall of the People with President of Syria Bashar al-Assad who is in China to attend the opening ceremony of the 19th Asian Games Hangzhou.

On September 26, the Ministry of Foreign Affairs held the fourth China-Arab States Forum on Reform and Development supported by the China-Arab Research Center on Reform and Development (CARC) in Shanghai. Experts and scholars from China and 17 Arab countries participated int the forum.

From October 17 to 18, the third Belt and Road Forum for International Cooperation was held in Beijing. President Xi Jinping attended the opening ceremony of the forum and delivered a keynote speech. He also held a welcome banquet and bilateral activities for the guests attending the forum.

On October 19, President Xi Jinping met at the Great Hall of the People with Prime Minister of Egypt Mostafa Madbouly who is in China to attend the third Belt and Road Forum for International Cooperation (BRF).

On October 22, the China-GCC Economic and Trade Cooperation Forum

leaders' important consensus and further deepening China-Mauritania practical cooperation on trade and investment, infrastructure, agriculture and green development, among others.

On July 30, Premier Li Qiang met with Mauritanian President Mohamed Ould Cheikh Ghazouani in Beijing who was in China to attend the opening ceremony of the 31st summer edition of the FISU World University Games, at the Great Hall of the People.

On August 10, Iraqi Prime Minister Mohammed S. Al-Sudani attended the ribbon-cutting ceremony for the Iraqi Amara 2×125MW single-cycle to combined-cycle power plant project, which was undertaken by Harbin Electric International.

On August 14, Minister of Commerce Wang Wentao met with CEO of Mubadala Investment Company and the UAE Presidential Special Envoy to China Khaldoon Khalifa Al Mubarak in Abu Dhabi, the UAE. The two sides exchanged in-depth views on implementing the important consensus reached by heads of state, furthering comprehensive strategic partnership and promoting Belt and Road cooperation between China and the UAE.

At about 2:00 on August 16, a SF Airlines freighter carrying more than 90 tons of cargo took off from Ezhou Huahu Airport, China's first cargo-focused airport and headed for Abu Dhabi, the capital of the United Arab Emirates. This marks the official opening of the Ezhou-Abu Dhabi international cargo route, and the further expansion of the cargo scope of Ezhou Huahu Airport.

On August 24, the completion and handover ceremony of the 7th Ring Road Project, constructed by POWERCHINA, was held in Farwaniyah Province, Kuwait.

At 11:40 on August 27, flight 3U3781 carrying more than 260 passengers flew from Yinchuan Hedong International Airport in Ningxia to Dubai, marking the resumption of direct flights from Yinchuan to Dubai.

From September 2 to 6, 2023 China International Fair for Trade in Services (CIFTIS) with the theme of "Opening-up leads development, cooperation delivers the future" was successfully held in Beijing. Middle Eastern countries actively participated in the Fair. The "Middle Eastern elements" became a beautiful landscape at this year's Fair.

On September 5, the Bank of China (BOC) opened its branch in Saudi Arabia's capital Riyadh. President of Bank of China Liu Jin, Ambassador to

Saleh Khabti attended the meeting and delivered speeches.

On July 6, the 29th China Lanzhou Investment and Trade Fair (Lanzhou Fair) was grandly opened in Jincheng, Lanzhou. This year's Lanzhou Fair invited Saudi Arabia and Thailand as guest countries, and Tianjin and Fujian provinces as guest provinces (cities). The host country and host province (city) held special economic and trade negotiation activities.

On July 8, 2023 China-Arab States Youth Leaders Dialogue was successfully held in Xi'an.

On July 13, the fourth China-Arab States Political Parties Dialogue, which was co-organized by the International Department of the CPC Central Committee (IDCPC), the Party School of the Communist Party of China (CPC) Central Committee (National Academy of Governance), the CPC Committee of Ningxia Hui Autonomous Region, was held in Yinchuan.

On July 13, CYVN Holdings, one of the United Arab Emirates sovereign wealth funds, completed a USD 1.1 billion strategic investment in NIO, the Chinese smart electric vehicle company, acquiring a 7% stake.

On July 13, the Sidi Aich Tunnel, part of the Bejaia Highway project built by the China Railway Construction Corporation Limited (CRCC) in northern Algeria, has opened to traffic.

On July 13, BYD held a brand launch event in Morocco, officially introducing three of its all-electric models, the Han EV, Tang EV, and Yuan PLUS (known as BYD ATTO 3 overseas), to the Moroccan market.

On July 18, President Xi Jinping held talks with Algerian President Abdelmadjid Tebboune, who is on a state visit to China, at the Great Hall of the People.

On July 21, Saudi Aramco completed a strategic investment of USD 3.4 billion in Chinese private refining company Rongsheng Petrochemical, acquiring a 10% stake in Rongsheng Petrochemical Co. Ltd..

On July 28, President Xi Jinping met in Chengdu with Mauritanian President Mohamed Ould Cheikh Ghazouani who is in China to attend the opening ceremony of the 31st summer edition of the FISU World University Games and pay a visit to the country.

On July 29, Minister of Commerce Wang Wentao met with Mauritanian Minister of Economy and Sustainable Development Abdessalam Ould Mohamed Saleh in Chengdu. The two sides exchanged in-depth views on implementing

On June 4, Director of China's National Energy Administration Zhang Jianhua, who led a delegation to visit Qatar, paid a visit to Qatar's Deputy Emir Abdullah bin Hamad bin Khalifa Al Thani in Doha and held talks with Saad bin Sherida Al Kaabi, the Minister of State for Energy Affairs of Qatar and the President and CEO of Qatar Energy Company.

On June 11, the 10th Arab-China Business Conference and the 8th Investment Seminar of the China-Arab States Cooperation Forum were held in Riyadh, the capital of Saudi Arabia, with over 3000 representatives from more than 20 countries attending the forum.

On June 11, the Ministry of Investment of Saudi Arabia signed a cooperation agreement worth USD 5.6 billion with Chinese innovative travel technology company Huayun Tong, planning to establish a joint venture company engaged in automotive research and development, manufacturing, and sales.

On June 14, President Xi Jinping held talks at the Great Hall of the People with Palestinian President Mahmoud Abbas who is on a state visit to China. The two heads of state announced the establishment of a strategic partnership between China and Palestine.

On June 19, Manaseer Group, the largest private company in Jordan, signed a strategic cooperation agreement with Chinese automotive company Great Wall Huaguan, planning to establish a joint venture company engaged in the production and sales of electric vehicles in Jordan.

On June 20, CNPC and Qatar Energy Corporation signed a cooperation document on the expansion project of northern Gas Field in Doha, capital of Qatar.

On June 25, a delivery ceremony for China-aided prototype satellites, the MisrSat II satellite project, was held at the satellite assembly, integration and test (AIT) center of the Egyptian Space Agency. It made Egypt become the first African country with the capacity to assemble, integrate and test satellites.

On June 29, Vice President Han Zheng attended and addressed the opening ceremony of the third China-Africa Economic and Trade Expo in Changsha, Hunan.

On July 6, the China (Gansu)-Saudi Arabia Desertification Control and Green Industry Cooperation Matchmaking Meeting was held in Lanzhou. Vice Chairman of the Gansu Provincial Political Consultative Conference Huo Weiping and deputy minister of the Ministry of Investment of Saudi Arabia

in the development of overseas renewable energy markets by engaging in the whole supply chain, strengthening the presence in the global market, and realizing a new breakthrough in the regional market of Northwest Africa.

On May 16, the "Malvern" ship, loaded with 65,000 tons of liquefied natural gas from the United Arab Emirates, completed unloading at the China National Offshore Oil Corporation's Guangdong Dapeng liquefied natural gas receiving station. This is China's first imported liquefied natural gas settled in RMB, marking a substantial step forward in China's exploration of cross-border RMB settlement transactions in the oil and gas trade field.

On May 16, the opening ceremony of a new branch of Industrial and Commercial Bank of China in Jeddah and the promotion of RMB business were held in Riyadh, the capital of Saudi Arabia.

On May 18, the opening ceremony of the 2023 China-Arab States Entrepreneurs Summit was held in Dubai.

On May 19, President Xi Jinping sent a congratulatory letter to King of Saudi Arabia Salman bin Abdulaziz Al Saud, the rotating president of the Council of the League of Arab States (LAS) at the Summit Level, on the convening of the Council's 32nd session in Jeddah.

On May 21, the 6th China-Arab States Expo Promotion Conference with the theme of "A Beautiful Era and a Common Vision" was held in Riyadh, the capital of Saudi Arabia.

On May 24, Saudi Vision Industries signed a strategic cooperation agreement with Chinese new energy technology company TCL Zhonghuan, planning to establish a joint venture and invest in the construction of a photovoltaic crystal chip factory project in Saudi Arabia.

On May 24, the 6th China-Arab States Expo Promotion Conference was held in Dubai, which was held by the Secretariat of the China-Arab States Expo and the Department of Commerce of Ningxia Hui Autonomous Region.

On May 29, the 18th Senior Officials' Meeting of the China-Arab States Cooperation Forum was held in Chengdu, Sichuan.

On June 1, the 2023 China-Arab States Enterprise Cooperation Fair, jointly organized by the Ningxia Council for the Promotion of International Trade, the Guangdong Council for the Promotion of International Trade, and the Guangzhou Council for the Promotion of International Trade, was held in Guangzhou.

and inspect AVIC Import and Export Co. Ltd.. A total of 20 ambassadors, chargé d'affaires, and diplomats from 17 Arab embassies and Arab League representative offices in China attended the activity.

On March 7, Capacity Middle East 2023, one of the largest telecommunications industry exhibitions in the Middle East was held in Dubai. During this exhibition, China Mobile International Limited (CMI) announced the successful launch of its Oman Muscat MC1 point of presence (PoP).

On March 15, Acting Chargé d'affaires of the Chinese Embassy in Sudan Zhang Xianghua met with Sudanese Minister of Energy and Oil Mohamed Abdullah Mahmoud. The two sides exchanged views on cooperation in the field of oil between China and Sudan.

On March 15, Haier Egypt Ecological Park, invested by Chinese enterprise Haier Smart Home, held a groundbreaking ceremony in the 10th of Ramadan City.

On March 16, Ambassador to Syria Shi Hongwei met with Syrian Minister of Local Administration and Environment Hussein Makhlouf to exchange views on strengthening bilateral cooperation and other issues.

On March 17, the "Investment China Year" and China-UAE Investment Forum, hosted by the Chinese Ministry of Commerce and the UAE Ministry of Economy, was held in Dubai, UAE. More than 70 companies from China and the UAE participated in the forum.

On March 22, Ambassador to Bahrain Ni Ruchi paid a visit to the chairman and president of Consultative Council of Bahrain Ali bin Saleh Al Saleh upon his arrival. Both sides exchanged in-depth views on China-Bahrain relations and deepening parliamentary cooperation between the two countries.

On March 22, Ambassador to Algeria Li Jian met with the chairman of the Algerian Economic Renewal Council (CREA) Kamel Moula. Commercial Counsellor of the Embassy Chen Zhong attended the meeting.

On March 28, President Xi Jinping had a phone call with Saudi Arabia's Crown Prince and Prime Minister Mohammed bin Salman Al Saud.

On April 12, China Energy Engineering Group Co., Ltd. (ENERGY CHINA) signed a memorandum of cooperation on green hydrogen projects in the southern region of Morocco with Saudi Arabia's Agilan Brothers and Morocco's Gaia Energy. Following the signing of the memorandum on the development of green hydrogen project in Egypt, China has made another milestone achievement

and Road" Initiative, and the implementation of the China-Arab States Summit.

On February 21, the Iraqi government signed deals with two Chinese companies and a United Arab Emirates (UAE) firm to develop six oil and gas fields.

On February 21, Ambassador to Kuwait Zhang Jianwei met with the Minister of Finance and Minister of State for Economic Affairs and Investments of Kuwait Abdulwahab M. Al-Rasheed to exchange views on promoting practical cooperation between China and Kuwait.

On February 23, Ambassador to Jordan Chen Chuandong attended the high-level partners' meeting on "Supporting the Palestinian National Employment Strategy" held in Amman.

On February 26, Ambassador to Syria Shi Hongwei met with the Chairman of Syrian Planning and International Cooperation Commission Dr. Fadi al-Khalil to exchange views on strengthening bilateral aid cooperation.

On February 28, Ambassador Zhang Yiming rang Nasdaq Dubai's market opening bell to celebrate the listing of carbon-neutrality-themed bonds by the Industrial and Commercial Bank of China Limited (ICBC), the world's largest bank by assets.

On March 2, the handover ceremony of medical supplies for the China-Mauritania "counterpart hospital" cooperation project was held at the National Hospital Center in Nouakchott, Mauritania. Under the witness of Ambassador Li Baijun, the director of Heilongjiang Eye Hospital Kan Ze, and the head of National Hospital Center Muktar signed a handover certificate for donating medical supplies such as medicine and equipment to Mauritania.

On March 3, Ambassador to Tunisia Wanli met with Tunisian Prime Minister Najla Bouden to exchange views on bilateral relations, practical cooperation, and international issues of common concern.

On March 5, Ambassador to Kuwait Zhang Jianwei and Acting CEO of KFH Abdel Wahab attended the China Auto Show held by Kuwait Financial Company (KFH).

On March 7, the first China Industrial Products Exhibition was grandly held at the Chinese-UAE Industrial Capacity Cooperation Demonstration Zone in Abu Dhabi.

On March 7, the Asia-Africa Department of the Ministry of Foreign Affairs organized a delegation of ambassadors from the Arab states to China to visit

A Al Nowaiser to exchange views on establishing closer economic and trade relations between the two sides.

From February 6th to 10th, Hong Kong Chief Executive Mr. John Lee paid an official visit to the United Arab Emirates. Organized by the Hong Kong Trade Development Council, over 30 high-level Hong Kong business representatives from different fields visited the UAE with the delegation.

On February 8, Ambassador to Algeria Li Jian met with President of MADAR Group Mr. Charaf-Eddine Amara and exchanged views on bilateral enterprise cooperation between China and Algeria.

On February 9, the first batch of medical supplies provided by the Chinese Red Cross to Syria arrived in Damascus. Ambassador to Syria Shi Hongwei, Deputy Minister of Local Administration and Environment Mr. Moutaz Douaji, and President of the Syrian Red Crescent Khalid Hboubati, went to the airport to extend the welcome.

On February 14, Ambassador Liao Liqiang met with Egyptian Minister of Agriculture El-Said Marzouq El-Qosair to exchange ideas on promoting cooperation between China and Egypt.

On February 15, the soft opening ceremony of Kuwait Health Assurance Hospital in Jahra Governorate was held, undertaken by Metallurgical Corporation of China Ltd., marking the initial delivery of the project as a whole.

On February 15, the 6th Egypt Petroleum Exhibition came to an end in Cairo, the capital of Egypt. During the exhibition, Chinese companies' booths attracted numerous visitors and are expected to further strengthen cooperation with oil and gas companies in the Middle East.

On February 16, Ambassador to Mauritanian Li Baijun met with the Minister of Health and Wellness Dr Kailesh Kumar Singh Jagutpal. The two sides exchanged views on further strengthening exchanges and cooperation in the medical and health fields between China and Mauritania.

On February 18, President Xi Jinping sent a message to the 36th African Union (AU) Summit, extending warm congratulations to African countries and the African people.

On February 20, Ambassador Liao Liqiang was invited to attend the China-Egypt Entrepreneurs' Seminar and made a keynote speech focusing on China's economic situation, the achievements and potential of China-Egypt economic and trade cooperation, the promotion of investment in Egypt under the "Belt

Chronicle of China-Arab States Economic and Trade Cooperation in 2023

On January 1, Minister of Transport and Logistic Services of Saudi Arabia Saleh bin Nasser Al-Jasser met with Ambassador Chen Weiqing. Both sides exchanged views on strengthening cooperation in the fields of transportation and logistics between the two countries.

On January 12, Ambassador to Mauritania Li Baijun met with Mauritanian Minister of Foreign Affairs, Cooperation and Mauritanians Abroad Salem Ould Merzoug, to exchange in-depth views on major issues of mutual concern and to promote the development of friendly relations between China and Mauritania.

On January 18, Ambassador to Kuwait Zhang Jianwei met with the Minister of State for Municipal Affairs of Kuwait Abdulaziz Waleed Al-Mujil to exchange views on implementing the consensus reached at the meeting between President Xi Jinping and Crown Prince Mishal, strengthening strategic docking and deepening practical cooperation between the two countries.

On January 19, Ambassador to Mauritania Li Baijun met with Mauritanian Minister of Interior and Decentralization Mohamed Ahmed Ould Mohamed Lemine to exchange in-depth views on issues of common concern and to promote the development of friendly relations between China and Mauritania.

On January 26, Head of the Office of the People's Republic of China to the State of Palestine Guo Wei, and Secretary General of the Council of Minister of Palestine Amjed Ghanim jointly signed the certificate of handover of Chinese Ministry of Foreign Affairs' assistance to Palestinian livelihood materials.

On February 5, Hong Kong Chief Executive Mr. John Lee began his visit to Saudi Arabia. He met with the Minister of Investment of Saudi Arabia Khalid Al Falih and Vice Chairman of the Public Investment Fund of Saudi Arabia Turqi

Chapter 12 Special Report on the Opening up of Ningxia

and cooperate with research institutions and universities in Saudi Arabia, the United Arab Emirates, Qatar, Iraq, Iran and other areas in fields including new materials, new energy, environmental protection technology, and food technology, so as to promote the sharing of scientific research resources and innovation achievements.

plan. Ningxia will also support Ningxia University in building first-class doctoral programs in chemical engineering technology, materials science and engineering materials, and regional and country studies, so as to comprehensively promote the sustainable and high-quality development of the export-oriented industrial system. Ningxia will also strengthen the cultivation of comprehensive human resource development in international trade, intellectual property, digital economy, e-commerce and with foreign language proficiency.

2. Enhancement of the Industrial chain and Construction of an Innovation Chain for Exports

Learning from Chongqing's successful experience in introducing foreign capital and cash technology, Ningxia aims to improve the added value and technical content of export products, and highlight the internal-development driving experience of economic growth. Ningxia will also further explore and improve the R&D investment mechanism of enterprises, cultivate first-class export innovative leading enterprises, and carry out the "fertile soil" action by cultivating export-oriented industries in the future.

Moreover, Ningxia plans to improve the coordination mechanism, build domestic and foreign "enclave" R&D centers, scientific and technological achievement incubation platforms and offshore incubators, and build a new mechanism for the implementation of scientific and technological achievements of "eastern and foreign (mainly Europe and the United States) R&D + Ningxia transformation." Ningxia will also promote the successful commercialization and industrialization achievements of Ningxia University's green technology innovation and advanced technology team for energy conservation and carbon reduction, and promote high-quality cooperation in green economy and green industries between China and Arab countries and Africa.

3. Concentration on the Export-oriented Industrial Chain and Optimization of the Education Chain

Ningxia plans to stimulate local universities to give efficient support to the development of export-oriented industries, and optimize disciplines focused on the export industry chain. Ningxia will also add and adjust related majors, and form an innovation platform matrix covering export-oriented industries. At the same time, Ningxia intends to support universities to establish joint laboratories,

financial institutions with considerable strength and influence, and strive to build an economic pilot zone with international standards, a concentration of financial institutions, and prosperous financial business. Moreover, Ningxia will obtain the consent of the People's Bank of China to set up a free trade account system in Ningxia National Open Industrial Park and strive to set up Sino-foreign joint venture financial institutions (mainly investment banks, insurance companies, funds, etc.). Ningxia will also provide policy support to serve the construction of inland pilot open zones, strive for the central bank to set up an offshore RMB settlement center, and give more freedom to offshore outlets and offshore amounts. In addition, Ningxia will set up an AIIB agency and a Silk Road Fund agency in Ningxia, focusing on supporting the construction of various export-oriented industrial parks.

3. Enhancement of the Construction of Comprehensive Bonded Zones

Ningxia is planning to strengthen the Yinchuan Comprehensive Bonded Zone and Shizuishan Bonded Logistics Center (B), and actively promote the interconnection of facilities, complementary industrial advantages, and efficient customs clearance. Ningxia will also focus on the development of export-oriented industries such as port customs clearance, bonded processing, and bonded logistics, and create a special customs supervision area with convenient trade and investment, outstanding functional characteristics, and efficient public services. In addition, Ningxia will also accelerate the development of the Yinchuan cross-border e-commerce comprehensive pilot zone, reasonably optimize the layout of the park, and strengthen cross-border service capabilities. Moreover, Ningxia aims to enhance the effect of industrial cooperation and unification, and speed up the construction of a cross-border e-commerce industrial chain and ecosystem integrating production, trade, settlement and logistics.

12.2.5 Improving the Core Competitiveness of Industry

1. Enhancement of the Export-oriented Industrial Chain and Layout of the High-qualified Personnel Chain

Focusing on the new track of export-oriented industries such as "six new, six special and six excellent" and "ten industrial chains", Ningxia will draw a roadmap for the development of high-level industrial personnel, and accelerate the implementation of a discipline-led and high-level personnel development

(Ningxia) Pilot Free Trade Zone, and two key points of the construction of the inland open economic pilot zone and the China Grape and Wine Open Development Comprehensive Pilot Zone. As such, Ningxia has committed to create a new engine for high-level opening up, make the national development zone bigger and stronger, and take the lead in implementing the management mode of tolerance and approval, notification and commitment system, and construction before inspection in the national development zone. Ningxia will also strengthen the function of the development zone as a platform for investment promotion, and cultivate and enhance new advantages and new momentum for foreign trade development, steadily enhancing the contribution of development zones to regional economic growth.

2. Enhancement of Institutional Innovation

Firstly, in line with the goal of the pilot free trade zone, Ningxia will strive to promote the institutional innovation of the inland open economic pilot zone, and enhance its status in the international division of labor and the international competitiveness of foreign trade. Drawing on Shanghai's "Regulations on the China (Shanghai) Pilot Free Trade Zone" and its successful implementation experience, Ningxia will further explore new rules and models for the opening up of all-factor foreign trade in line with international standards, introducing and gradually promoting relevant laws and regulations for the Ningxia Pilot Economic Zone, and taking the lead in the national economic development zone.

Secondly, in terms of tax system innovation, Ningxia plans to further learn from the fiscal and tax policies of the Shanghai Free Trade Zone, and fully promote the fiscal and tax policies that have been tried in the comprehensive bonded zone. Ningxia will also implement tax policies to promote investment and trade, draft tax policies that are different from those outside the pilot zone, and promote trade and investment facilitation. At the same time, Ningxia will experiment with the tax policies adopted in the Shanghai Free Trade Zone. For example, enterprises in the pilot zone will be rewarded with high-qualified personnel and personnel in short supply in the form of shares or capital contribution ratios.

Lastly, in terms of financial system innovation, Ningxia plans to further optimize the model of "internal training and external introduction", introduce cooperation and consultation mechanism with Inner Mongolia and Shaanxi, and open up clean energy complementary bundling and delivery channels. Thirdly, Ningxia intends to give full play to the role of platforms such as the Shaanxi-Gansu-Sichuan-Ningxia Adjacent Regional Economic Federation and the Joint Association of Hohhot-Baotou-Yinchuan-Chongqing Economic Zone, and strengthen cooperation with neighboring provinces and regions in the fields of industrial coordinated development, platform linkage and co-construction, and market information sharing. In the Yellow River Basin Bay Area, Ningxia will also promote exchange and cooperation in high-qualified personnel, industry, science and technology, investment, culture, information and other areas, fully integrating into the innovation chain, industrial chain, supply chain, capital chain and high-qualified personnel chain, so as to realize regional interconnection, share the fruits of development, and promote the process of economic integration.

2. Enhancement of the Cooperation with Major National Strategic Regions

Ningxia aims to strengthen cooperation in the coordinated development of the Beijing-Tianjin-Hebei region, the Yangtze River Economic Belt, and the Yangtze River Delta. Ningxia will also strengthen the construction of the Guangdong-Hong Kong-Macao Greater Bay Area, the Hainan Free Trade Port and other major national strategic docking, exchange and cooperation, and better involve into and support the new development pattern. In addition, Ningxia will also implement the plans of "internationally renowned enterprises entering Ningxia" and "central enterprises entering Ningxia", and promote the implementation of a number of good, large and high-tech projects with high scientific and technological content and both unifying and driving effects. Focusing on the mutual poverty alleviation cooperation between Fujian and Ningxia, Ningxia will fully implement the spirit of the East-West Poverty Alleviation Cooperation Symposium, and continuously expand cooperation and exchange in the fields of industrial docking, park co-construction, commercial and trade circulation, and exhibition activities, so as to create a new model of East-West mutual cooperation in the new era.

12.2.4 Actively Constructing a New Vehicle for Opening Up

1. Formulation of Good Target Designs

Ningxia is focused on the goal of striving for the establishment of the China

and cooperative ecosystem, promote the in-depth integration of production, education, research and application, and guide the effective connection and integrated development of upstream and downstream enterprises in the industrial chain. In addition, Ningxia will also accelerate the construction of an industrial ecology with coordinated development of software and hardware, strengthen exchange with the BRI countries, expand cooperation areas, enrich cooperation projects, and share the achievements of computing power innovation and development.

12.2.3 Expanding the Regional Economy, and Promoting Win-Win Development

1. Enhancement of the Cooperation among Urban Agglomerations along the Yellow River

Firstly, Ningxia will speed up infrastructure connectivity and promote economic integration. According to some research and development experiences, the impact of geographical location on urban development is crucial. Enterprises cluster near ports which in turn lead to higher labor productivity and thus higher wages. If the distance is more than 500 kilometers from the port, there is no significant correlation between the wage level and the distance to the port. This is one of the reasons why enterprises in the Yellow River Basin Bay Area are afraid of projects with high technology content and market demand, and instead, the resource-based and processing-oriented projects are highly pursued. Therefore, strengthening channel construction and regional cooperation is an important way to reduce the cost of factor flow and industrial gradient transfer. Ningxia also intends to accelerate the construction of the 5G network, expand the coverage of gigabit and above optical fiber, and establish the Internet of Things and industrial Internet infrastructure. Furthermore, Ningxia will increase the penetration rate of the industrial Internet, artificial intelligence, and big data, and promote the empowerment of traditional advantageous industries and their transformation to green, intelligent, and digital industries.

Secondly, Ningxia aims to cooperate with the four provinces to build a high-speed intercity railway network along the Yellow River, fill in the missing lines and open bottlenecked sections, and accelerate the formation of large corridors to the north, east, and south. In addition, Ningxia will optimize the coal

Certification Center, so as to make the exhibition a double-certified international high-quality professional exhibition of wine in China.

Thirdly, Ningxia aims to expand the influence of the exhibition and strive to invite guests including every session of China's national leaders, dignitaries from various countries, international and domestic wine industry chambers of commerce (associations), heads of important production and marketing enterprises, and important merchants such as international and domestic wine buyers and distributors. This will serve to make the exhibition an important event in the domestic and foreign wine industry. Lastly, Ningxia will strengthen exchange and cooperation with the world's major wine countries and domestic wine producing and sales areas, and continuously enhance the influence of the exhibition. In addition, Ningxia will hold the China (Ningxia) International Wine Expo in cooperation with countries such as France, the United States, Germany and other countries to so that more consumers at home and abroad can understand and pay attention to the wine producing area at the eastern foot of Helan Mountains in Ningxia. The future of Chinese wine is in Ningxia, and Ningxia will lead the Chinese wine industry to be better involved into the world.

3. "Western Digital Valley" Computing Industry Conference Platform

Firstly, with a global vision, computing power cooperation, value innovation, and driving future conferences, Ningxia plans to promote the deep integration of the computing industry, enhance the ability of scientific and technological innovation, and comprehensively contribute to the high-quality development of the computing industry in the western region and even the world. This will serve to make the exhibition an internationally renowned event that gathers industry elites and that offers a professional display stage for leading cutting-edge trends, and a business and trade cooperation platform that gathers global resources. Secondly, Ningxia will insist on directing internationalization, specialization and marketization, and closely focus on the latest development trends of the industry, cutting-edge technological achievements, and big data application scenarios and trainings of high-qualified personnel.

Moreover, Ningxia also plans to empower enterprises with "computing", and build a broad stage for enterprises to display products and promote cooperation, and enhance the innovation, competitiveness and influence of the computing industry in a comprehensive way. Lastly, Ningxia will focus on creating an open

high-qualified personnel. Thirdly, Ningxia will comprehensively improve the "Guest of Honor" mechanism between the China-Arab States Rotation Office and China, and establish the "Belt and Road China-Arab States Entrepreneurs Federation" under the China-Arab States Expo, so as to accelerate the exchange and cooperation between Chinese and Arab business elites, and effectively connect policies, resources and capital. Moreover, Ningxia plans to strengthen the systematic research on economics, trade, foreign-related laws and regulations and the industrial policies of the Arab countries, and establish the "China-Arab Countries Economic and Trade Law Research Center" to provide decision-making consultation for enterprises to "go global" and "bring in", learning from the experience of Guangxi and Chongqing on China-ASEAN research platforms.

Lastly, with the China-Arab States Expo as traction, Ningxia will closely coordinate with the China (Ningxia) International Wine Culture and Tourism Expo, the Western Digital Valley "Computing Industry Conference" and other high-level international cooperation platforms. In this way, Ningxia can accelerate the construction of a new development pattern for the international exhibition economy, deeply explore the industrial systems of West Asia, Central Asia, North Africa and ASEAN and other countries and the industrial cooperation potential of the "six new, six special and six excellent", and form a long-term mechanism to promote the cooperative development of Ningxia. Ningxia also plans to accelerate the construction of a new development pattern for the exhibition economy.

2. China (Ningxia) International Wine Culture and Tourism Expo Platform

Firstly, Ningxia plans to strengthen the overall design, fully promote its wine industry to the world, and involve the world wine industry into China. Ningxia will also promote mutual exchange and cooperation between the world wine industries and the in-depth integration of wine and culture, create an internationally renowned wine industry professional exhibition with Ningxia style, Chinese characteristics and world level, and make the exhibition an important platform to promote Ningxia's social and economic development and opening up. Secondly, Ningxia will strengthen the development of internal qualities, formulate exhibition quality development goals, and pass the certification of the International Association of the Exhibition Industry (UFI) and the ISO9001 quality management system certification of the China Quality

12.2.2 Striving for the Enhancement of Platforms for Opening Up

1. China-Arab States Expo Platform

Firstly, Ningxia plans to strengthen the top-level design, re-examine and reposition the China-Arab States Expo with a "global vision and China platform", and make better plans for medium and long-term development. Ningxia will also strive to build a general platform, hub and channel for political dialogue, economic and trade cooperation, commercial mediation, legal services and cultural and educational exchanges between China and Arab countries. In addition, Ningxia will also strive for the support of the National Development and Reform Commission, the Ministry of Commerce, the Silk Road Fund, the Asian Infrastructure Investment Bank and relevant central enterprises, and hold the BRI Trade and Investment Promotion Conference with a high level of quality. Ningxia aims to strengthen the coordination of docking with the Ministry of Foreign Affairs and the Ministry of Commerce, involve the economic, trade and investment activities of the China-Arab States Cooperation Forum into the China-Arab States Expo, and form a mechanism to operate and enhance the level of economic and trade cooperation at the China-Arab States Expo. The "two platforms, one center, and one engine" is an important service platform for a shared future for the China-Arab states community, a core platform for the organic connection of the BRI economic belt, a new investment and trade promotion center between China and Arab countries, and an important engine for promoting the development of the inland open economy. By building this platform, Ningxia will accelerate the formation of a new mechanism for "foreign investment + foreign trade" mutual assistance and cooperation, deepen and solidify economic and trade cooperation of China-Arab states, and promote new breakthroughs in economic and trade cooperation between China and Arab countries.

Secondly, in order to accelerate the negotiation of the China-GCC Free Trade Zone, it is imperative to pilot this zone in China. Ningxia intends to accelerate study of and reliance on the Yinchuan Comprehensive Bonded Zone to attract business associations between China and the GCC countries, well-known enterprises and international institutions, and provide services including business investment, legal services, finance, logistics, digital information, agricultural economic cooperation, cultural and tourism cooperation, and professional and

BRI channels, including loans from the Asian Infrastructure Investment Bank, investment in the central budget and other financial support. Ningxia will also accelerate the preparation of PPP projects for key infrastructure in the channels, and apply for inclusion in national demonstration. Secondly, Ningxia aims to cultivate and expand the main body of financial services, establish a financial service consortium and, carry out innovation of both financing products and bond financing to support the construction of the BRI channels, and explore the possibility of setting up a Sino-foreign joint venture channel construction investment (private equity) fund in the Ningxia Comprehensive Bonded Zone, some foreign trade base, and characteristic parks. Thirdly, Ningxia will strengthen the capacity for building channel financial operation coordination. On the basis of the existing cooperation in the new land-sea channels in the western region, Ningxia plans to explore a mechanism for sharing financial interests and resources, and promote a mechanism for coordination and compensation of interests among various regions and also for joint risk prevention.

4. Improving the Level of Air-Land Opening Channels

Firstly, as an important node of the China-Central Asia-West Asia Economic Corridor and the China-Mongolia-Russia Economic Corridor, Ningxia has committed to actively strive for national support to open and increase international routes to important cities in countries along the corridors, build a route network for countries along the Silk Road Economic Belt, connecting Northeast Asia and Southeast Asia and also China's central and western provinces and regions. Ningxia will also build Yinchuan Hedong International Airport into an important Chinese gateway airport for Central and West Asia. Secondly, the train operators of Ningxia will make full use of the "China-Kyrgyzstan-Ukraine" international logistics channel, building a "China-Arab States Express" from Ningxia-Irkeshtan to Central Asia, West Asia, and Europe and opening up a "second channel" for the five Central Asian countries, Afghanistan, Iran and other countries. In addition, Ningxia plans to continue to consolidate new support for the channels, and promote the transportation of Xinjiang coal to the east, the import of Mongolian coal and a new channel for energy and grain imports from Central Asia, actively engaging in the new land-sea corridor in the western region and promoting the construction of logistics hubs.

economy", and leverage docking strategies by integrating with countries from the east, west, north and south. Finally, Ningxia aims to amplify the effect of the China-Arab States Summit, strengthen contacts and dialogues with global international organizations such as the Belt and Road Summit Cooperation Forum and the Boao Forum for Asia, as well as regional international organizations such as ASEAN and the Shanghai Cooperation Organization. Within the business scope of these international organizations, Ningxia also will explore the possibility and feasibility of establishing cooperation platforms and strive to make new breakthroughs in the interconnection of international transportation facilities, the signing of international transport agreements, and the facilitation of cross-border direct customs clearance.

2. Accelerating the "Digital Silk Road"

Located inland, Ningxia must follow the "Digital Silk Road", a new path of high-level opening up under the new development pattern. Firstly, Ningxia plans to continue to lay a foundation for the development of the digital economy, align with international rules such as the Digital Economy Partnership Agreement (DEPA) and the Agreement for Trans-Pacific Partnership (CPTPP), build a competitive development system and demonstration zone in the western region for a digital economy, and find its voice in the development of the world's digital economy. Secondly, Ningxia aims to innovate digital cooperation mechanisms, build a national digital economy innovation and development pilot zone, accelerate the development of new models and business formats, vigorously develop financial and digital economy industries such as smart logistics, digital finance, and digital economy headquarters bases, and create an industrial diversification of the "Digital Silk Road".

Thirdly, Ningxia intends to carefully make plans for a new round of development planning and implementation, strengthen the overall guiding role of the China-Arab States Summit in digital economy cooperation, tap into the advantages of and common interests in cooperation among the countries of the Arab League in digital trade competition, and extend the value chain and industrial chain in the development of digital trade.

3. Strengthening the Ability of Financial Operation and Coordination of Channels

Firstly, Ningxia plans to work with relevant central departments in order to strengthen docking and strive to gain special funds for the construction of the

south and east, and the advantages of developing a higher-level open economy. Through 10 years of cumulative development, Ningxia's opening up has reached a new level, having improved the platforms, channels, carriers, scientific and technological innovation, foreign trade and foreign investment, all of which lays a solid foundation for deep integration into the BRI. In the future, Ningxia will follow the spirit of the 20th National Congress of the Communist Party of China and the important instructions given by president Xi Jinping's in speeches during his previous visits to Ningxia. Ningxia will also solidly promote the steady and long-term development of high-quality Belt and Road cooperation and the high-level opening up of the inland, building high-level channels and high-level platforms, actively integrating into a new pattern of domestic and international dual circulation, and building a more open policy system.

12.2 Prospects for Ningxia's Countermeasures for High-Level Opening up

12.2.1 Strengthening the Construction of the BRI Channels

1. Focusing on Top-level Designs

Firstly, a shift from "infrastructure thinking" to "channel thinking" is needed. In order to engage in the construction of the BRI channels, Ningxia has committed to adhere to the overall thinking, precise positioning, and differentiated development in cross-regional cooperation, and improve its own positioning in top-level design.

Secondly, Ningxia plans to accelerate the overall planning of the participation in the new western land-sea corridor and clarify its strategic positioning, development goals, spatial layout and main tasks. Ningxia also needs to strengthen regional and provincial-regional cooperation and linkage, promote the construction of channel infrastructure at a high level in accordance with the basic ideas of filling break points, strengthening internal connections, and resolving blockages, and share the development results of channel construction.

Thirdly, combining with the pattern of industrial parks and the actual development of logistics hubs in the autonomous region, Ningxia will accelerate the construction of key areas, projects, nodes and hubs, learn from the successful experience of Hangzhou Jinjiang Group's Abrasa Project from Yinchuan to Saudi Arabia, strive to promote the quality and upgrading of the "channel

Chapter 12　Special Report on the Opening up of Ningxia

Table 12.7　Proportion of R&D Expenditure in GDP in Ningxia and the Eight Provinces along the Yellow River (2019-2023)

	2023	2022	2021	2020	2019
Ningxia	1.57	1.56	1.56	1.51	1.45
Shaanxi	2.50	2.35	2.33	2.43	2.27
Inner Mongolia	0.93	0.20	0.20	0.93	0.86
Gansu	1.32	1.30	1.26	1.22	1.26
Qinghai	0.80	-	-	0.71	0.70
Shanxi	1.16	1.07	1.12	1.20	1.13
Sichuan	2.26	-	2.26	2.17	1.88
Henan	2.05	1.96	1.73	1.66	1.48
Shandong	2.59	2.49	2.34	2.31	2.10

Source: Official database of the National Bureau of Statistics, statistical yearbook of Ningxia and the eight provinces along the Yellow River, and data from the Ningxia Department of Science and Technology.

In 2023, the building of BRI entered a new decade and faced a new international and domestic environment. The signing of various international trade cooperation agreements is expected to promote the BRI as a new growth measurement for both the regional and the world economy. After the financial crisis, in order to extricate themselves from a sluggish economic recovery, countries are constantly seeking new economic growth points. In October 2023, in his keynote speech at the opening ceremony of the 3rd Belt and Road Forum for International Cooperation, President Xi Jinping announced China's eight actions to support high-quality Belt and Road cooperation. His remarks pointed Ningxia toward deeper integration into the BRI. As a fulcrum of the BRI, Ningxia shoulders the important task of building a highland for inland reform and opening up, and promoting high-level opening-up.

At the same time, Ningxia is in central position where major national strategies meet, including the development of the western region in the new era and the ecological protection and high-quality development of the Yellow River Basin. Ningxia is also a pioneer area for the later. In the building of BRI, Ningxia needs to form a new pattern of development in the western region, supported by ecological protection and high-quality development of the Yellow River Basin, with geographical advantages for the connecting regions to the north, west,

than the national average. This growth ranks 8th in the country, 4th in the west, 2nd in the northwest, and 1st in the nine provinces and regions along the Yellow River and completes the goal of "average annual growth of R&D investment of more than 10%." In addition, the intensity of R&D investment reached 1.57%, ranking 18th in the country. The proportion of R&D expenditure for enterprises reached 81.4%, 3.8 percentage points higher than the national average, and the proportion of industrial enterprises with R&D activities above the designated size reached 41.2%, 4 percentage points higher than the national average, ranking 8th in the country and 1st in the northwest provinces and regions. This data shows that Ningxia has achieved remarkable results in the innovation-driven development strategy, and the continuous growth of R&D expenditure has provided strong support for the region's scientific and technological innovation and economic development.

At the same time, Ningxia adheres to the principles such as cultivating fertile soil for high-qualified personnel, development is the first priority, and high-qualified personnel is the first resource, and constantly innovates policies and measures of the high-qualified personnel. Ningxia has successively issued some policies and measures, such as "Ningxia Hui Autonomous Region Interim Measures for Supporting Enterprises to Introduce and Cultivate High-qualified Personnel", "Ningxia Hui Autonomous Region Implementation Opinions on the Introduction of Scientific and Technological Innovation Teams", and "Ningxia Hui Autonomous Region Interim Measures for the Introduction of Overseas Chinese Experts." These police and measures have provided support of high-qualified personnel for the implementation of innovation-driven strategies and high-level opening-up in Ningxia and have achieved remarkable results. For example, Ningxia University has established a High-qualified Personnel sharing and exchange mechanism with Shanghai Jiao Tong University and Beijing University of Aeronautics and Astronautics, and has successively introduced a number of discipline leaders and added 15 candidates for major national projects of high-qualified personnel. All of these steps have served the development of chemical, material, energy and other industries in Ningxia, and leading to Ningxia University's ranking among the best universities in the west.

Thailand, Vietnam, Malaysia, Singapore and other countries (regions). The direct flight routes to Dubai and Hong Kong are running stably, and the reconstruction and expansion project (phase IV) of Yinchuan Hedong International Airport is steadily progressing. The approval of "Yinchuan Hedong International Airport General Plan" by the Civil Aviation Administration of China has already been obtained. The plan prepares for a volume of 28 million passengers and 200000 tons of cargo and mail in 2035, the building of a second runway of 3600 meters in length, a terminal of 220000 square meters, an expansion apron of 850000 square meters, and other facilities. Yinchuan Hedong International Airport will enter the ranks of modern western first-class airports after completion of these plans.

4. Rapid Construction of Digital Channels

Ningxia has persisted in taking the digital economy as a primary indicator of its development, and has built the only "dual center" of computing power and Internet exchange in western China. Yinchuan has formed more than 3000P of intelligent computing power, 500 million government data resources, and 8000 TB of data, striving to build a "Yinchuan Data Port". By 2023, over 100 companies, such as Ningxia Amazon, China Mobile, Meituan, and Xiyun, had established data centers or application data centers in Ningxia for data storage. At the same time, Ningxia has accelerated the construction of the national Yinchuan cross-border e-commerce comprehensive pilot zone. On the basis of making good use of the China-Arab States Expo and the China (Yinchuan) cross-border e-commerce comprehensive pilot zone, focusing on "six new, six special and six excellent" industrial layout, and with "two platforms and six systems" as the construction goal, Ningxia has created a cross-border e-commerce industry ecology with enterprise gathering, complete service system and innovative regulatory model, and has rented 19 overseas warehouses in 6 countries including Germany, Kazakhstan and Malaysia. So far, the number of cross-border e-commerce enterprises has reached 475.

12.1.3 Remarkable Innovation-driven Results

In 2023, Ningxia's R&D expenditure reached RMB7.938 billion, a year-on-year increase of 12.7%. This data not only shows the continuous growth of Ningxia's R&D expenditure but also that its growth rate is 2.6 percentage points higher

of people's living standards.

2. Solid Improvement in Railway Networks

By 2023, nine railway lines in Ningxia were included in the medium and long-term planning of the national railway network. In addition, "two horizontal and one vertical" of the "eight vertical and eight horizontal" high-speed railway networks planned by the state will pass through Ningxia, laying a good foundation for the construction of the Ningxia railway project. After the completion of the high-speed railways from Yinchuan to Xi'an, Zhongwei to Lanzhou, and Baotou to Yinchuan, the time from Yinchuan to Beijing, Xi'an, Sichuan and Chongqing, Lanzhou and other key cities will be limited to 2~5 hours. Subsequently, Ningxia will truly integrate into the national high-speed railway network, and greatly improve its ability to engage in the building of BRI and serve the national road network.

At present, the Yinchuan-Xi'an high-speed railway and the Zhongwei-Lanzhou section of Yinchuan-Lanzhou high-speed railway have been completely opened. In addition, the Huinong-Yinchuan section of the Baotou-Yinchuan high-speed railway has officially entered the operation test stage. As for the international rail channel, Ningxia has opened a Central Asian freight train from Yinchuan to Tehran, and with Tianjin Port opened a rail-water combined route. These accomplishments have opened up a low-cost and convenient land passage from North, Northwest and Northeast China to Central and West Asia. Ningxia has also opened westbound international freight trains from Yinchuan to Hungary in Europe, Mongolia, Russia and five Central Asian countries including Kazakhstan. Furthermore, Ningxia's southbound land-sea new corridor trains and eastbound rail-sea intermodal trains connect the markets of Central Asia, West Asia and South Asia. The new round of "Iron Machine", the National Logistics Demonstration Park, the Yinchuan-Xi'an National Integrated Freight Hub and other projects are under accelerated construction.

3. Ongoing Strengthening of Aviation Hubs

By 2023, Yinchuan Hedong International Airport completed its third phase of expansion, and the airfield rating was upgraded to 4E. The passenger volume of Yinchuan Airport has entered has reached the ten-millions, similar to large airports. Yinchuan Hedong International Airport has been authorized to have the third, fourth and fifth air rights of flying, with 79 navigable cities and more than 113 routes. It has opened 10 international routes from Yinchuan to

Chapter 12 Special Report on the Opening up of Ningxia

areas such as Beijing, Tianjin, Hebei, the Yangtze River Delta, Guangdong-Hong Kong-Macao Greater Bay Area, and key provinces along the Yellow River. From 2017 to 2023, more than 5000 investment projects were implemented, and the actual investment exceeded RMB 900 billion. Moreover, more than 100 companies from the world's top 500 and China's top 500 companies have been brought in. For many years, the fixed asset investments formed by investment promotion projects have accounted for approximately a 45% proportion of the total for the whole country. These investments have also strongly promoted the regulation of the economic structure and the transformation of growth momentum in Ningxia.

12.1.2 The Gradual Enhancement of the Function of Channels for Opening Up

1. Significant Improvement of the Smoothness of the Highway

By 2023, Ningxia had built a "three rings, four verticals and six horizontals" highway network, with 13 inter-provincial exits and was the second province in the west to connect counties with highways. In this way, the comprehensive three-dimensional transportation network has been accelerated. The density of the highway network is 56.59 km/100 square kilometers. It is higher than the national average and ranks 25th among the 31 provinces in China. The Ningxia highway network has been connected to border ports such as Alashankou and Khorgos to the west, and coastal ports in the east including in Tianjin and Shanghai.

Ningxia is also connected to the surrounding economic centers such as Lanzhou, Xi'an, Baotou and Taiyuan. In particular, the Ningxia section of the Yinchuan-Kunming Highway has been completely opened and has become a north-south corridor connecting Ningxia, Gansu and Shaanxi provinces, driving the development of transportation network resources and industrial development in the areas along the corridor, especially in the central and southern regions of Ningxia. At present, the total miles of roads in Ningxia have reached 39000 kilometers, and the miles of highways have exceeded 2300 kilometers. The national and provincial trunk road network has been improved. As the rural road infrastructure network has reached all villages, the resilience of the road network has been enhanced. These all provide a solid transportation foundation for the economic development of Ningxia and surrounding areas and the improvement

		Continued
	Amount of Actual Utilized Foreign Investment (Billion, USD)	Foreign Trade Dependence
2019	0.25	0.5
2020	0.27	0.5
2021	0.29	0.4
2022	0.34	0.5
2023	0.141	0.5

Source: Calculated from the Official database of the National Bureau of Statistics, the China and Ningxia Statistical Yearbook and Statistical Bulletin.

4. Significant Improvement of an Open Environment.

A series of policies and measures have been introduced to effectively enhance the leading role of the open economy, including participating in the building of the BRI, promoting the development of an open economy and new forms and models of foreign trade, actively utilizing foreign capital, supporting enterprises to "go global", and strengthening the construction of ports. Ningxia has also followed and promoted 260 projects of free trade zone reform, established a special class for key foreign-funded projects and a related mechanism for large-scale foreign-funded projects. Moreover, Ningxia has improved the trade facilitation mechanism which is composed of 10 departments and has built "Ningmaotong"(a comprehensive foreign trade services platform) and the Ningxia Digital Trade Platform. These comprehensive measures have served to promote a standard "single window" for international trade. Furthermore, Ningxia signed the "Framework Agreement on Cooperation and Joint Construction of the New Western Land-Sea Corridor" with 12 provinces, regions and cities in the west in order to effectively strengthen the financial guarantees and supply chain service capabilities of the export-oriented economy.

Regional economic cooperation and key investments have been upgraded effectively. Ningxia has focused on the investment and industrial transfer trends of large domestic and foreign enterprises and groups, key enterprises, competitive industries and key parks. In this way, Ningxia has organized and implemented a series of investment promotion activities, established regional cooperation mechanisms and built exchange and cooperation platforms in

(2) Utilization of Foreign Capital

From 2013 to 2023, Ningxia accumulated a total of USD 2.77 billion in foreign investment, with an average annual growth rate of 8.3%. Of this total, countries along the BRI have invested USD170 million, and 37 foreign direct investment enterprises have been established. So far,1127 foreign direct investment enterprises have been established in Ningxia.

The foreign investment mentioned above mainly comes from more than 50 countries and regions including Hong Kong, the United States, Singapore, Norway, Japan, South Korea, Malaysia, and Taiwan. It is mainly invested in equipment manufacturing, coal chemical industry, new energy, modern agriculture, business services, finance and other industries. Many Fortune-500 and well-known multinational companies have invested and built factories in Ningxia. These Amazon, Simpla, Louis Vuitton, Hennessy, Pernod Ricard, Schaeffler, Metro, Elkem of Norway, Schlumberger of Singapore, Carlsberg of Denmark, Mazakak of Japan, Hyosung of South Korea, Taekwang and others. Singapore, Malaysia, the United Arab Emirates, Iran and other countries along the BRI have set up a total of 124 foreign direct investment enterprises, with an actual investment of USD220 million, mainly in the areas of tourism, consulting, Internet and beverage production and processing.

On the whole, Ningxia's actual utilization of foreign capital is relatively small, and its ability to influence economic growth is limited. The structure of foreign investment is unevenly developed with investment mainly concentrated in traditional labor-intensive manufacturing industries and less involved in high value-added industries and service industries.

Table 12.6 Changes in the Amount of Actual Utilized Foreign Investment in Ningxia (2013-2023)

	Amount of Actual Utilized Foreign Investment (Billion, USD)	Foreign Trade Dependence
2013	0.2	0.6
2014	0.14	0.4
2015	0.22	0.6
2016	0.25	0.6
2017	0.31	0.7
2018	0.21	0.4

energy and other local products with its own characteristics. From "high energy consumption" to "high-tech", from "primary processing" to "fine processing" and "high-end", Ningxia injects strong internal power into the structure of export products. In 2023, monocrystalline silicon, dicyandiamide, tylosin, manganese metal, and lysine ester hydrochloride ranked among the top five of Ningxia's foreign trade exports.

From the perspective of the main trade markets, in recent years, Ningxia has actively explored the international markets and implemented the strategy of market diversification. It has carried out economic and trade exchanges with 60 countries along the BRI including Russia, India, Malaysia, Turkey, Uzbekistan, Saudi Arabia and the United Arab Emirates, and the pattern of market diversification has gradually taken shape. The main import commodities are bulk industrial raw materials, namely petroleum, manganese ore, wood pulp, machine tools and rubber. It is worth noting that since the BRI was proposed in 2013, Ningxia's imports from and exports to the European Union, ASEAN, the United States, India, and Singapore have all increased.

Table 12.5 The Development of Ningxia's Foreign Trade (2013-2023)

	Imports and Exports Total Value	Imports Total Value	Exports Total Value	Balance	Foreign Trade Dependence
	(Million)	(Million)	(Million)	(Million)	(%)
2013	19927.57	4120.93	15806.64	11685.71	8.6
2014	33391.68	6978.01	26413.67	19435.66	13.5
2015	23441.23	5028.24	18412.99	13384.75	9.1
2016	21478.37	5014.06	16464.31	11450.25	7.7
2017	34129.31	9358.52	24770.79	15412.27	10.7
2018	24916.09	6868.50	18047.59	11179.09	7.1
2019	24061.82	9169.94	14891.88	5721.94	6.4
2020	12316.65	3649.14	8667.52	5018.38	3.1
2021	21404.04	3922.80	17481.25	13558.45	4.7
2022	25737.94	6060.12	19677.82	13617.70	5.0
2023	20541.00	5560.00	14981.00	9421.00	3.9

Source: Calculated from the Official database of the National Bureau of Statistics, the China and Ningxia Statistical Yearbook and Statistical Bulletin.

structure is in the transition stage from primary to advanced, and its economic development is in the middle stage of industrialization.

Table 12.4 Changes of the proportion of the three industrial structures in Ningxia (2013 - 2023)

	1st Industry	2nd Industry	3rd Industry
2013	9.1	45.5	45.4
2014	8.8	45.0	46.2
2015	9.2	43.3	47.5
2016	8.7	42.4	48.9
2017	7.8	43.9	48.3
2018	8.0	42.4	49.6
2019	7.5	42.3	50.2
2020	8.5	41.2	50.3
2021	7.9	45.8	46.3
2022	8.0	48.3	43.7
2023	8.1	46.8	45.1

Source: Calculated from the Official database of the National Bureau of Statistics, the China and Ningxia Statistical Yearbook and Statistical Bulletin.

3. Rapid development of Foreign Trade and Investment

(1) Foreign Trade Development

Ningxia has more than 500 foreign trade business entities, carrying out trade with over 170 countries and regions. As can be seen from Table 12.5, from 2013 to 2023, Ningxia's total foreign trade development has been relatively fast.[1] In 2023, the total import and export volume was RMB 20.541 billion, 1.03 times that of 2013. Among them, the total import and export volume of the BRI countries was RMB 6.979 billion, accounting for 34%. There were 1,127 foreign direct investment enterprises, with a cumulative actual utilization in foreign capital of USD 2.77 billion, with an average annual growth rate of 8.3%.

In recent years, Ningxia has optimized the export structure, stepped up the adjustment of the industrial structure, focused on strengthening the export of biological products, agricultural and livestock products, new materials, new

---

[1] "2023, Let Ningxia 'Shine'," Ningxia News, February 21, 2023, https://www.nxnews.net/cj/cjtj/202302/t20230221_7863994.html.

	2023	2019	2013
Qinghai	24	22	26
Shandong	11	11	8
Shanxi	15	24	24
Shaanxi	12	12	13
Shanghai	2	2	2
Sichuan	20	16	21
Tianjin	6	5	4
Tibet	22	26	28
Xinjiang	16	20	14
Yunnan	23	23	27
Zhejiang	5	6	5
Chongqing	10	9	11

Source: Calculated from the official database of the National Bureau of Statistics.

2. Continuous Optimization of Industrial Structures

As can be seen from Table 12.4, the proportion of the three industrial structures in Ningxia has been gradually optimized from 2013 to 2023. The structure of the three industries changed from 9.1:45.5:45.4 in 2013 to 8.8:45.0:46.2 in 2014, realizing the transformation of the industrial structure from "231" to "321".[1] Moreover, in the ensuing 8 years until 2021, the industrial structure was 7.9:45.8:46.3 and the "321" pattern was relatively stable. Ningxia has embarked on an industrial development path with local characteristics. In 2022, due to the impact of Covid-19 on the 3rd industry, Ningxia's industrial structure was 8.0: 48.3: 43.7, that is, "231", but the proportion is not much different. In 2023, the first year after Covid-19, the industrial structure was 8.1:46.8:45.1. The industrial structure was continuously optimized and roughly equivalent to the national average and the two-wheel support pattern of industry and service has been basically formed. On the whole, according to the classification criteria of American economist Simon Kuznets, Ningxia's industrial

---

[1] *Ningxia Statistical Yearbook 2022*, compiled by Statistics Bureau of Ningxia Hui Autonomous Region and Ningxia Survey Team of National Bureau of Statistics, China Statistics Press, 2023.

Chapter 12   Special Report on the Opening up of Ningxia

Continued

	Fixed Asset Investment (Billion)	Growth Rate of Fixed Asset Investment (%)	Per Capita Fixed Asset Investment (RMB)	Growth Rate of Per Capita Fixed Asset Investment (%)
2020	290.62	4.8	40308.0	4.2
2021	298.47	2.7	41167.9	2.1
2022	322.94	8.2	44360.1	7.8
2023	339.09	5.0	46514.0	4.9

Source: Calculated from the Official database of the National Bureau of Statistics, the China and Ningxia Statistical Yearbook and Statistical Bulletin.

Table 12.3   2013-2023 National Per Capita GDP Ranking

	2023	2019	2013
Anhui	13	13	16
Beijing	1	1	1
Fujian	4	4	6
Gansu	31	31	30
Guangdong	7	7	7
Guangxi	29	29	29
Guizhou	28	28	31
Hainan	17	19	18
Hebei	26	27	23
Henan	25	18	20
Heilongjiang	30	30	25
Hubei	9	8	10
Hunan	14	14	15
Jilin	27	25	17
Jiangsu	3	3	3
Jiangxi	21	17	22
Liaoning	19	15	12
Inner Mongolia	8	10	9
Ningxia	18	21	19

in 2013 to 18th in 2023. The speed and total volume of economic development have accelerated, and the quality, efficiency and pattern have comprehensively improved.

Table 12.1   Changes in the Development of Ningxia's GDP (2004-2023)

	Ningxia's GDP	Growth Rate of Ningxia's GDP	Per Capita GDP	Growth Rate of Per Capita GDP
	(Billion)	(%)	(Yuan/person)	(%)
2013	232.77	9.8	35135	8.6
2014	247.39	8.0	36815	6.8
2015	257.94	8.0	37876	6.9
2016	278.14	8.1	40339	7.0
2017	320.03	7.8	45718	6.7
2018	351.02	7.0	49614	6.0
2019	374.85	6.5	52537	5.5
2020	395.63	3.9	55021	3.4
2021	458.82	6.7	63461	6.1
2022	510.46	4.0	70263	3.5
2023	53150	6.6	72957	6.3

Source: Calculated from the Official database of the National Bureau of Statistics, and the China and Ningxia Statistical Yearbooks. The per capita GDP growth rate in 2004, 2005, 2006, 2010, 2011 and 2020 is only estimated.

Table 12.2   Changes in Fixed Asset Investment in Ningxia (2013-2023)

	Fixed Asset Investment	Growth Rate of Fixed Asset Investment	Per Capita Fixed Asset Investment	Growth Rate of Per Capita Fixed Asset Investment
	(Billion)	(%)	(RMB)	(%)
2013	268.11	27.1	40257.4	25.8
2014	320.1	19.4	47212.2	17.3
2015	353.29	10.4	51651.0	9.4
2016	383.55	8.6	55186.5	6.8
2017	381.34	-0.6	54090.5	-2.0
2018	311.93	-18.2	43934.4	-18.8
2019	277.31	-11.1	38676.4	-12.0

Chapter 12 Special Report on the Opening up of Ningxia

Seizing opportunities, engaging in the building of the Belt and Road Initiative (BRI), and promoting advancement in opening up are the keys to Ningxia's healthy development. Since 2013, Ningxia has systematically set up the "1+X+6" policies on building the BRI and effectively promoting a wide, deep, and high level of opening up.

12.1 Current Situation of the Promotion of Ningxia's High-Level Opening Up

12.1.1 The Steady Improvement of an Open Economy

1. Comprehensive Improvement in Economic Quality and Efficiency

In 2023, Ningxia achieved its overall target at the best level in history. The regional GDP grew by 6.6%, ranking fifth in the country, and the growth rate of the added value of primary industry, secondary industry, and industry above designated size ranked second in the nation (with an increase of 7.7%, 8.5%, and 12.4% respectively). As can be seen from Tables 12.1, 12.2 and 12.3, the GDP of Ningxia was RMB232.77 billion in 2013 and RMB 531.50 billion in 2023, with a total growth rate of nearly 1.8-fold and an average annual growth rate of 8.61%. The per capita GDP increased from RMB 35135 in 2013 to RMB 46514 in 2023, with an absolute expansion of 1.32-fold and an average growth of 5.18%.

The investment in fixed assets has increased from RMB 268.11 billion in 2013 to RMB 339.09 billion in 2023, 1.26 times that of 2013, and remarkable achievements have been made in economic development. Looking across all provinces in the country, Ningxia's per capita GDP ranking has risen from 21st

overall national development strategy and foreign strategy. First, we shall give full play to the innovative advantages of market-oriented entities, accelerate the innovative application of exhibition forms, exhibition technologies, exhibition communication, exhibition services and other exhibition elements in the China-Arab States Expo, and build a digitalized and full-process exhibition ecosystem. Second, we should fully leverage the professional advantages of market-oriented entities, accurately match the supply and demand information of goods or services, reduce the transaction costs of domestic and foreign buyers, traders and suppliers, and comprehensively improve the level and ability of information, digitalization and intelligent services in the China-Arab States Expo. Third, we shall perform the international advantages of market-oriented entities, actively carry out trade promotion services, establish a cooperative and shared exhibition development mechanism, encourage market entities to cooperate with overseas professional exhibition agencies and mature exhibition projects, regularly hold professional exhibitions of the China-Arab States Expo abroad, continuously expand the influence and reputation of the China-Arab States Expo in Arab countries and countries along the Belt and Road, and build the China-Arab States Expo into a regional international exhibition brand.

Chapter 11 Special Report on the China-Arab States Expo

dual circulation linkage effect between Chinese and Arab countries' markets and resources.

In terms of the preparation work, we could consider the idea of government of the main driving force and market-oriented to hold the China-Arab States Expo well. Government of the main driving force mainly highlights the direction setting, rule setting and task setting. Direction setting refers to ensuring that all meetings, forums, exhibitions, and matchmaking activities focus on economic and trade cooperation during the process of scientifically formulating the strategic plan and overall plan for the China-Arab States Expo, always aiming to implement the strategies, plans, policies, and projects of China and Arab countries, always taking the consolidation of the sense of community of the Chinese nation as the main line, and leading the entire process of preparing for the China-Arab States Expo, and grasping the political direction. Rule setting refers to the government's research and introduction of policies and measures to promote the development of the China-Arab States Expo, following the laws of the exhibition industry, drawing on useful domestic and international experience, establishing open, fair and transparent market rules, and achieving the sustainable and healthy development of the Expo. It shall define the government's responsibilities for providing public services for exhibitions, and formulate rules and systems to promote the sustainable development of exhibitions in terms of strengthening financial incentives, optimizing the supervision of exhibits entering and leaving the country, improving financial and insurance services, enhancing the statistical system of the exhibition industry, and strengthening intellectual property protection. Task setting refers to the government's efforts to strengthen communication and coordination with Arabic government departments, national ministries, and local governments, striving for support from all parties, actively integrating national resources for economic and trade cooperation, and designing the indicators and outcomes to be achieved in the China-Arab States Expo in a practical and realistic manner. It also involves selecting market-oriented cooperation entities to ensure a pragmatic approach to the event and enhance the effectiveness of economic and trade cooperation.

The marketization mainly highlights innovation, professionalism and internationalization. Industry associations, chambers of commerce, intermediary organizations and enterprises are important partners in the institutional foreign-related forums and expositions, and play an irreplaceable role in serving the

Under the joint leadership of President Xi Jinping and the leaders of the Arab states, China-Arab relations are at the best level in history, and China-Arab all-round cooperation has ushered in major strategic opportunities. The China-Arab States Expo should take advantage of the opportunity and accelerate its development, build an important platform for high-quality cooperation of the BRI, and strive to play a more important role in the overall situation of China-Arab cooperation in the new era. First, we shall focus on serving the national economic and trade cooperation mechanisms and platforms. We will strengthen the cooperation with the Ministry of Commerce and the China Council for the Promotion of International Trade, actively play the role of bilateral and multilateral mechanisms such as the China-Arab Intergovernmental Economic and Trade Joint Committee and the China-Arab States Joint Chamber of Commerce, give full play to the platform function of the China-Arab States Expo, and promote mutual visits and exchanges between the governments and enterprises of China and Arab states. Second, we should focus on implementing China's investment and trade cooperation policy documents for Arab countries. Principles shall be adhered to, with enterprise as the main body, market as the leading factor, government as the driving force, and commercial operation. We shall connect China's production capacity advantages with the needs of Arab countries, carry out advanced, applicable, effective, employment-friendly, green and environmentally friendly production capacity cooperation with Arab countries, and support the industrialization process of Arab countries. Third, efforts shall be made to build a China-Arab intergovernmental cooperation platform for scientific and technological innovation. We shall build an integrated technology transfer collaboration network covering China and Arab countries, implement the China-Arab Science and Technology Partnership Program, and actively promote the application and promotion of scientific and technological achievements and advanced applicable technologies between the two sides. Fourth, we shall focus on promoting economic and trade cooperation between regions and Arab states. We shall innovate the organizational form of activities, hold investment and trade promotion activities in Arab countries on a regular basis, serve the provinces, autonomous regions and municipalities across the country to entering the Arab countries and open up markets, serve Arab countries' investment cooperation in various parts of China, expand the effectiveness of two-way economic and trade cooperation, and strengthen the

the building of a China-Arab community with a shared future in the new era, we shall focus on the key cooperation areas of the high-quality joint construction of the BRI between China and Arab countries, revitalize the overall resources of China's economic and trade cooperation with Arab countries, adapt to the development needs of Arab countries. Furthermore, the strategies, plans, policies and projects of China-Arab cooperation in the new era shall be implemented jointly, so as to build the China-Arab States Expo into an important platform for the high-quality joint construction of the BRI between China and Arab countries.

An important engine for boosting Ningxia's high-level opening up. Thoroughly implementing the spirit of the important speeches and instructions given by General Secretary Xi Jinping during his previous inspections in Ningxia, we shall consolidate the foundation of Ningxia's cooperation with Arab countries, give full play to the characteristics and advantages of cooperation with Arab countries, and improve the docking mechanism with the open platforms of other provinces and regions. In addition, we shall seize the major opportunities for the transfer of funds, technologies and industries from the eastern regions to the central and western regions, build a modern industrial system with characteristics and differentiation in line with local conditions, and form a development trend where high-level opening-up tasks are effectively integrated with the functions of the open platform of the China-Arab States Expo.

11.4 Paths to Successfully Host the China-Arab States Expo under the New Situation

As an extension and complement to the China-Arab Cooperation Forum in the economic and trade field, the China-Arab States Expo has, over the years, continuously optimized its operational mechanisms and top-level design. It has gradually established various exchange mechanisms, including opening ceremonies, guest-of-honor country and theme province series activities, exhibitions, investment and trade promotion events, and conferences and forums. The Expo has become an important platform for high-quality joint construction of the BRI between China and Arab countries, playing an increasingly significant and unique role in promoting economic and trade cooperation between the two sides.

industries with Arab countries, seek the converging points of interests and the greatest common divisor for cooperation, and form a coordinated development pattern featuring linkage between the higher and lower levels, connection between the domestic and foreign sectors, and mutual benefit and win-win results.

Combining the leading role of the market with the guidance of the government. We shall give full play to the dominant role of the market in the mechanism construction of the China-Arab States Expo, and better play the guiding and coordinating roles of the government in the preparatory work for the China-Arab States Expo, so as to jointly promote the effective and orderly operation of the China-Arab States Expo.

Combining goal orientation with problem orientation. We shall focus on the goal and requirement of high-quality joint construction of the BRI between China and Arab countries, accurately match the supply and demand structures in the fields of investment and trade, digital economy, scientific and technological cooperation, production capacity cooperation, and green development, study and solve the prominent problems existing in the development of the China-Arab States Expo, and enhance the synergy, linkage, integrity and effectiveness of development.

11.3.3　Functional Positioning

The main mechanism for serving China-Arab economic and trade cooperation. We shall strengthen the overall coordination of the China-Arab economic and trade cooperation mechanism at the national level, and clarify the functional positioning of the China-Arab States Expo as a centralized and unified economic and trade cooperation mechanism and a comprehensive service platform for both domestic and foreign exchanges with Arab countries. Moreover, we shall strengthen the coordination of the China-Arab economic and trade cooperation mechanism at the provincial level. Through establishing mutually beneficial cooperation relationships and the mechanism of holding events in turn, we shall optimize the allocation of economic and trade cooperation resources such as conference forums, and focus on enhancing the platform functions of the China-Arab States Expo.

An important platform for promoting the high-quality joint construction of the BRI between China and Arab countries. With the strategic goal of promoting

center on the cooperation pattern between China and Arab countries in the new era, and create characteristic incremental activities. Secondly, integrating the role of government and market. It shall adhere to the coordinated promotion principle of government guidance, market operation, enterprises as the main body, and win-win cooperation, and fully stimulate the enthusiasm of all sides to participate in the China-Arab States Expo. Thirdly, coordinating bilateral and multilateral aspects. It is to adhere to the working idea of negotiating cooperation multilaterally and facilitating implementation bilaterally. Jointly with the Arab side, we shall promote the implementation of the items agreed upon at the China-Arab Summit and the Ministerial Conference of the China-Arab States Cooperation Forum. Furthermore, we shall focus on improving the effective connection and synergy between the activities under the framework of the China-Arab States Expo and the bilateral economic and trade cooperation agenda by promoting multilateral cooperation through bilateral cooperation, enhancing the effectiveness of economic and trade cooperation in various forms such as bilateral cooperation, tripartite cooperation and multilateral cooperation. Fourthly, making comprehensive arrangements for scale and benefits. We shall steadily increase the scale and benefits of the China-Arab States Expo, prioritize small yet delicate projects in cooperation, carry out more projects with small investment, quick results and good economic, social and environmental benefits, and form more down-to-earth and people-centered cooperation achievements. Fifthly, balancing development and security. We shall firmly establish and practice the holistic view of national security, improve the risk prevention and control institutional mechanisms, strengthen overall coordination, clarify the responsibilities of all parties, ensure the guarantee of essential factors, and continuously improve the ability and level to respond to risks, meet challenges and turn risks into safety.

11.3.2 Basic Principles

Combing strategic alignment with coordinated development. We shall fully align with and implement the *Outline of the Comprehensive Cooperation between the People's Republic of China and Arab Countries*, the *Action Implementation Plan of the China-Arab States Cooperation Forum*, and the *Action Plan of the China-Gulf Cooperation Council Strategic Dialogue*. Upon this basis, we shall coordinate and align the economic and trade cooperation affairs of various departments and

11.3 Thoughts on Successfully Hosting the China-Arab States Expo under the New Situation

11.3.1 Overall Plan

In the next ten years, the China-Arab States Expo will uphold the banner of a community with a shared future for mankind, inherit and promote the Silk Road spirit, adhere to goal-oriented and action-oriented approaches, and be guided by the implementation of the Eight Joint Actions and the Five-pronged Cooperation Framework for China-Arab practical cooperation. It will actively build an upgraded version of the China-Arab States Expo with more refined functional positioning, practical innovation in the expo-organizing mechanism, significantly improved service levels, more solid cooperation foundations, and more prominent economic and trade results. It will steadily promote high-quality China-Arab cooperation in jointly building the BRI, continuously achieve new and greater results, and make greater contributions to Ningxia's high-level opening-up and high-quality development.

Under the strategic leadership of President Xi Jinping and Arab leaders, China-Arab relations are at their best in history, and the all-dimensional, multi-level, and wide-ranging cooperation pattern between China and Arab countries is continuously being enriched and deepened. The Eighth Plenary Session of the Thirteenth Central Committee of the Communist Party of Ningxia Hui Autonomous Region pointed out that we shall continuously raise the level of inland opening-up, serve and integrate into the joint construction of the BRI and the New Western Land-Sea Corridor, establish an industrial transfer undertaking cooperation mechanism, and steadily expand institutional opening-up. Against this backdrop, the China-Arab States Expo is facing significant strategic opportunities. It should follow the trend, strengthen internal capabilities, accelerate actions, strive to play a more important role in China-Arab cooperation in the new era, and focus on achieving the Five-pronged Overall Planning.

Firstly, making overall plans for inheritance and innovation. It shall maintain the good network of the China-Arab States Expo, consolidate the foundation for high-quality development, and refine and solidify the existing activities. Moreover, it is to focus on enhancing the ability of innovative development,

Samarkand Summit of the SCO in 2022, Egypt, Saudi Arabia and Qatar were approved as dialogue partners, while Bahrain, the United Arab Emirates and Kuwait were included in the new batch of dialogue partners that were agreed to be admitted[①].

Promoting the formation of a new pattern in the large-scale development of the western region in the new era has brought new opportunities for improving the platform functions of the China-Arab States Expo. On May 17, 2020, the *Guiding Opinions of the Central Committee of the Communist Party of China and the State Council on Promoting the Formation of a New Pattern in the Large-scale Development of the Western Region in the New Era* clearly stated that the western region should actively participate in and integrate into the construction of the BRI, strengthen the construction of open major transportation channels, build inland multi-level open platforms, successfully hold various national-level expositions, enhance the influence of the western region, develop a high-level open economy, and expand inter-regional interactive cooperation. On August 23, 2024, the Political Bureau of the Central Committee of the Communist Party of China held a meeting to review the *Several Policy Measures for Further Promoting the Formation of a New Pattern in the Large-scale Development of the Western Region*. The meeting pointed out that the large-scale development of the western region is a major strategic decision made by the Party Central Committee. It is necessary to deeply understand the strategic intention of the Party Central Committee, accurately grasp the positioning and mission of the large-scale development of the western region in promoting Chinese path to modernization, maintain strategic focus, consistently implement relevant work, focus on major protection, major opening up, and high-quality development, accelerate the construction of a new development pattern, and enhance the overall strength and sustainable development ability of the region[②].

---

① "Why Do Arab Countries Hope to Join the Shanghai Cooperation Organization," People's Daily Online, http://world.people.com.cn/n1/2023/0707/c1002-40030697.html, July 7, 2023.

② Xinhua News Agency, "The Political Bureau of the CPC Central Committee Holds a Meeting to Review Several Policy Measures for Further Promoting the Formation of a New Pattern in the Large-scale Development of the Western Region. General Secretary of the CPC Central Committee Xi Jinping Presides over the Meeting," the Official Website of Chinese government, https://www.gov.cn/yaowen/liebiao/202408/content_6970134.htm, August 23, 2024.

setting a benchmark for collective cooperation among developing countries[①]. On May 30, 2024, the 10th Ministerial Conference of the China-Arab States Cooperation Forum was held in Beijing. Both China and Arab states conducted in-depth discussions on stepping up the implementation of the outcomes of the First China-Arab Summit and accelerating the construction of the China-Arab community with a shared future, and signed cooperation documents such as the *Beijing Declaration* and the *Action Implementation Plan of the Forum from 2024 to 2026*.

The joining of Arab countries to multilateral mechanisms such as the BRICS Summit has brought new opportunities for innovating the operating mechanisms of the China-Arab States Expo. Arab countries are important cooperation partners for the international development of Global South countries[②]. The foundation of the rise of the Global South lies in long-term economic development. In the future, for playing more important role of the Global South on the international stage, continuous economic development will still be essential. Whether it is South-South cooperation or North-South dialogue, development has always been the core topic of the Global South[③]. Currently, the BRICS Summit has become the most powerful and dynamic international development cooperation mechanism among the Global South. Its influence in global governance has been continuously enhanced and it has exerted a huge attraction on a vast number of developing countries including those in the Middle East. At present, three Arab countries, namely Egypt, Saudi Arabia and the United Arab Emirates, have officially joined the BRICS family. Moreover, Arab countries are also actively applying to join the Shanghai Cooperation Organization (SCO). At the Dushanbe Summit of the SCO in 2021, the Secretariat of the SCO and the Secretariat of the League of Arab States signed a Memorandum of Understanding on cooperation, and it was decided at the meeting to admit Saudi Arabia, Egypt and Qatar as dialogue partners. At the

---

[①] Wang Yi, "Accelerating the Building of a China-Arab Community with a Shared Future for a New Era—*On* the Occasion of the Convening of the 10th Ministerial Conference of the China-Arab States Cooperation Forum," People's Daily Online, https://www.gov.cn/yaowen/liebiao/202405/content_6954208.htm, May 29, 2024.

[②] Liu Zhongmin, "The Middle East Segment of the 'Global South': Historical Logic and Practical Value," the International Cooperation Center, https://www.icc.org.cn/publications/internationaloberservation/2070.html, December 8, 2023.

[③] Xu Xiujun et al, "The Strategic Status and Role of the Global South Against the Background of the Transformation of the International Order," *International Forum*, 2024(2).

8.2%. The region has established 152 overseas direct investment enterprises in 36 countries and regions worldwide, with a total outbound investment of USD 4.39 billion. Among them, 23 overseas investment enterprises have been set up in six Arab countries, with a total investment of USD 435 million. From the perspective of trade markets, Ningxia has conducted economic and trade exchanges with 59 countries along the "Belt and Road," including Russia, India, Malaysia, and Saudi Arabia, gradually forming a diversified market landscape. In 2022, among Ningxia's major import and export markets, imports and exports to countries along the "Belt and Road" amounted to 8.02 billion yuan, representing a year-on-year increase of 23.7% and accounting for 31.2% of the region's total import and export value. Imports and exports to Middle Eastern countries reached 1.099 billion yuan, up 38.7%.

11.2 Multiple Development Opportunities under the New Situation of the China-Arab States Expo

The outcomes of the First China-Arab Summit and the 10th Ministerial Conference of the China-Arab States Cooperation Forum have brought new opportunities for innovating the content of the China-Arab States Expo. In December 2022, the First China-Arab Summit issued three important outcome documents. *The Riyadh Declaration of the First China-Arab Summit* announced that both sides unanimously agreed to make every effort to build a China-Arab community with a shared future for a new era. *The Outline of the China-Arab Comprehensive Cooperation Plan* put forward 182 cooperation measures in 18 fields such as politics, economy and trade, investment, and finance. The Document on *Deepening the China-Arab Strategic Partnership Oriented towards Peace and Development* covered important contents including the agreement of both sides to deepen the China-Arab strategic partnership, advocate multilateralism, strengthen cooperation within the framework of jointly building the BRI, and enhance the construction of the China-Arab States Cooperation Forum. Over the past two decades, the China-Arab States Cooperation Forum has established 19 important mechanisms such as the ministerial conference, the strategic and political dialogue, the forum on reform and development, and the energy cooperation conference. It has also released 85 important outcome documents, useful insights for local governments in establishing foreign economic and trade cooperation mechanisms. The sixth China-Arab States Expo created conditions for various provinces, regions, and municipalities, as well as domestic leading enterprises, to engage in "zero-distance" connections and "point-to-point" negotiations with Arab countries. As a result, 37 projects were signed with countries such as Saudi Arabia and Jordan, with a total signed amount of 20.62 billion yuan. Additionally, 24 domestic investment projects were facilitated, with an investment amount of 3.06 billion yuan. Guangdong, as the theme province, reached cooperation agreements on 37 projects with relevant sides such as Saudi Arabia and Shaanxi province, with a total signed amount of 10.04 billion yuan.

Fourth, Ningxia has reached a new level in its opening up to the outside world. Since 2013, Ningxia has fully utilized the China-Arab States Expo to actively integrate into and serve the construction of the BRI. It has built cooperation platforms, tapped into trade potential, optimized the investment environment, improved policy support, developed open carriers, facilitated external channels, and adhered to a combination of overall advancement and key breakthroughs, as well as a combination of mechanism innovation and policy guidance. Ningxia has achieved high-level opening up to the outside world on a larger scale and at a higher level, promoted the construction of a strategic highland for opening up to the west, and made phased achievements in participating in the BRI. The functionality of its opening-up channels has been gradually enhanced. As of the end of 2023, Yinchuan Hedong International Airport has opened 140 routes to 96 cities, including 85 domestic destinations with a 100% direct flight rate to provincial capital cities, and 11 international destinations with 12 international (and regional) routes already opened. Ningxia has strengthened cooperation with coastal ports and intensified exchanges with provinces and municipalities along the New Western Land-Sea Corridor. It has initially established a land-based open access pattern that connects the borders to the sea and links the south to the north. By building an international cargo system that integrates various transportation modes such as international railways and rail-sea intermodal transportation, Ningxia has formed a network of port passages for northwest outbound and southeast seaborne traffic, providing important support for the regional international logistics center. The level of open economy development has steadily improved. From 2013 to 2022, Ningxia cumulatively utilized foreign direct investment (FDI) of USD 2.36 billion, with an average annual growth rate of

Chapter 11 Special Report on the China-Arab States Expo

Arab States Expo in 2023, the number of signed projects reached 403, with a planned total investment and trade value of 170.97 billion yuan, representing a 75.32% increase in signed projects compared to the first Expo in 2013. The cooperation projects encompass various aspects such as commodity trade, investment cooperation, policy report releases, and friendship city construction. Investment cooperation extensively covers infrastructure development, capacity cooperation, high-tech, health and wellness, modern agriculture, logistics, playing a significant platform role in promoting the high-quality development of the BRI. In terms of technological cooperation, under the framework of the China-Arab States Expo, the cooperation forms between China and Arab countries in high-tech fields have become more diversified, with broadened cooperation areas tightened cooperation relationships. Through high-quality collaboration among multiple sides, the China-Arab Technology Transfer Center and the China-Arab Technology Transfer and Innovation Cooperation Conference have been elevated from local experiences to national and international mechanisms that promote policies and projects for China-Arab scientific and technological cooperation. In terms of industrial capacity cooperation, the China-Arab States Expo has facilitated the joint construction of industrial parks between China and Arab countries, and signing agreements between domestic enterprises and overseas industrial parks. This has provided a reference for domestic enterprises to explore international markets and establish a new model of two-way investment cooperation by going out and bringing in with Arab countries and other countries along the BRI, effectively promoting China-Arab industrial capacity cooperation.

The third aspect is the pragmatic development of cooperation between domestic provinces and regions with Arab countries. As an important platform for China and Arab countries to jointly build the BRI, the China-Arab States Expo connects the markets of both sides and creates a mutually beneficial and open platform. It actively mobilizes the domestic resources, greatly stimulating the enthusiasm for active participation from domestic provinces, regions, and municipalities. Since the sixth China-Arab States Expo, the scale of participation from domestic provinces, regions, and municipalities has continued to expand, with the quality and standard of participating enterprises constantly improving. This has deepened cooperation and exchanges in various fields between the relevant provinces, regions, and municipalities and Arab countries, and provided for policy communication between China and Arab countries. It serves as a platform for high-level dialogues and policy communication between China and Arab countries, promoting the continuous expansion of strategic cooperation between the two sides. Over the years, 112 countries and regions, 29 Chinese and foreign politicians, and 383 Chinese and foreign ministerial-level guests have participated in the Expo. The Expo has become an important platform for policy communication, negotiation, and information dissemination between Chinese and Arab governments, with the role of multi-field and multi-level exchanges becoming increasingly prominent. In December 2022, when President Xi Jinping traveled to Saudi Arabia to attend the "Three Summits" with Arab and Gulf Cooperation Council (GCC) leaders and the China-Saudi Arabia Summit, he specifically invited Saudi Arabia to be the guest of honor country at the sixth China-Arab States Expo, which was also included in the *China-Saudi Arabia Joint Statement* and the *China-Arab States Comprehensive Cooperation Plan*. This opened a new chapter for the Expo in serving presidential diplomacy. Arab countries have given high praise and positive responses, expressing their strong willingness to leverage the Expo to jointly build the BRI and promote economic and trade cooperation between China and Arab countries.

Secondly, economic and trade cooperation has been continuously deepened. The China-Arab States Expo has always focused on economic and trade cooperation, providing a platform for businessmen from China and Arab countries to engage in economic and trade communication, investment promotion, and achieving economic complementarity. This has facilitated rapid bilateral economic and trade growth and contributed to the economic development and well-being of both sides. In terms of signed projects, the China-Arab States Expo centers on enterprises and focuses on economic and trade cooperation. It organizes various exhibitions and forums centered around commodity trade, service trade, and technology trade to promote practical economic and trade cooperation between China and Arab countries. Looking at the economic and trade achievements of past China-Arab States Expos, the number of signed projects has gradually increased. In 2013, the Expo's economic and trade activities resulted in the signing of 158 cooperation projects with a total signed amount of 259.9 billion yuan, an increase of 34 projects and 18.82% in the signed amount compared to the Ningxia Investment and Trade Fair and China-Arab States Economic and Trade Forum in 2012. By the sixth China-

Chapter 11 Special Report on the China-Arab States Expo

President Xi Jinping pointed out that the China-Arab States Expo has become an important platform for serving the joint construction of the BRI between China and Arab countries.

11.1.2 The Achievements of the China-Arab States Expo under the Framework of the Joint Construction of the BRI by China and Arab countries

With comprehensive, multi-layered, and cross-sectoral cooperation between China and Arab countries, the China-Arab States Expo has always adhered to the goal of "serving national strategies and focusing on economic and trade cooperation." It has gradually developed into an international exposition with China and Arab countries as the main participants, integrating functions such as high-level dialogues, economic and trade promotion, exhibition negotiations, and opening up to the world. It has become an important platform for advancing and implementing pragmatic cooperation between China and Arab countries, exerting a broad and far-reaching influence in the international community. In September 2019, during an interview with Xinhua News Agency, Khalid Hanafi, Secretary-General of the General Union of Arab Chambers of Commerce, Industry, and Agriculture, stated that the China-Arab States Expo is an excellent platform for promoting economic and trade cooperation between China and Arab countries. China's open attitude towards the world, including Arab countries, will benefit both China and Arab countries[①]. The Expo has made positive contributions and achieved fruitful results in continuing the friendship between China and Arab countries, deepening friendly and cooperative relations, fostering consensus on cooperation in jointly building the BRI, promoting high-quality economic and trade cooperation, strengthening multi-field cooperation between provinces (autonomous regions and municipalities) and Arab countries, and accelerating Ningxia's opening-up and comprehensive economic development.

Firstly, high-level dialogues have been highly effective. As a high-level exchange platform between China and Arab countries, the China-Arab States Expo is not only a channel for commercial and trade cooperation but also

---

[①] "China-Arab Practical Cooperation Sets Sail towards New Areas: Interview with Khalid, Secretary-General of the Arab Federation for Agriculture, Industry and Commerce," Xinhuanet, http://www.xinhuanet.com/world/2019-09/06/c_1124968827.htm, September 6, 2019.

Promotion of International Trade (CCPIT) and the General Union of Arab Chambers of Commerce, Industry, and Agriculture. These efforts aim to closely facilitate mutual visits and exchanges between governments and enterprises from both China and Arab countries, actively promote trade and investment facilitation, and foster a positive trend of policy communication fostering consensus and economic and trade cooperation benefiting the people. Secondly, focusing on the implementation of China's policy documents on investment and trade cooperation with Arab countries, the China-Arab States Expo fully plays its role in facilitating enterprises' participation in overseas industrial park investment promotion and policy coordination. This helps to vitalize the investment advantages of some Arab countries and China's production capacity advantages, thereby promoting a dual circulation of industries and markets between China and Arab countries and driving sustainable development in bilateral investment, economy and trade. Thirdly, establishing a platform for scientific and technological innovation cooperation between China and Arab governments, People's government of Ningxia Hui Autonomous Region and the Ministry of Science and Technology took the lead in implementing the important initiative proposed by President Xi Jinping at the opening ceremony of the Sixth Ministerial Conference of the China-Arab Cooperation Forum to explore the establishment of the China-Arab Technology Transfer Center. In September 2015, they jointly founded the China-Arab States Technology Transfer and Innovation Cooperation Conference and established the China-Arab States Technology Transfer Center, which has become an important mechanism and pragmatic platform for promoting scientific and technological innovation cooperation between China and Arab countries. Fourthly, with the aim of enhancing the capacity to serve local economic and trade cooperation with Arab countries, innovative mechanisms for organizing conferences have been introduced, including the establishment of "dual guest-of-honor countries" and "dual theme provinces." High-quality cases of economic and trade cooperation between China and Arab countries are collected to comprehensively showcase local economic characteristics and strengths, while gathering the economic and trade cooperation needs of Arab countries. This serves to assist all provinces (autonomous regions and municipalities) in China in exploring markets in Arab countries and facilitates Arab investment and cooperation in various parts of China. In January 2016, during his visit to the headquarters of the Arab League,

Chapter 11   Special Report on the China-Arab States Expo

between governments and enterprises from both China and Arab countries. The second is to focus on implementing China's policy documents on investment and trade cooperation with Arab countries. Adhering to the principles of enterprise-centeredness, market orientation, government promotion, and commercial operation, it connects China's production capacity advantages with the needs of Arab countries to carry out advanced, applicable, effective, employment-friendly, and environmentally friendly production capacity cooperation with Arab countries, supporting the industrialization process of Arab countries. Thirdly, it focuses on establishing a platform for scientific and technological innovation cooperation between China and Arab governments. This includes constructing an integrated technology transfer and collaboration network that covers both China and Arab countries, implementing the China-Arab Science and Technology Partnership Plan, and actively promoting the application and communication of scientific and technological achievements as well as advanced and applicable technologies between the two sides. Fourthly, it strives to promote economic and trade cooperation between various local regions and Arab countries. It aims to innovate the organizational forms of activities to serve provinces (autonomous regions and municipalities) across China in their efforts to enter Arab countries and explore new markets, as well as to facilitate Arab investments and cooperation in various regions of China, thereby expanding the effectiveness of bilateral economic and trade activities.

From 2013 to 2023, the China-Arab States Expo has been successfully held for six consecutive times. In order to fully realize its functions and roles, the Expo has actively implemented the important speeches delivered by President Xi Jinping at the ministerial meetings of the China-Arab Cooperation Forum over the years. It has also actively cooperated with the implementation of China's policy documents towards Arab countries, resulting in the formation of a series of important mechanisms to promote economic and trade cooperation between China and Arab states. Firstly, focusing on the construction of national economic and trade cooperation mechanisms and platforms, the China-Arab States Expo fully leverages its role in economic and trade policy communication and project matchmaking and negotiation. It organizes national-level, international, and institutionalized China-Arab Business Summits, with participation from government departments, important chambers of commerce and industry, and various enterprises organized by the China Council for the

relations and build platforms for economic and trade cooperation is becoming ever more apparent. Based on Ningxia's geographical location, its history of exchanges with Arab countries, and the foundation for economic and trade cooperation, this important mission has historically been entrusted to Ningxia.

The China-Arab Economic and Trade Forum is characterized by a high degree of functional integration. Under its mechanism, its functional modules (activities) encompass economic and trade policy communication, investment and trade, infrastructure construction and energy, finance, agriculture, science and technology, education, radio and television, ecological and environmental protection cooperation, primarily serving three major functions. First, keeping in line with the national strategy and policy towards the Arab states. The main purpose is to invite national leaders to attend the opening ceremony of the China-Arab States Economic and Trade Forum and deliver keynote speeches, and actively undertake institutional activities under the framework of the China-Arab States Cooperation Forum in order to reflect its high-level and authoritative characteristics. The second is to widely promote cooperation between China and Arab countries in multiple fields. With the theme of "Inheriting Friendship, Deepening Cooperation, and Pursuing Common Development," the China-Arab Economic and Trade Forum establishes a high-level dialogue platform for governments, enterprises, and the private sectors to make economic and trade exchanges, and is committed to building a new international mechanism for China-Arab economic and trade cooperation. The third is to promote the development of Ningxia's inland open economy.

The functions of the China-Arab States Expo have gradually shifted from highly integrated multi-field cooperation to focusing on economic and trade cooperation. Its functional modules have been optimized and adjusted with a focus on economic and trade cooperation, including promoting economic and trade facilitation, production capacity cooperation, and technological cooperation under the framework of the joint China-Arab BRI. These modules primarily serve four major functions. The first is to focus on serving national economic and trade cooperation mechanisms and platform construction. It actively leverages the role of bilateral and multilateral mechanisms such as the Intergovernmental Joint Economic and Trade Committee and the Joint Chamber of Commerce of China and Arab Countries, and fully utilizes the platform functions of the China-Arab States Expo to facilitate mutual visits and exchanges

Chapter 11 Special Report on the China-Arab States Expo

Central Committee and the State Council, some local governments in China have started to hold regional foreign-related exhibition activities, undertaking the function of serving the country's overall diplomacy in the field of economic and trade cooperation. These exhibitions have been distinctive and effective. However, from both national and local perspectives, there has always been a lack of a national-level economic and trade exhibition platform mainly opening to cooperation with Arab countries. In 2004, the China-Arab States Cooperation Forum was established. With the purpose of enhancing dialogue and cooperation, and promoting peace and development, China and Arab states have extensively implemented exchanges and cooperation in the fields of politics, economy and trade, culture, environment, effectively functioning as a platform to promote economic and trade cooperation between China and Arab states. However, on the whole, there is still a lack of a China-Arab economic and trade cooperation platform that can fully leverage non-official forces and subsequently integrate government and civil sectors. From the Arabic perspective, changes in international, regional, and domestic political and economic situations have provided opportunities and scope for further China-Arab cooperation. At the international level, China's development model has been recognized by Arab countries, and there has been a widespread trend of looking eastward among Arab countries. After the 2008 international financial crisis, Arab countries have had more expectations for economic and trade cooperation and even political cooperation with China. At the regional level, at the end of 2010, the West Asia and North Africa were in turmoil, and the Arab world was generally in a historical stage of seeking stability, development, and benefit for the people in the midst of change. The transformation and upgrading of China's economy has provided greater space for China-Arab cooperation. In the process of exploring development paths that are in line with their respective national conditions, developing mutually beneficial cooperation with China is in line with the strategic interests of all countries. Domestically, Arab countries are confronted with the arduous tasks of vigorously strengthening infrastructure development, implementing strategies for industrial diversification, accelerating economic transformation, and improving people's livelihoods. Deepening economic and trade cooperation between China and Arab countries has become a strategic choice for both sides to achieve their respective economic development. Against this backdrop, the urgent need to explore the mechanisms to deepen China-Arab

11.1 Review of the Development of the China-Arab States Expo Since the Joint Construction of the BRI

The China-Arab States Expo is a national-level and international comprehensive exposition jointly hosted by the Ministry of Commerce of China, the China Council for the Promotion of International Trade, and the People's Government of Ningxia Hui Autonomous Region. Its predecessor was the China-Arab States Economic and Trade Forum held from 2010 to 2012. Since 2013, President Xi Jinping has sent congratulatory messages to the China-Arab States Expo for five consecutive times, repeatedly pointing out that the Expo has played a positive role in deepening pragmatic cooperation between China and Arab countries and promoting high-quality development of the joint construction of the BRI. This fully demonstrates the attention and support of the CPC Central Committee to the successful hosting of the China-Arab States Expo. With the in-depth development of China-Arab relations and the continuous accumulation of practical experiences in Ningxia, the functional orientation of the China-Arab States Expo has gradually shifted from "highly integrated cooperation in multiple fields between China and Arab countries" to "deepening economic and trade cooperation," and its service scope has expanded from promoting cooperation between Ningxia and Arab countries, China and Arab countries, to international cooperation under the BRI. In terms of mechanism building, activities in the science and technology sector have risen from local experience to a nationally recognized mechanism for science and technology exchange and cooperation between China and Arab countries. The Expo has become an important international economic and trade cooperation mechanism under the framework of the joint construction of the BRI between China and Arab countries.

11.1.1 The Joint Construction of the BRI Between China and Arab Countries Prompting a Transformation in the Functional Characteristics of the China-Arab States Expo, from "Highly Integrated Cooperation in Multiple Fields" to "Focusing on Economic and Trade Cooperation"

Since the beginning of the 21st century, with the approval of the CPC

position that these relations occupy in the century-long changes, as well as their crucial strategic importance for advancing the great cause of building a powerful country and realizing national rejuvenation. In the mid-December 2022, President Xi Jinping attended the first China-Arab States Summit in Riyadh, the capital of Saudi Arabia, leading the overall diplomacy and collective cooperation between China and Arab countries to a historic new height. Both China and Arab countries have vigorously and effectively implemented the outcomes of the first China-Arab Summit, with remarkable achievements in jointly building the Belt and Road Initiative (BRI). The full coverage of the BRI has been achieved among the 22 Arab countries of the League of Arab States (LAS), indicating that the BRI cooperation mechanism and path have been widely recognized and hold great appeal among Arab countries and the LAS. On October 18, 2023, President Xi Jinping attended the opening ceremony of the Third Belt and Road Forum for International Cooperation in Beijing and delivered a keynote speech, in which he elaborated on the original aspiration of the BRI, reviewed the achievements of its development, summarized the experience of cooperation, and announced eight actions. His speech received warm responses and active support from all sides. On May 30, 2024, President Xi Jinping attended the opening ceremony of the 10th Ministerial Meeting of the China-Arab Cooperation Forum and delivered a keynote speech, further proposing to build a "Five Major Cooperation Frameworks" with Arab countries, with a more vibrant innovation-driven pattern, a larger-scale investment and finance pattern, a more dimensional energy cooperation pattern, a more balanced economic and trade reciprocal pattern, and a broader dimension of humanistic exchanges pattern, in order to accelerate a China-Arab community with a shared future[①]. China-Arab relations are at their best level in history, and China-Arab comprehensive cooperation is facing significant strategic opportunities. The China-Arab States Expo shall seize this momentum and accelerate its actions, striving to play a more important role in the overall picture of China-Arab cooperation in the new era.

[①] "*President* Xi Jinping Attends the Opening Ceremony of the 10th Ministerial Meeting of the *China-Arab* Cooperation Forum and Delivers a Keynote Speech," People's Daily, May 31, 2024, p. 1.

Chapter 11   Special Report on the China-Arab States Expo

The medium and long-term major development strategy at the meeting of the Central Finance and Economics Commission proposed by Xi Jinping, general secretary of the Communist Party of China (CPC) Central Committee and Chinese president in April 2020, which is to create a new development paradigm with the domestic cycle as the mainstay, and domestic and international cycles reinforcing each other. It has overall guiding significance for promoting high-quality development and comprehensively building a modern socialist country. The report of the 20th National Congress of the Communist Party of China further proposed that endogenous dynamism and reliability of the domestic cycle, and the quality and standard of the international cycle shall be enhanced[①]. From China's development experience, actively participating in the international cycle has been a decisive factor in achieving long-term rapid economic development since the reform and opening-up, which is the fundamental basis for us to firmly participate in and continuously enhance international circulation. In the new development paradigm, the domestic cycle is the foundation and mainstay, while participating in the international cycle is an inevitable requirement under economic globalization and the international industrial division of labor.

General Secretary Xi Jinping's repeated efforts to promote leapfrog development in China-Arab relations fully demonstrate the special and significant

---

[①] Xi Jinping, *Upholding the Great Banner of Socialism with Chinese Characteristics, and Striving Together for the Comprehensive Construction of a Socialist Modernized Country — Report at the 20th National Congress of the Communist Party of China*, People's Press, First Edition, October 2022, p. 28.

Chapter 10 Special Report on China-Arab States Cooperation in Tourism

our historical sites. We will provide excellent services for Chinese travelers."[①]

Moreover, the Qatari government announced that the platform created for the Fan ID card during the World Cup has been transformed into a portal for tourists entering Qatar. Oman is also developing its first large-scale integrated facility project, Khazaen Economic City, which includes not only ports and economic infrastructure but also hotels, residential areas, and recreational zones.[②] Various Arab states have adopted multiple measures to welcome Chinese tourists and offer high-quality services to attract them.

The relationship between China and the Arab states has a long history, with peace, cooperation, openness, inclusivity, mutual learning, and mutual benefit being the consistent themes of their interactions. Over the past 70-plus years since the founding of the People's Republic of China, China and the Arab states have stood by each other in their pursuit of national independence and rejuvenation, remaining united and cooperative on the world's political and economic stage. This friendship and collaboration have achieved unprecedented breadth and depth. Today, as China and the Arab states face similar opportunities and challenges, it is even more necessary to continue this historic friendship, deepen strategic cooperation, and jointly build a China-Arab states community with a shared future for the new era, creating an even brighter future for China-Arab states relations.[③]

---

① "Tourism in the Middle East Accelerates Recovery," People's Daily, http://world.people.com.cn/n1/2023/0228/c1002-32632599.html, February 28, 2023.

② "Strong Recovery in Middle East Tourism Market; Sustainable Tourism Becomes a Focus," China News, https://www.chinanews.com/m/gj/2023/05-11/10005120.shtml, May 11, 2023.

③ "China-Arab States Cooperation Report in the New Era," Website of the Ministry of Foreign Affairs of China, https://www.mfa.gov.cn/web/ziliao_674904/tytj_674911/zcwj_674915/202212/t20221201_10983991.shtml, December 1, 2022.

Chinese-language signs at major attractions, encouraging the training of Chinese-speaking guides, and launching a Chinese tourism hotline. Since the signing of the visa-free agreement and the tourism cooperation memorandum of understanding between China and the UAE, both sides have actively promoted tourism collaboration under the China-Arab States "Belt and Road" Framework, strengthened airline partnerships, and improved decision-making for flight route openings. Unique and tailored transportation solutions have addressed urban and intra-urban transit challenges, greatly enhancing travel convenience between China and Arab states. In February 2023, the head of Dubai's Department of Tourism and Commerce Marketing expressed a warm welcome to Chinese tourists through a video message: "We are fully prepared to welcome back Chinese tourists. New attractions and experiences await you, and it's time to create new cherished memories here."① The General Manager of Ferrari World Abu Dhabi added, "We have missed our Chinese visitors greatly and cannot wait to welcome you."② In 2023, Abu Dhabi's airports recorded a total passenger volume of 23 million, marking a year-on-year growth of 44.5%. Within 60 days of its official renaming to Zayed International Airport, the airport handled 4.48 million passengers. As of December 2023, Zayed International Airport serves 117 travel destinations, an increase of around 20% from 100 cities in 2022.

In 2023, EgyptAir announced that it would increase the number of flights between Egypt and China to 13 per week starting in March. The Chairman of EgyptAir noted that both Egypt and China boast ancient civilizations with long histories, and Egypt looks forward to welcoming Chinese tourists. "We invite Chinese visitors to come and enjoy the local cuisine," said the manager of a traditional restaurant in the Zamalek district of Cairo, adding that the return of Chinese tourists would greatly boost the Egyptian tourism sector and contribute to the prosperity of global tourism. Egyptian Foreign Minister Sameh Shoukry stated, "We look forward to seeing more Chinese tourists visit Egypt and explore

---

① "Dubai Immigration Chief: Welcoming Chinese Tourists to the UAE," Sohu News, https://www.sohu.com/a/722460320_121124399, September 22, 2023.

② "Missing Chinese Tourists! After Three Years, UAE Rolls Out the Red Carpet for the Return of Chinese Tour Groups," Net Ease News, https://m.163.com/dy/article/HT53CJ050530WJIN.html, February 9, 2023.

Chapter 10 Special Report on China-Arab States Cooperation in Tourism

Environment of Albania, continuing to deepen tourism cooperation. This collaboration actively advocates for and pragmatically advances the establishment of a tourism community. Through the formation of alliance consultative bodies, a stable dialogue mechanism and regular meetings have been set up to conduct targeted research and to coordinate and promote fundamental concerns in tourism development within the alliance, such as visas, flights, talent exchange, and marketing promotion. Moreover, a communication platform for tourism enterprises has been established to strengthen personnel exchanges and promote project cooperation. Additionally, a tourism statistics and data system within the alliance has been created. Such initiatives enable countries to fully understand the development status of tourism and the achievements within the alliance.

In May 2023, the 30th edition of the Arabian Travel Market, themed "Working Towards Net Zero," was held at the Dubai World Trade Centre in the UAE.[①] This event brought together over 2,000 exhibitors and 34000 participants from more than 150 countries and regions. The Arabian Travel Market is the largest tourism trade show in the Arab world and the third largest globally. This year's exhibition covered various fields such as travel technology, aviation, hospitality, cruises, and attractions. It explored innovative and sustainable development trends in the global tourism industry and assessed growth strategies for key sectors.

In 2023, Saudi Arabia announced the construction of a new city spanning 19 square kilometers northwest of Riyadh, with its centerpiece being the New Murabba, a 400-meter-high cubical structure that correlates to the Old Murabba in the southern part of Riyadh. Once completed, it will be the world's largest standalone building. The New Murabba will leverage digital and virtual technology to create an immersive virtual space for visitors. In May, Saudi Arabia also unveiled plans for several mega-scale integrated cultural and tourism projects, including Neom, Amaala, Diriyah, the Red Sea, and Qiddiya.

Following the establishment of the "Hala China" Executive Committee in Dubai in 2018, and subsequent to the visa exemption agreement between the Chinese and UAE governments, a series of policies were implemented to attract Chinese tourists and enhance services. These measures included installing

---

① "May 1–4: Join the 30th Arabian Travel Market!" MENA Vision, https://zhuanlan.zhihu.com/p/625780274, April 28, 2023.

Many social media users expressed encouragement and approval of this initiative.

In addition, the "Chinese Language fever" in Arab states has been propelled by the rapid development of the "Online Silk Road." Several Chinese internet companies have actively participated in establishing online Chinese classrooms and mobile smart classrooms. Utilizing internet platforms, dedicated Chinese learning platforms tailored for Arab states have been created. These platforms offer a variety of courses suitable for Chinese learners in Arab states, including language learning, Chinese language exams, and "Chinese + vocational skills" programs, integrating advanced technologies such as artificial intelligence, virtual reality, and big data into innovative Chinese education models.[①]

Since 2013, China has trained 25000 various professionals for Arab states, provided approximately 11000 government scholarship opportunities, and dispatched 80 medical teams comprising nearly 1700 medical personnel. As of October 2022, four Arab states had announced the inclusion of Chinese in their national education systems, 15 Arab states had established Chinese language departments locally, and 13 Arab states hosted 20 Confucius Institutes and 2 independent Confucius Classrooms.

In 2023, China and Arab states further strengthened cooperation in training tourism professionals, jointly exploring the development direction and pathways for building core competencies for tourism professionals in the digital era. This included building a high-quality workforce skilled in tourism planning, design, operation, and management to improve the professionalism of tourism practitioners and cultivate more international, interdisciplinary talent for both sides. The collaboration between China and Arab states in the fields of tourism, education, and culture has been vibrant, broadening cultural exchanges and deepening mutual understanding.

10.3.4　Arab states Actively Engage in Tourism Cooperation with China

In February 2023, China and Albania signed a Memorandum of Understanding on Tourism Cooperation between the Ministry of Culture and Tourism of the People's Republic of China and the Ministry of Tourism and

---

① "'Chinese Language Fever' Reflects 'China-Arab States Cooperation Fever,'" People's Daily Overseas Edition, https://www.chinanews.com/m/gj/2023/05-11/10005120.shtml, May 11, 2023.

Chapter 10 Special Report on China-Arab States Cooperation in Tourism

pragmatic China-Arab states cooperation, enhances mutual understanding and trust through tourism, fosters civilizational exchange and mutual learning, and contributes to building a China-Arab states community with a shared future in the new era.

10.3.3 Continuously Deepened Cooperation Between China and Arab States in the Field of Education

In June 2023, the Confucius Institute in the Prince Sultan University, jointly established by Prince Sultan University in Saudi Arabia and Shenzhen University, was officially inaugurated in Riyadh, the capital of Saudi Arabia. This marked the operation of Saudi Arabia's first officially registered Confucius Institute. Several other Arab states also host multiple Confucius Institutes and independent Confucius classrooms. The Saudi education authorities have introduced a series of incentive measures to encourage the learning of Chinese. For example, students participating in Chinese courses are recognized as engaging in volunteer service; the Ministry of Education of Saudi Arabia will select outstanding students nationwide for commendation, with study tours to China being part of the rewards. In addition to the joint Confucius Institutes established with China, several Arab states have independently increased the proportion of Chinese language education in their national education systems. Currently, four Arab states—Saudi Arabia, Egypt, the UAE, and Tunisia—have integrated Chinese into their national education curricula.

The "Chinese Language fever" in Arab states continues to rise, demonstrating the increasingly close cooperation between China and Arab states. There are more and more Chinese classrooms in Arab states, with mandarin classes being incorporated into the curricula of students in states such as Saudi Arabia, Egypt, and the UAE. In Morocco and Jordan, many young people enjoy singing Chinese songs and choose to work in China. Numerous Arab youth have even adopted Chinese names for themselves. At King Fahd School in Saudi Arabia, students conduct morning assemblies in Chinese, with videos of these assemblies sparking widespread discussion not only within Saudi Arabia but also being reported by media across other Arab states. The UAE's *Gulf News* noted that this school's innovative approach of holding morning meetings in Chinese was introduced against the backdrop of the Saudi education department's initiative to enhance Chinese language teaching and improve students' Chinese proficiency.

Exchange event, themed "Creating New Platforms for Economic and Trade Exchange, Expanding New Fields for China-Arab States Cooperation," was held in Chaoyang District, Beijing. The event featured thematic promotions of the business environment in the UAE and Chaoyang District, deepened industry-specific cooperation with the UAE and Saudi Arabia, resulted in the signing of four cooperation projects, and conducted multiple China-Arab states project roadshows, covering various fields such as culture, tourism, and finance.[①]

In 2023, the China-Arab States Cultural and Tourism Cooperation Research Center was established at Beijing International Studies University.[②] It focuses on five areas: academic exchange, talent cultivation, training and research, think tank research, and industry promotion. The center aims to advance practical cultural and tourism cooperation and exchanges between China and Arab states through initiatives that promote interactions among cultural and tourism enterprises, training for cultural and tourism talent from Arab states, and cultural exchanges for youth of China and Arab states. By means of academic exchanges, expert seminars, and academic forums, the center provides effective support for the development of cultural and tourism industry cooperation between China and Arab states. Leveraging the university's disciplinary strengths, the center enrolls students from Arab states to pursue degrees in China, fostering high-level translators and multidisciplinary cultural and tourism professionals for both sides. Regular training programs for officials in the Arab cultural and tourism sectors are held to build bridges for civilizational exchange and mutual learning. The center facilitates interaction among industry, academia, and research, establishing a comprehensive cooperation mechanism and exchange platform for China-Arab states cultural and tourism industries. It encourages mutual visits and exchanges among China-Arab states cultural and tourism enterprises, promoting further institutionalization and normalization of bilateral exchanges and cooperation. The China-Arab States Cultural and Tourism Cooperation Research Center aspires to become a world-class platform for research and services in cultural and tourism development. It promotes the "Eight Joint Actions" for

---

[①] "2023 Beijing China-Arab States Economic, Trade, and Cultural Exchange Event Held," *Urban Civilization Net,* https://www.bjwmb.gov.cn/wmdt/cyq/10049277.html, December 6, 2023.

[②] "The China-Arab States Cultural and Tourism Cooperation Research Center Unveiled at Beijing International Studies University," China News, https://baijiahao.baidu.com/s?id=1773101283633289673&wfr=baike.

and published over 1,260 titles in six languages, including Arabic, Persian, and Urdu, for countries and regions involved in the "Belt and Road" Initiative. These publications span various genres, such as Chinese politics, economics, literature, and children's books, with nearly 2 million copies sold. Wisdom Palace has become the leading enterprise in China's book exports to Arab countries and the largest Chinese book publishing institution in the Arab world. The establishment of the China-Arab States Film and Television Service Centers (in Dubai and Hangzhou) facilitated the export of over 220 animated and film works to Arab states. The Arabic versions of TV dramas such as "The Story of Mountains and Seas" were broadcast on numerous television stations across Arab states, while the short video "Moroccan Girl Takes You to the Story Location of 'The Story of Mountains and Seas'" achieved a viewership of 10 million overseas.[1]

Additionally, in 2023, the launch ceremony for the "Shaanxi Shines on the Silk Road" International Cultural Exchange and the co-produced documentary "Impressions of Sanyuan" took place in Xianyang, Shaanxi Province. This initiative expressed a strong desire for in-depth, long-term exchanges and cooperation between China and Arab states. Based on the "Audiovisual China · Shaanxi Time" platform, the project aims to further explore the natural and historical cultural resources of various regions in Shaanxi. By employing rich audiovisual language, it seeks to better tell the stories of Shaanxi and China, showcasing the beautiful scenery, products, and attractions of the Shaanxi area to the Arab people, attracting more friends from Arab states and regions to come to Shaanxi for study, tourism, investment, and business, and ultimately fostering fruitful results in the cooperation between China and Arab states in broadcasting and television. This effort serves to establish a new platform for long-term cultural exchanges, injecting new momentum and vitality into China-Arab states cultural cooperation.[2]

In 2023, the 2023 Beijing China-Arab States Economic, Trade, and Cultural

---

[1] "The 10th Anniversary of Jointly Building the 'Belt and Road' Initiative – Adding Brilliance to the Inland Openness of Ningxia," Development and Reform Commission of the Ningxia Hui Autonomous Region, https://fzggw.nx.gov.cn/zwdt/202310/t20231012_4307691.html, October 12, 2023.

[2] "2023 'Shaanxi Shines on the Silk Road': China-Arab States International Cultural Exchange and Joint Documentary Production of 'Impressions of Sanyuan' Officially Launched," Sanqin Net, https://www.sanqin.com/2023-09/19/content_10368160.html, September 19, 2023.

create a green cultural tourism shoreline along the Yellow River and an ecological tourism purple corridor on the eastern foot of the Helan Mountains.[①]

10.3.2 Continuously Strengthened Interaction and Cooperation Between China and Arab States in Cultural Fields Such as Tourism and Broadcasting

In 2023, China's overseas investment destinations expanded from developed countries in Europe and the United States to countries of the "Belt and Road" Initiative such as Saudi Arabia, Kazakhstan, and Mongolia. The investment sectors diversified from mineral development and import-export trade to agriculture, manufacturing , and overseas industrial parks. As a result, exchanges and cooperation between China and Arab states in cultural, tourism, and broadcasting fields have been continuously strengthened.

In 2023, the 10th session of "Symposium on China-Arab Relations and China-Arab States Civilization Dialogue" was held in Abu Dhabi, UAE. The event was attended by Special Envoy of the Chinese Government on the Middle East Issue Zhai Jun, Minister of State to the UAE Cabinet Ahmed bin Ali Al Sayegh, Director of the Department of Culture and Dialogue of Civilizations of the League of Arab States Maha Gad and others. Representatives from the Chinese Ministry of Foreign Affairs, the Ministry of Culture and Tourism, as well as nearly 80 delegates from 18 Arab states and the Arab League also participated. The symposium aimed to strengthen cultural exchanges and cooperation, foster mutual understanding and connectivity between peoples, promote the exchange and mutual learning of civilizations, and advance the high-quality joint construction of the "Belt and Road" Initiative, while striving to create a community with a shared future for China and Arab states in the new era.[②]

In 2023, Wisdom Palace, a local private enterprise in Ningxia, was designated by the Publicity Department of the Communist Party of China as a key enterprise for national external publicity. To date, the company has translated

---

① "The China-Arab States Tour Operators Conference Will First Launch a 'Belt and Road' Cultural and Tourism Cooperation Promotion Conference," Ningxia News, https://whhlyt.nx.gov.cn/xxfb/hyxx/202309/t20230913_4262841.html, September 13, 2023.

② "10th session of 'Symposium on China-Arab Relations and China-Arab Civilization Dialogue' Held in the UAE," Xinhua News Agency, http://world.people.com.cn/n1/2023/1026/c1002-40103498.html, October 26, 2023.

10.3.1.4 Holding the "Belt and Road" Cultural and Tourism Cooperation Promotion Conference

In 2023, the "Belt and Road" Cultural and Tourism Cooperation Promotion Conference was jointly organized by participating countries and regions, including Arab states, as well as cultural and tourism departments from various provinces and regions in China. This conference marked the establishment of a new platform for the joint promotion of cultural tourism resources. Cultural and tourism departments from seven provinces, including Ningxia, Fujian, Gansu, Sichuan, and Xinjiang, along with representatives from several "Belt and Road" countries, conducted joint promotional activities for cultural tourism resources using a format of "creative video presentations of artistic programs + featured resources" to showcase local distinctive cultural tourism offerings. The conference effectively promoted cooperation between China and Arab states in areas such as tourism policy alignment, tourism industry collaboration, talent training in tourism, and tourism promotion. It contributed to the further implementation of the China-Arab States "Civilization Dialogue Action," enhanced the depth of cooperation within the tourism industry, and underscored the significant role of tourism in fostering exchanges and mutual learning between Chinese and Arab civilizations.[①]

10.3.1.5 Holding Ningxia Cultural Tourism Resource Promotion and Food Tasting Event

In 2023, the Ningxia Cultural Tourism Resource Promotion and Food Tasting Event utilized a format of "artistic programs + creative videos + featured resources" to creatively promote Ningxia's cultural tourism resources. The event showcased new achievements in the integration of "wolfberry + cultural tourism" through a combination of "video promotion + food tasting." During the "Incredible Ningxia - an Oasis in the Hinterland" Cultural and Tourism Resource Visit, participating guests were organized for visits to two new routes: the "Purple Dream - Intoxicating Helan Journey" and the "Yellow River Cultural Exploration Journey." These visits promoted and showcased some new cultural tourism projects and distinctive products launched by Ningxia in its efforts to

---

[①] "China and Arab States Tourism Sectors Discuss New Prospects for Cultural and Tourism Cooperation," The Website of the Central People's Government of the People's Republic of China, https://www.gov.cn/yaowen/liebiao/202309/content_6904932.htm, September 19, 2023.

facilitating broad and in-depth cooperation in tourism between the two sides. Zeng Bowe, Secretary-General of the Leisure and Holiday Branch of China Tourism Association and Director of the China Tourism Economics and Policy Research Center of Beijing Union University, addressed the new developments in China-Arab states tourism under the "Belt and Road" Initiative. He discussed the advancement of the "Belt and Road" Initiative and the background of international tourism cooperation between China and Arab states, providing suggestions for the internationalization, quality enhancement, and collaborative high-quality development of Ningxia tourism. He emphasized that developing inbound and outbound tourism is a key focus of China-Arab states international tourism cooperation. Zeng advocated for the formulation of a plan for international visitor exchanges between China and Arab states to expand the scale of international tourism on both sides. He believes that the friendly spirit of "mutual assistance, equality, mutual benefit, and inclusive learning" that has emerged between China and Arab states will become an important force in promoting world peace and development. Wu Ruoshan, President of the New Era Cultural Tourism Research Institute and Deputy Director of the Cultural Tourism Policy Research Center at the China University of Labor Relations, noted that against the backdrop of the continued expansion of international consensus on the "Belt and Road" Initiative, the achievements in Silk Road cultural and tourism cooperation are impressive. He highlighted that cooperative mechanisms and platform construction are steadily advancing, brand activities are fully launched, tourism exchanges are continuously deepening, and cultural heritage exchanges are closely knit. Under the new development framework, he suggested that to continuously enhance the development quality of China-Arab States Silk Road tourism cooperation, efforts should be made to strengthen Silk Road tourism brand building, implement precise marketing and promotion strategies, and improve the tourism service talent pool. He also recommended that both sides conduct joint research on international tourism-related topics to guide market behavior with theoretical outcomes, which will be a crucial step in deepening China-Arab states tourism cooperation.[①]

---

① "The China-Arab States Tourism Cooperation Forum is Held Today in Yinchuan, Ningxia," *China Daily*, https://baijiahao.baidu.com/s?id=1777461822242418804&wfr=spider&for=pc, September 19, 2023.

Chapter 10　Special Report on China-Arab States Cooperation in Tourism

international markets, promoting shared and win-win development opportunities in the international and domestic tourism sectors, facilitating mutual visits among tourists, and fostering people-to-people connections between China and Arab states.

10.3.1.3　Holding the China-Arab States Tourism Cooperation Forum

As an important component of the 2023 China-Arab States Tour Operators Conference, the China-Arab States Tourism Cooperation Forum aims to establish a high-end platform for exchange, sharing, and practical cooperation between China and Arab states, seeking to explore diverse pathways for tourism exchange and cooperation in the new era, thereby advancing the China-Arab states strategic partnership to a higher level. Centered on the theme "Diverse Pathways for China-Arab States Tourism Exchange and Cooperation in the New Era," the forum invites foreign diplomats stationed in China, as well as renowned experts and representatives from the domestic tourism industry, to engage in dialogue and exchange ideas.[①]

The Salvadoran Ambassador to China stated, "Culture is the soul of a nation, and cultural exchange is the source and important content of China-El Salvador relations. With the strong support of the governments of both sides, the friendship between our nations remains vibrant over time. I will continue to promote exchanges and cooperation in culture, economy, politics, and academia between the two sides to enhance mutual understanding." Tang Xiaoyun, Deputy Director of the China Tourism Research Institute (Data Center of the Ministry of Culture and Tourism), pointed out that tourism serves as a friendship bridge connecting China and Arab states and is an important channel for mutual learning and understanding in the exchange of civilizations in the new era. He noted that it brings new opportunities for deepening exchanges and cooperation between China and Arab states. To this end, he suggested promoting the establishment of a China-Arab States Tourism Cooperation Alliance, implementing more convenient comprehensive travel policies, deepening cultural exchanges between the peoples of China and Arab states, and advancing three-dimensional marketing and promotion led by new media, thus

---

[①] "The China-Arab States Tour Operators Conference will Build a New Platform for Promoting Cultural and Tourism Resources Between China and Other Countries," The Website of the Central People's Government of the People's Republic of China, https://www.gov.cn/yaowen/liebiao/202309/content_6903323.htm, September 11, 2023.

the culture-tourism integration enhancement and empowerment action plans, and promoting exchanges and mutual learning between Chinese and Arab civilizations. The conference is expected to further advance cultural and tourism exchange and cooperation between Ningxia and the countries and regions involved in the "Belt and Road" Initiative. Salvadoran Ambassador to China, Aldo Alvarez, and Moldovan Ambassador to China, Dumitru Braghiș, both stated in their speeches that they would seize opportunities under the "Belt and Road" Initiative to deepen cultural and tourism exchanges and cooperation with China. Officials from the Bureau of International Exchange and Cooperation of the Ministry of Culture and Tourism noted that the conference will undoubtedly enhance China-Arab states friendship, promote people-to-people connectivity, and contribute to the joint construction of the "Belt and Road" Initiative. The officials expressed hope that tour operators of both China and Arab states would use the conference as an opportunity to deepen cooperation in tourism policy alignment, industry collaboration, talent training, and market promotion, thereby leveraging the significant role of tourism in promoting exchanges and mutual learning between Chinese and Arab civilizations.

The Tour Operators Conference had the theme "Sharing Development Opportunities, Promoting Tourism Cooperation, and Building the 'Belt and Road' Together." It adopted a "1+4" format (where "1" stands for the opening ceremony of the China-Arab States Tour Operators Conference and "4" for activities held during the conference: the China-Arab States Tourism Cooperation Forum, the "Belt and Road" Cultural and Tourism Cooperation Promotion Conference, the Ningxia Cultural and Tourism Resource Promotion and Food Tasting Event, and the "Incredible Ningxia - an Oasis in the Hinterland" Cultural and Tourism Resource Visit). Tour operator representatives from China and Arab states signed multiple strategic cooperation agreements,[1] establishing an effective platform for enhancing practical cooperation in the tourism industry between China and other countries. It can be said that the China-Arab States Tour Operators Conference plays a significant role as a platform in strengthening the effective linkage of cultural and tourism resources between domestic and

---

[1] "Opening of the China-Arab States Tour Operators Conference at the 6th China-Arab States Expo," the Website of the Ministry of Culture and Tourism of the People's Republic of China, https://www.mct.gov.cn/preview/whzx/qgwhxxlb/nx/202309/t20230920_947360.htm, September 20, 2023.

Chapter 10 Special Report on China-Arab States Cooperation in Tourism

10.3.1.1 The China-Arab States Expo Continues to Play an Important Role in China-Arab States Cooperation in Tourism

In September 2023, the Ningxia Hui Autonomous Region successfully hosted the 6th China-Arab States Expo. The event welcomed guests from 65 countries, regions, and regional organizations, 20 central and national ministries and commissions, and 29 provinces (regions and municipalities). Participants from the business sector, enterprises, and trade associations accounted for 82% of the attendees, with a total of over 11200 participants and exhibitors. The event garnered 2.5 billion online views, with over 150 million views from overseas, and the total reading volume of two related Weibo topics exceeded 1.7 billion. The 2023 expo surpassed all previous ones in terms of guest specifications, exhibition scale, and coverage, earning widespread praise from the international community and attendees. The 6th China-Arab States Expo resulted in 403 cooperative achievements, with planned investments and trade amounting to 170.97 billion yuan. A total of 18 cultural and tourism cooperation agreements were signed between China and Arab states, leading to fruitful economic and trade cooperation and deepening tourism collaboration.① The role of the China-Arab States Expo in facilitating the co-construction of the "Belt and Road," enhancing trade and economic cooperation among domestic provinces, cities, and large enterprises, as well as promoting the high-quality development of Ningxia's economy and advancing high-level openness to the west, has become increasingly prominent.

10.3.1.2 Holding the China-Arab States Tour Operators Conference

In 2023, the China-Arab States Tour Operators Conference was held. It was attended by representatives from cultural and tourism administrative departments of relevant domestic regions and enterprises, as well as travel trade representatives from countries such as Iran, Saudi Arabia, Switzerland, Turkey, and Indonesia. Li Jinke, a member of the Standing Committee of the CPC Ningxia Hui Autonomous Regional Committee and Minister of the Publicity Department, stated that Ningxia is integrating the high-quality development of culture and tourism into the "Belt and Road" initiative, vigorously implementing

---

① "The China-Arab States Tour Operators Conference will Build a New Platform for Promoting Cultural and Tourism Resources Between China and Other Countries," *Xinhua News Agency*, https://www.gov.cn/yaowen/liebiao/202309/content_6903323.htm, September 11, 2023.

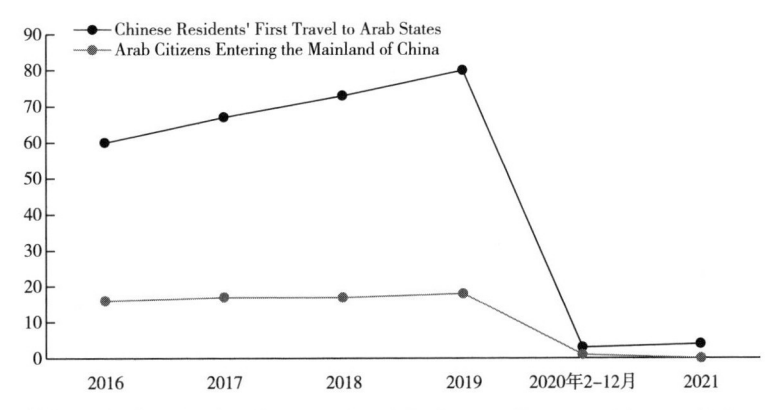

Figure 10.7 Trends of Inbound and Outbound Tourism Between China and Arab States (2016-2021)

Source: China Tourism Academy (Data Center of the Ministry of Culture and Tourism).

10.3.1 Continuously Strengthened New Platforms and Enhanced Impact of Opening Up

The open platforms such as the China-Arab States Expo, the China (Ningxia) International Wine Culture and Tourism Expo, and the "Western Digital Valley" Computing Power Industry Conference have been successfully implemented. Unique open brands such as the China-Arab States Expo, the Home of Wine, and the "Western Digital Valley" continue to enhance the influence and appeal of these platforms. The establishment of a comprehensive pilot zone for the open development of the grape and wine industry has led to the holding of three International Wine Culture and Tourism Expos. Wines from the eastern foot of Helan Mountains have won over 1100 international awards and are exported to more than 40 countries and regions, and are often presented as state gifts to leaders of various nations. Innovative efforts in the digital economy and computing power industry have been made, with two high-profile "Western Digital Valley" Computing Power Industry Conferences and the 2023 China Computing Power Conference being organized to establish a collaborative bridge for "East Data, West Computing Plan."[1]

---

[1] "The 10th Anniversary of Jointly Building the 'Belt and Road' Initiative – Adding Brilliance to the Inland Openness of Ningxia," The Website of the Development and Reform Commission of the Ningxia Hui Autonomous Region, https://fzggw.nx.gov.cn/zwdt/202310/t20231012_4307691.html, October 12, 2023.

Chapter 10 Special Report on China-Arab States Cooperation in Tourism

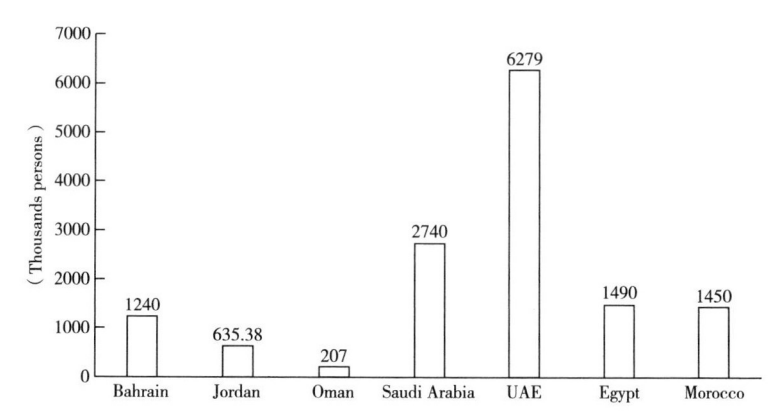

Figure 10.6 International Tourist Arrivals in Selected Arab States in 2023

Source: Oxford Economics, http://www.economics.ox.ac.uk.

10.3 Progress of China-Arab Tourism Cooperation in 2023

The year 2024 marks the 20th anniversary of the establishment of the China-Arab States Cooperation Forum. With the support of this forum, cooperation between China and Arab states in the tourism sector has gradually deepened. The trade volume between China and Arab states, including tourism service trade, has increased from $222.4 billion in 2012 to $431.4 billion in 2022, nearly doubling over the decade. From 2016 to 2019, the number of Chinese citizens traveling to Arab states as their first overseas destination maintained an average annual growth rate of 10%, reaching a historical peak in 2019; during this period, the number of Arab citizens entering the mainland of China also exhibited steady growth. Tourism plays an increasingly important role in the construction of the China-Arab states community with a shared future.

China is the world's largest domestic tourism market and has held the position of the world's largest outbound tourist source country for consecutive years. Before and after the COVID-19 pandemic, China has been a key player in the prosperity of the global tourism economy. Tourists are cultural carriers, and behind a thriving tourism economy lies cultural equality and cooperative exchange. Cultivating a more resilient tourism industry ecosystem and empowering China-Arab states cooperation through tourism has become one of the important ways to strengthen exchanges between China and Arab states.

in attracting foreign direct investment in tourism, accounting for 4.7% of the global total. Approximately 35% of new tourism projects in the Middle East are located in the UAE. From July to September 2022, the number of international tourists arriving in Egypt reached 3.4 million, a year-on-year increase of 52%, with a total of 11.7 million international visitors for the year. In 2023, the number of international tourists in Egypt rose to 14.9 million, reflecting a yearly growth of 27.35%. Qatar's tourism industry experienced rapid development, aided by the hosting of the 2022 FIFA World Cup. This was the first time that a World Cup event was held in the Middle East, attracting around 1.5 million visitors from around the globe. Statistics indicate that the World Cup generated approximately $17 billion in revenue for Qatar, and the infrastructure developments undertaken for the event will support the long-term growth of the tourism sector.[①]

In 2023, Morocco's tourism industry achieved a historic high, receiving a total of 14.5 million international tourists, which is a 12% increase compared to 2019 and a 33.02% increase from 2022.[②] Additionally, tourist arrivals in Bahrain and Jordan also saw an uptick. See Figures 10.5 and 10.6 for details.

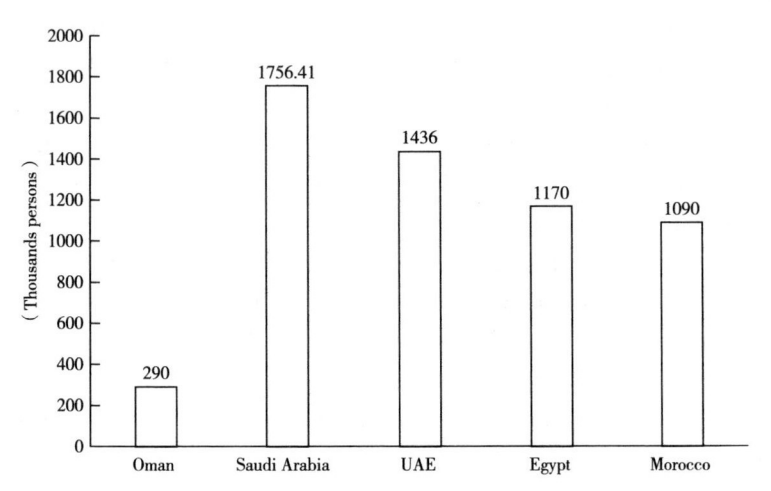

Figure 10.5 International Tourist Arrivals in Selected Arab States in 2022

Source: Oxford Economics, http://www.economics.ox.ac.uk.

[①] "The Tourism Industry in the Middle East Accelerates Recovery," *Guangming Online*, https://m.gmw.cn/baiia/2023-02/28/36396044.html, Feb. 28, 2023.

[②] Economic and Commercial Office of the Embassy of the People's Republic of China in the Kingdom of Morocco, http://ma.mofcom.gov.cn/article/jmxw/202402/20240203471621.shtml.

Chapter 10 Special Report on China-Arab States Cooperation in Tourism

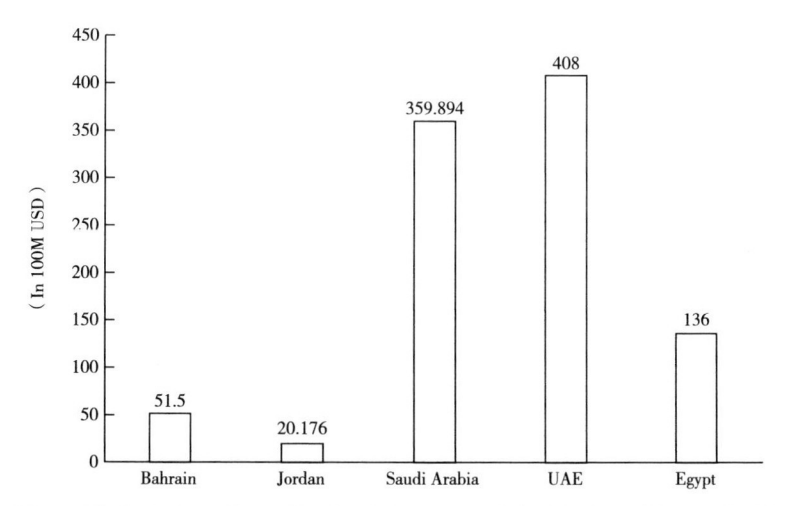

Figure 10.4 International Tourism Revenue of Selected Arab States in 2023

Source: Oxford Economics, http://www.economics.ox.ac.uk.

In 2022, Saudi Arabia welcomed 93.5 million tourists, a 121% increase compared to 2019, ranking first among Arab states and 13th globally with 17.56 million international visitors. It also received 77 million domestic tourists, a 21% growth compared to 2021. In the first quarter of 2023, Saudi Arabia hosted approximately 7.8 million international tourists, a 64% increase compared to 2019, setting a new historical record. Clearly, Saudi Arabia's overall strategies and initiatives have begun to yield results, significantly enhancing the contribution of tourism to GDP.[1]

In 2022, Dubai attracted 14.36 million international tourists, a remarkable 97% increase from 2021. In 2023, passenger traffic at UAE airports reached 62.79 million, reflecting a year-on-year growth of 46%. During the same period, the number of visitors to Dubai hit 8.55 million, up 20% year-on-year, setting a new historical record; the number of tourists visiting Abu Dhabi, Sharjah, and Ras Al Khaimah also saw double-digit growth. The rapid recovery of the UAE's tourism industry can be attributed to long-term investments and innovative initiatives in the sector. Statistics show that from 2018 to 2022, the UAE ranked fifth globally

---

[1] "Saudi Arabia Announces $800 Billion Investment in Tourism Development, Aiming to Welcome 100 Million Tourists by 2030," *Net Ease News*, htps://www.163.com/dy/article/IHTFQUEJ05198CJN.html? spss=dy_author, October 25, 2023.

totaled $13.6 billion, representing a significant 231.7% increase compared to the $4.1 billion in international tourism revenue in 2022, making it one of the fastest-growing states in the Arab tourism sector.① Jordan's international tourism revenue swiftly rose from $1.5837 billion in 2022 to $2.0176 billion in 2023, reflecting a growth rate of 27.39%. Morocco's total tourism revenue for 2023 amounted to $9.8 billion, up 15.8% from the previous year.② In 2022, the UAE performed well in international tourism, leveraging the Expo 2020 Dubai to attract over 24 million visitors from more than 192 countries and regions, achieving an international tourism revenue of $37.091 billion. In 2023, the UAE's international tourism revenue further increased to $40.8 billion, with a growth rate of nearly 9%.③ In 2022, Saudi Arabia ranked 11th globally in international tourism revenue; in 2023, its international tourism revenue reached $35.9894 billion, second only to the UAE among Arab states' tourism sectors.④ See Figures 10.3 and 10.4 for details.

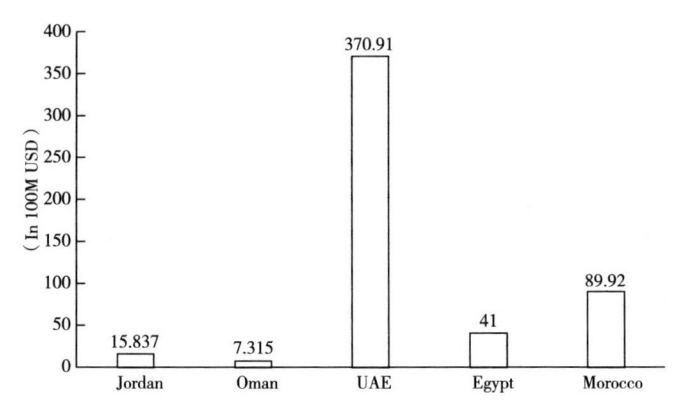

Figure 10.3 International Tourism Revenue of Selected Arab States in 2022

Source: Oxford Economics, http://www.economics.ox.ac.uk.

---

① "Middle East Tourism Industry Accelerates Recovery," *People's Daily*, https://m.gmw.cn/baijia/2023-02/28/36396044.html, February 28, 2023.

② "In 2023, Morocco welcomed 14.5 million tourists," The Website of the Economic and Commercial Office of the Embassy of the People's Republic of China in the Kingdom of Morocco, http://ma.mofcom.gov.cn/article/jmxw/202402/20240203471621.shtml, February 2, 2024.

③ "UAE Implements Multiple Measures to Develop Tourism Industry," *People's Daily*, https://baijiahao.baidu.com/s?id=1783122148757267659&wfr=spider&for=pc, November 21, 2023.

④ "Saudi Arabia Announces $800 Billion Investment in Tourism Development, Aiming to Welcome 100 Million Tourists by 2030," *Net Ease News*, https://www.163.com/dy/article/IHTFQUEJ05198CJN.html? spss=dy_author, October 25, 2023.

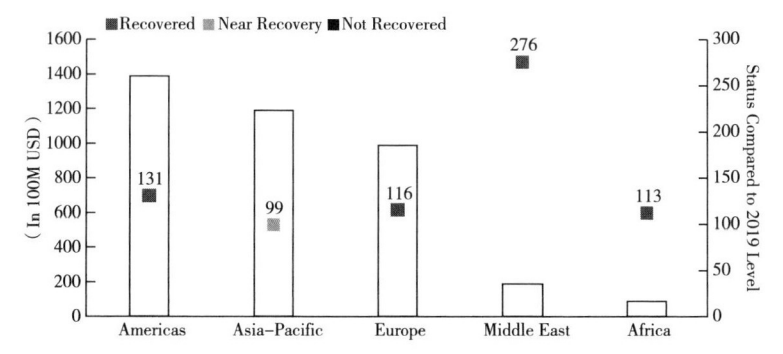

Figure 10.2 Comparison of Domestic Tourism Expenditure by Region in 2019 and 2023

Source: Oxford Economics, http://www.economics.ox.ac.uk.

10.2 Overview of Tourism Development in Arab States in 2023

10.2.1 Arab States' Tourism Industry Was the Fastest-Recovering Region Post-Pandemic

Compared to 2019, the number of international tourist arrivals in Arab states increased by 13% in 2023. Saudi Arabia and the UAE were the top two states in terms of international tourist arrivals, with increases of 66% and 21%, respectively, over 2019. Both states have treated tourism development as a national strategy, investing heavily in tourism infrastructure in recent years. Kuwait experienced the fastest growth in tourist arrivals, with a 90% increase in 2023 compared to 2019.[1]

International tourism expenditure in Arab states overall increased by 46% in 2023 compared to 2019, with all Arab states except Iraq surpassing their 2019 levels of inbound tourism expenditure. Evidently, Arab states have emerged as the fastest-recovering region in global tourism post-pandemic.

10.2.2 Strong Performance of Arab States' Tourism Industry in 2023

In 2023, most Arab states continued to show positive development trends in international tourism revenue and the number of tourist arrivals.

In the first quarter of 2023, Egypt's tourism revenue reached $4.1 billion, marking a 43.5% year-on-year increase. For the full year, Egypt's tourism revenue

---

[1] *Oxford Economics*, http://www.economics.ox.ac.uk.

10.1.2 Uneven Recovery Between International and Domestic Tourism

During the COVID-19 pandemic, strict restrictions on international travel led to a global shift where domestic tourism replaced outbound travel, an effect that continues to have an impact. In 2023, the three countries with the fastest growth in international tourist arrivals were Saudi Arabia, Albania, and Poland. However, in most countries, international tourism still lags behind domestic tourism.

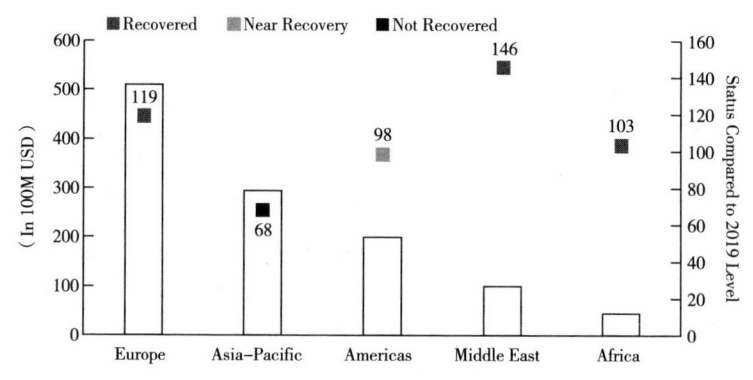

Figure 10.1 Comparison of Major Inbound Tourism Destinations by Region in 2019 and 2023

Source: Oxford Economics, http://www.economics.ox.ac.uk.

10.1.3 Continued Increase in Domestic Tourism Demand with Noticeable Substitution Effect

In 2023, domestic tourism expenditure in most regions globally returned to 2019 levels. The countries that experienced faster growth in their domestic tourism industry are those that are vast, populous, and have a significant number of people capable of affording travel. The most remarkable domestic tourism recovery was observed in the Middle East, where domestic tourism expenditure increased by 276% compared to 2019. The Americas followed with a 131% increase in domestic tourism expenditure, while Europe and Africa saw increases of 116% and 113%, respectively. Although the Asia-Pacific region had not fully recovered, it reached 99% of the 2019 level.① See Figure 10.2 for details.

---

① *Oxford Economics*, http:/www.economics.ox.ac.uk.

Chapter 10 Special Report on China-Arab States Cooperation in Tourism

10.1 Overview of Global Tourism Development

10.1.1 Global Tourism Shows a Strong Recovery Trend

In 2023, the number of international tourists globally reached approximately 1.29 billion, recovering to about 88% of the 2019 level. Global tourism revenue reached $1.4 trillion, equivalent to 93% of the 2019 level.[①] Overall, global tourism demonstrated a clear recovery trend.

Table 10.1 Comparison of International Tourist Arrivals in Different Regions, 2019 vs. 2023

Unit: Million

Region	2019	2023	Percentage Change
Americas	123	117	-4%
Europe	440	428	-3%
Asia-Pacific	213	149	-30%
Middle East	29	33	+0.13
Africa	49	43	-13%

Source: Oxford Economics, http://www.economics.ox.ac.uk.

[①] "Global Leisure Tourism Industry Report, November 8, 2023 (Annual Report 2023)," *Oxford Economics*, Sohu, https://www.sohu.com/a/736843840_118838.

should seize the opportunity presented by global environmental governance issues to advocate for enhanced communication and interaction with Arab states. While cooperating to develop economies, it is imperative to commit to environmental governance and protection and to construct a green "Belt and Road," facilitating the timely realization of carbon neutrality commitments, and promoting a collaborative endeavor among the peoples of Arab states to build a community with a shared future for mankind, thereby showcasing China's wisdom and sense of responsibility as a major power.

Although the construction of an ecological civilization is a shared challenge faced by the world, different countries encounter varying primary issues and stages in this process, resulting in diverse experiences shaped by national circumstances. As a developing major power, China must effectively manage both development challenges and ecological environmental protection. This necessitates viewing ecological environmental protection and socio-economic development as an organic whole rather than as opposing forces, achieving significant socio-economic advancement alongside prioritized ecological protection through coordinated efforts. In response to the "Belt and Road" Initiative, China and Arab states are continually deepening cooperation in new development concepts and fields, contributing robust support for the transformation of development in Arab states and reinforcing the construction of a China-Arab states community of shared destiny. Furthermore, China is providing its experiences, wisdom, and solutions to assist Arab states in effectively addressing the challenges of ecological civilization construction.

Chapter 9 Special Report on China-Arab States Cooperation in Ecological and Environmental Governance

consensus on protection in forests, grasslands, oceans, wetlands, and biodiversity. Strengthening technological exchanges and cooperation in the field of ecological protection will help build a long-term cooperation mechanism for the implementation of environmental treaties with Arab states. Third, there should be a vigorous push to foster collaboration between environmental protection NGOs and the Gulf Cooperation Council and the Arab League, leveraging their positive roles in regional ecological protection and governance.

9.3.4 Contributing Chinese Solutions and Wisdom to China-Arab States Cooperation in Ecological and Environmental Governance

The construction of an ecological civilization is intrinsically linked to the future of humanity, and the establishment of a green home is a shared dream for all people. Under the scientific guidance of Xi Jinping's thoughts on ecological civilization, we have achieved a significant transformation from focused remediation to systematic governance, as well as a shift from passive responses to proactive initiatives. China's accomplishments in ecological civilization construction have garnered global attention and have become a prominent symbol of the historic achievements and transformations attained by the Party and the state in the new era. The building of a community with a shared future for mankind provides direction and pathways for advancing global environmental governance and safeguarding ecological security worldwide. Among its key objectives is the collaborative pursuit of global ecological civilization and the creation of a clean and beautiful world, which are essential components of this community-building endeavor. China upholds a global governance perspective based on "Extensive consultation, joint contribution and shared benefits," advocates for the democratization of international relations, and maintains that all nations—regardless of size, strength, or wealth—should be treated equally. Additionally, China supports the active role of the United Nations and promotes the representation and voice of developing countries in international affairs. China will continue to play the role of a responsible major power, actively guiding the direction of international order reform and fostering solutions for global environmental protection and sustainable development.

In 2023, we mark the tenth anniversary of the "Belt and Road" Initiative. Against the backdrop of economic globalization and regional integration, China

turn, holds significant importance for deepening South-South environmental cooperation, pursuing shared green development, and promoting regional peace and stability.

9.3.3 A Modern Model of China-Arab States Ecological Protection and Governance for Win-Win Cooperation

Ecological prosperity leads to the advancement of civilization. China has consistently upheld the principles of ecological priority and green development, achieving a balance between development and protection, which serves as a valuable reference for many developing countries pursuing sustainable development. The construction of the "Belt and Road" ecological community is an essential part of building a community with a shared future for mankind. Over the past decade, guided by the concept of a community with a shared future, China has made significant progress in promoting the construction of the "Belt and Road" ecological community. Collaborative governance is essential for advancing the ecological community along the "Belt and Road." In the face of the ongoing threat of ecological degradation, Arab states must recognize their interconnected fates, overcome political obstacles to ecological cooperation and participate in regional ecological governance initiatives. The Chinese government has established a series of platforms and mechanisms for deepening exchanges and cooperation, leveraging existing bilateral and multilateral cooperation frameworks. Numerous dialogue and exchange activities themed around green "Belt and Road" construction have been organized to share experiences and promote cooperation in ecological civilization and green development with Arab states and regions.[①] First, the China-Arab States Cooperation Forum mechanism should be fully utilized to continuously advance the construction of cooperative mechanisms in ecological and environmental protection, jointly establishing a new framework for cooperation in this field. Second, efforts should be sustained to enhance collaborative governance with Arab states on issues such as greenhouse gas emissions, nuclear and radiation safety, water pollution, and soil contamination. It is important to promote the establishment of a systematic

---

① Yang Meiqin, Tang Ming, "Ecological Cooperative Governance: A New Driving Force for Promoting International Cooperation under the 'Belt and Road' Initiative," *Issues of Contemporary World Socialism*, Issue 1, 2020.

Chapter 9 Special Report on China-Arab States Cooperation in Ecological and Environmental Governance

with a systematic, multi-layered, and multidimensional communication approach. This would foster a framework for cultural exchanges involving governments, media, academia, and the public in dynamic interactions. Second, content that is universally relevant to Arab audiences should be created. It is important to select content that holds significant recognition in Arab states, shifting from rigid, formulaic narratives to flexible, compelling, and relatable storytelling. The value core of the "Belt and Road" ecological community should be promoted in a vivid, engaging, and vibrant way. Third, innovative communication platforms tailored for Arab audiences should be developed. Creating digital and audio-visual platforms that are easily accessible and appealing to the Arab public can enhance the dissemination of the "Belt and Road" ecological community concept. This approach breaks down national and cultural barriers, reaches the hearts of people along the route, and fosters international consensus for the high-quality construction of the "Belt and Road" ecological community.

9.3.2 Leveraging Multilateral Mechanisms to Gradually Improve China-Arab States Cooperation Mechanisms for Environmental Protection and Deepen South-South Ecological Cooperation

As developing nations, China and Arab states share similar positions and comparable responsibilities in addressing global environmental issues. Although cooperation in this field began relatively late, the complementary needs of both sides present significant potential for collaboration. Platforms such as the China-Arab States Cooperation Forum and the China-Arab States Expo should be fully utilized for strategic planning and thorough preparation to organize environmental cooperation meetings at appropriate times. Such initiatives would increase opportunities for exchange, actively promote the continuous deepening of China-Arab states environmental cooperation, and rely on these engagements to establish stable and effective communication channels, gradually refining the China-Arab states environmental cooperation mechanism.

From the perspective of bilateral relations, key Arab states such as Saudi Arabia, Egypt, Algeria, and Sudan have continuously enriched their strategic bilateral cooperation with China. Advancing bilateral environmental cooperation with these states at opportune moments would contribute to furthering equal, mutually beneficial, and sincere China-Arab states bilateral relations. This, in

address and resolve independently. In the construction of ecological civilization, no country can remain aloof or uninvolved; every one is a participant in the collective process of building a global ecological civilization. Each country should undertake its due international responsibilities, engage in deep exchanges and cooperation with others, bridge the deficit in international cooperation on ecological civilization, share the achievements of ecological progress, and jointly build a beautiful planet with a harmonious ecological environment. This collective endeavor should fully harness the dividends of ecological civilization, enabling people from all countries to attain high levels of ecological well-being.

The global governance approach with Chinese characteristics has been increasingly recognized by the international community. In May 2016, the United Nations Environment Programme released the report *Green is Gold: The Strategy and Actions of China's Ecological Civilization*, which fully acknowledged China's efforts and achievements in ecological civilization construction. In 2018, the joint statement of the 26th BASIC Ministerial Meeting on Climate Change for the first time incorporated the concept of "building a community of shared future for mankind" into a multilateral international document in the field of climate change response. In September 2020, President Xi Jinping declared, "China will scale up its nationally determined contributions by adopting more vigorous policies and measures, and aims to have CO_2 emissions peak before 2030 and achieve carbon neutrality before 2060."[①] At the Leaders' Summit on Climate in 2021, President Xi introduced the idea of building a "community of life for mankind and nature" for the first time.

Effectively telling China's story and enhancing the promotion of ecological concepts to Arab states are essential. Consolidating the public support and shared understanding for the joint construction of the "Belt and Road" ecological community, and overcoming "communication challenges" and "recognition barriers," are key steps in advancing the development of this community. First, a diversified communication system for Arab states should be constructed. In practice, the potential role of public diplomacy in the international dissemination of the "Belt and Road" ecological community concept should be emphasized,

---

① Xi Jinping, "Statement at the General Debate of the 75th Session of the United Nations General Assembly," *Qiushi* Online, http://www.qstheory.cn/yaowen/2020-09/22/c_1126527766.htm, September 22, 2020.

Chapter 9 Special Report on China-Arab States Cooperation in Ecological and Environmental Governance

9.3 Prospects for China-Arab States Cooperation in Ecological Governance

The relationship between China and Arab states has a long and profound history, characterized by peaceful cooperation, openness and inclusivity, mutual learning, and mutual benefits. In the new era, cooperation between China and Arab states in jointly building the "Belt and Road" aims to establish a path of open development, which must also be a path of green development. Throughout the process of jointly building the "Belt and Road," China has consistently prioritized ecological protection. Over the past decade, China has upheld the principle of green development in this initiative, strengthening international cooperation in areas such as ecological governance, biodiversity conservation, and climate change mitigation, with the goal of fostering an ecological civilization where humanity and nature coexist harmoniously. Projects in green infrastructure, green energy, green transportation, and green finance are continuously moving from the vision stage to tangible actions and outcomes, making green development the defining theme of the "Belt and Road" Initiative. China and Arab states, despite their distinct resource endowments and development paths, are both at a stage of transition toward green development. Both parties share common ground in their concepts and practices of ecological governance.

9.3.1 Promoting the Concept of a Community of Shared Future for China-Arab States Ecological Collaborative Governance and Strengthening the Promotion of Ecological Ideas to Arab States

President Xi Jinping stated, "Humanity and nature should coexist in harmony. Any harm we inflict on nature will eventually return to haunt us." [1] Human production and daily activities are exerting extensive impacts on the natural environment essential for survival. The problems caused by extreme weather and ecological degradation, affecting agriculture, the economy, environment, trade, and security, are beyond the capability of any single country or region to

---

[1] Xi Jinping, "Jointly Building a Community with a Shared Future for Mankind," *Qiushi*, Issue 1, 2021.

energy transitions. Beyond energy collaboration, China also provides support to Middle Eastern countries in sectors such as desalination, green finance, and sustainable agriculture, collectively addressing the challenges posed by climate change.

In addition, the "Eight Major Joint Actions" focus on green innovation, highlighting joint actions such as "leveraging China's Fengyun meteorological satellites and the World Meteorological Center Beijing to support Arab states in disaster prevention and mitigation," providing clear direction and pathways for China-Arab states meteorological cooperation. Chen Zhenlin, Director of the China Meteorological Administration, pointed out that China places great importance on meteorological cooperation with Arab states. In the first half of 2023, the China Meteorological Administration and the National Center of Meteorology of the UAE signed a bilateral government memorandum of understanding on meteorological technology cooperation. During the forum, both sides held further bilateral discussions, expressing their intention to deepen practical cooperation in areas such as artificial weather modification, meteorological satellite remote sensing monitoring and application, artificial intelligence, information and communication technologies, observational instruments and equipment, and education and training.

In recent years, extreme weather events such as heatwaves, typhoons, heavy rainfall, and sandstorms have occurred frequently worldwide, making climate change mitigation and disaster risk reduction a shared challenge for all of humanity. There is a growing call for enhanced international meteorological cooperation. Currently, China's Fengyun meteorological satellites are serving 129 countries, and the international emergency support mechanism for disaster prevention and reduction associated with these satellites has 32 registered countries. Among these, three Arab states have registered as members of the Emergency Support Mechanism for International Users of Fengyun Meteorological Satellites in Disaster Prevention and Mitigation, while ten Arab states have become international users of Fengyun satellite data. Additionally, China has provided short-term international meteorological training for over 2000 personnel from 22 Arab League member states, with many individuals pursuing master's or doctoral degrees in meteorology in China.

Chapter 9 Special Report on China-Arab States Cooperation in Ecological and Environmental Governance

and successful experiences, promoting the application of Chinese methods in agricultural water management across the Arab region. It provided technical support for sustainable development in agriculture and ecosystems, strengthened participating Arab states' resilience to climate risks, and improved agricultural water management systems. This initiative also promoted the reach of Chinese agricultural water management technologies and enterprises in "Belt and Road" partner Arab states, while creating valuable experience for similar future endeavors.

9.2.3 Addressing Extreme Climate Events and Meteorological Cooperation

Due to the intensifying effects of climate warming, extreme weather events are occurring with increasing frequency, significantly impacting human health, ecosystems, economies, agriculture, energy, and water supplies. As stated by Petteri Taalas, Secretary-General of the World Meteorological Organization, the growing frequency of extreme climate events poses ongoing threats to global economic and social development. Adapting to climate change and reducing carbon emissions not only test the governance capacity of Arab states but also present a macroeconomic challenge, requiring a green transition in development models, scientific and engineering support, and substantial economic investment.[1]

In December 2022, during the inaugural China-Arab States Summit, Chinese President Xi Jinping proposed the "Eight Joint Actions" for practical cooperation between China and Arab states, which included initiatives on green innovation and energy security. China suggested co-establishing the China-Arab States Clean Energy Cooperation Center, signaling a firm commitment to deepening cooperation in climate change mitigation. China, with the world's largest clean energy generation system—including leading capacities in hydropower, wind, and solar installations—leverages its technological advantages in clean energy to actively collaborate with Arab states in areas such as clean coal and solar energy. Chinese companies are extensively involved in large-scale clean energy projects in the UAE, Morocco, and Saudi Arabia, supporting local

---

[1] Yan Wei, Liu Aijiao, "The Compound Security Threats of Climate Change to the Middle East and Its Responses," *Social Sciences International*, vol. 4, 2023, p. 206.

from the State Key Laboratory of Remote Sensing Science at the Aerospace Information Research Institute, Chinese Academy of Sciences, leading a team in collaboration with Beijing Rainroot Technology Co., Ltd., the Remote Sensing Center of the National Council for Scientific Research - Lebanon, and the Lebanese Agricultural Research Institute. From June 9-16, 2023, the team completed site selection for four flux observation stations through field research and discussions.① At key sites—including the Kfrdan LARI farm (orchard) in northern Beqaa Valley, the Irrigation Experimental Station at the Lebanese Agricultural Research Institute in central Lebanon (farmland), and the field station of Research Center for Environment and Development, Beirut Arab University in the south (mixed forest and farmland)—they installed observation equipment such as eddy covariance systems and sap flow meters. Combined with existing lysimeters, weather stations, and Bowen ratio systems, these devices formed a water-heat flux observation network covering Lebanon's diverse surface types. During this period, the Chinese team also provided training for Lebanese technicians on routine maintenance, data reception, and data processing. From October 30 to November 10, 2023, the team held an online training course titled "Joint Laboratory's First Session on Evapotranspiration Remote Sensing Monitoring Methods and Ground Observation Technology, Agricultural Water Management for Irrigation Districts." Organized by the China Irrigation and Drainage Development Center, this course brought together experts from irrigation districts and related enterprises to provide training on agricultural water management to technicians from institutions in Lebanon, such as the National Remote Sensing Center, the Agricultural Research Institute, and the Ministry of Agriculture, as well as participants from the University of Lebanon, the Regional Centre for Space Science and Technology Education in Western Asia in Jordan, the Arab Organization for Agricultural Development in Tunisia, and relevant institutions in Yemen and Libya. This technical training provided Lebanon and "Belt and Road" partner Arab states with China's innovative evapotranspiration remote sensing monitoring and agricultural water management techniques

---

① "Completion of the Water-Heat Flux Observation Stations and Training for Diverse Surface Types in Lebanon by the National Key R&D Program 'China-Lebanon Joint Laboratory for Modern Agricultural Water Management' Project," The Website of the Aerospace Information Research Institute, Chinese Academy of Sciences, http://www.aircas.ac.cn/dtxw/hzjl/202306/t20230621_6784348.html, June 1, 2024.

Chapter 9 Special Report on China-Arab States Cooperation in Ecological and Environmental Governance

further share China's recent successes in desertification management, advancing transformation of technologies and collaboration on scientific projects.

9.2.2 Cooperation on Water-Saving Irrigation and Modern Agricultural Technology

In the digital era, technologies such as big data, cloud computing, and the Internet of Things have provided more countries with "new tools" for efficient water resource management. According to Ashwin Pandya, Secretary General of the International Commission on Irrigation and Drainage, countries worldwide should actively enhance the application of technology in water management, establishing systems and mechanisms tailored to their specific contexts. This includes increasing the exchange and sharing of water management knowledge to effectively assess global water security.

At the Water Resources Forum of the Sixth China-Arab States Expo, achievements in water resource cooperation between China and "Belt and Road" Initiative partner countries were presented. The forum, with the theme "Technological Empowerment for the Efficient and Intensive Use of Water Resources," used water as a central link to foster pathways for trade, investment, and improved living standards. Through innovative channels for international cooperation, the forum was designed to strengthen information exchange with "Belt and Road" Initiative partner countries on water resources, encourage technology transfer, and promote dialogue between governments and enterprises. By sharing Chinese approaches, standards, products, and services for water management, the forum facilitated trade agreements and project implementations. The aim was to make the China-Arab States Expo's Water Resources Forum a new platform for water cooperation, technology exchange, and economic collaboration in water-related fields.

Additionally, 2023 marks the tenth anniversary of the "Belt and Road" Initiative, with scientific and technological cooperation as a key component. In recent years, under the frameworks of the "Belt and Road" Science and Technology Innovation Action Plan and the China-Arab States Scientific and Technological Partnership Program, China and Arab states have broadened cooperation in science and technology, achieving practical results in areas such as agricultural water management, thus advancing joint "Belt and Road" projects between China and Arab states. Associate Researcher Zhu Weiwei

technology, and funding, focusing on technological innovation, transformation of technical achievements, and experience-sharing to promote advancements in governance concepts and practices. This collaboration will also facilitate the implementation of the United Nations Convention to Combat Desertification and support global compliance efforts, while advancing regional and global green development and improving livelihoods. This contributes to achieving the global targets of zero land degradation growth by 2030 and a 50% reduction in land degradation by 2040.① Looking ahead, China and Arab states will utilize the China-Arab States International Research Center on Drought, Desertification, and Land Degradation to hold international forums, conduct joint research on innovative technologies, establish a scientific think tank, develop a platform for technology sharing and result transfer, and undertake capacity-building initiatives in line with the memorandum.

China places significant emphasis on education, training, and technological exchange in environmental governance. From September 20-24, 2023, the International Seminar on Desertification Control Technologies and Practices was held in Yinchuan, Ningxia. Twenty international trainees from 13 countries, including Pakistan, Nigeria, and Algeria, along with nearly 50 local forestry and grassland technicians from Ningxia, participated in the training. The seminar coincided with the sixth China-Arab States Expo, providing attendees an opportunity to join the fifth Technology Transfer and Innovation Cooperation Conference of the China-Arab States Expo, where the head of the Technology Innovation Program of the United Nations Convention to Combat Desertification delivered a keynote speech on accelerating desertification control and promoting sustainable development. During an international seminar focused on desertification control and technical achievements, experts delivered presentations on this global challenge and participants engaged in discussions. The international trainees expressed appreciation for China's significant achievements in desertification control, noting their intent to apply best practices in their home countries. They also voiced interest in utilizing the platform of the International Knowledge Management Center on Combating Desertification to

---

① "Establishment of the China-Arab States International Research Center on Drought, Desertification, and Land Degradation," National Forestry and Grassland Administration Website, http://www.forestry.gov.cn, May 20, 2024.

Chapter 9 Special Report on China-Arab States Cooperation in Ecological and Environmental Governance

ecological protection. The conference also featured four technical matching and seminar sessions covering topics such as desertification prevention and green innovation, providing Chinese and Arab researchers a platform for scientific and technological exchange and collaboration.

9.2.1 Technical Cooperation on Desertification Control

Desertification, land degradation, and drought represent shared challenges for humanity. China has consistently been a strong advocate for global desertification control. On August 26, 2023, the Ninth Kubuqi International Desert Forum opened in Ordos, Inner Mongolia, under the theme "Technology-Empowered Desert Control for the Benefit of Mankind." At the forum, China's National Forestry and Grassland Administration and the Secretariat of the League of Arab States signed the Memorandum of Understanding on the Establishment of the China-Arab States International Research Center for Drought, Desertification and Land Degradation. The center was inaugurated and its initial projects officially launched. This research center aims to support and promote innovative research and international cooperation on drought, desertification, and land degradation between China and Arab states, striving to become a model of green development cooperation. China and the League of Arab States envision the center as a comprehensive international institution integrating scientific research, technological innovation, transformation of technical achievements, talent development, and capacity building. The focus will be on pooling resources in talent, technology, and funding from both sides, advancing critical technological innovation, applying research outcomes, and sharing experiences. This will provide scientific support, decision-making insights, and think tank resources for China and Arab states in addressing drought impacts, desertification control, and land degradation prevention.

The establishment of the China-Arab States International Research Center for Drought, Desertification, and Land Degradation was one of the "Eight Joint Actions" proposed by Chinese President Xi Jinping at the first China-Arab State Summit in December 2022. This initiative aims to enhance and deepen collaboration between China and Arab states in desertification control and related fields, providing scientific support, decision-making resources, and think tank services for combating the effects of drought, desertification, and land degradation. It seeks to integrate China-Arab states resources in talent,

owners. Due to the acute water deficit, Iraq's Ministry of Agriculture announced a nationwide suspension of rice cultivation in September 2023, turning many previously exported crops into import-reliant commodities. High temperatures were also prevalent in other parts of the region. In northwestern Syria, Idlib experienced record-breaking temperatures exceeding 46°C on August 13 and 14. Meanwhile, in North Africa, the capitals of Tunisia and Algeria and the Moroccan city of Agadir reached unprecedented highs of 49.0°C, 49.2°C, and 50.4°C, respectively. In the Gulf, the UAE also endured extreme summer temperatures, with parts of Abu Dhabi, Dubai, and other cities experiencing temperatures above 50°C in July and August. [1]

9.2 China-Arab States Cooperation in Ecological Environment Governance

Cooperation in ecological governance refers to a collaborative approach whereby, in response to increasingly complex and cross-regional ecological issues, political authorities strengthen their cooperation to break down narrow regional protectionism and to maximize both the holistic and synergistic effects of governance by using political means to encourage related entities to seek coordinated solutions to environmental challenges, ultimately achieving an overall improvement in ecological conditions. [2] China-Arab states cooperation in ecological governance has developed into a well-established framework with multi-level, multi-field cooperation. In 2023, the sixth China-Arab States Expo on Technology Transfer and Innovation Cooperation was held in Yinchuan, Ningxia, under the theme of "New Era, New Opportunities and New Future." During the conference, 300 advanced, applicable technologies were released to Arab states via video, spanning areas such as environmental protection, resource and energy utilization, and pollution control. In addition, eight cooperation agreements on technology transfer between China and Arab states were signed, including projects focused on desertification control, water-saving irrigation, and

---

[1] "Middle East 2023: Multiple States Face Threats from Extreme Weather, Urgent Response to Crisis is Imperative," *Beijing Daily,* December 24, 2023.

[2] Yang Meiqin, Tang Ming, "Ecological Cooperative Governance: A New Driving Force for Promoting International Cooperation in the 'Belt and Road' Initiative," *Issues of Contemporary World Socialism,* no. 1 (2020).

Chapter 9 Special Report on China-Arab States Cooperation in Ecological and Environmental Governance

health. The journal *Atmosphere* reported that recent annual economic losses due to sandstorms in the MENA region amount to nearly $150 billion, representing over 2.5% of the region's 2022 GDP.[①]

9.1.3 Extreme Weather

Throughout 2023, extreme weather events and severe natural disasters occurred repeatedly, causing immense losses to affected countries and their populations. These events underscored the importance of environmental protection and prudent use of Earth's resources. The MENA region, in particular, witnessed frequent extreme weather, exposing the pressing realities of global climate change. The impacts ranged from persistent drought and dust storms triggered by high temperatures to severe flooding caused by hurricanes. Climate change not only disrupts the lives of Middle Eastern populations but also threatens regional stability, sending a cautionary message to the world. In 2023, several countries across the Arab region experienced extreme high temperatures, with some nations reaching record-breaking heat. Many MENA states saw peak summer temperatures reaching unprecedented levels.

The World Meteorological Organization, in its *Provisional State of the Global Climate* report released ahead of the 28th Conference of the Parties to the United Nations Framework Convention on Climate Change, indicated that average temperatures in the MENA region rank as the highest globally. Since the summer of 2023, several states in this region have surpassed historical high-temperature records.[②] For instance, the Iraqi Meteorological Department, under the Ministry of Transportation, reported mid-August highs of 51°C in provinces such as Baghdad, Najaf, Diwaniya, Dhi Qar, and Muthanna, with temperatures in northern Iraq exceeding 44°C. Simultaneously, water scarcity intensified amid high temperatures and prolonged droughts. Although Iraq, located in the Tigris-Euphrates basin, traditionally enjoyed relative water abundance, conditions have sharply deteriorated in recent years. The summer of 2023 witnessed severe droughts in Diwaniya and Maysan provinces, where areas near the Tigris suffered from water shortages, leading to substantial financial losses for orchard

---

[①] Nasrat Adamo, "Climate Change: Droughts and increasing Desertification in the Middle East, With Special Reference to Iraq," *Engineering*, 2022, vol.14, p.239.

[②] "Multiple Climate Records Broken and Renewable Energy Becomes the Key to Solutions," The Website of the China Meteorological Administration, http://www.cma.gov.cn, March 26, 2024.

9.1.2 Drought and Desertification

The Arab region lies within low-latitude subtropical high-pressure zones, resulting in a predominantly arid climate. Its terrain consists mainly of plateaus, basins, and mountain ranges, lacking substantial water sources and receiving minimal rainfall. States such as Saudi Arabia, Yemen, Egypt, and the UAE frequently experience drought, arid conditions, and high temperatures. Weak water resource management, coupled with underdeveloped irrigation technology, results in low water use efficiency. With a growing population, rising water demand, and accelerated urbanization, the region's already fragile water infrastructure is under increasing strain, exacerbating humanitarian crises. [1] Drought also poses a significant risk of driving up the prices of food, water, and energy, worsening the situation further. In a 2023 report by the United Nations World Food Programme, over 12 million people in Syria faced hunger, with nearly 3 million at risk of food insecurity.

Due to the harsh climate conditions, soil and vegetation in the Arab region are continuously deteriorating, leading to severe desertification. This process is expanding rapidly, making the Arab region one of the most affected areas worldwide. States across the Arab world, plagued by desertification and relentless sandstorms, are keen to learn from China's successful desert control techniques to collectively address these issues. High temperatures, declining rainfall, and desertification have contributed to the region's frequent sandstorms. Between 15-20% of the world's sandstorms originate in the Middle East. In March 2020, Egypt experienced its most severe sandstorm in 26 years. Similarly, in March 2022, northern Algeria was struck by a sandstorm that impacted parts of the Mediterranean coast in Europe. Projections by Iraq's Ministry of Environment suggest that the number of sandstorm days within Iraq may increase annually from 272 days at present to nearly 300 by 2050. According to United Nations data, the frequency of sandstorms in the MENA region has significantly increased, impacting approximately 330 million people across 151 countries and causing substantial economic losses. Sandstorms deteriorate air quality, influence atmospheric circulation, and have harmful effects on ecosystems and human

---

[1] Yan Wei, Liu Aijiao, "The Compound Security Threats of Climate Change to the Middle East and Its Responses," *Social Sciences International*, vol. 4, 2023, p. 193.

Chapter 9 Special Report on China-Arab States Cooperation in Ecological and Environmental Governance

and Yemen.[①] The region's water resources are unevenly allocated, concentrated primarily in areas like the Nile Valley, the Tigris-Euphrates basin, and the Jordan River area. Many of these rivers span multiple countries, which has led to disputes over water usage. Additionally, even in areas with river and groundwater resources, distribution remains uneven. Regarding water usage, agricultural demand predominates, with most of the region's water devoted to irrigation. Issues such as excessive irrigation and inefficient water use are prevalent. Moreover, industrial and urban development are increasingly driving up water demand. Explosive growth in the urban population within the Arab region has further intensified the strain on water resources.

A World Bank report indicates that by 2050, the annual water deficit in the Arab region is expected to reach 25 billion cubic meters. In 2023, the World Bank published *The Economics of Water Scarcity in the Middle East and North Africa: Institutional Solutions*, which highlights an unprecedented water scarcity crisis across the region and offers various recommendations for water resource management and institutional reform to alleviate pressure on water resources. According to projections, by the end of 2029, the annual per capita available water in the Middle East and North Africa (MENA) region will drop below 500 cubic meters, the internationally recognized threshold for severe water scarcity. By 2050, the region's annual water deficit is projected to reach 25 billion cubic meters—equivalent to 65 times the output of the world's largest desalination plant built in Saudi Arabia. The report notes that in many MENA countries, water allocation across sectors such as agriculture and urban development is typically managed by central government agencies, which limits the ability of local governments to coordinate and address competing demands. To improve the distribution and use of water resources, the report recommends that Arab states adopt a national strategic water framework that grants local governments more authority in water allocation decisions, thereby enabling more effective coordination across sectors.[②]

[①] Jeannie Sowers, "Climate Change, Water Resources, and the Politics of Adaptation in the Middle East and North Africa," *Climatic Change*, 2011, Vol.2011, p.604.

[②] Guan Kejiang, "Middle East and North Africa States Step Up Efforts to Address the Water Crisis," *People's Daily*, May 18, 2023.

have become major issues widely faced by the Arab region.①

China has long been committed to promoting the building of a community with a shared future for humankind, enhancing international cooperation, upholding multilateral order and norms, and advancing the implementation of the Paris Agreement. As a responsible developing power, China has actively advocated and pragmatically engaged in South-South cooperation on climate change, continually providing support to other developing countries—particularly small island nations, the least developed countries, Arab states, and African countries—in addressing climate change.

9.1 Current State of the Ecological Environment in the Arab Region

The Arab region's ecological environment is highly fragile. The terrain is predominantly plateau, bordered by higher mountain ranges. The area of plains is minimal, mainly located in Egypt's Nile Valley and Delta, and in Iraq's Tigris and Euphrates river basins—cradles of ancient Egyptian and Babylonian civilizations. Geographically, the majority of the Arab region lies between 20° and 30° north latitude, with the Tropic of Cancer running through its center, resulting in a hot climate. The area is further influenced by subtropical high pressure and the northeast trade winds from Asia's arid interior, leading to persistently dry conditions with scarce rainfall. The plateau's isolated terrain prevents moist oceanic air from entering, exacerbating regional drought and reinforcing its characteristic tropical desert climate.

9.1.1 Distribution and Utilization of Water Resources

The Arab region is one of the most arid areas globally. In recent years, factors such as climate change, population growth, and shifts in economic and social conditions have led to a severe and escalating water scarcity across Arab states. Of the world's 17 most water-scarce countries, 14 are located in the Middle East and North Africa, including 12 Arab states such as Algeria, Libya, Saudi Arabia,

---

① Wang Lingling, "Research on Ecological and Environmental Cooperation Between China and Arab States/ Discussion on Cooperation in Desertification Prevention and Control and Technology Export," *Journal of Ningxia Communist Party Institute*, No. 6, 2013.

Chapter 9 Special Report on China-Arab States Cooperation in Ecological and Environmental Governance

Since the 18th National Congress of the Communist Party of China, under the guidance of Xi Jinping Thought on Socialism with Chinese Characteristics for a New Era, China has kept pace with the times and looked outward, shouldering its responsibilities as a major country and demonstrating its commitment on the global stage. China has promoted the building of a community with a shared future for humankind, achieving a major transformation from a participant in global environmental governance to a leader in this arena. Ecological civilization construction has become one of the central themes of this new era, and co-building ecological civilization is a core principle of Xi Jinping's thoughts regarding ecological civilization. On December 13, 2023, the 28th Conference of the Parties (COP28) to the United Nations Framework Convention on Climate Change concluded in Dubai, UAE. Negotiators from 198 parties gathered in Dubai for the first global stocktake under the Paris Agreement, and reached a consensus on increasing climate action efforts over the next decade.

The Arab states are located in arid and semi-arid regions, with diverse ecological environments characterized by dry climates and scarce rainfall, resulting in limited water resources and fragile ecosystems. Approximately 68% of the area consists of deserts and hills, with most regions experiencing hot, dry conditions that place the limited land resources at risk of desertification, leading to further degradation of soil and forests. Moreover, with the growing impacts of large-scale industrialization, oil extraction, marine pollution, and environmental degradation, ecological and sustainable development challenges

peaceful development, characterized by "joint consultation, joint contribution, and shared benefits," has garnered widespread acceptance among Arab states. As a key driver of global economic growth, China has witnessed a discernible "look to the East" trend among Arab states as they undergo strategic adjustments and developmental transformations.[1] Beyond China's technological prowess in fields such as clean energy, digital economy, high technology and new industrialization, its commitment to openness, inclusiveness, peaceful cooperation and independent development constitutes a significant attraction for Arab states. The current strategic landscape in the Middle East is characterized by complexity, volatility and intensifying great power competition across various domains, including politics, economics, diplomacy and security. Consequently, both China and Arab states face substantial strategic competitive pressures, potentially impacting China-Arab states scientific and technological cooperation. Under these circumstances, strengthening multilateral cooperation, maintaining strategic consensus and fostering strategic trust, with the aim of building a China-Arab states community with a shared future, become paramount for forging a more efficient, stable and enduring partnership in science and technology.

---

[1] Li, Weijian, *et al.*, "Abundant Fruits of the China-Arab States Cooperation Forum: A New Chapter in China-Arab Relations," *Arab World Studies*, 2023(1), pp.9-10.

Chapter 8 Special Report on China-Arab States Science and Technology Cooperation

enterprises have entered the Arab market, their limited scope, depth of engagement and partner diversity have hindered the development of a broad, grassroots ("bottom-up") market presence. Similarly, the Arab private sector faces challenges including limited technological innovation capacity, talent shortages, insufficient funding, information access barriers, and inadequate policy support. To overcome these limitations, China-Arab states scientific and technological cooperation should prioritize enhancing policy communication and technical exchanges between enterprises and research institutions at all levels, expanding cooperation to include a wider range of actors and leveraging market mechanisms and civil society engagement to forge a more dynamic and inclusive partnership.

8.3.3 Cultivating Talent and Promoting Long-Term China-Arab States S & T Cooperation

While China-Arab states scientific and technological cooperation has witnessed rapid expansion, it has predominantly featured a unidirectional flow of technology from China to Arab states. This asymmetry stems from the comparatively lower levels of scientific and technological development and smaller talent pools in many Arab nations, particularly those beyond the Gulf region. Consequently, fostering long-term, sustainable China-Arab states scientific and technological cooperation requires a concerted effort to develop robust research talent pipelines. The Arab world's substantial youth demographic, comprising approximately 370 million individuals (representing over 60% of the total population), is a decisive factor influencing the trajectory, level and future prospects of development in Arab states. Fundamentally solidifying the foundation of this cooperation hinges on prioritizing talent cultivation and team building. This can be achieved through initiatives such as the "10+10 Cooperation Plan" between Chinese and Arab universities, operating within the framework of the "China-Arab States Youth Development Action," and by intensifying exchanges among young researchers from higher education institutions and research organizations.b

8.3.4 Joint Consultation, Shared Benefits and Peaceful Promotion of China-Arab States S & T Cooperation

Since the inception of the Belt and Road Initiative (BRI), China's vision of

8.3.1 Deepening China-Arab States S & T Cooperation by Leveraging Respective Strengths

The robust growth of China-Arab states scientific and technological cooperation over the past decade is underpinned by the strong complementarity between the two sides. China's global technological leadership provides critical support for the Arab world's efforts in technological innovation and economic transformation, while the Arab world's abundant capital and vast markets offer an ideal platform for Chinese enterprises to "expand their global footprint." The United Nations' "Global Innovation Index 2023" projects China to maintain its leading position in numerous high-tech fields, including artificial intelligence, the Internet of Things, blockchain, 5G, 3D printing, robotics, drones, genetic engineering, nanotechnology, solar photovoltaic, biofuels, green hydrogen and electric vehicles.[①] On the other hand, Arab states, home to the world's largest sovereign wealth funds totaling $3.7 trillion (36% of global assets) and a high-income population of 60 million in Gulf states like Saudi Arabia, the United Arab Emirates, Qatar, Kuwait, Oman and Bahrain, are well-positioned to accelerate their investments in technological innovation. This is driven by the escalating demands of the knowledge economy and the imperative of a thoroughgoing national transformation on the part of the Arab states. Therefore, the future of China-Arab states cooperation is promising, with increasing alignment in technology, capital and market demands. Building on past successful cooperation, the two sides can further strengthen their partnership by closely integrating their supply chains and leveraging their respective advantages to create a win-win situation.

8.3.2 Deepening China-Arab States S & T Cooperation Through Multi-Stakeholder Partnerships and Market Mechanisms

While China-Arab states scientific and technological cooperation has recently seen significant advancements, largely driven by government entities and state-owned enterprises under the "Five Cooperation Patterns" framework, private sector involvement remains underdeveloped. This necessitates a deeper, more diversified and institutionalized approach. Although some Chinese private

---

① United Nations, "Technology and Innovation Report 2023," 2023, pp.136-151.

Chapter 8 Special Report on China-Arab States Science and Technology Cooperation

modern bio-breeding and pest control. Furthermore, in August 2023, China's National Forestry and Grassland Administration and the League of Arab States Secretariat signed a Memorandum of Understanding to establish the China-Arab States International Research Center for Drought, Desertification and Land Degradation. This joint initiative aims to leverage financial, technological and human resources to provide theoretical and practical support for combating land degradation in both regions. By collaborating on research and innovation, the two sides hope to contribute significantly to the global goals of achieving zero net land degradation by 2030 and a 50% reduction in land degradation by 2040.[1]

8.3 Prospects for China-Arab States Scientific and Technological Cooperation

The pursuit of China-Arab states scientific and technological cooperation is a strategic choice that aligns with the demands of our time, addresses pressing global challenges and serves the shared development goals of both China and the Arab world. In recent years, underpinned by robust scientific and technological collaboration, China-Arab states cooperation has evolved from traditional models centered on energy trade and engineering contracting to encompass emerging areas such as renewable energy, advanced technologies and aerospace communications. The first China-Arab States Summit proposed the "Eight Joint Actions" for practical China-Arab cooperation, which set higher standards and expectations for China-Arab states scientific and technological cooperation in multiple areas, including food security, public health, green innovation and energy security. Accordingly, the 10th Ministerial Meeting of the China-Arab States Cooperation Forum proposed the "Five Cooperation Patterns" led by innovation, outlining a visionary blueprint for China-Arab states relations in the new era, characterized by "a forward-looking and innovative approach." Looking ahead, China-Arab states scientific and technological cooperation is set to play a catalytic role in fostering a China-Arab states community with a shared future.

---

[1] Science and Technology Department of Ningxia Hui Autonomous Region, "Promotion and Matching Event for Desertification Control Technologies Held in Yinchuan," Retrieved from Ministry of Science and Technology of the People's Republic of China, https://www.most.gov.cn/dfkj/nx/zxdt/202310/t20231009_188350.html.

the "Youth Development Joint Action" under the eight joint actions for practical China-Arab states cooperation, China and Arab states have implemented the "China-Arab states Universities 10+10 Cooperation Plan", encompassing 39 universities including Tianjin University of Traditional Chinese Medicine, Capital Medical University and Tianjin Medical University, thus facilitating enhanced talent exchange, academic discourse and clinical practice in healthcare between the two sides.

Agro-ecological cooperation has enhanced food security for China and Arab states, emerging as a key area for Ningxia to leverage its regional strengths and foster cooperation with Arab states. From September 22 to 23, 2023, the 6th China-Arab States Expo hosted a cooperation conference on the quality development of modern agriculture. Themed "Deepening Practical Cooperation and Jointly Promoting Food Security", the conference aimed to foster China-Arab states agricultural technological innovation, investment cooperation and technological exchange, thereby further enhancing bilateral practical cooperation in agriculture. This conference successfully facilitated the implementation of 34 agricultural cooperation projects, spanning research and development, trade and investment. Specific initiatives include modern agricultural technology training and the introduction of new crop varieties and livestock breeds.[①] Notably, Ningxia Academy of Agricultural and Forestry Sciences and the National Research Center of Egypt signed a memorandum of understanding on scientific and technological cooperation in crop breeding, saline-alkali land improvement and agricultural biotechnology.[②] Beyond traditional areas like agricultural disaster prevention, water-saving irrigation and ecological enhancement, China-Arab states cooperation has expanded to include agricultural biodiversity. In March 2023, China and the United Arab Emirates signed a *Memorandum of Understanding on the Sustainable Development of Date Palm Cultivation*, committing to joint research and industrial cooperation in date palm regeneration, genetic transformation,

---

① "The 6th China-Arab States Expo Modern Agriculture High-Quality Development Cooperation Conference Held in Yinchuan," People's Daily Online, http://nx.people.com.cn/n2/2023/0922/c192493-40581410.html.

② Ningxia Academy of Agricultural and Forestry Sciences, "Delegation from the National Research Center of Egypt Visits Our Academy and Signs a Memorandum of Understanding on Science and Technology Cooperation," Retrieved from Ningxia Academy of Agricultural Sciences, https://www.nxaas.com.cn/xwzx/ynyw/202309/t20230928_4291969.html.

Chapter 8 Special Report on China-Arab States Science and Technology Cooperation

collaborative innovation project.[①] Furthermore, telecommunications providers such as Kuwait STC, UAE du and Kuwait Zain have established cooperative frameworks with Huawei in the 5.5G domain, facilitating joint endeavors in the research, development and field testing of 5.5G technology. In the same month, the Shenzhen Institute of Big Data Research, the Chinese University of Hong Kong (Shenzhen) and King Abdullah University of Science and Technology in Saudi Arabia signed a memorandum of understanding to establish a collaborative laboratory dedicated to scientific computing and machine learning. This initiative aims to foster in-depth cooperation in scientific research, talent cultivation and other areas, thereby stimulating the vitality of China-Arab states scientific and technological innovation. Additionally, Chinese e-commerce giants, including Alibaba, JD.com and Shein, have accelerated their expansion into Arab markets, propelling the "Silk Road e-commerce" initiative as a catalyst for economic revitalization in the Arab region. Currently, J&T Express has achieved comprehensive coverage across Saudi Arabia, processing over 100,000 parcels daily.

Healthcare cooperation has fostered the development of a smart "Internet+healthcare" platform between China and Arab states, emerging as a linchpin of practical bilateral cooperation. On September 22, 2023, the China-Arab States Expo convened a comprehensive health industry forum, delving into a wide range of topics such as Ningxia's "Internet+healthcare" initiative, national regional medical centers, maternal and child health, health management, telemedicine, smart healthcare, Traditional Chinese Medicine (TCM), intelligent medical equipment manufacturing and smart elderly care. Notably, the forum launched the China-Arab States Traditional Chinese Medicine "Internet+Healthcare" Smart Platform and the China-Africa Partner Hospital Cooperation Mechanism project, promoting collaboration between Chinese and Arab enterprises and medical institutions in regional medical center construction, the preservation and innovaton of TCM, chronic disease prevention and control and the intelligent advancement of the medical equipment industry. A memorandum of understanding was signed between Egypt's Ain Shams University and the Ningxia Health Commission. Moreover, in alignment with

---

① "Huawei: Leading the Next Phase of 5G Advances in the GCC," Middle East Economy, https://economymiddleeast.com/news/huawei-leading-5g-advances-gcc, 2023-12-19.

planning.① Furthermore, the fourth China-Arab States Beidou Cooperation Forum held in October 2023 underscored the growing importance of the Beidou Navigation Satellite System in the region. Arab nations expressed keen interest in leveraging the system's services through the China-Arab States Beiou/GNSS Center in Tunisia to enhance efficiency in precision agriculture, mineral exploration and fishery monitoring.② Since 2023, China has signed multiple memoranda of understanding with Arab states on the peaceful use of outer space, including *Memorandum of Understanding between the Government of the People's Republic of China and the Government of the Arab Republic of Egypt 1on Cooperation in the Peaceful Uses of Outer Space*, *Memorandum of Understanding between China and Sudan on Strengthening Cooperation in Space* and *Memorandum of Understanding between China and the United Arab Emirates on Cooperation in the Peaceful Uses of Outer Space*—laying a robust policy foundation for bilateral aerospace cooperation. These agreements, including those with Egypt, Sudan, and the United Arab Emirates, have solidified the commitment of both sides to deepening their partnership in space exploration.

Digital communications cooperation has fostered robust digital connectivity between China and Arab states, emerging as a pivotal area of bilateral scientific and technological collaboration. In recent years, Chinese companies have emerged as indispensable partners for Arab states in the realm of 5G communications, securing a dominant market position in nations such as Saudi Arabia, the UAE, Egypt, Oman and Bahrain. With substantial support from Chinese enterprises, 14 Middle Eastern countries have successfully deployed 5G networks. Notably, in March 2023, Saudi Telecom Company (STC) and Huawei forged a strategic partnership to construct a full-optical network infrastructure, laying the groundwork for the advent of the F5.5G era. Concurrently, Huawei and Zain KSA, Saudi Arabia's leading telecommunications operator, entered into a strategic cooperation agreement and jointly unveiled the "5.5G City"

---

① "Connected by Stars: A Chronicle of China-Arab States Space Cooperation," China Today, Retrieved from China-Arab States Cooperation Forum, http://www.chinaarabcf.org/chn/zagx/gjydyl/202406/t20240613_11435348.htm, 2024-6-13.

② "Exclusive Interview: China-Arab States Beidou Cooperation Adds a New Dimension to the Belt and Road Initiative— Interview with the Secretary-General of the Arab Information and Communications Technologies Organization," Retrieved from Sohu.com, https://www.sohu.com/a/733132535_121687414, 2023-10-26.

Chapter 8 Special Report on China-Arab States Science and Technology Cooperation

project in Dubai, UAE, constructed by Harbin Electric Group, was connected to the grid for the first time. As the Middle East's first clean coal-fired power plant, it is projected to supply 20% of Dubai's electricity upon full operation.[①] Similarly, the Al Dhafra PV2 Solar Power Plant in Abu Dhabi, the world's largest single photovoltaic power station, completed by China National Machinery Industry Corporation in November 2023, can supply electricity to 200,000 households, reduce carbon emissions by 2.4 million tons annually and increase the share of clean energy in the UAE's total energy structure to over 13%. By the end of 2023, this project had contributed a cumulative 3.6 billion kilowatt-hours of clean electricity to the UAE.[②] In addition, Noor III Concentrated Solar Power Plant in Morocco and the Al Kharsa Power Plant in Qatar, as important results of China-Arab states cooperation in the field of green energy, have also played an active role in the energy transition of Arab states.

Aerospace and satellite cooperation has propelled the construction of a "Space Silk Road" between China and Arab states, fostering new frontiers in bilateral scientific and technological collaboration. In recent years, China has provided Arab states with internationally competitive technologies and R&D support in remote sensing, navigation and communication, and deep space exploration. A prime example of this cooperation is the Egypt Satellite Assembly and Integration Test Center (AIT Center), completed in June 2023. Constructed by China Aerospace Science and Technology Corporation, the AIT Center is China's first foreign aid project for ground-based space infrastructure, empowering Egypt with the capability for independent satellite development. Subsequently, the successful launch of the jointly developed Egypt-2 low-orbit, high-resolution optical remote sensing satellite from the Jiuquan Satellite Launch Center in December 2023 marked a significant milestone in Sino-Egyptian cooperation, providing a robust technological foundation for Egypt to conduct environmental hazard assessments, land resource evaluations and urban

---

[①] Xinhua News Agency, "Overview: China and Middle Eastern Countries Join Hands to Address Climate Change," Retrieved from China Government Website, https://www.gov.cn/yaowen/liebiao/202312/content_6919310.htm, 2023-12-09.

[②] "China-Arab Countries Eye Technology Cooperation for High-Quality Development," Global Times, https://www.globaltimes.cn/page/202405/1313252.shtml, 2024-5-29.

research capabilities, China has inked scientific and technological cooperation agreements, 5G technology accords and talent cultivation pacts with nearly two dozen Arab nations. Furthermore, to enhance technological and industrial synergies, China and the Arab states have established numerous joint innovation laboratories and overseas scientific research centers in sectors such as aerospace, digital communications, agricultural ecology and healthcare, thereby facilitating the integration of their innovation, industrial and talent ecosystems. To promote scientific and technological cooperation, the two sides have undertaken extensive exchanges, with a particular focus on facilitating short-term research training for young Arab scientists in China, thus strengthening the scientific talent pipeline in the Arab world.

8.2.3 Key Areas of Cooperation

Against the backdrop of China and the Arab states' shared pursuit of development, and facilitated by platforms such as the China-Arab States Cooperation Forum and the China-Arab States Expo, China-Arab states scientific and technological cooperation has deepened and broadened significantly. Beyond traditional energy cooperation, new focal points have emerged in areas such as green energy, aerospace, digital communications, healthcare and agricultural technology. These collaborations have injected new vitality into the China-Arab states partnership.

Green energy cooperation has driven China and Arab states to build low-carbon energy systems and promote the transformation of energy patterns and economic structures in Arab states. As a key component of the "Eight Joint Actions," collaborative efforts in green innovation and energy security have significantly bolstered China-Arab states energy science and technology cooperation. Cooperation has spanned multiple sectors, including solar, hydrogen, wind and nuclear energy. Leveraging China's technological advancements in clean energy, Chinese enterprises have made substantial involvement in large-scale clean energy projects across the Arab world, particularly in Morocco, the United Arab Emirates and Saudi Arabia. In 2023, for instance, Chinese photovoltaic companies like Trina Solar Co. Ltd., China Sunergy Co. Ltd. and GCL Technology Holdings Ltd. announced significant investments in these countries, expanding their production capacities in silicon wafers, battery cells and polysilicon. In May 2023, the No. 4 unit of the Hassyan Clean Coal Power Plant

Chapter 8 Special Report on China-Arab States Science and Technology Cooperation

promoting China-Arab states scientific and technological cooperation over the past decade. As a national-level international technology transfer center, it has actively fostered the establishment of bilateral China-Arab states technology transfer centers, constructed a comprehensive domestic and international technology transfer cooperation network, developed a comprehensive information service platform for China-Arab states technology transfer, and organized various technology transfer training, promotion and matchmaking activities. The fifth China-Arab Technology Transfer and Innovation Cooperation Conference, held in Yinchuan, Ningxia, from September 21 to 24, 2023, with the theme of "Cooperating for innovation, creating a better future", invited over 700 participants, including representatives from the Arab League Secretariat, the Arab Organization for Agricultural Development, the Moroccan Ministry of Higher Education, Scientific Research and Innovation, and the Egyptian Research Institute. The conference facilitated the matchmaking activities for 300 advanced technological achievements and the signing of 10 key cooperation agreements.[1] Through various activities such as the China-Arab States High-Level Forum on Scientific and Technological Cooperation and the China-Arab States Green Innovation Development Technology Promotion Conference, the China-Arab States Technology Transfer Center has not only effectively promoted the transfer of advanced and applicable technologies and equipment overseas but has also successfully fostered a series of important innovation platforms, contributing to the implementation of numerous key scientific and technological demonstration projects. It has thus become an indispensable practical pathway for promoting China-Arab states scientific and technological cooperation.

China and the Arab states have made substantial strides in innovation cooperation, significantly boosting bilateral technological advancement. Beyond technology transfer, China and Arab states have actively engaged in innovative collaborations, leveraging their complementary advantages. Joint efforts have been made in multiple fields such as digital technology, renewable energy, environmental governance and healthcare, encompassing joint planning, collaborative research and development, and talent cultivation. To bolster mutual

---

[1] China-Arab Expo Secretariat, "China-Arab Technology Transfer and Innovation Cooperation Conference," Retrieved from https://www.cas-expo.org.cn/zh/cloudSummitDet.html?createTime=2023-09-21&id=730, 2023-9-21.

innovative partnerships in transportation, agriculture, government services, information communication, health, satellite navigation and environmental sustainability, offering vast opportunities for future collaboration.

Table 8.3 Distribution of Science and Technology Cooperation between China and Arab States or Regional Organizations

Country/ Regional Organization	Nuclear Energy	Energy Technology	Space Technology	Artificial Intelligence	Digital Economy	Agricultural Technology	Biomedicine	Intelligent Communication
AL	√	√	√	√	√	√	√	√
GCC	√	√	√	√	√	√	√	√
UAE	√	√	√	√	√	√	√	√
SA	√	√	√	√	√	√	√	√
Qatar		√		√	√	√	√	√
Algeria	√		√	√	√		√	√
Egypt	√	√	√	√	√	√	√	√
Tunisia	√	√	√		√			√
Iraq				√	√			
Jordan	√	√				√		
Sudan	√		√		√	√	√	
Oman		√	√	√		√		√
Morocco		√		√		√	√	
Lebanon	√					√		√
Kuwait					√		√	√
Bahrain			√					√

Data Source: This table is compiled from data provided by the Ministry of Commerce, the Ministry of Science and Technology, and a variety of public domestic and international sources.

8.2.2 Primary Channels for Cooperation

The China-Arab states technology transfer network has grown increasingly robust, facilitating bilateral scientific and technological cooperation. Established in 2015 under the joint efforts of the Chinese Ministry of Science and Technology and the People's Government of Ningxia Hui Autonomous Region, the China-Arab States Technology Transfer Center has played a pivotal role in

alignment, China-Arab states technological cooperation has been progressively expanding in terms of modalities, domains and depth, thereby unlocking substantial untapped potential.

The top-level design of China-Arab states technological cooperation has been steadily refined. At the inaugural China-Arab States Summit in December 2022, President Xi Jinping proposed "eight joint initiatives" for China-Arab states practical cooperation, elevating technological collaboration to an indispensable dimension of implementation. Subsequently, at the Third Belt and Road Summit Forum for International Cooperation in October 2023, Xi outlined eight actions to foster high-quality Belt and Road construction. Among these, building a three-dimensional connectivity network, promoting an open world economy and advancing green development have further solidified the strategic guidance for China-Arab states technological cooperation. As of now, bilateral economic, trade and technological cooperation agreements have been inked between China and 21 Arab countries, with the exception of Comoros, providing robust support for bilateral technological endeavors.[①] Overall, under the strong guidance of state leaders and within the context of the Belt and Road Initiative, China-Arab states technological cooperation has seen continuous improvement in terms of conceptual framework, policy support and developmental direction.

China-Arab states technological cooperation has yielded increasingly fruitful results. Firstly, the forms of technological cooperation have become increasingly diversified. Beyond traditional models, the two sides have engaged in mutually beneficial, co-constructed and shared initiatives in multiple dimensions, including technology transfer, joint science and technology park development, and scientific and technological personnel exchanges. Secondly, the scope of cooperation has expanded significantly, encompassing multiple fields (see Table 8.3) and extending to emerging areas such as new energy, aerospace, 5G, AI, drones and the digital economy.[②] Thirdly, the potential for cooperation continues to unfold. China-Arab states collaboration is not only addressing the current challenges of social informatization and economic globalization but also pioneering new frontiers in governance modernization. Both sides have explored

---

① Li, S. X. (Ed.), *2022 Annual Report on the Development of China-Arab States Economic and Trade Relations*, Social Sciences Documents Press, 2023, p.147.

② Sun, D. G., & Wu, T. Y., "The Fourth Industrial Revolution and China's Science and Technology Diplomacy towards Arab Countries," *West Asia & Africa*, 2020(6), p.115.

effectiveness and timeliness of their commercialization.[1]

Thirdly, the foundations for talent support and technological innovation industry models remain underdeveloped, resulting in a lack of internal momentum for long-term development. In an era of global competition for talent, the shortage of skilled professionals poses a significant challenge to all Arab states. Statistics reveal that less than 60% of young people in Arab states complete secondary education. Furthermore, only about one-third are proficient in mathematics, and less than two-thirds possess basic literacy skills. Approximately 30% of young people have attained a university degree, with only 28% majoring in science, technology, engineering and mathematics (STEM).[2] This severe shortage of skilled labor directly impedes the region's capacity for technological advancement. Concurrently, technological innovation and industrial transformation in Arab nations are predominantly driven by the public sector and state-owned enterprises, with limited private sector involvement. The private sector, as a pivotal force in driving innovation, commercializing research and fostering practical applications, is crucial for successful innovation-led transformations. However, beyond low participation rates, private enterprises face various challenges, including building talent pipelines, securing operational funding and aligning with government policies.

8.2 Specific Practices of China-Arab States Technological Cooperation

8.2.1 Overall Cooperation Trend

China-Arab states technological cooperation has become an integral part of the overall bilateral diplomatic relations. As a cornerstone in invigorating cooperative potential, expanding cooperation initiatives and fostering the construction of a China-Arab states community with a shared future, this collaboration has been instrumental in elevating the China-Arab states partnership to new heights. Both China and Arab states accord significant importance to technological cooperation. Based upon effective strategic

---

[1] International Monetary Fund. Promoting Inclusive Growth in the Middle East and North Africa: Challenges and Opportunities in a Post-Pandemic World, 2022, p.93.

[2] UN Economic and Social Commission for Western Asia. Annual SDG Review 2024: Skill Development, Innovation and the Private Sector in the Arab Region. February 2024, p.6.

have emerged as technological leaders in the Arab world, fueled by substantial investments in digital infrastructure, 5G and cloud technologies. Meanwhile, North African Arab countries like Egypt and Morocco have been actively seeking to leverage their demographic dividends and limited capital to advance their national technological innovation agendas. In contrast, Arab states such as Iraq, Lebanon and Syria lag significantly in terms of technological capabilities and development prospects, resulting in an imbalanced regional landscape for technological innovation and hindering the formation of a dynamic innovation partnership ecosystem with highly compatible collaborative relationships. According to the Global Innovation Index 2023, the UAE, Saudi Arabia and Kuwait rank among the top 50 globally, far outpacing other Arab countries. Conversely, Algeria and Mauritania rank at the bottom of the 132 participating countries, while Iraq and Yemen are not even included in the rankings.①

Secondly, the region's capacity for technological innovation remains limited, requiring significant efforts to enhance research output and industrial upgrading. Arab nations have traditionally relied heavily on international cooperation for major technological advancements, and their capacity for independent innovation is insufficient. Technological innovation is a cornerstone for national development and sustainable growth. Therefore, enhancing indigenous innovation capabilities is a pressing issue for Arab nations. Despite some fluctuations in recent years, the commercialization rate of technological achievements in most Arab states remains low. In 2022, global patent applications reached 3.46 million, while Arab nations collectively filed 17260 patents and were granted 5786. However, their share of global intellectual property patents was a mere 0.5%. Moreover, patent activities were concentrated in a few countries, namely Saudi Arabia (34%), Morocco (30%), the UAE (17%), Egypt (11%) and Algeria (6%), with other Arab nations showing limited contributions.② Globally, leading technological innovation patents are primarily held by private corporations such as IBM and Samsung, which exhibit higher rates of commercialization. In contrast, patents in Arab states are largely driven by public investment and state-owned enterprises, raising questions about the

---

① WIPO, Global Innovation Index 2023: Innovation in the Face of Uncertainty, 2023, pp.58-61.
② WIPO, World Intellectual Property Report 2022: The Direction of Innovation, 2022, pp.79-87.

scale solar photovoltaic project. The Dubai solar park, set for completion in 2030, is projected to become the world's largest solar park with a total installed capacity of 5 GW. Additionally, Arab states have commissioned blue hydrogen and experimental green hydrogen facilities, with other large-scale hydrogen projects underway.[1] In the domain of aerospace, Saudi Arabia committed a substantial $2.1 billion investment in 2020 to propel its space program forward. Concurrently, the National Space Technology Commission initiated a space startup alliance to cultivate a sustainable aerospace ecosystem. Furthermore, Bahrain and Kuwait successfully launched nanosatellites in 2021 and 2022 respectively, while the UAE successfully inserted its Hope Probe into Mars orbit, marking the region's inaugural interplanetary mission. Oman is also spearheading the development of the Middle East's first spaceport.[2]

8.1.3 Enduring Challenges in Innovation Prospects

Although Arab states have achieved notable strides in digital transformation and technological innovation, substantial challenges persist. The convergence of national fiscal capacity, effective governance and a skilled workforce is essential for sustained digital advancement. However, a closer examination of the region's industrial structure, governance models and societal foundations reveals significant obstacles to realizing its full technological innovation potential.

Firstly, the region grapples with significant disparities in technological development, impeding the formation of robust regional collaborative frameworks. Technological innovation, as a multifaceted development goal, demands concerted efforts and collaboration among neighboring countries across science, technology, politics, culture and security domains. To this end, the establishment of bilateral and multilateral cooperation frameworks is essential for fostering the sustainable development of technology. However, owing to diverse national contexts, the level of technological development among Arab states varies widely, with the "digital divide" poised to deepen. In recent years, Gulf Arab states such as Saudi Arabia, the United Arab Emirates, Bahrain and Qatar

---

[1] Zhang, R., & Xiang, J. Y., "The Energy Integration Transformation of GCC Countries: Connotation, Progress and Challenges," *Arab World Studies*, 2023 (4), pp.9-15.

[2] Omar Qaise. "Will Arab Countries Become the New Space-Tech Powerhouse?" https://interactive.satellitetoday.com/via/june-2023/will-arab-countries-become-the-new-space-tech-powerhouse/, 2023-05-23.

Chapter 8 Special Report on China-Arab States Science and Technology Cooperation

Table 8.2 Global Network Readiness Index Rankings of Gulf Countries (2023)

	UAE	Saudi Arabia	Qatar	Bahrain	Oman	Kuwait
Overall Score	62.4	56.1	54.2	52.5	52.1	48.4
Rank	30	41	46	51	54	64

Data source: Compiled based on data from the *Global Information Technology Report 2023*.

Specifically, Arab states have made significant strides in diversifying their technological endeavors and achieved remarkable accomplishments in fields such as information and communications technology (ICT), artificial intelligence, energy transition and aerospace. In the realm of ICT, Gulf Cooperation Council (GCC) nations have made substantial investments in 5G mobile networks to construct smart, interconnected cities, thereby enhancing connectivity across diverse sectors. Data from the second quarter of 2023 reveals that the United Arab Emirates has emerged as the world's fastest-growing 5G market, while Bahrain boasts one of the world's top 20 fiber optic penetration rates.[①] In the realm of artificial intelligence, AI-powered public administration is gaining significant traction across Arab nations, as highlighted in a recent report by Oliver Wyman. The consultancy estimates that this digital transformation will generate annual savings of over $7 billion for the GCC countries. Moreover, Arab states are poised to further expand their AI capabilities in 2023 and beyond. Projections indicate that AI technologies will contribute $45.9 billion to the GDP of Bahrain, Kuwait, Oman and Qatar by 2030.[②] Regarding energy transition, Arab states are committed to decarbonizing their oil and gas industries, with major energy companies in Saudi Arabia, Qatar and the UAE setting clear carbon reduction targets. Moreover, these countries are prioritizing the development of renewable energy sources, leading to substantial increases in renewable energy capacity. Landmark projects, completed and now fully operational, include the Mohammed bin Rashid Al Maktoum Solar Park in the UAE, Qatar's first full-capacity grid-connected solar photovoltaic project and Oman's first utility-

---

① Telecom Review, "From Deserts to Digital Dominance: Tech Transformation in the GCC," https://www.telecomreview.com/articles/reports-and-coverage/7409-from-deserts-to-digital-dominance-tech-transformation-in-the-gcc, 2023-10-09.

② Oliver Wyman, "7 Insights into Digital Trends in the GCC Digital Evolution," https://www.oliverwyman.com/our-expertise/insights/2024/apr/7-digital-trends-gcc.html, 2024-03-01.

Table 8.1 **Global Innovation Index Rankings of Arab States (2019-2023)**

	2019	2020	2021	2022	2023
United Arab Emirates	36	34	33	31	32
Saudi Arabia	68	66	66	51	48
Qatar	65	70	68	52	50
Kuwait	60	78	72	62	64
Bahrain	78	79	78	72	67
Oman	80	84	76	79	69
Morocco	74	75	77	67	70
Jordan	86	81	81	78	71
Tunisia	70	—	71	73	79
Egypt	92	96	94	89	86
Lebanon	88	87	92	—	92
Algeria	113	121	120	115	119
Mauritania	—	—	—	129	127
Iraq	—	—	—	131	—
Yemen	129	131	131	128	—

Data Source: Compiled from the World Intellectual Property Organization's Global Innovation Index

Note: Countries not included in a particular year's rankings are indicated by a blank cell.

Compared to other Arab states, the Gulf Cooperation Council (GCC) members have exhibited more rapid and significant advancements in technological innovation. As evidenced by the 2023 Global Network Readiness Index (Table 8.2), the six GCC states—the UAE, Saudi Arabia, Qatar, Bahrain, Oman and Kuwait—consistently occupy the top six positions among Arab nations and rank within the top 65 globally, reflecting a substantial competitive edge.① Furthermore, these countries consistently rank among the global leaders in indices such as the Global Talent Competitiveness Index, the Government AI Readiness Index, the Global Innovation Index and the United Nations E-Government Development Index.②

---

① Portulans Institwode, Network Readiness Index 2023, 2023, pp.32-40.

② P. Mokshita. "Digital Giants: GCC Countries Lead the Charge in Global Tech Rankings", https://www.sme10x.com/10x-industry/digital-giants-gcc-countries-lead-the-charge-in-global-tech-rankings, 2024-01-09.

Chapter 8 Special Report on China-Arab States Science and Technology Cooperation

all place scientific and technological innovation as a central component of their national development plans, providing clear strategic directions and roadmaps for the future. Second, to address specific needs, Arab states have also developed specialized strategic plans to serve national scientific innovation. For example, Bahrain launched the "Smart Programmer" initiative in 2023, aiming to train 10,000 programmers by 2027 to enter Bahrain's technology innovation industry. Similarly, the UAE's "Smart Digital" strategy, Saudi Arabia's "Open Big Data" strategy and Bahrain's "Open Data" strategy all focus on optimizing data utilization and information processing technology.

8.1.2 Remarkable Achievements in Science and Technology Innovation

In recent years, Arab states have experienced a surge in technological innovation, capturing global attention. According to the United Nations Economic and Social Commission for Western Asia's *Annual SDG Review*, the innovation landscape across the Arab region has undergone a significant transformation. Through concerted efforts involving governments, private sectors and academic institutions, these nations have delved into diverse fields such as clean energy, advanced technological infrastructure, aerospace and digital satellite technology, which has unlocked immense potential for socioeconomic development.[①] A comparative analysis of the *Global Innovation Index* over the past five years (Table 8.1) corroborates this trend. Saudi Arabia emerged as one of the top five global economies with the most rapid innovation growth between 2019 and 2023. The United Arab Emirates has maintained a steady ascent, nearing the top 30 globally by 2023. Notably, Saudi Arabia (climbing 20 places) and Qatar (climbing 15 places) successfully entered the top 50, while Bahrain (67), Oman (69), Jordan (71) and Egypt (86) also demonstrated significant improvements. Oman's progress was particularly noteworthy, with a 10-place jump between 2022 and 2023. These collective advancements underscore a systemic and holistic approach to innovation across the Arab world.[②]

[①] UN Economic and Social Commission for Western Asia. *Annual SDG Review 2024: Skill Development, Innovation and the Private Sector in the Arab Region*, February 2024, p.35.

[②] WIPO, Global Innovation Index 2023: Innovation in the Face of Uncertainty, 2023, pp.50-52.

technology has emerged as a vital pathway for Arab states seeking industrial transformation, economic growth and sustainable development. In response, Arab nations have placed substantial emphasis on developing comprehensive strategic frameworks at both regional and national levels to advance technological innovation and achieve strategic autonomy.

In 2018, the League of Arab States established the Arab Digital Economy Union[①], and subsequently released the *Arab Digital Economy Common Strategic Vision*. Serving as a roadmap for promoting digital economic development in the region, this vision outlined 50 planning initiatives to achieve 20 strategic objectives across five key areas: digital innovation, digital citizens, digital infrastructure, digital business and digital government.[②] The Gulf region has been at the forefront of scientific and technological development among Arab states, playing a pivotal role in the regional economic transformation. As a regional organization, the Gulf Cooperation Council has shifted its focus to economic diversification and digital transformation. In recent years, GCC sovereign wealth funds have prioritized investments in high-tech, renewable energy and digital intelligent industries. As of 2023, the total assets of these funds have reached US$3.6 trillion, representing a growth of over 70% compared to 2018, and laying a solid foundation for scientific innovation and economic transformation in the region.[③]

Beyond regional strategic support, Arab states have tailored their national scientific and technological innovation plans to align with their unique conditions and strategic objectives. First, scientific and technological innovation, as a crucial component of sustainable development in Arab states, plays a pivotal role in their comprehensive national development plans. For instance, the "Kuwait Vision 2035", "Saudi Vision 2030", "Oman Vision 2040", "UAE National Development Strategy for the Next 50 Years" and Egypt "Revitalization Plans"

---

① Founded in 2018, this organization operates under the League of Arab States and is directly overseen by its Secretary-General, aiming to promote collaboration among Arab states in the digital economy.

② Arab Commission for Digital Economy, *Arab Digital Economy Vision Towards A Sustainable Inclusive and Secure Digital Future*, January 2020.

③ "China Council for the Promotion of International Trade, "GCC Sovereign Wealth Funds Assets Reach $3.6 Trillion," Gulf Representative Office website, https://www.ccpit.org/gulf/a/20230927/20230927axs7.html.

Chapter 8   Special Report on China-Arab States Science and Technology Cooperation

China-Arab states science and technology cooperation represents a strategic development path that aligns with the mutual interests of both sides. In recent years, driven by the Belt and Road Initiative and responding to both China's expanding opening-up policy and Arab states' accelerated transformation needs, this cooperation has yielded substantial results. Since the first China-Arab States Summit, the "Eight Major Joint Actions" for China-Arab states pragmatic cooperation has provided clearer policy guidance and contemporary imperatives for scientific and technological collaboration. In 2023, China-Arab states science and technology cooperation gained momentum, achieving significant breakthroughs in cooperation models, fields and outcomes. In 2024, the 10th Ministerial Meeting of the China-Arab States Cooperation Forum proposed "Five Patterns of Cooperation" led by innovation-driven development, charting an inspiring blueprint for China-Arab relations in the new era under the banner of "Marching Forward Together." Looking ahead, China-Arab states science and technology cooperation is destined to become the primary driver of future bilateral relations and a catalyst for shared prosperity.

8.1   Current State of Scientific and Technological Development in Arab States

8.1.1   Gradual Maturation of Strategic Planning

As the 21st century unfolds, amid intensifying global technological innovation and competition, the pursuit of national development through science and

and utilization heavily rely on digital economy technologies and ideologies, making them a significant component of the digital economy landscape. New energy vehicles encompass smart Internet technology, big data analytics, artificial intelligence, intelligent manufacturing, and other domains, showcasing the broad applicability and profound impact of digital technology within the contemporary economic framework. Chinese electric car manufacturers prioritize enhancing the technological sophistication of their products by incorporating cutting-edge systems like intelligent assisted driving, interactive voice commands, smart body control systems, and seamless integration with mobile devices such as smartphones. These features cater to the preferences of consumers in the Arab market. Notably, the UAE and Chinese enterprises have collaboratively established the most extensive and robust Middle East service headquarters base for Chinese new energy vehicles in the region.[①] Moreover, over 20 Chinese automotive companies, including BYD, Chery, Changan, and Geely, have established their presence in the Middle East market.[②] Through the alliance in new energy vehicles, China and the UAE anticipate delving into more profound cooperation in upcoming digital economy frontiers, exemplified by intelligent networking, industrial Internet of Things, algorithmic recommendations, digital twin, and intelligent transportation.

[①] "China's New Energy Vehicle Service Headquarters Base in The Middle East Is Aiding Chinese New Energy Vehicle Brands in Accelerating Their Expansion Overseas," China Daily Online, https://qiye.chinadaily.com.cn/a/202208/24/WS6305c8aaa3101c3ee7ae556a.html, 2022-08-24.

[②] "Chinese Branded Cars Entering the Middle East Market," Huanqiu.com, http://www.xinhuanet.com/globe/2023-07/03/c_1310729581.htm, 2023-07-03.

Chapter 7　Special Report on China-Arab States Digital Economy Cooperation

delivery (COD)[①], digital payment trust in the region demands reinforcement. With evolving technologies and governmental support, digital transactions are gaining traction, witnessing a surge in e-wallets and payment applications. Chinese financial technology firms can actively pursue collaborations with local entities to address localization challenges in payments. Thirdly, accelerating digitalization and smart logistics innovation in the Middle East. Recent e-commerce regulations in some Arab states necessitate detailed product and delivery information. Chinese logistics enterprises can offer advanced technological solutions by integrating smart technologies with traditional logistics, thereby enhancing tracking mechanisms and data analytics capabilities. Fourthly, we can see the prospect of "her economy" for female consumers in the Middle East. Notably, the Middle East exhibits a promising landscape for female consumers. Young women constitute a significant user demographic within Arab region's e-commerce, showcasing robust purchasing power, particularly in segments like women's apparel, maternity and child products, and jewelry. This consumer segment holds substantial demand potential, offering lucrative opportunities for Chinese vertical e-commerce platforms specializing in beauty and apparel.

7.3.3　Nurturing Collaboration in Leading-edge Sectors: New Energy Vehicles as an Extension

In recent years, spurred by energy diversification efforts, the Arab region has emerged as a pivotal market for electric vehicles. Concurrently, Chinese electric vehicle firms are actively broadening their global footprint. Bolstered by mutual policy backing from China and Arab states and spurred by robust market demand in Arab regions alongside favorable policies concerning the new energy automotive industry, Arab states have evolved into a primary export market for China's electric vehicles. This has positioned the "new three items" of Chinese manufacturing—new energy vehicles, lithium batteries, and photovoltaic products (compared to the "old three items" of clothing, furniture, and home appliances) firmly in the limelight within the Arab world. While new energy vehicles are not inherently part of the digital economy, their evolution

---

① "Middle East E-Commerce Competition: Reaching A Tipping Point," The Paper.cn, https://www.thepaper.cn/newsDetail_forward_22400823, 2023-04-10.

such as 5G technology, Internet connectivity, big data centers, and cloud computing facilities, alongside promoting the digital evolution of traditional industries, serves as the pathway for China and Arab states to mutually reap the rewards of the digital economy. Collaborative efforts are essential to bridging the existing "digital divide." First, providing policy, financial, and technical aid to underdeveloped Arab states to expand broadband coverage, enhance service quality, and ensure the affordability of high-speed Internet access. Second, sharing China's successful digital transformation experiences with Arab states to bolster their autonomous development capacities leveraging China's expertise in digital economic advancement. Third, establishing a joint platform for cultivating digital technology talents, fostering personnel exchanges and communication, enriching digital literacy and practical skills among the populace in Arab states, and delivering long-term human capital support for the sustained cooperation and development of the digital economy between both sides.

7.3.2 Strengthening and Expanding Collaboration in Emerging Sectors: E-commerce as a Development Model

E-commerce, a burgeoning domain within the digital economy, intricately weaves through various facets of digital commerce, including data utilization, digital transactions, intelligent logistics, the subscription economy, and industrial digitalization. Its impact extends beyond the global economic landscape, reshaping both work dynamics and lifestyles while serving as a pivotal engine propelling China-Arab states cooperation within the new digital economy business sphere. In the forthcoming era, cross-border e-commerce cooperation between China and Arab states can concentrate on the following focal points: Firstly, "social media +" is an important breakthrough in the development of e-commerce. Introducing live e-commerce and KOL marketing not only addresses concerns regarding product trust but also caters to the entertainment preferences of consumers in Arab regions, promising a vast market. Leveraging technical tools and social platform influence, China's social e-commerce can pivot online shopping from mere functionality to experiential consumption, aligning with Arab customs and habits, thus crafting distinct brand value and competitive edges. Secondly, enhancing the trust of digital payment in the Arab region. While approximately 60% of online transactions in the Middle East rely on cash-on-

Chapter 7　Special Report on China-Arab States Digital Economy Cooperation

States' youth on scientific and technological innovations, green initiatives, and youth development.① Furthermore, on November 30, the inaugural China-Arab States Youth Development Forum successfully convened in Haikou under the theme of "Strengthening China-Arab States Youth Partnerships and Advancing the Construction of an Open Global Economy." During this forum, youths from China and Arab States actively engaged in discussions focusing on science and technology innovation, as well as sustainable green development.②

7.3　The Future of China-Arab States Cooperation in the Digital Economy

The collaboration between China and Arab states in the realm of the digital economy is steadily deepening. Particularly, Arab states, which have been trailing in digital economic advancements, are actively striving to enhance their digital economy development through international cooperative efforts in this arena. It is projected that the period from 2022 to 2027 will serve as the "digital economy acceleration phase" for the Middle East.③ With the backdrop of the Belt and Road Initiative's high-quality joint construction, there exists significant potential for cooperation between the two parties across traditional, emerging, and cutting-edge domains within the digital economy.

7.3.1　Bridging the Digital Divide in Traditional Sectors: Enhancing Digital Infrastructure and Talent Development

In the context of ensuring the sustainable growth of the digital "Belt and Road," establishing universal, secure, and cost-effective networks stands as the foundational pillar of the "Digital Silk Road." Advancing digital infrastructure,

---

① "Opening of the 6th China-Arab States Expo-China-Arab States Youth Innovation and Development Forum and 2023 China-Arab States Youth Exchange Camp," *China Youth Daily*, 2023-09-22, p.1.

② "First China-Arab States Youth Development Forum Focuses on Promoting Construction of Open World Economy," People's Daily Online, http://world.people.com.cn/n1/2023/1130/c1002-40129265.html, 2023-11-30.

③ "Middle East Countries Vigorously Develop Digital Economy (International Perspective)," People's Daily, 2023-11-22, p.14.

7.2.3 Youth Exchanges Are Infusing Fresh Vitality into Bilateral Cooperation

Collaboration between Chinese and Arab States' youth in science and technology benefits from significant human resource advantages. Presently, approximately three-quarters of China's scientific and technological workforce are aged 39 and below[1], with young talents leading the charge in driving China's innovation in this field. Similarly, Arab states boast a high proportion of young individuals, with a growing focus on nurturing young scientific and technological talents. Notably, the enrollment rates for higher education in certain Arab states have seen a substantial increase, empowering more young talents to play pivotal roles in advancing Arab states' industrialization and digital transformation efforts. The burgeoning population of young scientific and technological talents in both China and Arab states is ushering in a new wave of development momentum for digital economy cooperation between the two sides.

Young talents are emerging as the primary drivers of innovation in science and technology. The expansion of digital talent exchange, coupled with a focus on cultivating digital skills and fostering collaborative human resource development, stands as a critical foundation for China-Arab states digital economy cooperation. In December 2022, during the first China-Arab States Summit, President Xi Jinping introduced "eight common actions" for practical cooperation between the two sides. Among these actions, the initiative for "common actions for young talents" specifically highlighted the invitation of 100 young scientists from Arab states to China for collaborative scientific research exchanges.[2] Moreover, at the 6th China-Arab States Expo Youth Innovation and Development Forum in Yinchuan on September 21, 2023, under the theme of "China-Arab States Youth Joining Hands to Innovate and Thrive Together," various activities such as opening ceremonies, thematic forums, and interactive exchanges were organized. These events facilitated exchanges and dialogues between Chinese and Arab

---

[1] "CAST: China's Scientific and Technological Workforce Is Distinctly Marked by Its Youthful Composition," People's Daily Online, http://finance.people.com.cn/n1/2022/0625/c1004-32456472.html, 2022-06-25.

[2] "Xi Jinping Proposes 'Eight Common Actions' for China-Arab States Practical Cooperation at First China-Arab States Summit," the Central People's Government of People's Republic of China, https://www.gov.cn/xinwen/2022-12/10/ content_ 5731138.htm, 2022-12-10.

Chapter 7 Special Report on China-Arab States Digital Economy Cooperation

the six Gulf countries[①], propelling the growth of e-commerce in the Middle East to the forefront globally. Secondly, the proliferation of China's social e-commerce model has emerged as a key driving force for online shopping in the Middle East. With the maturation and diversification of e-commerce channels in the region, social platforms have swiftly become integral to the online shopping landscape, notably TikTok's introduction to the Middle East. This integration has infused great vitality into the local e-commerce sector, with live streaming gaining prominence and net influencers and Key Opinion Leader (KOL) marketing tactics gaining significant traction. Thirdly, China's cross-border e-commerce logistics sector is rapidly evolving in tandem with the e-commerce industry's growth. Prominent Chinese logistics firms specializing in digitalization are strategically expanding their e-commerce logistics networks in the Middle East. Companies such as iMile and J&T Express, representing Chinese express delivery services, have significantly broadened their customer base and market share in the region due to their extensive coverage, efficient logistics operations, and robust localized service capabilities. Fourthly, Chinese fintech companies are at the forefront of promoting mobile payment solutions and e-wallet services in the Middle East. For instance, in December 2022, Yiwu YiTe Network Technology Co., Ltd. successfully conducted its maiden cross-border RMB payment transaction with Saudi Arabia through its Yiwu Pay service, facilitating fast and seamless transactions.[②] Furthermore, in March 2023, Yiwu Pay completed cross-border payment transactions with the Industrial and Commercial Bank of China (ICBC) Abu Dhabi Branch, marking a milestone in conducting direct currency settlement for foreign trade orders in the Dubai market.[③]

---

① Shen Xiaoxiao, "E-commerce Development in the Middle East Gains Momentum (International Perspectives)," People's Daily Online, http://world.people.com.cn/n1/2022/0715/c1002-32475935.html, 2022-07-15.

② "Yiwu and Saudi Arabia Complete First Cross-Border RMB Payment Business, Ministry of Foreign Affairs: China-Arab States Economic and Trade Cooperation Continuously Steps Up to a New Level," China Daily website, https://cn.chinadaily.com.cn/a/202212/09/WS6393057ba3102ada8b226067.html, 2022-12-09.

③ "Yiwu Pay's First Cross-Border RMB Business in Dubai," Ministry of Commerce of the People's Republic of China website, http://ae.mofcom.gov.cn/article/ztdy/202403/20240303486777.shtml, 2024-03-28.

to new heights.① Moreover, in October 2023, the Huawei Digital Power Middle East & Central Asia hosted the Data Center Partner Connect 2023 conference in Dubai, where Huawei deepened collaborations with partners to develop eco-friendly and intelligent data centers, further enhancing digital infrastructure capabilities in the region.②

7.2.2 Distinct Development Features in Cross-Border E-Commerce Collaboration

E-commerce, a pivotal facet of the digital economy, stands out as one of the most dynamic and concentrated expressions of digital prowess. The seamless execution of online shopping, payment transactions, and marketing via the Internet and digital technologies serves as a vital catalyst propelling the robust advancement of China-Arab states digital economy cooperation. In recent years, the e-commerce landscape in Arab states has witnessed rapid growth, primarily owing to factors such as enhanced digital infrastructure, a tech-savvy youthful demographic, surging social media consumption trends, increasing public trust in digital payments, and supportive policies from local governments. China's wealth of expertise in e-payment solutions, digital ecosystems, and e-commerce practices has significantly propelled the expansion of China-Arab states cross-border e-commerce initiatives and overseas warehousing services. This has expedited the digital transformation of traditional trade practices, encompassing e-commerce platforms, logistics services, and electronic payment systems, thereby crystallizing distinct collaborative features.

Firstly, Chinese e-commerce platforms have emerged as a driving force behind the advancement of e-commerce in the Middle East. The Middle East region primarily engages in cross-border imports, and Chinese platforms like AliExpress, Shein, TikTok Shop, and Temu (the cross-border version of Pinduoduo) have emerged in the Middle East market. Statistics indicate that Chinese e-commerce platforms have achieved an impressive Internet user coverage rate of 80% across

---

① "The 6th China-Arab States Expo Special Issue-Silk Road," China-Arab States Expo website, https://www.cas-expo.org.cn/zh/newsDet.html?id=1841, 2023-09-24.
② "Middle East & Central Asia Data Center Partner Conference 'Partner Connect 2023' Successfully Held in Dubai," Huawei official website, https://digitalpower.huawei.com/cn/data-center-facility/news/detail/1393.html, 2023-10-24.

Chapter 7 Special Report on China-Arab States Digital Economy Cooperation

the execution of its "Vision 2030" to mitigate security risks associated with Western digital infrastructure equipment and components. Concurrently, China is overcoming Western barriers to its digital industry's global expansion, fostering an increasing willingness between China and Saudi Arabia to collaborate in the digital infrastructure domain. On April 10, 2023, FiberHome Communications, a subsidiary of China Information and Communication Technology Group, and CITIC Telecom Mobile finalized the handover of Saudi Arabia's 5G FWA network construction project. This milestone will pave the way for achieving the digitalization objectives outlined in Saudi Arabia's "Vision 2030."[1] Subsequently, on April 13, Saudi Arabia announced the establishment of four new Special Economic Zones to bolster its global technology industry presence and supply chain. Notably, the King Abdulaziz City for Science and Technology is poised to become a hub for cloud computing and cutting-edge technologies, enabling investors to establish data centers and cloud computing infrastructure, thereby creating new avenues for collaboration with Chinese enterprises.[2] Additionally, Huawei is actively involved in constructing 5G networks, backbone transmission networks, data centers, clouds and AI platforms for Saudi Arabia's NEOM.[3] In September 2023, the inauguration of the Huawei Cloud Riyadh node marked a significant milestone, establishing it as the central node for Huawei Cloud services across the Middle East, Central Asia, and Africa. This move accelerates Saudi Arabia's access to the boundless opportunities of the digital age.[4] In the same month, at the 6th China-Arab States Expo "Online Silk Road Conference" themed "Innovation Driven, Digital Leads to the Future," discussions focused on digital innovation, bolstering China-Arab states digital economy cooperation and elevating China-Arab states economic collaboration

---

[1] "Official Handover of Saudi Arabia's 5G FWA Network Construction Project Constructed by CITIC Group," China Economic Net, http://www.ce.cn/xwzx/gnsz/gdxw/202304/17/t20230417_38502964.shtml, 2023-04-17.

[2] "Saudi Arabia Officially Issues Licenses for 4 New Special Economic Zones," Ministry of Commerce of the People's Republic of China website, http://sa.mofcom.gov.cn/article/sqfb/202306/20230603414941.shtml, 2023-06-07.

[3] "Saudi Arabia's NEOM: 'A Place for Global Dreamers'," huanqiu.com, http://www.news.cn/globe/2023-04/27/c_1310711435.htm, 2023-04-27.

[4] "Go Global with Saudi Arabia — Huawei Cloud Officially Opens in Saudi Arabia," Huawei Cloud website, https://www.huaweicloud.com/news/2023/ 20230904160120957.html, 2023-09-04.

7.2 China-Arab States Cooperation in the Digital Economy

China-Arab states cooperation in the new era has deepened significantly, with digital economy collaboration emerging as a pivotal driver for this partnership. This collaboration encompasses crucial areas such as digital infrastructure development, cross-border e-commerce, and the nurturing of digital talent. On the one hand, the Fourth Industrial Revolution has prompted Arab states to devise digital transformation strategies, showcasing immense potential for development. On the other hand, Chinese enterprises have leveraged their expertise in big data, cloud computing, artificial intelligence, and e-commerce to engage with Arab states. This collaboration has propelled China-Arab states digital economy cooperation into a new phase, enhancing and broadening the partnership in terms of "facilities connectivity" and "trade facilitation."

7.2.1 Consistent and Trustworthy Collaboration in Digital Infrastructure Development

China has been at the forefront of the digital economy, and has seen major technological enterprises like Huawei and ZTE deeply engage in the Arab market. These Chinese tech giants have facilitated the extension of China-Arab states infrastructure construction cooperation into high-tech and digital sectors. By offering high-quality technologies and solutions, they have earned the trust and appreciation of Arab states, fostering a consistent and constructive collaboration in the digital economy realm. Simultaneously, Arab states have actively bolstered their investments in digital infrastructure development. Countries such as Saudi Arabia and the UAE have adopted a pragmatic approach towards high-tech applications, placing value on innovative digital infrastructures like 5G and its extensive potential applications. They stand against the high-tech dominance of Western powers, welcoming the involvement of Chinese enterprises in their own 5G infrastructure projects. Moreover, they acknowledge the positive contributions made by Chinese firms in bolstering the ICT industries within Arab states.

In March 2023, China played a pivotal role in facilitating the restoration of diplomatic ties between Saudi Arabia and Iran, a significant contribution to regional peace and stability. As Saudi Arabia advances its economy, it is expediting

Chapter 7 Special Report on China-Arab States Digital Economy Cooperation

highest in the region, with only the first three surpassing China. Regarding ICT service imports, Qatar, Egypt, Morocco, the UAE, and Lebanon rank highest in the region, with only Qatar exceeding China, while Egypt, Morocco, and China are at par. A closer examination of the high-tech manufacturing industry across Arab states in relation to the overall share of manufacturing reveals that only Morocco, Qatar, the UAE, and Saudi Arabia rank among the world's top 50, yet their development levels still lag behind China. This suggests that the subpar productivity in the high-tech manufacturing sector stands out as a key factor contributing to the underdeveloped state of digital industry trade in Arab states.

Table 7.5 Share of Digital Industry Trade and High-Tech Manufacturing in Arab States and China in 2023

Country	High-tech exports to total trade (%)		High-tech imports to total trade (%)		ICT services exports to total trade (%)		ICT services imports to total trade (%)		High-tech manufacturing to total manufacturing (%)	
	Share	Ranking	Share	Ranking	Share	Ranking	Share	Ranking	Share	Ranking
UAE	10.6	16	14.3	17	2	59	1.1	78	29.3	42
Saudi Arabia	0.8	76	7.5	74	0.6	98	0.5	111	26.3	47
Qatar	0.2	103	6	102	1.1	84	2.7	25	37.7	30
Kuwait	0.3	99	7.1	86	6.8	11	0.2	128	20.9	62
Bahrain	1.4	68	4.7	118	4.2	26	0.5	107	9.8	93
Oman	2.2	56	5	116	1.2	80	0.7	97	17	72
Morocco	2.1	57	8.1	68	3.7	30	1.2	75	42.8	23
Jordan	1.2	71	7.2	82	0.1	125	0.2	125	17.7	67
Tunisia	4.5	40	8.7	55	1.5	71	0.4	120	24.3	53
Egypt	0.7	81	7.4	75	1.7	65	1.2	72	22.6	57
Lebanon	0.4	94	5.1	113	2	58	0.9	89	N/A	N/A
Algeria	0	131	8.9	53	0.2	121	0.4	115	4.1	104
Mauritania	0	126	7.4	79	0.4	107	0.4	113	N/A	N/A
China	28	5	22.6	6	2.3	52	1.2	76	48.5	13

Note: "N/A" indicates missing values.

Source: Compiled from *Global Innovation Index 2023*.

Table 7.4 Innovation and Human Capital Indices & Rankings of Arab States and China in 2023

Country	Global Innovation Index	World Ranking	Human Capital Index	World Ranking	Country	Global Innovation Index	World Ranking	Human Capital Index	World Ranking
UAE	43.2	32	54.3	16	Jordan	28.2	71	26.8	82
Saudi Arabia	34.5	48	40.6	35	Tunisia	26.9	79	36.1	46
Qatar	33.4	50	33.8	54	Egypt	24.2	86	21.9	95
Kuwait	29.9	64	33.6	55	Lebanon	23.2	92	29.9	72
Bahrain	29.1	67	28.1	77	Algeria	16.1	119	16	113
Oman	28.4	69	34.2	52	Mauritania	13.5	127	14.2	119
Morocco	28.4	70	25.6	86	China	55.3	12	49.8	22

Source: Compiled from *Global Innovation Index 2023*.

7.1.3 Market Support for the Development of the Digital Economy: Import and Export Trade in the Digital Industry

The hard and soft power of digital economy development is primarily assessed by its internal growth. Import and export activities within the digital industry, particularly in high-tech and ICT sectors, play a crucial role in establishing connections between domestic and foreign markets, serving as a significant supporting force for the healthy and sustainable progression of a country's digital economy. On the one hand, importing advanced ICT equipment and technology elevates the competitiveness of the domestic digital industry, fostering its integration with other sectors. Simultaneously, exporting digital products and services to expand into international markets enhances a country's influence in the global digital economy and promotes the internationalization of its digital economy.

Based on the *Global Innovation Index 2023* findings (see Table 7.5), the leading five countries in the Arab region regarding the proportion of high-tech exports in total trade in 2023, in sequence, are the UAE, Tunisia, Oman, Morocco, and Bahrain. Despite this, all of them trail behind China. Similarly, the top five countries in the region concerning high-tech imports are the UAE, Algeria, Tunisia, Morocco, and Saudi Arabia, all falling short compared to China. In terms of ICT service exports, Kuwait, Bahrain, Morocco, Lebanon, and the UAE rank

Chapter 7　Special Report on China-Arab States Digital Economy Cooperation

by assessing both innovation potential and human capital.

The Global Innovation Index (GII), developed collaboratively by Cornell University, European Institute of Business Administration (INSEAD), and the World Intellectual Property Organization (WIPO), serves as a metric for assessing an economy's capacity for innovation. First introduced in 2007, the GII is released on an annual basis. The *Global Innovation Index 2023*[①] evaluates and categorizes 132 economies worldwide into four tiers: The first tier comprises ranks 1 to 33. The second tier encompasses ranks 34 to 66. The third tier includes ranks 67 to 99. The fourth tier covers ranks 100 to 132. Based on the survey data (see Table 7.4), only the UAE is positioned in the first tier among Arab states, securing the 32nd spot globally. However, there remains a significant gap compared to China's 12th ranking, the sole middle-income economy within the top tier. Saudi Arabia, Qatar, and Kuwait are placed in the second tier, while the remaining Ara countries are situated in the lower half globally. Scientific research and innovation play a fundamental role in propelling digital economy development. In recent years, Arab states within the first and second tiers have consistently emphasized heightened investment in innovation and research and development to foster progress in the digital economy landscape.

The human capital index within the Global Innovation Index is a composite of three key dimensions: basic education, higher education, and research and development. Generally, the level of human capital in Arab states is modest, with only the UAE outperforming China's global ranking in 2023. When considering Saudi Arabia as well, only two countries in the region are positioned within the top 1/3 globally. This deficiency in Arab states' digital talent can be attributed to three primary factors. Firstly, public education standards in the Arab region are generally subpar, particularly in fields like science, technology, engineering, mathematics, and other related disciplines. Secondly, the region faces a significant challenge with youth unemployment, with approximately 18% of young individuals categorized as being in a state of "neither in education, employment, nor training." Thirdly, digital literacy levels across the entire population are low, leading to a heavy dependence on expatriate technicians for technical expertise.[②]

[①]　WIPO, "Global Innovation Index 2023," https://www.wipo.int/edocs/pubdocs/en/wipo-pub-2000-2023-en-main-report-global-innovation-index-2023-16th-edition.pdf.

[②]　Wang Xiaoyu, "Foundations and Prospects of China-Arab States Digital Economy Cooperation in the New Development Landscape," *West Asia and Africa*, 2022(03).

speeds, five countries including the UAE, Qatar, Kuwait, Jordan, and Saudi Arabia exceed the global average Internet speed of 91.93 Mbps. However, none of them surpasses China's average Internet speed of 259.7 Mbps.

Table 7.3 Internet Speed and Rankings of Arab States and China in 2023

Country	Mobile networks		Fixed broadband		Country	Mobile networks		Fixed broadband	
	Speed /Mbps	World Ranking	Speed /Mbps	World Ranking		Speed /Mbps	World Ranking	Speed /Mbps	World Ranking
UAE	302.38	1	249.87	6	Somalia	21.8	112	13.63	151
Qatar	285.84	2	137.07	33	Algeria	20.86	115	12.28	158
Kuwait	196.94	3	158.68	26	Jordan	19.78	116	126.47	35
Bahrain	128.74	9	80.25	69	Libya	15.09	127	9.56	166
Saudi Arabia	126.14	11	107.19	44	Syria	11.35	134	3.48	179
Oman	71.58	38	61.18	86	Yemen	7.94	139	7.27	174
Morocco	35.51	68	26.58	130	Sudan	4.82	142	8.66	170
Lebanon	30.95	78	10.47	163	Palestine	N/A	N/A	62.87	83
Iraq	27.46	89	32.62	122	Djibouti	N/A	N/A	22.18	136
Egypt	24.26	106	62.94	82	Mauritania	N/A	N/A	21.77	137
Tunisia	22.25	111	9.02	168	China	164.58	4	259.7	5

Note: "N/A" indicates missing values.
Source: Compiled from SPEEDTEST.

7.1.2 Soft Power of Digital Economy Development: Innovation Potential and Human Capital

Innovation potential serves as the driving force behind digital economy advancement, directly influencing its sustainable growth. Only through consistent innovation can the utilization of digital technology be enhanced continuously. As the digital economy evolves, it necessitates a substantial pool of talented individuals with innovative capabilities to actively engage in its progression. Human capital emerges as the key element empowering nations to achieve technological innovation within the digital economy era, playing a critical role in bridging the technological disparity between countries. Accordingly, this chapter evaluates the soft power level in the digital economy development of Arab states

Chapter 7 Special Report on China-Arab States Digital Economy Cooperation

Continued

Country	Internet penetration (%)	Fixed Internet penetration (%)	Mobile broadband penetration (%)	3G and above mobile network penetration (%)	4G and above mobile network penetration (%)	Mobile phone penetration (%)
Libya	84.3†	N/A	120.9	72	40	85.4†
Mauritania	43.8†	N/A	70.8	43.7	34.7	60.9†
Morocco	88.1	86.2	82.6	99.3	99.1	96.2
Oman	95.2‡	94.4‡	112.6	100	97.8	97.1‡
Palestine	81.8	87.6†	20.1	59	0	77.8†
Qatar	99.7‡	95.0‡	144	100	99.8	99.6‡
Saudi Arabia	100	99.8	119.5	100	100	100
Somalia	19.9†	11.9‡	2.6	70	30	18.9†
Syria	N/A	N/A	17.4	97	42	N/A
Tunisia	71.9†	55.5†	81.3	99	95	86.4†
UAE	100	99.9	241.2	100	99.8	100
China	73.1	80.9†	101.6	99.9	99.9	81.5†

Note: "†" denotes ITU estimates; "‡" represents lagged values up to 2020; "N/A" indicates missing values.
Source: Compiled from *Measuring Digital Development: ICT Development Index 2023*.

According to the "Global Internet Speed Index"[①] published by SPEEDTEST, a well-known Internet speed measurement tool, 144 countries participated in mobile Internet speed assessments, while 181 countries took part in evaluating fixed broadband speeds. When considering the combined mobile and fixed broadband speed indicators (see Table 7.3), only the UAE ranks within the top 10 countries in the world. Qatar, Kuwait, and Saudi Arabia are among the top 50 countries globally. Further scrutiny of individual indicators reveals that the mobile Internet speeds in the UAE, Qatar, Kuwait, Bahrain, Saudi Arabia, and Oman exceed the global average of 50 Mbps, with the UAE, Qatar, and Kuwait securing positions among the top three countries globally, each surpassing China's average Internet speed of 164.58 Mbps. Regarding fixed broadband

---

① SPEEDTEST, Speedtest Global Index (Median Country Speeds January 2024), https://www.speedtest.net/global-index.

(2) National level

The ITU's *Measuring Digital Development: ICT Development Index 2023*[1] survey reveals significant disparities in ICT levels across various countries in the Arab region (see Table 7.2). Concerning Internet penetration rates, countries like Algeria, Iraq, Djibouti, Mauritania, and Somalia fall below the global average of 70.5%. Together with Egypt and Tunisia, they also lag behind China's level of 73.1%. In terms of fixed Internet penetration, Djibouti, Tunisia, and Somalia are below the world average of 70.8%. Additionally, Iraq, Algeria, Lebanon, and Egypt all rank lower than China's level of 80.9 %. Regarding mobile broadband penetration, countries such as the UAE, Qatar, Kuwait, Bahrain, Libya, Saudi Arabia, and Oman surpass China's average of 101.6%. Algeria, on the other hand, exceeds the global average of 92.5%. For 4G mobile network penetration, Kuwait, Bahrain, and Saudi Arabia outperform China's average of 99.9 %. Conversely, countries like Algeria, Syria, Libya, Mauritania, Somalia, and Palestine fall below the global average of 82.9%. In terms of mobile phone penetration, only Palestine, Iraq, Djibouti, Mauritania, and Somalia are below both China's rate of 81.5% and the world average of 80.7%.

Table 7.2 ICT Fundamentals in the Arab States and China in 2023

Country	Internet penetration (%)	Fixed Internet penetration (%)	Mobile broadband penetration (%)	3G and above mobile network penetration (%)	4G and above mobile network penetration (%)	Mobile phone penetration (%)
Algeria	66.2†	78.3†	97.1	98.2	79.9	83.3†
Bahrain	100	100	135.2	100	100	100
Djibouti	64.0†	65.9†	35.9	90	90	74.3†
Egypt	71.9‡	73‡	61.6	99.5	98	99.4‡
Iraq	65.0†	79.8†	47.5	96.9	95.9	75.3†
Jordan	86	90.1	65.3	99.8	99	89.9†
Kuwait	99.7	99.4	136.6	100	100	99.2
Lebanon	87.9†	75.8†	76.8‡	99.6‡	99.2‡	89.1†

---

[1] ITU, "Measuring digital development ICT Development Index 2023," https://www.itu.int/itu-d/reports/statistics/IDI2023/.

Chapter 7 Special Report on China-Arab States Digital Economy Cooperation

In the Arab region, various forms of the "digital divide" exist concurrently. For instance, the urban Internet penetration rate was 81.6% in the Arab region in 2023, notably higher than the 50.8% observed in rural areas. Regarding gender discrepancies, the Internet penetration rate stands at 63.8% for females and 73.7% for males. Globally, the gender parity score[1] for Internet penetration increased from 0.9 to 0.92 between 2019 and 2023, whereas in the Arab region, this metric only rose from 0.79 to 0.87 during the same period.

Although the demographic makeup of Internet users in the Arab region skews towards the youth, there has been a significant uptick in Internet penetration rates among other age groups, climbing from 58% in 2020 to 66.4% in 2023. This shift constitutes a pivotal factor contributing to the overall growth in Internet penetration levels in the Arab region.

In addition to penetration rates, broadband accessibility[2] serves as a crucial indicator of ICT development. While the cost of mobile broadband usage in the Arab region has decreased and is below the global average from 2021 to 2023, there remains significant potential for reducing fixed broadband fees. For instance, mobile broadband affordability in the Arab region was 1.2%, 1%, and 0.9% from 2021 to 2023, lower than the world average of 1.9%, 1.5%, and 1.3%, respectively, and demonstrating a consistent year-on-year decline. In contrast, fixed broadband affordability stood at 3.5%, 3.7%, and 3.1%, respectively, which is on par with or higher than the global average of 3.5%, 3.2%, and 2.9%.

---

[1] A gender parity score (defined as the percentage of females divided by the percentage of males) below 1 suggests that males are more inclined to use the Internet compared to females, whereas a score above 1 signifies the opposite. When the score falls within the range of 0.98 to 1.02, it indicates that gender parity has been attained.

[2] Broadband accessibility is a key objective outlined by the United Nations Broadband Commission for Sustainable Development (the "UN Broadband Commission"). By 2025, the Commission aims to ensure that entry-level broadband services in developing nations are affordable, with costs not exceeding 2 percent of their monthly per capita Gross National Income (GNI). For more information, please refer to the official website of the Broadband Commission, "Targets to be achieved by 2025 by the Broadband Commission for Sustainable Development," https://broadbandcommission.org/Documents/Translated%20Documents/Targets/Targets2025%20Chinese.pdf.

world average of 111%. Similarly, the active mobile broadband subscription rate was 75.4%, trailing behind the world average of 87%. A closer look at the penetration rates of various mobile network types in the Arab region in 2023 reveals that the 3G and above mobile network penetration rate reached 95.4%, slightly exceeding the global average of 95%. However, the penetration of 4G and above mobile networks was at 77.3%, lower than the world average of 90%, and the penetration of 5G and above networks was merely 12.2%, significantly below the global average of 38%. Furthermore, the fixed broadband network, often referred to as the "information highway," serves as a direct reflection of a nation's ICT development level and a crucial indicator of its overall national strength[1]. In the Arab region, the fixed broadband subscription rate stands at 11.7%, indicating a notable gap from the global average of 19%.

Table 7.1 Summary of ICT Fundamentals in the Arab Region

ICT (2019-2023)		2019	2020	2021	2022	2023
Internet penetration rate (%)		55.3	61.6	64.2	66.9	68.9
Urban /Rural Areas	Urban areas	N/A	73.7	76.4	79.1	81.6
	Rural areas	N/A	44.6	46.7	49.4	50.8
Gender	Female	49.4	55.6	58.6	61.5	63.8
	Male	62.2	67.2	69.5	71.9	73.7
Age	Youth population (15-24)	N/A	74.5	76.5	77.8	78.4
	Population beyond the youth demographic	N/A	58.0	61.7	64.1	66.4
Fixed telephone subscription rate (%)		8.4	8.7	9.0	9.1	9.2
Fixed broadband subscription rate (%)		7.5	8.6	9.7	10.5	11.7
Mobile cellular subscription rate (%)		96.7	96.2	99.2	101.6	103.1
Active mobile broadband subscription rate (%)		60.8	64.0	67.6	71.4	75.4
Mobile cellular network penetration rate (%)		96.8	97.1	97.1	97.6	97.6
3G and above mobile network penetration rate (%)		91.2	92.5	94.1	94.5	95.4
4G and above mobile network penetration rate (%)		61.8	73.6	74.8	76.4	77.3
5G and above mobile network penetration rate (%)		N/A	N/A	7.3	8.5	12.2
Mobile phone penetration rate (%)		75.4	77.2	79.2	81.0	82.6

Note: "N/A" indicates missing values.

Source: Compiled from *Measuring Digital Development: Facts and Figures 2023*.

[1] "China Unicom Releases 'White Paper on High-quality Development of Home Networking Terminals', Kicking off High-quality Development of Home Networks," Sina Finance, https://finance.sina.com.cn/tech/roll/2022-12-21/doc-imxxmspu4037828.shtml, 2022-12-21.

Chapter 7 Special Report on China-Arab States Digital Economy Cooperation

dimensional indicator system to provide robust support for advancing the high-quality growth of the digital economy, crafting informed and strategic digital policies, and bolstering the digital competitiveness of both the nation and the region. Considering factors like the credibility and accessibility of indicator data, this chapter primarily examines the current digital economy landscape in Arab states across three key dimensions: hard power, soft power, and the market support environment for digital economy advancement.

7.1.1 Hard Power in Digital Economy Development: ICT Infrastructure

The Information and Communication Technology (ICT) sector stands as a vital component of the digital economy, serving as the bedrock of digital transformation. The level of ICT advancement within a nation significantly influences its digital transformation process and the potential for digital economy growth[1], acting as a critical foundation for assessing a nation's progress in digital economy development. The rapid development of digital infrastructure has emerged as a key agenda for countries globally, enabling the reshaping of productivity paradigms, the exploration of new application scenarios, and the innovation of novel business models.[2]

(1) Regional level

The Arab region demonstrates a relatively low overall level of ICT development, as highlighted in the ITU's annual report *Measuring Digital Development: Facts and Figures 2023.*[3] While recent indicators have shown an upward trend, they still lag behind global averages in several key areas (see Table 7.1). In 2023, the Arab region exhibited an Internet penetration rate of 68.9%, slightly surpassing the world average of 67%. However, the fixed telephone subscription rate stood at 9.2%, below the global average of 11%, while the mobile cellular subscription rate was at 103.1%, falling short of the

---

[1] Cai Yuezhou and Niu Xinxing, "Analysis of the International Competitiveness of China's ICT Industry — Comparative Advantage and Technology Content Measurement Based on the Accounting of Trade Value Added," *Reform*, 2021(04).

[2] Jiao Yong and Qi Meixia, "Digital Economy Empowers the Development of New Productivity," *Economic and Management Review*, 2024(03).

[3] ITU, "Measuring digital development: Facts and Figures 2023," https://www.itu.int/en/ITU-D/Statistics/Pages/facts/default.aspx.

Chapter 7　Special Report on China-Arab States Digital Economy Cooperation

The digital economy is a novel economic model where digitized knowledge and information serve as pivotal production factors, digital technology acts as the primary driving force, and modern information networks function as vital conduits. Through the seamless integration of digital technology into the real economy, we enhance the levels of digitalization, networking, and intelligence across both economic and societal realms.① Positioned as a key element of the *"One Belt, One Road"* initiative and a frontier for future international collaboration, the digital economy has emerged as a new arena for global cooperation and competition.② Given this context, China needs to pay close attention to the evolving landscape and trends of the digital economy in Arab states, foster deeper exchanges and partnerships in digital economy sectors with Arab states, and collectively drive the growth and prosperity of both economies. This collaborative endeavor will inject fresh impetus into the overall advancement of the global digital economy.

7.1　The Digital Economy Development in Arab States

Accurate measurement of the digital economy is essential for assessing its current state of development. It is crucial to employ a comprehensive, multi-

---

① "Activating the New Engine of Foreign Trade Development with Digital Trade," People's Daily Online, http://finance.people.com.cn/n1/2021/0719/c1004-32161520.html, 2021-07-19.

② Institute of Finance, Chinese Academy of Social Sciences (CASS), National Laboratory for Finance and Development (NLFD), and China Social Science Press (CSSP), "Report on the Development Index of the Global Digital Economy (TIMG 2023)," Website of the Institute of Finance, CASS: http://ifb.cass.cn/newpc/sjk/202306/ P020230601501807198861.pdf.

Chapter 6 Special Report on China-Arab States Energy Cooperation

Arab states and delivering extensive economic benefits.

By fostering sustainable economic and fiscal development, both sides reap economic gains while laying a solid foundation for future cooperation. As new energy projects continue to advance and mature, China–Arab collaboration will become even closer and more profound in both economic and fiscal dimensions, not only enhancing their status and influence in the global new energy market but also providing robust support for the stability and prosperity of the global energy landscape.

and maximize returns. In 2023, collaboration in the new energy market further boosted the influence of both sides in the global new energy arena. As Chinese enterprises invest in solar and wind projects in Arab states, they foster the growth of local new energy markets while simultaneously broadening their own market space. Looking ahead, as cooperation in energy technology R&D and innovation continues to deepen and expand, China and Arab states will jointly address global energy market challenges and opportunities, enhance competitiveness in the global new energy market, and gain strong momentum for economic growth.

6.4.3 Promoting Sustainable Economic and Fiscal Development

Promoting sustainable economic and fiscal development is one of the key objectives of China–Arab states energy cooperation. Through new energy cooperation, Arab states have effectively improved their fiscal positions, achieving more diversified and stable revenue streams. For instance, Saudi Arabia has partnered with China to develop multiple large-scale solar and wind projects, supplying clean energy, creating a substantial number of jobs, and driving local economic growth. Statistics show that in 2023, fiscal revenue derived from new energy projects accounted for 10% of Saudi Arabia's total fiscal income, an increase of three percentage points compared to 2022. From China's perspective, investments made in Arab states yield long-term, stable returns, stimulating domestic economic growth and facilitating industrial upgrading while enhancing the international competitiveness of Chinese enterprises. In 2023, the average return on China's new energy investments in Arab states reached 12%. Some projects, such as the solar power project in Qatar, achieved returns as high as 15%, far surpassing the global average.

The creation of employment opportunities and social stability represents another significant social benefit arising from new energy cooperation. China–Arab energy projects have generated numerous jobs, improved local living standards, and contributed to social stability and prosperity. Sustainable economic and fiscal development is also reflected in the positive ripple effects on related industries. The growth of new energy projects has stimulated expansion in manufacturing, services, and other sectors, thereby improving regional economies more broadly. According to statistics, in 2023, China–Arab states new energy cooperation projects collectively created more than 400000 direct and indirect jobs, effectively promoting social stability and economic development in

China stand as exemplary models within the new energy sector.

Technology transfer and investment cooperation are key instruments for realizing a diversified energy supply chain. China's global leadership in renewable energy technologies and equipment manufacturing can, through technology transfer and investment cooperation, facilitate R&D exchanges in areas such as photovoltaic power generation, energy storage, and smart grids. This will help Arab states upgrade their local technical capabilities, strengthen management skills, and train a substantial number of technical professionals, thereby driving the growth of their local new energy industries. Establishing a cooperative model for building a diversified energy supply chain not only enables both sides to share experience and technology—effectively addressing current and future energy security challenges and uncertainties in the global energy market—but also fosters mutual benefit in the energy domain. In doing so, it contributes to the stability and sustainable development of the global energy landscape.

6.4.2 Promoting Two-Way Investment and Market Expansion

Promoting two-way investment and market expansion represents one of the core elements of China–Arab states energy cooperation. Through two-way investment, both sides not only share the fruits of economic development but also achieve technology exchange and industrial upgrades. In 2023, total bilateral investment in new energy projects between China and Arab states reached US$15 billion, covering multiple areas including solar, wind, and energy storage. For example, the photovoltaic power station project invested in and constructed by PowerChina in Abu Dhabi has not only supplied a substantial amount of clean energy locally, but also created about 5,000 direct jobs and tens of thousands of indirect employment opportunities. For Arab states, cooperation with China enables more effective utilization of abundant natural resources and facilitates economic diversification. Initiatives like Saudi Arabia's "Vision 2030" and the UAE's "2050 Energy Strategy" underscore the importance of economic diversification and sustainable development. Through two-way investment, cooperation in energy technology research, development, and innovation will be further deepened.

Market expansion is a crucial safeguard for realizing the benefits of two-way investment. By exploring and developing markets, enterprises from both China and Arab states can enhance their competitiveness, optimize resource allocation,

In November 2023, Jinko Power Technology Co., Ltd. signed a power purchase agreement with the Saudi Power Procurement Company for the 400-MW Tabarjal solar PV project. Located approximately 17 km northeast of Tabarjal city in Saudi Arabia's Al Jouf Province, the project is slated for completion and commercial operation within two years after construction commences. Once operational, it is expected to reduce CO_2 emissions by over 7.17 million tons annually.

In November 2023, China Machinery Engineering Corporation completed the Al Dhafra PV2 Solar Power Plant in the UAE. Currently the world's largest single-site solar plant, it covers about 21 square kilometers and includes a 2.1 GW solar PV generation area, a 33/400 kV step-up substation, and a 400-kV switching station. Its output can meet the electricity needs of about 200000 households in the UAE, reducing more than 2.4 million tons of CO_2 emissions annually and increasing the share of clean energy in the UAE's overall energy mix to over 13%.

6.4 Prospects for China–Arab States Energy Cooperation

6.4.1 Jointly Building a Diversified Energy Supply Chain

China and Arab states are poised to forge a win-win scenario of energy security and green development, demonstrating enormous potential in jointly building a diversified energy supply chain. Deeper and more diversified cooperation in renewable energy highlights their shared commitment to tackling climate change. Arab states, such as Saudi Arabia, Qatar, and the United Arab Emirates, not only possess abundant oil and gas resources but also enjoy exceptional solar and wind conditions. China, as the world's largest energy consumer, exhibits substantial and varied energy demands. These complementary resource endowments provide a solid foundation for long-term energy cooperation and green transitions, with renewable energy cooperation serving as a new focal point of China–Arab energy relations. Through this collaboration, Arab states can leverage their abundant natural resources more effectively, diversify their energy mix, and advance economic diversification and sustainable development. Concurrently, China can diversify its energy supply sources, reduce reliance on a single energy import channel, and enhance its overall energy security. Solar power projects jointly developed by Saudi Arabia, the UAE, and

energy cooperation, reflecting their joint efforts in economic diversification, technological innovation, policy support, and environmental protection.

In May 2023, China National Petroleum Corporation (CNPC) and QatarEnergy signed cooperation documents for the North Field Expansion project. In November, China Petrochemical Corporation (Sinopec) and QatarEnergy signed an agreement for the second phase of the North Field expansion project. Under these agreements, over the next 27 years, QatarEnergy will supply CNPC and Sinopec with 4 million tons and 3 million tons of LNG per year, respectively, while transferring 1.25% and 1.875% of the project's equity to the two companies.

In May 2023, the 18th Senior Officials' Meeting of the China–Arab States Cooperation Forum (CASCF) was held in Chengdu, Sichuan Province. In June, the 10th China–Arab Businessmen Conference and the 8th Investment Seminar of the Forum were convened in Riyadh, Saudi Arabia. In September, the 7th China–Arab States Energy Cooperation Conference took place in Haikou, Hainan. In October, the 10th China–Arab Relations and China–Arab Civilization Dialogue Symposium was held in Abu Dhabi, UAE. During these meetings, participants conducted in-depth discussions on cooperation in solar, wind, and energy storage technologies, resulting in a series of energy cooperation agreements. These covered renewable energy project investment, technology transfer, and joint R&D, further deepening China–Arab states new energy cooperation.

In June 2023, Saudi Arabia's Ministry of Investment and the Chinese electric vehicle manufacturer Human Horizons signed an agreement worth US$5.6 billion. The two parties will cooperate in the development, manufacturing, and sales of HiPhi-branded electric vehicles.

In October 2023, a wind power demonstration project in the UAE, constructed by Power Construction Corporation of China (Power China), commenced operations. With a total installed capacity of 117.5 MW across four wind farms, it can supply electricity to more than 23,000 households and reduce carbon dioxide emissions by 120000 tons per year. As the first completed wind power project in the UAE, it is significant for verifying wind energy availability and performance indicators nationwide. It also exemplifies how China–Arab cooperation promotes the export of Chinese technology and equipment.

renewable energy, and create new employment opportunities and growth drivers, thereby achieving energy diversification and sustainable economic development. Among Arab states, wealthy oil and gas producers such as the UAE and Saudi Arabia lead the energy transition, while major regional countries like Egypt and Morocco are also moving forward actively. These states are key partners for China–Arab states cooperation in the new energy sector.

Second, the complementarity of technology and investment acts as a catalyst for accelerating China–Arab states new energy cooperation. The new energy sector is closely intertwined with emerging technologies, and trends such as greening, electrification, marketization, and digitalization in the energy domain are driving transformative changes in energy systems. China is developing new types of productive capacity. Among the eight initiatives supporting the high-quality co-construction of the Belt and Road, it calls for "promoting green development" and deepening cooperation in green infrastructure, green energy, and green transportation. Projects like Red Sea public infrastructure have been included on lists of practical cooperation initiatives. China has established a globally leading new energy industrial system, holding advantages in photovoltaic, wind, and energy storage technologies, as well as extensive experience in project implementation. It can offer advanced technology and management support to Arab states, helping them rapidly develop their new energy industries. In terms of resource endowment, Arab states possess abundant and evenly distributed solar and wind resources, providing ideal conditions for large-scale new energy projects. Moreover, the region's openness to foreign investment and relatively accommodating market environment offer opportunities for Chinese enterprises. Given the significant potential, "resources plus technology" is a critical field in China–Arab states new energy cooperation. Joint efforts underscore this synergy: The China–Saudi Renewable Energy Technology Research Center focuses on the research, development, and application of photovoltaic and energy storage technologies, and a photovoltaic power plant project constructed by Power China in Abu Dhabi supplies the UAE with substantial clean energy. This collaboration exemplifies the promising prospects of China–Arab states new energy cooperation.

6.3.2 New Developments in China–Arab States New Energy Cooperation

In 2023, China and Arab states made significant strides in the field of new

6.3 Current State of New Energy Cooperation Between China and Arab States

6.3.1 Driving Forces Behind China–Arab States Energy Cooperation

Climate change continues to draw global attention. From November 30 to December 12, 2023, the 28th Conference of the Parties (COP28) under the United Nations Framework Convention on Climate Change (UNFCCC) will convene in Dubai, United Arab Emirates (UAE). Following the previous conference in Sharm El Sheikh, Egypt, this marks the second consecutive year that the global climate summit is held in the Arab region, highlighting the Arab states' strong commitment to global climate governance. At present, green energy transition has become an overarching trend, and cooperation in the new energy sector aligns with the shared vision of both China and Arab states, increasingly emerging as a mutual priority.

First, the need for energy transition and economic diversification serves as a fundamental driver of China–Arab states new energy cooperation. Accelerating a green and low-carbon transition is a unified response to climate change. To date, about 140 countries have proposed carbon neutrality targets, covering 88% of global greenhouse gas emissions, 90% of the world's economy, and 85% of the world's population. As an active participant in global climate governance, China has consistently advanced efforts in low-carbon development. Its share of non-fossil energy consumption rises yearly, its energy efficiency improvements rank among the world's fastest, and it has built the largest electricity supply network and clean power generation system worldwide. For many years, China has held the top global position in the scale of hydropower, wind power, photovoltaic power, biomass power generation, and nuclear power under construction. Arab states widely share a pressing need for development and energy transition. They have put forward various medium- and long-term national development plans, exemplified by Saudi Arabia's "Vision 2030," the UAE's "Vision 2071 Centennial Plan," and Oman's "Vision 2040." These policies indicate that several Arab oil- and gas-rich nations are pursuing economic transformation strategies characterized by "de-petrolization," market liberalization, privatization, and internationalization. The goal is to reduce dependence on oil and gas, expand

with ExxonMobil, paving the way for ExxonMobil's exit from the West Qurna-1 oilfield. CNPC (China National Petroleum Corporation) holds the largest share in this oilfield and will formally become the lead contractor on January 1, 2024. In May 2024, Iraq will hold its 5th+ and 6th rounds of oil and gas bidding. Five Chinese oil companies—Zhenhua Oil, CNOOC, Anton Oil, Zhongman, and Sinopec—have each won multiple blocks. Among them, ZhenHua Oil secured the Abu Khema and Qurnain blocks; CNOOC secured Block 7; Anton Oil obtained the Dbufriyah block; and Zhongman secured the Middle Furat (Euphrates) and Northern Extension of East Baghdad blocks.

In the downstream refining and petrochemical sector, on March 26, 2023, Saudi Aramco joined forces with China North Industries Group and Panjin Xincheng Industrial Group to establish Huajin Aramco Petrochemical Co., Ltd. With shareholdings of 30%, 51%, and 19% respectively, the joint venture plans to build a large-scale integrated refining and chemical complex in Panjin, Liaoning Province, including a refinery with a capacity of 300,000 barrels per day and a chemical plant producing 1.65 million tons of ethylene and 2 million tons of paraxylene per year. On March 27, Saudi Aramco announced the purchase of a 10% stake in China's Rongsheng Petrochemical for RMB 24.6 billion. In January 2024, Rongsheng Petrochemical announced plans to acquire a 50% stake in the SASREF refinery in Jubail, Saudi Arabia, and to expand its capacity. Meanwhile, both parties are also discussing Saudi Aramco's acquisition of up to a 50% stake in Rongsheng Petrochemical's subsidiary, Ningbo Zhongjin Petrochemical, as well as potential joint efforts to upgrade existing facilities and develop the downstream Rongsheng New Materials Jintang project.

6.2.3　Other Energy Infrastructure Construction

In June 2023, a consortium formed by Petrofac-HQC (a UK-China joint venture) signed an Engineering, Procurement, and Construction (EPC) contract with Step Polymers Spa, a wholly owned petrochemical subsidiary of Sonatrach, Algeria's national oil company. Valued at US$1.5 billion, this petrochemical project is located at the Port of Arzew in Algeria, covering an area of 88 hectares and boasting a polypropylene production capacity of 550000 tons per year. The project is scheduled to be operational 42 months from the start date.

Chapter 6   Special Report on China-Arab States Energy Cooperation

6.2.2 Comprehensive Oil and Gas Industry Chain Investment Cooperation Between China and Arab States

Beyond oil and gas trading, China and the Arab states also engage in comprehensive investment cooperation across oilfield development, oil and gas infrastructure construction, and oil refining and petrochemical sectors.

In the upstream exploration and development segment, China cooperated with several key Arab states in 2023, including Qatar, Saudi Arabia, Algeria, and Iraq, resulting in the signing of numerous cooperation agreements.

In April 2023, Sinopec and QatarEnergy signed an agreement for a 5% equity stake in the North Field East (NFE) expansion project. With a total investment of US$28.75 billion, upon completion, Qatar's annual LNG export capacity will rise from the current 77 million tons to 110 million tons. In June, CNPC (China National Petroleum Corporation) signed an agreement with QatarEnergy, becoming the first value-added partner in the North Field expansion project. Under the agreement, QatarEnergy will supply CNPC with 4 million tons of LNG per year over a 27-year period, while transferring a 1.25% equity stake in the project to CNPC. In November, Sinopec and QatarEnergy signed an integrated cooperation agreement for the second phase of the North Field South (NFS) expansion project, which includes a 27-year long-term LNG sales and purchase agreement and an upstream equity agreement. According to this deal, QatarEnergy will supply Sinopec with 3 million tons of LNG per year and transfer a 5% stake in the joint venture company to Sinopec (equivalent to a 1.875% stake in the NFS project). This marks the third long-term LNG sales and purchase agreement between the two companies, and their second integrated cooperation deal following the first phase of the North Field expansion project.

In May 2023, Sinopec, TotalEnergies, and Saudi Aramco engaged in negotiations concerning the Jafurah natural gas development project in Saudi Arabia. The parties are expected to reach an investment agreement worth US$10 billion, which may include the construction of LNG export facilities. The Jafurah gas field is one of the world's largest undeveloped gas fields and is pivotal to Saudi Arabia's strategy to increase its natural gas production. Negotiations remain ongoing, and no final investment decision has been made yet.

In November 2023, the Iraqi Ministry of Oil reached a settlement agreement

Table 6.9   China's Crude Oil Imports from Arab States (2019-2023)

Unit: 10000 tons

Country	2019	2020	2021	2022	2023
Saudi Arabia	8332.12	8492.20	8757.58	8750.01	8598.38
Iraq	5179.72	6011.62	5412.45	5548.47	5924.35
UAE	1528.89	3117.51	3194.94	4281.84	4180.63
Oman	3386.99	3784.38	4479.36	3938.43	3915.95
Kuwait	2268.86	2749.58	3016.37	3327.93	2453.07
Qatar	85.83	619.89	785.17	770.44	1046.40
Libya	940.43	169.67	613.78	374.20	333.67
Algeria	54.14	40.44	3.99	0.00	14.69
Yemen	175.52	182.57	94.30	84.05	0.00
Egypt	79.55	132.41	49.00	18.94	0.00

Source: GTT.

In terms of natural gas imports, China imported 165.6 billion cubic meters of natural gas in 2023, a year-on-year increase of 9.5%. Of this, liquefied natural gas (LNG) accounted for 59.4%, with import volumes growing by 12.35% year-on-year. China's natural gas imports from Arab states primarily consist of LNG. In 2023, China imported 19.0735 million tons of LNG from Arab states, up by 10.69% year-on-year, which comprised 26.55% of China's total LNG imports. Qatar is China's predominant LNG supplier among Arab states, with imports from Qatar accounting for 87.65% of China's LNG imports from Arab states in 2023.

Table 6.10   China's LNG Imports from Arab States (2019-2023)

Unit: 10000 tons

Country	2019	2020	2021	2022	2023
Qatar	832.90	816.75	907.96	1573.33	1671.85
Oman	109.21	106.95	165.37	96.28	104.52
UAE	11.99	30.09	72.87	11.92	67.49
Algeria	6.16	12.24	25.14	6.83	34.65
Egypt	18.55	6.43	132.87	34.85	28.84

Source: GTT.

Continued

Country	2019	2020	2021	2022	2023	Share in 2023 (%)
Lebanon	76	90	190	875	1005	0.07
Mauritania	88	88	88	89	123	0.01
Libya	5	5	6	6	8	0.00
Morocco	734	774	854	854	934	0.07
Oman	26	129	155	655	672	0.05
Palestine	82	117	178	192	192	0.01
Qatar	5	5	5	805	805	0.06
Saudi Arabia	109	109	439	440	2285	0.16
Somalia	7	16	24	47	51	0.00
Sudan	80	117	136	190	190	0.01
Syria	2	12	33	60	60	0.00
Tunisia	80	95	95	197	506	0.04
UAE	1935	2333	3002	3588	5925	0.42
Yemen	254	258	258	264	290	0.02
Arab States (Total)	6598	7829	9445	12593	17544	1.24
World	595492	728405	873858	1073136	1418969	100

Source: International Renewable Energy Agency (IRENA).

6.2 Current Status of Traditional Energy Cooperation Between China and Arab States

6.2.1 China-Arab States Oil and Gas Trade

Oil and gas trade serve as the cornerstone of trade cooperation between China and Arab states. Arab states are key suppliers of oil and gas to China. In 2023, China's total crude oil imports reached 564.2911 million tons. The top 10 sources were Russia, Saudi Arabia, Iraq, Malaysia, the United Arab Emirates, Oman, Brazil, Angola, Kuwait, and the United States. Of these, five were Arab states—Saudi Arabia, Iraq, the United Arab Emirates, Oman, and Kuwait—together making up 44.43% of China's total crude oil imports.

Table 6.7 Wind Power Generation Capacity in Arab States (2019-2023)

Unit: MW, %

Country	2019	2020	2021	2022	2023	Share in 2023 (%)
Algeria	10	10	10	10	10	0.00
Bahrain	1	1	1	3	3	0.00
Egypt	1132	1380	1640	1643	1890	0.19
Jordan	384	529	632	614	614	0.06
Kuwait	12	12	12	12	12	0.00
Lebanon	3	3	3	3	3	0.00
Mauritania	34	34	34	34	137	0.01
Morocco	1225	1435	1471	1558	1858	0.18
Oman	50	50	50	50	50	0.00
Saudi Arabia	3	3	3	403	403	0.04
Somalia	4	4	4	4	4	0.00
Syria	1	1	1	1	1	0.00
Tunisia	245	245	245	245	245	0.02
Yemen	0	0	0	0	104	0.01
Arab States (Total)	3104	3707	4106	4580	5334	0.52
World	622773	733719	824602	901231	1017199	100

Source: International Renewable Energy Agency (IRENA).

Table 6.8 Photovoltaic (PV) Generation Capacity in Arab States (2019-2023)

Unit: MW, %

Country	2019	2020	2021	2022	2023	Share in 2023 (%)
Algeria	366	366	366	451	451	0.03
Bahrain	10	10	21	46	57	0.00
Egypt	1647	1643	1663	1724	1856	0.13
Iraq	37	37	37	42	42	0.00
Jordan	971	1541	1811	1966	1990	0.14
Kuwait	84	84	84	102	102	0.01

Table 6.6 Hydropower Generation Capacity in Arab States (2019-2023)

Unit: MW, %

Country	2019	2020	2021	2022	2023	Share in 2023 (%)
Algeria	228	209	129	129	129	0.01
Egypt	2832	2832	2832	2832	2832	0.20
Iraq	1797	1797	1797	1797	1797	0.13
Jordan	6	6	4	4	4	0.00
Lebanon	282	282	282	282	282	0.02
Morocco	1770	1770	1770	1770	1770	0.13
Sudan	1482	1482	1482	1482	1482	0.11
Syria	1490	1490	1490	1490	1490	0.11
Tunisia	66	66	66	66	66	0.00
Arab States (Total)	9953	9934	9852	9852	9852	0.70
World	1313071	1335280	1360923	1395266	1407754	100

Source: International Renewable Energy Agency (IRENA).

Wind power capacity in Arab states is currently still modest. In 2023, their installed wind power capacity stood at 5334 MW, a share of just 0.52% of the global total (see Table 6.7). The West Asia and North Africa region is one of the world's richest areas in terms of solar resources, making solar energy a key focus within renewable energy resource development in Arab states. In 2023, photovoltaic (PV) capacity accounted for 54.10% of their total renewable energy generation capacity. From 2019 to 2023, PV capacity in Arab states grew from 6598 MW to 17544 MW, with an impressive average annual growth rate of 41.47%, outpacing the global average annual growth rate of 34.57%. However, solar resource development is significantly uneven among Arab states. In 2023, PV generation was dominated by the United Arab Emirates, Saudi Arabia, Jordan, Egypt, and Lebanon. These five countries together represented 74.45% of the total PV generation capacity in Arab states (see Table 6.8).

lack hydropower resources. In 2023, hydropower capacity in Arab states reached 9852 MW, accounting for only 0.70% of global hydropower capacity (see Table 6.6).

Table 6.5 Renewable Energy Generation Capacity in Arab States (2019-2023)

Unit: MW, %

Country	2019	2020	2021	2022	2023	Share in 2023 (%)
Algeria	604	585	505	590	590	0.02
Bahrain	10	11	22	48	59	0.00
Egypt	5690	5934	6258	6322	6709	0.17
Iraq	1594	1594	1594	1599	1599	0.04
Jordan	1374	2088	2460	2597	2621	0.07
Kuwait	97	97	97	114	114	0.00
Lebanon	368	382	482	1167	1297	0.03
Mauritania	122	122	122	123	260	0.01
Libya	5	5	6	6	8	0.00
Morocco	3272	3522	3638	3725	4105	0.11
Oman	76	179	205	705	722	0.02
Palestine	82	118	178	192	192	0.00
Qatar	24	24	24	824	824	0.02
Saudi Arabia	113	113	443	843	2689	0.07
Somalia	11	19	27	51	54	0.00
Sudan	1761	1798	1817	1871	1871	0.05
Syria	1500	1509	1530	1557	1557	0.04
Tunisia	391	406	406	508	817	0.02
UAE	1936	2334	3003	3597	6052	0.16
Yemen	254	258	258	264	290	0.01
Arab States (Total)	19284	21098	23075	26703	32430	0.84
World	2550319	2822931	3088809	3396323	3869705	100

Source: International Renewable Energy Agency (IRENA).

					Continued
Country	2020	2021	2022	2023	Share in 2023 (%)
Jordan	2	2	2	2	0.00
Kuwait	173	181	191	157	0.37
Mauritania	0.00	0.00	0.00	0.00	0.00
Libya	124	145	148	153	0.36
Morocco	1	1	1	1	0.00
Oman	354	389	406	430	1.00
Qatar	1753	1780	1833	1820	4.25
Saudi Arabia	1068	1105	1228	1252	2.92
Sudan	0.00	0.00	0.00	0.00	0.00
Syria	35	35	27	32	0.07
Tunisia	13	22	23	20	0.05
UAE	551	557	574	603	1.41
Yemen	5	5	4	1	0.00
Arab States (Total)	5819	6256	6395	6428	15.01
World	40228	42295	42485	42824	100

Source: ETRI.

6.1.3 Other Energy Development and Utilization in Arab States

With regard to traditional energy resources, Arab states have very limited coal reserves. In 2023, global proven coal reserves stood at 1258.18 billion tons, whereas Arab states' proven coal reserves amounted to 552 million tons, representing a mere 0.04% of the world's total.

Beyond traditional energy, as global pressures to address climate change intensify, Arab states have actively advanced the development of renewable energy. From 2019 to 2023, their renewable energy generation capacity expanded from 19284 MW to 32430 MW, achieving an average annual growth rate of 17.04%, surpassing the global average growth rate of 12.93% (see Table 6.5).

Among various forms of renewable energy, the development of hydropower in Arab states is limited due to the region's hot, arid climate and scarcity of water resources. Apart from hydroelectric facilities in the Nile River basin of Egypt and Sudan, the Tigris River basin in Iraq, and facilities in Syria, most Arab states

Table 6.3 Proven Natural Gas Reserves in Arab States (2020-2023)

Unit: trillion cubic meters, %

Country	2020	2021	2022	2023	Share in 2023 (%)
Algeria	4.50	4.50	4.50	4.50	2.25
Bahrain	0.00	0.00	0.00	0.00	0.00
Egypt	2.14	2.14	2.14	2.14	1.07
Iraq	3.53	3.53	3.53	3.53	1.76
Jordan	0.00	0.00	0.00	0.00	0.00
Kuwait	1.70	1.70	1.70	1.70	0.85
Mauritania	0.00	0.00	0.00	0.00	0.00
Libya	1.50	1.50	1.50	1.50	0.75
Morocco	0.00	0.00	0.00	0.00	0.00
Oman	0.67	0.67	0.67	0.67	0.33
Qatar	24.67	24.67	24.67	24.67	12.31
Saudi Arabia	6.02	6.02	6.50	6.66	3.32
Sudan	0.08	0.08	0.08	0.08	0.04
Syria	0.27	0.27	0.27	0.27	0.13
Tunisia	0.07	0.07	0.07	0.07	0.03
UAE	5.94	6.30	6.31	6.31	3.15
Yemen	0.27	0.27	0.27	0.27	0.13
Arab States (Total)	51.36	51.72	52.21	52.37	26.14
World	192.20	193.45	199.51	200.37	100

Source: ETRI.

Table 6.4 Natural Gas Production in Arab States (2020-2023)

Unit: 100 million cubic meters, %

Country	2020	2021	2022	2023	Share in 2023 (%)
Algeria	851	1050	1005	1063	2.48
Bahrain	184	184	184	184	0.43
Egypt	585	678	645	615	1.44
Iraq	120	122	124	95	0.22

					Continued
Country	2020	2021	2022	2023	Share in 2023 (%)
Jordan	0.00	0.00	0.00	0.00	0.00
Kuwait	13112	13000	13505	13500	3.01
Mauritania	0.00	0.00	0.00	0.00	0.00
Libya	2000	5960	5100	6018	1.34
Morocco	0.00	0.00	0.00	0.00	0.00
Oman	4233	4212	4350	4754	1.06
Qatar	7587	7850	7753	7884	1.76
Saudi Arabia	52316	51750	52530	52493	11.69
Sudan	310	320	310	255	0.06
Syria	285	289	474	502	0.11
Tunisia	170	210	180	180	0.04
UAE	16562	16649	18129	18123	4.04
Yemen	408	408	267	224	0.05
Arab States (Total)	127198	130364	135053	136124	30.32
World	417905	423717	438278	448929	100

Note: Includes crude oil and condensates.
Source: ETRI, EIA.

6.1.2 Natural Gas Reserves and Production in Arab States

Arab states possess abundant natural gas resources; however, both their share of global reserves and production are significantly lower than those of their oil resources. In 2023, the proven natural gas reserves of Arab states totaled 52.37 trillion cubic meters, representing 26.14% of the world's total. Their overall natural gas output reached 642.8 billion cubic meters, accounting for 15.01% of global production (see Tables 6.3 and 6.4).

Among Arab states, Qatar leads in both proven natural gas reserves and production. In 2023, Qatar's proven natural gas reserves constituted 47.11% of the Arab states' total, while its production accounted for 28.31% of their aggregate output. In addition to Qatar, countries such as Saudi Arabia, the United Arab Emirates, Algeria, and Iraq also hold substantial natural gas resources.

Table 6.1　Proven Crude Oil Reserves in Arab States (2020-2023)

Unit: billion barrels, %

Country	2020	2021	2022	2023	Share in 2023 (%)
Algeria	12.20	12.20	12.20	12.20	0.71
Bahrain	0.09	0.19	0.19	0.19	0.01
Egypt	3.30	3.30	3.30	3.30	0.19
Iraq	145.02	145.02	145.02	145.02	8.47
Jordan	0.00	0.00	0.00	0.00	0.00
Kuwait	101.50	101.50	101.50	101.50	5.93
Mauritania	0.02	0.02	0.02	0.02	0.00
Libya	48.36	48.36	48.36	48.36	2.82
Morocco	0.00	0.00	0.00	0.00	0.00
Oman	5.37	5.37	5.37	5.37	0.31
Qatar	25.24	25.24	25.24	25.24	1.47
Saudi Arabia	267.03	258.60	258.60	260.67	15.22
Sudan	1.25	1.25	1.25	1.25	0.07
Syria	2.50	2.50	2.50	2.50	0.15
Tunisia	0.43	0.43	0.43	0.43	0.03
UAE	97.80	97.80	99.56	100.45	5.86
Yemen	3.00	3.00	3.00	3.00	0.18
Arab States (Total)	713.12	704.78	706.54	709.50	41.42
World	1661.91	1703.11	1706.88	1712.92	100

Source: ETRI, EIA.

Note: Includes crude oil and condensates.

Table 6.2　Crude Oil Production in Arab States (2020-2023)

Unit: 10000 tons, %

Country	2020	2021	2022	2023	Share in 2023 (%)
Algeria	5760	5820	6360	6137	1.37
Bahrain	874.50	874.50	874.50	874.50	0.19
Egypt	3110	2960	2990	2966	0.66
Iraq	20470	20061	22230	22213	4.95

Chapter 6 Special Report on China-Arab States Energy Cooperation

6.1 Overview of Arab States' Energy Resources

6.1.1 Oil Reserves and Production in Arab States

Currently, the Arab states account for 41.42% of the world's proven crude oil reserves, and their crude oil production makes up 30.32% of the global total (see Tables 6.1 and 6.2). In terms of proven reserves, the scale of proven crude oil reserves in Arab states and their share of the global total have both seen a modest rebound in recent years. With regard to production, influenced by the global energy crisis triggered by the Ukraine conflict, demand for Russian crude oil has partially shifted toward oil-producing Arab states, driving an increase in their production. As a result, Arab states have increased their crude oil output for two consecutive years since 2022.

Although the Arab states collectively possess abundant oil resources, these reserves are unevenly distributed, primarily concentrated in Saudi Arabia, Iraq, Kuwait, and the United Arab Emirates. By the end of 2023, these four countries accounted for a combined 85.64% of the Arab states' proven crude oil reserves and 35.48% of the world's proven crude oil reserves. In terms of production, in 2023, the combined annual crude oil output of these four countries reached 1063.29 million tons, representing 78.11% of the total crude oil production of Arab states and 23.69% of the global total (see Tables 6.1 and 6.2).

also faces some difficulties. Firstly, the long-standing "century-old-problem" of the Israeli-Palestinian conflict has had a negative impact on the normal economic activities of the Arab countries, increasing external risks to economic development and cooperation. In particular, the spillover of the Israeli-Palestinian conflict is evident, and the risk of war is gradually increasing, directly threatening the security, stability, and development of regional countries. Meanwhile, the geopolitical competition in the Middle East is fierce, with frequent interventions by Western powers such as the United States, and a resurgence of terrorist activities, all of which pose severe challenges to the stability and economic development of regional countries. In this context, China and the Arab states should work together to address various challenges such as regional uncertainties, in order to create a favorable environment for agricultural cooperation. Secondly, agricultural cooperation has the characteristics of a long-time span and slow results. Therefore, before agricultural enterprises go abroad to the Arab region, they should strengthen on-site research on the target countries of cooperation, take risk prevention measures, formulate corresponding agricultural cooperation plans, and avoid blindly going abroad and investing.

drones and share development achievements. China helps the Arab countries improve existing agricultural irrigation systems, enhances agricultural water-saving capabilities, and achieves self-sufficiency in grain and strategic agricultural products, and finally overcomes food security dilemma.

Thirdly, continue to expand China-Arab States trade in agricultural products. In the "Eight Major Common Actions," it is pointed out that a "green channel" should be established for the export of high-quality agricultural and food products from the Arab states to China. In recent years, the Arab countries have been optimizing their commodity structure, implementing economic diversification policies, and increasing exports of non-oil commodities such as fresh oranges and grapes from Egypt, dates from Saudi Arabia, and so on. The Third Plenum of the 20th Central Committee of the Communist Party of China pointed out that China would expand high-level opening-up to the world, which meant more opportunities for cooperation for developing countries, including the Arab states. China's huge market size provides new business opportunities for agricultural products from the Arab states to enter China. By leveraging international cooperation platforms such as the China-Arab States Cooperation Forum, the China-Africa Cooperation Forum, the China-Arab States Expo, and the China International Import Expo, we will expand the import of non-energy products, especially agricultural and food products, from the Arab countries. For example, China has a strong demand for olive oil and mainly relies on imports. Olive oil is an important specialty agricultural product in Jordan, which provides broad cooperation space for China-Jordan olive oil cooperation.

Fourth, promote the establishment of a ministerial level dialogue mechanism on agriculture between China and the Arab states. Agriculture is an important foundation for national economic development and a key factor in ensuring food supply. In recent years, under the framework of China-Arab States Expo, China and the Arab states have established cooperation in agricultural economy, trade, and technology. However, under the framework of China-Arab States Cooperation Forum, a ministerial level dialogue mechanism between China and the Arab states in agriculture has not yet been established, which added difficulties to high-level exchanges and interactions in agriculture, restricted the exchange of agricultural governance experience, and China-Arab States agricultural cooperation.

China-Arab States agricultural cooperation has broad cooperation space, but exchanges in areas such as dryland agriculture, comprehensive utilization of saline alkali land, and animal disease prevention and control. At the same time, we can strengthen the exchange of agricultural talent and experience with the Arab states to promote sustainable agricultural development. As of 2022, China has actively organized training courses for nearly 10,000 agricultural officials and technicians from the Arab League member states. The "Eight Major Common Actions" also pointed out that China is willing to send 500 experts in agricultural technology to the Arab side to help increase grain yield, improve its ability to harvest and store grain and reduce losses, and improve agricultural productivity. 2) strengthen the construction of joint laboratories and research centers. Both the "Eight Major Common Actions" and the "Five Cooperation Frameworks" indicate that China is willing to jointly build a modern agriculture joint laboratory with the Arab states and establish a China-Arab States International Research Center on Drought, Desertification, and Land Degradation. 3) strengthen research on agriculture in the Arab states, explore the agricultural needs of different Arab countries and realize precise docking. 4) establish agricultural technology cooperation projects. By utilizing the China-Arab States Technology Transfer Center, promote China's mature agricultural technology to the Arab countries. For example, the Mauritania Livestock Technology Demonstration Center, jointly invested and assisted by the Chinese Ministry of Commerce and Ningxia, has successfully planted nearly a thousand acres of forage grass on the edge of the Sahara Desert in Africa, creating an oasis on barren land. The center also shares soil improvement, water-saving irrigation and other technologies with agricultural technicians from Mauritania, the UAE, Sudan and other countries, driving these countries to plant tens of thousands of acres of forage grass. It has become a shining business card for China-Arab States agricultural cooperation.[①]

Secondly, expand new growth points for agricultural cooperation. China and the Arab states have carried out extensive cooperation in smart agriculture, dryland agriculture, desert agriculture, water-saving irrigation, animal husbandry and veterinary medicine, green agriculture, and achieved positive results. In the future, China and the Arab states should actively expand new growth points in soil health, hydroponic agriculture, soilless cultivation, and the use of agricultural

---

① "China-Arab States Agricultural Cooperation Turns Desert into Oasis," Xinhua News Agency, https://finance.sina.com.cn/jjxw/2023-09-24/doc-imznuqqi0383278.shtml, September 24, 2023.

Chapter 5 Special Report on China-Arab States Agricultural Cooperation

trade continues to grow, China-Arab States agricultural science and technology cooperation and exchanges are becoming increasingly close. The China-Arab States Agricultural Technology Transfer Center has demonstrated and achieved results in multiple Arab countries such as Mauritania and Morocco. As of the end of 2022, China has held nearly 500 training courses for 10,000 agricultural officials and technicians from 22 Arab League member states, covering desert agriculture, aquaculture, and smart agriculture and so on.[①]

5.3 Prospects for China-Arab States Agricultural Cooperation

Under the strategic guidance of the head-of-state's diplomacy, political mutual trust between China and the Arab states continues to strengthen, and economic and trade cooperation continues to deepen. As an important part of China-Arab States practical cooperation, China-Arab States agricultural cooperation maintains a good development momentum. Looking ahead, China-Arab States agricultural cooperation should take the opportunity of the Global Development Initiative and the high-quality "Belt and Road" cooperation, benchmark the "Eight Major Common Actions" and "Five Cooperation Frameworks," and jointly promote China-Arab States agricultural cooperation to a new level.

Firstly, strengthen the exchange and cooperation of modern agricultural technology. Besides the objective factors, the lack of modern agricultural technology is also an important reason for the decline of agricultural production in the Arab countries. The world is experiencing unprecedented changes. The most prominent manifestation in agriculture was the severe shortage of global food supply chains, leading to the deterioration of food security, especially in the Arab countries. Therefore, the Arab countries must fully utilize all existing capabilities in the region, provide all agricultural land, and utilize advanced technological resources to achieve food self-sufficiency. This also provides an opportunity for China-Arab States agricultural cooperation. 1) strengthen exchanges of agricultural technical personnel from both sides. China can dispatch technical experts to focus on agricultural science and technology

---

① Pramod Kumar, "China and Arab States Sign $471m Worth of Agri Deals," https://www.agbi.com/agriculture/2023/09/china-and-arab-states-sign-471m-worth-of-agri-deals/, September 25, 2023.

the Arab states, stating that China is willing to take the implementation of the Global Development Initiative as an opportunity to strengthen dialogue and exchanges with the Arab states, deepen the integration of interests, continuously improve the level of national and regional food security through joint research and development, technology demonstration and promotion, and capacity building. Promoting China-Arab States agricultural cooperation makes positive contributions to building a China-Arab community with a shared future. In September 2023, the "International Training Course on Combating Desertification in Developing Countries under the Background of Climate Change" organized by the Gansu Desert Control Research Institute was held in Lanzhou. Officials from the Science and Technology Department of Gansu Province and the Forestry and Grassland Bureau of Gansu Province, as well as 15 experts and scholars from the United Nations Food and Agriculture Organization (FAO) representative office in Saudi Arabia and the Center for Vegetation Cover and Desertification Control in Saudi Arabia, participated in the opening ceremony with the aim of improving the level of desertification control and utilization in Saudi Arabia. Through on-site inspections and learning, they gained a deeper understanding of the mature sand barrier control and afforestation technologies in Gansu, and widely promote the application, which showcased the achievements of China's ecological environment construction in all aspects, enhanced mutual understanding, and laid a solid foundation for future cooperation and exchanges.[1] On November 23, 2023, the opening ceremony of the Dubai China Agricultural, Animal Husbandry and Fishery Products (Orwell) Wholesale Market, a key agricultural project of the "Belt and Road," and the China-Middle East International Agricultural Products Circulation Seminar were held in the Orwell Wholesale Market in Dubai. Ma Hongtao, Director of the Agricultural Trade Promotion Center of the Ministry of Agriculture and Rural Affairs of China, led the Chinese agricultural trade delegation to participate in the event and promote products. A total of 16 intention contracts for supply and procurement docking were signed by Chinese and foreign enterprises in attendance, with the contract amount up to 9.7 billion yuan. As agricultural

---

[1] Gansu Provincial Department of Science and Technology, "Gansu Province Holds International Training Course on Desertification Control under the Background of Climate Change," https://www.most.gov.cn/dfkj/gs/zxdt/202309/t20230908_187800.html, September 8, 2023.

Chapter 5 Special Report on China-Arab States Agricultural Cooperation

construction of the Moroccan overseas branch center for agricultural technology transfer between China and the Arab states, and the introduction of excellent new varieties in the plantation and animal husbandry. Focusing on the "six special"①industries. 26 domestic interregional investment, trade and cooperation projects were signed to further deepen the bilateral and multilateral exchanges and cooperation in agriculture of the "Belt and Road" partner countries and expand the international and domestic marketing channels of agricultural products with Ningxia characteristics.②

On August 15-16, 2023, Minister of Agriculture and Rural Affairs Tang Renjian met with Egyptian Minister of Agriculture and Land Reclamation Mohamed El-Quseir and Assistant Secretary General of the Arab League Hossam Zaki in Cairo. During the meeting with Mohamed El-Quseir, Tang Renjian stated that in recent years, under the strategic guidance of President Xi Jinping and President Sisi, the comprehensive strategic partnership between China and Egypt has achieved leapfrog development, and agricultural cooperation has yielded significant results. China is willing to implement the "Nine Projects"③ and "Eight Major Common Actions" proposed by President Xi Jinping, and work with Egypt to strengthen the construction of joint laboratories in agriculture, expand exchanges of agricultural technology and management personnel, and bilateral agricultural economic and trade cooperation around comprehensive protection and utilization of soil, breeding of salt-alkali tolerant crop varieties and high-yield cultivation, integrated water-fertilizer irrigation, and green growth of agriculture, so as to promote the continuous advancement of food production and agricultural sustainable development capabilities to a new level. Both sides jointly signed the *Action Plan for Agricultural Cooperation between China and Egypt for the Period of 2023-2025*. During the meeting with Hossam Zaki, Tang Renjian highly praised the agricultural relations between China and

---

① Six special: grape wine, wolfberry, milk, cattle, Tan sheep (a kind of sheep raised in Ningxia and known for its fine pelt), and cold climate vegetables.

② "The Sixth China-Arab States Expo Modern Agriculture High-quality Development Cooperation Conference was Successfully Held in Yinchuan," Autonomous Region Agricultural International Cooperation Project Service Center, https://nynct.nx.gov.cn/xwzx/zwdt/202309/t20230927_4290401.html, September 27, 2023

③ Nine projects: health, poverty alleviation and benefitting farmers, trade promotion, investment drive, digital innovation, green development, capacity building, people-to-people exchanges, and peace and security.

5.2.2 Progress of China-Arab States Agricultural Cooperation

China-Arab States agricultural cooperation is not only reflected in agricultural product trade, but also in new progress made in technical training, exchange and cooperation, and agreement signing.

China-Arab States Expo is an important platform for economic and trade cooperation between China and the Arab states, and has become an important platform for the joint construction of the "Belt and Road" Initiative between China and the Arab states. The agricultural sector is an important component of the China-Arab States Expo. The 6th China-Arab States Expo, with the theme of "New Era, New Opportunities, New Future," was held in Yinchuan, Ningxia from September 21 to 24, 2023. As an important part of the Expo, Conference on High-quality Modern Agricultural Development and Cooperation gathered officials, experts and scholars from more than 40 countries to discuss agricultural technology, trade and investment, food security and so on. The conference has built an important platform for further deepening China's practical agricultural cooperation with the Belt and Road partner countries, tapping new potential and opening up new space for cooperation. More than 350 guests were invited to attend the conference, including 110 foreign guests and 240 domestic guests. Senior officials, experts, scholars, key business associations, enterprise representatives from more than 40 countries such as Mauritania, Pakistan, and Egypt, and leaders of the Ministry of Agriculture and Rural Affairs as well as experts, scholars, key business association representatives, and key enterprise representatives from well-known domestic research institutions, participated in the conference. Focusing on the theme of "deepening practical cooperation and jointly ensuring food security," seven activities were held, including the opening ceremony, signing ceremony, keynote speech, high-end dialogue, round table on "Belt and Road" food security and agricultural cooperation, research and training of senior officials from developing countries, and modern agriculture investigation and exchange. Focusing on the theme of "promoting agricultural cooperation and ensuring food security," the round table on "Belt and Road" food security and agricultural cooperation was held, forming five cooperation consensuses, which further promoted the agricultural exchanges and cooperation of the "Belt and Road" partners, including Ningxia, China and the Arab states. Eight international cooperation projects were signed, such as the

Chapter 5 Special Report on China-Arab States Agricultural Cooperation

parts of plants" were the most exported agricultural products to the Arab states. The main destinations for the export of "(09) Coffee, tea, mate and spices" are North African Arab countries, including Morocco (USD 197.515416 million), Mauritania (USD 67.161799 million), Algeria (USD 81.021551 million), Libya (USD 32.21468 million), Tunisia (USD 9.911156 million), and Djibouti (USD 3.093944 million). The main export destinations for "(20) Preparations of vegetables, fruit, nuts or other parts of plants" were Iraq (USD 237865549), Saudi Arabia (USD 153284990), Yemen (USD 4930.4593), Jordan (USD 41.160956), Oman (USD 22.947081), Syria (USD 2.884201), and Comoros (USD 8276400).

Table 5.4 Destination Countries of Agricultural Products Exported to the Arab States in 2023

Unit: USD 10000

Country	Rank	Export value in 2022	Export value in 2023	Year-on-year Change (%)
UAE	1	91242.9	103323.3	13.2
Saudi Arabia	2	36762.8	54154.6	47.3
Iraq	3	24005.9	49581.6	106.5
Morocco	4	32846.4	33408.0	1.7
Egypt	5	31776.0	24791.2	-22.0
Algeria	6	14999.6	22888.8	52.6
Jordan	7	13703.2	13496.9	-1.5
Libya	8	5742.3	11155.5	94.3
Tunisia	9	10608.1	11004.7	3.7
Kuwait	10	10858.9	10031.2	-7.6
Lebanon	11	8551.0	8508.6	-0.5
Yemen	12	8174.0	8329.8	1.9
Mauritania	13	6542.0	7669.8	17.2
Oman	14	5513.4	6377.3	15.7
Bahrain	15	4003.2	5372.0	34.2
Sudan	16	4171.3	5178.3	21.2
Qatar	17	3798.2	4422.0	16.4
Syria	18	1060.7	1261.2	18.9
Somalia	19	1072.0	1204.2	12.3
Djibouti	20	1298.7	825.8	-36.4
Palestine	21	383.7	702.8	83.1
Comoros	22	212.6	200.8	-5.6

Source: Ministry of Commerce of the People's Republic of China, "China's Monthly Import and Export Statistical Report - Agricultural Products," December 2023, pp. 15-17.

Continued

Country	Rank	Import Value in 2022	Import Value in 2023	Year-on-year Change (%)
Morocco	6	3327.6	5803.5	74.4
Lebanon	7	507.7	967.9	90.6
Somalia	8	665.7	469.1	-29.5
Algeria	9	181.6	173.0	-4.8
Tunisia	10	274.6	139.3	-49.3
Jordan	11	60.3	69.2	14.6
Iraq	12	14.5	60.7	317.6
Syria	13	188.4	37.2	-80.2
Oman	14	22.6	13.4	-40.6
Comoros	15	4.8	6.4	33.9
Yemen	16	0.0	4.6	105097.7
Bahrain	17	0.1	0.6	434.1
Libya	18	0.2	0.3	34.9
Kuwait	19	0.4	0.2	-44.5
Qatar	20	1.2	0.1	-88.5
Palestine	21	—	—	—
Djibouti	22	—	—	—

Source: Ministry of Commerce of the People's Republic of China, "China's Monthly Import and Export Statistical Report - Agricultural Products," December 2023, pp. 23-25.

It can be seen from Table 5.4 that the top ten destinations for China's exports to the Arab states in 2023 were the UAE, Saudi Arabia, Iraq, Morocco, Egypt, Algeria, Jordan, Libya, Tunisia, and Kuwait, accounting for 86.96% of the total exports of the Arab states. The UAE has been the top destination for China's agricultural exports to the Arab states for several consecutive years, with an export value of USD 1033.233 million in 2023, an increase of 13.2% year on year, accounting for 26.91% of the total exports to the Arab states. China's exports to Iraq increased by 106.5%, making it the third largest destination for China's export from the Arab states.

In terms of the structure of agricultural products, in 2023, "(09) Coffee, tea, mate and spices," as well as "(20) Preparations of vegetables, fruit, nuts or other

Chapter 5 Special Report on China-Arab States Agricultural Cooperation

included," with an increase of 77.80%, and the largest decrease was "(15) Animal or vegetable fats and oils and their cleavage products; prepared animal fats; animal or vegetable waxes," with a decrease of 30.43%.

5.2.1.3 Source and Destination Countries of China-Arab States Trade in Agricultural Products

As is shown in Table 5.3, the main Arab countries that China imported agricultural products from were Sudan, the UAE, Egypt, Mauritania and Saudi Arabia. In 2023, the trade value of agricultural products imported from the above five countries accounted for 96.08% of the total imports from the Arab states. From the perspective of importing countries in terms of the structure of agricultural products, Saudi Arabia (USD 87.36863 million), Somalia (USD 3.160422 million), and Comoros (USD 0.9462 million) were the main importing countries for "(03) fish and crustaceans, molluscs and other aquatic invertebrates." Egypt (USD 101.712559 million) and Iraq (USD 60.0956 million) were the main importing countries for "(08) Fruit and nuts, edible; peel of citrus fruit or melons." Sudan (USD 60706.0305 million) was the main importing country for "(12) oil seeds and oleaginous fruits; miscellaneous grains, seeds and fruit, industrial or medicinal plants; straw and fodder." Morocco (USD 28.890461 million) and Syria (USD 227821 million) were the main importing countries for "(15) animal or vegetable fats and oils and their cleavage products; prepared animal fats; animal or vegetable waxes." Lebanon (USD 8.786603 million) was the main country for "(18) cocoa and cocoa preparations." Mauritania (USD 101.841530 million) was the main country for "(23) food industries, residues and wastes thereof; prepared animal fodder."

Table 5.3 Source Countries of Agricultural Products Imported from the Arab States in 2022 and 2023

Unit: USD 10000

Country	Rank	Import Value in 2022	Import Value in 2023	Year-on-year Change (%)
Sudan	1	81265.3	77294.5	-4.9
UAE	2	50500.2	53955.0	6.8
Egypt	3	33412.3	31883.0	-4.6
Mauritania	4	16044.9	16554.2	3.2
Saudi Arabia	5	11645.5	9996.2	-14.2

	Import		Export	
(Product Code) Product Name	value (Unit: USD 10000)	Year-on-year Change (%)	value (Unit: USD 10000)	Year-on-year Change (%)
Type III Animal or vegetable fats and oils and their cleavage products; prepared animal fats; animal or vegetable waxes				
(15) Animal or vegetable fats and oils and their cleavage products; prepared animal fats; animal or vegetable waxes	36838.73	15.96	2259.60	-30.43
Type IV Prepared food stuffs; beverages, spirits and vinegar; tobacco and manufactured tobacco substitutes				
(16) Meat, fish or crustaceans, molluscs or other aquatic invertebrates; preparations thereof	8.23	-86.29	12681.51	5.03
(17) Sugars and sugar confectionery	600.60	-52.46	15404.38	35.00
(18) Cocoa and cocoa preparations	1094.27	105.67	3232.39	12.39
(19) Preparations of cereals, flour, starch or milk; pastrycooks' products	293.33	107.99	5348.70	33.21
(20) Preparations of vegetables, fruit, nuts or other parts of plants	222.48	192.97	69979.82	50.70
(21) Miscellaneous edible preparations	92.30	-27.78	17619.95	14.96
(22) Beverages, spirits and vinegar	711.72	227.86	5140.91	11.58
(23) Food industries, residues and wastes thereof; prepared animal fodder	42340.84	-14.22	3249.83	-18.58
(24) Tobacco and manufactured tobacco substitutes	998.65	27.71	45132.11	37.12

Data Source: calculated per statistics from the General Administration of Customs of China.

In 2023, the top five categories of agricultural products exported to the Arab states were as follows: "(20) Preparations of vegetables, fruit, nuts or other parts of plants," "(09) Coffee, tea, mate and spices," "(24) Tobacco and manufactured tobacco substitutes," "(12) Oil seeds and oleaginous fruits; miscellaneous grains, seeds and fruit, industrial or medicinal plants; straw and fodder," "(07) Vegetables and certain roots and tubers; edible," with an export value over USD 200 million. The least exported agricultural product was "(01) Animals; live," with an export value of only USD 91300. Compared with 2022, the largest increase in 2023 was "(14) Vegetable plaiting materials; vegetable products not elsewhere specified or

imports was "(14) Vegetable plaiting materials; vegetable products not elsewhere specified or included," with a decrease of 91.78%.

Table 5.2 China's exports and imports of agricultural products to/from the Arab states in 2023

(Product Code) Product Name	Import		Export	
	value (Unit: USD 10000)	Year-on-year Change (%)	value (Unit: USD 10000)	Year-on-year Change (%)
Type I Live animals; animal products				
(01) Animals; live	0	0	9.13	34.66
(02) Meat and edible meat offal	0	0	2373.41	35.44
(03) Fish and crustaceans, molluscs and other aquatic invertebrates	15938.79	8.49	8451.93	7.91
(04) Dairy produce; birds' eggs; natural honey; edible products of animal origin, not elsewhere specified or included	118.81	118.81	1922.30	-15.41
(05) Animal originated products; not elsewhere specified or included	226.86	-5.17	840.38	-22.23
Type II Vegetable Products				
(06) Trees and other plants, live; bulbs, roots and the like; cut flowers and ornamental foliage	0.74	0.74	2243.38	48.52
(07) Vegetables and certain roots and tubers; edible	5.27	-27.41	29275.05	29.91
(08) Fruit and nuts, edible; peel of citrus fruit or melons	11631.85	15.31	25912.58	38.44
(09) Coffee, tea, mate and spices	150.68	-23.26	63388.41	17.87
(10) Cereals	0	0	13631.25	-24.56
(11) Products of the milling industry; malt, starches, inulin, wheat gluten	0	0	1904.11	9.65
(12) Oil seeds and oleaginous fruits; miscellaneous grains, seeds and fruit, industrial or medicinal plants; straw and fodder	60996.80	-7.57	39000.95	6.46
(13) Lac; gums, resins and other vegetable saps and extracts	647.10	-42.17	2348.76	20.80
(14) Vegetable plaiting materials; vegetable products not elsewhere specified or included	14.02	-91.78	343.60	77.80

year. Some Arab countries have also become important source and destination countries for the imports and exports of China's agricultural products. For example, Moroccans have preference for Chinese green tea, and Morocco is also the largest target country for Chinese green tea exports. In 2023, Morocco is the third largest market for China's tea exports, with a quantity of 59830.5 tons with the value of USD 1900.65 million. In 2022, it was 75439.9 tons with the value of USD 239.498 million, a decrease of 20.7% and 20.6% year on year. Syria is the third largest market for China's wheat exports, exporting 2336.0 tons in 2023 with the value of USD 1.329 million. The United Arab Emirates is the third largest export market for tobacco in China, exporting a total of 27400.0 tons with the value of USD 71.304 million in 2023 and 31005.1 tons with the value of USD 79.884 million in 2022, a decrease of 11.6% and 10.7% year on year. In 2023, the UAE is also the second largest market for China's rapeseed oil imports, importing 284257.4 tons of rapeseed oil with the value of USD 319.218 million. In 2022, it was 185410.1 tons worth of USD 279.217 million, an increase of 53.3% and 143.3% year on year respectively.[①]

5.2.1.2 Structure of China-Arab States Trade in Agricultural Products

From Table 5.2, it can be seen that in 2023, the main agricultural products imported from the Arab states were as follows: "(12) Oil seeds and oleaginous fruits; miscellaneous grains, seeds and fruit, industrial or medicinal plants; straw and fodder," "(23) Food industries, residues and wastes thereof; prepared animal fodder," "(15) Animal or vegetable fats and oils and their cleavage products; prepared animal fats; animal or vegetable waxes," with an import value over USD 300 million. The import value of "(03) Fish and crustaceans, molluscs and other aquatic invertebrates" and "(08) Fruit and nuts, edible; peel of citrus fruit or melons" exceeded USD 100 million. Four categories weren't imported. Compared with 2022, in 2023, the largest increase in imports was "(22) Beverages, spirits and vinegar," with an increase of 227.86%, and four categories of agricultural products with an increase over 100%. The largest decrease in

---

① Department of Foreign Trade, Ministry of Commerce of the People's Republic of China, "China's Monthly Import and Export Statistical Report Agricultural Products (December 2023)," February 8, 2024, http://wms.mofcom.gov.cn/cms_files/filemanager/1077459795/attach/20247/fc1e6d92 7252464ab24b9e53b391c4a1.pdf?fileName=%E4%B8%AD%E5%9B%BD%E5%86%9C%E4%B A%A7%E5%93%81%E8%BF%9B%E5%87%BA%E5%8F%A3%E6%9C%88%E5%BA%A6%E7 %BB%9F%E8%AE%A1%E6%8A%A5%E5%91%8A2023%E5%B9%B412%E6%9C%88.pdf.

Chapter 5 Special Report on China-Arab States Agricultural Cooperation

agrifood products to China.[①] In May 2024, at the 10th Ministerial Conference of the China-Arab States Cooperation Forum, President Xi Jinping proposed to build a "Five Cooperation Frameworks."[②] In establishing a more balanced mutually beneficial economic and trade pattern, China welcomes the Arab states actively participate in the China International Import Expo and is willing to expand import of non-energy products from the Arab side, especially agricultural products. All these important documents provide crucial direction and blueprint for future agricultural cooperation between China and the Arab states. In recent years, China and the Arab states have continuously strengthened agricultural trade exchanges and deepened agricultural science and technology cooperation. With the establishment of platforms and mechanisms such as the China-Arab States Cooperation Forum, the China-Arab States Expo, and the "Belt and Road" Initiative, China-Arab States agricultural cooperation has continued to reach new levels, adding new momentum to the agricultural development of both sides. The China-Arab States agricultural cooperation mainly includes trade in agricultural products, agricultural technology cooperation, agricultural talent exchange and training, and the signing of agricultural cooperation projects.

5.2.1 China-Arab States Trade in Agricultural Products

5.2.1.1 Scale of China-Arab States Trade in Agricultural Products

According to the statistical report on agricultural product released by the Ministry of Commerce in December 2023, China's total import and export value reached USD 333.03 billion in 2023, a decrease of 0.4% year on year. Of the total amount, the export value reached USD 98.93 billion, an increase of 0.7% year on year; the import value reached USD 234.11 billion, a decrease of 0.8% year on year. Among them, the total trade value of China-Arab States agricultural products countries was USD 5.666 billion, an increase of 12.8% year on year. The export value amounted to USD 3.692 billion, an increase of 21.4% year on year; the import value reached USD 1.974 billion, a decrease of 0.3% year on

---

① Ministry of Foreign Affairs, Xi Jinping proposed "Eight Major Common Actions" for China-Arab States Practical Cooperation at the First China-Arab States Summit, December 10, 2022.

② Five Cooperation Frameworks consist of a more dynamic framework for innovation, an expanded framework for investment and finance cooperation, a more multifaceted framework for energy cooperation, a more balanced framework for mutually beneficial economic and trade ties, and a broader framework for people-to-people exchanges.

agricultural and food security issues.[①] China-Arab States agricultural cooperation is an important component of practical cooperation and an important area of exchange between China and the Arab states.

In the *14th Five-Year Plan for International Cooperation in Agriculture and Rural Areas* released by Ministry of Agricultures and Rural Affairs of People's Republic of China in 2022, it is pointed out that during the 14th Five-Year Plan period, China will carry out cooperation with West Asian countries in the fields of food security, disaster prevention and loss reduction, and trade and investment, enrich the forms of agricultural economic and trade cooperation, and enhance the comprehensive agricultural development capacity of both sides. China will continue to promote the import of date seedlings from the UAE, enrich the supply of date products in our domestic market, and deepen cooperation in modern agriculture, grass and livestock integration, and food security. China will promote in-depth cooperation with North African countries in the fields of food security, sustainable agriculture and digital agriculture in the form of economic and trade cooperation, experience sharing, capacity building and technology transfer.[②] At the first China-Arab States Summit in December 2022, President Xi Jinping proposed Eight Major Common Actions[③] for China-Arab States practical cooperation. For the cooperation initiative on food security, China is ready to help the Arab side enhance its food security and comprehensive agricultural production capacity. China will, together with the Arab side, build five joint laboratories of modern agriculture and carry out 50 demonstration projects in agricultural technology cooperation, and send 500 experts in agricultural technology to the Arab side to help increase grain yield, improve its ability to harvest and store grain and reduce losses, and improve agricultural productivity. China will establish a "green channel" for the Arab side to export quality

---

① Sun Degang, *Research on China's Overall Diplomacy towards Arab Countries under the Framework of the China-Arab States Cooperation Forum*, Xinxing Publishing House, 2024, p. 393.

② Ministry of Agriculture and Rural Affairs, "14th Five-Year Plan for International Cooperation in Agriculture and Rural Areas," http://www.moa.gov.cn/zxfile/reader?file=http://www.moa.gov.cn/govpublic/GJHZS/202201/P020220128632546567867.pdf, January 18, 2022, pp. 22-23.

③ Eight Major Common Actions: first, to support common action for development; second, joint action on food security; third, joint health action; fourth, joint action on green innovation; fifth, joint action on energy security; sixth, dialogue among civilizations and joint action; seventh, young people should act together; eighth, joint action on security and stability.

Chapter 5 Special Report on China-Arab States Agricultural Cooperation

children suffering from severe malnutrition.① In addition, Russia's withdrawal from the Black Sea Grain Initiative② disrupted global food supply, especially the wheat market. Meanwhile, India decided to halt exports of non-Basmati varieties since July 2023. These resulted that global rice prices skyrocketed. External uncertainty has led to continuous deterioration of food security in many low-and middle-income countries. The most vulnerable countries include Tunisia, Libya, Lebanon, Iraq, and Egypt, not to mention war-torn Syria, Sudan, and Yemen. Egypt and Lebanon heavily rely on imported rice and wheat, and are currently facing challenges in food financing, while Sudan, deeply mired in famine and internal conflict, is unable to import expensive food. The rupture of the food agreement will only exacerbate the supply challenges and price pressures that these countries are already facing. Lebanon, Egypt and Syria have experienced significant currency depreciation, leading to a triple digit increase in food prices, and now face greater risks. In fact, due to conflicts and climate-related challenges such as droughts, the number of food insecure people in the Middle East has surged by 20% in the past three years.

5.2 Current Situation of China-Arab States Agricultural Cooperation

From both the perspective of national stability and economic development, food security and agricultural development are key concerns in the governance of the Arab states. However, slow agricultural development and food insecurity have been one of the characteristics in the Arab region. Major countries with significant influence in the region do not have the ability to gather forces from all parties to build a regional food security mechanism to address common security issues. Therefore, agricultural cooperation with other countries outside the Arab region has become an effective path for the Arab states to collectively address

---

① "Crisis in Sudan: What is Happening and How to Help," International Rescue Committee, June 24, 2024, https://www.rescue.org/article/crisis-sudan-what-happening-and-how-help.

② In July 2022, the United Nations and Turkey brokered a Black Sea Grain Initiative. According to the agreement, about one-third of the grain crossing the Black Sea is shipped to Egypt, Libya, Israel, Tunisia, Algeria, Turkey and Iran. Just one year after the agreement came into effect, Russia announced its withdrawal from the agreement.

the highest in low-income countries, reaching 31.1 percent, and Arab States least developed countries (LDCs) with 28.8 percent. The gap in undernourishment between countries affected by conflict and countries not affected by conflict in the region continued to increase in 2023 as the increasing number and magnitude of conflicts are significant drivers of food insecurity in the region. The PoU was four times higher in countries affected by conflict (26.4 percent) than in countries not affected by conflict (6.6 percent). Somalia had the highest PoU (51.3) percent, followed by Yemen (39.5 percent), the Syrian Arab Republic (34 percent), and the Comoros (16.9 percent). In 2023, moderate or severe food insecurity in the Arab region reached 39.4 percent (186.5 million individuals), a 1.1 percentage point increase from the previous year. 15.4 percent of the population (72.7 million people) faced severe food insecurity in 2023.① Wars and conflicts have also greatly affected the food access to the Arab countries. *The 2023 Global Food Crisis Report* shows that from January to May 2022, 17.37 million people in Yemen faced severe food insecurity.② In Syria and Iraq, wars, resistance, and conflicts often lead to delays or cancellations of food aid missions.③ The "Early Warning for Famine Hotspots (November 2023-April 2024)" jointly released by the Food and Agriculture Organization of the United Nations and the World Food Programme points out that food insecurity caused by internal conflict in Sudan in 2023 will have spillover effects on neighboring countries, and the food security problem in Palestine may worsen with the escalation of the Israeli-Palestinian conflict.④ The conflict in Sudan has seriously affected food production and grain harvest. 18 million people (37% of the total population) are experiencing severe food insecurity. Compared to the conflict before, the number of people facing severe food security has increased by 10 million, including 5 million at risk of catastrophic hunger and over 0.7 million Sudanese

---

① Food and Agriculture Organization of the United Nations, International Fund for Agricultural Development, United Nations Children's Fund, World Food Programme & World Health Organization, "2024 Regional Overview of Food Security and Nutrition: Financing the Transformation of Agrifood Systems", Cairo, 2024, p.1.

② Food Security Information Network, 2023, Global Report on Food Crisis, Online Publishing, 2023, p.149.

③ Food Security Information Network, 2023, Global Report on Food Crisis, Online Publishing, 2023, pp.43-44.

④ WEP and FAO, Hunger Hotspots, FAO-WFP Early Warnings on Acute Food Insecurity: November 2023 to April 2024 Outlook, Rome: FAO, 2023, pp.5-8.

Chapter 5 Special Report on China-Arab States Agricultural Cooperation

to 11th and Morocco dropped from 8th to 10th. 14 Arab countries ranked among the top 100 global wheat importers. Only Iraq experienced a 90.4% increase in wheat imports. This is mainly due to water scarcity and desertification, which have led to a decrease in local wheat production, forcing Iraq to make up for the shortfall through imports. The lack of rainfall in winter is the biggest challenge for the production of crops such as wheat, rice, and barley in Iraq.

Table 5.1 Wheat Imports of Some Arab Countries in 2023

Global Rank	Importer	Import Value (USD 100 million)	Range of Change (%)
2	Egypt	37.73	-11.6
10	Morocco	19.11	-25.3
11	Algeria	18.41	-31.3
24	Tunisia	7.92	-10.8
31	Saudi Arabia	5.63	-66.1
32	Yemen	5.59	-44.7
33	Iraq	5.45	+90.4
43	UAE	3.30	-49.1
60	Mauritania	1.82	-43.7
64	Jordan	1.47	-65.2
65	Kuwait	1.30	-19.4
70	Sudan	1.21	-76.8
80	Lebanon	0.85	-62.7
87	Oman	0.65	-81.8

Source: Wheat Imports by Country,

https://www.worldstopexports.com/wheat-imports-by-country/?expand_article=1.

Undernourishment in the Arab States has reached a new height. The prevalence of undernourishment (PoU) increased by 0.6 percent in 2023 from the previous year and reached 14 percent. There were 66.1 million undernourished people in 2023, an increase of 4 million from 2022. PoU was

and export olive oil. Non-food producing countries, represented by the GCC countries, have transferred part of their agricultural industries to other countries for development and used the rich land resources of other countries to develop their own agriculture, thereby providing their people with the necessary food and alleviating the food security crisis. The contribution of the agricultural sector to the economy of the Arab countries varies from country to country. For example, in Saudi Arabia, the contribution rate of the agricultural sector is about 3.2%, while in the United Arab Emirates, the contribution rate of the agricultural sector represents about 15.3 billion dirhams in the year 2022, and is expected to grow by 28% in 2025 and reach to 19 billion dirhams, while in Egypt, its contribution rate is 15% in 2022.[①]

Agriculture in the Arab region is generally underdeveloped. The total area of the Arab states is approximately 1.402 billion hectares, accounting for 10.2% of the world's total land area, with the arable land area of approximately 197 million hectares. One major obstacle to restrict sustainable agricultural development in the Arab region is the shortage of agricultural land and water resources. In addition, the region is also facing serious problems of natural resource degradation caused by soil erosion, desertification, waterlogging, and salinization. Due to insufficient arable land, severe water scarcity, climate change, and ongoing geopolitical conflicts, the Arab region is facing significant food security issues, which are exacerbated by rapid population growth. The annual population growth rate in the Arab region exceeds 2%, which is higher than the average level of middle-income countries worldwide (1.3%).

The Arab countries are highly dependent on food imports, especially wheat. Population growth and climate change increase their dependence on wheat imports, making the Arab countries more vulnerable to international market fluctuations. Therefore, ensuring food security is not only solving the problem of people's food and clothing, but also maintaining the foundation of rulers' governance. As is shown in table 5-1, Egypt is the second largest importer of wheat in the world. In 2023, Egypt, Morocco, and Algeria ranked among the top 15 wheat importers. Compared to 2022, the ranking of Algeria dropped from 6th

---

① Ali Mohamed Al-Khouri, "The Agricultural Sector, the Interest and Challenges It Faces in the Middle East," *Al Wafd Newspaper*, October 12, 2023, https://arab-digital-economy.org/language/en/9095.

Chapter 5 Special Report on China-Arab States Agricultural Cooperation

Agricultural cooperation is an important component of China-Arab States economic and trade cooperation. Under the guidance of the head-of-state diplomacy, China-Arab States practical cooperation is becoming more and more solid. Agricultural cooperation is continuously bearing fruitful results, with the trade value of agricultural products continuing to grow, agricultural science and technology cooperation steadily advancing, and exchanges and cooperation constantly strengthening.

5.1 Current Situation of Agricultural Development in the Arab States

Agriculture is the foundation of the national economy and the cornerstone of social stability. Agriculture can not only eliminate many crises, but also increase many economic and strategic advantages. Agriculture has important strategic significance, and agricultural production is regarded as a key focus of the national economy by the Arab countries, which is also reflected in their national development strategies, such as Egypt's "2030 Vision," Saudi Arabia's "2030 Vision," Oman's "2020 Vision Plan," Sudan's "Five-Year Programme for Economic Reform (2015-2019)," Djibouti's "Accelerated Growth and Employment Promotion Strategy 2015-2019," Comoros's "Accelerated Economic Growth Strategy 2017-2021." Those strategies regard promoting agricultural production as a major issue in their national economic construction and improving people's livelihoods. For example, Tunisia mainly produces grains and olive oil and is one of the major countries in the world to produce

trust and a strong mutual desire to boost economic trade and investment but also elevates practical cooperation across various sectors to new heights. It provides lasting momentum for bilateral relations, enhancing the voice of developing countries and promoting more balanced and diversified global financial governance.

Chapter 4 Special Report on China-Arab States Financial Cooperation

In the context of digital transformation, Chinese enterprises have expanded digital payment technologies and financial services to Arab merchants, gaining greater market prospects by offering services such as cross-border mobile payments, digital technology solutions, merchant payment services, digital payment and financial services for cross-border trade, as well as digital wholesale banking. For instance, the rapid expansion of Dubai's fintech ecosystem presents Chinese fintech companies with opportunities to collaborate with local institutions and test new products. iPayLinks, a Chinese company with mature payment solutions, became the first in China to receive a service investment license in Saudi Arabia. As Arab states' commercial and capital markets open to China, leading innovative enterprises are offered fiscal incentives and support for investors. China actively encourages and supports enterprises and financial institutions to deepen cooperation with Arab states in new technology sectors, gradually expanding project operations and collaboration scale. This also helps Chinese companies improve global industrial chains, enhancing their international competitiveness and influence.

Attracting Arab capital—represented by sovereign wealth funds—to play a greater role in China's domestic financial market is another key focus. Sovereign wealth funds, known for their high risk tolerance, have rapidly emerged as a significant force in 21st-century global financial markets. Traditionally focused on Europe and the U.S., Arab sovereign wealth funds have recently shown increased interest in China's financial markets and a positive outlook on China's long-term economic growth prospects. For example, Saudi Arabia's Public Investment Fund invested approximately $12.2 billion in Chinese equities between 2017 and 2021, accounting for about one-fifth of its total overseas equity investments. Similarly, Abu Dhabi's Mubadala Investment Company aims to increase its Asian assets from the current 12% of total assets to 25% by 2030, driving hundreds of billions of dollars into Asian markets. In terms of industrial manufacturing, China's well-established technological and supply chain systems offer a distinct advantage over Arab states. Many Chinese companies, backed by Arab capital, can leverage extensive networks and resource advantages to foster synergies, supporting economic transformation and technological advancement in Arab states. This facilitates mutual benefits and win-win outcomes.

The financial cooperation between China and Arab states showcases immense potential and promise. Strengthening this collaboration not only reflects deep

the commodity trade sector grew significantly, with the total amount reaching 985.73 billion RMB. All of the deliverable foreign crude oil contracts on the Shanghai Futures Exchange are sourced from Arab states, and in 2022, the total trading volume of crude oil futures reached 53.58 million lots, making it the third-largest crude oil futures trading center globally. The influence of RMB-denominated crude oil futures is steadily growing. Middle Eastern oil-producing states are actively seeking to reduce their reliance on the U.S. dollar and enhance currency cooperation with major global economies, including China. With the solid foundation of energy cooperation between China and Arab states, there are increasing opportunities for expanding the use of the RMB in international settlements and transactions. As commodity settlement and pricing mechanisms are restructured, the role of the RMB as an international currency will be continuously strengthened.

In line with the demands of Arab states for energy transition and financial technology advancements, China should enhance bilateral financing and policy environments with Arab states, accelerating the international expansion of enterprises and seizing opportunities in emerging industries globally. Many Arab states are currently pushing for economic diversification and digital transformation, seeking to reduce their dependence on oil by shifting towards a digital economy and high-tech sectors. As a result, the renewable energy and fintech sectors have been growing rapidly, while many traditional industries are also undergoing rapid transformation. The Middle East, with abundant renewable energy resources, has launched several cutting-edge projects of global significance. China and Arab states are continually exploring financial cooperation in emerging fields such as new energy and the digital economy and actively promoting energy transition under the global green development agenda. This collaboration unlocks potentials in clean energy sectors like solar power, wind energy, nuclear energy, hydrogen energy, biomass energy, and electric vehicle industries (such as battery technology and charging infrastructure). For example, on May 1, 2023, Baosteel partnered with Saudi Aramco and the Public Investment Fund to build the world's first low-carbon full-process thick plate plant in Saudi Arabia. On June 19, 2023, Great Wall Haval, the parent company of Qiantu Motors, signed a strategic cooperation agreement with Jordan's largest private company, Manaseer Group, to establish a joint venture serving the Middle East and North African electric vehicle market.

Chapter 4 Special Report on China-Arab States Financial Cooperation

members, fortifying mechanisms for trade and economic cooperation, leveraging platforms such as the China-GCC Economic and Trade Ministers' Meeting and joint (mixed) bilateral economic and trade committees. This helped deepen cooperation in areas such as trade investment, digital economy, sustainable development, and infrastructure, and drive the operation of the China-Gulf Joint Investment Commission. Secondly, cooperation under the BRICS framework turned out to be equally critical. At the 15th BRICS Summit held in South Africa on August 24, 2023, the mechanism announced its second expansion, adding Saudi Arabia, Egypt, the UAE, Iran, and Ethiopia as BRICS members, effective January 1, 2024. Among these, Saudi Arabia is a vital pivot for China's investments and trade in the Middle East and North Africa region, while the UAE, as a major entrepôt hub, has greater influence on surrounding Arab states. Egypt, overseeing the Suez Canal, holds critical geographic significance, bridging the Red Sea and the Mediterranean. By enhancing dialogue and coordination, and utilizing the BRICS framework, financial market opening can be accelerated, enabling Saudi Arabia, the UAE, and Egypt to act as conduits for fostering high-efficiency trade, investment, and financial ties between China and the Arab world.

Promoting market connectivity through financial technology innovation and establishing a smoother onshore-offshore RMB circulation mechanism will accelerate the internationalization of the RMB, with energy cooperation serving as a foundational pillar. Facilitating trade and payment systems will effectively reduce foreign exchange risks, providing greater convenience for China-Arab states economic and trade exchanges. Continuously advancing the pilot applications of the central bank digital currency (CBDC), actively participating in the integration of multilateral payment systems, establishing regional settlement platforms, and promoting interconnected cross-border payments within the framework of multilateral currency bridges, will help reduce reliance on the current U.S. dollar-based payment system. In November 2023, the People's Bank of China and the Central Bank of the UAE signed a Memorandum of Understanding on enhancing cooperation in CBDCs, and the Bank of China signed a digital currency cooperation agreement with the First Abu Dhabi Bank, with both parties collaborating in financial technology innovation and CBDC development. In the commodity trading sector, the role of the RMB as a settlement currency is deepening. In 2022, cross-border RMB settlements in

4.4 Prospects of China-Arab States Financial Cooperation

The deepening financial cooperation between China and Arab states is one of the key achievements in the broader collaboration between the two parties. Driven by the Arab states' aspirations to expand their overseas investment markets, reduce dependence on oil economies, improve their financial systems, and promote domestic industrial upgrades, their willingness to engage in financial cooperation with China has continuously increased. This aligns with China's strategy of further opening up its economy. By advancing the "Belt and Road" Initiative, China-Arab states economic cooperation, and the BRICS mechanism in alignment with Arab states' long-term economic development visions and strategies, the deepening of financial cooperation will help both sides achieve mutual industrial upgrades and economic development.

At present, China-Arab states financial cooperation is primarily composed of business activities such as trade settlement, cross-border investment, and syndicated loans conducted by Chinese financial institutions. However, the participation of financial market players is still at an early stage, and financial support for SMEs venturing abroad remains limited. Looking ahead, the focus should be on strengthening cooperation in financial regulation and risk prevention, further opening capital markets, and constructing multi-level financial service platforms, including securities and bond issuance. Additionally, enhancing arrangements for currency swaps and establishing offshore RMB clearing centers will deepen financial cooperation and promote trade and investment.

While building more layers of financial mechanisms, it is crucial for China to align with the financial policies of key Arab states. Historically, China has largely viewed the Arab world as a collective entity, but the reality is that Arab states vary significantly in their levels of development. Most China-Arab states financial cooperation projects have been concentrated in economically vibrant nations with well-developed financial systems. Beyond platforms like the China-Arab States Cooperation Forum and the "Belt and Road" Initiative, China's smaller-scale cooperation with key Arab states can serve as a foundation to extend financial cooperation to other Arab states. First, we have strengthened the China-GCC efforts, aligning the development strategies of China and GCC

accelerate industrial deployment and achieve economic diversification. China's new economy enterprises are increasingly favored by sovereign wealth funds and large corporations from Arab states, with active investment projects in high-tech sectors such as new energy, digital technology, and healthcare. For example, in the field of NEVs, Arab states are accelerating their cooperation with Chinese NEV companies to achieve faster development. On October 9, BAIC BJEV reached a cooperation consensus with the UAE-based Bin Omeir Holding Group to upgrade and improve vehicle models with intelligent technology and to deeply cooperate in market promotion. On October 11, Xiling Power disclosed the signing of a "Strategic Cooperation Framework Agreement" with Bin Omeir Holding Group, under which Bin Omeir will serve as a strategic investor, and both parties plan to establish a joint venture company with a 700 million RMB investment to develop NEV components. Cooperation in the financial sector will provide stronger support for pragmatic industrial collaboration between the two parties.

Hong Kong, taking a leading step in advancing financial openness, has become an important conduit for capital connectivity between the mainland of China and major Gulf countries. The demand for RMB interest rate risk management among foreign participants has continued to grow, and the two-way opening of China's financial market has been steadily advancing. In July 2022, the People's Bank of China, the Securities and Futures Commission (SFC) of Hong Kong, and the Hong Kong Monetary Authority (HKMA) issued a joint announcement, stating that the Mainland-Hong Kong Interest Rate Swap Connect (referred to as "Swap Connect") was being developed. On May 15, 2023, "Swap Connect" was officially launched, facilitating foreign investors' participation in the domestic RMB interest rate swap market and supporting the construction of a high-level financial opening framework. Since 2023, Hong Kong and Saudi Arabia have made significant progress in deepening the interconnection of capital markets between the two regions. In 2023, the Abu Dhabi Investment Office partnered with Hong Kong's Arte Capital to help Chinese companies expand into the Middle East and North Africa, further strengthening the economic ties between China and Arab states. Hong Kong has established closer cooperation in financial services with Middle Eastern states, particularly Saudi Arabia and the UAE, fostering dialogue and understanding at the regulatory level, thus laying a solid foundation for deeper capital market collaboration in the future.

financial wealth and accelerate economic diversification. Egypt, the third-largest economy in Africa, has undertaken economic reforms in recent years to enhance its macroeconomic resilience under the pressure of inflation and debt burden. As Arab states have continued to launch industrial transformation and opening-up policies in recent years, they have improved the financing and policy environment, aiming to create more room for international financial investment and achieve their goals of economic diversification.

China-Arab states financial cooperation continues to empower infrastructure and energy projects. Under the "Belt and Road" Initiative, Chinese companies have invested in and constructed numerous infrastructure projects worldwide. These projects include 5G cellular network technology, high-speed railways, roads, ports, and energy, thereby providing a strong industrial foundation for developing countries. Many Arab states are at a critical stage of national transformation, but their domestic funding and financial services are insufficient to support the necessary economic and social development. Chinese technology and expertise have helped fill these gaps, promoting infrastructure construction and industrial upgrades in these countries. Multiple financial cooperation projects between China and Arab states centered on energy infrastructure are ongoing. On October 9, 2023, Sinosure insured the first medium- to long-term renewable energy financing project, providing long-term export buyer's credit insurance support for the 500 MW Manah II Solar PV IPP Project in Oman. In the same month, the Hassyan power plant in Dubai, jointly invested by the Silk Road Fund, Harbin Electric Corporation, and UAE investment institutions, became fully operational. This plant— the Silk Road Fund's first investment in the Middle East—will provide 20% of Dubai's electricity, supporting the region's energy diversification goals. By the end of 2023, the China Development Bank had issued loans totaling more than $6.48 billion in Egypt to support major infrastructure projects, including the 500 kV transmission line project and the China-Egypt TEDA Suez Economic and Trade Cooperation Zone.

Forward-looking industries such as new energy and other high-tech sectors have emerged as new highlights of Arab states' investment in China. The objectives of Arab capital entering China's financial markets have become clearer, with a more proactive and assertive approach. China-Arab states financial cooperation has also become an important channel for Arab capital to

Chapter 4 Special Report on China-Arab States Financial Cooperation

Establishment of Offices in China: Middle Eastern sovereign wealth funds have established branch offices within China to monitor the latest developments of Chinese high-tech enterprises and make investment decisions. Currently, several Middle Eastern sovereign funds, including Abu Dhabi Investment Authority, Kuwait Investment Authority, Qatar Investment Authority, and Saudi Public Investment Fund, have set up offices in China. The recently established UAE 42X Fund opened an office in Shanghai, and Mubadala's China office was established in Beijing in September 2023. The Ministry of Investment for Saudi Arabia (MISA) is in the process of setting up an office in the Guangdong–Hong Kong–Macao Greater Bay Area.

4.3 Trends in China-Arab States Financial Cooperation

In July 2018, at the opening ceremony of the eighth ministerial meeting of the China-Arab States Cooperation Forum, China proposed that cooperation between China and Arab states should firmly grasp the "handle" of connectivity and actively promote the cooperation of oil and gas, and of low-carbon energy – the "dual rotation," striving for the "dual wings" of financial and high-tech collaboration. Practical cooperation in finance between China and Arab states is based on aligning the "Belt and Road" Initiative with the development strategies of Arab states. By deepening infrastructure construction and capacity development, mechanisms and platforms are being built from a national strategic level to attract a broader range of participants in the financial market and solidly promote China-Arab states financial cooperation through various innovative forms.

The long-term development strategies of major Arab states have created more opportunities for China-Arab states financial cooperation. Economic diversification and sustainable growth are major development goals for Arab states in the coming years. As one of the world's largest oil exporters, Saudi Arabia has strong economic power, and accelerating the transformation of its financial sector is a key component of "Saudi Vision 2030." It is working towards establishing Riyadh as the financial hub of the Middle East. The United Arab Emirates has developed a highly competitive financial services sector and advanced infrastructure to reduce its reliance on oil. Qatar's "National Vision 2030" outlines a strategy to convert natural resources into national

Continued

Chinese Enterprise	Time	Industry	Arab Investor	Financing Situation
Shein	May 2023	E-commerce	Mubadala Investment Company (MIC)	Led a new round of $2 billion financing
Guodong Group	May 2023	Communications R&D	Mubadala Investment Company (MIC)	Investment of $150 million from MIC Capital Management
NIO	July 2023	Electric Vehicles	Abu Dhabi CYVN Holdings	Completed strategic investments totaling approximately $1.1 billion
	December 2023			Strategic investments totaling approximately $2.2 billion
B.Duck	July 2023	Entertainment	Saudi Public Investment Fund (PIF)	Total investment of $250 million
China Life Science Industry Facilities Fund	October 2023	Healthcare	Mubadala Investment Company (MIC)	Led fundraising of $875 million
Pony.ai	October 2023	Autonomous Driving	NEOM Investment Fund (NIF)	Total investment of $100 million
eWTP Arabia Capital	December 2023	Investment Institution	Saudi Public Investment Fund (PIF)	Total investment reaching approximately $200 million

Source: Compiled from public reports.

In addition to private equity investments in the primary market, such sovereign wealth funds from the Middle East also allocate assets in China's A-share and H-share markets. Mubadala Investment Company tends to participate directly in equity financing for Chinese high-tech enterprises, while its investment activities in the A-share securities market are relatively limited. Prominent Middle Eastern investment institutions, such as the Abu Dhabi Investment Authority and the Kuwait Investment Authority, frequently appear among the top ten shareholders of A-share listed companies. These two major funds exhibit significant differences in industry selection, with the Abu Dhabi Investment Authority placing a stronger emphasis on the energy sector.

Table 4.4 Representative Cases of Arab Sovereign Wealth Funds Investing in Chinese Enterprises

Chinese Enterprise	Time	Industry	Arab Investor	Financing Situation
Didi	December 2017	Ride-hailing	Mubadala Investment Company (MIC)	Participated in a new round of over $4 billion financing
Lufax	March 2019	Wealth Management	Qatar Investment Authority (QIA)	Led a $1.33 billion Series C financing
Megvii Technology	May 2019	Artificial Intelligence	Abu Dhabi Investment Authority (ADIA)	Led a $750 million Series D financing
Xpeng Motors	August 2020	Electric Vehicles	Qatar Investment Authority (QIA), Mubadala Investment Company (MIC)	MIC and QIA subscribed to $100 million in preferred shares in Xpeng Motors' C++ financing
Transcenta Holding	December 2020	Biopharmaceuticals	Qatar Investment Authority (QIA)	QIA participated as a new investor in $105 million crossover financing
SenseTime	September 2022	Artificial Intelligence	Saudi Company for Artificial Intelligence (SCAI)	Reached a cooperation agreement to invest 776 million Saudi Riyals in SenseTime MEA, a joint venture with PIF
VSPO	February 2023	Entertainment	Savvy Games Group	Savvy Games Group, a subsidiary of PIF, invested $265 million, becoming the single largest shareholder
JD Industrial Technology	March 2023	Distribution	Mubadala Investment Company (MIC), Abu Dhabi Growth Fund's 42X Fund	Led a $300 million financing
Yuanqi Bio	March 2023	Biopharmaceuticals	Qatar Investment Authority (QIA)	Led a $45 million Series B1 financing
Hasten Bio	April 2023	Biopharmaceuticals	Mubadala Investment Company (MIC)	Led a $315 million financing by C-Bridge Capital and MIC

Table 4.3 Global Top Ten Sovereign Wealth Funds Ranking

Rank	Sovereign Wealth Fund	Total Assets (Billion USD)	Region
1	Government Pension Fund Global (Norway)	1,631.4	Europe
2	China Investment Corporation	1,350.0	Asia
3	SAFE Investment Company Limited	1,090.0	Asia
4	Abu Dhabi Investment Authority	993.0	Middle East
5	Public Investment Fund (Saudi Arabia)	925.0	Middle East
6	Kuwait Investment Authority	923.45	Middle East
7	GIC Private Limited	770.0	Asia
8	Qatar Investment Authority	526.1	Middle East
9	Hong Kong Monetary Authority Investment Portfolio	514.2	Asia
10	Temasek Holdings	492.2	Asia

Source: Sovereign Wealth Fund Institute (SWFI), data accessed in June 2024.

<u>Asset Allocation in China</u>: China is a participant and leader in technology innovation and new economic fields. As China's achievements in innovation continue to grow, major sovereign wealth funds in the Middle East have increased their investments in China's venture capital and startup markets, providing funding support and more opportunities for new economic enterprises with growth potential. To seek diversified economic development and industrial upgrades, these sovereign funds are accelerating capital allocation in China's primary market. According to SWFI data, the direct mergers and acquisitions and investment amount of sovereign wealth funds from the GCC states in China reached $2.3 billion in 2023. In terms of industry distribution, the most attractive investment areas are biotechnology, artificial intelligence, and electric vehicles (see Table 4.4). The strong financial capacity of such sovereign wealth funds from the Middle East enables them to directly participate in equity financing for high-tech Chinese enterprises. This not only offers substantial investment returns but also helps attract Chinese high-tech companies to develop businesses in Arab states, supporting the upgrade of local technology industries.

Chapter 4 Special Report on China-Arab States Financial Cooperation

market of the Saudi Stock Exchange can apply for secondary listings in Hong Kong. In November 2023, the Shanghai Stock Exchange signed a memorandum of understanding with the Dubai Financial Market to jointly explore the development of ESG (Environmental, Social, and Governance) and sustainable development-related products. The Hong Kong Stock Exchange introduced the region's first ETF tracking Saudi stocks by the end of 2023, marking a significant step in enhancing international cooperation and promoting the development of capital markets.

<u>Credit Insurance Business:</u> On October 9, 2023, China Export & Credit Insurance Corporation (Sinosure) underwrote its first medium- and long-term insurance financing project for renewable energy, providing medium- and long-term export buyer credit insurance support for the 500 MW Manah II Solar PV IPP Project in Oman.

<u>Digital Currency Bridge:</u> Since participating in the pilot program for the digital currency bridge in 2022, the ICBC Abu Dhabi Branch has utilized the currency bridge platform to conduct central bank digital currency pilots in scenarios such as goods trade, service trade, interbank fund transfers, and funding borrowing, achieving positive results. Among these, the cross-border RMB payroll services conducted through the digital currency bridge have expanded the practical application scenarios of the RMB internationally, better serving the overseas development of Chinese enterprises.

4.2.4 Sovereign Wealth Funds

As investment entities of the national public sector, the rapid development of sovereign wealth funds signifies that developing countries are gaining increasing influence and importance within the international financial system. The latest ranking from the Sovereign Wealth Fund Institute (SWFI) shows that the Public Investment Fund (PIF) of Saudi Arabia, the Abu Dhabi Investment Authority (ADIA), the Kuwait Investment Authority (KIA), and the Qatar Investment Authority (QIA) rank among the top globally (see Table 4.3). In recent years, sovereign wealth funds from Arab states have been increasing their investments in China.

the total issuance of Panda Bonds in 2022 reached 85.07 billion RMB, and increased to 155.45 billion RMB in 2023. In 2018, the UAE successfully issued the first sovereign "Panda Bond" in the Chinese interbank bond market, totaling 2 billion RMB. In October 2023, Egypt successfully issued a 3.5 billion RMB sustainable "Panda Bond," marking the first "Panda Bond" in Africa. In November 2023, ICBC's "Belt and Road" themed green bonds were successfully listed on the Nasdaq Dubai, bringing the total value of bonds listed by ICBC on this exchange to 7.4 billion USD, making it a leading issuer of Chinese bonds on the exchange. The successful issuance of these bonds demonstrates the cooperation potential between China and Arab states in capital raising and investment.

RMB Loans: In March 2023, the Export-Import Bank of China and the Saudi National Bank completed their first cooperation on RMB loans, with funds prioritized for facilitating bilateral trade between China and Saudi Arabia. This initiative promotes the smooth flow of financing, trade, and investment between China and Arab states. In October 2023, the Export-Import Bank of China signed a cooperation agreement with the Bank of Africa in Morocco, aiming to actively promote economic and trade exchanges and financial cooperation through project financing, parallel financing, and trade financing, while strengthening information sharing and personnel exchanges, and exploring the use of RMB loans. This marks a diversification of the trade and payment systems between China and Arab states, which will help reduce dependence on the US dollar and mitigate foreign exchange risks, providing greater convenience for business transactions between the two countries.

Capital Market Platform Cooperation: In February 2023, the Hong Kong Stock Exchange signed a memorandum of cooperation with the Saudi Tadawul Group to explore collaboration in various fields, including arrangements for cross-listing. On September 3, 2023, the Shanghai Stock Exchange signed a memorandum of cooperation with the Saudi Tadawul Group in Riyadh, aiming to promote corporate listings and dual listings of ETFs. On September 28, 2023, the Shanghai Stock Exchange, along with the Hong Kong Stock Exchange's wholly-owned subsidiary, Hong Kong Exchanges and Clearing Limited, announced the inclusion of the Saudi Stock Exchange in its list of recognized securities exchanges. Consequently, companies listed on the main

Bank of China (ICBC) Doha Branch and the Agricultural Bank of China Dubai Branch serve as the only RMB clearing banks in Qatar and the UAE, respectively, so they play a significant role in meeting the cross-border RMB fund clearing needs of clients in the Middle East and North Africa. The Cross-Border Interbank Payment System (CIPS) operates smoothly, providing fund clearing and settlement services for domestic and foreign financial institutions. As of the end of 2023, there were 139 direct participants, including Bank of China (Djibouti) Co., Ltd., Bank of China Dubai Branch, Bank of China Abu Dhabi Branch, Bank of China Qatar Financial Centre Branch, ICBC Doha Branch, ICBC Riyadh Branch, Agricultural Bank of China Dubai Branch, and Agricultural Bank of China Dubai International Financial Centre Branch.

4.2.3 Development of Financial Institutions and Businesses

Establishment of Branches: In 2023, ICBC and Bank of China opened branches in Saudi Arabia, becoming the second and third Chinese banks to operate in the country. The establishment of these branches further expands the coverage of Chinese financial services, demonstrating China's high recognition of Saudi financial regulations, investment environment, and geographical advantages. This marks a new level of cooperation in the financial sector between the two parties and provides stronger support for the deep integration of the "Belt and Road" Initiative and "Saudi Vision 2030".

Bond Issuance: The issuance of "Panda Bonds"[①] steadily enhances the RMB's financing capability and promotes the internationalization of the RMB. In recent years, against the backdrop of significant interest rate hikes in major developed economies, the financing costs in RMB have relatively decreased. With the growth and increased openness of China's bond market, the convenience and regulation for foreign entities to issue bonds in the domestic market have further improved, leading to rapid growth in the issuance of RMB-denominated "Panda Bonds" by issuers registered abroad. According to Wind Data Service,

---

[①] "Panda Bonds" refer to bonds issued by overseas institutions in China that are denominated in RMB. For more information, please refer to the "Panda Bond Product Handbook" published by the National Association of Financial Market Institutional Investors (NAFMII) at the following link: Panda Bond Product Handbook, 2024, p.3, https://www.nafmii.org.cn/xhdt/202407/P020240705533954859021.pdf.

4.2.2 Central Bank Cooperation

China and Arab states have further strengthened bilateral currency swap and RMB clearing cooperation between their central banks, facilitating direct currency exchange settlements. This collaboration alleviates trade financing pressures and effectively addresses issues of short-term liquidity fluctuations, while actively promoting trade and investment exchanges between the two parties. It has also played a positive role in maintaining regional financial stability and healthy development.

Bilateral Currency Settlement: In 2023, in the interbank foreign exchange market, the RMB/Saudi Riyal transaction volume reached RMB 2.85 billion, down from RMB 3.32 billion in 2022. The RMB/UAE Dirham transaction volume was RMB 720 million, 3.5 times higher than the RMB 160 million in 2022.[①]

Bilateral Currency Swap Agreements: By the end of 2023, the People's Bank of China had signed bilateral currency swap agreements with central banks or monetary authorities from 41 countries and regions, amounting to over 4 trillion RMB. Effective agreements with Arab states include the following:

On February 20, 2023, the People's Bank of China renewed its bilateral currency swap agreement with the Central Bank of Egypt, valued at 18 billion RMB/80.7 billion Egyptian Pounds;

On November 20, 2023, the People's Bank of China signed a bilateral currency swap agreement with the Central Bank of Saudi Arabia, with a swap scale of 50 billion RMB/26 billion Saudi Riyals, effective for three years;

On November 28, 2023, the People's Bank of China renewed its bilateral currency swap agreement with the Central Bank of the UAE, with a swap scale of 35 billion RMB/18 billion UAE Dirhams and a validity of five years.

These bilateral currency swap arrangements help strengthen financial cooperation between the two parties, expand the use of local currencies, and facilitate trade and investment.

Overseas Clearing Mechanisms: In 2023, the number of countries and regions with RMB clearing banks increased to 33. The Industrial and Commercial

---

① The People's Bank of China: *Report on RMB Internationalization 2024*, http://www.pbc.gov.cn/huobi zhengceersi/214481/3871621/5472873/index.html, September 30,2024.

investment cooperation agreements worth more than 70 billion RMB were signed between the two parties. In August 2023, during the Saudi-Chinese Business Forum, the two parties signed 12 cooperation agreements worth over 5 billion Saudi Riyals (1.3 billion USD). On December 15, 2023, the Chinese-Saudi Investment Conference was held in Beijing, resulting in the signing of more than 60 cooperation agreements and memoranda involving numerous sectors, including energy, agriculture, tourism, mining, finance, logistics, and healthcare.

The Middle East has become a target region for Shenzhen as the city aims to establish itself as an international wealth management center and facilitate business linkages and industrial layout. In January 2023, to accelerate the development of an international wealth management hub, explore multi-channel approaches to increase residents' property income, and uphold the spirit of China-Arab states friendship featuring "reciprocal support, equality and mutual benefit, inclusiveness, and mutual learning," Shenzhen introduced the Public Investment Fund for the first time, establishing Blue Ocean Taiku (Shenzhen) Private Equity Investment Fund Co., Ltd. in China and initiating the first Middle East Cooperation Fund, with initial funding exceeding 1 billion USD.

Hong Kong, with its unique international financial position, is facilitating connections between the mainland of China and the Saudi market. In February 2023, after the Chief Executive of the Hong Kong Special Administrative Region, John Lee Ka-chiu, led a delegation to visit Saudi Arabia, both parties actively promoted economic and trade cooperation, witnessing a successful kickoff. During the visit to Hong Kong of Abdullah Al-Swaha, the Saudi Minister of Communications and Information Technology, 11 companies from the mainland of China and Hong Kong signed memorandums of cooperation with eWTP Arabia Capital to enter the Saudi market and join the Saudi-Chinese Business Council, aiming to promote the entry of Hong Kong's leading financial and technology companies into the Saudi market. The Saudi-Chinese Business Council connects the mainland of China, Hong Kong, and Saudi Arabia through its Hong Kong office, enhancing talent exchange, business cooperation, and collaboration in innovative technologies, while promoting the listing of Saudi companies on the Saudi and Hong Kong stock exchanges. In September 2023, Hong Kong hosted the "Belt and Road Summit," which for the first time included a Middle East Forum.

in the financial sector. In the GFCI 34 sub-index rankings, Dubai ranks 13th globally in investment management, 15th in professional services, and 11th in financial technology, making it the leading financial center in the Arab region and attracting a significant number of multinational corporations and foreign investors.

4.2 Progress in China-Arab States Financial Cooperation

China and Arab states have further strengthened financial connectivity under the framework of the China-Arab Cooperation Forum and the "Belt and Road" Initiative. The forms and scope of cooperation are continuously expanding, and efforts are underway to enhance platforms and mechanisms for financial collaboration. Positive results have been achieved in areas such as central bank cooperation, the internationalization of the RMB, and attracting Arab sovereign wealth funds for financing in China.

4.2.1 Platform Construction

Cooperation between China and the GCC is steadily advancing. On October 22, 2023, the China-GCC Economic and Trade Ministers' Meeting was held in Guangzhou, China. The meeting focused on the implementation of the economic and trade initiatives of the first China-GCC Summit. They reached a broad consensus on topics such as jointly maintaining a multilateral trading system, promoting bilateral investment, deepening cooperation in industrial and supply chains, enhancing connectivity, and advancing energy transition. The meeting resulted in the adoption of the "Joint Statement on Deepening China-GCC Economic and Trade Cooperation."

The number of communication platforms for businesses from both sides across various fields is increasing, playing a positive role in driving investment and financing. In February 2023, during the LEAP Summit 2023 held in Riyadh, Saudi Arabia, the Saudi-Chinese Business Council was officially established to connect high-level government agencies, enterprises, non-profit organizations, and academic institutions from both countries. The 10th session of the Arab- Chinese Businessmen Conference, and the 8th session of the Investments Symposium were held in Riyadh in June 2023, where discussions focused on trade, finance, energy, and green industries. Over 30 economic and

Chapter 4 Special Report on China-Arab States Financial Cooperation

as well as Palestine and Libya, which are affected by regional conflicts, are particularly vulnerable, with fragile financial systems. Additionally, U.S. economic sanctions on Syria have led to stagnation in its economic development, making it challenging for the country to integrate into the international financial system.

4.1.2 The Increasing Prominence of International Financial Centers in Arab States

Arab states boast several significant international financial hubs, with their rankings showing an upward trend. According to the Global Financial Centers Index (GFCI 34) report, published in September 2023, among the 121 global financial hubs, seven are in Arab states. Apart from Casablanca in Morocco, which is in Africa, the other six major financial centers are located in Asia (see Table 4.2). The financial sector in the UAE is highly developed, with Dubai and Abu Dhabi being the most influential financial centers in the Arab world, ranking first and second regionally. Dubai's financial market is also one of the most active stock markets in the Middle East. Saudi Arabia is actively transforming its capital, Riyadh, into a financial center for the region.

Table 4.2 Ranking of Financial Centers in Arab States

Financial Center	GFCI 34 Regional Ranking	GFCI 34 Global Ranking	GFCI 34 Score	Rank Change	Score Change
Dubai	1	21	719	↑1	↑17
Abu Dhabi	2	35	702	0	↑13
Casablanca	3	54	682	↑3	↑40
Bahrain	4	74	660	↑8	↑51
Riyadh	5	75	659	↑13	↑56
Doha	6	78	656	↓14	↑28
Kuwait City	7	82	646	↑20	↑57

Source: Global Financial Centers Index (GFCI).

In terms of scores, all seven Arab financial centers have shown improvements, with an overall average score increase of 5.9% compared to the previous period. This reflects a continuous rise in comprehensive competitiveness related to the business environment, human capital, infrastructure, taxation, and reputation

The financial development of Arab states exhibits a distinct polarization. The Chinn-Ito Financial Openness Index is a commonly used measure of the degree of capital account openness among countries. The GCC member states, categorized as high-income economies, generally have high financial openness indices, along with countries like Djibouti and Jordan, which also show relatively high levels of capital account openness (see Table 4.1). In contrast, most other Arab states have low levels of financial openness. From the perspective of external financing, a high and increasing burden of external debt may affect a country's sovereign creditworthiness and its ability to withstand external shocks, particularly for low-income countries, where external financing can become unsustainable. The debt ratio of a country is measured by the proportion of its external debt stock to Gross National Income (GNI), while the debt service pressure is assessed by the ratio of debt service payments to export value. The internationally recognized safe line for the former is 20%, while the latter is generally set within the range of 15% to 25%. Overall, Egypt, Jordan, Djibouti, and Lebanon stand out with significant external debt burdens, with Egypt's external debt stock ranking first among Arab states at USD 163.1 billion.

As the burden of external debt and debt servicing costs rise, developing countries find their financing options increasingly limited, especially for middle- and low-income countries, which often have poor overall economic resilience due to prolonged economic underdevelopment and insufficient fiscal strength. When large amounts of foreign currency exit and the local currency depreciates sharply, liquidity crises often arise, potentially leading to sovereign debt distress. The World Bank's "2024 International Debt Report" reveals that in 2023, the total external debt of low- and middle-income countries (LMICs) in the world reached USD 8.8 trillion, up 2.4 percent from the previous year. The rise in global interest rates has increased the debt burden, and the total debt repayment expenditure in that year reached USD 1.4 trillion, of which interest payments reached USD 272.3 billion, an increase of 41.7 percent. Many developing countries are facing heavy debt repayment pressure. Among Arab countries, Sudan has long been among the top ten countries with the highest concentration of sovereign default debts in the world, and countries such as Iraq and Lebanon also have a high risk of sovereign debt default. These heavily indebted Arab states struggle not only to achieve smooth financing internationally but also find it impossible to secure international aid. Low-income countries such as Somalia, Sudan, and Yemen,

allocate external financial assets. The primary drivers of financial development in Arab states stem from the capital-rich members of the Gulf Cooperation Council (GCC), which have achieved world-leading per capita GDP levels and substantial capital accumulation and fiscal surpluses. In contrast, middle- and low-income Arab states display relatively weak overall financial development and generally low levels of financial system openness.

Table 4.1 Financial Openness and Debt Levels of Arab States

Country	Financial Openness Index	Total External Debt (Million USD)	External Debt as % of GNI Debt	Service as % of Exports
High-Income Economies				
Bahrain	1.00			
Kuwait	0.70			
Oman	0.94			
Qatar	1.00			
Saudi Arabia	0.70			
UAE	1.00			
Upper-Middle-Income Economies				
Libya	0.16			
Algeria	0.16	7129	3.7	0.4
Iraq	—	22588	8.6	5.3 (2021)
Lower-Middle-Income Economies				
Comoros	0.16	368.7	29.5	2.7
Djibouti	0.70	3170	88.5	1.6
Egypt	0.42	163104	35.4	23.2
Jordan	1.00	41204	85.6	21.4
Lebanon	0.45	67109	309.4 (2021)	32.7
Tunisia	0.16	39652	88.0	17.8
Mauritania	0.16	4604	47.4	8.0
Morocco	0.16	64713	50.1	10.1
Low-Income Economies				
Somalia	—	4164	40.1	1.1
Sudan	0.55	22433	44.2	2.9
Syria	0.00	4848	58.8 (2021)	3.1 (2010)
Yemen	1.00	7351	32.6 (2018)	14.6 (2016)

Note: The Financial Openness Index is updated to 2021, and debt-related data is updated to 2022. If 2022 data is missing, the most recently available data has been cited, with the year indicated in parentheses.

Source: Chinn-Ito Financial Openness Index, World Bank International Debt Statistics (IDS) database, World Development Indicators (WDI) database. Data accessed in September 2024.

Chapter 4　Special Report on China-Arab States Financial Cooperation

China and Arab states have formed a complementary relationship in terms of industry and technology, and financial cooperation plays a critical role in promoting the development of trade, infrastructure, and capacity-building projects between the two parties. Thanks to the China-Arab States Cooperation Forum and the "Belt and Road" Initiative, financial collaboration between the two parties has become increasingly close, achieving significant progress and continuous innovation breakthroughs. Arab states are persistently seeking diversified investment markets to the east, are committed to reducing reliance on oil revenues and are optimizing their financial structures. Their willingness to enhance capital allocation in the Chinese market is continually growing; financially strong Arab states are not only important supplemental sources of financing for China's emerging industries but also key partners in furthering the internationalization of the RMB. Looking ahead, there is immense potential for further development in financial cooperation between the two parties.

4.1　Financial Situation in Arab States

4.1.1　Polarization in Financial Development among Arab States

In the international financial sector, the flow of capital transcends national borders. A country's financial system is not isolated; macroeconomic factors such as the sustainability of domestic economic growth, stability of financial policies, and security of the financial system determine the intrinsic driving force for financial development. Equally important, the level of openness to external markets and the country's international reputation influence its capacity to

Chapter 3 Special Report on China-Arab States Investment Cooperation

modernization proposes to accelerate the development of new quality productive forces and further increase the pace of opening up to the outside world. The first China-Arab States Summit was held in December 2022 to mark a new era of China-Arab cooperation, and at the opening ceremony of the Eighth Ministerial Meeting of the China-Arab Cooperation Forum in May 2024, President Xi Jinping pointed out, "On the basis of promoting the eight common actions of China-Arab practical cooperation, we will build five major patterns of cooperation with the Arab side, and push the building of the China-Arab community of a shared future to run at an accelerated pace."[①] The cooperation space between China and Afghanistan has further opened up, whether in the traditional energy, infrastructure, economic and trade fields, or in new fields such as artificial intelligence, investment and financing, new energy, etc., which all reflect the new potential and new momentum of China-Arab cooperation, continue to promote the leapfrog development of China-Arab relations, and will inject a strong impetus to promote the building of the China-Arab community of a shared future.

---

① First, a more dynamic innovation-driven pattern. The second is a larger investment and financial pattern. Third, a more three-dimensional energy cooperation pattern. Fourth, a more balanced pattern of economic and trade reciprocity. Fifth, a broader pattern of humanistic exchanges.

Investment has become the Middle East countries' access to technology, talent, and the idea Middle Eastern people are "rich fools" is unrealistic, Arab's long-lasting business culture makes them more professional, pragmatic, and they will pay more attention to whether the investment will be helpful to the national development strategy.If Chinese enterprises want to expand their businesses to the Middle East, they must have an international vision and cross-cultural competence, and be able to understand each other's ideas.

The "two-way efforts" between China and the Arab states are accelerating. In the past few decades, China-Arab economic relations were dominated by one-way investment from China to Arab states, with huge amounts of petrodollars from Arab states being invested mainly in European and American markets. But in the last two years the situation has changed significantly, China has become an emerging destination for Arab capital, and the two-way investment flow between China and Arabia is basically flat. What is more noteworthy is that this change is not a temporary tactical adjustment, but a long-term strategic shift, behind both political reasons and economic considerations.① Looking ahead, the trend of China-Arab investment boom and cooperation will continue. The intensifying political and economic cooperation between China and Arab states is the objective result of the superposition of various factors, including global geopolitical developments, China's huge economic development potential, the diversification and transformation of Arab states, the global energy transition, the highly complementary economic and industrial structures of China and Arab states, as well as China's longstanding and relative friendship and identification with Middle Eastern countries.These trends will continue and deepen in the coming years. At present, China's economy is facing both internal and external pressures and structural factors superimposed on the Chinese enterprises have more incentives to develop new markets in the Middle East. The "China Solution Plus Local Production Capacity" is conducive to a win-win situation for China's investment in the Middle East.②

At present, development, reconciliation and cooperation and balanced diplomacy have become the priority of Arab governments, and Chinese

---

① Niu Xinchun, "Arab states' investment surge in China has both economic and political accounts," *China Daily*, April 2,2024.
② Li Mingzhu, "Deepening Middle East Investment: Chinese Solution Plus Local Production Capacity Achieves Win-Win," *Securities Times*, March 13, 2024.

Chapter 3 Special Report on China-Arab States Investment Cooperation

Sino-Arab cooperation. For Middle Eastern capital, these games may increase the risk of uncertainty and political costs of its investment in China. The impact of US-China relations on the high-tech sector is particularly significant. In the long term, changes in US-China relations present both challenges and opportunities for Middle Eastern capital to invest in China. The "decoupling" of the U.S. and the West from China has led to increased downward pressure on China's foreign investment and capital markets. Arab states are increasingly aware of the potential risks of dollar hegemony. In order to promote its industrial diversification and get rid of dependence on the United States , Arab financial capital increased its investment in China. Optimistic about China's huge potential for economic development, it accelerates "Looking east" to "Going to east". In addition, Arab states have high investment thresholds and tend to favour European standards, and Chinese enterprises are facing fierce competition from Europe, America, India, Japan, South Korea and other emerging economies.

It is important to set reasonable expectations for enterprises that are considering investing in Arab states. At the same time, due to significant cultural differences, investors need to be alert to possible cognitive biases and potential risks during the decision-making process. Chinese companies face the following four main risks. First, political risk, which is often reflected in the political stability of the host country. Second, policy and legal risk, the development of an industry is closely related to the support of policies and laws. Therefore, the stability of policies and laws plays an important role in determining the long-term development opportunities and risks, as well as integrating and optimizing the allocation of resources. At the same time, the legal system in the Arab region is different from the civil law system and the common law system, and overseas enterprises should avoid falling into the circle of past experience. Third, we should take into consideration the mounting uncertainties caused by the commercial risk, exchange rate risk and other changes to the domestic enterprises. Fourth, compliance risk. Chinese enterprises face a series of challenges in the process of "going overseas", such as overseas market entry strategy, tax planning, cost control, cultural integration, localization, data security compliance and so on. Although Arab sovereign wealth funds are seen as a superior alternative to U.S. LPs (limited partners), in reality, their current investment focus is still in Europe and the U.S., and the amount of money invested in China is not commensurate with its attractiveness to Chinese GPs.

that China will host the second China-Arab Summit in China in 2026. Arab people are full of expectations, believing that the China-Arab States Summit will further lead the building of the Arab-Chinese community with a shared future to move forward.

3.3.2 New Challenges for China-Arab States Investments Cooperation

At present, China's development is faced with a complex and severe international environment and the arduous and heavy task of domestic reform, development and stability. With weak momentum in global economic growth, sticky inflation, frequent geopolitical conflicts, international trade friction and other issues, insufficient effective domestic demand, greater pressure on business operations, and more hidden risks in key areas, the promotion of stable economic operation faces many difficulties and challenges. At the same time, Arab states are also facing greater downside risks and uncertainties, including the escalation of the Palestinian-Israeli conflict and the continuation of the armed conflict in the Sudan, the Red Sea crisis, the surge in the debt crisis, the reduction in oil production and tight fiscal policies, the high cost of living and slow growth rates. Affected by gloomy global growth prospects, trade and geopolitical tensions, industrial policy adjustments and supply chain reshaping, the international investment climate will remain challenging in 2024.

The new challenges to China-Arab investment cooperation are mainly in the areas of geopolitics, international competition, and integration into mainstream international ESG (environmental, social and corporate governance) standards. Uncertainty over the new round of the Palestinian-Israeli conflict and potential military escalation in the region has cast a shadow over the startup ecosystem, prompting a wait-and-see approach by regional and international venture capital firms, and negatively affecting the inflow of foreign investment to Arab states. US-China relations are an important geopolitical factor affecting China-Arab investment cooperation. The tension between China and the US is not only reflected in the political and security fields, but also has an indirect impact on the economic cooperation between the two countries. The United States upholds the cold war thinking, the economic and trade issues "politicization" and "security", and has increased the scrutiny of Arab sovereign wealth funds, especially in the field of high-tech financing projects, financial science and technology, to hamper

Chapter 3　Special Report on China-Arab States Investment Cooperation

progress.[①] On May 30, 2024, as a member of the Political Bureau of the CPC Central Committee and Foreign Minister ,Wang Yi, while attending the 10th Ministerial Meeting of the China-Arab States Cooperation Forum (CASCF), said that since the first China-Arab States Summit, under the guidance of President Xi Jinping and the leaders of the Arab states, the building of the China-Arab community with a shared future has made obvious progress, and the China-Arab relationship is now at its best in history. On May 30, the 10th Ministerial Meeting of the China-Arab States Cooperation Forum (CASCF) was successfully held in Beijing, achieving fruitful results.The meeting adopted three outcome documents, namely the *Beijing Declaration*, *The CASCF Execution Plan for 2024-2026*, and *China-Arab States Joint Statement on the Palestinian Issue*. The execution plan makes plans for the next two years for China and the Arab states to strengthen the construction of the forum mechanism and promote multi-bilateral cooperation in various fields such as politics, economy and trade, investment, finance, infrastructure, resources and environment, humanistic exchanges, aviation and aerospace, education and health, and so on. During the meeting, China also signed a number of bilateral and multilateral cooperation documents with participating countries and the secretariat of the Arab League. President Xi Jinping attended the opening ceremony of the 10th Ministerial Meeting of the China-Arab Cooperation Forum and delivered a keynote speech, proposing four goals and building a "five patterns of cooperation", which triggered a warm response from people from all walks of life in Arab states. China will continue to build a high-quality Belt and Road with the Arab states, injecting fresh impetus into the ancient Silk Road. China will work with Arab states to further strengthen the main axis of energy cooperation and enhance the partnership between energy supply and demand. China welcomes Arab states to invest more in China's development, and will continue to support the implementation of landmark projects and "small but beautiful" projects in Arab states, and work with the Arab side to create a high-tech industrial growth pole with more scientific and technological content.[②] President Xi Jinping announced

---

① Wang Yi, "Being an Action-oriented Practitioner of a Sino-Arab Community of a Share Future," Speech by Wang Yi at the 10th Ministerial Meeting of the China-Arab Cooperation Forum, http://www.chinaarabcf.org/chn/zyfw/202405/t20240531_ 11366647.htm, published on June 8,2024.

② Wang Yi, "Accelerating the Building of a China-Arab Community with a Shared Future for a New era," *People's Daily*, May30, 2024.

but is also an inevitable move that grasps the laws of economic development and conforms to the trend of the times, demonstrating its determination and commitment to share opportunities with the world.

The Arab states have continued to demonstrate their openness to foreign investors, and the overall trend in the investment environment has been favourable. Development has become the first priority of Arab states, and governments have formulated ambitious economic development strategies, introduced a series of preferential policies to attract investment, endeavored to improve the business environment and actively attracted the inflow of foreign investment. According to the *The Investment Climate in Arab Countries 2024* issued by The Arab Investment and Export Credit Guarantee Corporation (Dhaman) in July 2024, the volume of capital inflows into Arab states over the past three decades increased significantly from an average of USD 6.6 billion from 1994 to 2003 to about USD 45 billion between 2004 and 2013, and then declined slightly to USD 44.6 billion from 2014 to 2023. The Arab states' share in total FDI inflows attracted by developing countries averaged 5.7 percent between 2004 and 2013 (reaching 7.8 percent in 2023)[1]. Currently, the Arab states' attraction of FDI is characterized by two features: firstly, the increasing share of investment from the global South; secondly, the areas attracting FDI have become more diversified, and in addition to the traditional areas of energy and infrastructure fields, new energy, big data, artificial intelligence, artificial satellites and other fields have become new hot areas for investment in recent years.[2]

China and the Arab states have complementary economic structures. China has a broad consumer market and a complete industrial system, while Arab states are rich in energy resources and their economic diversification is on the rise. They are the natural partners. With the in-depth promotion of the Belt and Road Initiative, China-Arab economic and trade cooperation is expanding, and cooperation in green economy and high-tech fields is ushering in new development.

Building a China-Arab community with a shared future has made positive

---

[1] Dhaman, *The Investment Climate of Arab States in 2024*, July 2024, p. 8.
[2] "Arab States' Magnetism to Attract Foreign Investment Grows," *People's Daily (Overseas Edition)*, August 10, 2023.

Chapter 3   Special Report on China-Arab States Investment Cooperation

has brought new opportunities for investment cooperation. The demographic dividend and economic diversification and transformation of Arab states have brought golden opportunities for Chinese enterprises to go overseas. China is an important engine of global economic growth, possessing advanced technology and experience as well as advantageous production capacity, and it remains an important investment destination for all foreign capital, including Arab capital.

3.3.1   New Opportunities for China-Arab States Investments Cooperation

China will release more opening dividends to the world. The Third Plenary Session of the 20th CPC Central Committee attracted much attention both at home and abroad. *Resolution of the Central Committee of the Communist Party of China on Further Deepening Reform Comprehensively to Advance Chinese Modernization* (hereinafter referred to as the *Resolution*), deliberated and adopted at the meeting, is tightly focused on the theme of Chinese modernization and has made a comprehensive deployment of comprehensively deepening reforms. With a total of more than 300 important reform initiatives, the *Resolution* has further elaborated China's propositions and proposals, and conveyed China's ideas and Chinese voices to the world. The *Resolution* also proposes that all these reform tasks should be completed by 2029, and the dividends of the system will be further released.This will bring new opportunities and new impetus to the Chinese economy. The development of new quality productive forces has become an important driver of economic growth, and one important aspect of this is the construction of a modernized industrial system. A key focus of this meeting is to expand China's high-level opening up to the outside world. The *Resolution* makes special arrangements for opening up to the outside world, proposing that opening up is the distinctive mark of Chinese modernization, and that it is necessary to adhere to the basic state policy of opening up to the outside world, to promote reform through opening up, and to build a higher level of a new open economic system. At present, economic globalization is facing huge challenges, and it is the common responsibility of all countries to oppose unilateralism and protectionism, and maintain the global economic order and the security and stability of the industrial chain and supply chain. China's promotion of high-level opening up to the outside world not only comes from the successful practice of opening up to promote reform and development,

Middle Eastern countries have begun to accelerate the layout of Chinese assets due to the need for industrial diversification. Middle Eastern capital investing in the secondary market may be more for financial returns. However, sovereign wealth funds, whether they invest directly or as LPs (limited partners), pay more attention to whether the invested companies are helpful to their own countries' industries. For example, the Abu Dhabi Sovereign Wealth Foundation focuses on new energy, cutting-edge technology, new materials and healthcare.

Arab capital will continue to enhance its layout in China. As Niu Xinchun, executive director of the China Institute for Arab Studies at Ningxia University, said, "Getting rid of the over-dependence on oil, getting rid of the single dependence on the United States, and embracing emerging countries, emerging industries and emerging markets are the root causes of the Arab countries' investment redirection."[①] This strategic shift will last for decades, and with China's huge potential for economic development as the world's second-largest economy, its increasingly perfect business environment, and its growing investment attractiveness, Arab countries' investment in China is bullish in the long term.

3.3 Opportunities and Challenges for China-Arab States Investment Cooperation

At present, changes unseen in a hundred years are advancing. The world has entered a new period of turbulence and change, and the complexity, severity and uncertainty of the external environment are on the rise. Political, economic, legal, security, public opinion, and operational risks are superimposed, so the situation faced by the development of outward investment and cooperation is still intricate and complex. At the same time, the fundamentals of China's long-term economic improvement have not changed, and the industrial structure has been optimized and upgraded; new quality productivity has given rise to new business forms, new modes and new kinetic energy, thus its international influence, appeal and shaping power have been continuously enhanced, and the relevant countries are eagerly looking forward to sharing the dividends of China's development, which

---

① Niu Xinchun, "Arab States' Investment Surge in China Has Both Economic and Political Accounts," *China Daily*, April 2, 2024.

invest, including renewable energy, electric vehicles and battery technology. In November 2022, PIF announced it would partner with Foxconn to launch its first electric vehicle brand, Ceer, and build a one million square metre factory there. A month later, new energy vehicle company Enovate announced that it would set up a joint venture with Saudi company Sumou Holding to jointly invest USD 500 million in Saudi Arabia to set up a manufacturing and R&D base for new energy vehicles. In June 2023, CYVN Holdings, the investment arm of Abu Dhabi's sovereign fund, made a strategic investment in Nio by way of a targeted issuance of new shares and a transfer of old shares strategic investment totalling approximately USD 1.1 billion, becoming the majority shareholder with a 7 percent stake. Currently poorly run Hiphi, Evergrande ,as well as Xpeng , Pony.ai , CH-AUTO, BeyonCa and Enovate , have all been favored by Middle Eastern capital. In June 2024, Saudi Aramco also acquired a 10 percent stake in HORSE, a global powertrain technology company that is a joint venture between Geely and Renault Powertrain Limited, and it will focus on fuel engine and hybrid powertrain technologies. Arab investors hope to bring expertise and technological experience in China's automotive manufacturing sector back to their home countries through investment and the return of their joint venture partners to promote the development of the country's automotive industry. For example, Pony.ai received a USD 100 million investment from Saudi Arabia's New Future City Investment Fund (NIF), and as a condition, Pony.ai needs to set up a joint venture with NEOM, with the Robotaxi fleet, self-driving manufacturing and R&D centre all landing in New Future City. Enovate has set up a joint venture with Sumou Holding, a Saudi company, and plans to set up a new energy vehicle manufacturing and R&D base in Saudi Arabia, with an annual production capacity of about 100000 new energy vehicles.

In terms of the Arab capital investment direction in China, it mainly focuses on new energy, major consumption, biomedicine, information technology and other fields. It tends to allocate to industrial structure related fields as manufacturing, public utilities, raw materials and essential consumption and so on .With the promotion of industrial upgrading strategies in major Arab economies, it is expected to increase the layout in China's advantageous industries such as new energy and advanced manufacturing, which will echo its own development strategy. As the world's second largest economy, China has a huge market and potential consumption capacity attracting investors from all over the world.

Saudi Aramco has become one of the foreign companies with the largest investment in China by way of equity investment, distributed in the upstream and downstream of traditional energy, AI and new energy sectors .[①] Saudi Aramco acquired a 10 percent stake in Rongsheng Petrochemical for 24.6 billion yuan, and signed a contract with Zhejiang Petrochemical to supply 480,000 barrels of oil per day (20-year term). In July 2024 , Saudi Aramco and Rongsheng Petrochemical signed a cooperation framework agreement to mutually acquire a 50 percent stake in each of each other's subordinate entities and to expand the project at a cost of USD 12.2 billion to set up a joint venture with NORINCO and SINCEN, to construct a large-scale refining and chemical joint unit with a capacity of 300,000 barrels per day. Subsequently, Saudi Aramco and the other three petrochemical giants (Sheng Hong Petrochemical, Hengli Group, and Yulong Petrochemical) reached an agreement to purchase 10 percent of Sheng Hong Petrochemical, Hengli Group, and Yulong Petrochemical, aiming to nail down long-term crude oil supplies for downstream refiners and expand their strategic partnership with Sinopec.The cooperation between Chinese refiners and Saudi Aramco is conducive to leveraging the resource advantages of both sides for mutual benefits. At present, Saudi Aramco has the advantage of upstream resources, while China has the advantage of mature supporting industries and a wide range of market advantages, which can not only integrate resources, reduce costs, and gain value in market competition, but also drive the domestic refining and chemical enterprises to usher in the revaluation of asset value. The 260000 tonnes per annum polycarbonate plant invested by Saudi Basic Industries Corporation (SABIC) has commenced commercial operation in Tianjin. Cooperation between Qatar and China in the oil and gas sector is also extending. Qatar Energy and Chinese partners signed two agreements in Beijing: firstly, China State Shipbuilding Corporation Ltd. (CSSC) will build 18 ultra-large liquefied natural gas (LNG) carriers to meet the transport needs of Qatar's expanded northern gas fields; secondly, Qatar Energy and three Chinese shipowners, including China Merchants Shipbuilding (CMS), signed long-term transport charters for nine ultra-large LNG vessels.

  China's new energy vehicles are also areas where Arab capital is keen to

---

① In 2024, Saudi Aramco signed a letter of intent with Geely Group, investing in ZhiPu. etc. laying out the new energy and AI industry.

Chapter 3　Special Report on China-Arab States Investment Cooperation

the requirements of the strategic transformation of the national economy and the continuous development of the Chinese market, PIF has begun to expand its investment to China in recent years. PIF has publicly stated that "China is an important strategic market", and its investment volume in China has reached USD 22 billion, focusing on sustainable development, science and technology, automobiles, health care, recreation and entertainment, and other consumer sectors.[①] PIF's investment in China mainly includes channels such as becoming a mutual fund manager, investing indirectly through Saudi entities, and investing in the secondary market. However, at present, PIF directly allocates fewer assets to China's private equity primary market, and PIF's investment orientation is consistent with the Saudi "Vision 2030" — to promote energy transformation and change Saudi Arabia's economic structure and international image. PIF's investment objective is not only to make profits, but also to realize the strategic objectives of the country.

Mubadala and Abu Dhabi Investment Authority (ADIA), Qatar Investment Authority (QIA) and Kuwait Investment Authority (KIA) have already invested in China, and they plan to tap into the Chinese market in the long term. Mubadala focuses on business models linked to the Internet, and has already invested in companies such as Kuaishou, BOSSZhipin, Xpeng, SenseTime and Ziroom, covering a wide range of sectors, including technology, consumerism, healthcare, and life services. Abu Dhabi Investment Authority invested USD 2.2 billion in Nio in December 2023 through its investment fund CYVN. The Qatar Investment Authority announced in December of the same year that it had invested approximately USD 200 million to subscribe for ordinary shares in Kingdee International, and in June 2024 it announced that it would acquire a 10 percent stake in China's second-largest public fund company, Huaxia Funds, via Primavera Capital Group, to become its third-largest shareholder. Kuwait Investment Authority increased its stake in Shenzhen Airport Group in the fourth quarter of 2022. In the secondary market, Middle Eastern sovereign wealth funds have maintained a high level of activity in China, with large holdings in A-share listed companies through the QFII channel.

Co-operation in traditional energy and petrochemical fields has deepened.

[①] Wu Juanjuan, "Saudi Public Investment Fund: China is an Important Strategic Market," China Fund News, July 12, 2024.

in China, with a focus on the chemical industry, digital technology innovation and new energy. Previously, Middle Eastern funds were mostly involved in China as LPs (limited partners) through head VC/PE (venture capital/private equity). Instead, they are now bypassing investment institutions and directly setting up offices in China, building local investment teams and conducting direct investment business. Previously, Kuwait Investment Authority (KIA), Qatar Investment Authority (QIA) and Abu Dhabi Investment Authority (ADIA) have all set up offices in China. In September 2023, Mubadala set up an office in Beijing, and the Saudi Public Investment Fund (SPIF) is also planning to set up an office in Beijing by the end of 2024 or the beginning of 2025 to carry out its direct investment business, following the opening of an office in Hong Kong, China.

Global sovereign wealth funds (SWFs) invested a total of USD 124.7 billion in 2023. Among the top ten SWFs in terms of investment size, five are from Arab states: Abu Dhabi Investment Authority (ADIA), UAE; Kuwait Government Investment Authority (KIA); Saudi Public Investment Fund (PIF); Qatar Investment Authority (QIA); and UAE's Dubai Investment Company (ICD).In 2023, the Saudi Public Investment Fund (PIF), the UAE's Mubadala Investment Company (Mubadala), Abu Dhabi Investment Authority (ADIA), Abu Dhabi Development Holding Company (ADQ) and Qatar Investment Authority (QIA) invested a total of USD 74 billion, accounting for 58.34 percent of total global sovereign wealth fund investments. The Saudi Public Investment Fund (SPIF) invested USD 31.6 billion, ranking first globally. Global SWF data shows that of the nearly USD 89 billion invested by Arab sovereign wealth funds in 2022, USD 51.6 billion went to Europe and North America, with only 1-2 percent going to Asia, mainly China. Up to 2023, the five largest sovereign wealth funds in the Middle East have USD 4.1 trillion in assets under management, of which the cumulative investment in China is about USD 40 billion.[1]

Saudi Arabia's Public Investment Fund (PIF) has made multiple layouts in China. Since its establishment in 1971, PIF has invested in hundreds of companies, with an asset management scale of more than USD 925 billion, and it is an important driver of the Saudi government's "Vision 2030". Attracted by

---

[1] Zhang Chuanjie, "Opportunities and Challenges of Middle Eastern Countries' Investment in China," *World Affairs*, September, 2024.

Chapter 3 Special Report on China-Arab States Investment Cooperation

in 2023.①

In terms of investment stock, by the end of 2023, the stock of Arab states' FDI in China increased to USD 7.29 billion from USD 4.99 billion in 2022, with the top three sources of investment being the UAE (USD4.5 billion, accounting for 61.7 percent of the total), Saudi Arabia (USD 1.89 billion, accounting for 25.9 percent of the total) and Kuwait (USD 0.33 billion, accounting for 4.5 percent of the total). Despite the significant increase in Arab states' direct investment in China, which accounts for 0.5 percent in 2022 to 1.5 percent in 2023. Arab states' direct investment in China is still in its infancy due to its low starting point, and the share of Arab states' direct investment stock in China will only be 0.26 percent in 2023, and it is mainly concentrated in the GCC countries such as the UAE, Saudi Arabia and Kuwait. countries.②

3.2.2 Frequently Planned Big Moves of Arab Investment in China

National sovereign wealth funds, family offices, and corporate investment departments are more common among the Arab capital. The earliest investment in China by Middle Eastern capital can be traced back to 2006, when the Kuwait Investment Authority and the Qatar Investment Authority participated in the subscription of ICBC, the world's largest IPO at that time. In recent years, large entrepreneurs in the Middle East have increasingly favoured investment opportunities in China's new economy. In terms of choosing the investment direction in the Chinese region, Arab Capital has maintained its own long-standing tendency to integrate its own national industrial development plans with China's advantageous industries, focusing mainly on artificial intelligence, biomedicine, new energy and smart cars, while habitually focusing on traditional energy projects (mainly refining and chemical integration projects). In June 2023, at the 10th Entrepreneurs' Conference of the China-Arab States Co-operation Forum, Chinese companies and Middle Eastern investors signed about 30 investment agreements with a total value of USD 10 billion. In March 2024, the president of Saudi Aramco delivered a speech at the first landmark event of "Invest in China", stressing that Saudi Aramco will increase its investment

---

① Ministry of Commerce of the People's Republic of China, *2024 Statistical Bulletin of China's Foreign Investment*, China Commerce and Trade Press, September 2024, p. 28.

② Ministry of Commerce of the People's Republic of China, *2024 Statistical Bulletin of China's Foreign Investment*, China Commerce and Trade Press, September 2024, pp. 27-37.

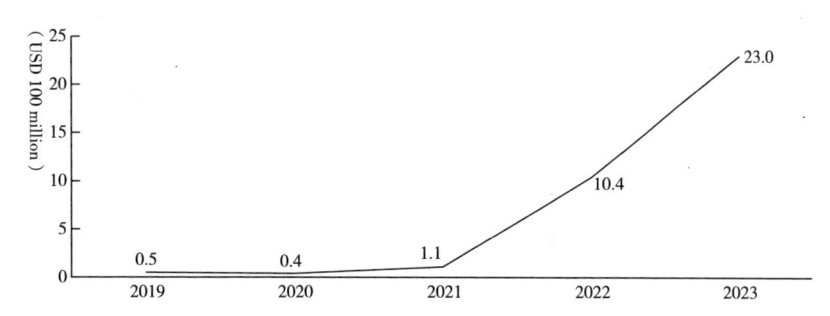

```
                                                          23.0
                                               10.4
       0.5        0.4        1.1
       2019      2020       2021      2022      2023
```
(Y-axis: USD 100 million)

Figure 3.3   Arab Direct Investment Flows to China (2019-2023)

Source: Ministry of Commerce of the People's Republic of China, National Bureau of Statistics, State Administration of Foreign Exchange, *2024 Statistical Bulletin of Foreigh Investment in China*, pp. 27-30.

Between 2003-2022, the UAE has made a substantial investment in China totalling USD 11.4 billion in key sectors such as real estate, financial services, green energy and transport.[①] With the strengthening of relations between the two countries, the UAE's direct investment in China increased sharply to USD 2.2 billion in 2023 from USD 960 million in 2022, a year-on-year increase of 129.2 percent, and accounted for 95.7 percent of the investment flows from Arab states to China.[②] China has become one of the most important investment destinations for Saudi capital. The huge Saudi consortium, which is actually highly concentrated in its movements when it acts abroad, relies on two pillars for its foreign investment - the Public Investment Fund (PIF), the Saudi sovereign wealth fund, and Saudi Aramco, corresponding to capital investment and industrial investment, respectively. After the establishment of a comprehensive strategic partnership between China and Saudi Arabia, Saudi capital gradually began to enter China directly, and the scope of investment has gradually switched from an early focus on Internet unicorns and start-up technology enterprises to real industries such as petrochemicals and new energy. Due to the special investment method of Saudi capital, Saudi direct investment in China is still relatively low. In 2022, the flow of Saudi direct investment into China slightly increased to USD 80 million from USD 0.7 billion in 2021, and USD 90 million

---

① Hussein Bin Ibrahim Al Hamadi, UAE Ambassador to China, "40 Years of Sino-UAE Diplomatic Relations: Towards Global Cooperation and Economic Growth," *China Daily*, 19 June 2024.

② Ministry of Commerce of the People's Republic of China, *2024 Statistical Bulletin of China's Foreign Investment*, China Commerce and Trade Press, September 2024, p. 28.

Chapter 3　Special Report on China-Arab States Investment Cooperation

82.7 percent; the amount of direct investment in China was USD 17.6 billion, a decrease of 16.7 percent. The actual use of foreign investment in high-tech industries amounted to USD 61 billion, down 10.8 percent.[①] China's actual use of FDI amounted to USD 189.13 billion in 2022, a year-on-year increase of 4.5 percent.The UAE ranked 13th among the top 15 countries as a major source of investment in 2022, with USD 960 million of FDI in China, accounting for 0.5 per cent of the total.[②] In 2023, the UAE ranked 10th with USD 2.2 billion in direct investment in China, accounting for 1.4 percent of China's total attraction of foreign investment flows that year.[③]

3.2.1　Significant Increase of Direct Investment of the Arab States in China

In the past two years, Chinese modernization has accelerated the development of new quality productivity, continuously accelerated the pace of reform and opening up, and gradually improved the business environment and attracted more and more foreign investment.At the same time, along with the increase in Arab states' petrodollar income and the great recognition of China's market potential, the trend of Arab states' looking eastward has been highlighted and there has been a substantial increase in direct investment in China. In 2022, China attracted a significant increase in direct investment flows from Arab states from USD 110 million in 2021 to USD1.04 billion in 2022, a year-on-year increase of nearly 10 times (See Figure 3.3). It continued to rise sharply in 2023, reaching USD 2.30 billion, more than tripling year-on-year[④], approaching or even exceeding the scale of Chinese investment in Arab states in recent years. It took only three years for Arab investment in China from scratch to rival Chinese investment in the Arab world.[⑤]

[①] Ministry of Commerce of the People's Republic of China, *2024 Statistical Bulletin of China's Foreign Investment*, China Commerce and Trade Press, September 2024, p.1.

[②] Ministry of Commerce of the People's Republic of China, *2023 Statistical Bulletin of China's Foreign Investment*, China Commerce and Trade Press, September 2023, p.7.

[③] Ministry of Commerce of the People's Republic of China, *2024 Statistical Bulletin of China's Foreign Investment*, China Commerce and Trade Press, September 2024, p.7.

[④] Ministry of Commerce of the People's Republic of China, *2024 Statistical Bulletin of China's Foreign Investment*, China Commerce and Trade Press, September 2024, pp.27-30.

[⑤] Niu Xinchun, "Arab states' investment surge in China has both economic and political accounts", *China Daily*, April 2,2024.

USD one billion investment platform to invest in high-growth companies in the Gulf region and China, with a focus on consumer goods, healthcare, logistics and business services.This follows Investcorp's partnership with Hong Kong-based private investment firm Fung Capital in 2022 to launch a USD 50 billion fund dedicated to investing in medium-sized companies in China's Greater Bay Area.

The focus of Chinese enterprises on investment in the Middle East is closely related to the accelerated pace of internationalization of Chinese enterprises. At the same time, the Middle East states are actively promoting economic diversification, accelerating the pace of energy transition, and reducing dependence on the oil industry, while China continues to maintain its position as the world's top manufacturing and exporting country, and possesses advanced 5G and new energy technologies ,etc., and close cooperation between the two sides is expected to achieve a win-win situation. Seeking closer political, economic and trade relations with China, as well as energy diversification and economic transformation through technological cooperation are the main reasons for Arab states to increase investment in China. In addition, due to the transformation of the global geopolitical and economic landscape, the growth rate of investment in China from Europe and the United States has slowed down, while the economic and trade ties between China and the Arab states have become closer, and the Arab states' investment in China has shown a rapid growth momentum.

3.2 Trends of Investment of the Arab States in China

In 2023, global cross-border investment continued to decline by 1.8 percent after a strong rebound in 2021 and a downturn in 2022. Influenced by multiple factors such as changes in global FDI trends and industrial structure, as well as the reverse globalization of manufacturing, China's overall performance in attracting FDI in 2020-2023 was not weak , but the pressure to fall back from a high level was obvious. In 2023, 53766 new enterprises were established by FDI, up 39.7 percent year-on-year. The actual use of foreign direct investment amounted to USD163.25 billion (down 13.7 percent), accounting for 12.3 percent of the global share, ranking second in the world. Among them, 13649 enterprises were newly set up in countries involved in the Belt and Road Initiative (including those investing in China via some free ports), an increase of

Chapter 3 Special Report on China-Arab States Investment Cooperation

(002493.SZ) and many other A-share listed companies will focus their attention upon the Middle East, to start strategic investment and market layout. Rich in oil resources and new energy, Middle East is becoming China's major clean energy overseas expansion destination. A number of listed companies signed hefty overseas orders, which is hailed as the "two-way efforts" of China's new energy industry, a new round of overseas demand and thirst of Middle East green transition .[①]Three giants of China's new energy industry JinkoSolar, TZE and Envision Group announced that they had signed a strategic agreement with the Saudi Arabia's Public Investment Fund to establish a joint venture in Saudi Arabia to promote the clean energy transition in the Middle East.

The layout of Chinese companies in the Arab states falls into two main categories. One is the pursuit of diversified sources of financing to enhance the activity and financing capacity of the secondary market, and some companies are considering expanding into the Middle East; the other is those companies seeking growth opportunities in overseas markets, which are achieved through successful business and internationalization. In the primary market, several well-known domestic venture capital institutions have established offices in the Arab states with three demands: first, to find more exit channels to meet the challenges of the exit situation in the domestic market; second, to explore new sources of funding, and third is to assist Chinese companies in conducting and expanding their business in the Middle East. [②]In the field of public funds, the Southern East British Saudi Arabia ETF was listed on the Hong Kong Stock Exchange with an initial investment of more than USD1 billion on November 29, 2023. The first two domestic ETFs investing in the Saudi market were listed on the SSE and the SZSE respectively in June 2024, which meets the needs of Chinese investors to lay out the Saudi market and diversify their investments, and also helps to diversify Saudi Arabia's capital market and enhance its attractiveness to foreign investors. Chinese sovereign wealth funds have also been active in the Middle East. In April 2024, China's sovereign wealth fund CIC and Bahrain-based investment company Investcorp. launched Investcorp. Golden Horizon, a

---

① Yang Yang, "Four major clean energy companies announced on the same day to win the heft order of Saudi Arabia," ThePaper.cn. , https://m.thepaper.cn/newsDetail_forward_28098736, July,17, 2024.

② Cai Yuekun, "Nearly 10 Listed Companies Made Official Announcements in This Month, Chinese Enterprises Investing in the Middle East in a Rising Tide," *The Economic Observer*, July 27 , 2024.

conducive to win-win investment and cooperation between China and Arab states. China's investment in the Middle East focuses on the two traditional areas of energy and infrastructure. State-owned enterprises (SOEs) are the mainstay of China's investment in Arab states, focusing on energy, infrastructure and building materials. Private enterprises are also catching up, mainly investing in information technology, manufacturing, construction, trade services and life services. New investment areas including finance, new energy, aerospace, biopharmaceuticals, digital economy and modern agriculture also emerged. The export of China's high value-added production capacity and technological solutions is also bringing positive changes to the Middle East. More and more Chinese enterprises are accelerating their overseas expansion efforts in the Middle East. The world's largest single photovoltaic power plant contracted by Chinese enterprises has been fully completed in the United Arab Emirates. The J&T Express in the United Arab Emirates and Saudi Arabia has opened up the "last kilometre" service for Chinese e-commerce enterprises to go overseas to provide online purchases; and a number of high-tech enterprises such as Huawei Cloud and Sense Time are expanding their business to the Middle East market. LONGi has participated in the construction of a number of photovoltaic power stations in Saudi Arabia's Red Sea New City and New Future City. Meituan has entered the Saudi Arabia market, and domestic gaming companies have laid out the Middle East market in full .[①] The UAE, Saudi Arabia, Egypt and Iraq are the Arab markets where Chinese investment is more active and has greater potential.

Arab states are attracting A-share listed companies with their unique advantages to invest. According to incomplete statistics from the *Economic Observer*, in the first half of 2024, more than 15 listed companies have said that they will increase the width of investment layout in the Middle East region . This number hit a new high in the same period of the last five years. Since July in 2024, POWER CHINA (601669.SH), Maxvision Technology (002990.SZ),Fengguang (301100.SZ), SUNGROW(300274.SZ), JinkoSolar (688223.SH), TZE (002129.SZ), Hainan Mining (601969.SH), Rongsheng Petrochemical

---

① Chinese enterprises take 12 seats in the top 30 of the popularity rankings of the Top Apps in Saudi Arabia, and 13 seats in the top 39 of the popularity rankings of the Top Apps in the United Arab Emirates.

Chapter 3 Special Report on China-Arab States Investment Cooperation

the top three destinations for Chinese direct investment in the Arab states in 2023, followed by Algeria, Egypt and Sudan (See Figure 3.2). In 2023, except for Egypt, China's investment in the above-mentioned Arab countries has achieved a significant increase. The UAE has always been the largest investment destination for China's investment in the Arab states, accounting for 67.3% of the total direct investment flow of China to the Arab states. In terms of investment stock, in 2023, China's direct investment stock in the UAE is USD 8.91 billion, accounting for 41.1 percent of the total direct investment stock of China in the Arab states. It was followed by Saudi Arabia with USD 3.186 billion, Iraq with USD 2.169 billion, Algeria with USD 1.699 billion and Egypt with USD 1.287 billion.[①]

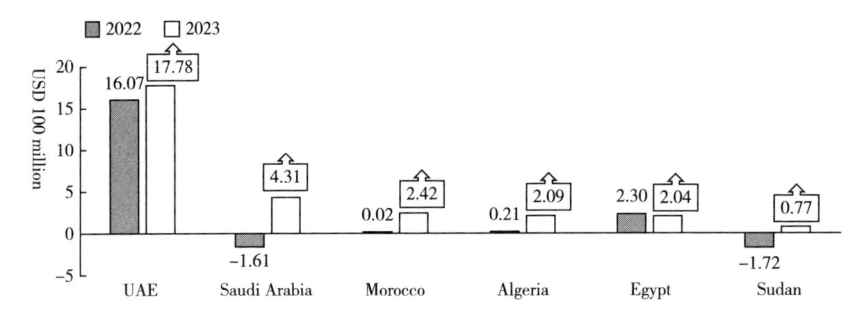

Figure 3.2 Main Destinations of China's Direct Investment Flows to Arab States in 2022 and 2023

Source: Ministry of Commerce of the People's Republic of China, National Bureau of Statistics, State Administration of Foreign Exchange, *2023 Statistical Bulletin of China's Outward Foreign Direct Investment*, China Commerce and Trade Press, pp. 47-54.

China's investment in the Arab states has become increasingly diversified. Since 2023, China and the Arab states have accelerated and deepened their interactions, which have become increasingly comprehensive and diversified. China-Arab relations have moved beyond the economic and trade sphere into a second phase. The flow of capital, talent and technology has become a new theme in the relationship. The "Chinese Solution + Local Production Capacity" is

---

[①] Ministry of Commerce of the People's Republic of China, National Bureau of Statistics, State Administration of Foreign Exchange, *2022 Statistical Bulletin of China's Outward Foreign Direct Investment*, pp. 53-54.

Table 3.2 China's FDI in Major Economies in the World in 2023

Unit: USD 100 million

Economy	Flow			Stock	
	Amount	YoY(%)	Percentage(%)	Amount	Percentage(%)
Globe	1772.9	8.7	100	29554.0	100
Hong Kong, China	1087.7	11.5	61.3	17525.2	59.3
ASEAN	251.2	34.7	14.2	1756.2	5.9
EU	64.8	-6.1	3.7	1024.2	3.5
USA	69.1	-5.2	3.9	836.9	2.8
Austrilia	5.5	-80.4	0.3	347.7	1.2
Arab States	26.4	29.6	1.5	216.9	0.7
Total	1504.7	11.3	84.9	21707.1	73.4

Source: National Bureau of Statistics of China, *2023 Statistical Buletin of Outbound Direct Investment*, China Commerce and Trade Press, p. 30.

GCC countries and Arab countries such as Egypt and Sudan are the main destinations of Chinese direct investment in the Arab states. By the end of 2023, the UAE ranked 10th among the top 20 countries in China's outward FDI flows, with an investment flow of USD 1.78 billion, accounting for 1 percent.[1] The UAE maintains its position as the second largest trading partner, the first investment destination, the first export market, and the third largest engineering market in China among these Arab states as well. Bilateral co-operation has been all-round and extensive, with more than 8000 Chinese-funded enterprises investing in the UAE, covering sectors such as infrastructure, finance and currency, new energy, life sciences, artificial intelligence, etc.[2] Surprisingly, capital and currency-based investment cooperation are becoming a new highlight and growth point. China has become the third largest source of investment in the UAE. In terms of investment flow, the UAE, Saudi Arabia and Morocco were

---

[1] Ministry of Commerce of the People's Republic of China, *2023 Statistical Bulletin of China's Outward Foreign Direct Investment*, China Commerce and Trade Press, September 2024, p.15.

[2] Xinhua, "2024 China-Arab Entrepreneurs Summit Opens in Abu Dhabi," http://www.xinhuanet.com/world/20240516/770238424adf4460b7d43274c12344f8/c.html, May 16, 2024.

Chapter 3 Special Report on China-Arab States Investment Cooperation

3.1.2 Continuous Increasement of the Investment Layout in the Arab States

China's investments are spread all over the world. China's outward FDI flow amounted to USD 177.29 billion in 2023 , an increase of 8.7 percent over the previous year, the stock of outward FDI was USD 2955.4 billion, distributed in 189 countries (regions) around the world, with nearly 80 percent of the flow going to the fields of business services, wholesale and retailing, manufacturing, and finance.[1] In the face of the severe international situation, China has actively been building the new development paradigm, actively participated in the reform and construction of the global investment governance system, deepened investment cooperation under the Belt and Road Initiative, and improved the mechanism of multi-bilateral investment cooperation. According to UNCTAD's *2024 World Investment Report,* global outward FDI flows will be USD 1.55 trillion in 2023, with an end-of-year stock of USD 44.38 trillion.[2] Based on these statistics, China's outward FDI in 2023 will account for 11.4 percent and 6.7 percent of the global investment flow and stock respectively, and will rank third in the global ranking of countries (regions).[3]

Despite the adverse factors such as geopolitical tensions and the global downturn in direct investment, China's direct investment in the Arab states has increased by 29.6 percent year-on-year from USD 2.03 billion in 2022 to USD 2.64 billion in 2023. By the end of 2023, China's direct investment was USD21.69 billion. At the same time, the share of China's direct investment in the Arab states in China's total outward investment flow and stock remains low, at 1.5 percent and 0.7 percent respectively in 2023 (See Table 3.2).

---

[1] Ministry of Commerce of the People's Republic of China, *2023 Statistical Bulletin of China's Outward Foreign Direct Investment*, China Commerce and Trade Press, September 2024, pp. 3-4.
[2] UNCTAD, *2024 Word Investment Report*, June 2024, p.157.
[3] Ministry of Commerce of the People's Republic of China, *2023 Statistical Bulletin of China's Outward Foreign Direct Investment*, China Commerce and Trade Press, September 2024, p.5.

percent from 2022, with an average of 113 jobs created per project.[①] In terms of capital expenditure on greenfield projects, the UAE ranked first with USD 43.7 billion in investment, accounting for 24.1%. In terms of the number of greenfield projects, the U.S. ranked first with 302 projects (capital expenditure of about USD 6.4 billion), accounting for 16.8 percent of the total number of projects. China's greenfield investment in the Arab states ranked fifth in terms of the number of projects (87 projects, or 4.3 percent) and second in terms of capital expenditure (USD 36.4 billion in capital expenditure, or 20.1 percent), but topped the list in terms of job creation, with 65,423 jobs created, or 28.8 percent .(See table 3.1)

Table 3.1 Source Countries (regions) of Greenfield Investment in the Arab States in 2023

Rank	Country	Number	Percentage (%)	Country	Capital Expenditure	Percentage (%)	Country	Job created	Percentage (%)
1	USA	302	15.1	UAE	437	24.1	China	65423	28.8
2	UK	269	13.4	China	364	20.1	USA	16801	7.4
3	India	234	11.7	Hong Kong, China	197	10.9	UAE	13132	5.8
4	UAE	144	7.2	UK	131	7.2	UK	13116	5.8
5	China	87	4.3	Qatar	112	6.2	Germany	12090	5.3
6	France	86	4.3	Ireland	98.9	5.5	France	11362	5.0
7	Germany	65	3.2	USA	64	3.5	Turkey	10453	4.6
8	Italy	60	3.0	Saudi Arabia	63	3.5	Hong Kong, China	9960	4.4
9	Switzerland	56	2.8	India	44	2.4	India	8040	3.5
10	Singapore	55	2.7	France	41	2.2	Italy	6541	2.9

Source: Dhaman, *The Investment Climate in Arab Countries 2024*, July 2024, p.63.

---

① Dhaman, *The Investment Climate in Arab Countries 2024*, July 2024, p.60.

Chapter 3 Special Report on China-Arab States Investment Cooperation

regional situation. According to data from a report released by the United Nations Conference on Trade and Development in June 2024, FDI inflows to Arab states declined by 12.4 percent to USD 67.7 billion in 2023, accounting for 7.8 percent of total inflows to developing countries and 5.1 percent of the global total of about USD 1.33 trillion (See figure 3.1). FDI inflows to Arab states continued to be concentrated in five countries, with a share of over 95 percent. The highest total inflows were to the UAE, which attracted USD 30.7 billion, or 45.4 percent ; followed by Saudi Arabia, which attracted USD 12.4 billion, with a share of 18.2 percent; Egypt, which ranked third with USD 9.8 billion, or 18.2 percent of the total inflows to the Arab states; Bahrain, which ranked fourth with USD 6.8 billion, or 10 percent of the total, then Oman with USD 4.7 billion and Kuwait with USD 2.1 billion, or 7 percent and 3.1 percent of the total, respectively.[①]

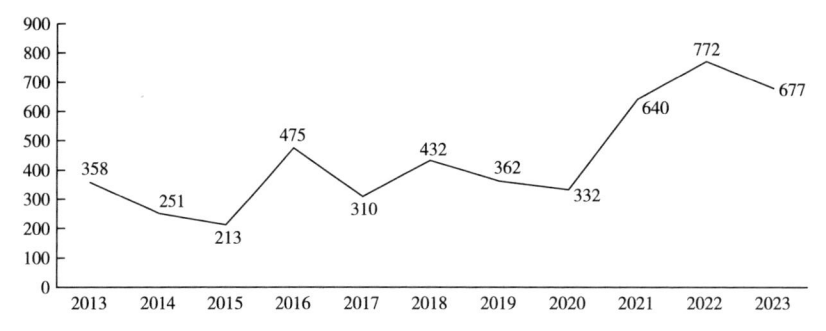

Figure 3.1 Net FDI inflows to the Arab States

Source: UNCTAD, *2024 World Investment Report*, June 2024, pp.152-156.

According to the *The Investment Climate in Arab Countries 2024*, released by the Arab Investment and Export Credit Guarantee Corporation (Dhaman) in July 2024, the Arab states are emerging as a major destination for enterprises and business investors from all sectors seeking growth opportunities. The number of greenfield FDI projects flowing into the Arab states grew by 20.3 percent in 2023 to 2001, with the total capital expenditure of USD181 billion (13.6 percent of global capital expenditure on greenfield projects). Greenfield projects created more than 266000 jobs (8.1 percent of the global total), an increase of 17.7

---

① UNCTAD, *2024 World Investment Report*, June 2024, p.156.

resilient, with the non-oil sectors gradually becoming an important support for economic growth in the region.In recent years, China and Arab states have accelerated industrial and investment cooperation, which has also provided vigorous momentum for economic transformation.[①]China-Arab investment cooperation goes beyond energy and trade and gradually expands to renewable energy, construction, finance, internet technology (e-payment, cloud computing, data centers), and culture (video games and entertainment), becoming more and more comprehensive and diversified.

3.1.1 Continuous Improvement of the Investment Environment in the Arab States

According to *The World Investment Report* released by the United Nations Trade and Development Organization in June 2024, global foreign direct investment (FDI) declined by 2 percent in 2023 to USD 1.3 trillion. For the second consecutive year, global foreign investment (both direct and indirect) fell by more than 10 percent. Tighter financing conditions, uncertain investor sentiment, financial market volatility and tougher regulatory measures were the main reasons for this trend. FDI flows to developing countries fell by 7 percent to USD 867 billion.[②] The report also notes that the international investment environment will remain challenging in 2024. FDI patterns keep changing dramatically due to gloomy growth prospects, trade and geopolitical tensions, industrial policy adjustments and supply chain remodelling , which leads to a more cautious attitude held by those multinational enterprises toward overseas business expansion .

In the process of economic diversification in the Arab states, the continuous improvement of infrastructure, open policies and economic and trade environment are bringing new opportunities for the development of the region. The governments are actively guiding the flow of foreign investment to emerging technologies and strategic industries. Since the first half of this year, international institutions have remained optimistic about the economic growth prospects of the Arab states, despite the impact of fluctuating oil prices and the turbulent

---

① Yang Xiaolin, "Many Middle Eastern Countries Push for Economic Diversification, China-Arab Cooperation Upgrades Quality", *ECONOMIC DAILY,* June 7, 2024.

② UNCTAD, *2024 World Investment Report,* June 2024, p.3.

Chapter 3 Special Report on China-Arab States Investment Cooperation

Global foreign direct investment (FDI) continued to decline in 2023 as a result of slower global economic growth and intensified trade friction. In the process of economic diversification in Arab states, the continuous improvement of infrastructure, open policies and economic and trade environment will bring new opportunities for the development of the region. Economic and trade cooperation is the "ballast" and "propeller" of China-Arab relations, and China has been the largest trading partner of Arab states for many years. Due to the high complementarity of both economic structures and development strategies, cooperation between the two sides in many fields has shown vitality. The Arab states increasingly turn to the East. They actively seek to cooperate with fast-growing economies such as China and India. In recent years, China and Arab states have accelerated production capacity and investment and financing cooperation, and investment cooperation has shown new development characteristics and trends. In 2023, Chinese technology, energy and other enterprises began to develop overseas markets in the Middle East, domestic GP (general partners) have gone to the region to raise capital. Arab capital including Saudi Aramco, sovereign wealth funds and other Arab capitals began to invest in China's primary and secondary markets. All of these moves show that the "two-way efforts" between China and the Middle East is still continuing in 2024. However, due to historical reasons, China-Arab mutual investment is still in its infancy and has great potential for future development.

3.1 Trends of Chinese investment in the Arab States

The process of economic diversification in the Arab states has remained

Intelligent Water-Saving," establishing two international joint labs for water-saving irrigation and training Arab technical personnel. These innovations have been widely applied in arid regions of Oman, the UAE, and Egypt. Notably, the university's water-saving technology, used on the turf for the 2022 Qatar World Cup stadiums, gained global attention.

China-Arab States clean energy cooperation has accelerated, establishing a "dual-wheel" model that integrates oil and gas partnerships with low-carbon energy collaboration to support Arab States in energy transition and sustainable development. In 2023, China and Saudi Arabia launched the Red Sea Integrated Smart Energy Project—the world's largest off-grid smart energy and energy storage initiative. China Energy Engineering Corporation signed green hydrogen development MOUs with Egypt's New and Renewable Energy Authority, while SPIC Huanghe Hydropower Development Company secured similar agreements with companies in Oman and Morocco. Additionally, China National Nuclear Corporation signed peaceful nuclear energy agreements with the UAE, Saudi Arabia, and Algeria.

E-commerce in the Middle East is booming, with rapid market expansion and strong growth momentum. Chinese e-commerce brands like Xiyin have capitalized on this trend, quickly establishing a foothold with innovative business models and technological strengths in the Middle East market. E-commerce giants like JD.com and Alibaba have expanded their reach by partnering with local platforms and upgrading cross-border logistics services. Chinese logistics firms, such as J & T Express, have also made significant progress, boosting regional logistics efficiency and supporting the circulation of Chinese products. Looking ahead, cooperation prospects remain promising as China aims to further support the growth of the Middle Eastern e-commerce market while opening new avenues for its own e-commerce globalization.

Chapter 2 Special Report on China-Arab States Trade Cooperation

seen significant breakthroughs, with notable progress in recent years through closer alignment of development strategies. Within the China-Arab States Technology Partnership framework, both sides have advanced the "Belt and Road" Science, Technology, and Innovation Cooperation Action Plan. On September 21, 2023, the Fifth China-Arab States Technology Transfer and Innovation Cooperation Conference took place in Yinchuan, Ningxia, under the theme "China-Arab States Science and Technology Cooperation: Sharing an Innovative Future." The conference introduced 300 advanced, applicable technologies to Arab States through video, spanning fields such as environmental protection, resource and energy utilization, and pollution control. Additionally, eight key China-Arab States projects in science and technology cooperation and technology transfer were signed collectively.

In 5G communications, Chinese companies have become critical partners in Arab States, holding substantial market shares in Egypt, Saudi Arabia, the UAE, Oman, and Bahrain. China's digital technology supports these countries in accelerating digital transformation across sectors like transportation, energy, education, and AI. A prime example is China's assistance to Saudi Arabia in building data centers and providing internationally leading cloud services. In nuclear energy, Chinese companies have signed peaceful applying nuclear energy agreements with the UAE, Saudi Arabia, and Sudan, encompassing uranium exploration, nuclear fuel supply, and nuclear plant operations and maintenance. In aerospace and satellite cooperation, China and Arab States launched the China-Arab States Beidou Cooperation Forum, establishing the first overseas Beidou Satellite Navigation System center—the China-Arab States Beidou/GNSS Center—in Tunisia. China has signed multiple cooperation agreements in aerospace and satellite technology with Algeria, Sudan, Egypt, and Saudi Arabia, resulting in successful launches of satellites, including Algeria's Alcomsat-1, SaudiSat-5A/5B, and Sudan's first scientific experimental satellite.

Significant progress has also been made in ecological and agricultural technology cooperation. Western provinces like Ningxia and Gansu are leveraging their expertise through the China-Arab States Cooperation Forum and China-Arab States Technology Transfer Center to advance partnerships with Arab States in environmental protection, water conservation, agriculture, and desertification control. Ningxia University has implemented projects such as the "China-Arab States Key Technology Research and Demonstration of Green

2.3.3　Service Trade Cooperation Between China and Arab States

China-Arab States service trade has grown steadily, largely fueled by commodity trade and initiatives like the Belt and Road, the China-Arab States Cooperation Forum, and the China-Arab States Expo. This expansion has driven significant breakthroughs, particularly in finance, high-tech services, new energy development, and e-commerce, highlighting substantial cooperation potential on both sides.

Currency and financial cooperation between the two parties has deepened steadily. Since 2012, China has signed and renewed bilateral currency swap agreements with countries like the UAE, Qatar, and Saudi Arabia. By 2023, the local currency swap agreement between China and Saudi Arabia alone had reached a scale of 50 billion RMB. In December 2022, Yiwu in Zhejiang and Saudi Arabia completed the first cross-border RMB payment transaction. Concurrently, the People's Bank of China, the UAE Central Bank, and other institutions joined the m-CBDC (the multilateral Central Bank Digital Currency) Bridge project to explore the use of central bank digital currencies (CBDCs) for cross-border payments. The share of RMB-settled transactions in China-Arab States trade in goods and services rose from 11% in 2013 to 25% in 2022, signaling increasing acceptance of RMB internationalization in the Middle East. Financial cooperation mechanisms has strengthened steadily, with 16 Arab States joining the Asian Infrastructure Investment Bank (AIIB) by July 2022. In August 2023, Saudi Arabia, the UAE and Egypt joined the BRICS New Development Bank, marking a significant milestone in China-Arab States financial collaboration. Financial institutions on both sides have expanded, with the UAE's First Abu Dhabi Bank upgrading its Shanghai office to a branch in 2022, and branches of the National Bank of Kuwait and Qatar National Bank also operating in Shanghai. Cooperation in capital market continues to grow. In December 2022, the Bank of China's USD300 million bond was officially listed on Nasdaq Dubai, and the Agricultural Bank of China, Industrial and Commercial Bank of China, and Bank of China each issued bonds in Dubai. The UAE's sovereign wealth fund has also actively participated in H-share listings and overseas IPOs of major Chinese banks, including the Bank of China, ICBC, and Agricultural Bank of China, fostering deeper trade and industrial cooperation.

High-tech and technology cooperation between China and Arab States has

Chapter 2 Special Report on China-Arab States Trade Cooperation

base of Arab States, with limited manufacturing and agricultural sectors. The oil industry remains the primary economic pillar, highlighting the need for further diversification and improvement of their industrial systems. In recent years, Gulf oil-producing countries have prioritized economic diversification and modernization, with notable progress led by the UAE in building modern service sectors such as finance, tourism, and exhibiting events. Countries like Egypt and Morocco are also attracting foreign investment to expand light manufacturing and textiles, enhancing their production capabilities. Cooperation between these countries and China has extended beyond trade to investment and finance, fostering productive partnerships that drive capacity building and economic growth.

Table 2.12 Structure of China's Import Products from Arab States (2019-2023)

Unit: USD 100 million

Product Code	Major Product Category	Import Amount in 2019	Import Amount in 2020	Import Amount in 2021	Import Amount in 2022	Import Amount in 2023
27-27	Mineral Fuels and Oils	1205.03	941.58	1524.2	2307.86	1926.25
28-38	Chemical Products	100.44	78.36	106.92	95.73	81.32
39-40	Plastic and Rubber Products	91.24	83.98	92.79	92.05	69.14
25-26	Mineral Products	26.73	20.75	36.54	31.92	31.83
72-83	Metal Products	9.69	14.5	35.6	21.85	22.10
06-15	Vegetables	6.85	10.9	12.39	10.93	11.03
84-85	Machinery and Electrical Products	4.37	4.76	5.91	7.87	9.17
68-71	Ores and Glass	2.46	0.62	2.55	2.03	4.99
50-63	Textiles and Apparel	4.17	3.82	3.76	4.28	4.74
16-24	Food Products	2.19	3.66	5.15	5.27	4.68
01-05	Animal Products	2.16	0.65	1.05	1.47	1.58
90-99	Miscellaneous Manufactures	0.33	0.43	0.68	0.61	0.65
41-43	Leather and Fur Products	0.39	0.28	0.57	0.50	0.54
86-89	Transport Equipment	0.21	0.17	0.19	0.17	0.18
44-49	Wood and Wood Products	0.51	0.94	0.44	0.09	0.15
64-67	Footwear Products	0.05	0.04	0.04	0.04	0.05

Note: China as the reporting entities.

Classification Basis: HS2007.

Source: Data compiled and calculated based on the United Nations International Trade Database.

consistent with 2022 (see Table 2.11).

Table 2.11 Structure of China's Export Products to Arab States (2019-2023)

Unit: USD 100 million

Product Code	Major Product Category	2019 Export Amount	2020 Export Amount	2021 Export Amount	2022 Export Amount	2023 Export Amount
84-85	Machinery and Electrical Products	368.35	387.76	443.16	518.82	590.08
72-83	Metal Products	146.26	144.64	174.41	242.08	244.91
50-63	Textiles and Apparel	192.32	180.57	207.08	204.24	202.30
90-99	Miscellaneous Manufactures	127.02	161.57	187.07	195.10	196.35
86-89	Transport Equipment	72.59	68.04	95.8	137.12	159.94
39-40	Plastic and Rubber Products	76.63	79.47	98.62	121.21	121.68
28-38	Chemical Products	41.89	46.02	85.79	89.10	80.11
68-71	Ores and Glass	57.65	54.52	56.31	67.38	60.84
64-67	Footwear Products	37.68	32.92	41.01	45.81	43.21
44-49	Wood and Wood Products	29.25	27.85	30.53	44.48	40.18
41-43	Leather and Fur Products	18.67	12.31	16.84	20.58	20.71
06-15	Vegetables	14.34	14.84	14.98	15.84	18.03
27-27	Mineral Fuels and Oils	9.93	6.28	9.63	14.50	15.70
16-24	Food Products	9.34	8.5	7.99	11.24	14.45
25-26	Mineral Products	1.13	1.65	1.82	1.38	1.42
01-05	Animal Products	2.14	1.04	1.17	1.27	1.33

Note: China as the reporting entities.

Classification Basis: HS2007.

Source: Data compiled and calculated based on the United Nations International Trade Database.

In 2023, mineral fuels and oils continued to be the top import category, totaling USD192.625 billion and comprising 88.83% of China's total imports from Arab nations—a 16.54% decrease from USD230.786 billion in 2022. Chemical products were the second-largest category at USD8.132 billion, down 15.05% from USD9.573 billion in 2022, followed by plastics and rubber products at USD6.914 billion (see Table 2.12). In summary, apart from the top three import categories, other imported products from Arab States have remained minimal. This trade structure reflects a relatively narrow industrial

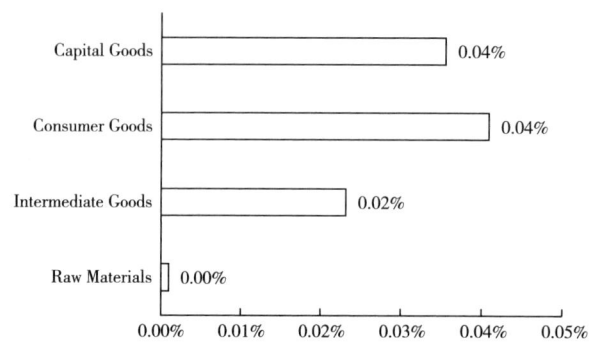

Chapter 2 Special Report on China-Arab States Trade Cooperation

Figure 2.15 Proportion of Four Major Categories of China's Exports to Arab States in 2023

- Capital Goods: 0.04%
- Consumer Goods: 0.04%
- Intermediate Goods: 0.02%
- Raw Materials: 0.00%

Classification Basis: HS2007.

Source: Compiled and calculated based on data from the United Nations International Trade Database.

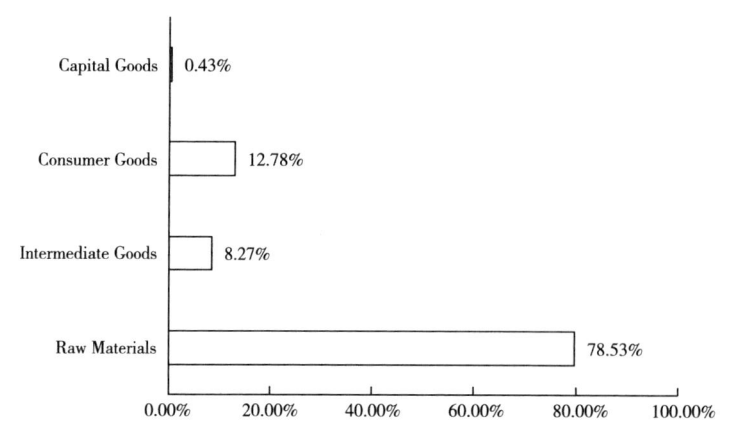

Figure 2.16 Proportion of Four Major Categories of China's Imports from Arab States in 2023

- Capital Goods: 0.43%
- Consumer Goods: 12.78%
- Intermediate Goods: 8.27%
- Raw Materials: 78.53%

Classification Basis: HS2007.

Source: Compiled and calculated based on data from the United Nations International Trade Database.

In specific product categories, China's main exports to Arab States in 2023 included machinery and electrical products, metal products, textiles and apparel, and various manufactured goods, which represented 32.58%, 13.52%, 11.17%, and 10.84% of total exports, respectively, amounting to 68.11% overall. China also exported plastic and rubber products, transport equipment, ores and glass, and chemical products to Arab States. The export structure in 2023 remained

totaling USD170.018 billion, or 78.53% of total imports from the region. Consumer goods followed at USD27.665 billion, making up 12.78%, with intermediate goods and capital goods comprising 8.27% and 0.43% of total imports, respectively. Since 2017, the bilateral trade structure between China and Arab States has remained stable, consistently reflecting these characteristics (see Table 2.10, Figures 2.15 & 2.16).

Table 2.10 Trade Structure of Major Commodity Categories Between China and Arab States (2019-2023)

UNCTAD Product Classification	Trade Volume and Share	2019	2020	2021	2022	2023
Raw Materials	Export Value (USD 100 million)	13.15	13.22	13.78	14.87	17.46
	Share (%)	1.11	1.09	0.94	0.87	0.99
	Import Value (USD 100 million)	1090.45	858.22	1378.79	2047.38	1700.18
	Share (%)	74.94	73.85	75.39	79.37	78.53
Intermediate Goods	Export Value (USD 100 million)	236.02	224.92	327.45	420.57	407.34
	Share (%)	19.86	18.60	22.23	24.87	23.04
	Import Value (USD 100 million)	207.85	185.84	244.54	215.58	178.99
	Share (%)	14.28	15.99	13.37	8.40	8.27
Consumer Goods	Export Value (USD 100 million)	549.84	569.63	636.41	722.68	718.24
	Share (%)	46.27	47.11	43.20	42.73	40.63
	Import Value (USD 100 million)	152.44	113.38	195.40	308.76	276.65
	Share (%)	10.48	9.76	10.68	11.97	12.78
Capital Goods	Export Value (USD 100 million)	389.39	401.29	465.29	533.00	624.56
	Share (%)	32.77	33.19	31.59	31.52	35.33
	Import Value (USD 100 million)	4.35	4.68	5.92	7.84	9.24
	Share (%)	0.30	0.40	0.32	0.30	0.43

Product Classification: Calculated based on the classification by the United Nations Conference on Trade and Development (UNCTAD).

Note: China as the reporting entities.

Classification Basis: HS2007.

Source: Compiled and calculated based on data from the United Nations International Trade Database.

Chapter 2　Special Report on China-Arab States Trade Cooperation

Overall, compared to 2022, there were no significant changes in China's top ten trading partners among Arab States in 2023. The only shift was a swap in rankings between Kuwait and Qatar, with Qatar surpassing Kuwait to become the fifth-largest trading partner in terms of trade volume with China.

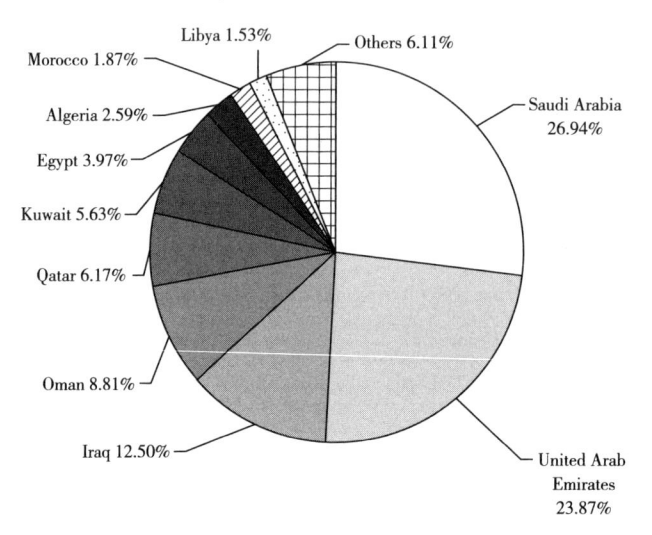

Figure 2.14　Share of Trade Volume of China's Top Ten Trading Partners Among Arab States in Total China-Arab States Trade in 2023

Classification Basis: HS2007.

Source: Data compiled and calculated based on the United Nations International Trade Database.

2.3.2　Bilateral Trade Structure Between China and Arab States

An analysis of the 2023 bilateral trade structure between China and Arab States, based on the United Nations Conference on Trade and Development's classification of trade goods, reveals the following characteristics.

In 2023, China's exports to Arab States were dominated by consumer goods and capital goods, valued at USD71.824 billion and USD62.456 billion, respectively. These categories combined reached USD134.280 billion, accounting for 75.96% of China's total exports to the region, marking a 2.29% increase from 2022. This underscores China's competitive edge and trend toward product upgrading in manufactured goods. Chinese products have met the rising consumer demands of Arab States.

In 2023, China's imports from Arab States were predominantly raw materials, with a trade volume of USD107.216 billion, followed by the United Arab Emirates, with a trade volume of USD94.992 billion. Iraq, Oman, Qatar, Kuwait, Egypt, Algeria, Morocco, and Libya ranked 3rd to 10th, respectively. Trade volumes with China exceeded USD10 billion for Iraq, Oman, Qatar, Kuwait, Egypt, and Algeria, reaching USD49.752 billion, USD35.077 billion, USD24.564 billion, USD22.389 billion, USD15.816 billion, and USD10.304 billion, respectively. Among the top ten, Algeria recorded the highest trade growth with China, increasing by 38.87%.

In terms of exports, China's largest export destination among Arab States in 2023 was the United Arab Emirates, with exports totaling USD55.683 billion, followed by Saudi Arabia at USD42.855 billion. Egypt, Iraq, and Algeria ranked next, with export values of USD14.935 billion, USD14.286 billion, and USD9.458 billion respectively. Among the top ten trading partners, China's exports to Libya saw the highest growth, surging by 64.41%.

In terms of imports, China's largest source in the region was Saudi Arabia, with imports totaling USD64.361 billion, followed by the United Arab Emirates, Iraq, Oman, Qatar, and Kuwait, with imports valued at USD39.309 billion, USD35.466 billion, USD31.279 billion, USD20.928 billion, and USD17.165 billion respectively. Of the top ten trading partners, Morocco recorded the highest import growth, at 7.68% (see Table 2.9).

Table 2.9 Overview of China's Top Ten Trading Partners Among Arab States in 2023

No.	Country	Amount (USD 100 Million)			YoY Growth (%)		
		Import & Export	Export	Import	Import & Export	Export	Import
1	Saudi Arabia	1072.16	428.55	643.61	-7.60	12.81	-17.53
2	United Arab Emirates	949.92	556.83	393.09	-4.31	3.38	-13.43
3	Iraq	497.52	142.86	354.66	-6.79	2.13	-9.95
4	Oman	350.77	37.98	312.79	-13.27	-9.68	-13.69
5	Qatar	245.64	36.36	209.28	-7.47	-8.85	-7.23
6	Kuwait	223.89	52.25	171.65	-28.88	5.12	-35.25
7	Egypt	158.16	149.35	8.81	-13.05	-13.02	-13.59
8	Algeria	103.04	94.58	8.47	38.87	50.70	-26.00
9	Morocco	74.34	64.54	9.80	11.77	12.42	7.68
10	Libya	61.01	39.01	21.99	14.96	64.41	-25.02

Note: China as the reporting entities.

Classification Basis: HS2007.

Source: Data compiled and calculated based on the United Nations International Trade Database.

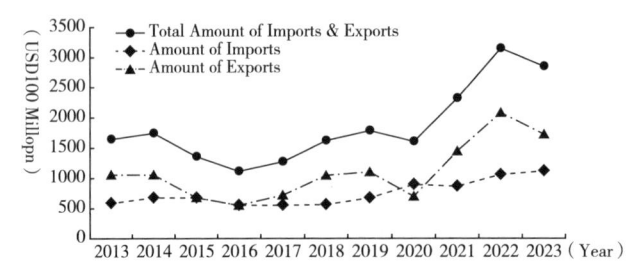

Chapter 2 Special Report on China-Arab States Trade Cooperation

Figure 2.12 Trade Trends Between GCC Countries and China (2013-2023)

Note: GCC countries as the reporting entities.

Classification Basis: HS2007.

Source: Data compiled and calculated based on the United Nations International Trade Database.

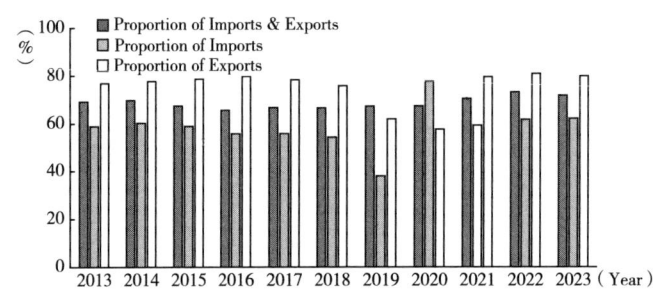

Figure 2.13 Proportion of GCC Countries' Trade in Total China-Arab States Trade (2013-2022)

Note: GCC countries as the reporting entities.

Classification Basis: HS2007.

Source: Data compiled and calculated based on the United Nations International Trade Database.

2.3 Trade Relations Between China and Arab States

China-Arab States trade cooperation is a key aspect of building a China-Arab States community with a shared future in the new era. China is currently the largest trading partner of Arab States, while Arab States are the largest source of energy imports for China.

2.3.1 Trade Relations Between China and Major Trade Partners Among Arab States

In 2023, China's largest trading partner among Arab States was Saudi Arabia,

China and the GCC (Gulf Cooperation Council) countries have strong economic and trade synergies, with the GCC serving as a major energy supplier to China. In recent years, their economic and trade relations have grown closer, with cooperation deepening and expanding. In 2023, trade between the GCC and China totaled USD 285.977 billion, representing 71.83% of China-Arab States trade. GCC exports to China reached USD 173.233 billion, making up 79.90 % of Arab States' exports to China, while imports from China were USD 112.744 billion, accounting for 62.19 % of Arab States' imports from China (see Table 2.8, Figures 2.12 and 2.13). The GCC countries thus play a pivotal role in China-Arab States trade cooperation.

Table 2.8   Overview of Trade Between GCC Countries and China (2013-2023)

Year	Imports and Exports Trade		Imports Trade		Exports Trade	
	Total Amount (USD 100 million)	Proportion (%)	Amount (USD 100 million)	Proportion (%)	Amount (USD 100 million)	Proportion (%)
2013	1653.47	69.21	596.77	58.88	1056.70	76.83
2014	1751.83	69.78	685.90	60.30	1065.93	77.67
2015	1366.15	67.45	678.10	58.98	688.05	78.63
2016	1122.8	65.65	561.73	55.83	561.08	79.75
2017	1280.29	66.77	551.13	55.89	729.16	78.33
2018	1628.91	66.60	572.88	54.40	1056.03	75.83
2019	1792.59	67.34	681.50	38.02	1111.06	61.98
2020	1614.06	67.44	905.78	77.72	708.28	57.68
2021	2328.97	70.53	874.15	59.34	1454.82	79.55
2022	3158.00	73.22	1067.88	61.72	2090.12	80.93
2023	2859.77	71.83	1127.44	62.19	1732.33	79.90

Note: GCC countries as the reporting entities.

Classification Basis: HS2007.

Source: Data compiled and calculated based on the United Nations International Trade Database.

Chapter 2　Special Report on China-Arab States Trade Cooperation

actively responded to the Initiative and fully leveraged their resource endowments and industrial complementarities with China, resulting in rapid growth in trade cooperation. In 2022, bilateral trade between China and Arab States saw a strong surge, with total trade volume exceeding USD431.284 billion for the first time. Arab States' exports to China reached USD258.269 billion, a 41.22% increase compared to 2021, while imports from China amounted to USD173.014 billion, a 17.45% rise from the previous year. In 2023, the total bilateral trade between China and Arab States amounted to USD398.1 billion. Exports stood at USD216.8 billion, a 15.97% decrease compared to 2022, while imports reached USD181.3 billion, a 4.79% increase from the previous year. Although the total trade volume and exports declined in 2023 compared to 2022, on average, the trade growth rate between China and Arab States from 2013 to 2023 was higher than China's overall foreign trade growth rate. Additionally, the average growth rate also surpassed that of China's trade with other Belt and Road Initiative partner countries, indicating strong momentum in bilateral trade growth. Since 2013, China has been the largest trading partner of Arab States. Trade with China accounted for 12.00% of the total trade volume of Arab States, increasing to 27.10% in 2022 and further to 28.02% in 2023 (see Figure 2.11). Their trade partnership continued to be strengthened and enhanced.

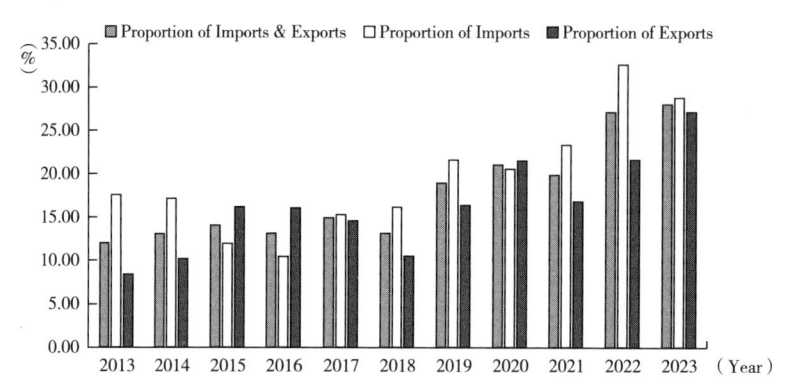

Figure 2.11　Proportion of Arab States' Trade with China in Total Trade Volume (2013-2023)

Note: Arab States as the reporting entities.

Classification Basis: HS2007.

Source: Data compiled and calculated based on the United Nations International Trade Database.

In 2022, the UAE remained the leading importer of service trade, with imports amounting to USD73.21 billion. Saudi Arabia followed in second place, recording USD47.986 billion in imports, while Qatar ranked third with USD23.259 billion. Egypt held the fourth position, and Iraq overtook Kuwait to claim fifth place, with imports of USD22.072 billion and USD12.951 billion respectively. The Gulf Cooperation Council (GCC) continued to dominate as the regional integration organization with the largest share of total service trade imports among Arab States, accounting for 71.96%. Excluding missing data, Comoros recorded the lowest service trade imports in 2022, totaling only USD142 million (see Table 2.7).

Table 2.7　Import Amounts of Arab States' Service Trade (2015-2022)

Unit: USD 100 million

Country	2015	2016	2017	2018	2019	2020	2021	2022
Algeria	110.77	108.81	115.99	104.52	—	80.03	66.64	68.67
Bahrain	65.92	75.3	76.42	79.39	80.83	92.63	102.89	84.32
Comoros	0.83	—	—	—	—	0.97	1.14	1.42
Djibouti	2.30	1.99	—	2.02	6.20	—	—	8.73
Egypt	175.19	170.32	173.99	178.34	209.32	181.99	229.51	200.72
Iraq	126.20	100.37	—	177.85	244.93	137.96	132.55	129.51
Jordan	45.28	45.65	46.70	46.62	47.85	30.10	41.08	45.95
Kuwait	237.96	263.48	285.66	335.67	300.67	189.92	206.75	112.01
Lebanon	136.93	132.80	138.53	143.38	144.49	57.46	—	—
Libya	46.58	28.83	—	—	62.67	—	—	44.09
Mauritania	6.41	6.05	—	—	—	8.45	7.82	9.82
Morocco	79.13	86.04	97.94	92.97	101.84	70.88	85.26	99.59
Oman	102.14	99.46	—	—	—	55.39	—	93.54
Qatar	307.75	315.41	314.27	307.35	354.16	346.98	343.40	232.59
Saudi Arabia	880.36	702.67	768.18	554.77	749.73	538.83	732.81	479.86
Somalia	13.28	13.35	14.52	14.78	—	—	—	21.53
Sudan	17.79	15.07	19.06	6.07	14.23	13.22	13.91	6.00
Syria	—	—	—	—	—	—	—	—
Tunisia	30.76	30.11	29.62	29.41	30.98	23.67	25.83	25.89
United Arab Emirates	818.79	838.39	855	709.87	740.64	595.23	761.06	732.10
Yemen	12.75	—	—	—	—	—	—	14.01

Note: "—" indicates missing data.

Source: Data compiled and calculated based on the WTO (World Trade Organization) website.

2.2.3　The Export Status of Arab States to China

Since the launch of the Belt and Road Initiative in 2013, Arab countries have

Chapter 2　Special Report on China-Arab States Trade Cooperation

In 2022 the top five Arab States in service trade exports were the UAE, Qatar, Saudi Arabia, Egypt and Kuwait. The UAE remained the largest exporter in the region, with service trade exports totaling USD93.472 billion, reflecting a slight decrease of 0.82% from 2021. Qatar moved up one spot to second place with exports reaching USD29.409 billion, representing a substantial growth of 60.30% from the previous year. Saudi Arabia climbed four positions to third, with an export value of USD22.688 billion, showing a remarkable increase of 120.21% compared to 2021. Egypt dropped two places to fourth, with exports amounting to USD16.7 billion, a decrease of 23.73%. Kuwait secured fifth place, rising one spot, with exports totaling USD11.943 billion, an increase of 10.20%. Excluding missing data, Comoros had the lowest service trade exports among Arab States in 2022, amounting to just USD18 million (see Table 2.6).

Table 2.6　Export Amounts of Arab States' Service Trade (2015-2022)

Unit：USD 100 million

Country	2015	2016	2017	2018	2019	2020	2021	2022
Algeria	34.55	34.33	32.61	30.40	—	32	30.25	48.53
Bahrain	91.13	109.98	111.3	119.15	115.78	114.68	132.25	109.37
Comoros	0.84	—	—	—	—	0.68	0.51	0.18
Djibouti	4.55	4.06	—	2.09	11.04	—	—	8.85
Egypt	185.39	136.06	200.33	229.06	209.32	150.53	218.97	167.00
Iraq	62.60	48.35	—	53.06	66.37	38.03	43.73	65.20
Jordan	62.69	60.35	67.20	70.21	79.65	24.59	44.03	21.50
Kuwait	60.56	55.29	51.63	76.17	82.39	72.55	108.38	119.43
Lebanon	159.1	151.93	160.8	152.95	150.68	50.06	—	—
Libya	4.83	0.86	—	—	1	—	—	12.40
Mauritania	2.46	2.70	—	—	—	1.83	1.93	2.33
Morocco	146.74	153.79	172.61	178.94	193.7	138.55	154.61	112
Oman	33.79	36.04	—	—	—	18.30	—	40.70
Qatar	149.97	151.76	177.06	177.80	190.80	194.29	183.46	294.09
Saudi Arabia	144.74	172.53	180.21	173.86	241.82	102.48	103.03	226.88
Somalia	3.55	3.73	3.93	4.05	—	—	—	2.79
Sudan	17.27	15.45	15.17	14.86	13.68	12.30	18.80	1.87
Syria	—	—	—	—	—	—	—	—
Tunisia	32.94	32.49	32.60	36.43	42.73	22.75	27.18	20.1
United Arab Emirates	607.76	655.96	704.97	708.78	734.65	621.38	1018.38	934.72
Yemen	7.28	—	—	—	—	—	—	2.06

Note: "—" indicates missing data.

Source: Data compiled and calculated based on the WTO (World Trade Organization) website.

US$26.537 billion, a 60.10% decrease compared to 2021. In terms of export structure, Arab States' service trade exports are primarily concentrated in transportation (34.02%), trade-related services (26.94%), insurance and financial services (17.13%), and telecommunications, computer and information services (10.26%). For the import structure, Arab States' service trade imports are largely composed of transportation services (36.85%), insurance and financial services (25.58%), trade-related services (17.21%), other business services (11.45%), and telecommunications, computer and information services (5.84%).

Table 2.5   Service Trade Volume and Growth Rate of Arab States (2013-2022)

Year	Exports & Imports		Exports		Imports		Trade Balance (USD 100 million)
	Total amount (USD 100 million)	YoY Growth (%)	Amount (USD 100 million)	YoY Growth (%)	Amount (USD 100 million)	YoY Growth (%)	
2013	4220.32	3.5	1324.40	1.4	2895.92	4.5	-1571.52
2014	5268.17	24.8	1792.08	35.3	3476.09	20.0	-1684.00
2015	5029.84	-4.5	1812.73	1.2	3217.12	-7.5	-1404.39
2016	4859.74	-3.4	1825.64	0.7	3034.10	-5.7	-1208.46
2017	4846.27	-0.3	1910.41	4.6	2935.87	-3.2	-1025.46
2018	4810.82	-0.7	2027.81	6.1	2783.01	-5.2	-755.20
2019	5263.35	9.41	2174.80	7.25	3088.54	10.98	-913.74
2020	4018.71	-23.65	1595.00	-26.66	2423.71	-21.53	-828.71
2021	4836.16	20.34	2085.51	30.75	2750.65	13.49	-665.14
2022	4555.35	-5.81	2144.99	2.85	2410.36	-12.37	-265.37

Source: Data compiled and calculated based on the WTO (World Trade Organization) website

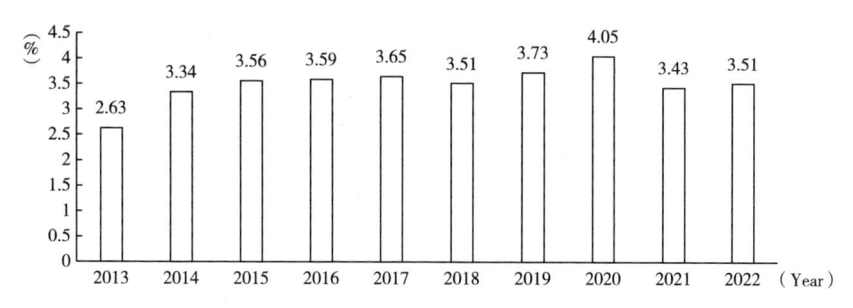

Figure 2.10   Proportion of Arab States' Service Trade Exports in Global Service Trade Exports (2013-2022)

Year	2013	2014	2015	2016	2017	2018	2019	2020	2021	2022
%	2.63	3.34	3.56	3.59	3.65	3.51	3.73	4.05	3.43	3.51

Source: Data compiled and calculated based on the WTO (World Trade Organization) website.

Chapter 2 Special Report on China-Arab States Trade Cooperation

and 4.35% of the total trade volume respectively, making up a combined 33.74% of the total trade (see Figure 2.9). Compared to 2022, there were no changes in the rankings of these top four trading partners.

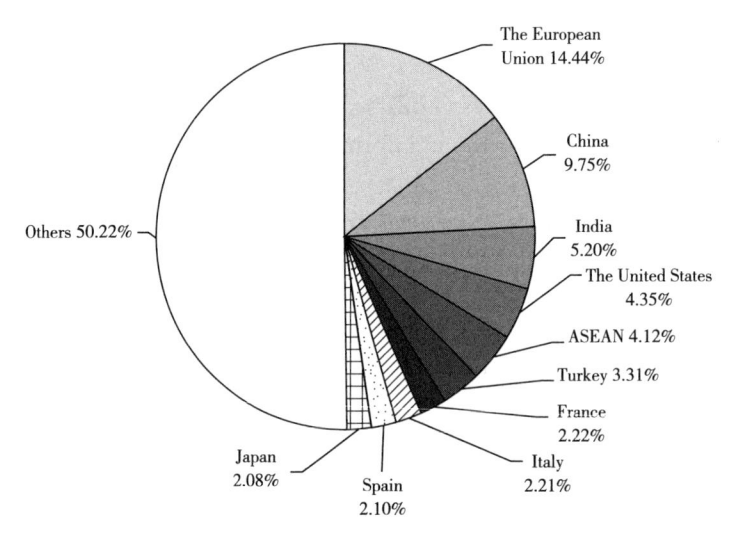

Figure 2.9 Proportion of Arab States' Total Trade with the Top Ten Trading Partners in 2023

Note: Arab States as the reporting entities.

Classification Basis: HS2007.

Source: Data compiled and calculated based on the United Nations International Trade Database.

2.2.2 Overview of Service Trade in Arab States

In 2022 the total value of service trade in Arab countries was USD455.535 billion, with exports amounting to USD214.499 billion and imports reaching USD241.036 billion. Compared to 2021, both the total service trade value and imports saw a decline. The total trade value decreased by 5.81%, while imports fell by 12.37% year-on-year. Service trade exports performed well, growing by 2.85% in 2022 compared to the previous year (see Table 2.5, Figure 2.10). In 2022 Arab States' service trade exports accounted for 3.51% of the global total, a slight increase of 0.08% from 3.43% in 2021, showing overall stability with minimal change.

Since 2013 Arab States have consistently experienced a trade deficit in services. The deficit peaked at USD168.4 billion in 2014, but it has gradually decreased amid fluctuations. By 2022 the service trade deficit had reduced to

Table 2.4 Foreign Trade Volume and Growth Rate of Arab States (2013-2023)

Year	Import & Export Trade		Export Trade		Import Trade		Trade Balance	
	Total amount (USD 100 million)	YoY Growth (%)	Amount (USD 100 million)	YoY Growth (%)	Amount (USD 100 million)	YoY Growth (%)	Amount (USD 100 million)	YoY Growth (%)
2013	19903.86	2.35	12088.30	-1.64	7815.56	9.21	4272.74	-16.76
2014	19208.59	-3.49	11205.41	-7.30	8003.18	2.40	3202.23	-25.05
2015	14392.32	-25.07	7091.00	-36.72	7301.32	-8.77	-210.33	-106.57
2016	13007.05	-9.63	6264.12	-11.66	6742.93	-7.65	-478.80	-127.64
2017	12838.43	-1.30	6744.69	7.67	6093.74	-9.63	650.95	235.95
2018	18598.23	44.86	9974.09	47.88	8624.14	41.52	1349.95	107.38
2019	14080.79	-24.29	7335.58	-26.45	6745.21	-21.79	590.37	-143.73
2020	11398.47	-19.05	5712.96	-22.12	5685.51	-15.71	27.45	-95.35
2021	16607.35	45.70	8749.95	53.16	7857.40	38.20	892.55	3151.52
2022	15916.44	-4.16	8002.35	-8.54	7914.10	0.72	88.25	-90.11
2023	14205.02	-10.75	6667.90	-16.68	7537.13	-4.76	-869.23	-10.85

Note: Arab States as the reporting entities.

Classification Basis: HS2007.

Source: Data compiled and calculated based on the United Nations International Trade Database.

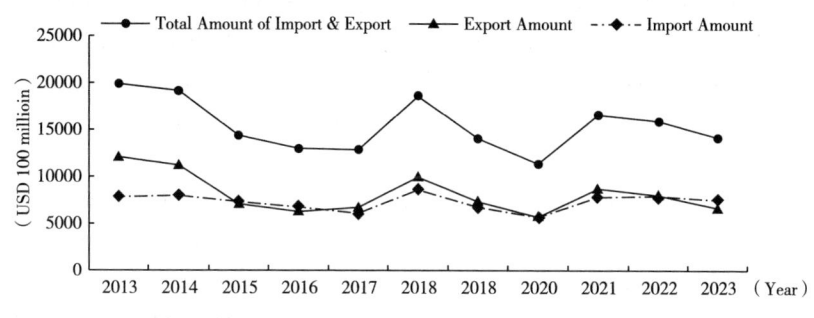

Figure 2.8 Trade Trends of Arab States (2013-2023)

Note: Arab States as the reporting entities.

Classification Basis: HS2007.

Source: Data compiled and calculated based on the United Nations International Trade Database.

The top four trading partners of Arab States in 2023 were the European Union, China, India, and the United States, accounting for 14.44%, 9.75%, 5.20%,

Chapter 2 Special Report on China-Arab States Trade Cooperation

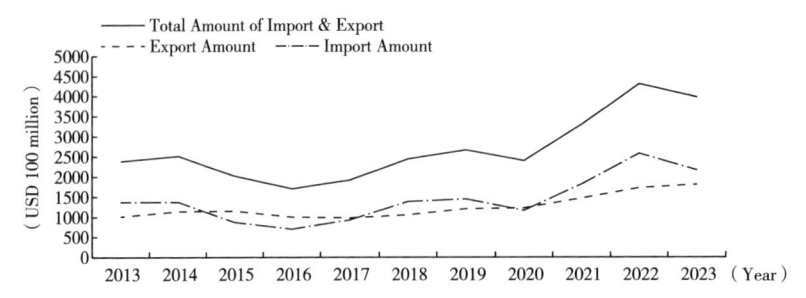

Figure 2.7 Trends of Trade between China and Arab States (2013-2023)

Note: China as the reporting country.

Classification Basis: HS2007.

Source: Data from 2013 to 2022 compiled and calculated based on the United Nations International Trade Database, data of 2023 released by the Ministry of Commerce of the People's Republic of China.

2.2 Trade Status of Arab States with China

2.2.1 Overview of Arab States' Foreign Trade

The foreign trade volume of Arab States peaked at USD1.990386 trillion in 2013. However, their foreign trade declined for four consecutive years from 2014 to 2017 due to falling oil prices and regional instability (see Table 2.4). After falling for several years, oil prices had an increase in 2018, and then declined again in 2019 and 2020 due to ongoing instability and the impact of the COVID-19 pandemic. The total trade volume of Arab States rose sharply in 2021 as the global economy began to recover and oil prices trended upward. The foreign trade volume reached USD1.660735 trillion in 2021, a 45.70% increase compared to 2020, likely driven in part by oil production cuts. In 2022, the total foreign trade volume of Arab States decreased to USD1.591644 trillion, a 4.16% decline from 2021. Exports, in particular, dropped by 8.54% to USD800.235 billion. In 2023 the total foreign trade of Arab States continued to decline, reaching USD1.420502 trillion, a 10.75% decrease from 2022. And exports fell by 16.68% to USD666.79 billion, while imports decreased by 4.76% to USD753.713 billion.

Arab States trade cooperation continued to advance steadily with both sides deepening trade relations. In 2023, China's total trade with Arab States amounted to USD 398.1 billion, a 7.69 % decrease from 2022. Exports to Arab States rose by 4.79 % to USD181.3 billion, while imports dropped by 16.06% to USD 216.8 billion compared to the previous year (See Table2.3). As shown in Figure 2.7, although China's total trade and imports with Arab States saw a slight decline in 2023, the overall trend of China-Arab States trade remains upward with fluctuations. Despite global challenges from unprecedented changes and the pandemic, China-Arab States cooperation has continued to thrive with China remaining the Arab States' largest trading partner for several consecutive years.

Table 2.3　China's Trade Volume with Arab States (2013-2023)

Year	Import & Export Trade		Export Trade		Import Trade		Net Export Value	
	Total amount (USD 100 million)	YoY Growth (%)	Amount (USD 100 million)	YoY Growth (%)	Amount (USD 100 million)	YoY Growth (%)	Amount (USD 100 million)	YoY Growth (%)
2013	2388.97	7.41	1013.52	11.03	1375.45	4.88	-361.93	-9.20
2014	2510.51	5.09	1138.21	12.30	1372.30	-0.23	-234.09	-35.32
2015	2025.41	-19.32	1150.40	1.07	875.01	-36.24	275.38	117.64
2016	1710.29	-15.56	1006.74	-12.49	703.56	-19.59	303.18	10.10
2017	1917.57	12.12	986.73	-1.99	930.84	32.30	55.89	-181.57
2018	2445.67	27.57	1053.10	6.70	1392.57	49.60	-339.47	-807.39
2019	2662.01	8.85	1205.21	14.44	1456.82	4.61	-251.61	-25.88
2020	2393.43	-10.09	1227.99	1.89	1165.44	-20.00	62.55	124.86
2021	3301.90	37.96	1473.12	19.96	1828.78	56.92	-355.66	-668.60
2022	4312.84	30.62	1730.14	17.45	2582.69	41.22	-852.55	139.71
2023	3981.00	-7.69	1813.00	4.79	2168.00	-15.97	-355.00	-58.36

Note: China as the reporting country.

Classification Basis: HS2007.

Source: Data from 2013 to 2022 compiled and calculated based on the United Nations International Trade Database，data of 2023 released by the Ministry of Commerce of the People's Republic of China.

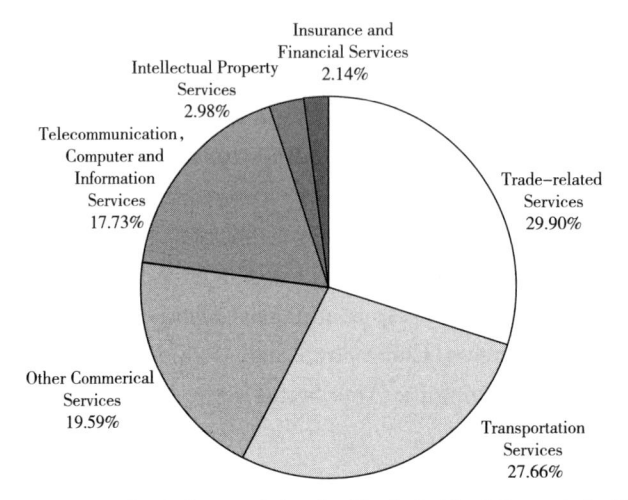

Figure 2.5　China's Share of Service Trade in Total Exports in 2022

Note: China as the reporting country.

Source: Data compiled and calculated based on the WTO (World Trade Organization) website.

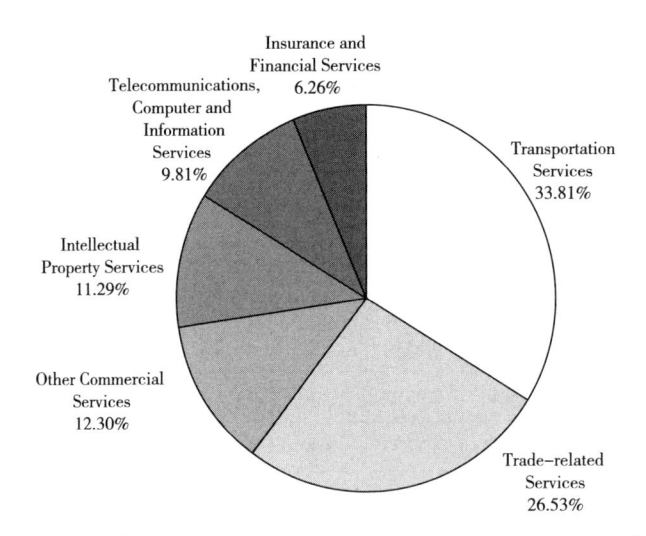

Figure 2.6　China's Share of Service Trade in Total Imports in 2022

Note: China as the reporting country.

Source: Data compiled and calculated based on the WTO (World Trade Organization) website.

2.1.3　Basic Status of China's Trade to Arab States

Despite the complex and volatile foreign trade environment in 2023, China-

Table 2.2　China's Service Trade: Import and Export Volumes with Growth Rates (2013-2022)

Year	Imports & Exports Trade		Exports Trade		Imports Trade		Net Exports Value	
	Amount (USD 100 million)	YoY Growth (%)	Amount (USD 100 million)	YoY Growth (%)	Amount (USD 100 million)	YoY Growth (%)	Amount (USD 100 million)	YoY Growth (%)
2013	5376	11.3	2070	2.7	3306	17.5	-1236	55.08
2014	6520	21.3	2191	5.9	4329	30.9	-2138	72.98
2015	6541	0.3	2186	-0.2	4355	0.6	-2169	1.45
2016	6616	1.1	2095	-4.2	4521	3.8	-2426	11.85
2017	6957	5	2281	8.9	4676	3.4	-2395	-1.28
2018	7822	12.4	2636	15.5	5186	10.9	-2550	6.47
2019	7839	0.2	2832	7.4	5007	-3.5	-2175	-14.71
2020	6617	-14.9	2806	-0.9	3811	-23.9	-1005	-53.79
2021	8335	24.9	3922	39.8	4413	25.8	-491	-51.14
2022	8477	1.7	4543	15.8	3934	-10.8	-609	24.03

Source: Data compiled and calculated based on the WTO (World Trade Organization) website.

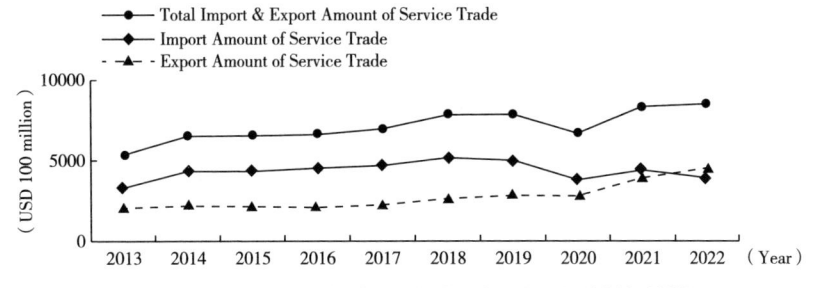

Figure 2.4　Trends in China's Service Trade (2013-2022)

Source: Data compiled and calculated based on the WTO (World Trade Organization) website.

2.1.2　China's International Trade in Services

In 2022, China's service trade achieved steady growth, reaching a record high in scale. As shown in Table 2.2, the total import and export volume of China's service trade from 2013 to 2022 generally followed an upward trend, with the overall scale of continuous expansion in service trade. According to data from the World Trade Organization (WTO), China's total service trade in imports and exports reached USD847.7 billion in 2022, a year-on-year increase of 1.7%. Exports rose by 15.8% to USD454.3 billion, while imports declined by 10.8% to USD393.4 billion. China's service trade primarily focuses on services related to trade, transportation services, other commercial services, telecommunications, computer and information services, intellectual property service, and insurance and financial services. The structure of service trade categories showed little change compared to the previous year.

In terms of exports, trade-related services held the largest share at 29.90%, followed by transportation services at 27.66%, other commercial services at 19.59%, telecommunications, computer, and information services at 17.73%, intellectual property at 2.98%, and insurance and financial services at 2.14%. For imports, transportation services led with 33.81%, followed by trade-related services at 26.53%, other commercial services at 12.30%, intellectual property at 11.29%, telecommunications, computer, and information services at 9.81%, and insurance and financial services at 6.26%.

Due to factors such as its stage of economic development and technological level, China's service trade has been less competitive compared to developed countries in Europe and the United States, resulting in a persistent trade deficit. As shown in Table 2.2, China's service trade deficit was USD123.6 billion in 2013, peaking at USD255 billion in 2018. However, since 2019 the deficit has been narrowing, with the service trade deficit decreasing significantly to USD60.9 billion in 2022 compared to that in 2018.

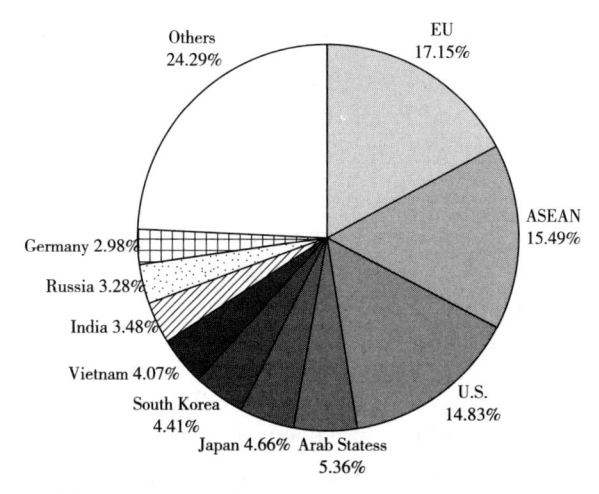

Figure 2.2 Proportion of China's Export Value to Top 10 Trade Partners as a Percentage of Total Exports in 2023

- Others 24.29%
- EU 17.15%
- ASEAN 15.49%
- U.S. 14.83%
- Arab Statess 5.36%
- Japan 4.66%
- South Korea 4.41%
- Vietnam 4.07%
- India 3.48%
- Russia 3.28%
- Germany 2.98%

Note: China as the reporting country.

Classification Basis: HS2007.

Source: Data compiled and calculated based on the United Nations International Trade Database.

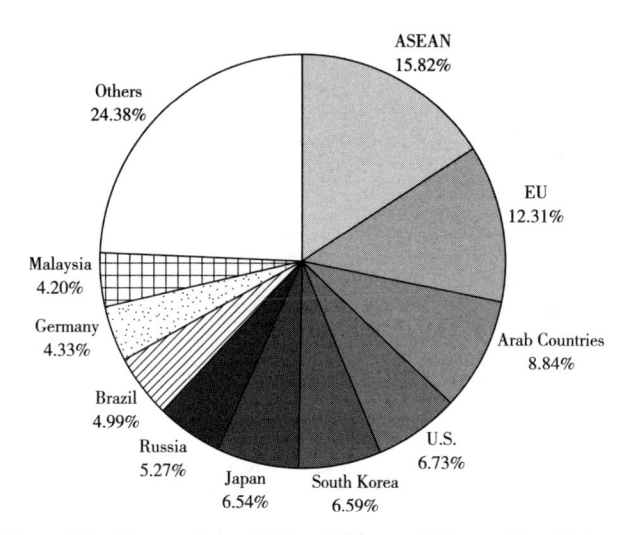

Figure 2.3 Proportion of China's Import Value to Top 10 Trade Partners as a Percentage of Total Exports in 2023

- Others 24.38%
- ASEAN 15.82%
- EU 12.31%
- Arab Countries 8.84%
- U.S. 6.73%
- South Korea 6.59%
- Japan 6.54%
- Russia 5.27%
- Brazil 4.99%
- Germany 4.33%
- Malaysia 4.20%

Note: China as the reporting country.

Classification Basis: HS2007.

Source: Data compiled and calculated based on the United Nations International Trade Database.

Chapter 2 Special Report on China-Arab States Trade Cooperation

Since 2023 China has made significant strides in market diversification, enhancing regional cooperation and expanding trade scale with countries participating in the Belt and Road Initiative. The top ten trading partners for China in 2023 were ASEAN, the European Union, the United States, Arab States, Japan, South Korea, Russia, Vietnam, Australia and Germany. The trade volume with these partners accounted for 75.31% of China's total trade. Specifically, trade with ASEAN, the EU, the U.S., and Arab States comprised 15.63%, 15.11%, 11.43%, and 6.82% of the total trade volume respectively, making up a combined 48.99%. Compared to 2022, Arab States remained to be China's fourth-largest trade partner, while Russia rose to the seventh.

China's largest export destination remains the European Union, with ASEAN overtaking the United States for the second place. The U.S., Arab States and Japan rank the third, fourth, and fifth respectively, with Arab States consistently occupying the fourth position. Regarding imports, ASEAN tops the list, followed by the EU, Arab States, the U.S., South Korea, Japan, Russia, Brazil, Germany, and Malaysia. Arab States continue to be China's third-largest import trade partner.

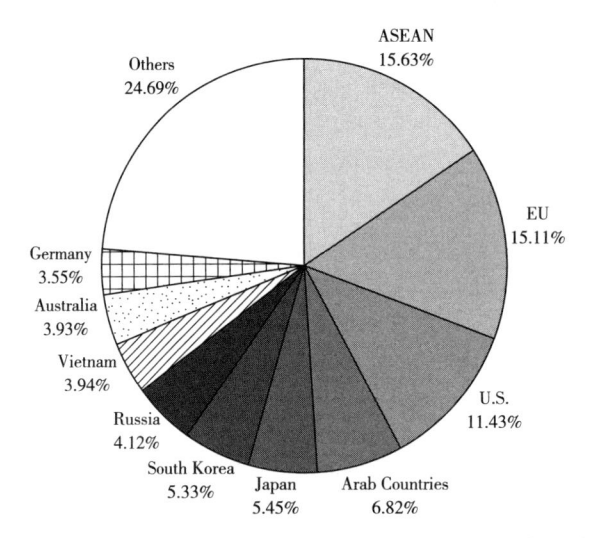

Figure 2.1 Proportion of Total Trade Volume with China's Top Ten Trade Partners in 2023

Note: China as the reporting country.

Classification Basis: HS2007.

Source: Data compiled and calculated based on the United Nations International Trade Database.

positively contributing to the ongoing recovery and enhancement of the national economy.

In 2023, China's total import and export volume reached USD5.8322 trillion, surpassing the U.S. by USD0.75 trillion and maintaining its position as the world's largest goods trader for the seventh consecutive year. Specifically, China's exports totaled USD3.3797 trillion, reflecting a 5.95% year-on-year decline, but it still accounted for 14.2% of the global market, holding steady compared to 2022 and remaining the world's top exporter for 15 years. China's imports amounted to USD2.4525 trillion, down 5.42% with a 10.6% global market share, slightly up from 2022, and ranking second in global imports for 15 years. Amid the challenging global economic recovery, China has maintained overall stability in its market share, demonstrating strong resilience in development.

Table 2.1 China's Foreign Trade Volume and Growth Rate (2013-2023)

Year	Import & Export Trade		Export Trade		Import Trade		Trade Balance	
	Total amount (USD 100 million)	YoY Growth (%)	Amount (USD 100 million)	YoY Growth (%)	Amount (USD 100 million)	YoY Growth (%)	Amount (USD 100 million)	YoY Growth (%)
2013	40014	7.45	22090.07	7.82	17924.51	6.99	4165.56	11.52
2014	41566	3.88	23422.93	6.03	18143.54	1.22	5279.39	26.74
2015	38096	-8.35	22734.68	-2.94	15361.95	-15.33	7372.73	39.65
2016	36855	-3.26	20976.37	-7.73	15879.21	3.37	5097.16	-30.86
2017	39747	7.85	22633.71	7.90	17114.24	7.78	5519.47	8.29
2018	44828	12.78	24942.30	10.20	19886.01	16.20	5056.29	-8.39
2019	45675	1.89	24985.78	0.17	20689.50	4.04	4296.20	-15.03
2020	46462	1.72	25906.01	3.68	20555.91	-0.65	5350.10	24.53
2021	60467	30.14	33623.02	29.79	26843.63	30.59	6779.39	26.72
2022	61867	2.31	35936.01	6.88	25931.14	-3.40	10004.87	47.58
2023	58322	-5.73	33797.48	-5.95	24524.67	-5.42	9272.81	-7.32

Note: China as the reporting country.

Classification Basis: HS2007.

Source: Data compiled and calculated based on the United Nations International Trade Database.

Chapter 2 Special Report on China-Arab States Trade Cooperation

Since 2023 the global economy and demand recovery have lagged behind expectations, leading to disrupted multilateral trade rules and a rise in protectionism. This has prompted a rapid restructuring of global industrial and supply chains, resulting in a volatile and unstable trade pattern. Geopolitical tensions, particularly from the Ukraine crisis, the Israel-Palestine conflicts, and their spillover effects have further complicated the international economic environment, sharply increasing the risks and costs of international trade. Following the shock of the COVID-19 pandemic, China's economic operations have gradually improved. However, cyclical and structural issues have become more pronounced, marked by weak domestic demand and declining external demand. Consequently, China's foreign trade development faces significant challenges and uncertainties. In this complex and challenging environment, China has bolstered its top-level design, refined its foreign trade policy framework, enhanced the vitality and resilience of trade enterprises, and cultivated new competitive advantages and actively driven its transformation. As a result, both the scale and quality of China's foreign trade have steadily improved, leading to new breakthroughs.

2.1 China's Trade with Arab States

2.1.1 Fundamental Overview of China's Foreign Trade

Despite the complex and challenging external environment, China's foreign trade has continued to progress under pressure, demonstrating a stable development trend. It has exhibited strong resilience and innovative vitality,

financed by the special loans in support of industrialization in the Middle East as well as by the credit line for China-Arab financial cooperation. China supports closer cooperation between financial institutions from the two sides, welcomes Arab states to issue panda bonds in China, and welcomes Arab banks to join the Cross-border Interbank Payment System. China is also ready to deepen exchanges and cooperation on central bank digital currency with the Arab side." Financial institutions from both China and Arab countries can explore more flexible and diverse cooperation modes in this regard, providing more convenient and efficient financial service support for pragmatic cooperation in trade, investment, and infrastructure.

Chapter 1 Overall Situation of China-Arab States Economic and Trade Cooperation

and refining. In response to the demand for clean energy transformation in Arab countries, the Chinese side will explore cooperation opportunities in the field of new energy, strengthen cooperation in clean and low-carbon energy technologies such as hydrogen energy, energy storage, wind power, photovoltaics, and smart grids, as well as cooperation in localized production of new energy equipment, and jointly promote the transformation and upgrading of the energy structure to achieve green and sustainable development for both parties.

President Xi Jinping further stated that "China will build with the Arab side ten joint laboratories in such areas as life and health, AI, green and low-carbon development, modern agriculture, and space and information technology. We will enhance cooperation on AI to make it empower the real economy and to promote a broad-based global governance system on AI. We also stand ready to build with the Arab side a joint space debris observation center and a Beidou application, cooperation and development center, and step up cooperation in manned space mission and passenger aircraft." With this framework, China will continue to strengthen "industry-academia-research" integrated cooperation with Arab countries in the fields of digital economy such as cross-border e-commerce, smart cities, and information and communication, as well as high-tech fields such as artificial intelligence, biopharmaceuticals, aerospace, and promote common development in high-tech fields between China and Arab countries.

In terms of mutually beneficial economic and trade ties, President Xi Jinping put forward that "China will continue to implement vigorously the development cooperation projects with a total worth of RMB 3 billion yuan. It stands ready to accelerate the negotiations on bilateral and regional free trade agreements and advance the dialogue mechanism for e-commerce cooperation. It welcomes active participation of the Arab side in the China International Import Expo, and is willing to expand import of non-energy products from the Arab side, especially agricultural products." Both China and Arab countries will strive to improve the bilateral trade structure and promote balanced trade development; enhance the level of trade liberalization and facilitation, creating broader space for development in bilateral trade and investment.

With regard to investment and finance cooperation, President Xi Jinping said, "We are ready to establish with the Arab side an industry and investment cooperation forum, continue to expand the China-Arab states interbank association, and implement at a faster pace the cooperation projects that are

may transfer and increase the costs of commercial activities such as trade and investment for foreign enterprises in the region, adversely affecting Sino-Arab economic and trade cooperation.

Thirdly, there are risks of external interference. The US Middle East strategy aims to serve great power competition, promoting initiatives such as the "India-Middle East-Europe Economic Corridor (IMEC)" to construct an anti-China encirclement in the Middle East and encouraging multiple Arab countries to decouple from China in areas such as high-tech, military industry and trade, and critical infrastructure. Under US coercion and inducements, some Arab companies have been forced to divest from China and withdraw from the Chinese market. In the next phase, how the US adjusts its Middle East strategy and its strategy to suppress China in the region, and whether regional powers such as Saudi Arabia, the UAE, and Egypt will reduce cooperation with China under the US's carrot and stick policy, will undoubtedly have a non-negligible impact on Sino-Arab economic and trade cooperation, meriting close attention.

1.3.3 Prospects for China-Arab Economic and Trade Cooperation

Looking ahead, the prospects for economic and trade cooperation between China and Arab countries are broad. Both parties will continue to uphold the principle of mutual benefit and win-win cooperation, strengthen trade exchanges and investment cooperation, continuously explore the potential for cooperation in traditional and renewable energy, digital economy, high-tech, and other fields, and improve the trade structure and investment cooperation to achieve high-quality development of bilateral economic and trade cooperation.

In his keynote speech at the opening ceremony of the 10th Ministerial Conference of the China-Arab Cooperation Forum, President Xi Jinping stated, "China will further enhance strategic cooperation with the Arab side on oil and gas, and integrate supply security with market security. China is ready to work with the Arab side on new energy technology R&D and equipment production. We will support Chinese energy companies and financial institutions in participating in renewable energy projects in Arab states with total installed capacity of over 3 million kilowatts." Under this guidance, China will strengthen cooperation with Arab countries in traditional fields such as oil and natural gas, continue to expand imports of oil and natural gas, and enhance cooperation in upstream oil and gas development, engineering services, storage, transportation,

Chapter 1 Overall Situation of China-Arab States Economic and Trade Cooperation

driven development, investment and finance, energy cooperation, mutual benefit for economic and trade ties, and people-to-people exchanges. These frameworks not only coordinate the areas of cooperative strength between the two sides but also further tap into the new potential for China-Arab cooperation, expanding the depth and breadth of cooperation and helping Sino-Arab cooperation continuously achieve new breakthroughs.

1.3.2 Risks and Challenges Facing China-Arab Economic and Trade Cooperation

Looking ahead to 2024, the fundamental complexity and multilateralism of the Middle East situation have not changed, with uncertainty and instability remaining prominent. China-Arab economic and trade cooperation still faces many difficulties and challenges.

Firstly, there are security risks. The new round of Israeli-Palestinian conflict broke out in October 2023 remains unresolved, with lingering impacts and ongoing concerns. Meanwhile, the resurgence of civil war in Sudan, and the stalemates in Yemen and Libya, have led to a continued deterioration of the regional security. In particular, critical shipping routes such as the Red Sea face severe security crises, posing threats to Sino-Arab trade in goods and energy. The protection of China's interests, including investments and the safety of personnel and property in some Arab countries, has become increasingly challenging.

Secondly, there are policy risks. From the perspectives of economic development and social stability, Gulf Arab countries such as Saudi Arabia and the UAE are accelerating economic diversification, but due to relatively low international oil prices, their economic growth has slowed. Egypt, Tunisia, Lebanon, and other countries are struggling with currency depreciation, high inflation, and soaring debt, leading to severe development issues. Morocco has experienced a rare earthquake, and Libya has been hit by hurricanes; the frequent occurrence of natural disasters poses threats to the survival of multiple Arab countries. From the political landscape and social trends, the resurgence of strongman politics in Arab countries is prominent, with intense party factional struggles and accelerated differentiation and combination among various old and new political forces. These overlapping factors have led to an increase in trade and investment protectionism and inward-looking economic policies in Arab countries, with high tax levels and localization requirements for labor, which

development through deepening reforms and expanding openness. Major development strategies such as the "Vision 2030" of the UAE, Saudi Arabia, and Egypt, Qatar's "Vision 2035," Oman and Kuwait's "Vision 2040," and Morocco's "Economic Take-off Plan" continue to be implemented. Arab countries are more determined to improve their trade and investment environments, enhance their openness to the outside world, and advance secular social reforms. Their endogenous development momentum and self-development capabilities are continuously enhanced.

In the coming period, Arab countries will still have strong external demand and internal drive in areas such as infrastructure, energy transition, digital economy, and healthcare. Their high degree of complementarity and fit with Chinese industries will become the driving force and new frontier for high-quality development in Sino-Arab economic and trade cooperation. At the opening ceremony of the 10th Ministerial Conference of the China-Arab Cooperation Forum held in May 2024, President Xi Jinping delivered a keynote speech emphasizing that China is willing to work closely with Arab countries as good partners and in the spirit of equality, mutual benefit, inclusiveness and mutual learning, to build the China-Arab relationship into a benchmark for maintaining world peace and stability, a model for high-quality joint construction of the Belt and Road, a paradigm of harmonious coexistence between civilizations, and a model for promoting global governance[①]. President Xi Jinping also proposed in his speech that China is ready to work with Arab countries on the basis to put in place the "Five Cooperation Frameworks"[②] to step up the building of a China-Arab community with a shared future. The "Five Cooperation Frameworks" align with the common wishes and needs of both China and Arab countries, systematically proposing new initiatives and measures for pragmatic cooperation between China and Arab countries in areas such as innovation-

---

① "Keynote speech by President Xi Jinping at the opening ceremony of the 10th Ministerial Conference of the China-Arab States Cooperation Forum, the State Council People's Republic of China," https://www.gov.cn/yaowen/liebiao/202405/content_6954511.htm, 2024-05-30.

② "Five Cooperation Frameworks": refer to a more dynamic framework for innovation, an expanded framework for investment and finance cooperation, a more multifaceted framework for energy cooperation, a more balanced framework for mutually beneficial economic and trade ties, and a broader framework for people-to-people exchanges. Reference: Xi says China ready to work with Arab side to put in place "Five Cooperation Frameworks", Xinhua News, http://www.news.cn/politics/leaders/20240530/4d0361664d6f4348aeb2f15b7bb17a91/c.html, 2024-05-30.

dates, and Omani aquatic products have successively obtained access to the Chinese market; China and Arab countries have reached an agreement on the protocol for the export of Emirati oysters to China, paving the way for future large-scale trade.

1.3 Trends in China-Arab States Economic and Trade Cooperation

2024 marked the 20th anniversary of the establishment of the China-Arab Cooperation Forum, and the 10th Ministerial Conference of the Forum was held in Beijing. At the conference, the Beijing Declaration was adopted, which reviewed the important consensuses reached at the First China-Arab Summit and the progress in implementing the summit outcomes, and outlined the practical path for advancing the construction of a China-Arab community with a shared future. Additionally, the "Action Plan for the China-Arab States Cooperation Forum 2024-2026" was approved, outlining plans for the next two years to strengthen the forum's mechanism, and promote cooperation in various fields including multilateral and bilateral politics, economy and trade, investment, finance, infrastructure, resources and environment, people-to-people exchanges, aerospace, education, and health. Standing at a new historical starting point, China and Arab countries will continue to deepen economic and trade cooperation and actively promote high-quality joint construction of the Belt and Road, injecting new impetus and writing a new chapter in the development of the China-Arab strategic partnership and the construction of a China-Arab community with a shared future.

1.3.1 New Development Opportunities for China-Arab Economic and Trade Cooperation

Currently, Arab countries are at a historical juncture marked by the overlapping of the "post-America era" and the "post-oil era." With the decline of American influence in the Middle East, the momentum of Arab countries "looking eastward" has become more evident. After years of geopolitical conflicts and ideological confrontations, Arab countries have a more urgent desire for stability and development, prioritizing economic development as their top task and primary concern. They hope to achieve "overtaking on a curve" in industrial

enterprises have provided important support for development strategies such as Saudi Arabia's "Economic Vision 2030" and Algeria's New Algeria. China contributed to several significant development projects, particular in construction and infrastructure, such as the tallest building in Africa within the Central Business District of Egypt's new administrative capital, the world's largest energy storage project in Saudi Red Sea New City, the 1,216-kilometer East-West Highway in Algeria, and power station projects in Missan, SalahAl-din and Rumaila in Iraq, the social housing project in East Sitra, Bahrain, which has greatly improved the living conditions of local residents. In addition, China's Beidou Satellite Navigation System provides quality application services to Arab countries, facilitating local people in transportation, precision agriculture, land surveying and mapping, environmental monitoring, and other fields. Companies such as Huawei actively participate in the construction of telecommunications infrastructure such as 5G networks in countries like Egypt, and leverage artificial intelligence, information and communication technology, and other technologies to help the UAE, Algeria, and other countries build smart cities and engage in international digital industry cooperation.

1.2.6 Continuous Optimization of Trade Structure

Through joint efforts by China and Arab countries, the scale of trade has continued to expand, and the commodity structure has become increasingly rational. High-value-added goods from China, such as electromechanical products and high-tech products, have become increasingly popular in Arab markets. In 2023, China's exports of the "new three items" (electric vehicles, lithium batteries, and solar products) to Arab countries totaled USD 4.8 billion, up 10.4% year-on-year, marking a new growth point in China-Arab trade. Among them, exports of solar cells and lithium batteries increased by 21.3% and 6.6% respectively, while electric vehicle exports grew by 32.7%. Statistics from Jordanian customs show that nearly half of the imported cars in 2023 were electric vehicles, 80% of which were produced in China.

China has actively expanded imports of non-oil and gas products from Arab countries. In 2023, China imported USD120 million worth of fruits and vegetables from Arab countries, up 21.1% year-on-year, with Arab specialty agricultural products such as Egyptian citrus continuing to sell well in the Chinese market. Currently, Egyptian mangoes, Emirati camel milk, Saudi dried

Chapter 1 Overall Situation of China-Arab States Economic and Trade Cooperation

other countries, effectively contributing to the diversification of local industries. CMOC Group plans to invest USD 1.5 billion to build a 500,000-tonne electrolytic aluminum project in Saudi Arabia, while GCL Group plans to jointly invest RMB 16 billion with Saudi Arabia to launch a granular silicon project, both pending approval from the Saudi government. In April 2023, Huaxin Cement completed the acquisition of a 59.58% stake in Oman Cement Company for USD 190 million and optimized its production organization and processes, significantly increasing Oman Cement Company's production capacity from 4,300 tons per day before the acquisition to 5,400 tons per day.

1.2.5 Steady Progress of Cooperation on Major Infrastructure Projects

Arab countries are among the earliest and most important markets for Chinese enterprises to carry out contracted engineering business. In recent years, to improve people's livelihood and increase employment, Arab countries have generally increased their investment in infrastructure, leading to rapid development in China-Arab cooperation in contracted engineering projects.

Contract values show steady growth. Under the framework of cooperation on infrastructure construction for the BRI, Chinese enterprises have witnessed steady growth in the value of newly signed project contracting contracts in Arab countries. In 2023, the signed contract value amounted to USD 47.2 billion, marking a year-on-year increase of 28.8% and accounting for 17.8% of the total newly signed contracts by Chinese enterprises overseas. Saudi Arabia, Algeria, the UAE, Iraq, and Egypt are the top five markets, with Saudi Arabia ranking first among Arab countries, where the newly signed contract value reached as high as USD16.8 billion, representing a year-on-year increase of 72.6%. Chinese enterprises won the bid for a major real estate project in Riyadh, Saudi Arabia, with a total contract value of USD 2.05 billion, signed an EPC general contracting contract for an Iraqi refinery worth USD 2 billion, and participated in a consortium that won a bid for a USD 1.5 billion petrochemical project in Algeria.

Positive progress has been achieved in key projects. In 2023, Chinese enterprises completed a turnover of USD 27.7 billion in Arab countries, up 9.5% year-on-year, accounting for 17.2% of the total turnover completed by Chinese enterprises overseas. The large-scale projects undertaken by Chinese

in groups." The China-Egypt TEDA Suez Economic and Trade Cooperation Zone has emerged as Egypt's industrial park with the best overall environment, highest investment density, and highest unit output. It has attracted a cumulative investment of 1.8 billion from China, with nearly 150 enterprises setting up operations. Preliminary industrial clusters have formed in areas such as new building materials, petroleum equipment, and high and low voltage electrical appliances, with cumulative sales exceeding USD 4.3 billion and taxes paid to Egypt government exceeding USD 200 million. The zone has directly created more than 5,000 jobs locally and indirectly driven employment for about 50,000 people. Haier has obtained the Gold License from the Egyptian government and invested USD 106 million to build a home appliance eco-park locally. The main construction has been completed, and upon commencing operations in the first quarter of 2024, it will further drive the entire Chinese home appliance industry's upstream and downstream enterprises to go global. Ningxia's first-phase project of the China-Oman (Duqm) Industrial Park in Oman's Duqm Special Economic Zone has a clear focus, prioritizing the oil and gas equipment industry. After an initial investment of USD 6 million, Hong Tong Property, a key enterprise in the park, invested another USD 2 million in 2023 for the second-phase expansion project, adding a new production line for composite oil pipelines. Tianjin Rongheng Group plans to invest USD 2 million in the park to build a project with an annual output of 2,000 special oilfield pumps and has obtained an investment license from the Omani government.

The entities involved in industrial cooperation are becoming more diversified. In 2023, China's industrial investment cooperation with Arab countries featured a collaborative effort between state-owned and private enterprises. China Energy Engineering Corporation, United Energy Group, and China Glass Holdings, among others, signed capacity cooperation agreements with Egypt's Suez Canal Economic Zone, involving key projects such as the construction of potassium chloride plants, with a planned total investment of USD 15 billion. Baoshan Iron & Steel Co., Ltd (Baosteel) held a ground breaking ceremony for a joint venture of steel plate mill project with Saudi Arabia, which was worth of USD 4.154 billion. Companies such as China Jushi, Haier Smart Home, Aotecar New Energy Technology, and Ningbo Aierkelin Electronic Technology invested in production and processing projects for glass fibers, washing machines, automotive parts, and air-conditioning copper pipes in Egypt, Jordan, Morocco, Bahrain, and

Chapter 1 Overall Situation of China-Arab States Economic and Trade Cooperation

New breakthroughs have been achieved in cooperation areas. China UnionPay actively expanded its payment market presence in Arab countries, achieving full coverage of UnionPay card POS terminals and over 90% coverage of ATMs in countries like Qatar. It also promoted the acceptance of UnionPay credit card payments in the public transportation systems of some Arab countries and enrolled Arab commercial banks such as the National Bank of Kuwait as UnionPay members. The Dubai branch of ICBC listed green bonds with a Belt and Road theme on Nasdaq Dubai, while the Dubai branches of Bank of China and China Construction Bank successfully issued USD 534 million and USD 600 million in green floating-rate bonds, respectively. Sovereign wealth funds from Gulf Arab countries expanded their presence in China, with Mubadala Investment Company's Beijing office officially established in September 2023. Sovereign wealth funds from Kuwait, Qatar, Saudi Arabia, and the UAE conducted intensive direct investments and mergers and acquisitions in China, with a total investment amount of USD 2.3 billion throughout the year. In the fourth quarter of 2023, NIF, a fund under Saudi Arabia's NEOM, invested USD 100 million in Pony.ai, while the UAE tech company G42, through its fund CYVN, invested a total of over USD 3 billion in NIO on two occasions. The Qatar Investment Authority announced an investment of approximately USD 200 million to subscribe for ordinary shares of Kingdee International.

1.2.4 Orderly Development of High-Quality Industrial Cooperation

Cooperation in industrial and manufacturing sector is an important component of China's pragmatic cooperation with Arab countries, and it is also a key area for achieving breakthroughs in their collaboration. In recent years, as Arab countries have accelerated their economic diversification strategies and industrialization processes, both China and Arab nations have leveraged important cooperation platforms such as overseas economic and trade cooperation zones established by Chinese enterprises. They have continuously expanded the scope of cooperation and witnessed the emergence of new trends and highlights in cooperation, focusing on the high-quality development of industrial cooperation.

The industrial agglomeration effect is gradually becoming evident. By the end of 2023, China and Arab countries had jointly established over 16 economic and trade cooperation zones, assisting Chinese enterprises in various fields such as light industry, heavy industry, agriculture, and logistics to "go overseas

agreements will play a positive role in facilitating bilateral trade and investment and maintaining financial system stability. The CBUAE and the PBOC signed a *MOU on Strengthening Cooperation in Central Bank Digital Currencies* (CBDCs), deepening cooperation in fintech innovation and CBDCs. The Export-Import Bank of China and the National Commercial Bank of Saudi Arabia completed the first RMB loan cooperation, with loan funds preferentially used to meet the financing needs under the China-Saudi Arabia trade. In October 2023, the Export-Import Bank of China and Bank of Africa Morocco signed a cooperation agreement, actively promoting economic and trade exchanges and financial cooperation through project financing, parallel financing, and trade financing, while strengthening information sharing and personnel exchanges and jointly exploring the use of RMB loans. In terms of capital market cooperation, the Hong Kong Exchange and Saudi Stock Exchange signed an MoU to explore cooperation opportunities in areas such as fintech and dual listing. The Shanghai Stock Exchange and Dubai Financial Market signed an MOU on cooperation, planning to jointly explore and develop ESG (Environmental, Social, and Governance) and sustainable development-related products, as well as cross-border indexes, exchange-traded funds (ETFs), and other financial products.

Financial cooperation has reached a new level. The Chinese and Egyptian governments signed an MOU on debt-for-development cooperation. Bank of China assisted Egypt in successfully issuing RMB 3.5 billion in sustainable development panda bonds. The China Development Bank completed the full disbursement of a RMB 7 billion loan agreement with the Central Bank of Egypt, focusing on supporting special loans for small and medium-sized enterprises in Africa by the National Bank of Egypt and the Bank of Egypt, the 500 KV transmission line project in Egypt, and the China-Egypt TEDA Suez Economic and Trade Cooperation Zone. China Export & Credit Insurance Corporation underwrote the first medium- and long-term insurance policy for a renewable energy power financing project, providing medium- and long-term export buyer's credit insurance support for Oman's Manah II 500 MW photovoltaic power station project. The Saudi Ministry of Finance appointed the Industrial and Commercial Bank of China (ICBC) as the sole lead arranger to raise USD 11 billion for infrastructure construction projects and conducted multiple rounds of negotiations with the Export-Import Bank of China on mixed loan financing for the Land Bridge railway project.

Trade and investment drive technology transfer. Approximately 95% of the traditional energy buses of Kuwait's public transportation are imported from China. The electric buses produced by Kinglong Company of China were officially put into use in Kuwait on January 1, 2023, contributing to the development of local green transportation. In Qatar, over 80% of the pure electric buses are made in China. Chinese enterprises are no longer satisfied with mere trade cooperation and intend to deepen their cooperation with Arab countries in the field of green energy through investment in factories, technology transfer, and other upgraded cooperation models. They hope to play an important role in reducing carbon emissions and promoting energy strategic transformation in Arab countries. Yutong Bus plans to jointly invest USD 20 million with Qatar's public transport company to build a new energy bus assembly plant within the Qatar Free Zone, with a designed annual production capacity of 500 electric buses. In Morocco, Chinese enterprises are actively arranging cooperation across the entire electric vehicle industry chain, involving various links such as battery cathode and anode materials, electrolytes, and separators. Gotion High-Tech has signed a MOU with the Moroccan government to invest USD 6.4 billion in the construction of an electric vehicle megafactory project. CNGR Advanced Material Co., Ltd. plans to build a green new energy industrial park in Morocco and has formed a joint venture with Moroccan partners. Shanghai AEOLON Wind Power has entered the geological survey stage for factory construction. Companies such as CATL and Huayou Cobalt have also begun exploring market potential in Morocco.

1.2.3 Vibrant Financial Cooperation

Financial cooperation is a multifaceted highlight of China-Arab joint efforts in building the BRI. In 2023, China achieved remarkable progress in financial cooperation with multiple Arab countries, providing robust support for pragmatic cooperation across various fields and mutual development between China and Arab countries.

New steps have been taken in mechanism building. In terms of currency swap and RMB clearing cooperation, the Saudi Central Bank, the Central Bank of the UAE (CBUAE), and the People's Bank of China (PBOC) signed new or renewed bilateral currency swap agreements, with swap sizes reaching RMB 50 billion/SAR 26 billion and RMB 35 billion/AED 18 billion, respectively. These

Max class. Leveraging its leading design and construction capabilities, Hudong-Zhonghua Shipbuilding (Group) Co., Ltd. secured all 18 orders for QC-Max LNG carriers, totaling over USD 5.9 billion, making it the largest single order of ships ever won by a single Chinese ship builder.

1.2.2　Green Energy Cooperation as a Highlight

Both China and Arab countries face the challenges of energy structure transformation and green development. Cooperation in the field of green and clean energy not only helps to promote the diversification of their respective energy structures but also contributes to the global effort to address climate change. In 2023, China and Arab countries have continuously expanded their cooperation in clean energy fields such as photovoltaics, wind energy, hydropower, hydrogen energy, and nuclear power, demonstrating the bright prospects of cooperation in this area.

Large-scale cooperative projects are emerging. Photovoltaic power stations and wind power stations built by Chinese enterprises in Arab countries have become the main force in local clean energy supply. The 500-megawatt (MW) photovoltaic power station in Kom Ombo, Egypt, the 500-MW wind power station in the Suez Bay, and the two 500-MW photovoltaic power stations, Manah I and Manah II, in Oman, have started construction as scheduled. The 100-MW photovoltaic power station project in Kairouan, Tunisia, has entered the temporary construction phase. The 2.6-gigawatt (GW) photovoltaic project in Al Shubah, Saudi Arabia, is progressing smoothly. The Abu Dhabi Wind Power Demonstration Project, the Abu Dhabi Al Dhafra Photovoltaic Power Station Project, and the Phase 4 of Dubai's Mohammed bin Rashid Al Maktoum Solar Park have been completed successively. The four units of the Hassyan Clean Coal Power Station in Dubai have been completed and entered the commercial operation stage, while the 34-MW photovoltaic project in Tangier, Morocco, has started commissioning and grid connection. In addition, Chinese enterprises are actively seeking for new projects. China Energy Engineering Corporation Limited and China Southern Power Grid have signed intention agreements with local partners in Egypt on green hydrogen projects and pumped storage projects, respectively. CNPC and China Energy Engineering Group are discussing the formation of a consortium to participate in the bidding for a green hydrogen project in Oman.

Chapter 1 Overall Situation of China-Arab States Economic and Trade Cooperation

Corporation (CNPC), China National Offshore Oil Corporation (CNOOC), and Zhenhua Oil have participated in the development of oilfields in countries like Iraq, the UAE, and Oman, achieving substantial equity production. In November 2023, ExxonMobil sold its stake in the West Qurna-1 oilfield in Iraq, and CNPC became the lead operator of the field, further deepening oil cooperation between China and Iraq. In April and November 2023, Sinopec signed two agreements with Qatar Energy, acquiring a 1.25% equity stake in the eastern expansion of the North Field LNG and a 1.875% equity stake in the southern expansion. This marks the first time that Chinese oil and gas company has entered the upstream LNG development sector in Qatar and will lead to an increase in imports of approximately 11 million tons of LNG per year from Qatar starting from 2028.

Downstream cooperation has seen a noticeable rise. In March 2023, Chinese company Rongsheng Petrochemical and Saudi Aramco signed a strategic cooperation agreement, in which Saudi Aramco acquired a 10% stake in Rongsheng for USD 3.4 billion in cash. Additionally, a package of agreements was signed covering crude oil and raw material supply, crude oil storage, and the sharing of downstream advanced petrochemical technology. Saudi Aramco also signed framework agreements with companies such as Eastern Shenghong and Yulong Petrochemical, expressing interest in acquiring a 10% strategic equity stake in these Chinese private refining and petrochemical enterprises, continuously increasing its efforts to establish an integrated downstream industrial layout in China. In April 2023, the SABIC Fujian Petrochemical Complex, an ethylene project between China and Saudi Arabia kicked off construction, marking the official launch of the project with a total investment of approximately RMB 44.8 billion. Jointly invested and developed by Fujian Energy and Petrochemical Group and Saudi Basic Industries Corporation (SABIC), this project is the province's largest investment to date, with an expected annul ethylene capacity of up to 1.8 million metric tons.

The results of complementary cooperation have been impressive. Hudong-Zhonghua Shipbuilding (Group) Co., Ltd. and Qatar Petroleum have established a good cooperative relationship since 2022. They are currently executing an order for 12 conventional LNG tankers with a carrying capacity of 174000-cubic-meter LNG, worth a total of USD 2.4 billion. In addition, Qatar launched tenders in the second half of 2023 for 44 conventional 174000-cubic-meter LNG carriers and 18 ultra-large LNG carriers of 270000-cubic-meter capacity in the QC-

The bilateral exchange mechanism is becoming increasingly mature. In May 2023, Mr. Zhang Jianhua, Director of China's National Energy Administration, was invited to visit the UAE, Saudi Arabia, and Qatar, where he exchanged in-depth opinions with government departments and company heads in the oil and gas fields. In September 2023, the 7th China-Arab Energy Cooperation Conference was successfully held in Haikou, Hainan Province of China. During the conference, the Chinese and Arab participants exchanged in-depth views on the theme of "Adhering to High Quality and High Standards for Sustainable Development and Creating the Golden Period of China-Arab Energy Cooperation." A report, "Review and Outlook of China-Arab Energy Cooperation" was release during the conference, which comprehensively reviewed the course and achievements of Sino-Arab energy cooperation, summarized experience and lessons learned, analyzed the current situation of China-Arab energy cooperation, and planned future cooperation.

Traditional trade has seen a decline in oil and an increase in gas. Oil and gas trade cooperation has always been the cornerstone of China-Arab trade and economic cooperation. In 2023, China imported approximately 260 million tons of crude oil from Arab countries, a year-on-year decrease of 2.29%, accounting for 47% of China's total crude oil imports globally. Among China's top ten source of crude oil imports, five are Arab countries, including Saudi Arabia (2nd), Iraq (3rd), the UAE (5th), Oman (6th), and Kuwait (9th). In terms of natural gas, China imported 18.98 million tons of liquefied natural gas (LNG) from Arab countries, a year-on-year increase of 10.5%, accounting for 26% of China's total global imports, with a total value of USD 11.89 billion. Qatar has become China's second-largest source of LNG imports, exporting 16.66 million tons of LNG to China, second only to Australia (24.16 million tons). More importantly, the unloading of 65000 tons of LNG from the UAE was completed at the Dapeng LNG Terminal, Guangdong province in May 2023, marking the first import of LNG in RMB settlement, which signifies a substantial step forward in China's cross-border RMB settlement transactions for the oil and gas trade. The Abu Dhabi National Oil Company (ADNOC) signed a 15-year LNG supply contract with ENN Group to supply 1 million tons of LNG annually to China from 2028.

Upstream cooperation has made steady progress. In terms of upstream resource development, companies such as China National Petroleum

2.3 billion, representing a year-on-year increase of 120%. Ninety-nine percent of the new investment came from Gulf Arab countries. Arab countries generally value China's huge market size and have increased their investment in the petrochemical industry. They are optimistic about the market space and development potential of China's high-tech industries and digital economy, and are actively expanding their asset allocation in sectors such as semiconductors, new materials, and renewable energy. The UAE and Saudi Arabia are the most active and significant Arab investors in China. At the corporate level, Saudi Arabian Oil Co., or Saudi Aramco has accumulatively invested more than RMB 100 billion in China, becoming the foreign enterprise with the largest cumulative investment in China.

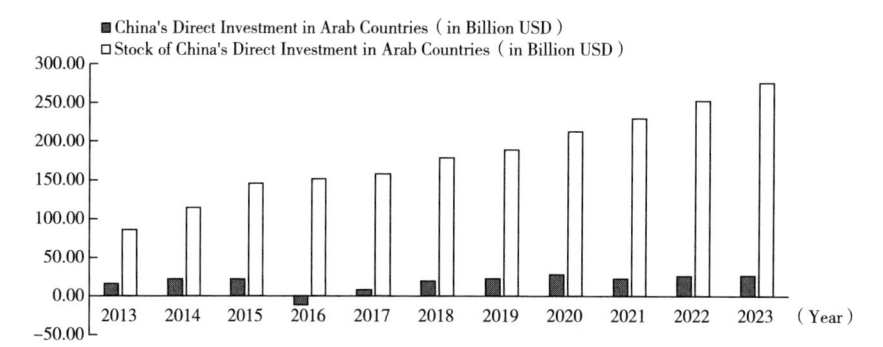

Figure 1.2 Flow and Stock of China's Direct Investment in Arab Countries (2013-2023)

Data Source: Annual Statistical Bulletins on China's Outward Direct Investment published by the Ministry of Commerce.

1.2 Current Trends of China-Arab States Economic and Trade Cooperation

1.2.1 Continuous Consolidation of Oil and Gas Upstream and Downstream Cooperation

In 2023, China and Arab countries worked together to actively implement the outcome of the first China-Arab Summit and the China-Gulf Summit held in December 2022, and continued to expand cooperation in the traditional energy fields of oil and gas, continuously elevating the cooperation levels.

of 4.69%. Despite an overall contraction of 4.6% in China's exports, it achieved export growth to 12 Arab countries, delivering a remarkable performance. In particular, the export growth rates to Saudi Arabia, Algeria, Morocco, Libya, and Mauritania all reached double digits, with Algeria and Libya experiencing significant increases of 52.4% and 68.2%, respectively.

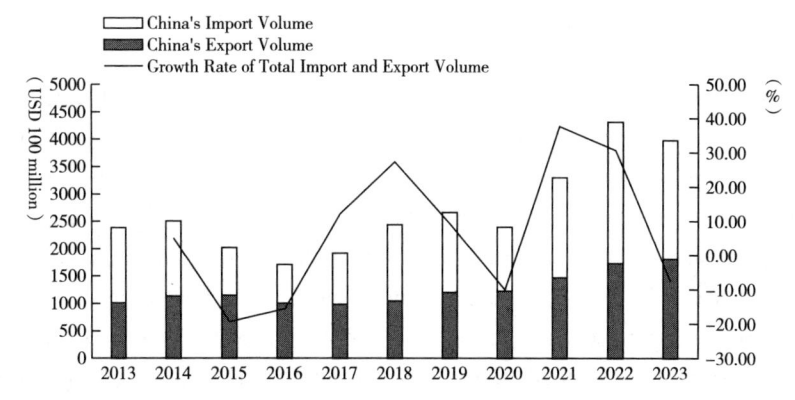

Figure 1.1 Total Import and Export Volume Between China and Arab Countries (2013-2023)

Data Source: General Administration of Customs.

1.1.4 Continuous Growth in Two-Way Investment

In 2023, China's new direct investment across all industries in Arab countries amounted to USD 2.69 billion, marking a year-on-year increase of 2.7%, continuing the trend of growing investment in Arab countries. The UAE, Saudi Arabia, and Egypt were China's top three investment destinations in Arab countries in 2023, with new direct investments of USD 1.789 billion, USD 279 million, and USD 203 million respectively. Additionally, countries such as Algeria, Morocco, and Mauritania have become increasingly attractive to Chinese enterprises for investment, with new investments in 2023 showing year-on-year growth rates of 86.47%, 20.22%, and 79.92% respectively. Oil and gas projects and processing and manufacturing projects invested in by Chinese enterprises in Arab countries have been operating smoothly, and the construction and operation of industrial parks have been steadily advancing.

In 2023, Arab countries increased their actual investment in China to USD

Chapter 1 Overall Situation of China-Arab States Economic and Trade Cooperation

medical healthcare, the Expo premiered exhibitions for State-owned enterprises, smart meteorology, and equipment manufacturing and technology, further showcasing the cooperative advantages between China and Arab countries in economy, trade, energy, infrastructure, and other fields, and achieving fruitful results. The Expo generated 403 cooperation outcomes, with a total planned investment and trade volume reaching RMB 170.97 billion. Among them, there were 50 cooperation projects, 218 investment projects totaling RMB 157.1 billion in investment, and 135 trade projects totaling RMB 13.87 billion in trade. During the Expo, 36 cooperation agreements, including the "China-Qatar Cooperation Agreement on the Construction of 'One Park and Two Centers' and Technology Transfer in Photovoltaic Smart Agriculture" and the "Strategic Cooperation Agreement for Gizan Industrial Cluster", were signed, facilitating 58 projects with a total value of RMB 52.82 billion. Saudi Arabia, as the guest of honor at this Expo, sent a large economic and trade delegation of over 150 people to participate. During this period, China and Saudi Arabia conducted a series of promotion, exchange, and negotiation activities focusing on financial cooperation, energy cooperation, and international cooperation in industrial parks, reaching 15 cooperation projects with a total value of RMB 12.4 billion[①].

1.1.3 Slight Decline in Sino-Arab Trade Volume

Influenced by factors such as the decline in international oil prices, the Sino-Arab trade volume in 2023 amounted to USD 398.1 billion, representing a year-on-year decrease of 7.7%. China has continued to maintain its position as the largest trading partner of Arab countries, with Saudi Arabia, the UAE, Iraq, Oman, and Qatar being China's top five trading partners among Arab countries. In terms of imports, China's imports from Arab countries totaled USD 216.79 billion, a year-on-year drop of 16.06%. Despite a slight decrease of 2.29% in the total volume of crude oil imported from Arab countries, the cumulative value of China's crude oil imports from Arab countries amounted to USD 164.909 billion, a year-on-year decline of 17.25%. On the export front, China exported goods to Arab countries worth USD 181.297 billion, marking a year-on-year increase

---

① "The 6th China-Arab States Expo Secures 403 Cooperation Achievements Totaling Over 170 Billion Yuan", CCTV News, https://news.cctv.com/2023/09/24/ARTIGsUsNVvohybnYmZYYBpR230924.shtml, September 24, 2023.

1.1 General Status of China-Arab States Economic and Trade Cooperation

1.1.1 Cooperation under the Belt and Road Initiative Being Expanded to Cover All Areas

2023 marks the 10th anniversary of the Belt and Road Initiative (BRI). Over the past decade, Arab countries have increasingly become an important strategic fulcrum, a region rich in achievements, and an area with significant growth for the BRI. On October 18, 2023, the Third Belt and Road Forum for International Cooperation was held in Beijing, attended by the Prime Minister of Egypt, the Special Representative of the President of the United Arab Emirates (UAE) and other Arab leaders. On November 29, 2023, a memorandum of understanding (MOU) on jointly promoting the construction of the Belt and Road was signed by China and Jordan, marking that China has signed cooperation agreement on jointly building the Belt and Road with all 22 Arab countries and the Arab League, achieving "full coverage". In addition, the National Development and Reform Commission of China and the Ministry of Foreign Affairs of Bahrain signed a letter of intent on jointly formulating a cooperation plan for the BRI, which would deeply align the BRI with the "Economic Vision 2030" of Bahrain, charting a roadmap for pragmatic cooperation between the two countries in such fields as finance, information and technology (ICT), logistics, advanced manufacturing and renewable energy. It will help promote higher-quality development of bilateral relations.

1.1.2 The China-Arab States Expo, a Bridge and Tie

After a decade of development, the China-Arab States Expo has yielded a series of influential and exemplary achievements in economic and trade cooperation between China and Arab countries, establishing itself as a significant platform for jointly building the BRI between China and Arab states. The sixth China-Arab States Expo, held from September 21st to 24th, 2023, fully resumed offline operations, focusing on implementing the "Eight Joint Actions" for pragmatic cooperation between China and Arab countries and the five key areas of cooperation between China and the Gulf states for the next 3-5 years. Building on its existing exhibitions of emerging materials, branded goods, and

Chapter 1 Overall Situation of China-Arab States Economic and Trade Cooperation

The year 2023 has witnessed a global economic slowdown, fast adjustment of geopolitical landscape, frequent outbreaks of regional conflicts, deterioration of humanitarian situation, and the overlap of traditional and non-traditional security risks such as food, energy, disasters and ecology. This year, the situation in the Middle East was also evolving in a complex way amidst twists and turns. On one hand, diplomatic reconciliations marked by the Saudi-Iranian rapprochement and Syria's reinstatement in the Arab League progressed steadily; on the other hand, the regional conflicts centered on the new round of Palestinian-Israeli conflict continued to escalate. Against the backdrop of intertwined reconciliation and turmoil, led by head-of-state diplomacy, and with the follow-up implementation of the economic and trade outcomes of the First China-Arab States Summit (hereinafter referred to as the "China-Arab Summit") and the First China-Gulf Cooperation Council Summit (hereinafter referred to as the "China-GCC Summit") as the guideline, China's economic and trade cooperation with Arab countries in 2023 achieved steady and healthy development. The trade volume between China and Arab countries remained stable and of high quality, and the two-way investment continued to heat up. Cooperation in infrastructure construction proceeded steadily, while cooperation in emerging fields such as finance, green economy, and digital economy continued to expand and deepen. The economic and trade cooperation between China and Arab countries made an important contribution to promoting the high-quality development of the Belt and Road Initiative and building a new era of the China-Arab community of shared future.

CONTENTS

    8.3   Prospects for China-Arab States Scientific and Technological Cooperation / 167

Chapter 9   Special Report on China-Arab States Cooperation in Ecological and Environmental Governance / 171

    9.1   Current State of the Ecological Environment in the Arab Region / 172

    9.2   China-Arab States Cooperation in Ecological Environment Governance / 176

    9.3   Prospects for China-Arab States Cooperation in Ecological Governance / 183

Chapter 10   Special Report on China-Arab States Cooperation in Tourism / 189

    10.1   Overview of Global Tourism Development / 189

    10.2   Overview of Tourism Development in Arab States in 2023 / 191

    10.3   Progress of China-Arab Tourism Cooperation in 2023 / 195

Chapter 11   Special Report on the China-Arab States Expo / 210

    11.1   Review of the Development of the China-Arab States Expo Since the Joint Construction of the BRI / 212

    11.2   Multiple Development Opportunities under the New Situation of the China-Arab States Expo / 221

    11.3   Thoughts on Successfully Hosting the China-Arab States Expo under the New Situation / 224

    11.4   Paths to Successfully Host the China-Arab States Expo under the New Situation / 227

Chapter 12   Special Report on the Opening up of Ningxia / 231

    12.1   Current Situation of the Promotion of Ningxia's High-Level Opening Up / 231

    12.2   Prospects for Ningxia's Countermeasures for High-Level Opening up / 244

Chronicle of China-Arab States Economic and Trade Cooperation in 2023 / 256

Postscript / 272

Chapter 4 Special Report on China-Arab States Financial Cooperation /072

- 4.1 Financial Situation in Arab States /072
- 4.2 Progress in China-Arab States Financial Cooperation /076
- 4.3 Trends in China-Arab States Financial Cooperation /085
- 4.4 Prospects of China-Arab States Financial Cooperation /088

Chapter 5 Special Report on China-Arab States Agricultural Cooperation /093

- 5.1 Current Situation of Agricultural Development in the Arab States /093
- 5.2 Current Situation of China-Arab States Agricultural Cooperation /097
- 5.3 Prospects for China-Arab States Agricultural Cooperation /109

Chapter 6 Special Report on China-Arab States Energy Cooperation /113

- 6.1 Overview of Arab States' Energy Resources /113
- 6.2 Current Status of Traditional Energy Cooperation Between China and Arab States /121
- 6.3 Current State of New Energy Cooperation Between China and Arab States /125
- 6.4 Prospects for China–Arab States Energy Cooperation /128

Chapter 7 Special Report on China-Arab States Digital Economy Cooperation /132

- 7.1 The Digital Economy Development in Arab States /132
- 7.2 China-Arab States Cooperation in the Digital Economy /142
- 7.3 The Future of China-Arab States Cooperation in the Digital Economy /147

Chapter 8 Special Report on China-Arab States Science and Technology Cooperation /151

- 8.1 Current State of Scientific and Technological Development in Arab States /151
- 8.2 Specific Practices of China-Arab States Technological Cooperation /158

CONTENTS

Chapter 1 Overall Situation of China-Arab States Economic and Trade Cooperation / 001

1.1 General Status of China-Arab States Economic and Trade Cooperation / 002

1.2 Current Trends of China-Arab States Economic and Trade Cooperation / 005

1.3 Trends in China-Arab States Economic and Trade Cooperation / 015

Chapter 2 Special Report on China-Arab States Trade Cooperation / 021

2.1 China's Trade with Arab States / 021
2.2 Trade Status of Arab States with China / 029
2.3 Trade Relations Between China and Arab States / 037

Chapter 3 Special Report on China-Arab States Investment Cooperation / 047

3.1 Trends of Chinese Investment in the Arab States / 047
3.2 Trends of Investment of the Arab States in China / 056
3.3 Opportunities and Challenges for China-Arab States Investment Cooperation / 064

Preface

Cooperation Forum and delivered a keynote speech. He proposed building Five Cooperation Frameworks with the Arab side, accelerating the construction of the China-Arab Community with a Shared Future, which has pointed out the direction and provided the fundamental guidance for China-Arab states cooperation in the next stage. The China-Arab States Expo, as a national-level and international comprehensive exposition, has become an important platform for China and the Arab states to jointly build the "Belt and Road" after a decade of development. It has played a positive role in deepening practical cooperation between China and the Arab states and jointly promoting high-quality development of the "Belt and Road" cooperation. The 6th China-Arab States Expo held in 2023 produced 403 formal cooperations including 50 cooperative projects, 218 investment projects, and 135 trade projects in modern agriculture, clean energy, medical and health care, digital economy and tourism cooperation, with the total value of 170.97 billion yuan.

In view of this, the China-Arab States Research Institute of Ningxia University has organized authoritative experts and scholars in relevant fields to compile the *Development Process of China-Arab Economic and Trade Relations Annual Report 2023*. It introduces the development process and achievements of economic and trade cooperation between China and the Arab states in 2023, and analyzes the existing opportunities and challenges. We hope that this book could provide valuable references for government decision-making departments, scholars, entrepreneurs and students.

Finally, we would like to show our appreciation to all the people who have contributed to the writing, translating, editing and proofreading of this book and also thank the readers for your attention and support.

Li Shaoxian
December 2024, Ningxia

development of the Belt and Road Initiative (BRI) and the implementation of the Three Initiatives(Global Development Initiative, Global Security Initiative and Global Civilization Initiative), and continuously advanced the building of the China-Arab Community with a Shared Future.

Economic and trade cooperation is the "ballast stone" and "roll booster" for deepening Chinese-Arab relations. The Arab states are important cooperation partners for China in promoting the construction of the BRI. With the joint efforts of both sides, by the end of 2023, China had signed the BRI cooperation documents with all 22 Arab countries and the League of Arab States, achieving full coverage. Within the framework of jointly building the BRI, the two sides have implemented more than 200 large-scale projects, and the results of cooperation have benefited nearly 2 billion people on both sides. In terms of trade, China has remained the largest trading partner of Arab countries for many consecutive years. The trade volume between China and the Arab states increased from $238.89 billion in 2013 to a record high of $431.4 billion in 2022, with an 80.6% growth in ten years. China's investment stock in the Arab states grew from $8.57 billion in 2013 to $27.6 billion in 2023, an increase of 2.2 times. Meanwhile, the Arab states are also intensifying their investment in China. In 2023, the direct investment from Arab countries in China reached $2.3 billion, a year-on-year increase of 120%. The United Arab Emirates and Saudi Arabia are the most active Arab countries in terms of investing in China. By the end of 2023, the cumulative investment from Arab countries in China had exceeded $7 billion. In terms of infrastructure construction, in 2023, Chinese enterprises signed new contracts worth $47.2 billion in this region, a year-on-year increase of 28.8%, accounting for 17.8% of the total value of newly signed contracts. The completed business turnover was $27.7 billion, a year-on-year increase of 9.5%, accounting for 17.2% of the total completed business turnover. Among them, the value of newly signed contracts in Saudi Arabia reached $16.8 billion, a year-on-year increase of 72.6%, ranking first among Arab countries. From the perspective of specific fields, China and Arab countries have achieved fruitful results in many areas such as Energy, production capacity cooperation, agriculture, digital economy and aerospace. Cooperation in emerging fields like finance, green development, and digital economy has been continuously expanded and deepened, becoming new highlights. In May 2024, President Xi Jinping attended the 10th Ministerial Conference of the China-Arab States

Preface

Against the backdrop of profound changes in the global landscape and intertwined chaos and changes in the international environment, the Middle East region is also undergoing profound changes of the times and historical shifts. In 2023, the countries in the Middle East region witnessed a continuous increase in their aspirations for stability and development, and they have successively given top priority to development. Saudi Arabia and Iran achieved a historic reconciliation under China's mediation, which gave rise to a "wave of reconciliations" in the Middle East region: relations among Arab countries warmed up, relations between Iran and the member states of the Gulf Cooperation Council (GCC) significantly eased, and Turkey improved its relations with Arab countries and Iran. President Recep Tayyip Erdogan successively visited the United Arab Emirates, Qatar and Saudi Arabia, promoting the establishment of new security and diplomatic partnerships with relevant countries. Turkey also restored diplomatic relations at the ambassadorial level with Egypt, and the overall regional situation showed a trend of relaxation. However, at the same time, a new round of the Palestinian-Israeli conflict broke out on October 7, 2023 and continued to escalate. The conflict has had a significant impact on the global economy and exerted a profound influence on the regional pattern in the Middle East.

The year 2023 was also the first year after the first China-Arab States Summit. Under the strategic guidance of head-of-state diplomacy, China-Arab States relations have been continuously improved and upgraded. The relationship between China and the Arab states are at their best in history. The political mutual trust between the two sides has been continuously strengthened, high-level exchanges have continued to expand, economic and trade cooperation has continued to expand, and exchanges and mutual learning among civilizations have continued to deepen. Together, they have promoted the high-quality

Editorial Committee for *The Development Process of China-Arab States Economic and Trade Relations Annual Report 2023*

Director

Xu Xiaoping

Deputy director

Yang Wenhui, Nie Dan, Li Shaoxian

Members (Arranged by the number of strokes in the Chinese characters of each surname)

Ding Long, Wang Guangda, Wang Lincong, Niu Xinchun, Mao Xiaojing, Zhu Dong, Li Shaoxian, Su Hong, Yang Wenhui, Yang Chunquan, Wu Sike, Zhang Qianjin, Lu Ruquan, Tang Zhichao, Xu Xiaoping, Nie Dan, Cui Yanxiang

Editor-in-chief

Li Shaoxian

Deputy editor-in-chief

Su Hong, Zhang Qianjin

The Development Process of China-Arab States Economic and Trade Relations Annual Report 2023

The Secretariat of China-Arab States Expo /Edit
Li Shaoxian /Editor in Chief

中阿经贸关系发展进程 2023年度报告

社会科学文献出版社
SOCIAL SCIENCES ACADEMIC PRESS (CHINA)